Latinos

The publisher gratefully acknowledges
the generous contribution to this book
provided by the General Endowment of the
University of California Press Associates.

Latinos

Remaking America

EDITED BY

Marcelo M. Suárez-Orozco
and Mariela M. Páez

UNIVERSITY OF CALIFORNIA PRESS

Berkeley   Los Angeles   London

DAVID ROCKEFELLER CENTER FOR
LATIN AMERICAN STUDIES

Harvard University

University of California Press
Berkeley and Los Angeles, California

University of California Press, Ltd.
London, England

Library of Congress Cataloging-in-Publication Data

Latinos : remaking America / edited by Marcelo M. Suárez-Orozco
and Mariela M. Páez.
    p.   cm.
  "David Rockefeller Center for Latin American Studies, Harvard
University."
  Papers originally presented at the conference entitled Latinos in
the 21st century : mapping the research agenda, held in April 2000
at Harvard University.
  Includes bibliographical references and index.
  ISBN 0-520-23486-3(alk. paper).—ISBN 0-520-23487-1
(pbk. : alk. paper)
  1. Hispanic Americans—Social conditions—21st century—
Congresses. 2. Hispanic Americans—Politics and government—
21st century—Congresses. 3. Hispanic Americans—Economic
conditions—21st century—Congresses. 4. United States—Social
conditions—1980—Congresses. 5. United States—Ethnic relations—Congresses. I. Suárez-Orozco, Marcelo M., 1956– II. Páez,
Mariela. III. David Rockefeller Center for Latin American
Studies.

E184.S75 L37 2002
305.868073—dc21   2001053492

Manufactured in the United States of America
10 09 08 07 06 05 04 03 02
10 9 8 7 6 5 4 3 2 1

The paper used in this publication meets the minimum requirements of ANSI/NISO Z39.48-1992 (R 1997) (*Permanence of Paper*).∞

For John H. Coatsworth

CONTENTS

ACKNOWLEDGMENTS

Books have complex social lives. This one is no exception. It is our pleasure to name and thank some of the dedicated individuals who were involved in the making of this collective effort. The book is based on papers originally presented at the conference *Latinos in the 21st Century: Mapping the Research Agenda*, which was held in April 2000 at Harvard University. Harvard graduate students Irene Bloemraad (sociology), Guiomar García (education), Paul Hernández (anthropology), Madga Hinojosa (government), Jill Jefferis (education), Blanca Quiroz (education), Wendy Roth (sociology), Eric Shaw (education), and Chris Tirres (religion) acted as conference amanuenses. Their precise and exhaustive work was critical in helping us provide systematic feedback to the authors as they turned their conference presentations into scholarly chapters. John Coatsworth, Monroe Gutman Professor of Latin American Affairs and director of Harvard's David Rockefeller Center for Latin American Studies, supported this initiative with his characteristic warmth, enthusiasm, and gusto for things Latin American—Latino included. Neida Jiménez, conference coordinator at the David Rockefeller Center, did an exemplary job managing with precision and diplomacy the complex logistics of a conference involving over fifty presenters. Steve Reifenberg, executive director of the Rockefeller Center, provided strategic support—and wise counsel—just when we needed it most. Harvey Fineberg, then provost at Harvard University, and Jerome T. Murphy, then dean of the Harvard Graduate School of Education, gave us two important grants early in the development of this initiative. Dottie Engler of the Harvard Graduate School of Education flawlessly organized the activities around the conference's keynote address delivered by the Honorable Henry Cisneros. Various foundations also supported this effort. We are grateful to the Spencer Foundation, Hewlett Foundation, the W. T. Grant

Foundation, and the National Science Foundation for the grants that made various phases of this work possible. Carola Suárez-Orozco, co-director of the Harvard Immigration Project, read and reread several sections of the book. Carola's tactful and wise feedback substantially improved the final version of the book. We are also grateful to the anonymous reviewers for the University of California Press. Naomi Schneider shepherded the project with her legendary professionalism and diplomacy. Finally, we want to thank our colleagues throughout the country, many of whom were involved in the conference and the book, for their extraordinary generosity in sharing with us their enthusiasm and *buena voluntad.* *¡Mil gracias!*

Introduction

The Research Agenda

Marcelo M. Suárez-Orozco and Mariela M. Páez

During the closing decades of the twentieth century, the process of gradual demographic transformation that had begun on the eve of World War II gained extraordinary momentum. At the end of the war, the population of the United States was largely of white European origin. By the year 2000, more than a quarter of the U.S. population was composed of members of ethnically marked minorities, including African Americans, Latinos, and Asian Americans, and the future augurs even more startling changes.[1] In a widely cited report, scientists at the U.S. Bureau of the Census concluded that by the year 2050, some 50 percent of the U.S. population would be members of ethnic minorities—making the term minority somewhat anachronistic (Fig. I-1). This and other census projections are somewhat uncertain. After all, the terms *Latino* and *Asian American* did not even exist fifty years ago; who is to say the terms as they are now used will have currency fifty years from now? These data nevertheless suggest an unequivocal social fact: the United States is now in the midst of unprecedented change.[2]

This increasingly obvious demographic reality makes it evident that the United States is becoming a country that is no longer largely white and of European origin (U.S. Census Bureau 1999). Indeed, the future of the United States will be in no small measure linked to the fortunes of a heterogeneous blend of relatively recent arrivals from Asia, from the Caribbean, from other parts of the world, and above all from Latin America.

At the dawn of the new century, the more than 35 million Latinos in the United States make up roughly 12.5 percent of the total population. It is estimated that in just two generations, the United States will have the second largest number of Latinos in the world—after Mexico. More Latinos than African Americans are currently attending U.S. schools. Indeed, Latinos may already have surpassed African Americans as the nation's largest minority

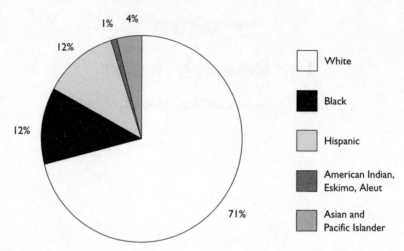

Figure I.1. Resident Population Estimates of the U.S. by Race and Hispanic Origin: U.S. Census Bureau, October 2000.

group. The U.S. Census Bureau claims that by the year 2050, a full quarter of the U.S. population will be of Latino origin; that is, nearly 100 million people will be able to trace their ancestry to the Spanish-speaking, Latin American, and Caribbean worlds.

This book brings together some of the leading minds in the scholarly study of the Latino population of the United States. Because of the extraordinary dimensions and recentness of the phenomenon under consideration—from 1990 to 2000 the Latino population grew by 58 percent—this effort can serve only as an initial and somewhat tentative exploration. By necessity, we must ask many more questions than we can possibly answer with any degree of certainty. We must heed Francis Bacon's "double use" of doubt.

Three general principles guided the making of this book. First, we define Latino studies broadly as the scholarly study of the Latino population of the United States and its transnational links to the Caribbean and Latin American worlds. It is an emerging field that must tolerate—indeed thrive—on ambiguities. We envision the field of Latino studies as a big tent covering a broad range of social science and humanistic scholarship. Thus the contributors to this volume include scholars who feel at home doing positivistic social science with large data sets as well as scholars in cultural studies who focus on post-modern theory and literary criticism.

Second, the book performs and telecasts a call for interdisciplinary work as a matter of necessity. Interdisciplinary work can succeed when it slows down—or, better yet, altogether stops—"the taken-for-granted practices that can bureaucratize disciplinary work. Interdisciplinary work imposes certain mutual calibrations of theoretical models, methodological strategies, and analytic perspectives. By definition interdisciplinary work subverts the reductionistic impulses common to many disciplinary enterprises" (Suárez-Orozco and Robben 2000, p. 3). Although each discipline must, of course, cultivate its own garden, periodic disciplinary crossings can open fertile new terrains. Something unique can happen when a psychoanalyst and a political scientist come together and are encouraged to develop and sustain a scholarly conversation. This volume brings together an unprecedented assembly of anthropologists, education scholars, health and medical scientists, historians, linguists, political scientists, psychoanalysts and psychologists, sociolinguists, and sociologists who share a scholarly interest in the Latino population of the United States.

Third, the book is comparative in nature. It examines the varieties of the Latino experience by considering all the major subgroups that make up the Latino population of the United States—Mexican, Puerto Rican, Cuban, Central and South American, and Dominican. We examine Latinos in context: the Florida experience (Stepick and Stepick, this volume) differs from that of New York (Smith, this volume), and both differ from California (Vigil; Gándara, this volume) and Texas (Chapa, this volume).

The Latino population of the United States is a highly heterogeneous population that defies easy generalizations. As Stepick and Stepick, Torres-Saillant, and others in this volume suggest, the tired and facile "Latinos-are-a-big-family" glosses over the contradictions, tensions, and fissures—around class, race, and color—that often separate them. Indeed, most of the authors in this book would reject any essentializing—that is, any attempt to discuss all Latinos as one seamless whole. Bluntly, what does an English-speaking third-generation upper-status white Cuban American in Florida have in common with a Maya-speaking recent immigrant from Guatemala? What, precisely, warrants collapsing their distinct histories, current socio-cultural predicaments, and probable destinies under the same rubric? To complicate matters further, as Jorge Domínguez suggests (this volume), Latinos are not from the other side of the moon: in some important respects they are not particularly distinguishable from other Americans. How, then, are we to proceed? Cautiously.

In this book we have opted for the broadest, most inclusive, and most generous definition of Latinos: that segment of the U.S. population that traces its descent to the Spanish-speaking, Caribbean, and Latin American worlds. The term *Latino* is a new and ambiguous invention. It is a cultural category that has no precise racial signification. Indeed, Latinos are white, black, indigenous, and every possible combination thereof. Yet, as a number of authors in this book discuss, upon entering the United States, Latinos undergo a rapid regime of racialization.

The term *Latino* also lacks the specificity regarding national origin that terms such as *Irish American* and *Italian American* convey. Latinos come from over a dozen countries as varied as Mexico, Colombia, and the Dominican Republic (Fig. I-2). They also include Puerto Ricans, who may move freely between the island and the mainland as U.S. citizens. Nor does the term *Latino* evoke any particular period in U.S. history. Latinos are among the "oldest" Americans—the ancestors of some settled in the Southwest and spoke Spanish, making it their home well before there was a United States. They did not come to the United States; the United States came to them. Latinos are also among the "newest" Americans, for two-thirds of all Latinos in the United States are either immigrants or the children of immigrants. Because the vast majority of Latinos in the United States come from Latin America—the number of Latinos from Central and South America grew by over 100 percent between 1990 and 2000 (U.S. Census Bureau 2001b)—we chose the term *Latino* over *Hispanic*—a term that emphasizes the population's link with "Hispania," or Spain.

Latinos have varied histories, cultural sensibilities, and current social predicaments. The vectors of race and color, gender, socioeconomic status, language, immigrant status, and mode of incorporation into the United States shape their experiences. Latinos are a work in progress; they are a people in the process of becoming as they settle, in unprecedented numbers, in the United States. The very term *Latino* has meaning only in reference to the U.S. experience. Outside the United States, we don't speak of Latinos; we speak of Mexicans, Cubans, Puerto Ricans, and so forth. Latinos are made in the USA.

Given this heterogeneity, this ambiguity, and these internal fissures, what arguments can be advanced for a Latino panethnic construct? Are Latinos in the United States poised to achieve Bolívar's dream of unity that for centuries escaped their brothers and sisters in Latin America? Or will each Latino subgroup follow its own path—Cubans in one direction, Mexicans in another, and Dominicans in another still? Is it not wiser, empirically sounder, and more promising to keep our gaze on individual groups such as Cuban Americans, Mexican Americans, Dominican Americans, and so forth? Yes and no.

Systematic scholarly work at the subgroup level has generated important empirical data and theoretical insight. The work by sociologist Alejandro Portes and anthropologist Alex Stepick is a case in point (Portes and Stepick 1993). By focusing on the somewhat unique features of the Cuban ethnic enclave in Florida, they have broadened considerably our theoretical understanding of the dynamics of immigrant insertion into the U.S. economy and society (Stepick and Stepick, this volume). Indeed, to date the vast majority of the scholarship on Latinos has tended to focus on individual subgroups.[3] It is now time to extend the conversation.

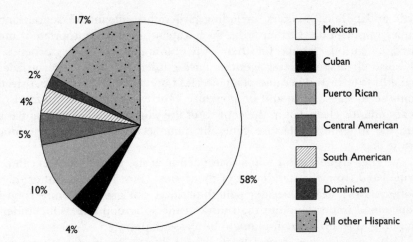

Figure I.2. Latinos, by Type of Origin: Current Population Survey, 2000.

The case for broader scholarly analysis at the panethnic level can be made along at least three general principles: one based on politics, one based on theoretical considerations, and one based on sociohistorical themes. At the political level, the panethnic construct has emerged as significant. Latinos are entering the United States in large numbers at a time when the nation's ethos is dominated by a "culture of multiculturalism" (Suárez-Orozco and Suárez-Orozco 2001; Glazer 1997). The social practices and cultural models that we have come to call multiculturalism shape the experiences, perceptions, and behavioral repertoires of immigrant and native-born Latinos in ways not seen in previous eras of large-scale immigration. A hundred years ago, there certainly was no culture of multiculturalism celebrating—however superficially and ambivalently—ethnicity and communities of origin.[4] "Passing" was the name of the game. In the words of Berkeley cultural psychologist George De Vos, we have all noticed now the "passing of passing" (De Vos 1992).

Latinos today are players in social spaces where racial and ethnic categories have high-stakes political and economic implications. The largest wave of immigration in U.S. history—the wave responsible for the current Latino-ization of the country—took place after the great struggles of the civil rights movement.

One reason why racial and ethnic categories are relevant is that they have become critical tools in the workings of the state apparatus. Nation-states use these categories for various purposes, such as census enumeration, taxation, and apportionment for political representation. Racial and ethnic categories as generated by state policy are relevant to a variety of civic and political matters, including civil rights, affirmative action, and equal opportunity; furthermore, such categories are appropriated and used by various groups for their own emotional and strategic needs.[5] Because all major federal agencies have chosen to employ the broader panethnic term and because of a powerful bureaucratic and market-driven impulse to standardize and homogenize (Torres-Saillant, this volume), it is abundantly clear that in the context of the workings of the state apparatus, the subgroup labels are generally quite secondary to the panethnic construct.[6]

Another argument for scholarly reflection at the panethnic level can be articulated from the standpoint of theoretical considerations rather than politics. Work at the broader panethnic level can generate more robust conceptual understandings than work at the subgroup level. Our understanding of transnationalism might be a case in point.

Caribbean Latinos, especially mainland Puerto Ricans and immigrant Dominicans, have been depicted as paradigmatic examples of groups engaged in deep transnationalism, an analytic concept that is often used to refer to economic, political, and cultural strategies articulated by diasporic peoples across national spaces (Basch, Schiller, and Blanc 1995; Smith and Guarnizo 1998). Significant numbers of Puerto Ricans and Dominicans are said to lead dual lives—engaging in double consciousness, cultivating dual loyalties, living serially between their islands and the mainland. Recent studies, for example, suggest that Dominican immigrants have developed political, economic, and cultural adaptations that involve high levels of transnationalism. They remit large sums of money to their homeland, they remain substantially engaged in political processes there, and they return periodically with their children to nourish social and cultural ties in their island home (Levitt 1997; Guarnizo 1994; Pessar 1995). Research on mainland Puerto Ricans suggests a slightly different version of this general transnational dynamic. Although they are less likely than Dominicans to send dollars to the island,[7] mainland Puerto Ricans remain socially, culturally, and at times politically involved in island affairs (Torre, Vecchini, and Burgo 1994).

It seems clear that our theoretical understanding of transnationalism might benefit from placing what the Caribbean pattern suggests in the context of a larger Latino framework. If we examine the Caribbean experience against the backdrop of, for example, the Mexican experience, a more subtle understanding of transnationalism is likely to emerge.

Mexican immigration to the United States has over the last two decades undergone a profound transformation. Historically, U.S. immigration policies, market forces, and the social practices of Mexican immigrants did not encourage their long-term integration into American society (Suárez-Orozco 1998). A sojourner pattern of largely male-initiated circular migration, characterized by efforts to earn dollars during a specific season, dominated the Mexican experience for decades into the 1980s (Durand 1998). After concluding their seasonal work, large numbers of Mexicans returned south of the border, eventually to resume the cycle the following year. In that context, Mexican immigrants engaged in dual lives, displaying the kinds of proto-transnational behaviors now more fully developed among Caribbean Latinos. Like Puerto Ricans and Dominicans today, the Mexican immigrants of yesterday lived both "here" and "there."

Yet data on various aspects of Mexican immigration suggest the intensification, over the last two decades, of a trend toward permanent settlement in the United States. Wayne Cornelius (1998) has argued that Mexican immigrants are rapidly moving away from transnational strategies. For example, over time and across generations, Mexicans tend to remit less money, become less involved in Mexican politics, and visit there less often (Cornelius 1998). Will Dominicans, over time and across generations, follow the Mexican pattern? Or will they adopt the Puerto Rican version of transnationalism, which by some indicators has intensified rather than decreased over time (Bonilla 1989)? The answer is uncertain, but its implications for our theoretical understandings are significant.

In the context of the broader Latino framework, transnationalism turns out to be a more complex set of social adaptations, which seems to take different forms and serve different purposes. Furthermore, it becomes increasingly obvious that transnational adaptations need to be systematically examined over time and across generations. This implies the value of a research agenda that would examine the varieties of transnationalism across sites, social groups, and generations to track longitudinal as well as transgenerational continuities and discontinuities in behaviors and adaptations.

There are other arguments for choosing a panethnic level of analysis. In striking contrast to the other major new immigrant group, Asians, most Latinos share a common language, Spanish.[8] Not all Latinos are Spanish speakers, but the Spanish language has become ubiquitous. On Wednesday, September 13, 2000, CBS aired to a national audience of over 7.4 million viewers several Spanish-language commercials—with English subtitles—during a prime-time show, the Latin Grammy Awards. In May 2001, President George W. Bush made history when he delivered his weekly radio address to the nation in Spanish—a move that was applauded by some as a shrewd strategy to court Latino support and condemned by others as encouraging linguistic and ethnic divisions. The president was surely aware that Spanish is now the nation's second language, spoken by nearly 20 million people. More important, it is itself a world language shared by over 265 million people. Thus although Latinos, like other groups, are divided by factors such as race and color, class, and national origin, the Spanish language generates a powerful gravitational field bringing them together.

Studies of language maintenance and shift suggest that Latinos, more than any other ethnic group, tend to remain loyal to their native language, with Mexicans being the most committed Spanish speakers (Portes and Rumbaut 1990). Even third-generation bilingualism is relatively higher among Latinos than among other ethnic groups (Portes and Rumbaut 1990).

Indeed, Latino families are distinct in their extensive use of Spanish at home. Recent data show that in their homes, about 83 percent of immigrant Latino youth use their native language primarily or exclusively; the comparable figure for immigrant Asians is 68 percent. Among native-born Latino youths of foreign-born parents, 58 percent still speak primarily Spanish at home; the figure is about 43 percent for native-born Asians with immigrant parents. Some 39 percent of Latino native-born youths of native-born parents report speaking only English at home, whereas 82 percent of their Asian counterparts do so. These patterns suggest that Latino families are more likely to retain their native language than other groups, such as Asians (Kao 1999).

Language is intrinsically involved in the processes of education, including literacy development, and identity formation (Darder, Torres, and Gutierrez 1997). Within the last two decades, language in education has become a subject of heated debate among government officials, policy makers, educators, parents, and concerned citizens. Most recently bilingual education—ever controversial in the United States—has been under a microscope as new initiatives for English-only instruction have been proposed throughout the nation (Gándara; Moll and Ruiz, this volume). Indeed, language is at the core of the Latino educational experience in this country, but as many of the authors in this volume point out, discussion of educating Latino youths should not be reduced to issues of language alone. It requires a full understanding of the social, political, cultural, and racial context in which language is embedded (Zentella; Moll and Ruiz, this volume).

Like Latinos themselves, the language of Latinos in the United States presents a complicated picture. There are many dialects, intonations, and varieties of Spanish, "Spanglish," and English. For many Latinos Spanish is a lingua franca, but specific words, folk sayings, and accents often produce different meanings and values within the different Latino communities. Language varieties act as a way of signifying subethnic identifications and marking subgroup identities (Zentella, this volume). Language is also implicated in the social construction and conditions that shape class, racial, gender, and sexual identities. Thus the Spanish language in all its varieties plays a central role in the construction and transformation of the Latino community in the United States. Will Spanish follow the path of previous immigrant languages such as German, Italian, and Japanese and be asphyxiated in the United States? (Lieberson, Dalto, and Johnston 1975). Or will it be the exception to the rule? Will the sheer force of Latino demographics—the fact that there is now a highly elaborate social infrastructure to support the Spanish language, the availability of new information technologies, and the continuing flows of Latin American immigration—provide the oxygen needed for Spanish to flourish in the United States? If Spanish does endure here, will its persistence be an asset or a hindrance for Latinos? Will globalization give an edge to Latino bilinguals? These broad questions set the stage for the theoretical and empirical work discussed in various chapters in this book (Pearson; Zentella; Gándara; Carlo and Snow, this volume).

Language is only one of the cultural building blocks crucial to any understanding of Latino identities. Latinos also tend to share cultural models, social practices, and religious sensibilities that shape and give meaning to their lives. Peggy Levitt (this volume) examines how Latino immigrants are transforming the nature of organized religion in the United States. They are now the largest ethnic group in the Catholic Church, making up over two-thirds of all Catholics in Florida, Texas, and New Mexico. She explores how their involvement in religion in turn shapes their social and political incorporation into the United States. Related to their Catholic affiliation is the importance of fictive kinship patterns (*compadrazgo* and *comadrazgo*—godparenthood) in structuring social relations among Latinos.

SOCIOHISTORICAL THEMES

The most robust case for the analytic use of the panethnic Latino construct emerges from various shared sociohistorical processes that are at the heart of the Latino experience in the United States (see Sanchez, this volume). This book identifies three such themes: the experience of immigration; the changing nature of U.S. relations with Latin America; and the processes of racialization as Latinos enter, and complicate, the powerful "black-white" binary logic that has driven U.S. racial relations. In the words of Silvio Torres-Saillant (this volume), "We share the experience of being uprooted by large socioeconomic forces from our original homelands. We come from societies with a history of unequal association with the United States, a country that has influenced and sometimes even dictated political behavior in Latin America."

Immigration

The Latino experience in the United States has been profoundly shaped by immigration (Cornelius; Hondagneu-Sotelo; Falicov, this volume). The vast majority of Latinos are either immigrants or the children of immigrants. In 1980 there were roughly 14 million Latinos in the United States (Delgado and Stefancic 1998, p. xvii). Twenty years later, there were over 35 million, most of them new immigrants. Large-scale immigration from Mexico, Central and South America, and the Caribbean has been the backbone of what U.S. scholars of immigration now call "the new immigration" (Suárez-Orozco and Suárez-Orozco 2001; Edmonston and Passel 1994; Hing 1993).

According to Suárez-Orozco (1999), three distinct social formations lie at the heart of an emerging Inter-American Immigration System (IIS): (1) more or less uninterrupted flow of large-scale legal (as well as undocumented) immigration from Mexico, which rapidly intensified after 1980 and is structured by powerful economic forces and sociocultural practices that seem unaffected by unilateral policy initiatives; (2) more time-limited "waves" (as opposed to uninterrupted "flows") of large-scale immigration from Central and South America—by the early 1980s, El Salvador and Guatemala replaced Cuba as the largest source of asylum seekers arriving from the Spanish-speaking world; and (3) a Caribbean pattern of intense circular migration typified by the Puerto Rican and Dominican experiences in New York, where Dominicans are now the largest immigrant group.

By the 1990s, there were more legal immigrants from Mexico alone than from all of Europe combined. By the end of the twentieth century, well over seven million Mexican immigrants resided in the United States (González Baker et al. 1998). More than one-fourth of all Mexican immigrants to the United States arrived in the first half of the 1990s (Binational Study on Migration 1997, p. ii). Mexican immigrants constitute nearly half of the total Mexican origin population of the United States.

The history of Mexican immigration makes it quite distinct from other immigration to the United States: Most remarkable is the "immigration" that occurred when Mexico lost roughly half of its northern territory to the United States. Consider also the joint U.S.-Mexican border, the critical mass of Mexican citizens and Mexican Americans now residing on the U.S. side of "the line," and their heavy concentration in a handful of states. The large number of undocumented Mexican immigrants (it is estimated that nearly 40 percent of illegal immigrants in the U.S. today are Mexicans) also sets them apart from other immigrant groups—although perhaps not from the experiences of Central Americans.

By the early 1980s, the intensification of cold-war tensions in Central America and increased direct U.S. involvement in the conflict generated unprecedented population displacements and new migratory flows. During the 1960s, and again briefly in 1980,[9] Cubans had dominated the Latin American refugee experience in the United States, but the 1980s were characterized by large-scale emigration from war-torn areas in El Salvador, Guatemala, and Nicaragua. By the year 2000, some 1.7 million Central Americans made the United States their home (U.S. Census Bureau 2001b, 3). By one account "one in every six Salvadoreans now lives in the United

States" (Mahler 1995. p. 37; see also Mahler 1995b). Also, the escalation of the war in Colombia and the sharp intensification of U.S. involvement in the conflict revealed the beginnings of a large-scale migratory wave as growing numbers of Colombians began leaving their war-ravaged country, many of them to head north to the United States (Krauss 2000, p. 1). Indeed, Colombians are the largest group of the "new, new Latinos" originating in South America; approximately half a million Colombians now live in the United States.

The Dominican-Caribbean experience is paradigmatic of what sociologists and anthropologists of immigration have called transnational migratory circuits (Hondagneu-Sotelo, this volume; Basch, Schiller, and Blanc 1995). This pattern of immigration is typified by intensive back-and-forth movement, not only of people but also of goods and information, principally between the islands of Hispaniola and Manhattan. Although the 3.4 million Puerto Ricans who live on the mainland are U.S. citizens and thus not considered immigrants, their sociocultural and linguistic adaptations resemble those of immigrant Latinos. Puerto Ricans, too, display intense levels of transnationalism; in the felicitous worlds of Luis Rafael Sánchez, many of them live "en la guagua aérea" (the air-bus) (Sánchez 1994; Torre, Vecchini, and Burgos 1994).

Another relevant feature of the new transnational framework is that even as Latinos enmesh themselves in the social, economic, and political life of their new lands (Cornelius 1998; Durand 1998), they remain powerful protagonists in the economic, political, and cultural spheres in the countries they left behind. Latinos are emerging as "hemispheric citizens." Latino remittances and investments have become vital to the economies of varied countries of emigration, such as the Dominican Republic, Mexico, and El Salvador. In the latter country, remittances in the 1990s became the largest source of foreign exchange, averaging over a billion dollars a year. Likewise, the Binational Study on Immigration estimates that remittances to Mexico were "equivalent to 57 percent of the foreign exchange available through direct investment in 1995, and 5 percent of the total income supplied by exports" (Binational Study on Migration 1997, p. vii).[10]

Politically, Latinos are also becoming increasingly relevant actors with influence in political processes both "here" and "there." Some observers have noted that the outcomes of Dominican elections are routinely determined in New York City, where Dominicans are the largest group of new immigrants (Pessar 1995). Likewise, Mexican politicians have recently "discovered" the political value of the more than seven million Mexican immigrants living in the United States. Mexican President Vicente Fox underscored a new official attitude toward expatriates when he toured the border region in December 2000 to welcome back personally a few of the estimated one million Mexicans traveling south for Christmas. The new Mexican dual-nationality initiative, whereby Mexican immigrants who become nationalized U.S. citizens would retain a host of political and other rights in Mexico, is also the product of this emerging transnational framework.

Culturally Latinos not only are significantly reshaping the ethos of their new communities but also are responsible for significant social transformations in their countries of origin. Peggy Levitt (1997) has argued that Dominican and Brazilian "social remittances" affect the values, cultural models, and social practices of those left behind. Immigrant Latinos today are more likely to be at once "here" and "there," bridging increasingly unbounded national spaces (Basch, Schiller, and Blanc 1995), and in the process to transform both home and host countries.

Several features characterize the new Latin American immigration to the United States. First, a growing body of research suggests that the economic restructuring and sociocultural changes taking place in the Americas virtually ensure that Latin American immigration to the United States will be a long-term phenomenon. Globalization and economic restructuring have intensified inequality in Latin America, generating unemployment and underemployment—and hence new migratory waves (Dussel 2000). Beyond Mexico and Central America, the contours of a large-scale South American exodus became increasingly clear by the end of the year 2000 when large numbers of Ecuadorians, Peruvians, Venezuelans, and Argentineans headed north (*Washington Post* 2000, p. A1) (see Table I.1).

On the U.S. side of "the line," there is a voracious and enduring demand—indeed, *addiction* might be a more appropriate term—for immigrant workers in both the service sector and the knowledge-intensive sector of the economy (Cornelius 1998). The extraordinary Latino population growth in Nevada, Georgia, Arkansas, and North Carolina during the 1990s (see Table I.2) is tied to the explosion of new jobs in the construction, service, meat, and poultry industries in those states (*New York Times* 2000, 15). It is likely that the extremely high flows of Latin American immigration to the United States during the last two decades will eventually decrease (Binational Study on Migration 1997), but it is safe to assume that Latin Americans will continue to dominate immigration to the United States over the next decades.

Second, new data suggest that the immigration momentum we are currently witnessing cannot be easily contained by unilateral policy initiatives, such as the various border control efforts and theatrics that have intensified over the last decade (Chavez 2001; Andreas 2000). Transnational labor-recruiting networks, family reunification, and wage differentials continue to act as a powerful impetus to Latin American immigration to the United States.

Third, new data suggest that Latin American immigrants are in the United States to stay. Today's Latin American immigrants, especially Mexicans

TABLE I.1. Hispanic Population by Type: 2000

Subject	Number	Percent
Hispanic or Latino Origin		
Total population	281,421,906	100.0
Hispanic or Latino (of any race)	35,305,818	12.5
Not Hispanic or Latino	246,116,088	87.5
Hispanic or Latino by Type		
Hispanic or Latino (of any race)	35,305,818	100.0
Mexican	20,640,711	58.5
Puerto Rican	3,406,178	9.6
Cuban	1,241,685	3.5
Other Hispanic or Latino	10,017,244	28.4
Dominican (Dominican Republic)	764,945	2.2
Central American (excludes Mexican)	1,686,937	4.8
Costa Rican	68,588	0.2
Guatemalan	372,487	1.1
Honduran	217,569	0.6
Nicaraguan	177,684	0.5
Panamanian	91,723	0.3
Salvadoran	655,165	1.9
Other Central American	103,721	0.3
South American	1,353,562	3.8
Argentinean	100,864	0.3
Bolivian	42,068	0.1
Chilean	68,849	0.2
Colombian	470,684	1.3
Ecuadorian	260,559	0.7
Paraguayan	8,769	0.0
Peruvian	233,926	0.7
Uruguayan	18,804	0.1
Venezuelan	91,507	0.3
Other South American	57,532	0.2
Spaniard	100,135	0.3
All other Hispanic or Latino	6,111,665	17.3
Checkbox only, other Hispanic	1,733,274	4.9
Write-in Spanish	686,004	1.9
Write-in Hispanic	2,454,529	7.0
Write-in Latino	450,769	1.3
Not elsewhere classified	787,089	2.2

SOURCE: U.S. Census Bureau, Current Population Survey, May 2001.

TABLE 1-2. Hispanic Population by Type for Regions, States, and Puerto Rico: 1990 and 2000

(For information on confidentiality protection, nonsampling error, and definitions, see *www.census.gov/prod/www/abs/decenial.html*)

	1990			2000						
	Total Population	Hispanic Population		Total Population	Hispanic Population		Hispanic Type			
		Number	Percent		Number	Percent	Mexican	Puerto Rican	Cuban	Other Hispanic
United States	248,709,873	22,354,059	9.0	281,421,906	35,305,818	12.5	20,640,711	3,406,178	1,241,685	10,017,244
Region										
Northeast	50,809,229	3,754,389	7.4	53,594,378	5,254,087	9.8	479,169	2,074,574	168,959	2,531,385
Midwest	59,668,632	1,726,509	2.9	64,392,776	3,124,532	4.9	2,200,196	325,363	45,305	553,668
South	85,445,930	6,767,021	7.9	100,236,820	11,586,696	11.6	6,548,081	759,305	921,427	3,357,883
West	52,786,082	10,106,140	19.1	63,197,932	15,340,503	24.3	11,413,265	246,936	105,994	3,574,308
State										
Alabama	4,040,587	24,629	0.6	4,447,100	75,830	1.7	44,522	6,322	2,354	22,632
Alaska	550,043	17,803	3.2	626,932	25,852	4.1	13,334	2,649	553	9,316
Arizona	3,665,228	688,338	18.8	5,130,632	1,295,617	25.3	1,065,578	17,587	5,272	207,180
Arkansas	2,350,725	19,876	0.8	2,673,400	86,866	3.2	61,204	2,473	950	22,239
California	29,760,021	7,687,938	25.8	33,871,648	10,966,556	32.4	8,455,926	140,570	72,286	2,297,774
Colorado	3,294,394	424,302	12.9	4,301,261	735,601	17.1	450,760	12,993	3,701	268,147
Connecticut	3,287,116	213,116	6.5	3,405,565	320,323	9.4	23,484	194,443	7,101	95,295
Delaware	666,168	15,820	2.4	783,600	37,277	4.8	12,986	14,005	932	9,354
District of Columbia	606,900	32,710	5.4	572,059	44,953	7.9	5,098	2,328	1,101	36,426
Florida	12,937,926	1,574,143	12.2	15,982,378	2,682,715	16.8	363,925	482,027	833,120	1,003,643
Georgia	6,478,216	108,922	1.7	8,186,453	435,227	5.3	275,288	35,532	12,536	111,871
Hawaii	1,108,229	81,390	7.3	1,211,537	87,699	7.2	19,820	30,005	711	37,163
Idaho	1,006,749	52,927	5.3	1,293,953	101,690	7.9	79,324	1,509	408	20,449
Illinois	11,430,602	904,446	7.9	12,419,293	1,530,262	12.3	1,144,390	157,851	18,438	209,583
Indiana	5,544,159	98,788	1.8	6,080,485	214,536	3.5	153,042	19,678	2,754	39,062
Iowa	2,776,755	32,647	1.2	2,926,324	82,473	2.8	61,154	2,690	750	17,879
Kansas	2,477,574	93,670	3.8	2,688,418	188,252	7.0	148,270	5,237	1,680	33,065
Kentucky	3,685,296	21,984	0.6	4,041,769	59,939	1.5	31,385	6,469	3,516	18,569

State									
Louisiana	4,219,973	2.2	93,044	4,468,976	2.4	107,738	32,267	7,670	8,448	59,353
Maine	1,227,928	0.6	6,829	1,274,923	0.7	9,360	2,756	2,275	478	3,851
Maryland	4,781,468	2.6	125,102	5,296,486	4.3	227,916	39,900	25,570	6,754	155,692
Massachusetts	6,016,425	4.8	287,549	6,349,097	6.8	428,729	22,288	199,207	8,867	198,367
Michigan	9,295,297	2.2	201,596	9,938,444	3.3	323,877	220,769	26,941	7,219	68,948
Minnesota	4,375,099	1.2	53,884	4,919,479	2.9	143,382	95,613	6,616	2,527	38,626
Mississippi	2,573,216	0.6	15,931	2,844,658	1.4	39,569	21,616	2,881	1,508	13,564
Missouri	5,117,073	1.2	61,702	$595,211	2.1	118,592	77,887	6,677	3,022	31,006
Montana	799,065	1.5	12,174	902,195	2.0	18,081	11,735	931	285	5,130
Nebraska	1,578,385	2.3	36,969	1,711,263	5.5	94,425	71,030	1,993	859	20,543
Nevada	1,201833	10.4	124,419	1,998,257	19.7	393,970	285,764	10,420	11,498	86,288
New Hampshire	1,109,252	1.0	11,333	1,235,786	1.7	20,489	4,590	6,215	785	8,899
New Jersey	7,730,188	9.6	739,861	8,414,350	13.3	1,117,191	102,929	366,788	77,337	570,137
New Mexico	1,515,069	38.2	579,224	1,819,046	42.1	765,386	330,049	4,488	2,588	428,261
New York	17,990,455	12.3	2,214,026	18,976,457	15.1	2,867,583	260,889	1,050,293	62,590	1,493,811
North Carolina	6,628,637	1.2	76,726	8,049,313	4.7	378,963	246,545	31,117	7,389	93,912
North Dakota	638,800	0.7	4,665	642,200	1.2	7,786	4,295	507	250	2,734
Ohio	10,847,115	1.3	139,696	11,353,140	1.9	217,123	90,663	66,269	5,152	55,039
Oklahoma	3,145,585	2.7	86,160	3,450,654	5.2	179,304	132,813	8,153	1,759	36,579
Oregon	2,842,321	4.0	112,707	3,421,399	8.0	275,314	214,662	5,092	3,091	52,469
Pennsylvania	11,881,643	2.0	232,262	12,281,054	3.2	394,088	55,178	228,557	10,363	99,990
Rhode Island	1,003,464	4.6	45,752	1,048,319	8.7	90,820	5,881	25,422	1,128	58,389
South Carolina	3,486,703	0.9	30,551	4,012,012	2.4	95,076	52,871	12,211	2,875	27,119
South Dakota	696,004	0.8	5,252	754,844	1.4	10,903	6,364	637	163	3,739
Tennessee	4,877,185	0.7	32,741	5,689,283	2.2	123,838	77,372	10,303	3695	32,468
Texas	16,986,510	25.5	4,339,905	20,851,820	32.0	6,669,666	5,071,963	69,504	25,705	1,502,494
Utah	1,722,850	4.9	84,597	2,233,169	9.0	201,559	136,416	3,977	340	60,226
Vermont	562,758	0.7	3,661	608,827	0.9	5,504	1,174	1,374	310	2,646
Virginia	6,187,358	2.6	160,288	7,078,515	4.7	329,540	73,979	41,131	6,332	206,098
Washington	4,866,692	4.4	214,570	5,894,121	7.5	441,509	329,93	16,140	4,501	90,934
West Virginia	1,793,477	0.5	8,489	1,808,344	0.7	12,279	4,347	1,609	453	5,870
Wisconsin	4,891,769	1.9	93,194	5363,675	3.6	192,921	126,719	30,267	2,491	33,444
Wyoming	453,588	5.7	25,751	493,782	6.4	31,669	19,963	575	160	10,971
Puerto Rico[1]	3,522,037	NA	NA	3,808,810	98.8	3,762,746	11,546	3,623,392	19,973	107,835

SOURCE: U.S. Census Bureau Census 2000, Summary File 1.
NA Not available.
[1] Census 2000 was the first to ask a separate question on Hispanic origin in Puerto Rico.

and Central Americans, are more likely to settle permanently in the United States than those who arrived in the previous eras of immigration (Cornelius 1998). Latinos, therefore, are an enduring, rather than a transient, feature of the new American social landscape.

The Latino presence in the United States is largely defined by immigration. The vast majority of Latinos have been directly or indirectly touched by the experience of immigration. It is part of a shared experience and history that brings together the various distinct paths Latinos have taken in their journey to the United States. Although there have been differences in modes of incorporation and patterns of immigration, every Latino subgroup shares the experience of settling in this country and engaging in a process of social, economic, and cultural adaptation.

Dangerous Liaisons: U.S. Relations with Latin America

The eclipse of European ascendancy and dominance in the Americas as the nineteenth century came to a close and the parallel rise of the United States as the hemisphere's unrivaled hegemonic nation figured prominently in the making of the Latino experience in the United States. The story of the Latino population of the United States can be fully articulated only against the backdrop of the historical, political, and economic relationships between the United States and Latin America. The United States and Latin America have never been equal partners. U.S. relations with Latin America can be characterized as an asymmetrical liaison between a dominant power and a weaker, often reluctant partner. The history of U.S.–Latin American relations is, of course, complex and beyond the scope of this introduction (Smith 1996; Schoultz 1998; Bulmer-Thomas and Dunkerley 1999). We must, however, briefly mention a few themes that are especially relevant to an understanding of the Latino experience.

The first theme involves U.S. territorial expansion, a phase in U.S. relations with Latin America that historian Peter Smith (1996) has argued is best characterized as "imperial" in nature. It is at the heart of the nation-building process by which the United States emerged from the original thirteen colonies to become the continent's sole transoceanic power. This nation building was driven by an ideological apparatus with equal parts of pseudoscientific racism and cultural arrogance (laced with a good dose of Puritan zeal), along with a voracious appetite for Latin American land and other resources. It was achieved, largely via direct military confrontation and a series of territorial annexations, appropriations, and purchases (including the 1803 Louisiana Purchase for 15 million dollars and the Florida Purchase from Spain in 1819). But the choice prize of this imperial campaign surely was the territory that is now the U.S. Southwest. The aftermath of the 1846–1848 Mexican War resulted in the annexation of roughly half of Mexico's territory.

The transfer of lands stretching west of Texas all the way to the Pacific Ocean—formally decreed in the 1848 treaty of Guadalupe Hidalgo—is the most obvious example of how this expansionist phase was implicated in the making of the Latino population of the United States (Chavez 1984; McWilliams 1968; Acuña 1981; Anaya 1976; Montejano 1999; Weber 1973). Without taking a step Mexicans residing north of the Rio Grande found themselves living in a different country. Similarly, the seeds for the making of the mainland Puerto Rican community were planted in 1898 when the island of Puerto Rico became a U.S. possession in the aftermath of the Spanish American War (Silén 1989).

By the beginning of the twentieth century, relations with Latin America would no longer be dominated by U.S. territorial expansionist impulses. They gave way to a new set of dynamics and policy objectives. The well-known history of U.S. economic and cultural hegemony in the region—including countless direct and indirect military interventions in Latin American affairs—is at the heart of events during this era. It is beyond the scope of this introduction to examine systematically this phase in U.S. relations with Latin America. It has been extensively treated in the scholarly literature within the frameworks of Marxist theory, dependency theory, and world systems theory (see, for example, LaFeber 1984; Cardoso and Faletto 1979; Wallerstein 2000).

But there is no question that various U.S. militacy interventions in Latin America and the Caribbean during the twentieth century have substantially contributed to the making of the Latino population of the United States. Likewise, U.S. economic and cultural hegemony have contributed to uprooting Latinos from the Caribbean and Latin American contexts and to their resettlement in the United States.

In the aftermath of World War II, the Cold War came to drive U.S. intervention in Latin America. Whereas in the earlier era, hemispheric relations were shaped by a U.S. ideology of racism and cultural superiority, by the mid-twentieth century a relentless—at times fanatical—anticommunism dominated U.S. policy toward Latin America. Harvard political scientist Jorge Domínguez (1998, p. 33) has argued that the Cold War emerged

as significantly distinctive in U.S. relations with Latin America because ideological considerations acquired a primacy over U.S. policy in the region that they had lacked at earlier moments. From the late 1940s until about 1960, ideology was just one of the important factors in the design of U.S. policy towards Latin America. The victory and consolidation of the Cuban revolutionary government changed that. In its subsequent conduct of the key aspects of its policy towards Latin America, the U.S. government often behaved as if it were under the spell of ideological demons.

Chasing its demons led the United States to intensify overt and covert military interventions in the Caribbean and in Central and South America from the 1950s until the dismantling of the Berlin Wall in 1989. Cold War tensions in the Latin American context took the form of various insurgency and counterinsurgency campaigns stretching south of the U.S. border all the way to Patagonia. They left sequelae of death, displacements, and devastation. In Central America alone, there were some 100,000 politically motivated killings in Guatemala and 75,000 in El Salvador, much of the killing taking place in the 1980s.

United States involvement in these conflicts intensified them, swelling the ranks of new refugees and immigrants. A decade after U.S. intervention, one million asylum seekers, refugees, and immigrants from that area of the world had fled Central America and now make the United States their home (Suárez-Orozco 1989). (This situation can be compared to the effects of the earlier U.S. involvement in Vietnam.[11]) The intensification of the Soviet-American conflict during the Cold War also contributed to the development of a robust Cuban diaspora to the United States numbering over one million people. Likewise, earlier (1960s) interventions in the Dominican Republic and elsewhere fed migration to the United States. That is why many Latinos of Guatemalan, Salvadoran, Nicaraguan, and other origin can tell their American friends, "We are here because you were there."[12]

The end of the Soviet Union—and with it, the Cold War—ushered in a new set of priorities in U.S. relations with Latin America, except for Cuba. U.S. military interventions would no longer be driven by fear of communism and competition with the Soviet Union. New security concerns emerged: drugs, undocumented immigration, and after September 11, 2001—terrorism, and economic restructuring (Bulmer-Thomas and Dunkerley 1999). The 1990s saw a remilitarization of U.S. policy in Latin America (Domínguez 1999). The new focus was drugs, with extraordinary increases in U.S. military involvement in Colombia by the year 2000. The militarized antinarcotics effort is likely to deepen the upheaval in Colombia, where over two million citizens have been displaced from their homes—more than the war in Kosovo displaced (Krauss 2000). It is safe to predict that the size of the Colombian diaspora to the United States will grow exponentially as U.S. policy intensifies the conflict in their native land.

Ongoing concerns about undocumented immigration from Latin America and the Caribbean led to a slightly different militarized front pertinent to U.S.–Latin American relations. The 1990s saw an unprecedented security buildup at the southern sector of the U.S. international border—now the most heavily guarded border in the world (Chavez 2001; Andreas 2000). It is designed to deter drug trafficking and, especially, undocumented immigration from Latin America. A related effort was the 1994 U.S. military intervention in Haiti, theoretically executed to stabilize the country but actually the first U.S. military intervention ever undertaken to contain undocumented immigration—specifically, the growing number of Haitian rafters arriving on the shores of Florida in the early 1990s.

The end of the Cold War, along with the development of new information and communication technologies, intensified the U.S.-led globalization that had been taking place over the course of the century (Sen 2000). It is now clear that globalization made U.S. hegemony more overwhelming than ever (Suárez-Orozco 2001). Indeed, some French intellectuals now call the United States the world's only "hyperpower." How will this new hyperpower affect Latin America?

In Latin America, globalization, economic liberalization, and restructuring have directly contributed to deepening inequality and the intensification of migratory flows. New regional trade agreements have also contributed to this process. The recent Mexican experience with the North American Free Trade Agreement (NAFTA) is a case in point. The theory behind NAFTA was that the liberalization and restructuring of the Mexican economy—along with massive foreign investments taking advantage of raw materials and cheap labor—would generate economic growth, creating new jobs in export manufacturing and increasing wages. It was assumed that the growth generated by these economic restructuring and liberalization strategies would reduce the pressures for Mexicans to migrate to the United States in search of better jobs at better wages. In practice, the liberalization of the Mexican economy has so far produced mixed results. Growth has been uneven, with some regions of Mexico and some sectors of the economy benefiting much more than others. There has also been a rapid growth in inequality (Dussel 2000).

The recent Mexican experience also suggests that an increase in wages may paradoxically increase rather than decrease migratory pressures. As John Coatsworth (1998, 76) has noted, "Over the course of the twentieth century, the proportion of the Mexican population earning enough to cover [migratory] expenses [has] increased substantially. Should Mexican wages begin to rise again in the coming years, rates of undocumented migration to the United States will probably increase . . . as more people manage to save what they need to immigrate." This is in part because an increase in wages "stimulates consumerism and consumption and raises expectations regarding the standard of living . . . [which,] combined with easy access to information and migration networks, in turn create tremendous pressure for emigration" (Zhou and Gatewood 2000, 10). In short, there is reason to suspect that globalization will continue to be closely associated with large-scale immigration flows.[13]

Globalization is now the dominant vector structuring U.S. relations with Latin America. It is a postideological, market-driven process of economic and regional integration and interdependence. It is at the core of the "complex and interlocking forms of interdependence emerging between the United States and Latin America, involving the movement of capital, modes of industrialization, trade, migration, and growing inequality" (Bonilla et al. 1998, p. x). This new phase represents a continuation of the asymmetrical relationship between the most powerful country in the world and its poor neighbors to the south. But in contrast to the previous two phases, Latinos today are emerging as significant actors in contemporary U.S. relations with Latin America. It will be an important item in the scholarly program of the next generation of scholars of U.S.-Latin American relations to examine how, if at all, the Latino factor mediates the new U.S.-Latin American agenda.

Racialization

Much of the scholarly work on minorities in the United States has centered either on the concept of ethnicity or, conversely, on the concept of race. The theoretical work on ethnicity has focused largely on the study of white European immigrants and the transgenerational process of change as their children became "white ethnic" Americans (Doucette-Gates, Brooks-Gunn, and Chase-Lansdale 1998). A parallel current of theoretical work has examined the experiences of African Americans in the United States within the paradigm of race, exploring their unique experiences with the legacy of slavery, segregation, and "the one drop rule."[14] These two independent scholarly projects proceeded along parallel lines without much systematic and meaningful cross-fertilization. As Nathan Glazer astutely observed (1993), the vast majority of scholarly work on immigration and the making of white ethnics failed to consider the preexisting racial polarization so central to any understanding of American social structure. The new immigration, a human wave dominated by Latinos and other immigrants of color, is finally bringing the two conceptual paths together (Waters 1999). Will the experiences of Latinos best be captured by the paradigm of ethnicity or by the paradigm of race? Will they follow the pattern of yesterday's white European ethnics or will the process of racialization lead to a remaking of the color line? The jury is still out.

We can envision several different long-term scenarios for Latinos. One scenario is that Latinos simply replicate the European immigrant experience and, over the course of a few generations, become, en masse, a version of yesterday's "white ethnics."

Another scenario would have the racially heterogeneous Latinos follow different paths as a function of skin color, human and "social capital." In this scenario, lighter-skinned Latinos who are able to settle in integrated neighborhoods maximize their opportunities for status mobility and, over the course of two or three generations, "disappear," becoming *de facto,* if not *de coeur,* sociologically white (that is, like whites in terms of major demographic and social indicators). In the census of 2000, roughly half of all Latinos self-identified as "white" (U.S. Census Bureau 2001a, p. 10). Conversely, poorer and darker skinned Latinos, who settle in highly segregated neighborhoods culturally dominated by African Americans tend, over the generations, to disappear in the other direction, joining the black side of the U.S. "color line."

In yet a third scenario, Latinos, by the sheer force of their numbers, finally break the black-white binary mold. Unlike previous waves of (European) immigrants, Latinos prove able, in the long term, to maintain certain vital cultural sensibilities and social practices via the replenishment generated by ongoing immigration, proximity to Latin America, and new communication and information technologies. In this scenario, Latinos manage to create a sociocultural space of their own. New Latino immigrants may be able en masse to articulate new strategies of adaptation beyond the tired old model of straight-line or unilineal assimilation driven by the "either/or" logic of acculturation (Suárez-Orozco 2000). As Falicov (this volume) perceptively argues, Latinos are pursuing and performing "both/and" identity styles and cultural adaptations. In the process they are redefining double consciousness, interacting with the institutions of the mainstream culture, and with their coethnic cultures in the United States, and acting transnationally by maintaining linguistic, social, economic, political, and cultural links with their relatives and other compatriots in Latin America and the Caribbean.

No one can say which of these tentative scenarios will prove most accurate in the long term, but three themes in the racialization process Latinos now face are likely to shape their future. These are (1) long-held stereotypes that mainstream Americans have of Latin Americans, (2) the low levels of education and skill of many Latin Americans as they join a thoroughly globalized U.S. economy, and (3) the intense forms of segregation—in schools, in neighborhoods, and in the workplace—that Latinos are experiencing. What are the dominant contours of these concurrent processes?

Negative Stereotypes.   In his exquisite history of U.S. policy toward Latin America, Lars Schoultz has argued that U.S. political elites have long held the "pervasive belief that Latin Americans are an inferior branch of the human species" and, furthermore, that the "belief in Latin American inferiority is the essential core of United States policy towards Latin America."

Here is a sampling of quotations through which Schoultz traces the way the United States related to Latin America for over two centuries. From John Quincy Adams: "The people of South America are the most ignorant, the most bigoted, the most superstitious of all Roman Catholics" (quoted in Schoultz 1998, p. 5). From Senator John Clarke: "To incorporate such a disjointed and degraded mass into even limited participation with our social and political rights, would be fatally destructive to the institutions of our country. There is a moral pestilence attached to such a people which is contagious—a leprosy that will destroy" (quoted in Schoultz 1998, p. 14). From Joel Poinsett, the first U.S. proconsul to Latin America—the man who brought the poinsettia to the United States from Latin America: "[Mexicans are] an ignorant and immoral race...[in] constant intercourse with aborigines, who were and still are degraded to the very lowest class of human beings" (quoted in Schoultz 1998, p. 19). From President Teddy Roosevelt: "[Colombians are] contemptible little creatures...jackrabbits...foolish and homicidal corruptionists.... [T]o the worst characteristics of 17th Century Spain, and of Spain at its worst under Phillip II, Colombia has added a squalid savagery of its own, and it has combined with exquisite nicety the worst forms of despotism and anarchy, of violence, and of fatuous weakness, of dismal ignorance, cruelty, treachery, greed, and utter vanity" (quoted in Schoultz 1998, p. 164). From Assistant Secretary of State Huntington Wilson: "Nature, in its rough method of uplift gives sick nations strong neighbors" (quoted in Schoultz 1998, p. 205). From Secretary of State John Foster Dulles: "You have to pat them a little bit and make them think you are fond of them" (quoted in Schoultz 1998, p. 332).

Schoultz's data suggest that U.S. opinion makers and leaders have been remarkably consistent in their views on Latin Americans from colonial times up to the present. In this ideological structure, Latin Americans are depicted as racially and culturally inferior, ignorant, degraded, filthy, childlike, and essentially unable to govern themselves.

It is not surprising, then, that in U.S. public opinion polls, Latinos rank among the least favored of all new Americans (Cornelius, this volume). Princeton University sociologists Thomas Espenshade and Maryann Belanger (1998, pp. 370–371) examined data on American public opinion about immigration basing their conclusions on surveys by twenty different organizations over a thirty-year period. They found that

Latin American and Caribbean immigrants in general, and Mexican immigrants in particular, rank somewhere near the bottom in terms of how Americans view immigrants from different parts of the world. European immigrants are most favored, and Asians fall in the middle. In comparison with Latin American immigrants, Asian immigrants are perceived as less likely to use welfare or to commit crimes, and more likely to work hard, to have strong family values, and to do well in school.

Wayne Cornelius (this volume) advances an "ethno-cultural" hypothesis to account for the specifically anti-Latino sentiment found in public opinion surveys and other data. According to Cornelius, the anti-Latino sentiment cannot be explained by the usual economic factors. Theorists of the anti-immigrant sentiment have argued that the best predictor of its intensity is the state of the macroeconomy—most specifically, the unemployment rate (Espenshade and Belanger 1998, p. 367). When the economy is weak and unemployment is high, public opinion generally turns against immigration. According to Cornelius's hypothesis, there is an "ethno-cultural objection to the most recent wave of Latino immigration that underlies persistent U.S. public concern about immigration levels, regardless of the state of the macroeconomy" (Cornelius, this volume). Cornelius focuses his analysis on American objections to Latino ethnicity, language, and culture—along with their growing numbers—as an explanation for the persistence of such "ambivalent reception."

The pervasive view, found among policy leaders as well as the general public, that Latin Americans in general are inferior and specifically are more likely to "commit crimes and take advantage of welfare, and less likely to work hard, do well in school, and have strong family values" (Jones-Correa 1998, p. 407) powerfully shapes the Latino experience in ways that we are only recently beginning to understand (C. Suárez-Orozco 2000, pp. 194–226). Most at risk are Latino youths who struggle to develop a healthy identity and sense of self in the context of such toxic attitudes and beliefs, an obstacle that further complicates the already arduous task of adapting to the institutions of American society.

Poverty. Over the past century, Latinos have been leaving a continent rich in culture, natural resources, and beauty but poor in terms of economic and social development (see Table I.3). It is also a continent of startling inequalities. Social and economic indicators reveal the breadth of the "distribution of sadness" south of the Río Grande (Vélez-Ibáñez 1996). For example, in 1995 the GNP per capita was $2,521 for Mexico, $1,671 for El Salvador, $1,438 for the Dominican Republic, and $379 for Nicaragua, compared to $27,550 for the United States (see Table I.3, Wilkie, Alemán, and Ortega 2000). It has been estimated that the "average U.S. cat eats more beef than the average person in Central America" (Barry and Preusch 1986, p. 142). In 1995, life expectancy was 67.8 years for males and 73.9 years for females in Mexico, 50.7 years for males and 63.9 years for females in El Salvador, and 67.6 years for males and 71.7 years for females in the Dominican Republic, compared to 72.2 years for males and 78.8 years for females in the United States (Wilkie, Alemán, and Ortega 2000). Over 60 percent of the Guatemalan population, over half of the Nicaraguan population, 40 percent of the Dominican population, and over

TABLE 1.3. Selected Demographic Characteristics
for Latin American Countries,* 1995

	Population (millions)	GNP per capita	Life Expectancy Male/ Female	Highest Level Attained Postsecondary (% of total population)	No Schooling† (% of total population)	Illiteracy (% of total population)
Mexico	83.226	2,521	67.8 / 73.9	6.5	21.4	10.4
Dominican Republic	7.110	1,438	67.6 / 71.7	1.9	40.1	17.9
Cuba	10.628	2,068	72.9 / 76.8	5.9	3.7	4.3
El Salvador	5.110	1,671	50.7 / 63.9	5.3	38.5	28.5
Colombia	34.970	2,107	66.4 / 72.3	10.3	11.8	8.7
Peru	21.569	2,363	62.7 / 66.6	18.2	23.4	11.3
Guatemala	8.749	1,337	55.1 / 59.4	1.2	61.6	44.4
Ecuador	10.264	1,476	67.3 / 72.5	11.1	1.8	9.9
Nicaragua	3.827	379	64.8 / 67.7	—	53.9	34.3
Honduras	4.879	672	65.4 / 70.1	3.3	33.5	27.3
United States	249.907	27,550	72.2 / 78.8	44.6	0.6	—

*The selected countries correspond to the top ten countries in number of immigrants coming to the United States. The countries are listed in descending order. That is, the highest number of Latin American immigrants who entered the United States in 1999 were from Mexico.

†Data for "No Schooling" correspond to different years: Mexico, 1990; Dominican Republic, 1970; Cuba, 1981; El Salvador, 1992; Colombia, 1993; Peru, 1993; Guatemala, 1981; Ecuador, 1990; Nicaragua, 1971; Honduras, 1983.

20 percent of the Mexican population have had no schooling, compared to 0.6 percent of the U.S. population (Wilkie, Alemán, and Ortega 2000). Increasing inequalities, coupled with the extraordinary burden of meeting foreign debt payments, have meant that "most of Latin America was still staggering" at the beginning of the new century (Skidmore and Smith 1992)

As a consequence, new Latino arrivals tend to be poorly educated and little skilled. A comparison of the average years of schooling for the top three immigrant groups reveals significant differences. In 1990 the average Mexican immigrant to the United States had 7.6 years of schooling, the average Filipino had 12.3 years of schooling, and the average Chinese had 12.8 years of schooling (Statistical Yearbook of the Immigration and Naturalization Service 1997, pp. 27–28). By the year 2000, inequalities had intensified: only 11.2 percent of the U.S. population of Latin American origin had a bachelor's degree or higher, compared to 44.9 percent of the

TABLE I.4. Selected Characteristics of
Hispanic and Non-Hispanic Population

	Hispanic	Non-Hispanic	Non-Hispanic Whites
Total Population (millions)	35.3*	240.1	193.1
Median Age (years)	26.1	36.1	37.5
Educational Attainment			
Less than high school	43.9%	13.8%	12.3%
High school or more	56.1%	86.2%	87.7%
Bachelor's degree or more	10.9%	26.7%	27.7%
Percentage in Labor Force			
Male	78.4%	73.3%	74.3%
Female	55.8%	60.7%	60.3%
Percentage of unemployed	6.7%	4.3%	3.6%
Median earnings: 1998			
Male	$18,430	$30,468	$31,486
Female	$12,910 ·	$18,510	$18,987
Household Income: 1998 (median income in dollars)	$28,330	$40,251	$42,439
Type of Family			
Married couple	68.0%	77.5%	82.2%
Female-headed	23.7%	17.2%	13.0%
Male-headed	8.2%	5.3%	4.8%
Families below the Poverty Line: 1998	22.7%	8.6%	6.1%
Children below the Poverty Line: 1998	34.4%	32.4%	10.6%

SOURCE: U.S. Census Bureau, Current Population Survey, March 1999.
*U.S. Census Bureau, Current Population Survey, May 2001.

U.S. population of Asian origin. Because all U.S. workers other than those with college degrees have been losing ground in terms of real wages, Latinos today earn substantially lower salaries than other Americans.

As noted in Table I.4, Latino males on average earn $18,430, compared with an average of $31,486 for non-Hispanic whites. More worrisome is the prevalence of poverty in the Latino population. Despite the high percentage of labor force participation, 22.7 percent of Latino families live below the poverty line. For non-Hispanic whites, the corresponding number is 6.1 percent. In addition, some 34.4 percent of all Latino children now live below the poverty line, compared to 10.6 percent of non-Hispanic whites. Deep and concentrated poverty is powerfully implicated in a variety of long-term educational, social, and health outcomes (Massey and Denton 1993).

Latinos, we must again emphasize, are not a monolith (see Table I.5). Significant differences exist in these broad demographic characteristics and social conditions. In terms of education and socioeconomic standing, Cubans tend to have an advantage over all other groups. Stepick and Stepick (this volume) eloquently examine the social origins of the Cuban advantage. They document how the unprecedented investment of federal, state, and local resources by a U.S. government bent on rewarding the foes of a communist regime enabled Cubans in exile to develop an extraordinarily powerful economic, social, and political base. Partly as a result of the largest investment ever made by the U.S. government in a refugee group, Cubans today are the best educated and wealthiest of all Latinos. For example, whereas 50.3 percent of all Mexican Americans have less than a high school education, only 29.7 percent of Cuban Americans have not completed high school. Nearly one in four Cuban Americans has a bachelor's degree or more, whereas only 7.1 percent of Mexicans have comparable educational credentials. Whereas nearly 25 percent of all Mexican families live below the poverty line, the corresponding number for Cubans is 11 percent. Note that Puerto Ricans have the highest rate of poverty of any Latino group; fully 43.5 percent of Puerto Rican children live below the poverty line. It is worth noting that Mexicans have one of the highest labor force participations of all groups. They nevertheless face difficult odds as they try to penetrate the better-rewarded sectors of the U.S. economy.

Over the last twenty years, Latino immigrants have been entering a country that is economically unlike the country that absorbed—however ambivalently—previous waves of European immigration. Economically, the previous large wave of immigrants arrived on the eve of the great industrial expansion, in which immigrant workers and consumers played a significant role (Higham 1975). European immigrants got into an elevator that was going up fast: a U.S. economy that was in the process of raising the standard of living for all workers. By contrast, recent immigrants are actors in a thoroughly globalized and rapidly changing economy that is increasingly taking an "hourglass" shape. The elevator now has two destinations: "up" to the top of the hourglass and "down" to its bottom. Well-educated, highly skilled immigrants are moving into well-remunerated, knowledge-intensive industries at a heretofore unprecedented rate (Waldinger and Bozorg-mehr 1996). Nearly 40 percent of all new businesses in California's famed Silicon Valley are owned by immigrants. On the other hand, low-skilled immigrants, many of them Latinos, are finding themselves sinking into the

TABLE 1.5. Selected Characteristics of Hispanics by Type of Origin

	Hispanic	Mexican	Puerto Rican	Cuban	South/ Central American	Other Hispanic
Total Population (millions)	35.3*	20.7	3.0	1.4	4.5	2.1
Median Age (years)	26.1	24.2	27.5	41.3	29.9	28.3
Educational Attainment						
Less than high school	43.9%	50.3%	36.1%	29.7%	36.0%	28.9%
High school or more	56.1%	49.7%	63.9%	70.3%	64.0%	71.1%
Bachelor's or more	10.9%	7.1%	11.1%	24.8%	18.0%	15.0%
Percentage in Labor Force						
Male	78.4%	80.4%	66.3%	73.4%	80.8%	72.3%
Female	55.8%	55.2%	52.6%	49.2%	61.8%	57.1%
Percentage of Unemployed	6.7%	7.0%	7.3%	4.9%	5.9%	6.4%
Median Earnings: 1998						
Male	$18,430	$17,395	$22,711	$22,864	$18,961	$21,146
Female	$12,910	$11,995	$16,444	$20,673	$13,309	$14,832
Household Income: 1998 (median income in dollars)	$28,330	$27,361	$26,365	$32,375	$31,636	$30,463
Type of Family						
Married couple	68.0%	69.9%	56.7%	79.2%	66.6%	61.7%
Female-headed	23.7%	21.3%	37.2%	17.0%	23.7%	30.6%
Male-headed	8.2%	8.7%	6.1%	3.7%	9.7%	7.8%
Families below the Poverty Line: 1998	22.7%	24.4%	26.7%	11.0%	18.5%	18.2%
Children below the Poverty Line: 1998	34.4%	35.4%	43.5%	16.4%	26.6%	31.6%

SOURCE: U.S. Census Bureau, Current Population Survey, March 1999.
*U.S. Census Bureau, Current Population Survey, May 2001.

low-wage sector. And some scholars have argued that, unlike the low-skilled industry jobs of yesterday, the jobs now typically available to large numbers of low-skilled Latino immigrants offer little prospect of upward mobility (Portes 1996).

Segregation. Another important feature of the Latino experience is the increasingly segregated concentration of large numbers of Latinos in a handful of states in large urban areas polarized by racial tensions. By the year 2000, half of all Latinos lived in two states, California (11 million) and Texas (6.6 million) (see Table I.2). Over 70 percent of all Mexican Americans reside in three states (California, Texas, and Illinois). A number of distinguished sociologists have argued that as a result of an increasing segmentation of the economy and of society, many low-skilled Latino immigrants "have become more, not less, likely to live and work in environments that have grown increasingly segregated from whites" (Waldinger and Bozorgmehr 1996, p. 20). Quite alarming are the recent findings of the Harvard Civil Rights Project, which established that Latino children are now facing the most intense segregation (by race and poverty) of any ethnic and racial group in the United States: "American schools continue the pattern of increasing racial segregation for black and Latino students. . . . Latino segregation by both measures has grown steadily throughout the past 28 years, surpassing the black level in predominantly non-white schools by 1980 and slightly exceeding the proportion in intensely segregated schools (90–100% minority) in the 1990s. . . . [S]chool segregation statistics show that the next generation of Latinos are experiencing significantly less contact with non-Latino whites; 45% of Latinos were in majority white schools in 1968 but only 25% in 1996" (Orfield and Yun 1999, p. 14). Indeed, by 1999 over 35 percent of all Latino students were enrolled in schools where 90 to 100 percent of their peers were other minority students.

School segregation is strongly linked to inequalities in schooling opportunities, processes, and outcomes. Forced to attend inferior schools, living in deep poverty and in heavily segregated neighborhoods, many Latino children struggle educationally against the odds (Moll and Ruiz, this volume). Most worrisome is the unacceptable rate of school dropout. In 1998, 29.9 percent of Latino youths dropped out of high school, compared to 7.7 of white, non-Latino youths and 13.8 percent of African American youths (U.S. Department of Education 2000). The future looms even more troubling, as schools throughout the country are instituting achievement tests as a prerequisite for graduation. Recent data suggest that large numbers of Latino youngsters are failing these tests. For example, in 1999 over one-third of all Latino students failed the Massachusetts Comprehensive Assessment System (MCAS). Of course, whether or not achievement tests are administered, Latino youngsters who are leaving school without the skills demanded by an increasingly unforgiving global economy face dim prospects on the job front.

Latinos, we claim, are the offspring of these three broad sociohistorical processes: large-scale immigration, U.S.-Latin American relations, and racialization. These momentous social and historical vectors have shaped the experiences of Latinos in the United States. Although each Latino subgroup—indeed, each Latino individual—is unique, the lives, struggles, dreams, and deeds of Latinos in the United States can be fully understood only in reference to these formations and their enduring legacies.

ABOUT THE BOOK

The origin of this book was a three-day conference under the auspices of the David Rockefeller Center for Latin American Studies and the Harvard Graduate School of Education. With the generous support of the Spencer Foundation, the Hewlett Foundation, the David Rockefeller Center for Latin American Studies, the Harvard Graduate School of Education, and the Office of the Provost at Harvard University, more than fifty scholars from around the country convened at Harvard to examine the state of research in the emerging field of Latinos in the United States. The Harvard conference identified and named the major themes in the scholarly study of Latinos in the United States. It also established general parameters for charting an agenda for new basic research on Latino studies. All of the authors included in this volume presented original, heretofore unpublished materials.

This volume is unique. First, unlike previous publications, the chapters in the present volume were all commissioned to follow rather strict thematic guidelines. Two broad questions were at the heart of the original invitation: What do we know, and what do we need to know, about the Latino population in the United States? After identifying the topics most urgently in need of scholarly attention, we invited the leading scholars in the relevant fields (health, education, political science, and so on) to write original papers. For example, the scholars in the field of health were invited to reflect upon the complex scholarship on (1) the epidemiological paradox (Latino immigrants tend to be healthier than their nonimmigrant counterparts), (2) Latino access to health care, and (3) the problem of health and disease as a function of time and immigrant generation in the United States.

Second, the majority of the scholars involved in this project are themselves Latinos. Latino scholars have emerged as leading researchers in the field. The authors were invited because of the quality of their scholarship, the uniqueness of their perspective, and their passion and energy in pursuing important research topics in this field of inquiry. The extraordinary success of the Harvard conference and the comprehensive scope of this volume are evidence of the growing role of Latino intellectuals in identifying, naming, and shaping this emerging domain of scholarly, political, and community work. Lest we be misunderstood, we reject the claim that only Latinos can or should study Latino issues. A number of the extraordinary pieces included in this volume were not written by Latinos. The notion that only Latinos can or should study Latinos is based on an anachronistic perspective on ethnicity that lacks scholarly currency and moral authority. It also suggests a reductionistic project for scholarship that is certain to undermine more ambitious interdisciplinary conversations and broader theoretical efforts. We echo Jorge Domínguez's warning (this volume) that the Latino population of the United States is too important to leave to Latino scholars alone.

Third, the chapters included in this volume grew out of a scholarly process involving many intra- and interdisciplinary conversations. The original papers were circulated ahead of time and presented in different panels addressing broad areas of inquiry (immigration, language, education, and the like). The Harvard conference was designed to allow authors to make brief presentations of their papers, with substantial time then devoted to commentary by various senior Harvard scholars, responses by the authors, and discussions among panelists. Harvard doctoral students from various faculties and schools were responsible for taking copious notes during the emerging discussions. On the basis of these discussions, we provided detailed and extensive editorial suggestions for each author revising the original paper for inclusion in this volume. We would like to think that all chapters benefited from this lengthy process. The chapters that follow offer a sampling of some of the most influential research in this emerging scholarly domain. The authors present original data and identify new theoretical and emperical problems suggesting areas in need of further scholarly work. Taken together the chapters can also be read as a plea for much-needed collaborative and interdisciplinary work. It is our intention and hope that the book will help broaden understanding—not only among scholars and policy makers—but also in the general audience about the profound demographic and cultural changes taking place in their communities.

NOTES

1. Throughout the book, the various authors represented here use terms: Latino, Latinos, Latina, Latinas, Latin@, Latin@s, Latina/o, and Latino/as. We, the editors, have encouraged the authors to use the term or terms of their choice.

2. Nor do these projections take into account the increasingly fertile field of transethnicity: Latinos, very much like other immigrants before them, are marrying

out of their various groups of national origin in large numbers. According to some estimates, nearly 30 percent of all married people of Mexican origin are married to non-Mexicans (Jiménez, 2000 ["Immigration, Assimilation and the Mexican Origin Population." Filed Statement, Department of Sociology, Harvard University]).

3. See, for example, Alvarez 1987; Ambert and Alvarez 1992; Camarillo 1979; Chavez 1991; Cruz 1998; Flores 1993, 2000; Gomez-Quiñones 1990; Grasmuck and Pessar 1991; Guarnizo 1994; Gutierrez 1995; Levitt 1997; Mahler 1995a, 1995b; Massey and Liang 1989; Nieto 1995, 2000; Pachón and DeSipio 1994; Pérez y González, 2000; Pessar 1995; Portes and Bach 1985; Portes and Stepick 1993; Rodríguez 1995; Rodríguez and Sánchez Korrol 1996; Romo 1983; Sánchez 1993; San Miguel 1987; Suárez-Orozco 1998; Suárez-Orozco 1989; Suárez-Orozco and Suárez-Orozco 1995; Torres-Saillant and Hernández 1998; Velez-Ibáñez 1996.

4. Indeed, the defining ritual at Ellis Island was the mythical renaming ceremony wherein immigration officers—sometimes carelessly and sometimes purposefully—renamed new arrivals with more Anglicized names—a cultural baptism of sorts. Others chose to change their names because of racism or anti-Semitism or simply to blend in. Hence, Israel Ehrenberg was reborn as Ashley Montague, Meyer Schkolnick was reborn as Robert Merton, and Issur Danielovitch Demsky was reborn as Kirk Douglas (Friedman 1999).

5. An outcome of our culture of multiculturalism is that new immigrants must be socialized into preexisting racial and ethnic categories, becoming, for example, "Latino" or "Asian." Over the course of basic research among immigrant Latino youths, we have witnessed the disorientation they feel when they discover that their regional or national identities have little relevance in the U.S. context (Suárez-Orozco and Suárez-Orozco 2001). A boy from El Salvador, will, depending on where he settles down, soon discover that what matters now is that he is a Latino, not that he is a Central American or Salvadoran—because the category *Salvadoran* will be irrelevant to most of his teachers, peers, and neighbors. These categories, although they are quite powerful, seem to have little resonance with new immigrants as they enter the country. Over time, however, they become increasingly relevant, particularly for children as they begin to struggle with identity formation, especially during the period of adolescence.

6. Peggy Levitt (this volume) also explores how in recent years the Catholic Church has strategically used a non-nation-specific approach, instead embracing a panethnic "Latino" construct to attract new immigrants from the Dominican Republic and elsewhere into the fold.

7. After all, Puerto Rico is a dollar economy.

8. Recent Latino immigrants are, of course, more likely to be Spanish speakers than more established Latinos. Over time and across generations, Latinos tend to become English-language-dominant. Furthermore, those who trace their origins back several generations in the United States may have little or no knowledge of the Spanish language.

9. In 1980, more than 129,000 Cuban *Marielitos* arrived in Florida over the course of a few weeks.

10. Cornelius (1998), however, argues that over time, Mexican immigrants in the United States are less likely to invest in capital improvements in their sending

communities. In fact, he argues that a new feature of the Mexican experience in the United States is that as Mexican immigrants become increasingly rooted in the United States, they go back to their communities mainly for rest and relaxation.

11. The fact that there are over one million Southeast Asians in the United States today can be directly traced to U.S. intervention in this region.

12. North African youth in France and elsewhere in Europe often respond to xenophobic assaults and identity threats with the saying "We are here because you were there."

13. Zhou and Gatewood (2000, p. 10) point out that: "globalization perpetuates emigration from developing countries in two significant ways. First, direct U.S. capital investments into developing countries transform the economic and occupational structures in these countries by disproportionately targeting production for export and taking advantage of raw material and cheap labor. Such twisted development, characterized by the robust growth of low skilled jobs in export manufacturing, draws a large number of rural, and particularly female workers, into the urban labor markets. Increased rural-urban migration, in turn, causes underemployment and displacement of the urban workforce, creating an enormous pool of potential emigrants. Second, economic development following the American model in many developing countries stimulates consumerism and consumption and raises expectations regarding the standard of living. The widening gap between consumption expectations and the available standards of living within the structural constraints of the developing countries, combined with easy access to information and migration networks, in turn create[s] tremendous pressure for emigration. Consequently, U.S. foreign capital investments in developing countries have resulted in the paradox of rapid economic growth and high emigration from these countries to the United States."

14. Here we must point to a disciplinary bifurcation in the use of the term race. Sociologists and psychologists have continued to use the term, but anthropologists are more skeptical and view race as a folk construct that, although powerful in its social and cultural implications, is devoid of any scientific (biological or cultural) foundation.

REFERENCES

Acuña, R. (1981). *Occupied America: A history of Chicanos.* 2nd ed. New York: Harper & Row.

Alvarez, R. M. (1987). *Familia: Migration and adaptation in Baja and Alta, California, 1800–1975.* Berkeley: University of California Press.

Ambert, A. N., and Alvarez, M. D., eds. (1992). *Puerto Rican children in the mainland: Interdisciplinary perspectives.* New York: Garland Publishers.

Anaya, R. (1976). *Heart of Aztlan.* Berkeley: Editiorial Justa Publications.

Andreas, P. (2000). *Border games: Policing the U.S.–Mexico divide.* Ithaca: Cornell University Press.

Barry, T., and D. Preusch. (1986). *The Central American fact book.* New York: Grove.

Basch, L., N. G. Schiller, and C. S. Blanc (1995). *Nations unbound: Transnational projects, postcolonial predicaments and deterritorialized nation-states.* Switzerland: Gordon and Breach Science Publishers.

Binational Study on Migration. (1997). *Binational study: Migration between Mexico and the United States.* Washington, DC: U.S. Commission on Immigration Reform.

Bonilla, F. (1989). La circulación migratoria de la década actual. *Centro de Estudios Avanzados Bulletin,* 2(3): 55–59.

Bonilla, F., E. Meléndex, R. Morales, and M. Torres, eds. (1998). *Borderless borders: U.S. Latinos, Latin Americans and the paradox of interdependence.* Philadelphia: Temple University Press.

Bulmer-Thomas, V., and J. Dunkerley, eds. (1999). *The United States and Latin America: The new agenda.* Cambridge: Harvard University Press.

Camarrillo, A. (1979). *Chicanos in a changing society: From Mexican pueblos to American barrios in Santa Barbara and Southern California, 1848–1930.* Cambridge, MA: Harvard University Press.

Cardoso, F. H., and E. Faletto, (1979). *Dependency and development in Latin America.* Berkeley: University of California Press.

Chávez, J. R. (1984). *The lost land: The Chicano image of the Southwest.* Albuquerque: University of New Mexico Press.

Chavez, L. (1991). *Out of the barrio: Toward a new politics of Hispanic assimilation.* New York: Basic Books.

Chavez, L. R. (1992). *Shadowed lives: Undocumented immigrants in American society.* Fort Worth: Harcourt Brace.

Chavez, L. R. (2001). *Covering immigration: Popular images and the politics of the nation.* Berkeley: University of California Press.

Coatsworth, J. H. (1998). Commentary. In *Crossings: Mexican immigration in interdisciplinary perspectives,* M. Suárez-Orozco, ed. Cambridge, MA: Harvard University Press.

Cornelius, W. A. (1998). The structural embeddedness of demand for Mexican immigrant labor. In *Crossings: Mexican immigration in interdisciplinary perspectives,* M. Suárez-Orozco, ed. Cambridge, MA: Harvard University Press.

Cruz, J. F. (1998). *Identity and power: Puerto Rican politics and the challenge of ethnicity.* Philadelphia: Temple University Press.

Darder, A., R. D. Torres, and H. Gutiérrez, eds. (1997). *Latinos and education: A critical reader.* New York: Routledge.

Delgado, R., and J. Stefancic, eds. (1998). *The Latino/a condition: A critical reader.* New York: New York University Press.

De Vos, G. (1992). *Social cohesion and alienation: Minorities in the United States and Japan.* Boulder: Westview Press.

Domínguez, J. I. (1999). U.S.–Latin America relations during the Cold War and its aftermath. In *The United States and Latin America: The new agenda,* V. Bulmer-Thomas and J. Dunkerley, eds. Cambridge, MA: Harvard University Press.

Doucette-Gates, A., J. Brooks-Gunn, and L. P. Chase-Lansdale (1998). The role of bias and equivalence in the study of race, class, and ethinicity. In *Studying minority adolescents: Conceptual, methodological, and theoretical issues,* V. McLoyd and L. Steinberg, eds. Mahwah, NJ: L. Erlbaum, 211–236.

Durand, J. (1998). Migration and integration. In *Crossings: Mexican immigration in interdisciplinary perspectives,* M. Suárez-Orozco, ed. Cambridge, MA: Harvard University Press.

Dussel, P. E. (2000). *Polarizing Mexico: The impact of liberalization strategy.* New York: Lynne Rienner Publishers.

Edmonston, B., and J. S. Passel, (1994). *Immigration and ethnicity: The integration of America's newest arrivals.* Washington, DC: The Urban Institute Press.

Espenshade, T. J., and M. Belanger, (1998). Immigration and public opinion. In *Crossings: Mexican immigration in interdisciplinary perspectives*, M. Suárez-Orozco, ed. Cambridge, MA: Harvard University Press.

Flores, J. (1993). *Divided borders: Essays on Puerto Rican identity.* Houston: Arte Público Press.

Flores, J. (2000). *From bomba to hip-hop: Puerto Rican culture and Latino identity.* New York: Columbia University Press.

Friedman, L. (1999). *Identity's architect: A biography of Erik H. Erikson.* New York: Scribner.

Glazer, N. (1993). Is assimilation dead? *Annals of the American Academy of Social and Political Sciences* 530: 122–136.

Glazer, N. (1997). *We are all multiculturalists now.* Cambrige, MA: Harvard University Press.

Gómez-Quiñonez, J. (1990). *Chicano politics: Reality and promise, 1940–1990.* Albuquerque: University of New Mexico Press.

González Baker, S., F. D. Bean, A. E. Latapi, and S. Weintraub (1998). U.S. immigration policies and trends: The growing importance of migration from Mexico. In *Crossings: Mexican immigration in interdisciplinary perspectives.* M. Suárez-Orozco, ed. Cambridge, MA: Harvard University Press.

Grasmuck, S., and P. R. Pessar, (1991). *Between two islands: Dominican international migration.* Berkeley: University of California Press.

Guarnizo, L. (1994). Los Dominicanyork: The making of a binational society. *Annals of the American Academy of Social and Political Science*, 533:70–86.

Gutiérrez, D. (1995). *Walls and mirrors: Mexican Americans, Mexican immigrants, and the politics of ethnicity.* Berkeley: University of California Press.

Higham, J. (1975). *Send these to me: Jews and other immigrants in urban America.* New York: Atheneum.

Hing, B. O. (1993). *The making and remaking of Asian America through immigration policy, 1850–1990.* Stanford: Stanford University Press.

Jiménez, P. (2000). *Immigration, assimilation, and the Mexican origin population.* Field statement, Department of Sociology, Harvard University.

Jones-Correa, M. (1998). Commentary on immigration and public opinion. In *Crossings: Mexican immigration in interdisciplinary perspectives.* M. Suárez-Orozco, ed. Cambridge, MA: Harvard University Press.

Kao, G. (1999). Psychological well-being and educational achievement among immigrant youth. In *Children of immigrants: Health, adjustment, and public assistance*, D. J. Hernández, ed. Washington, DC: National Academy Press.

Krauss, J. (2000). War in Colombia creates a nation of victims. *New York Times*, 31 August.

LaFeber, W. (1984). *Inevitable revolutions: The United States in Central America.* New York: Norton.

Levitt, P. (1997). Transnationalizing civil and political change: The case of transnational organizational ties between Boston and the Dominican Republic. Ph.D. diss., Massachusetts Institute of Technology.

Lieberson, S., G. Dalto, and M. E. Johnston. (1975). The course of mother tongue diversity in nations. *American Journal of Sociology* 81:34–61.

Mahler, S. (1995a). *American dreaming: Immigrant life on the margins.* Princeton: Princeton University Press.

Mahler, S. (1995b). *Salvadorans in suburbia: Symbiosis and conflict.* Boston: Allyn & Bacon.

Massey, D., and N. Denton, (1993). *American apartheid.* Cambridge, MA: Harvard University Press.

Massey, D. S., and Z. Liang (1989). The long-term consequences of a temporary worker program: The U.S. bracero experience. *Population Research and Policy Review* 8:199–226.

McWilliams, C. (1968). *North from Mexico: The Spanish-speaking people of the United States.* New York: Greenwood Press.

Montejano, D., ed. (1999). *Chicano politics and society in the late twentieth century.* Austin: University of Texas Press.

New York Times. (2000). Hispanic and Asian populations expand. August 30.

Nieto, S. (1995). A history of the education of Puerto Rican students in the U.S. mainland schools: "Losers," "Outsiders," or "Leaders"? In *Handbook of research on multicultural education,* J. A. Banks and C. A. McGee, eds. New York: Macmillan, 388–411.

Nieto, S., ed. (2000). *Puerto Rican children in U.S. schools.* Mahwah, NJ: Lawrence Erlbaum Associates.

Orfield, G., and J. T. Yun (1999). *Resegregation in American schools.* Cambridge, MA: The Civil Rights Project, Harvard University.

Pachón, H. C., and L. DeSipio (1994). *New Americans by choice: Political perspectives of Latino immigrants.* Boulder: Westview Press.

Pérez y González, M. E. (2000). *Puerto Ricans in the United States.* Westport, CT: Greenwood Press.

Pessar, R. R. (1995). *A visa for a dream: Dominicans in the U.S.* Boston: Allyn & Bacon.

Portes, A. (1996). *The new second generation.* New York: Russell Sage Foundation.

Portes, A., and R. L. Bach (1985). *The Latin journey: Cuban and Mexican immigrants in the United States.* Berkeley: University of California Press.

Portes, A., and R. G. Rumbaut (1990). *Immigrant America: A portrait.* Berkeley: University of California Press.

Portes, A., and A. Stepick (1993). *City on the edge: The transformation of Miami.* Berkeley: University of California Press.

Rodríguez, C. E. (1995). *Puerto Ricans born in the U.S.A.* Boulder: Westview Press.

Rodríguez, C. E., and V. Sánchez Korrol, eds. (1996). *Historical perspectives on Puerto Rican survival in the United States.* Princeton: Markus Wiener Publishers.

Romo, R. (1983). *East Los Angeles: History of a barrio.* Austin: University of Texas Press.

Sanchez, G. (1993). *Becoming Mexican American: Ethnicity, culture, and identity in Chicano Los Angeles, 1900–1945.* New York: Oxford University Press.

Sánchez, L. R. (1994). *La guagua aérea.* San Juan, PR: Editorial Cultural.

San Miguel, G. (1987). *"Let all of them take heed": Mexican Americans and the campaign for educational equality in Texas, 1910–1981.* Austin: University of Texas Press.

Schoultz, L. (1998). *Beneath the United States.* Cambridge, MA: Harvard University Press.

Sen, A. (2000). Commencement speech at Harvard University.

Silén, J. A. (1989). *Historia de la nación puertorriqueña*. Río Piedras, PR: Editorial Edil.

Skidmore, T. E., and P. H. Smith (1989). *Modern Latin America*. New York: Oxford University Press.

Smith, M. P., and L. E. Guarnizo, eds. (1998). *Transnationalism from below*. New Brunswick: Transaction Publishers.

Smith, P. H. (1996). *Talons of the eagle: Dynamics of U.S.–Latin American relations*. New York: Oxford University Press.

Statistical Yearbook. Immigration and Naturalization Service (1997). Washington, D.C.: U.S. Department of Justice.

Suárez-Orozco, M. (1989). *Central American refugees and U.S. high schools: A psychosocial study of motivation and achievement*. Stanford: Stanford University Press.

Suárez-Orozco, M., ed. (1998). *Crossings: Mexican immigration in interdisciplinary perspectives*. Cambridge, MA: Harvard University Press.

Suárez-Orozco, M. (1999). Latin American immigration to the United States. In *The United States and Latin America: The new agenda*, V. Bulmer-Thomas and J. Dunkerley, eds. Cambridge, MA: Harvard University Press.

Suárez-Orozco, M. (2000). Everything you ever wanted to know about assimilation but were afraid to ask. *Daedalus Journal of the American Academy of Arts and Sciences*. 129(4): 1–30.

Suárez-Orozco, M. (2001) Globalization, immigration, and education: The research agenda. *Harvard Educational Review*. 71(3): 345–365.

Suárez-Orozco, M., and A. C. G. Robben, (2000). Interdisciplinary perspectives on violence and trauma. In *Cultures under siege: Collective violence and trauma in interdisciplinary perspectives*, A. C. G. Robben and M. Suárez-Orozco, eds. Cambridge: Cambridge University Press.

Suárez-Orozco, C., and M. Suárez-Orozco (1995). *Transformations: Migration, family life, and achievement motivation among Latino adolescents*. Palo Alto: Stanford University Press.

Suárez-Orozco, C., and M. Suárez-Orozco (2001). *Children of immigration*. Cambridge: Harvard University Press.

Torre, C. A., H. Vecchini, and W. Burgos (1994). *The commuter nation: Perspectives on Puerto Rican migration*. Río Piedras, PR: Editorial de La Universidad de Puerto Rico.

Torres-Saillant, S., and R. Hernández (1998). *The Dominican Americans*. Westport, CT: Greenwood Press.

U.S. Census Bureau (2001a). *Overview of race and hispanic origin*. Washington, DC: Internet release date, March 2001.

U.S. Census Bureau (2001b). *The Hispanic Population*. Washington, DC: Internet release date, May 2001.

U.S. Census Bureau, Current Population Survey (March 1999). *Ethnic and Hispanic Statistics Branch, Population Division*. Washington, DC: Internet release date, March 8, 2000.

U.S. Department of Education. National Center for Education Statistics (2000). *Digest of education statistics, 1999*. NCES 2000–01, by Thomas D. Snyder. Washington, DC: Government Printing Office.

Vélez-Ibáñez, C. G. (1996). *Border visions: Mexican cultures of the Southwest United States*. Phoenix: University of Arizona Press.

Waldinger, R., and M. Bozorgmehr (1996). *Ethnic Los Angeles*. New York: Russell Sage Foundation.

Wallerstein, I. (2000). Globalization on the age of transition? A long-term view of the trajectory of the world-system. *International Sociology* 15(2): 249–265.

Washington Post (2000) South America's exodus. November 29.

Waters, M. (1999). *Black identities: West Indian dreams and American realities*. Cambridge, MA: Harvard University Press.

Weber, D.J., ed. (1973). *Foreigners in their native land: Historical roots of the Mexican Americans*. Albuquerque: University of New Mexico Press.

Wilkie, J. W., E. Alemán, and José G. Ortega, eds. (2000). *Statistical abstract of Latin America* (36). Los Angeles: UCLA Latin American Center Publications.

Zhou, M., and J. V. Gatewood, eds. (2000). *Contemporary Asian American: A miltidisciplinary reader*. New York: New York University Press.

PART ONE

Histories, Migrations, and Communities

The first section of the book examines Latino histories and migrations, as well as the making and remaking of Latino communities. The first three chapters place contemporary Latino predicaments in the context of broad sociocultural and political processes that have unfolded over the course of several centuries. Historian George Sanchez examines the nature of the historical forces behind Latino racialization, focusing on contemporary racial discourse, *mestizaje,* and racial blending as they are related to the Mexican American experience. The eminent cultural theorist, Juan Flores, discusses the processes that shaped the experiences and sensibilities of the Caribbean Latino diaspora via a creative interpretation of popular music and literary traditions. He examines the diverse modalities and adaptations of Cuban, Puerto Rican, and Dominican immigrants and refugees who settled in large numbers on the east coast of the United States over the last century. He reflects on the promise and elusiveness of solidarity among Caribbean Latinos—a promise that is often subverted by internal tensions revolving around race and color, class, and other cultural factors that have worked to destabilize the emergence of a pan-Caribbean Latino solidarity. Anthropologists Alex Stepick and Carol Dutton Stepick describe the extraordinary journey of Miami Cubans, the so-called "golden exiles," in a dynamic, cultural, and historical perspective. They examine the political, economic, and social processes that have transformed Miami from a sleepy retirement community to a vibrant, multinational Latino metropolis known throughout the world as Latin America's capital.

The next three chapters focus on the making of Latino communities. Urban anthropologist Diego Vigil explores the nature of the development of the largest Latino community in the United States—Los Angeles, a county that today has more than four million Latinos. Vigil examines the historical, ecological, and socioeconomic factors that have structured the growth of Mexican Los Angeles. He identifies various processes of racialization and multiple marginalities that have endured over the past century and that continue to shape forms of community life. He pays special attention to the continuing dynamics that have given rise historically, just as today, to street gangs among Mexican and, more recently, Central American youths.

Sociologist Robert C. Smith examines new Latino community dynamics currently unfolding in New York City, one of the recent U.S. destinations for immigrants from Mexico. Smith broadens the theoretical field by privileging gender as a key factor in his analysis of the school and work outcomes in the second-generation Mexican American community. He finds, perhaps not surprisingly, that girls tend to do much better than boys in their schooling and thus to have better prospects in the opportunity structure. His careful analysis of the psychological, social, and cultural processes that mediate these distinct outcomes represents an important advancement in our understanding of this increasingly obvious pattern: gender matters.

John Trumpbour and Elaine Bernard, directors of the Harvard Trade Union Program, present a broad overview of the role of unions in the Latino work experience. The Latino community, they argue, is on the cutting edge of labor activism in the new millennium. Their analysis explores how Latinos are profoundly transforming the American labor movement and how, in turn, it is shaping the nature of the Latino insertion into the American workforce.

Religion is another decisive force that shapes Latino experiences in the United States. Religion is emerging as a powerful vector of social cohesion in Latino communities. But beyond bringing Latinos together in the United States, it is also generating powerful new webs of contact and communication with the countries they left behind. Sociologist Peggy Levitt examines how Latino communities and their ongoing transnational relationships with Latin America are shaped by religion. Levitt analyzes the role of the Roman Catholic Church as a site for social and political incorporation into the United States and for continuing involvement with the countries of origin. She shows how Latinos are transforming the Roman Catholic Church and how it, in turn, is transforming the nature of their participation in American society and beyond.

Latinos are generating profound changes in the American setting by their sheer numbers, linguistic practices, and cultural affinities to the lands they left behind. The momentous changes brought about by the Latino-ization of the United States are disorienting to many established citizens and sometimes create fear and anxiety. Political scientist Wayne A. Cornelius examines the sources of public resistance to Latino immigration. He goes beyond the usual economic determinants of anti-immigrant sentiment and reflects on the ethnocultural factors that may shape the specifically anti-Latino public attitudes that are prevalent in California and other places where Latino communities are visibly transforming the local landscape.

Public anxieties about the new immigration have, in turn, led to a series of legislative initiatives. Sociologists Jacqueline Hagan and Nestor Rodríguez document the negative impact of the 1996 U.S. immigration reform law on Latino communities and families in the Texas border region and throughout Mexico and El Salvador. Their data suggest that Latino communities have been disproportionately affected by these new initiatives. They identify three areas of concern: (1) the negative effects of these initiatives on community solidarity, which result from increased INS policing and the militarization of border neighborhoods and communities; (2) the fragmentation and destabilization of Latino families as a result of large-scale deportations; and (3) the hardships generated by the new sponsorship requirements make it more difficult for low-income Latinos to legally sponsor family members to join them in the United States.

Chapter 1

"Y tú, ¿qué?" (Y2K)

Latino History in the New Millennium

George J. Sanchez

Recently I became involved in a series of fascinating conversations with students enrolled in a Mexican American history class I teach at the University of Southern California.[1] About eighteen of the twenty-one students enrolled were Latino, and the entire class was focused on the similarities and differences between the present-day status of Mexican immigrants and Mexican Americans in the United States and that of people of Mexican origin in the past. What captured our attention was the census form that all U.S. families had been asked to fill out and in particular, the questions regarding race and ethnic identity. All Americans were asked whether they had "Hispanic ancestry" and then, in a separate question, what their own racial background was. This second question allowed (for the first time) for multiple responses, but it did not include a category for Mexican or Latino as a race, even though separate "racial" categories were included for specific Asian countries, such as China, Japan, and the Philippines.

My Latino students and their families found these questions puzzling and inconsistent with their own sense of ethnic and racial identities. Unlike many Anglo Americans, who now take offense at having to answer any question regarding their racial background, my students were perplexed by the odd positing of a "Hispanic" category that was not considered racial and by the implication that people of Mexican origin fell comfortably into another racial category, or multiple categories, or the ubiquitous "other." One student, in particular, explained that all the members of her family had answered the racial question differently, depending on their own self-identities. Her father checked "white" under the racial question, whereas her mother checked both "white" and "Indian." She herself had checked the "other" category and filled in "Mexican" as her racial designation. Other students in the class reported similarly wide-ranging decisions among their family members about how to fill out the racial categorization.[2]

I raise the issue of the census form to highlight the way in which the Latino population's sense of self and its collective history are still far from having a definitive impact on the understanding of race, ethnicity, and nationhood in the United States. The same disjuncture that appears on the census form persists in studies of race and nation in U.S. history, my own field. Although the Harvard conference celebrated the demographic explosion of the Latino population of the United States, the intellectual transformation necessary to accord the Latino condition its rightful prominence in U.S. history is just beginning and will be the centerpiece, I believe, of the work of Latino historians in the twenty-first century. In this chapter, I will outline several critical areas of development in the field of Latino history that I see emerging in recent work, particularly work by younger scholars. In short, I use a different meaning for the abbreviation "Y2K." Rather than a pesky computer bug, I want to make it mean a call to Latino academicians to answer the query, "Y tú, ¿que?" with a resounding attempt to move Latinos to the center of our academic specialties and interdisciplinary discussions.

Let me begin by noting two general tensions that have marked the late-twentieth-century development of Latino history and that will continue to have a profound impact on the field in this twenty-first century. The first is the difference in outlook and direction among historians of Latinos in the United States, depending on whether their training was rooted in Latin American or U.S. history. Most Latinos who entered the historical profession in the 1960s trained in Latin American history, mainly because the study of U.S. history totally ignored the Latino presence in this nation's past.[3] It was only the hiring of Latino historians to teach in U.S. history programs, primarily in the western states, that made it possible to train in U.S. Latino history at UCLA, the University of Texas at Austin, and other institutions. This second wave of Latino historians in the 1970s and 1980s, led by individuals such as Albert Camarillo at Stanford University and Mario García at the University of California, Santa Barbara, institutionalized Latino history solidly within an American historical framework. It also fueled efforts to legitimate the study of the Latino past by vigorously pursuing archival collecting, building a cadre of Latino graduate communities in American history programs, and contributing to interinstitutional efforts such as the IUP, the Inter-University Program for Latino Research.[4]

The results of this change of emphasis have been both positive and negative. The scholars who emerged from the 1980s era of graduate historical training tended to place their work solidly within frameworks of U.S. history, particularly the reinvigorated subfields of the new Western history, urban history, labor history, women/gender history, and immigration history.[5] According to Alberto Camarillo, Mexican American history went from "a nascent, relatively unknown subfield of mainstream U.S. history" to a growing, respected body of scholarship, which "has served as the spring-board for studies that pose new, provocative questions and open new areas of inquiry."[6] On the other hand, as Yale historian Stephen Pitti has recently acknowledged, "graduate students in Chicano history today probably know less about Latin America than those that entered the field in the 1960s and early 1970s."[7] Although this situation is certainly a result of a strategic choice by many Chicano historians to get solid training in U.S. history, it is also a sad result of the bifurcation of most history Ph.D. programs, which have tended to train students in largely isolated regional contexts.

This development also highlights the uneven quality of progress in diversifying the historical profession with Latinos of various ethnic groups. Overwhelmingly, the group discussed above that was trained in the 1980s and 1990s has consisted of historians of the Mexican American experience in the United States. Puerto Rican and Cuban American historians, much fewer in overall numbers, continued to emerge primarily from programs that stressed Latin American and Caribbean history. Yet, in none of these subfields of U.S. or Latin American history did Latino historians come close to dominating the ranks of practitioners. For example, according to a study conducted by Rubén Rumbaut, historians of immigration to the United States continue to be almost entirely of European origin, unlike the more substantial percentages of Latino and Asian American immigration specialists working in sociology and political science.[8] Indeed, as the numbers of Central American and South American immigrants to the United States increased in the 1980s and 1990s, new scholars of these groups tended to enter social science fields in which they could investigate these recently formed communities; the field of history continued to seem quite distant from the experiences of these Latino newcomers.

This brief history of the uneven generations of Latino historians in terms of national origins leads to the second critical question that marks the development of the field in the late twentieth and early twenty-first centuries: Is there such a thing as Latino history? Clearly, the vast majority of monographs and essays that fall comfortably under the rubric of "Latino history" are, upon closer inspection, focused on one particular national group, be it Cuban American, Puerto Rican, Chicano, or another. Historical writings about Latinos have tended to concentrate on one particular geographic area at one particular time, and given the spatial concentration of national-origin groups within the nation, this has led to a body of work in which ethnic specificity still reigns supreme. Other fields in Latino studies, such as literature, have been much more able and willing to stretch across national boundaries and periods of time.[9] Several of the social sciences, especially sociology, have developed comparative approaches, which have allowed for greater pan-Latino efforts than history.[10] Even in areas where more than one Latino group lived in close proximity, such as Chicago, the tendency of historians has been to write about only one of those groups.[11]

Recently, however, younger scholars have begun to write dissertations or first books that take comparative historical approaches quite seriously. John Nieto-Phillips has broadened his historical work on ethnic identity formation of New Mexicans at the turn of the twentieth century by comparing the policies and postures of New Mexicans with the colonial discourse surrounding Puerto Rico after 1898.[12] His work illuminates the important role that colonialism played in decision making about language policy, citizenship, and race in both areas at a time when U.S. lawmakers determined the proper direction of acquired colonial possessions and their populations in a wider framework. Similarly, Adrian Burgos investigates the meaning of race and the color line in the world of professional baseball by looking at the lives of Latino ballplayers as they negotiated among the U.S. major leagues, the Negro leagues, and several venues in the Caribbean and Latin America.[13] Concentrating on the period before Jackie Robinson "broke the color line" in major league baseball, Burgos is able to show how Mexican, Puerto Rican, Venezuelan, Dominican, and other Latino ballplayers were engaged in fluid discourse on race in which their placement was not necessarily predetermined by their appearance but instead was socially constructed to meet the needs of teams and players alike.

Indeed, as a teaching practice, Latino history—as opposed to Mexican American history or Puerto Rican history—is taught only at a few schools in the Midwest and Northeast where both the student population and the intellectual climate justify that framework.[14] On these campuses, the dilemma is how to structure a course that can deal with the wide diversity of experiences that mark the various ethnic histories within the Latino population, while equipping students with enough grounding in each group to understand the larger narrative trajectory of Latino history. I was able to do this by concentrating on two characteristics that nearly all Latino groups in the United States share: having experienced a colonial relationship to the United States as a people and having come to the continental United States as an immigrant/migrant group. The colonial background is critical to an understanding of the incorporation of various Latino groups in the nineteenth and early twentieth centuries; the migrant experience becomes the basis for comparative understandings of all groups in the twentieth century up to the present.

By first focusing on the varied colonial relationships between Latino groups and the United States, one invariably focuses on the nineteenth century wars that brought Latin American countries into direct contact with the growing power of the United States. Beginning with the Monroe

Doctrine of 1820, the United States launched a foreign policy committed to eventually replacing European powers as the major colonial overloads among Latin American nations throughout the American continent. Through the Texas Rebellion of 1836, the Mexican American War of 1848–1850, and the Spanish American War of 1898, the United States positioned itself as the dominant power in the Western Hemisphere, both adding physically to the U.S. land base and developing neocolonial economic ties throughout the region. It was this colonial relationship that shaped the incorporation of the earliest groups of Latinos in the United States during the nineteenth century, installing U.S. governmental powers as direct overseers of Mexican, Cuban, and Puerto Rican populations, now incorporated to varying degrees into the American orbit.

The second experience of commonality between Latino groups is the largely twentieth-century experience of migration to the continental United States from the various nations of Latin America. Although stories of immigration to the United States often portray ambitious immigrants crossing the seas to take advantage of opportunities for advancement, the picture of migration from Latin America is complicated by ongoing neocolonial economic ties to the United States and the varying categories of immigrant status that mark different Latino groups in the twentieth century. The differences among the illegal and extralegal status of many Mexican immigrants to the American Southwest, the refugee status of Cuban migrants in the post-Castro period, and the citizenship status of Puerto Ricans in the continental United States must have far-reaching implications for the nature of these groups' entry and incorporation into U.S. society, but few studies have directly addressed this issue.[15] The overriding historical reality of the twentieth century for all Latino groups, however, is that communities in the United States have been profoundly enriched and transformed by migrants from Latin America.

A third critical area, which I believe needs to be explored to enhance our understanding of Latinos' place in U.S. society, is the complicated role of race and racial formation (see Suárez-Orozco and Páez, this volume). The racial identities and ascriptions of Latinos present an often confusing picture to most U.S. citizens because of the particular history of race in the United States, where a strict dichotomy between black and white governed law and politics. The racially mixed background of most Latinos in the United States, coupled with more fluid ascriptions of racial categories in Latin America, has left Latino understanding of race at odds with U.S. racial descriptions. Moreover, issues of race in the United States, and the contribution of Latino history to a new understanding of race, stand as a critical arena that can potentially bridge the division between Latin American and U.S. history, as well as serve as an important point of comparison between the histories of various Latino groups in the United States.

Because growth in the field of Latino history and recognition of the demographic realities of the twenty-first century have much to contribute to changing intellectual understandings of race in the United States, the remainder of this chapter is devoted to these issues of racial formation. In particular, it addresses the question of the 2000 U.S. census and the place of *mestizaje* in contemporary racial discourse in the United States.

During the 1990s, this nation prepared for its decennial census in a unique and important way. Various census officials, academic consultants, and racial advocacy organizations debated the efficacy of adding a mixed-race designation to the census form. This debate, although it settled on the solution of allowing Americans to check off more than one racial category, was as important for the various positions taken by the debate participants as for the final resolution. Two multiracial organizations—"Project R.A.C.E.," based in Atlanta and composed of interracial married couples who were worried about their children's designation, and the "Association of Multiethnic Americans," consisting of mixed-race adults—fought for two different census solutions. They were often in conflict with racial advocacy organizations, especially the NAACP and MALDEF, who worried that a "multiracial" category on the census form would dilute the demographic strength of the black and Latino populations, respectively. Most sociologists and demographers involved in this debate agreed that some change in the census form was needed to acknowledge the multiracial population, and they were critical in crafting the final solution.[16]

I am principally concerned not with the actual debate that took place around the census but, rather, with the symbolic value of the multiracial human body around which both popular and academic discussions often revolved. I will argue that the multiracial body has been appropriated for use as a symbol of multiethnic America, often representing the nation's hope for the future and its potential for overcoming racial strife. Rather than being a "monstrous" depiction—one has only to think back to literary depictions of the "tragic mulatto"—the multiracial body appeared in the 1990s as an angelic savior for our age. But investing that sort of utopian power in the genetic mixing of our era only serves to heighten a new form of racial essentialism and once again to frame the process of overcoming racial hierarchy as a fundamentally biological one. Moreover, although historians have been among its most avid proponents, this new fascination with multiracial bodies is ahistoric in being unable to look at the particular ways in which racialization occurs *despite* and *alongside* racial mixing.

Probably the most famous interracial image of the 1990s was a virtual person, the computer-generated woman who graced the cover of *Time*'s 1992 special issue on immigration.[17] Abandoning a tradition of magazine covers that had depicted immigration and race by showing a multitude of different faces, *Time* chose to combine the races into one face, a young adult woman of uncertain origins but with striking features and an olive skin tone. This image, rather than evoking concern over the nation's future, as many previous covers had, was supposed to comfort us as Americans. If this is what diversity brings—a multiracial beauty whose own body encompasses all the different strands of newcomers to America—we should embrace this future.

Rather than a virtual image, the male equivalent of this future for the 1990s has been golfing star Tiger Woods, born to African American and Thai parents. Woods broke into the golfing scene when corporations were looking for a new spokesperson for multiracial America. Thus Woods, in his famous Nike commercials, is used to represent the future and becomes almost a Pied Piper among children, encouraging the multiracial legions to join him in taking over one of this nation's whitest of sports. His image, of course, is generally used in this country to stress his black roots. In Asia, however, Nike uses Woods's image to promote golf among that region's middle class, and it is his Asian roots that are played up. The multiracial body, therefore, becomes an excellent vehicle for globalization—an image made to order for multinational corporate capital.[18]

The multiracial body has also become the favorite symbol of a host of liberal and neoliberal writers who call on Americans to move beyond race, ethnicity, and identity politics toward a "new American nation" where difference is minimized and cosmopolitanism and toleration loom large. From historian Gary Nash's call, in his 1995 presidential address to the Organization of American Historians, for a deliberate *mestizaje* to rein in the divisions of contemporary America to social commentator Michael Lind's argument in *The Next American Nation* that the rise of intermarriage will contribute to a new America based on multiraciality, committed liberals have increasingly offered answers to the supposed problems of living in an era of multiculturalism by advocating racial mixing to break down racial difference.[19]

All of these published works point to the increasing rate of interracial marriage since the striking down of antimiscegenation laws in the 1950s and 1960s—and the increase in the numbers of children born to these unions. "Sixty percent of the babies born in Hawaii in 1991 were of 'mixed' race," declares Lind, adding that nearly one of three Hispanics marries a non-Hispanic and that "half of all Asian-Americans born in the United States marry outside of their official racial 'nation.'"[20] Even the numbers of children born to a black and a white parent grew fivefold, to 51,000, from 1968 to 1988. Nash reports that 70 percent of American Indians marry people who are not Indian; that outside the South, 10 percent of all African American males marry nonblack women; and that black-white marriages overall have tripled since 1970. For Nash, this means that "Mestizo America is a happening thing. A multiracial baby boom is occurring in America today."[21]

Both authors point approvingly to the changes that have occurred over the last thirty years, but they also note that these changes are not altogether new. Nash reminds us that the very word *miscegenation* did not appear until the late nineteenth century and that most of the American colonies saw no reason to ban intermarriage with Native Americans. He chronicles a host of "racial boundary jumpers," from John Rolfe and Pocahontas to Sam Houston, who took a Cherokee wife, to fur traders throughout North America, including the fabled Kit Carson. For Nash, U.S. history is awash with folks who illustrate a racial "in-betweenness," including a long history of Indo-Africans such as Crispus Attucks; Spanish mixing with both Indians and Africans to produce individuals like the Spanish-African Pio Pico, the last Mexican governor of California; and the Punjabi-Hispanic couplings of the early twentieth century in agricultural California. According to Nash, "about three-quarters of African Americans today are multiracial, and perhaps one-third have some Indian ancestry. Virtually all Latino Americans are multiracial, so are nearly all Filipino Americans, so are a majority of American Indians, and millions of whites have multiracial roots."[22]

With all this historical intermingling, and with the recent upturn in interracial marriage, why is the present moment one in which the products of these unions can be vested with such power? Clearly, for these authors and others it is, as Nash puts it, "the specters of Sarajevo, Sri Lanka, and Somalia" that force us "to ask about the costs of the rigidifying of ethnoracial particularisms." For him, to transcend "America's Achilles' heel of race requires that we embrace hybridity—not only in physical race crossing but in our minds as a shared pride in and identity with hybridity."[23] For Michael Lind, these trends point to the conclusion that "conventional categories promise to become increasingly meaningless, as whites, Asians, and Hispanics intermarry in the Pacific-oriented America of tomorrow." Whereas Lind calls for racial amalgamation and "altogether eliminating race as a category from law and politics," Nash believes that "racial blending is undermining the master idea that race is an irreducible marker among diverse peoples."[24]

Having a background in Chicano history and a working knowledge of Latin American history, I, however, can only respond to these U.S. scholars, "Welcome to the Americas!" Racial mixing has never in itself destroyed racial privilege, as the place of Africans and natives throughout nearly all Latin American countries has proved. Moreover, new racial formations out of mixed-race people, such as the mestizos who make up the vast majority of Mexicans in this country and to the south, are ever-present possibilities that certainly change the meaning of race, but not necessarily the privilege of whiteness in our society. If recent work in Asian American, Latino, and Native American studies has shown us anything over the past thirty years, it is that racialization projects can encompass various strategies for assigning difference: outright exclusion, processes of making the native foreign, creating "noble savages" to emphasize the inevitability of (white) progress, the exoticism that creates desire. It has been primarily the white-black binary character of racialization (particularly that created within U.S. slavery with its formal taboo against white-black unions, all the while producing offspring of such illicit unions that would be recategorized as black) that has blinded U.S. scholars to the range of racialization projects that have captured the vivid imagination of Americans in different regions at different times.

Indeed, if recent work in American studies is considered, which encourages us to think of "the cultures of U.S. imperialism," these calls for "positive miscegenation" take on a new and troubling dimension. Many of the historical examples of racial blending occurred in the time of U.S. growth as a continental empire, incorporating Indians and Mexicans through conquest, both territorial and sexual. This is *not* to deny the human emotions involved in individual unions; rather, it is to place these unions in the historical context that enables us to understand their potential for societal transformation. In the twentieth century, many interracial unions were shaped by the U.S. military presence in Asia—from the Philippines, to the occupation of Japan and Korea, to Vietnam. Not only were these unions highly gendered, as in most imperial situations, but they also produced migrations to the United States that gave us the mixed-raced individuals to whom all these authors refer. Our era, at the turn of the twenty-first century, is producing mixed-race individuals in the context of globalization, particularly the hegemonic role played by U.S. military and economic interests, which will help produce international networks of capital and trade without necessarily benefiting those left behind in our inner cities, who, though they too are involved in racial mixing, are left both "darker" and poorer.

Scholars of the imperialism of other nations would not be surprised by an upturn in mixed-race individuals. The histories of Britain and France are full of narratives of new racial formations that have helped perpetuate empires, while at the same time leading to new migrations to the imperial centers, particularly after World War II. Demonstrating, as Nash does, that "human emotions—the attraction of people to each other regardless of race and religion and much else—has run ahead of ideology and has often caused identity confusion and anxiety" does not address the many ways in which desire is structured by our own historical moments.[25] As recent work on "orientalism" has shown us, desire—even when it enjoys state and ideological sanction—can produce as powerful an "othering" process as that which emphasizes separation and containment.[26]

There is more that is troubling to me in this recent fascination with mixed-race unions and individuals than their detachment from our current historical moment. Ironically, the emphasis on biological mixing reinscribes essentialist categories of difference. Indeed, for racial boundary crossings to matter at all, difference has to be consistently maintained so that the act of crossing bears significance to the society. The emphasis on the *unique* role of mixed-race people in challenging America's racial assumptions also makes me wary of returning to biological interpretations linking race and culture. Mixed-race individuals must not only confront our racial assumptions because they exist; they must also act on the basis of their biology. They must serve as bridges and symbols for the rest of us.

No stronger example of this troubling perspective exists than the epilogue to David Hollinger's important book *Postethnic America: Beyond Multiculturalism.* Hollinger emphasizes that the offspring of interracial unions are of critical importance to a society that can move beyond race and ethnicity. "Mixed-race people are a powerful symbol for an opportunity long said to distinguish American society from that of most societies in Europe and Asia: the making of new affiliations. . . . Mixed-race people are performing a historic role at the present moment: they are reanimating a traditional American emphasis on the freedom of individual affiliation, and they are confronting the American nation with its own continued reluctance to apply this principle to ethno-racial affiliations."[27] Because his book is a call to move away from affiliations based solely on descent and toward one based on consent (à la Werner Sollors), mixed-race people seem uniquely positioned to have choice in their racial affiliations. But Hollinger's argument also portrays mixed-race individuals as being biologically forced to choose. The reason why their choice is so "historic" is that their mixed gene pool forces them to make a decision about something that other Americans take for granted when they assume that their racial being is shaped by forces out of their control—their skin color and their parents' homogeneous culture.

Of course, the choice available to people of mixed race is also a burden as a consequence of America's racial hierarchy and emphasis on difference. In today's neoliberal, post-civil-rights world, this supposed choice is squandered if individuals do not recognize the duality of their racial position. If they choose solely a white racial position, they reinscribe white racial supremacy; if they choose solely a nonwhite racial position, they reinscribe an ethnic nationalism or a racialized condition that endorses a world where the races live apart. For the world envisioned by Hollinger, Nash, or Lind to exist, these individuals must choose a *dual* existence in which their very bodies serve as a bridge between races and cultures.[28] What a burden for these super-Americans to shoulder! What an abandonment of responsibility by those of us who appear to be bounded by one racial identity!

If this role is starting to sound a lot like a traditional role played by people of color, I think it is. DuBois's double consciousness was an acknowledgment that as long as racial hierarchy exists, as it has throughout the twentieth century he was foreshadowing, both a national and a racial identity would wreak havoc in the consciousness of African Americans. The "choice" of affiliation presented by Hollinger begins to look like the "choice" of African Americans: no choice at all. Others may be reminded of the classic collection of writings by radical women of color, *This Bridge Called My Back*, which in 1981 discussed the highly contested position of radical feminists, particularly lesbian feminists, in serving as bridges for whatever dialogues on race, gender, and sexual oppression arise in the feminist community. In that work, Gloria Anzaldúa spoke for a much more highly conflictual position than that described in the other works I have discussed so far. "I am a wind-swayed bridge, a crossroads inhabited by whirlwinds . . . this task—to be a bridge, to be a fucking crossroads for goddess' sake . . . the pull between what is and what should be . . . the mixture of bloods and affinities, rather than confusing or unbalancing me, has forced me to achieve a kind of equilibrium. Both cultures deny me a place in *their* universe. Between them and among others, I build my own universe, *El Mundo Zurdo*. I belong to myself and not to any one people."[29]

Anzaldúa herself is speaking from a position of multiple identities, but one fully engaged in specific communities of Chicanas, feminists, lesbians, and women of color. Moreover, she continually acknowledges the inner war that affects a *mestiza* conscious-ness, which sounds so different from the less complicated mestizo world described earlier by Gary Nash. Six years later Anzaldúa writes, "Cradled in one culture, sandwiched between two cultures, straddling all three cultures and their value systems, *la mestiza* undergoes a struggle of flesh, a struggle of borders, an inner war. Like all people, we perceive the version of reality that our culture communicates. Like others having or living in more than one culture, we get multiple, often opposing messages. The coming together of two self-consistent but habitually incompatible frames of reference causes *un choque*, a cultural collision."[30] Mestizo America, I would agree with Anzaldúa, is just as likely to produce cultural conflict as it is to generate individual liberation and collective equality. Whatever symbolic value continues to be placed on multiracial bodies, those bodies will continue to be sites of struggle—places where the visions of America's racial future are contested, both by the individuals who inhabit those bodies and society as a whole.

At one level, these two visions of "*mestiza* America" have a great deal in common. They both celebrate the crossing of racial boundaries and look forward to a time in which race does not determine social condition as much as it does today. But they also have fundamental disagreements that reflect conflicts over the very definitions of race and power in our contemporary and historical United States. One camp believes that the dismantling of racial categorization, in and of itself, will contribute mightily to a more equitable society; this is the vision of racial liberals and conservatives alike, one that links the neoliberals described here with those involved in the dismantling of affirmative action and ethnic studies programs in California. The other camp believes that white racial privilege must be attacked, because it continues to exploit racial difference and the distribution of political and economic power in our society. This attack usually emanates from specific communities whose disempowerment would only delay the elimination of racial privilege in society. Multiracial human bodies, for all their symbolic value in our contemporary world, cannot replace multiracial coalitions of individuals and organizations as the engines that are likely to transform American society. And it is *all* the boundaries that govern privilege in the United States—those shaped by race, class, gender, sexuality, and nation—that must be crossed to bring about a truly equitable society. My hope is that the field of Latino history will contribute mightily, in the next century, to that form of border crossing.

NOTES

1. The class was History 472, "The History of the Mexican American," at the University of Southern California, in spring semester 2000.

2. To understand the problems with categorizing the Mexican American population that plague the U.S. census, see José Hernández, Leo Estrada, and David Alvirez, "Census Data and the Problem of Conceptually Defining the Mexican American Population," *Social Science Quarterly* 53 (March 1973): 671–687.

3. This generation would include Juan Gómez-Quiñones, who was trained as a Latin American historian at UCLA; Rodolfo Acuña, whose first book was on the Mexican state of Sonora; and Ramón Eduardo Ruiz, whose distinguished career remained focused on Mexican history at the University of California, San Diego.

4. Albert Camarillo, *Chicanos in a Changing Society: From Mexican Pueblos to American Barrios in Santa Barbara and Southern California* (Cambridge, MA: Harvard University Press, 1979 and 1996) and Mario T. Garcia, *Desert Immigrants: The Mexicans of El Paso, 1880–1920* (New Haven, CT: Yale University Press, 1981).

5. This group includes Vicki Ruiz, Antonia Castañeda, David Gutiérrez, and George Sanchez, all trained at Stanford University under Alberto Camarillo in the late 1970s and 1980s; Deena González, trained at the University of California, Berkeley, in U.S. history; and Camille Guerin-González, trained at the University of California, Riverside. This was less the case among the group of Chicano labor and political historians trained under Juan Gómez-Quiñones at UCLA in the 1970s and 1980s—Devra Weber, Antonio Ríos-Bustamante, Luis Arroyo, Francisco Balderrama, and Emilio Zamora, who tended to straddle the borderland between U.S. and Mexican history more directly.

6. Alberto Camarillo, "Reflections on the Growth of Chicana/o History," in *Voices of a New Chicana/o History*, Refugio I. Rochin and Dennis N. Valdes, eds. (Lansing, MI: Michigan State University Press, 2000): 237.

7. Stephen J. Pitti, "Ernesto Galarza Remembered: A Reflection on Graduate Studies in Chicano History," in *Voices of a New Chicana/o History*, op. cit., 234.

8. Rubén G. Rumbaut, "Immigration Research in the United States: Social Origins and Future Orientations," in *Immigration Research for a New Century: Multidisciplinary Perspectives*, Nancy Foner, Rubén G. Rumbaut, and Steven J. Gold, eds. (New York: Russell Sage Foundation; 2000): 34.

9. See, for example, the essays in *José Martí's "Our America": From National to Hemispheric Cultural Studies*, Jeffrey Belnap and Raul Fernandez, eds. (Durham, NC: Duke University Press, 1998), and the work of Jose David Saldivar, especially *The Dialectics of Our America: Genealogy, Cultural Critique, and Literary History* (Durham, NC: Duke University Press, 1991) and *Border Matters: Remapping American Cultural Studies* (Berkeley: University of California Press, 1997).

10. One example is Alejandro Portes and Robert L. Bach, *Latin Journey: Cuban and Mexican Immigrants in the United States* (Berkeley: University of California Press, 1985).

11. Compare, for example, the work of sociologist Felix Padilla in *Latino Ethnic Consciousness: The Case of Mexican Americans and Puerto Ricans in Chicago* (Notre Dame, IN: University of Notre Dame Press, 1985) with the work by historian Gabriella Arrendondo, "'What! the Mexicans, Americans?'": Race and Ethnicity, Mexicans in Chicago, 1916–1939" (Ph.D. diss., University of Chicago, 1999) and earlier work by historians Louise Año Nuevo Kerr and Francisco Arturo Rosales, all of which concentrate exclusively on Mexican Americans.

12. See John Nieto-Phillips, "Citizenship and Empire: Race, Language, and Self-Government in New Mexico and Puerto Rico, 1898–1917," *Journal of the Center for Puerto Rican Studies* (Fall 1999): 5174.

13. See Adrian Burgos, Jr., "Playing America's Game: Latinos and the Performance and Policing of Race in North American Professional Baseball, 1868–1959" (Ph.D. diss., University of Michigan, 2000).

14. I, for example, taught Latino history at the University of Michigan, but since returning to California, I have taught a course labeled "History of the Mexican American" at the University of Southern California.

15. One study that does is Silvia Pedraza-Bailey's *Political and Economic Migrants in America: Cubans and Mexicans* (Austin: University of Texas Press, 1985).

16. See Juanita Tamayo Lott, *Asian Americans: From Racial Category to Multiple Identities* (Altamira Press, 1999): 99; and Charles Hirschman, Richard Alba, and Reynolds Farley, "The Meaning and Measurement of Race in the U.S. Census: Glimpses Into the Future," *Demography* 37:3 (August 2000): 381–393.

17. *Time*, Special issue on immigration (1992), cover page.

18. See Henry Yu, "How Tiger Woods Lost His Stripes: Post-Nationalist American Studies as a History of Race, Migration, and the Commodification of Culture," in *Post-Nationalist American Studies*, John Carlos Rowe, ed. (Berkeley: University of California Press, 2000): 223–246.

19. Gary B. Nash, "The Hidden History of Mestizo America," *The Journal of American History* 82:3 (December 1995): 941–962; Michael Lind, *The Next American Nation: The New Nationalism and the Fourth American Revolution* (New York: The Free Press, 1995).

20. Lind, see note 19: 294.

21. Nash, see note 19: 959.

22. Nash, see note 19: 941–943, 949.

23. Nash, see note 19: 961–962.

24. See note 19: Lind: 294, 295–96; Nash: 960.

25. Nash, see note 19: 959–960.

26. For the classic work on "orientalism," see Edward W. Said, *Orientalism* (New York: Pantheon Books, 1978).

27. David Hollinger, *Postethnic America: Beyond Multiculturalism* (New York: Basic Books, 1995): 166.

28. According to John Womack, in his "Latinos in the 21st Century" commentary at the Harvard Conference, the idea that mestizos would be natural leaders and the leading missionaries in society comes straight from 19th-century positivist and authoritarian notions. This theme surfaces in the work of José Vasconcelos, particularly *Raza Cósmica*, and resonates with anthropologists Franz Boas and Gilberto Friere.

29. Cherrie Moraga and Gloria Anzaldúa, eds., *This Bridge Called My Back: Writings by Radical Women of Color* (Watertown, MA: Persephone Press, 1981): 205–209.

30. Gloria Anzaldúa, *Borderlands: The New Mestiza/La Frontera* (San Francisco: Spinsters/Aunt Lute Press, 1987): 78.

Chapter 2

Islands and Enclaves

Caribbean Latinos in Historical Perspective

Juan Flores

La música de Borinquen, y la música cubana, y la quisqueyana,
[coro]: que sabe a ron, sabe a miel, sabe a caña
Que lindas son, que lindas son, las tres isletas hermanas,
por eso yo, por eso yo, las adoro con el alma
lo lei lo lei, [etc.]
Es el tabaco cubano el mejor del universo,
Y el café de Puerto Rico ni hablar mi hermano de eso
[coro, lei lo lei . . .]
De Cuba es el son guajiro, de Puerto Rico la danza,
de Quisqueya es el merengue que a todo el mundo le encanta
[coro, lei lo lei . . .]
Fue en Cuba José Martí quien luchó su libertad,
y Duarte fue por Quisqueya, y por Borinquen ¿quién será?
[coro . . .]
Son tres, son tres, las islas hermanas
Son tres, son tres, las islas hermanas
Que las quiero ver, las quiero ver, las tres soberanas
Son tres . . .
Que no me quiero morir sin ver la unión antillana
Son tres . . .

The music of Borinquen, and music from Cuba, and from Quisqueya,
[chorus] it tastes like rum, tastes like honey, tastes like sugar cane
How beautiful they are, how beautiful, the three little sister islands,
And that's why I, that's why I, adore them with all my heart
[chorus]
Cuban tobacco is the best in the whole universe,
And coffee from Puerto Rico, please, brother, let's not even talk about that
[chorus]
From Cuba the son guajiro, from Puerto Rico la danza,
and from Quisqueya the merengue that everyone loves
[chorus . . .]
In Cuba it was José Martí who fought for its freedom,
and Duarte was for Quisqueya, and for Borinquen, who will it be?
[chorus . . .]
And I do want, I want to see, the three of them sovereign,
I don't want to die without seeing the Antillean union.
DAVILITA, *"Son Tres Las Islas Hermanas"*

Davilita sings "las Antillas": "Son tres, las islas hermanas." The three islands—Cuba, Puerto Rico, and the Dominican Republic—are sisters, bound together in deep cultural and historical affinity. In his beautiful song of that title, the legendary Puerto Rican vocalist Pedro Ortíz Dávila ("Davilita") evokes the distinctive flavors and rhythms of his Spanish Caribbean, "el Caribe hispano," "las Antillas." He sings adoringly of their physical beauty, their seductive music, and their world-renowned cigars and coffee, all to the delicious "sabor" of rum, honey, and sugar cane, whose praise he sings in the lilting refrain. Davilita also voices great pride in the three countries' struggles for freedom and in national leaders of the stature of José Martí and Juan Pablo Duarte. But when he turns to the historical experiences of the island sisters, the seams in that sibling kinship begin to show, and the great singer's adoration gives way to uncertainty and to the forceful proclamation of an unfulfilled political ideal.

Davilita was a Caribbean Latino. With all the heartfelt love he expresses for the islands and although he was born in Puerto Rico, he spent nearly all of his adult life in El Barrio in New York—where he arrived at age fourteen in 1927—and did not return to Puerto Rico until the 1950s. Through the 1930s and 1940s, the formative decades in the history of New York's Latino community, he established himself and was widely recognized as the premier vocalist in Puerto Rican music. Shortly after his arrival, in 1929, he joined up with Rafael Hernández and was lead voice in Hernández's Trío Borinquén, renamed the Cuarteto Victoria, during the height of its immense international popularity. Davilita also sang, both in the chorus and as a lead singer, with the variously named groups of Pedro Flores for many years, and he was the first to record many of the compositions of both Rafael Hernández and Pedro Flores, who are among the foremost composers in twentieth-century Latin American music. His associations and achievements were boundless in the music of that period and included collaboration with musicians of the magnitude of Manuel Jiménez ("Canario"), Alberto Socorrás, Plácido Acevedo, Noro Morales, Pedro ("Piquito") Marcano (the composer of "Son Tres"), and, after his return to Puerto Rico, Felipe Rodríguez ("La Voz"). His first recording, in 1930, was Rafael Hernández's "Lamento Borincano," and thanks to the prodding of Canario, Davilita became the first to record that international anthem of the Latino migrant population, a composition that José Luis González considered the first protest song in the history of Latin American popular music. It was the voice of Davilita, a nineteen-year-old *boricua* from East 100th Street, that resounded from the record stores and tenement windows of El Barrio, and from many Latino working-class barrios, on the ominous eve of the Great Depression.[1]

Musically, "Son Tres" is a *canción*. Although it incorporates traces of Cuban *son montuno* and Puerto Rican *plena*, makes boastful mention of the

Dominican *merengue* ("que a todo el mundo le encanta") and has a fade-out chorus of traditional *lei-lo-lei*, Davilita and composer Marcano are careful to choose a more generic, hybrid song form like the *canción* so as to encompass all three Caribbean traditions without unduly emphasizing any one national style. After all, Davilita is intent on marveling at the symbiosis and cohesion of the three-part cultural family, and as long as he lingers on the delights they all offer—kindred tastes, smells, sights, and sounds—and on expressive traditions, he is able to sustain that confident sense of harmony. But when it comes to political history, the dissonance sets in, or, more precisely, the three sisters take divergent paths. For whereas Cuba and the Dominican Republic achieved national sovereignty and can claim as their founding leaders Martí and Duarte, Davilita must ask, suggestively, of his own *patria*, "y por Borinquén ¿quién será?" His Borinquén alone remained in direct colonial bondage, and thus, despite their deeper affinities, stood apart from the other sisters. Because the song dates from around mid-century, and because Davilita was known for his strong affiliation with the Puerto Rican nationalist cause, one could surmise that the question "¿quién será?" might well be posed in veiled reference to Pedro Albizu Campos, who was then languishing in a federal penitentiary while his fellow combatants carried on the intense militant struggle for national independence. Or perhaps it is a sarcastic allusion to Luis Muñoz Marín, the country's first elected governor, who in those years was compromising the very goals of sovereignty to which he had earlier dedicated himself.

But when Davilita contemplates the sorry political state of his homeland in the present, rather than sinking in defeat, he thinks of the future and of the past. The song ends with an emphatic pronouncement of the singer's own longing for the sovereignty of all three sister islands, and for the realization, in his own lifetime, of the historical ideal held since their national formation in the nineteenth century, "la unión antillana." That final phrase evokes the names of Martí, Hostos, Betances, Máximo Gómez, Sotero Figueroa, and countless other patriotic leaders, as well as that of the great Lola Rodríguez de Tío, who penned the lines on Spanish Antillean unity, "Cuba y Puerto Rico, de un pájaro las dos alas." In the same mellifluous tones, but with noticeably greater urgency, Davilita shows that his hope for the cultural unity of his native region extends to the broader field of political struggle and beyond the present to the region's rich and challenging historical legacy. In his warm embrace of the three sisters, he does not shy away from the obstacles they face or from the bifurcations in their political trajectories.

Of course, Davilita might have been more befuddled had he reflected on "las islas hermanas" at a time closer to our own, after the Cuban Revolution and the Trujillo nightmare in the Dominican Republic. His concern over the divergent historical destinies of his three related islands might have reached a crisis pitch had he pondered the three emigrant enclaves that had taken such divergent shapes in the United States at the century's end. As remote from each other as "las tres hermanas" now stand in the community of nations, the three "islands" of Caribbean Latino immigrants offer up radically different modalities of Latino presence in the new millennium. The familiar "sabor" is still there, of course, and Dominicans, Puerto Ricans, and Cubans still enjoy that distinctive bond at the sensual, performatory, and expressive levels, especially when their taste is contrasted with the stylistic sensibilities and traditions of that other major component of present-day Latino life, the Mexican American. And it is meaningful to nourish that family kinship, in the manner of Davilita, as the basis of deep cultural solidarity. As for their sociological placement and perspectives in contemporary U.S. society, however, the three Caribbean Latino enclaves may appear to be cousins, and distant ones at that, but hardly sisters. On the other hand, because Hispanic Caribbean politics are now being played out so actively in the public field of U.S. culture, it may well be that today, like a century ago, the diaspora setting will serve to catalyze a renewal of the ongoing ideal of "la unión antillana."

The media hype surrounding the current "Latino explosion" lends the booming Latino presence an air of novelty, as though these throngs of new Americans had just begun to land during the present generation. In the case of Caribbean Latinos in particular, this sense of recency is pervasive. The Cuban community dates from 1959, the Dominican from the mid-sixties at the earliest, and even the Puerto Rican enclave, though admittedly of older vintage, is often treated as a post–World War II phenomenon sparked by the industrialization of the island economy in the 1940s and 1950s. U.S. Antillanos, like Caribbeans and Latin Americans in general, are presented as a paradigmatic case of the "new immigration"—an influx of tribal peoples from the Third World issuing from the worldwide process of decolonization and the restructuring of global, regional, and local economies.[2]

The reach of Caribbean Latino history is, of course, much longer than that; it actually predates and then coincides with the waves of European immigration of the later nineteenth and early twentieth centuries. Bernardo Vega, certainly the most substantive source of information about that history, transports us as far back as the early nineteenth century. (A case could be made for extending the story to Alvar Núñez Cabeza de Vaca's expedition to *La Florida*, although it is hard to talk about the life of U.S. Latinos before there was a United States.) Bernardo Vega, with his tale of interlocked autobiography and political history, gives ample reason for dating the conditions for a Caribbean Latino presence in the United States to the 1820s, when complete independence of the continent from Spanish rule opened the door to U.S. regional hegemony as manifest in the Monroe Doctrine of 1823. By means of the recollections of his long-lost uncle Antonio Vega, who had been in New York since 1857 and whom Bernardo met up with a few years after his own arrival in 1916, the revolutionary *tabaquero* was able to reconstruct his own family's genealogy. His great-great-grandfather had fled into exile from Spain to take part in the lively smuggling trade that brought munitions and other aid to the independence wars raging in Venezuela and the other Latin American republics. Bernardo established his own subversive pedigree in this way, while at the same time placing the history of the Caribbean Latino diaspora in a broad and momentous political context. For indeed, rather than being the product of recent, late-twentieth-century changes in the economic and political map, people from the Spanish Caribbean began gravitating toward the northern cities as soon as the United States assumed its regional hegemonic role and became a counterpole to the stubbornly lingering Spanish empire.[3]

What Bernardo fails to mention, although it would certainly support his case more convincingly than the doses of "myth," as he calls them, that infuse his biographical version of events, is that in the 1820s, the documentary and literary presence of Caribbean Latinos in New York had already begun. In 1823, the twenty-year-old Cuban poet and patriot José María de Heredia arrived in Boston for several years of exile in the American Northeast, mostly in New York City. Fleeing the Spanish and colonial authorities because of his avid clamor for the independence of his beloved homeland, Heredia founded and edited a newspaper, continued to write prolifically, and published his first book of poems, *Poesías*, in New York in 1825. Most memorably, he had occasion to visit Niagara Falls, to which he paid emotional and philosophical homage in his long poem "Niágara," one of the canonical texts of Cuban literature. This poem can also be considered one of the founding works of Caribbean Latino literature in the United States. Although it contains little description of American society of the time, much less of any Cuban exile settlement, it is nevertheless of cardinal importance as an early reflection, written on North American soil, by a Caribbean on the metaphysical significance of the United States. In this way it anticipated the profound and prolific reflections of Martí, Hostos, and others later in the century.[4]

Although "Niágara" is something of a literary and historical chronicle, Heredia was not alone in his early exiled state, nor was he the only one to give literary expression to that condition. In fact, another of his poems, "Himno del desterrado," became an anthem among exiled Cuban writers of the period and served as the signature text in the first anthology of such writing, *Laúd del desterrado*, which was published in 1858. The poems of this collection, which was recently republished as part of the

Hispanic Literature Recovery project,[5] were written in the rather conventional romantic and neoclassical forms and meters then in favor, but at the same time they presented an entirely new perspective on a Spanish-language "New World" reality and thus paved the way for the later, powerfully ambivalent visions of Martí and Rubén Darío.

Another gap in Bernardo's fanciful tale of early Latino history is its omission of the towering figure of Félix Varela y Morales (1788–1853), the Catholic leader and early proponent of the Cuban national idea who spent nearly all of his life in the United States, including many years (1837–1853) as the Vicar General of the Catholic Archdiocese of New York. Another source describes Padre Varela as

> one of the most innovative and foresighted thinkers of Cuba. He was the first to propose the abolition of slavery and the complete independence of Cuba. He introduced reforms to the educational system of Cuba, and he was elected as one of the Cuban representatives to the Cortes of Spain. [In the United States] he built up a social health ministry, founding day-care centers for working mothers, orphanages, and schools for boys and girls. He ministered to the sick in hospitals and helped the underprivileged. A prolific author, publisher, and editor of journals and magazines in English, he became a civil rights advocate for Native Americans, as well as immigrant groups then entering New York, such as Italians, Poles, Hispanics, and especially, Irish. He defended the human and civil rights of Catholics and non-Catholics alike.[6]

To this impressive array of accomplishments, we might add that Félix Varela contributed to the beginnings of U.S. Latino literature with his novel *Jicoténcal*, which is based on the Spanish conquest of Mexico and has been referred to as "the first historical novel in the New World."[7]

As Padre Varela's example shows, New York shared the stage in this early period of Caribbean Latino history with Florida, where once again, as is also true in more recent times, "La Florida" took its distinctive place in the Latino imagery. Varela entered the United States through Florida, living his early years in historic St. Augustine, where he later died and where a monument to his memory was unveiled on the 200th anniversary of his birth, in 1988. It was in Florida—not so much Miami as Tampa, Key West, and Ybor City—that the drama of Caribbean Latino life took on discernible shape during the middle half of the nineteenth century, a process that has been well documented in the works of Gerald Poyo and Winston James.[8] James especially, in his book *Hold Aloft the Banner of Ethiopia*, illuminates the place of the tobacco industry in the formation of a Spanish and Cuban community and traces the racial and class divisions that unfolded in that context. In contrast to the sporadic and numerically insignificant numbers of *antillano* exiles of the preceding decades, the Florida enclaves were the earliest evidence of a relatively dynamic and numerous population.

Very little of this important prehistory finds its way into Bernardo Vega's account, which tends to leap over the midcentury period to the entrance of Hostos and Martí on the New York scene in the later decades of the century.

Bernardo acknowledges, of course, the selective functioning of his aging uncle's memory and comments on Tío Antonio's tendency to highlight and lend uncritical preference to Puerto Rican actors in the drama. Bernardo even justifies this *boricua*-centric bias by pointing to the subordinate role accorded to Puerto Ricans in international affairs. Although he admits that Antonio's nationalist tributes call for qualifications and "more careful criteria," in a memorable pronouncement he defends his uncle's remarks as a "valid response to the foolish idea that Puerto Rico exists in a historical vacuum. Without a doubt," he continues, "in order to stand on our own two feet Puerto Ricans of all generations must begin by affirming our own history. It is as if we are saying we have roots, therefore we are!"[9] But in spite off all Tío Antonio's emphasis on early Puerto Rican achievements, the nineteenth century is no doubt the Cuban century in Caribbean Latino presence in the United States, from the earliest signs and articulations of an exile location to the tumultuous activism and vocal community presence in New York, Philadelphia, and Florida that had evolved by the end of the century. As the principal Puerto Rican leaders and thinkers themselves recognized, the Cuban presence made up the bulk of the community in formation, and it was to the Cuban struggle that the Puerto Rican remained integrally tied. If in Lola Rodríguez de Tío's vision Puerto Rico and Cuba were "two wings of a bird," then that bird was admittedly lopsided. But in those heady times, the ideal of Antillean unity was at the peak of its popularity, and such contrasts and contentions along national lines were not of overriding concern. The metaphoric binational bird, however awkward, would surely find its equilibrium and soar to new heights of solidarity and sovereignty.

There is a wing missing, of course, from Lola's emblematic *antillano* mascot: the Dominican Republic, a reflection of the divergent historical experience throughout the entire period. Although some Dominicans played a noteworthy role in the struggle against Spain, and although Santo Domingo itself was a significant location of exile activity (one thinks, above all, of the immense significance of Hostos in Dominican intellectual history), no sizable Dominican presence can be established in U.S. settings, much less any evidence of a distinctive Dominican enclave. Much research remains to be done, but it appears that the same can be said of the Dominican exile and emigrant experience throughout most of the twentieth century. Important exceptions, such as members of the illustrious Henríquez Ureña family, have been identified, as have numerous individuals and *conjuntos* in the New York musical scene of the 1920s and 1930s.[10] Bernardo even mentions that a winner of the prestigious *Juegos Florales* literary prizes in 1919—according to him "the most outstanding event in the Spanish-speaking community in New York since the turn of the century"—was a Dominican author, the esteemed Manuel Florentino Cestero.[11] And although the Dominican part in the building of the Latino community would await the final decades of the century, it would be a mistake to discount the ongoing Dominican role in the conceptualization of a pan-*antillano* ideal. One need only recall the dramatic opening lines of Pedro Mir's masterwork *Contracanto a Walt Whitman*, written in the mid-twentieth century, to recognize the coconspiracy of Dominicans in opposition to U.S. domination over the region and its cultures. Mir begins his majestic "countersong" by asserting his own personal full-scale pan-Spanish Caribbean identity, a "yo" that he then goes on to counterpose to that of the formidable Whitman: "Yo," he begins,

> Yo
>> un hijo del Caribe
> precisamente antillano.
> Producto primitivo de una ingenua
> criatura borinqueña
>> y un obrero cubano,
> nacido justamente, y pobremente,
> en suelo quisqueyano.[12]

In the early years of the twentieth century, it was the Spaniards who figured most prominently in that community, along with the Cubans and Puerto Ricans. Whatever one thinks about the inclusion of Spanish immigrants and their descendants in the present-day "Latino" configuration, there can be no doubt as to their presence and importance in the Florida and New York Latino settlements prior to the first World War and even earlier. This was particularly the case in the decades just before and after the turn of the century, and it was most evident in the world of tobacco. Bernardo's entire account, from his first New York years through the Spanish Civil War of the 1930s, makes constant mention of Spanish comrades and cultural activity, and he even counted the Sephardic Spaniard Jacobo Silvestre Bresman as an influential intellectual and political mentor and one of his most faithful friends. The Spanish role in the anarchist and labor movements, including those in New York and Florida, is well known and has been cited by Bernardo himself, José Yglesias, and others.

What often goes unmentioned in accounts of Spanish immigrants in early Latino history, however, is the issue of class and racial differences in those multi-Latino interactions, where the seams of that panethnic enclave life showed through. Winston James tells of such conflicts, recounting how Spaniards and white Cubans played an increasingly dominant role in the ownership and managerial operations of the cigar trade in later-nineteenth-century Florida and how the class and black-white divide took an ever greater toll on the earlier unity among the Spanish-speaking *tabaqueros.* James documents the emergence of an Afro-Cuban consciousness among the black cigar workers, with the obvious implication that subsequent Caribbean Latino history needs to be studied, and told, with that crucial observation in mind.[13] In her book on Puerto Rican musicians in New York through the 1940s, *My Music Is My Flag,* Ruth Glasser offers further evidence of the racist dimension of Latino community formation, especially the role of Spanish cultural presence in that kind of discrimination. On the basis of extensive interviews, Glasser tells of the exclusionary policies of the Asturian, Valencian, and Gallician clubs and cultural centers, which often refused admittance to black Latinos. The Club Asturiano, for example, a benevolent society founded in 1923 "to serve Asturians, was later opened to include all Spanish speakers, as long as they were white."[14]

With the Depression and interwar years, the tobacco industry declined, and the Spanish role in the New York Latino community receded in both volume and significance. The Cuban and Puerto Rican components of the multi-Latino diaspora took central stage, which they held until recent decades. Although Cubans continued to prevail in Florida and in pockets in the Northeast, the Puerto Rican population finally surpassed all of the other groups, particularly after U.S. citizenship was given to Puerto Ricans in 1917. By 1930, in New York there were twice as many Puerto Ricans as Spaniards, Cubans, and Dominicans combined.[15] During those decades and throughout the 1950s, the latter two groups found themselves in similar positions as exiles from long-term dictatorial rule, a situation that was further complicated by the overt and covert exercise of U.S. imperial power, including direct military occupation. Puerto Ricans, meanwhile, empowered as U.S. citizens to travel to U.S. cities and encouraged to seek work there in response to unemployment resulting from the industrialization of the island, saw their numbers increase geometrically in the post–World War II years. This development brought their presence to nearly a million by the 1960s and made them the second largest Latino group in the country (after the Mexican Americans).

But prior to this divergence in their paths, marked emphatically by the Cuban Revolution of 1959, Puerto Ricans and Cubans during the 1920s, 1930s, and 1940s constituted the core of the Caribbean Latino community in the United States. General social and cultural interaction can be documented and is particularly conspicuous, for example, in popular music. Throughout those years, musicians of both nationalities proliferated, dominated all the major bands and orchestras, and shared musical repertoires and audiences. Styles were preponderantly Cuban, reflecting the far greater visibility of things Cuban in the mass culture. As a telling example, of the fifteen "Afro-Cubans" in Machito's unsurpassed orchestra of the 1940s, nine were Puerto Ricans. It was the Cuban image that stood for the tropical Spanish-speaking Caribbean in the many popular dances, particularly with the entry of Desi Arnaz into American living rooms during the 1950s. The Cuban American critic Gustavo Pérez-Firmat offers a sensitive analysis of this phenomenon in his book *Life on the Hyphen.*[16]

Even though the swelling Puerto Rican demographic presence was thus typically eclipsed by the Cubans' stylistic influence in the public sphere, the relationship between the two cultures was one not of contention but of remarkable creative symbiosis and confluence. Davilita's songs resound with these fusions and blendings. His repertoire comprised mainly Cuban song traditions of the *son, bolero,* and *guaracha,* but most of them were written by the major Puerto Rican composers Rafael Hernández, Pedro Flores, and Plácido Acevedo. As was evident in his own rendition of "Son Tres," there is great continuity between Puerto Rican and Cuban traditions; both create and partake equally of "el sabor." (What better evidence than the music that came to be called "salsa" in the last quarter of the twentieth century?)

The Cuban–Puerto Rican continuum, which has formed the crux of Caribbean Latinos' cultural history, is intimately associated with blackness in the U.S. context. The shared African moorings of their national and popular cultures carry over strongly to the diasporic context, so that just as they share language and culture with other Spanish speakers, they share deep cultural heritages, and deeply racialized social histories, with people of African descent. *Afroantillanos* constitute by far the largest non-English-speaking black population in U.S. history, and Caribbean Latino history thus substantively overlaps the history of Afro-Latinos in this country.[17]

To a significant degree, in fact, what sets off *antillanos* within the Latino panethnicity is precisely this interface with blackness and an Afro-Atlantic imagery—and its compatibility with the notion of Latino identity in the United States. Although in their dominant and "consumer" version, Latino realities are often walled off from or counterposed to blackness and Afro-diasporic cultural experience, the *antillano* perspective encompasses the continuity and mutuality between them. This more porous border, of course, has made for a far more active reciprocity with African Americans. After half a century of close social interaction, Caribbean Latinos, and *afroantillanos* in particular, are the Latinos who have most directly encountered antiblack racism in the United States, even on the part of other Latinos. They are also those who have enjoyed the most productive sharing and exchange with black Americans. Music history provides ample evidence of the latter dimension. As Winston James points out, the figures of Afro–Puerto Ricans Arturo Alfonso Schomburg and Jesús Colón illustrate, in different historical periods, the strong and complex attachments between the two populations at the intellectual and political levels and their unity in facing up to U.S. racism.[18]

As relevant as it may be to recent issues, this difference within the pan-Latino cultural configuration is not new to our times. The racial and color divide was clearly evident over the long stretches of Caribbean Latino history in the twentieth century. The great Davilita is once again a key source on *antillano* experience in this regard. That renowned black Puerto Rican emigrant of long standing recalled the hierarchy he witnessed in the musical field, where Puerto Ricans and Cubans were typically paid less than other Spanish-language artists. "Victor never treated us like they did the Mexicans, the South Americans when it came to money...Venezuela,... and Argentina and all those countries charged a lot of money and [the company] paid them.... [Xavier] Cugat was Spanish, [but he] charged as if he were an American, wherever he went. But the Puerto Ricans, no."[19] Cubans and Puerto Ricans, inhabiting as they do the darker end of the Latino chromatic spectrum, most frequently find themselves at the bottom of the pan-Latino pecking order. And it would seem that Davilita's observations of the world of popular music would also apply to all other areas of U.S. society, and to almost any historical era.

The implications of Davilita's comments run deeper still and perhaps point to yet another distinction, this time within the *antillano* diaspora experience itself. With his emphasis on the Puerto Ricans as those most devoid of any cultural preference and least likely to be treated equitably, we are reminded again of the line from "Son Tres": "y por Borinquén ¿quién será?" All of the other Latino groups, even the other *antillanos*, have their diplomatic representation, and their home countries—Argentina, Venezuela, Mexico—stand up for them, however feebly and selectively at times, in the U.S. context. They have some recourse to their native republics, as corrupt or tyrannical as these may be. Not so the Puerto Ricans, whose unique status as U.S. citizens has proved a mixed blessing. Those who reside in the states are alone among the Latinos in lacking any governmental or institutional support from their home nation. An editorial column of the same period makes a similar point about inter-Latino relations in New York; the Spanish-language weekly *Gráfico*, under the editorship of Bernardo Vega, included the following comment in 1927: "The most vulnerable group of those which comprise the large family of Ibero-Americans (in New York City) is the Puerto Rican. Truly it seems a paradox that being American citizens these should be the most defenseless. While the citizens of other countries have their consulates and diplomats to represent them, the children of *Borinquen* have no one."[20]

This paradoxical character of the Puerto Ricans as "orphans" is directly attributable to the island's colonial condition and the ramifications of that status in the diaspora in the form of internal colonialism. And if the colonial relationship drew visible lines of differentiation between Puerto Ricans and other Latinos (including *antillanos*) in earlier times, the same continues to be true today. This is most starkly evident in the chapter "The Puerto Rican Exception" in Linda Chavez's infamous *Out of the Barrio*.[21] In the Puerto Rican case, class and racial subordination is compounded by ongoing colonial dependence, a dimension of collective social experience that puts to a severe test these emigrants' inclusion in the prevailing Latino concept. Within the *antillano* subset, the Puerto Rican presence is thus of a very different order from both the Cuban and the Dominican, as divergent as those two also are from one another. Fidel Castro once referred to Puerto Rico as the "perfumed colony," and that it certainly is with respect to relative degrees of economic misery and political authoritarianism. But in the U.S. setting, the community forged of a colonial labor migration stands in greater long-term disadvantage than that which has issued from political exile, or even from the more recognizable Third World immigration seen in the Dominican case. The sheer relative volume of the Puerto Rican emigration movement, where the diaspora is nearly equal in size to the island population, is another indication of this disparity. The "perfume" and the sugar-cane legacy turn bittersweet in the racialized, pathologized circumstance of the colonial minority citizen.

On the other hand, Puerto Ricans are for related reasons the U.S. *antillano* group that lived through and participated in the formative 1960s and 1970s in U.S. history. The ethnic affirmation and political stridency of those years were of constitutive importance for the emergence of Latino identity in the context of U.S. minority struggles. This period also saw the emergence of coalitions across national lines with African Americans, Native Americans, and Asian Americans, as well as the connection of these domestic social movements to political and cultural developments at an international level. In this respect, the social positioning and group history of Puerto Ricans would seem to approximate that of Mexican Americans more closely than that of the other Caribbean Latinos, whose cultural location and sense of group identity took shape after that dramatic and definitive stage. It is important to call attention to this differential political history and social placement of the groups, because such critical considerations are omitted from many discussions of Latino panethnicity, especially those that limit the focus to immigration or to language background and other cultural commonalities.

As we enter the new millennium then, the three Caribbean Latino enclaves exhibit as many disjunctures and discontinuities in the U.S. context as do their respective "islas hermanas" in the contemporary Caribbean regional and international settings. The anachronistic direct colony, the beleaguered neocolony, and the foundering experiment in dependent socialism issue markedly divergent diasporas, whose principal commonality would seem to be the degree to which their current configurations mirror, and are defined by, the status of their home countries in world affairs. Despite their obvious affinities within the full Latino composite, and despite the long-term historical congruencies that underlie the persistent Antillean ideal, no facile assumption of intimate family loyalties or automatic political cohesion among U.S. Cubans, Dominicans, and Puerto Ricans is in order, at least for the foreseeable future.

However, historical experience shows these relations and disparities to be in continual flux, and it is therefore important not to fix our analytic gaze too squarely on the immediate present. Just as the island nations themselves can undermine and refigure the familiar patterns of international demarcation, so too the enclaves may recognize new grounds for rapprochement and cultural coalescence along the contentious U.S. ethnic queue. Certainly the shared Afro-Latino background that tends to distinguish them most within the pan-Latino composite, along with the attendant complementary relationship to blackness, promises to have unifying repercussions within the U.S. racial formation, where the significance of the color line seems to be in no way declining.

The sociocultural location of Caribbean Latinos is thus defined by their relationship to non-Caribbean Latinos on the one hand and to non-Latino Caribbeans on the other. A key question is whether the prevailing Latino concept will have the effect of perpetuating, in the enclave context, the Caribbean's long and tragic history of balkanization along the lines of languages and cultures, or whether it will help foster the kind of pan-Caribbean solidarity that shared life in the United States has engendered in earlier historical periods. Of course the transnational linkages and interrelations between diaspora and homeland politics are central to any prognostic view, as illustrated at the turn of the millennium by such prominent issues in U.S. headlines as the Puerto Rican political prisoners and the Vieques situation, and, in the Cuban context, the tragicomic deadlock over the custody of Elián González. Dominicans in the United States also found themselves embroiled in a controversy of international dimensions over the raising of the national flag in Newark in commemoration of their independence day when they encountered the opposition of Mayor Sharpe James. An interesting *antillano* twist to this dispute is that the most vehement spokesman for the Dominican symbolic cause, Councilman Luis Quintana, is a New Jersey Puerto Rican.[22]

But the global dimension of Caribbean Latino experience and prospects transcends even the island–enclave nexus. One of the most striking examples for me brings me back, once again, to Davilita. His magnificent rendition of "Son Tres" is available to contemporary listeners only on a CD, titled "Guide to Puerto Rican Music," which was released by SONY Columbia in Japan strictly for Japanese consumption. I was delighted to find a CD compilation of Davilita's recordings from his peak years of the 1930s, although

"Son Tres" was not included. When I examined the cover of that collection, which includes songs by a variety of *antillano* composers, I was intrigued to read, "Product of Interstate Music, Ltd., East Sussex, England" and after the date, 1998, "Made in the Czech Republic." So much for sovereignty, and "la unión antillana," and that sweet pan-Caribbean "sabor," in the new, global millennium!

I will conclude with the words of another renowned Caribbean, whose voice might not be as mellifluous as Davilita's but is equally resounding and says much of how the island sisterhood can extend to the metropolitan enclaves of our times. Speaking of the kindred linguistic, musical, and dance expressions in the Caribbean, and of their extension in far-flung diasporas, the great Barbadian writer George Lamming arrives at the following intriguing observation:

> From Cuba to the Guyanas and across every inflection which language confers on the chosen tongue of each territory, this style of performance is evident and travels whenever this island people, and those islanded on the mainland, migrate without any loss of innocence to forge exotic and subversive enclaves in cities whose prestige once made them certain of their names. London, Paris, New York, Amsterdam. These are the Caribbean external frontiers.[23]

NOTES

1. Frequent discussion of the life and work of Davilita may be found in Ruth Glasser, *My Music Is My Flag: Puerto Rican Musicians and Their New York Communities* (Berkeley: University of California Press, 1995). José Luis González's comments on "Lamento Borincano" appear in his essay "Razón y sentido del 'Lamento Borincano,'" in González, *El país de cuatro pisos y otros ensayos* (Río Piedras, Puerto Rico: Ediciones Huracán, 1989), 131–8. (The English version appears in *Boricuas*, Roberto Santiago, ed. (New York: Ballantine, 1995), 49–52.

2. A recent example of this identification of Latinos as "new immigrants" may be seen in Juan González, *Harvest of Empire: A History of Latinos in America* (New York: Viking, 2000). See also Roberto Suro, *Strangers Among Us: How Latino Immigration Is Transforming America* (New York: Knopf, 1998).

3. See *Memoirs of Bernardo Vega*, César Andreu Iglesias, ed. (New York: Monthly Review Press, 1984), esp. 39–79.

4. On Heredia, see William Luis, *Dance Between Two Cultures: Latino Caribbean Literature Written in the United States* (Nashville, TN: Vanderbilt University Press, 1997), 6–7.

5. See *El laúd del desterrado*, Matías Montes-Huidobro, ed. (Houston, TX: Arte Público, 1997).

6. Jorge L. Sosa, "Padre Félix Varela: Defender of Human Rights," in *Hispanic Presence in the United States*, Frank de Varona, ed. (Miami: Mnemosyne, 1993), 153–7 (quote is from p. 144). On Félix Varela, see also González, *Harvest of Empire*, 217–8.

7. Rodolfo J. Cortina, "Cuban Literature in the United States: 1824–1959," in *Recovering the U.S. Hispanic Literary Heritage* (Houston, TX: Arte Público, 1993), 69–88 (quote is from p. 79).

8. See Gerald Poyo, *"With All, and for the Good of All": The Emergence of Popular Nationalism in the Cuban Communities of the United States, 1848–1898* (Durham, NC: Duke University Press, 1989), and Winston James, *Hold Aloft the Banner of Ethiopia: Caribbean Radicalism in Early Twentieth-Century America* (London: Verso, 1998).

9. *Memoirs of Bernardo Vega*, 43.

10. See Daisy Cocco de Filippis, *Documents of Dissidence: Selected Writings by Dominican Women* (New York: Dominican Studies Institute, 2000). See also Silvio Torres Saillant, *El retorno de las yolas: Ensayos sobre diáspora, democracia y dominicidad* (Santo Domingo: Librería La Trinitaria, 1999).

11. See *Memoirs of Bernardo Vega*, 108.

12. Cited in Pedro Mir, *Countersong to Walt Whitman and Other Poems* (Washington, DC: Azul Editions, 1993), 46–7.

> I
>   a son of the Carribean
> Antillean to be exact.
> The raw product of a simple
> Puerto Rican girl
>   and a Cuban worker,
> born precisely, and poor,
> on Quisqueyan soil.

13. See James, 32–57.

14. Glasser, 101.

15. For data on comparative Latino immigration to New York, see Gabriel Haslip-Viera, "The Evolution of the Latino Community in New York," in *Latinos in New York*, Haslip-Viera and Sheri Baver, eds. (Terre Haute, IN: Notre Dame University Press, 1996), 3–28. On page 8, the figure for the Puerto Rican population of New York City in 1940 is given as 61,463, that for "Cuba and West Indies" as 23,124, and that for "Central and South America" as 19,727.

16. Pérez-Firmat, *Life on the Hyphen: The Cuban-American Way* (Austin: University of Texas Press,1994), see esp. 1–20.

17. See my article "Afro-Latino Culture in the United States" in *Africana: The Encyclopedia of the African and African American Experience*, Henry Louis Gates and Anthony Appiah, eds. (New York: Basic Civitas Books, 1999).

18. See James, 195–231. On the musical interactions between New York Puerto Ricans and African Americans, see my essay "'Cha Cha with a Backbeat: Songs and Stories of Latin Boogaloo," in *From Bomba to Hip-Hop: Puerto Rican Culture and Latin Identity* (New York: Columbia University Press, 2000), 79–112.

19. Glasser, 149.

20. Cited in Virginia Sánchez-Korrol, *From Colonia to Community: The History of Puerto Ricans in New York* (Berkeley: University of California Press, 1994), 73. I have developed this argument about the institutional differentiation among Latinos in my essay "Life off the Hyphen: Latino Literature and Nuyorican Traditions," in *From Bomba to Hip-Hop*, op. cit., 167–88.

21. Linda Chavez, *Out of the Barrio: Toward a New Politics of Hispanic Assimilation* (New York: Basic Books, 1992), 139–59. Chavez's book stands out among accounts by a Latino author in adopting an openly neo-conservative, assimilationist position, and especially in its pathologizing treatment of Puerto Ricans.

22. See Roberto Bustamante, "Controversia por celebración de la Independencia Dominicana," *El Diario/La Prensa*, 26 February 2000, p. 5.

23. *Enterprise of the Indies*, George Lamming, ed. (Port of Spain: Trinidad and Tobago Institute of the West Indies, 1999), vii.

Chapter 3

Power and Identity

Miami Cubans

Alex Stepick and Carol Dutton Stepick

INTRODUCTION

On April 30, 2000, close to one hundred thousand Latinos, overwhelmingly Miami Cubans,[1] marched through the streets of Little Havana. Miami Cubans, along with significant numbers of other Latinos, were united. And they had become united in response to what they perceived as discrimination from the larger society, what has been called "reactive ethnicity" (Portes and Bach 1984). They were protesting the U.S. government's treatment of a six-year-old Cuban rafter boy who had been staying with his Miami Cuban relatives. His Cuban father wanted the boy back, but the Miami Cuban relatives and their supporters refused to give him up, claiming that he would suffer incomparably in Castro's Cuba. The U.S. government forcibly removed the child, much to the horror of Miami Cubans. They could not understand how the United States could side with Castro's government. After the boy was seized, the community was left stunned by the sense that the U.S. government had ignored the claims of Miami Cubans who had so stalwartly opposed communism and had become so successful in the United States.

First-generation Miami Cuban immigrants have achieved economic and political power unprecedented in the entire history of U.S. immigrants. They have come to expect success. Not only are Cubans the most economically successful Latinos in the United States, but for forty years they have evinced an extraordinary solidarity based upon an identity as intransigent anticommunist Cuban patriots.

Up close, however, the vivid picture of Miami Cuban power and success dissolves into multiple conflicting and confusing images. By the end of June 2000, two months after one hundred thousand demonstrated in the streets, cracks in Miami Cuban solidarity slowly, fitfully reemerged—fractures that had developed over the past fifteen years of the twentieth century but that the Elián González case had temporarily bridged. At the beginning of the twenty-first century, Miami's Cuban and Latino communities are undergoing a sluggish transformation in which Miami Cuban power is becoming diffused. Cuban identity and solidarity are eroding under the stress of non-Cuban, Latino demographic diversity and the maturation of second-generation Miami Cubans, who care less about Castro and more about "making it" in America. This chapter examines first the forces that constructed a seemingly monolithic, powerful community and then the processes that have undermined that solidarity.

THE BUILDING OF CUBAN MIAMI

We Cubans made Miami. Before us, Miami was nothing but a decaying winter vacation spot and swamp. Now, it's the capital of Latin America. And, we Cubans did it!

A MIAMI CUBAN BUSINESSMAN

Indeed, Cubans do deserve much of the credit for shifting Miami's economic focus from northern tourists to international southern trade. But their stories of self-congratulation usually fail to acknowledge the critical political context that encouraged them—even permitted their success.

Cubans fleeing Castro's Cuba began arriving in significant numbers in the 1960s, following the failure of the Bay of Pigs invasion.[2] Their arrival reflected both the failure of a U.S.-backed military invasion of Cuba and the failure of a socialist revolution to retain those who had the most skills and resources for reconstructing Cuba. The Cubans' arrival also coincided with the construction of Great Society programs that provided extensive benefits to minority populations and that were quickly expanded to include Cuban refugees. The U.S. government created the Cuban Refugee Program, which spent nearly $1 billion between 1965 and 1976 (Pedraza-Bailey 1985). Through this program, the federal government paid transportation costs from Cuba and offered financial assistance to needy refugees and to state and local public agencies that provided refugee services. Even in programs not especially designed for them, Cubans seemed to benefit. From 1968 to 1980, Latinos (almost all Cubans) received 46.9 percent of all Small Business Administration loans in Dade County (Porter and Dunn 1984).

Even more important was indirect assistance. Through the 1960s, the private University of Miami had the largest Central Intelligence Agency (CIA) station in the world, outside of the organization's headquarters in Virginia. With perhaps as many as twelve thousand Cubans in Miami on its payroll at one point in the early 1960s, the CIA was one of the largest employers in the state of Florida. It supported what was described as the third largest navy in the world and over fifty front businesses: CIA boat shops, gun shops, travel agencies, detective agencies, and real estate agencies (Didion 1987). Ultimately, this investment did much more to boost Cubans in Miami economically than it did to destabilize the Castro regime.

The state of Florida also passed laws that made it easier for Cuban professionals to recertify themselves to practice in the United States. At the county level, in the late 1970s and early 1980s, 53 percent of minority contracts for Dade County's rapid transit system went to Latino-owned firms. Dade County Schools led the nation in introducing bilingual education for the first wave of Cuban refugees in 1960. The Dade County Commission also designated the county officially bilingual in the mid-1970s. With about 75 percent of Cuban arrivals before 1974 directly taking advantage of some kind of state-provided benefits, and with virtually everyone profiting from indirect aid, the total benefits available to the Cuban community appear to surpass those available to any other U.S. minority group (Pedraza-Bailey 1985).

The first wave of Cubans has been labeled the "Golden Exiles," the top of Cuban society who were most immediately threatened by a socialist revolution (Portes, 1969). These new arrivals were different from other minorities in the United States. They were not only white but also predominantly middle or upper class. The presence of entrepreneurs and professionals in the Cuban refugee flow provided a trained and experienced core who knew how to access and use the extraordinary benefits provided by the U.S. government. Some had already established a footing in the United States and, when the revolution came, abandoned one of their residences for another across the straits of Florida. A Cuban shoe manufacturer, for example, produced footwear for a major U.S. retail chain before the Cuban revolution. He obtained his working capital from New York financial houses. After the revolution, the only change was that the manufacturing was done in Miami rather than Havana. He even was able to keep some of the same employees.

The earlier-arriving, higher-status refugees created the first enterprises in what came to be known as the Cuban enclave and allowed Miami to be the only U.S. city where Latino immigrants created a successful and self-sustained ethnic enclave economy. Miami has proportionally the largest concentration of Latino businesses (over fifty-five thousand) and of large Latino enterprises in the country. Although Miami-Dade County has only 5 percent of the total U.S. Latino population, thirty-one of the top one hundred Latino businesses in the United States are located there. U.S. Cubans' rate of business ownership is more than three times that of Mexicans and nearly six times that of Puerto Ricans.

The Cuban enclave benefits not only Cuban business owners but also the broader Miami Cuban community. Most later-arriving Cuban immigrants from more modest origins than the Golden Exiles are employed by Cuban Miami enclave firms in various entry-level positions, which may offer low wages but can often be apprenticeships rather than dead-end jobs. Miami Cuban employers frequently provide training to their Miami Cuban workers and may even help them establish their own independent businesses. Miami Cuban garment workers become subcontractors, establishing informal workshops in their homes. Miami Cuban construction workers become contractors or subcontractors, also working out of their homes. For financing, workers who have turned entrepreneurs can go to banks (sometimes owned by Miami Cubans and certainly staffed by Miami Cubans) where they are likely to find sympathetic loan officers. For markets, they rely on the Miami Cuban community's loyalty and preference for buying from "their own."

The result has been a most economically successful immigrant community. A comparison of Cubans and Mexicans who came to the United States in the mid-1970s, for example, revealed that the Cubans not only had higher wages than the Mexicans, even Cubans with the same educational level as Mexicans received higher wages (Portes and Bach 1985).[3]

Miami Cubans also transformed Miami by attracting investment and migration from the rest of Latin America and the Caribbean, turning Miami into a diverse, dynamic Latino economic center of the Americas. Only New York has more foreign-owned banks than Miami. Nearly 50 percent of U.S. exports to the Caribbean and Central America and over 30 percent of U.S. exports to South America pass through Miami. Miami's Free Trade Zone is the first and largest privately owned trade zone in the world. With more non-stop cargo flights to Latin America and the Caribbean than Orlando, Houston, New Orleans, Atlanta, Tampa, and New York's Kennedy combined, Miami's airport is the top U.S. airport for international freight. The airport has more airlines than any other in the Western hemisphere; it is frequently easier to get from one Latin American country to another by going through Miami than by going directly. Miami also has the largest cruise port in the world, ironically transporting primarily U.S. passengers on vacations throughout the Caribbean and Latin America while many of the citizens of those countries are immigrating to Miami. Miami may not be a global city equal to New York or London, but it is assuredly the economic capital of Latin America (Nijman 1996a), and its Cuban immigrants made it so.

The economic transformation has also altered much of Miami's culture. For example, at a 1998 event held by the University of Miami and the state of Florida to discuss plans for educating a "multilingual workforce for the 21st Century," the university's newly installed dean of education, an import from a university up north, spoke of language diversity as a problem that people where he came from would soon be encountering. The faculty member who was moderating the conference gently reminded the dean that in Florida multilingualism is viewed as an asset and promised to continue to educate him.

Antibilingual-education measures such as those that passed in the late 1990s in California no longer have a chance in Miami.[4] It is easier to find a job, to shop, and just to get things done if one knows Spanish. It is also much easier to advance economically if one knows English. Miami is truly bilingual and multicultural (Garreau 1981; Levine 1985; Portes and Stepick 1993). Miami Dade Community College has more foreign students, mostly Latino, than any other college or university in the nation. One of the three Spanish-language local television newscasts has more viewers than any of the local English-language television stations. The main Spanish-language daily, *El Nuevo Herald*, reprints articles from eleven Latin American newspapers. The 1990 census showed that Spanish had replaced English in Miami-Dade as the language most often spoken at home. Even at work, the language most frequently spoken by Latinos in South Florida is Spanish (42.2 percent).

It is not just the number of Latinos and the pervasive use of Spanish that makes Miami the *de facto* capital of Latin America. Latinos are also the demographic majority in some Texas cities, such as Laredo, El Paso, and San Antonio, and in other border areas such as California's Imperial Valley, but there they lack the political and economic clout exercised by Miami Cubans.

Miami Cubans translated the favorable reception by the U.S. government and the millions of dollars of resettlement assistance not only into a self-sufficient economic enclave and thriving international economic city but also into a "direct line" to the centers of political power in Washington. Despite considerable political diversity among Miami Cubans in the early 1960s, by the 1970s politics and profits had become fused. Anti-Castro, anticommunist Miami Cubans invested locally and also enforced political consensus by harassing, boycotting, and even terrorizing their more liberal political and economic compatriots (Forment 1989), a process referred to as enforceable solidarity (Portes 1987).

The outcome was a profound economic and political solidarity. From the 1960s on, most Miami Cubans, despite their diverse class origins and social views, patronized other Miami Cuban-owned businesses and preferred conationals as business associates at the same time that they shared a coherent anti-Castro, anticommunist ideology. Expelled and despised by the government of their country, abandoned at the Bay of Pigs by a supposedly friendly host government, bartered away during the 1962 Cuban missile crisis, and ridiculed by Latin American intellectuals, the exiles had few to trust but each other. As illustrated in a full-page advertisement in the *Miami Herald* that was paid for by the most powerful Miami Cuban organization, the Cuban American National Foundation, resentment and a sense of persecution had evolved:

> All our achievements have been accomplished with a national press coverage that has often portrayed us as extremists. This has been the most unfair and prejudiced perception we have experienced in America.... The *Miami Herald* is aggressive in its ignorance of our people. It refuses to understand that Cuban Americans see the struggle between totalitarianism and democracy as a personal, ever-present struggle. We live the struggle daily because our friends and families enslaved in communist Cuba live it daily. (Cuban American National Foundation 1987)

Unlike other minorities, which usually adopt antiestablishment, progressive positions, Miami Cubans have been militant conservatives on foreign policy, specifically on anticommunism issues. As a result, anticommunist policy positions and anticommunist rhetoric are de rigueur for local political candidates. For example, in the mid-1980s the City Commission passed a resolution barring any expenditure of "funds of the City of Miami ... where representatives of Communist-Marxist countries have either been scheduled to participate or invited to attend." Subsequently, Miami-Dade County passed a similar resolution. In an effort to win Miami Cuban readership, the *Miami Herald* created an entirely new Spanish-language edition run almost exclusively by Cuban exiles who seldom have a favorable word for the Castro government (O'Connor 1992).

The Miami Cubans' solidarity has produced tangible political results. Miami's city and county mayors are foreign-born Cuban immigrants, as are the superintendent of the public schools (the fourth largest district in the nation), the president of the community college (the largest in the nation), and the president of the local state university (one of the country's most rapidly growing). In the wake of the Elián crisis, the Miami Cuban mayor fired the Anglo police chief and the Anglo city manager. They were replaced by Miami Cubans. Also Cuban-born are the Miami-Dade County police chief, the state prosecutor for Miami-Dade County, two congressional representatives, and the majority of the Miami-Dade County state legislative contingent. Nationally, the two Miami Cubans in the U.S. House of Representatives,[5] along with the Cuban American National Foundation, successfully promoted Radio and T.V. Martí, which broadcasts to Cuba, as well as the Cuban Democracy Act, which tightened U.S. economic sanctions against Cuba. More generally, Miami Cubans have emerged as a group whose support is actively courted by a growing number of officeholders from outside the state—from presidential candidates to members of Congress seeking campaign contributions (Moreno 1996).

These victories have not been without costs to the image of Miami Cubans and the well-being of the overall community. In response to an intolerance concerning political opinions about Cuba, the Inter-American Press Association and the human rights group Americas Watch in 1992 condemned the Miami exile community for violations of civil liberties (Garcia 1996; Rohter 1992). There have been many other lost opportunities. The most recent examples: An international music market conference that focused on the Americas had met in Miami Beach for several years, but in 1998 the county blocked the conference because Cuban musicians were scheduled to attend. Also in 1998, the Miami Light Project, a leading local arts group, had to forgo presenting a Cuban musical group in order not to lose $60,000 in county funding. The July 1999 Junior Pan American Games track and field meet was moved to Tampa after Miami-Dade refused to support it because Cuba would be represented in the games. The Latin Grammys scheduled for September 2000 pulled out of Miami. For similar reasons, a local group bidding to hold the 2007 Pan Am Games in Miami-Dade pulled out after realizing that the county would not support the games because Cuban athletes would participate.

Achieving both economic and political success as a Miami Cuban did not necessarily shield individuals from prejudice and discrimination. Certainly during the early stages of Cuban settlement in the 1960s, Cubans confronted significant prejudice when apartment owners, for example, posted signs declaiming, "No Pets, No Kids, No Cubans." Moreover, in an effort to prevent the political empowerment of Cubans, local Anglo politicians in the 1960s and 1970s successfully urged federal officials to relocate new Cuban refugees outside of Dade County. Public resentment against Cuban Americans mounted, especially in the wake of the 1980 Mariel boatlift when the *Miami Herald* editorialized repeatedly against Cubans and when national polls listed Cubans as the least desirable immigrants. This was largely a reaction to Castro's propaganda about those leaving Cuba in the boatlift. As late as 1993, a USA Today/CNN/Gallup poll found that only 19 percent of the respondents believed that immigration from Cuba has benefited the United States (Moreno 1996). Dade County was also the birthplace of the English-only movement in the United States during the 1980s (Castro, Haun, and Roca 1990; Castro 1992).

By the late 1980s, after the election of a Cuban-born mayor, a majority on the city council, numerous state representatives, and a congressional representative, and recognizing the business elite's inability to advance their agenda without the support of the Cuban business community, Miami's old-line, non-Hispanic white political and business elite switched to a policy of incorporation. In the meantime, the Cuban enclave had been forging itself into the staging ground for a profound Latinoization of Miami.

EROSION OF MIAMI CUBAN SOLIDARITY
Demographic Dilution of Cuban Hegemony

Undoubtedly, Miami is an immigrant city. By 1990 Miami had the highest proportion of foreign-born residents of any U.S. metropolitan area. Over 70 percent of Miami's population is either a first-generation (48.6 percent) or a second-generation (22.9 percent) immigrant (Rumbaut 1998a).

Cubans are the largest of Miami's immigrant groups, but perhaps not by quite so great a margin as one might expect. Although over 25,000 Cuban immigrants settle in Miami yearly, Cubans constitute only 35 percent of the county's total population and 60 percent of the area's Latino population (Miami-Dade County, 1999). The Cuban percentage has been declining since the mid-1980s. Fleeing first the Sandinista regime and then the Contra war against the Sandinistas, Nicaraguan immigrants form the second largest Miami Latino population. By the late 1980s, they made Miami the largest Nicaraguan settlement in the United States, at an estimated 105,000 in 2000. Every Latin American and Caribbean country has a presence in Miami, which is also home to nearly 100,000 Puerto Ricans (Boswell 1994).

Whereas rifts between Cubans and non-Hispanic whites dominated during the 1980s, since then, divisions between Cubans and other Latinos have begun to emerge. One Miami Nicaraguan insists that "Cubans get more opportunities. Cubans think they are better than Nicas. Cubans are able to move up in the work place easier. We Nicas get treated differently at work. They think we are less competent. They make rude remarks about us, call us indios and tira flechas, make us feel unwelcome in public places" (Konczal 1999).

The impetus for Nicaraguans coming to Miami paralleled that of the original Cuban migration. Like Cubans, Nicaraguans were fleeing a radical, left-wing revolution. Accordingly, Miami Cubans first welcomed them as fellow anticommunists, and many Nicaraguans consciously attempted to replicate the Cuban economic enclave and political solidarity.

However, they found their way impeded by obstacles that Cubans had not confronted. First, in a general national atmosphere that was more restrictive toward immigrants, the U.S. government was far less welcoming toward Nicaraguans than it had been toward Cubans. Only after prolonged political battle did selected Nicaraguans qualify for a legal immigration status, and in their struggles for immigration benefits, Nicaraguans have been treated much more similarly to Salvadorans and Haitians than to Cubans.[6] The compressed time frame of Nicaraguan immigration (less than ten years compared to the forty years for Cuban immigrants) also contributed to the more negative reaction to their arrival. The U.S. hostility toward permanent Nicaraguan resettlement diverted Nicaraguans' resources and focus, thus weakening their voice in local affairs.

Unlike the many Cuban entrepreneurs who had firm ties to the U.S. economy, Nicaragua's economy had been less linked to the United States, so Nicaraguan entrepreneurs could not so easily reestablish themselves (Rodríguez 1999). The Nicaraguan exodus also lacked the finality of the Cubans' migration. The electoral defeat of the Sandinistas in the late 1980s made the Nicaraguan community far more transnational than settled in Miami.

Our ethnographic work[7] among immigrant youths has revealed that the local dominance of Cubans dramatically affects Nicaraguan youths. When Nicaraguans first arrive, they confront the prejudice and discrimination thrown at all *refies* ("refugees") or new arrivals. They learn the epithets of *indio* (Indian) and *tira flecha* (spear thrower). They realize that not only can they not speak English but they also dress wrong and are barred from hanging out with the "in" people. They also take education too seriously.

Being young, however, they quickly adapt. They learn and come to prefer English, or at least Miami's Spanglish, within a couple of years. They change their manner of dress in an effort to merge with their new Cuban-dominated peer culture. Many refer to themselves as Hispanics (and a few as Latinos), instead of Nicaraguans. And many suppress their interest in and respect for education. A few years later, however, most evolve further still. They come to realize their specific, peculiar role of being Nicaraguans in Miami. As reflected in both our own ethnographic work and the survey research of Portes and Rumbaut (2000), many resurrect a Nicaraguan identity label. Overall, this survey found, the number of individuals who self-identify simply as "American" declines dramatically for all immigrant youths as they grow older.

In short, the increased diversity of Latino immigrants in Miami has not promoted the adoption of a Latino identity; rather, it reinforces national identities. The dominance of Cubans, for example, prompts Nicaraguan youth first to shed or camouflage their culture and then to readopt a national identity label.

Nicaraguans also recognize that being a Latino in Latino-dominated Miami can be better than being Latino elsewhere in the United States. As one high school senior in our study stated, *"I think here in Miami we're not going to have a problem, but I think if we move probably to Colorado, Michigan and stuff, they'll discriminate against any Hispanics. Okay, if you go up north in Orlando, they do discriminate; the white guy [does]."*

Increased immigration diversity, then, has diluted Cuban demographic dominance, but it has had a mixed effect on identity. Non-Cuban Latinos in Miami learn to assert their national identities locally at the same time that they realize that being Latino in Miami, even if Cubans dominate, is better than being Latino outside of Miami.

Generational Dissolution of Solidarity

Miami Cubans in the aggregate are becoming increasingly dissimilar. Cubans have one of the highest naturalization rates of all immigrant groups, and they vote frequently. They have voted as an ethnic block in local elections and have consistently supported Republicans in state and national elections (Moreno and Warren 1992). Moreover, according to a 1997 survey, 70 percent say that in local political elections, a candidate's position on Cuba is important in determining whether they vote for that candidate (Grenier and Gladwin 1997). The Elián González affair at the beginning of 2000 demonstrated Miami Cubans' solidarity and force. Tens of thousands demonstrated in the streets. Media attention was unceasing. Numerous commentators labeled the event a watershed for the community. We argue, however, that the attention surrounding Elián and the solidarity displayed were transitory experiences that veiled a longer-term, more fundamental generational dissolution of solidarity among Cubans.

Through the 1990s, fissures began to emerge, especially along generational lines. In the early 1990s, for example, I [Alex] taught a freshman honors course on ethnicity in Miami, and the students read Joan Didion's *Miami* (1987), which focuses on the extreme Cuban right wing. The book details the case of Orlando Bosch, a former medical doctor accused of numerous terrorist activities, including the bombing of a Cuban airliner over Venezuela. About half of the students were of Cuban descent, almost all born in the United States of parents who were born in Cuba. Nearly all had close-knit families, including grandparents with whom the students discussed the readings. Almost unanimously, the Cuban grandparents celebrated Bosch's terrorism as the work of a *freedom fighter*. The parents, referred to as the 1½ generation because most migrated to the United States when they were children, were ambivalent. They were strongly anti-Castro, but they did not endorse the murder of innocent human beings. The children, who were overwhelmingly second-generation immigrants, had never even heard of Orlando Bosch. They viewed his acts as terrorism and were shocked by them. These generational differences have been reinforced repeatedly in our five-year ethnographic project.

In many respects, the children of Cuban immigrants have been assimilated in characteristic American fashion. They have abandoned the self-identity label of American, but neither do they identify as Cuban. Instead, they strongly prefer the hyphenated label Cuban-American. Our ethnographic work reveals Miami Cuban high school students to be the most Americanized in terms of teenage celebration of drinking, drugs, sex, car culture, and the disparagement of education (Konczal 1997), and they have the highest dropout rate among immigrant students attending public schools (Portes and Rumbaut 2000). Miami Cubans also are the least likely of all immigrant youths to report experiencing discrimination (Rumbaut 1997b; Rumbaut 1998b).

Younger Miami Cubans truly are living on the hyphen (Perez Firmat 1994). They prefer to speak English, watch English-language television, listen to English-language radio, dress in American styles, and adopt the attitudes of typical mainstream American adolescents. At the same time, they understand and speak Spanish, often have close extended-family ties, and are at least aware of why their parents and grandparents are so passionate about Cuba. Their grandparents remain fixated on recapturing their lost status and property in Cuba. Their parents have focused on establishing new lives in a new country. The younger generation cares little about lost status and property. For Miami Cuban youth, Cuba is primarily a memory constructed through the stories their grandparents repeat at every family gathering. They often take for granted the accomplishments of their parents. For Miami Cuban youth, economic security is often something assumed, rather than something to be recovered or created again. Miami Cuban youth know that they belong to the locally dominant group, and they act on this knowledge.

Miami Cuban youth may agree with their parents' and grandparents' assessment that Fidel Castro is a dictator who has ruined Cuba. They also will respond to what they perceive as violence against their community. But they are unlikely to be as profoundly passionate in their anti-Castro sentiments as their parents and grandparents.

LOSING POWER

Fissures within Miami Cuban unity are also visible in politics, both in public discussions and governmental policies. *El Nuevo Herald* was created by the *Miami Herald* largely to appeal to the political sensitivity of anticommunist Cubans (Portes and Stepick 1993), but this newspaper now has a Cuban-born columnist, who consistently supports more dialogue and closer relations with the Castro government and condemns Miami Cuban right-wing fanaticism. Although this columnist has received numerous death threats, he and his column persist, a condition that probably would not have existed fifteen years ago.

Survey results confirm emerging divisions among Miami Cubans. The Latino National Political Survey in the early 1990s revealed that 45.5 percent of naturalized Cubans identified themselves as "moderate" or "liberal." Furthermore, even those who favor a hard line against Castro are often liberal on domestic issues (Garcia 1996:122). A 1997 survey of Miami Cubans found that over 51 percent would support a dialogue with the Cuban government, a significant increase over a 1991 poll. Seventy-one percent felt that all points of view on how to deal with Castro were not being heard in Miami. And, younger residents were more likely to oppose military action and instead favor opening up relations (Grenier and Gladwin 1997).

Even large-scale public events reflect a diminution of right-wing Miami Cuban power and influence. Throughout the 1980s, university-sponsored debates and public forums to discuss foreign policy relative to Cuba or Nicaragua routinely elicited large protests, threats, and sometimes acts of violence. In March 2000, however, the Latin American Studies Association held their meetings in Miami. *El Nuevo Herald* trumpeted the expected arrival of over 120 Cuban scholars from Cuba, the largest contingent ever to visit in the United States. Conference organizers from the local state university (Florida International University) feared massive public demonstrations and disruptions of the meetings, but fewer than five protesters carried placards across the street from the hotel, and not a single conference event was disrupted.

The case of Elián González reflects both the inertia of right-wing Miami Cuban power and its dissolution. Miami Cubans mounted an impressive effort to keep Elián in the United States, including the introduction of legislation by Cuban American members of Congress to offer Elián instant U.S. citizenship, a move supported by Florida's Republican and Democratic non–Miami Cuban senators. On the other hand, whereas demonstrations in favor of Cuban rafters in 1994 garnered tens of thousands of supporters, before federal authorities snatched Elián, the vigil outside his relatives' Miami house seldom numbered more than twenty, and most of the stalwarts were over 60 years old. The broader Miami Cuban community did not coalesce until the U.S. government threatened to, and then eventually did, forcibly remove Elián from the custody of his extended family in Miami and restore him to his father, who had come from Cuba to retrieve him. Many of the Cubans and other Latinos who then came out into the streets were motivated less by anticommunism than by the U.S. government's powerful show of force.

Although extreme right-wing Cuban hegemony is declining, the political and media structures of power created by that hegemony were able to catapult Elián into our daily consciousness, while only occasionally mentioning those Miami Cubans and other Latinos whose views reflect emerging generational and demographic changes. The anti-Castro, anticommunist Miami Cuban faction clearly remains the most visible and the most vocal. It still has the greatest influence on local politics, and the national media seem not yet to have recognized the slow decline in its constituent base.

THE FUTURE

Miami Cubans have always been an exceptional case, both among Latinos in the United States and among minorities in general. They are a first-generation immigrant minority that has vaulted past native minorities to attain both economic and political power based upon exceptional community solidarity.

A few academics and many Miami Cubans themselves attribute Miami Cuban success to hard work and intelligence (Moncarz 1978; Botifol 1985), maintaining that "We Cubans made Miami!" A similar explanation at the other end of the political scale is the Cuban government's and *its* academics' assertion that Miami Cubans are mafia, scum, worms, and traitors to the revolution (Hernandez and Gomis 1986). Political scientists (such as Moreno 1996) point out that Cubans do not fit the standard profile for minority politics—they have no legacy of internal colonialism (García 1988), nor did they have to engage in coalition building in order to attain power (Browning, Marshall, and Tabb 1984). Sociological explanations tend to emphasize the immigrants' upwardly skewed social background (Portes 1969), their European, non-African, nonindigenous racial status (Stepick and Grenier, 1993), their intact, extended families with many workers (Perez 1986), and especially the positive reception offered them by the U.S. government (Pedraza-Bailey 1985; Masud-Piloto 1996; Stepick and Grenier, 1993; Portes and Manning 1986; Portes and Rumbaut 1990).

The tremendous community solidarity that propelled Miami's Cuban community, however, is slowly and fitfully eroding. Cubans are no longer Miami's only visible immigrants. Non-Cuban Latinos have diluted Cubans' demographic majority. Miami Cuban voices have begun to challenge the hegemonic anti-Castro obsession, and the formerly hegemonic anti-Castroites have not been able to terrorize them into silence as they intimidated dissidents in the 1960s and 1970s.

The power established by the older Miami Cubans, however, exhibits an inertia that will probably mask the community's evolution for some time to come. Although the younger Miami Cubans have different agendas than the older Miami Cubans, the defining issue of older Cubans, anti-Castroism, still remains the primary political issue of the broader Miami Cuban community, as the Elián González case demonstrates. In hopes of maintaining the momentum generated by the Elián affair, the most important Miami Cuban lobby, the Cuban American National Foundation, appointed a new, younger executive director. The media continue to concentrate disproportionately on the visible, contentious issues surrounding Miami Cubans' interest in their homeland, rather than on the more mundane, mainstream domestic issues of concern to the emerging second generation. Like any group, whenever Miami Cubans feel threatened and believe that issues important to them are ignored, they are likely to demonstrate solidarity across all generations. But apart from these episodic occasions, solidarity will be more elusive.

The second generation, the ones who define themselves as Cuban Americans and whose attitudes and concerns are easily as much American as Cuban, will eventually shift political attention away from Cuba to domestic issues. They are likely to replicate the political attitudes and behaviors of the second- and third-generation European immigrants of the twentieth century. The meaning of their Cuban roots will be more nostalgic than activist as they come to see Miami, not Cuba, as their homeland. Miami has become the center of immigrant Cuban life for all generations of Cubans. Even if Cuba does one day welcome back the exiles who have politically opposed the current regime for so long, few of the second generation are likely to consider relocating in Cuba. Some grandparents will return to die in their homeland. Many parents, those of the 1 ½ generation, will return to visit family and explore economic opportunities. But even if they do establish businesses in Cuba, these are likely to be transnational businesses with their base in Miami and a branch in Cuba.

The increased demographic diversity of Miami's immigrants will further challenge Miami Cubans' hegemony. Nicaraguans have been clamoring for a social and political voice for more than a decade. Haitians, who are identified as black Caribbean immigrants and not Latinos, are beginning to field local political candidates. African Americans openly voice their resentment of Miami Cubans' economic and political success. The voices of other Latino communities are also likely to emerge. There are nearly as many Puerto Ricans in Miami as Nicaraguans. Political instability in Colombia has generated a strong immigrant flow into Miami. And other Latin immigrants also continue to arrive daily.

The key will be how Miami Cuban leaders react. Some Miami Cuban politicians and opinion leaders have responded by broadening their agenda to incorporate the concerns of other groups. Other Miami Cubans, especially radio talk show hosts, however, remain preoccupied with anti-Castro sentiments. In the process, they alienate both other Latinos and non-Latinos. The anti-Castro fixation in the Elián González affair created a backlash both locally and nationally. The U.S. Congress refused to grant a legal immigration status to Elián, and Congress voted to end the U.S. medicine and food embargo on Cuba.[8] Soon after Elián returned with his father to Cuba, a Miami federal district judge ruled unconstitutional Miami-Dade County's ordinance that prohibited the county from officially dealing with any firm that does business with anyone in Cuba.

In the wake of Elián's brief sojourn and departure, public discourse in Miami has concentrated on how to improve relations between Miami Cubans and the rest of the community. Because Miami Cubans are locally dominant, whether Miami remains marked by Cuban conflict with the broader community or comes together across its ethnic components will largely depend on the course chosen by Miami Cuban leaders—whether, that is, they remain absorbed by homeland politics or refocus on Miami.

NOTES

1. Most narrowly, *Miami* refers to the City of Miami, which has over 365,000 residents and is the largest of thirty municipalities in Miami-Dade County. The county, which changed its name from Dade County to Miami-Dade County in 1997, has slightly over 2 million residents and is the eighth largest county in the United States. Although not all of the county is urban, it is frequently referred to as Metropolitan Miami. This paper uses the term *Miami* to refer to the broader area of Miami-Dade County. We refer to Miami Cubans specifically to avoid the confusing *Cuban* or *Cuban American* or the more wordy *people of Cuban descent*. Miami's Cuban population is a mix of first- and second-generation immigrants, along with a few third-generation ones. We use *Miami Cubans* to refer to people of Cuban descent, regardless of generation, who reside in Miami.

2. Numerous accounts detail the history of Cuban immigration to the United States, inter alia, see Masud-Piloto 1996; Pedraza 1996; and Portes and Bach 1984.

3. The most severe challenge to the absorptive capacity of the Cuban enclave came with the 1980 Mariel boatlift that brought 125,000 new arrivals within a few months. In spite of having educational and occupational characteristics similar to earlier-arriving Cuban refugees of the 1970s, the Mariel refugees were severely stigmatized by Fidel Castro's characterization of them as the dregs of Cuban society. As a result, 27 percent were unemployed three years after their arrival, twice as many as among Cuban refugees arriving in the 1970s (Portes and Clark 1985). Two years later, however, their unemployment rate had declined by half. More significantly, 18 percent of those who were gainfully employed had managed to establish their own private practice or small business, and 45 percent of those employed were working in Cuban-owned firms (Portes and Clark 1987).

4. Miami-Dade County did pass an antimulticultural ordinance in 1980 when non-Latinos were still the majority. In the early 1990s, that ordinance was reversed.

5. There is also a Cuban American representative in Congress who represents New Jersey.

6. Admittedly, U.S. policy toward Cuban undocumented immigrants became increasingly restrictive following the Guantánamo rafter crisis of 1994, after which the United States claimed the right to return to Cuba those who had not made it to U.S. shores (referred to as the wet feet versus dry feet policy). Still, those Cubans who make it to U.S. shores are allowed to remain, although U.S. law grants no special privileges to Cubans just because they make it to U.S. soil. The Cuban Adjustment Act, nevertheless, does grant permanent residency to Cubans once they have been in the United States for one year, regardless of how they arrived—a legal benefit denied to all other immigrants. The United States also admits approximately 25,000 Cubans legally to the United States via the U.S. Interests Section in Havana.

7. With funding from NSF (SBR-9511515), the Andrew Mellon Foundation, the Carnegie Corporation, and the Spencer Foundation, we began following cohorts of immigrant and native minority youths in the fall of 1995 when these individuals entered high school. We have remained in contact with them ever since. Lisa Konczal (1997, 1999) has worked most closely with the Nicaraguan youth.

8. Miami Cuban congressional representatives, however, did manage to maintain significant restrictions on U.S. corporate and individual involvement with Cuba that would enhance European trade relations with Cuba.

REFERENCES

Boswell, Thomas. 1994. *The Cubanization and Hispanicization of Metropolitan Miami.* Miami, FL: Cuban American Policy Center.

Botifol, Luis J. 1985. *How Miami's New Image Was Created.* Miami, FL: University of Miami, Institute of Interamerican Studies.

Browning, Rufus P., Dale Rogers Marshall, and David H. Tabb. 1984. *Protest Is Not Enough: The Struggle of Blacks and Hispanics for Equality in Urban Politics.* Berkeley: University of California Press.

Castro, Max. 1992. "The Politics of Language." In *Miami Now!,* G. Grenier and A. Stepick, eds. pp. 109–132. Gainesville, FL: University Press of Florida.

Castro, Max J., Margaret Haun, and Ana Roca. 1990. "The Official English Movement in Florida." In *Perspectives on Official English,* K. L. Adams and D. T. Brink, eds. pp. 151–160. Berlin: Mouton de Gruyte.

Cuban American National Foundation. 1987. The Cuban-American Community and the Miami Herald, paid political announcement. In the *Miami Herald,* p. 11A.

Didion, Joan. 1987. *Miami.* New York: Simon and Schuster.

Forment, Carlos A. 1989. "Political Practice and the Rise of an Ethnic Enclave: The Cuban American Case, 1959–1979." *Theory and Society* 18:47–81.

García, Chris. 1988. *Latinos and the Political System.* Notre Dame, IN: University of Notre Dame Press.

Garcia, Maria Cristina. 1996. *Havana USA: Cuban Exiles and Cuban Americans in South Florida, 1959–1994.* Berkeley: University of California Press.

Garreau, Joel. 1981. *The Nine Nations of North America.* Boston: Houghton Mifflin.

Grenier, Guillermo, and Hugh Gladwin. 1997. *FIU 1997 Cuba Poll.* Miami: Institute for Public Opinion Research, Florida International University.

Hernandez, Rafael, and Redi Gomis. 1986. "Retrato del Mariel: el ángulo socio-económico." *Cuadernos de Nuestra America* 3 (January–June):138–139.

Konczal, Lisa. 1997. *Immigrant Identity and Academic Orientation: Nicaraguan and Cuban Adolescents in Miami.* Washington, DC: American Anthropological Association.

Konczal, Lisa. 1999. *Assimilating into Hispanic America: The Case of Nicaraguan Immigrant Adolescents.* Miami, Florida: Immigration and Ethnicity Institute, Florida International University.

Levine, Barry B. 1985. "The Capital of Latin America." *Wilson Quarterly* (Winter): 46–73.

Masud-Piloto, Felix Roberto. 1996. *From Welcomed Exiles to Illegal Immigrants: Cuban Migration to the U.S., 1959–1995.* Totowa, NJ: Rowman and Littlefield.

Miami-Dade County, Department of Planning and Zoning. 1999. *Population by Race and Hispanic Origin, Miami-Dade County, 2000.* Miami: Miami-Dade County.

Moncarz, R. 1978. "The Golden Cage: Cubans in Miami." *International Migration Review* 16:160–173.

Moreno, Dario. 1996. "Cuban-American Political Empowerment." In *The Politics of Minority Coalitions: Race, Ethnicity, and Shared Uncertainties*, W. C. Rich, ed. Westport, CT: Praeger.

Moreno, Dario, and Christopher L. Warren. 1992. "The Conservative Enclave: Cubans in Florida." In *Latinos in the 1988 Elections*, R. de la Garza, ed. Boulder, CO: Westview Press.

Nijman, Jan. 1996. "Ethnicity, Class, and the Economic Internationalization of Miami." In *Social Polarization in Post-Industrial Metropolises*, John O'Laughlin and J. Friedrichs, eds. Berlin and New York: Walter de Gruyter: 283–300.

O'Connor, Anne-Marie. 1992. "Trying to Set the Agenda in Miami." *Columbia Journalism Review* 31(1).

Pedraza, Sylvia. 1996. "Cuba's Refugees: Manifold Migrations." In *Origins and Destinies: Immigration, Race, and Ethnicity in America*, S. Pedraza and R. Rumbaut, eds. pp. 263–279. Belmont, CA: Wadsworth.

Pedraza-Bailey, Sylvia. 1985. *Political and Economic Migrants in America: Cubans and Mexicans*. Austin: University of Texas Press.

Perez, Lisandro. 1986. "Immigrant Economic Adjustment and Family Organization: The Cuban Success Story Reexamined." *International Migration Review* 4(1):1–20.

Perez Firmat, Gustavo. 1994. *Life on the hyphen: The Cuban-American Way*. Austin: University of Texas Press.

Porter, Bruce, and Marvin Dunn. 1984. *The Miami Riot of 1980: Crossing the Bounds*. Lexington, MA: D.C. Heath and Company.

Portes, Alejandro. 1969. "Dilemmas of a Golden Exile: Integration of Cuban Refugee Families in Milwaukee." *American Sociological Review* 34:505–518.

Portes, Alejandro. 1987. "The Social Origins of the Cuban Enclave Economy of Miami." *Sociological Perspectives* 30(October):340–371.

Portes, Alejandro, and Robert L. Bach. 1985. *Latin Journey: Cuban and Mexican Immigrants in the United States*. Berkeley: University of California Press.

Portes, Alejandro, and Juan Clark. 1987. "Mariel Refugees: Six Years After." *Migration World Magazine* 15(5):14–18.

Portes, Alejandro, Juan M. Clark, and Robert D. Manning. 1985. "After Mariel: A Survey of the Resettlement Experiences of 1980 Cuban Refugees in Miami." *Cuban Studies* 15(2):37–59.

Portes, Alejandro, and Robert D. Manning. 1986. "The Immigrant Enclave: Theory and Empirical Examples." In *Competitive Ethnic Relations*, S. Olzak and J. Nagel, eds. Orlando, FL: Academic Press.

Portes, Alejandro, and Rubén Rumbaut. 2000. *Legacies: The Children of Immigrants in America*. Berkeley: University of California Press.

Portes, Alejandro, and Rubén G. Rumbaut. 1990. *Immigrant America: A Portrait*. Berkeley: University of California Press.

Portes, Alejandro, and Alex Stepick. 1993. *City on the Edge: The Transformation of Miami*. Berkeley: University of California Press.

Rodríguez, Margarita. 1999. "Different Paths, Same Destination: U.S.-bound Nicaraguan and Cuban Migration in a Comparative Perspective." Ph.D. diss., University of Miami.

Rohter, Larry. 1992. "Miami Leaders Are Condemned by Rights Unit." In *New York Times*, p. A18.

Rumbaut, Rubén. 1994. "The Crucible Within: Ethnic Identity, Self-Esteem and Segmented Assimilation among Children of Immigrants." *International Migration Review* 18(Winter):748–794.

Rumbaut, Rubén. 1998a. "Transformations: The Post-Immigrant Generation in an Age of Diversity. American Diversity: Past, Present, and Future." *Eastern Sociological Society*, Philadelphia.

Rumbaut, Rubén G. 1997b. "Paradoxes and Orthodoxies of Assimilation." *Sociological Perspectives* 40(0731-1214):1–22.

Rumbaut, Rubén G. 1998b. "Pinos Nuevos? Growing up American in Cuban Miami." *Cuban Affairs* IV(3–4):4–5.

Stepick, Alex. 1992. *Social, Political and Cultural Capital: Haitians and Cubans in Miami*. Middlebury, VT: Middlebury College Conference on Immigration, 1992.

Stepick, Alex. 1998. *Pride against Prejudice: Haitians in the United States*. Boston: Allyn & Bacon.

Stepick, Alex, and Guillermo Grenier. 1993. "Cubans in Miami." In *The Barrios: Latinos and the Underclass Debate*, J. Moore and R. Rivera, eds. New York: Russell Sage Foundation.

Commentary

John H. Coatsworth

The interesting and provocative essays by George Sanchez, Juan Flores, and Alex Stepick and Carol Stepick raise significant issues that confront Latino historiography in the twenty-first century. They are also wonderfully self-conscious examples of the current interpretive and analytic preoccupations of the best scholars in this field. I will first comment on the issues that their essays address. Then I will point out five areas of potentially fruitful historical research that these essays suggest but do not touch on explicitly.

These authors are representative of one of the major strengths of Latino history and of Latino studies more generally. They are important "public intellectuals," whose words are read and carry weight well beyond the academy. Their work combines analysis and advocacy, scientific detachment in research and a constant awareness of how history is communicated and how it can affect Latino culture identity as well as large U.S. (and even international) political processes. In Latino studies, as in other fields, taking this posture has yielded great creativity and insight, though it can also entail both personal and intellectual risks.

Juan Flores and the Stepicks focus on Caribbean–Latinos. Flores restores the hyphen to a term invented precisely to escape hyphenation. He cites evidence of collaboration among Cuban, Puerto Rican, and Dominican immigrants in music, occasional appeals to unity in their national and disaporic literatures, the cultural and historical ties of all three groups to a common Afro-Caribbean past, the domination of their former homelands by the same U.S. government and private corporations, and their shared experience of immigration and of racism in the United States.

Flores concludes in his paper, as he does in his important new book,[1] that the three immigrant "enclaves," as he calls them, "have taken such discrepant shape" in the twentieth century that they have become isolated from each other. The obstacles to "la unión antillana" mirror those that have made the twentieth-century evolution of the three countries so different. Although he concludes with some suggestive references to U.S. racism, "pan-Caribbean solidarity," and globalization, he tells us that Latino political cohesion is not likely "at least for the foreseeable future." He thus concurs with the Stepicks, who emphasize the divisions emerging in Miami's recent history as the Latino population becomes increasingly diverse. They explore how more recent arrivals from Central and South America are challenging the hegemony of the old Cuban exile community.

Flores has won well-deserved recognition for the sophistication and realism with which his work addresses the distinct historical trajectories represented in the Spanish-speaking Caribbean and for the way he uses these differences to deepen understanding of the unique cultural, artistic, and musical achievements of each country. But for two reasons I hope he is wrong about the obstacles that impede the development of pan-Caribbean or pan-Latino identities. First, if he is right, then his own celebration of this cause collapses into a tradition of utopian appeals for unity that have proved in the past to be as futile as they were beautiful. This, of course, is the generic curse of the public intellectual—aesthetically memorable irrelevance.

Second, I think a different curse may be more likely. The pace of change, especially in the Caribbean and among Caribbean–Latinos, is accelerating. (This topic is well addressed in the Stepicks' elegant analysis of the recent transformation of Miami.) One fascinating aspect of this acceleration is the development of multiple, complementary, and even competing identities and personas among a continuously mobile population that has somehow managed to cope with, adapt to, and even reshape cultures and societies at ends of the migration path. A single individual, for example, can now exist as a Dominican, a Caribbean–Latino, a "Latino," and a U.S. citizen all at once and still preserve a mental landscape ready to incorporate much more.

George Sanchez's paper addresses issues in the historiography of Latinos within the larger field of U.S. history. He rightly praises recent trends in writing Latino history, particularly efforts to compare the histories of the various Latino and Latin American immigrant groups. Comparative history of this kind is crucial, of course, if we are to deepen our understanding of each of the distinct Latino diasporas in the United States. Sanchez's main focus, however, is on race. He reminds us that the meaning of race and of racial identity has nothing to do with biology and everything to do with history—with social and cultural practice. He argues, again I think rightly, that biological mestizaje is therefore no substitute for (and indeed may be partly a result of) political struggles against racism and intolerance . . . "and all the boundaries that govern privilege in our society."

Sanchez's argument, and especially his conclusion, suggests a research agenda broader than either his paper or that of Juan Flores addresses explicitly. In my view, at least five sets of issues could become significant for Latino history and historiography as the twenty-first century advances.

First, as Sanchez implies, I think it will be important for Latino history to emancipate itself from the conditions of U.S. national historiography. It is useful to compare the history of diverse Latino groups within the United States to that of Latin Americans in Latin America. From the perspective of the United States, Latin American immigrants and the Latino population in general constitute a disadvantaged minority. From the Dominican or Mexican perspective, they look different: younger, better educated, more entrepreneurial, luckier, with money to invest and family contacts that enable them to travel where others cannot. These contrasts have long shaped the immigrant and Latino experience of the United States.

Second, Latino history is also traditional history. Many Latin American immigrants return to their home countries or send money home. They are transforming not only the United States but their home countries as well. Latino history is being made *in Latin America*, not just in the United States. Latino historians and Latin American historians need to work more closely together.

Third, these papers suggest to me that historians of the United States, and of the Latino and African American experience specifically, have much to offer historians of Latin America. I think it likely that the historiography of Latin America, at least for the first decades of the twenty-first century, will be characterized by the discovery or perhaps rediscovery of the significance of race and racism. Historians of the Latino and African American and Asian American experiences in the United States could contribute to this trend by learning more about Latin America. They could also deepen their understanding of racial and ethnic discrimination in U.S. history by subjecting it to comparison with notable Latin American cases, as previous generations of U.S. historians from Frank Tannenbaum to Eugene Genovese did so effectively.[2]

Fourth, we can deepen our understanding of Latino history in the United States by extending the comparisons that George Sanchez cited in his essay to include comparative history of Latino and non-Latino immigrants and their descendants. Indeed, I believe such a move will be crucial if Latino history is ever to attain a central place in the historiography of the United States as a whole, not to mention the curriculum of U.S. history and American studies in our universities. The contemporary social science literature suggests quite strongly that recent Latin American immigrants and their children are not experiencing the intergenerational assimilation and upward mobility that immigrants in the late nineteenth and early twentieth centuries experienced.

Finally, vast under-researched areas in the (more or less conventional) political, economic, social, and cultural history of Latinos in the United States still remain to be explored. I was reminded of this the other day when I finally got around to reading a 1998 paper by Peter Temin, an economic historian of the United States, entitled "The Stability of the American Business Elite."[3] Temin showed that among the 500 largest companies "that have dominated economic life in this country for the past 100 years," 80 percent of the CEOs in 1900 were "male, white, and mostly native-born Protestants from good families." Using 1996 data, Temin then estimated that between 75 and 88 percent of today's CEOs at the top 500 were also "male, white, and mostly native-born Protestants from good families." He then looked at the 400 richest individuals in the United States in 1996 and discovered that at least 83 percent of them were "male, white, and mostly native-born Protestants from good families." This leads me to conclude that George Sanchez is surely right about the need to work on "all the boundaries that govern privilege." As the Stepicks remind us, boundaries are also an integral part of the Latino experience, which is why I hope that Juan Flores is not so utopian as he imagines in his vision of Latino unity.

NOTES

1. Juan Flores, *From Bomba to Hip-Hop: Puerto Rican Culture and Latino Identity—Popular Cultures* (New York: Columbia University Press, 2000).

2. Frank Tannenbaum, *Slave and Citizen: The Negro in the Americas* (New York: Vintage Books, 1946); Eugene Genovese, "The American Slave Systems in World Perspective," Part One of *The World the Slaveholders Made: Two Essays in Interpretation* (New York: Vintage Books, 1969). See also Carl Degler, *Neither Black Nor White: Slavery and Race Relations in Brazil and the United States* (New York: Macmillan, 1971).

3. Peter Temin, "The Stability of the American Business Elite" (Unpublished paper, National Bureau of Economic Research, Historical Paper 110, December 1998).

Chapter 4

Community Dynamics
and the Rise of Street Gangs

Diego Vigil

The roots of Chicano gangs in Los Angeles can be traced to the settlement patterns Mexican immigrants typically had to follow in a city that was ill prepared for their integration. Being forced into isolated and physically substandard neighborhoods (barrios and colonias) had a series of repercussions; for example, Mexicans were socially distanced and made to feel inferior and marginal. Thus the children of the immigrants started off socially and psychologically marginalized, and conventional socialization routines were largely unavailable to them. This chapter outlines why ecological and socioeconomic factors figure prominently in the segregation and isolation of Mexicans and examines how the rate and direction of acculturation were undermined by these conditions. In the wake of maladaptation from such strains and pressures, a street youth population emerged and evolved into a gang subculture. The power of place and that of space are noteworthy in these developments.

These changes date from the aftermath of the 1910 Mexican Revolution. After large-scale immigration from Mexico, street groups of second-generation Mexican American youths began to emerge. More established gangs can be traced from at least the 1930s (Bogardus 1926, 1934; Vigil 1993b). Youth street groups that began rather innocuously as loose assemblages of wayward children had solidified and evolved within twenty years into formal gangs with a more destructive, violent bent to their routines and rhythms. Why did these transformations occur in such a short period of time? Much of what is recounted here about developments in the early decades of the twentieth century is reminiscent of what scholars several decades later have noted about "shantytown" migrant enclaves in various Latin American nations (Lomnitz 1977; Leeds 1974). Indeed, similar types of youth street groups have been noted in Mexico City (Lomnitz 1978) and

97

along the border (Castro 1981; Valenzuela 1988). In recent decades, as more rural migrants have flocked to the cities, gangs have become a transnational phenomenon (Hazlehurst and Hazlehurst 1998).

Los Angeles was undergoing rapid industrial and technological changes in the early twentieth century, and urban planning was unable to keep up and accommodate the growth in the population. Thus a makeshift and uneven integration of Mexican immigrants and their families occurred. This adaptation process was especially difficult because the newcomers were poor, came from a rural background, and fit into a familiar and devalued stereotype as "Indian-looking" Mexican workers. In short, the community dynamic that generated street gangs stemmed from the way Los Angeles grew and developed and from the way racism toward Mexicans segregated and isolated them from most sectors of society.

Indeed, the rapidity and unevenness of such changes affected the urbanization process, particularly where Mexicans were to work, live, raise their families, and gain access and exposure to, and identification with, the dominant Anglo American culture and institutions. The manner in which these changes unfolded has tended to marginalize the Chicano population. In fact, multiple marginality prevailed. That is, at every point of entry or contact and at every level of integration and adjustment, Chicano adaptation to the United States was outside of mainstream consideration (Vigil 1988; Vigil and Yun 1996, 1998). Traditional institutions of social control were undermined in this context, causing many youths to spend most of their time on the streets rather than at home or in school. Street socialization was the result for many barrio (neighborhood) youths, sometimes seriously affecting at least 4 to 14 percent of the children who formed street gangs (Vigil 1990).

ECOLOGICAL ASPECTS

Where Mexican immigrants settled contributed to a number of problems. Some of these problems reflected inadequate infrastructure and public amenities, and others had a more long-lasting geo-social imprint. First, let's consider the ecological aspects. Low-paying jobs, of course, necessitated settlement in areas where land values and rent were low. Barrio enclaves, then, can be traced in part to the fact that immigrants who earned little pay were forced to settle in areas that they could afford. Mexican immigrants, like other ethnic groups, also gravitated to communities that reflected their own customs and patterns, for this lessened the effects of culture shock and gave them a sense of community and security.

However, the negative treatment immigrants received from the host cultural group also reinforced this choice. Discrimination forced Mexican immigrants to congregate in locations separate from the dominant Anglo majority. As one early researcher (Douglas 1928, p. xiv) noted, Mexican barrios in Santa Ana were characterized by inferior locations, poor housing, and segregation and discrimination. In combination, these influences led to the spatial separation of immigrant settlers from the surrounding community and to the creation of visually distinct neighborhoods. The common implications of the phrase *across the tracks* (or irrigation canals, highways, river, or freeway) reflect this spatial separation and visual distinctiveness (Bogardus 1934, p. 70). In addition, most barrios are characterized by homes that are smaller in size, are occupied by more people per household, and are generally lacking in adequate public services.

Discrimination and residential segregation helped developers and landlords make a profit without considering immigrants' needs. Additionally, rapid technological and economic changes often resulted in poor city planning: inferior land sites for development, unsurveyed and unpaved streets, lack of public utilities such as lights and sewers, and so on. Settlement patterns in southern California attest to this fact, as numerous barrios or colonias (rural colonies) were founded in the most neglected interstices of the cities and outlying rural areas.

Los Angeles has had a barrio since the nineteenth century, located just east of the town center (Romo 1983). Before large-scale immigration in this century, there were also colonias or pockets of Mexican American residents in outlying rural districts. Some of the latter, such as Los Nietos and Cucamonga, date from early Mexican rancho (ranch) days. By the 1920s and 1930s, these urban and rural barrios were filled with newcomers, and new barrios had been established. Most were of the interstitial variety in the urban area, such as El Hoyo Maravilla. Gustafson, a Methodist minister, reported that "El Hoyo" looked like a "hobo jungle" (1940, p. 43). Several decades later, Moore (1978) found that things had remained largely unchanged in El Hoyo Maravilla, home to one of the oldest and most deeply rooted gangs in East Los Angeles.

Rural colonias were usually situated next to the workplace. Cucamonga is an example of such a place. At first the Mexican settlements were scattered in small pockets throughout the area (Guasti, Ontario) when they arrived as unskilled farm laborers to work in the citrus and vineyard industries. As the industries expanded, the need for more seasonal workers (and more year-round regulars) increased, the Mexicans eventually filled one particular neighborhood—Northtown (situated across the tracks and flood canal). This enclave had once been peopled largely by non-Mexican (Italian) semiskilled and skilled workers who eventually bought land of their own and moved out of the neighborhood. By the 1930s it was a Mexican barrio, and it has remained so to the present. In the mid-1980s, many of the streets were still unpaved, and those that were paved had no curbs or sidewalks. Most of the homes were small, graying, brownish clapboard structures with only a bedroom to contain an entire family. Outhouses, some sturdy and others dilapidated, dotted back yards in what was obviously a socially and physically isolated human congregation of fifteen hundred people.

Railroad section workers and their families settled in Watts, agricultural workers in Cucamonga, and so on. Romo underscored how Mexican workers and their families had to settle in labor camps near train track lines (1983, p. 69). Whether old or new, urban or rural, all of the camps exhibited the qualities noted earlier: spatial separation and visibly inferior housing. Kienle (1912, p. 8) early made this connection between workplace and liveplace, emphasizing how the railroad companies built long rows of sheds and deducted the rent from the workers' earnings. Other contemporary reports (such as Culp 1921) also noted these conditions.

ECOLOGICAL SIDE EFFECTS: GEO-SOCIAL RAMIFICATIONS

Researchers of the Chicago School of Urban Sociology have achieved a general understanding of the ways in which urbanism (the structure) and urbanization (the process) work to make certain segments of the city (ethnic groups, social classes, or residential areas, singly or in combination) more subject to human disorganization (Thrasher 1963 [1927]; Shaw and McKay 1942). Studies of early Mexican immigration to Los Angeles show that these new residents settled in neglected and inferior locations (Fuller 1974 [1920]). Bogardus (1926, 1934), trained at the University of Chicago, directed his USC students in this type of ecological work. These investigations found that areas that were initially bypassed in the development of urban Los Angeles—the "flats" or lowlands; the areas underneath bridges; and the undesirable gulches, ravines, and hollows—subsequently were developed with poor street planning and limited public services (Gustafson 1940; Ginn 1947).

Many of these "interstices" became marginal areas of the city, in which problems of social disorganization originated and grew. Gustafson (1940) underscored that it was poor racial groups that lived there, and further, that the "lowlands (the Flats; an area that gradually produced at least three gangs: Primera [First St.] Flats, Tercera [Third St. Flats] and Cuatro [Fourth St.] Flats) have always been occupied by Mexican laborers and less favored classes" (p. 40). As a result, the police were always looking for criminals there. Ginn (1947) concurs and adds that isolated neighborhoods were very crowded and without outlets for youths. This is one of the reasons why so many Mexican youths congregate on street corners and subsequently become delinquents. Although some of these observers' conclusions (especially on crime and delinquency) are overstated (or perhaps prophetic, given that these areas are still trouble spots), they nevertheless seem to reflect a general consensus on the problematic qualities of these neglected interstices, including emergent gangs. Bogardus had earlier warned that "these gangs are not yet of the fixed type" and urged that the city "solve its boy gang problem while it is still comparatively easy to cope with it" (1926, p. 89). In time, Bogardus and others became resigned to the way that isolated, crowded, and inadequately organized communities set Mexicans apart from the rest of southern California society (1934, p. 19).

With the expansion and growth of older barrios and the development of new ones, concomitant with the spread of metropolitan Los Angeles, ecological conditions had taken their toll. Within two decades of his warning of a "boy gang problem," Bogardus (1943) was writing of the urgent need to recognize the problems generated by these settlement patterns. When the federal government stepped in to establish public housing developments, it was too late. Street youth groups had successfully taken root and were increasingly taking a more destructive route. East Los Angeles has five such projects. Many of these have become barrios in their own right. Although intended to curb urban social disorganization, the projects were engulfed by the larger barrio world that existed all around them. Gustafson (1940, p.112) recognized this problem at a public housing development being built in the early 1940s. Confirming those fears, the tract later became the territory of Barrio Nuevo Estrada Courts, one of the bigger gangs in the area during the early 1980s.

Ecological conditions in the barrios of Los Angeles and adjacent rural areas have improved since those neighborhoods were first established in the 1930s and 1940s, but some, such as White Fence, still bear the marks of a backwater enclave. Public housing developments and the expansion of barrios into working-class areas have brought major changes. Even the oldest barrios have often upgraded their own housing, and roads have been paved, and gas, water, power, and sewer services have been introduced. Notwithstanding these changes, neither older nor more recent urban barrios in the area compare in quality of residential amenities to most other areas of the city. Suburban developments have surrounded rural and semi-rural colonia pockets, which have thus come to resemble urban barrios. However, many of the colonias still exhibit signs of underdevelopment, lacking adequate sewer systems, major retail centers, paved sidewalks, and/or adequate housing.

Social and spatial isolation resulted from these strains and stresses, disrupting social networks and breeding dysfunctional forces. As neglected, underserved sections of the larger community, the barrios took on the appearance of underdeveloped backwashes. Although most of the residents are law-abiding citizens, they are regularly exposed to vices and antisocial activities, even if only as victims. This is particularly true for those who are concentrated in densely populated, rapidly decaying areas (Clinard 1960, 1968; Shaw and McKay 1942).

Barrio residents are aware of these variations among barrios and of the usually more salient difference between barrios and other neighborhoods (Achor 1978). They are equally aware of the discrepancies in official and commercial attitudes that go with that difference. Typically this awareness is expressed as discontented grumbling, but increasingly in recent years it has been articulated in organized and quasi-organized protest. Some protest and resistance efforts have included pressuring auto insurance companies to lower insurance rates; other initiatives are aimed at improving school facilities. In one memorable event known as the 1968 Blow-Outs, over seven thousand students walked out of Eastside high schools. Many outlying rural colonias have lodged similar protests.

HOW ISOLATION AND SEGREGATION CONTRIBUTES TO GANGS

The specific areas that will be addressed in this assessment are economic restraints, the rate and direction of acculturation, a sense of inferiority, isolation and implosion, and the effect of an encapsulated "pocket"-type of community.

Economic restraints on families and children are undoubtedly the most important in understanding the emergence of street gangs. The obvious features are nutrition and health needs and practices, as well as unsanitary housing conditions. The adjustment from a rural, peasant background to living in the United States also took its toll. Many immigrants raised large families under squalid conditions, in a modern version of the hacienda and debt peonage, and gender roles became redefined. In this context, most immigrant heads of households moved their families right next to or close to the work site, becoming a permanent workforce near a field or factory. Poor pay and working conditions went alongside job insecurity, as oppressive bosses and unpredictable economic cycles sometimes turned immigrant workers out into the streets. Many women had by now joined the industrial workforce and they, especially the single mothers among them, were acutely affected by these forces. Most of the unemployed workers were confined to their only known world, the little island of a "barrio." To seek and find another job somewhere else was difficult if not impossible. Family life was thus often severely strained, and the repercussive effect was to undermine the stability of the household and the social control necessary to supervise the children. Street socialization resulted when households became crowded and family life was disrupted, leading children to spend more and more of their time out on the streets. As Robert Smith has noted in another context (see Chapter 5 in this volume), male socialization is affected by work conditions and expectations, and if routes to employment and to the respectability associated with having a job are undermined, then young men seek other ways to get money and gain respect.

Even for those fortunate enough to find a good job, then there was the additional restraint of living in a segregated community, which limited both social mobility and residential mobility. Most of the workers were locked into their job and social status, with little possibility of moving up. For many, the job site and home site were synonymous. Housing covenants and restrictions ensured that anyone who did manage to move up would still find it nearly impossible to move out. Those who did upgrade on their skills, knowledge, and pay usually purchased a home in the barrio and made improvements on it. In that respect, they joined the ranks of the most prosperous in the barrio and were recognized as lower-class role models.

The rate and direction of acculturation to dominant values and norms are also affected by living in such an isolated environment. Having access to, and a mode of identification with, the dominant Anglo social world and cultural repertoire is essential for integration into society (Vigil 1997). Labor from Mexico was sought after, but Mexicans themselves were unwelcome and were relegated to second-class status. Thus adjustment to American society and integration into it were thwarted and slowed. At the job site and at home it was customary to speak primarily in Spanish. Most theaters and recreational facilities were off limits, so workers and their families could hardly travel outside the barrio. Mass media in the form of television was not yet a factor, so entertainment and social outlets within or near the barrio evolved. Here again, contact and interaction with people and institutions of the dominant culture were limited. Children of immigrants were subject to additional pressure from two sources: from Anglo teachers in schools who reprimanded them for speaking Spanish and from Mexican parents to whom they returned home and with whom they spoke (of necessity) in Spanish. *Choloization* is an apt term for this linguistic and cultural conflict and confusion. The term is derived from *cholo,* a word used for centuries in Latin America to describe cultural or racial marginality (Vigil 1988, 1990). The latter is a key aspect of the processes leading to the formation of gangs and the shaping of gang members. *Cholo* is a self-descriptive label that street youths use on a regular basis. It reflects their cultural marginality and tendency to create their own language and style, sometimes called Spanglish.

Barriers stemming from location or place are so pervasive that the cumulative effect is the development of a sense of inferiority. This occurs on both a personal and a social level for barrio dwellers. For the second-generation children, the schooling experience adds a dimension that deepens ambiguity of self-image. The gender aspect of this conflict with schools has recently been noted in New York City (see Chapter 5). Females often have been able to take advantage of opportunities, whereas males, just as in earlier times, have become more alienated from American institutions. Schools had a notoriously poor record in the early years of barrio settlement (Valencia 1991). For example, segregated schools were quite common in rural areas; the docu-drama on the Lemon Grove incident near San Diego, California, in 1930 serves as a reminder of this era—separate and unequal schools (Alvarez 1988; Gonzales 1990). Urban schools also failed in this regard, and even to this day, the dropout rate in inner-city Mexican American neighborhoods is close to 50 percent (Vigil 1997). With stressed family situations and poor schooling experiences, many youths are pushed out into the streets for their education. In fact, it is important to underscore that the street gang, now as then, remains the socializer of last resort and fills the voids in parenting, schooling, and policing. Inferior law enforcement, of course, is also a factor in the sense of inferiority that emerges among barrio dwellers, particularly when police brutality and harassment are part of the historical record (Escobar 1998).

Finally, the development of this type of "pocket" settlement creates problems within the community. Rather than facilitating an open and fluid adaptation and adjustment to American society, the insulated, isolated, closed community that emerges implodes on itself. Sometimes this kind of settlement fosters a distinctively separatist identity, where each barrio begins to think only of itself: Cuca(monga), Hoyo, Lomas, Pacoima. Rather than networks and bridges among Mexican immigrants, there are gulfs and moats, each enclave a castle unto itself. The more isolated and poverty-stricken the barrio, the more "boundedness" and the more likely that the children there have severe problems that lead inexorably to prolonged and deep street socialization. A similar pattern has been noted for Mexican youth in other cities (see Chapter 5). These factors appear to generate the toughest, most active, and most violent of the street gangs. Law enforcement historical accounts of gangs in East Los Angeles often refer to old country village rivalries carried over to the new barrios as the initial source of gang conflicts in the 1930s, but this view is shortsighted. The ecological factor and its manifestations always escape such observers who look for the causes of gang behavior elsewhere than in the United States.

CONCLUSION

In sum, the settlement of Mexicans in segregated, visually inferior locations made adaptation difficult. A life of poverty in the hollows, at the bottom of ravines, and across the tracks did little to enhance the adjustment of new groups of Mexican immigrants to American society. Mexicans residing in the United States felt unwanted and discriminated against in the aftermath of the American takeover of Texas, California, and the Southwest. Thereafter, the large-scale Mexican immigration to densely populated areas in this century created the conditions for major social problems. The early "boy gang problem" that observers noted in the 1920s has now become a "gang subculture problem" with subsequent generations of Mexican youths (Vigil 1988).

In the following decades, street gangs emerged in other populations in Los Angeles (Vigil 2001). Sharing many of the same characteristics of the Mexican American gangs, these other groups had migrated to the city and settled in neighborhoods separate from the dominant society and had struggled with the barriers associated with a low-income life. African American gangs followed those of Mexican Americans and by the 1980s received widespread media coverage (including the film *Colors*). The imagery of ghetto violence and drug trafficking captured the public eye. Soon the Vietnamese and Central American immigrant groups, both escaping the horrors of war, generated street youth gangs. Although the great majority of these populations were able to avoid the destruction and violence born of the streets, those who became street-socialized were pulled into a life that gangs dominated. Ecological stressors and the ill effects of where people lived and worked affected these other ethnic groups much as they did the Mexican immigrants.

In the late twentieth century, gangs became a transnational problem, first in European countries such as Germany, the Netherlands, and Denmark, and now in places like Brazil, El Salvador, Guatemala, and Mexico. The explanation for this phenomenon can be traced in part to media and popular music, as in the case of "gangster rap" generating the "wigger" (a word derived from the racist term *nigger* and applied to white youths who have embraced black rap) subculture in Denmark. Occasionally, the dissemination of gang culture is more direct. Salvadoran immigrants' children forged their own gangs in Los Angeles, and after the 1992 riots, immigration authorities, in collusion with law enforcement, deported hundreds of gang members back to El Salvador. In so doing, American authorities inadvertently exported gang culture. At present, street gangs are an unavoidable presence in places like San Salvador, capital of El Salvador. Street gangs also appear to be emerging in Chiapas, Mexico, where I have been examining how local Indian migration to the city has affected families and children.

Ecological influences exert a strong shaping force on all humans. All children in a place that is isolated and "different" are affected by this knowledge. For example, barrio gang and nongang youth know that their self-identities are shaped by barrio life, for they know that a spatial and social distance separates them from their more affluent neighbors and that this distinctiveness affects their quality of life, job prospects, educational opportunities, and the like. Poverty, discrimination, and social/cultural cohesiveness helped create Mexican barrios, but the effects of urbanization—along with poor city planning and neglectful and uncaring authorities—made the barrios an ecologically inferior place to raise a family.

The community dynamics that created gangs and shaped gang members stemmed from the nexus of immigration, rapid industrial and capitalist development, and poor urban planning. Sociocultural and sociopsychological repercussions emerged from where Mexicans lived and worked. Externally imposed restrictions resulted in the establishment of visually distinct and spatially separate communities. From this crucial marginalized beginning, the ripple effects of marginality consumed residents and their children. People there knew that they were in the backwaters of the city or area, and they understood that they were a low-status people. The seeds of resistance and protest were thus sown at that time, although decades passed before they bore fruit. School officials and other public servants began to think of these barrios and their people as a drain on resources and a nuisance. This disparaging attitude has become so ingrained that mention of the barrio, or of any low-income Mexican American neighborhood, usually involves social distancing ("They're from Northtown") or opprobrium ("They're from the projects").

Moreover, in the early decades of the last century, Los Angeles was undergoing rapid changes, developing from a Mexican pueblo to a major U.S. city in just a few short decades. Technological expansion and the need for a nearby, steady, exploitable, and cheap labor pool made it imperative that workers and their families settle in readily available and cheap locations. The ecological niches that constituted the new Mexican settlements reflected policies based on expedience with little concern for the residents or their needs. Workers were paid poorly and in turn paid less for rent in substandard housing; consequently, social and residential mobility were severely compromised, and barrios became pressure cookers with no way out.

In most instances, city planners failed to monitor and address the environmental effects of haphazard settlement patterns. In fact, private developers and city planners had a "gentlemen's agreement" to ignore restrictions and codes, and they regularly selected sites that had been bypassed for previous development projects. For example, a Santa Ana development was built on swamp land and included plumbing fixtures with no sewer outlet. East Los Angeles had numerous barrios sprout up in undesirable and unsafe niches that were outside regular sewage, electric, and gas services and beyond bus routes. The result was an appendage rather than an integrated part of the larger community. In short, immigrant adaptation to Los Angeles during a time of rapid industrial changes and poor, uneven urban planning wreaked havoc for the Mexican people. The newcomers were often engulfed in a sense of isolation and exclusion. Moreover, the marginal nature of the immigrants' limited contact with both city institutions and the Anglo ethnic group precluded their learning the ways of urban life and the language and customs of the dominant culture. Even Americanization learning programs failed because they were steeped in the racist assumption that Mexicans were culturally (read: racially) deficient (Gonzales 1990). Schools and law enforcement did not ameliorate these problems and, for the most part, exacerbated them. Left with little institutional assistance in their marginalized situations, Chicano youths created (and subsequently strengthened and expanded) street gangs to address, on their own, the voids in their socialization.

REFERENCES

Achor, Shirley. 1978. *Mexican Americans in a Dallas Barrio.* Tucson: University of Arizona Press.

Alvarez, Robert. 1988. "National Politics and Local Responses: The Nation's First Successful Desegregation Court Case." In *School and Society: Learning Content Through Culture,* H. T. Trueba and C. Delgado-Gaitan, eds. New York: Praeger.

Bogardus, Emory S. 1943. "Gangs of Mexican American Youth." *Sociology and Social Research* 28:55–66.

Bogardus, Emory S. 1934. *The Mexican in the United States.* U.S.C. Social Science Series, #8. Los Angeles: University of Southern California.

Bogardus, Emory S. 1926. *The City Boy and His Problems.* Los Angeles: House of Ralston, Rotary Club of Los Angeles.

Burgess, E. W. 1925. "The Growth of the City: An Introduction to a Research Project." In *The City,* R. E. Park, E. W. Burgess, R. O. McKensie, eds. pp. 47–62. Chicago: University of Chicago Press.

Castro, Gustavo López. 1981. *El Cholo: Origen y desarrollo.* Mexicali: Universidad Autónoma de Baja California.

Clinard, M. 1960. "Cross-Cultural Replication of the Relation of Urbanism to Criminal Behavior." *American Sociological Review* 25: 253–257.

Clinard, M. B. 1968. *Sociology of Deviant Behavior.* New York: Holt.

Culp, Alice Bessie. 1921. *A Case Study of the Living Conditions of Thirty-five Mexican Families of Los Angeles with Special Reference to Mexican Children.* Master's thesis, University of Southern California, Department of Sociology.

Douglas, Helen W. 1928. *The Conflict of Cultures in First-Generation Mexicans in Santa Ana, California.* Master's thesis, University of Southern California, Department of Sociology.

Escobar, Edward. 1998. *Race, Police, and the Making of a Political Identity: Mexican Americans and the L.A.P.D.* Berkeley: University of California Press.

Fuller, E. 1974. "The Mexican Housing Problem in Los Angeles" [originally published 1920]. In *Perspectives on Mexican American Life,* C. E. Cortez, ed., New York: Arno Press.

Ginn, M. D. 1947. *Social Implications of the Living Conditions of a Selected Number of Families Participating in the Cleland House Program.* Master's thesis, University of Southern California, Department of Sociology.

Gonzales, Gilbert. 1990. *Chicano Education in the Era of Segregation.* Philadelphia: The Balch Institute Press.

Gustafson, C. V. 1940. *An Ecological Analysis of the Hollenbeck Area of Los Angeles.* Master's thesis, University of Southern California, Department of Sociology.

Hazlehurst, K., and C. Hazlehurst, eds. 1998. *Gangs and Youth Subcultures: International Explorations.* New Brunswick, NJ: Transaction.

Kienle, John Emmanuel. 1912. *Housing Conditions Among the Mexican Population of Los Angeles.* Master's thesis, University of Southern California, Department of Sociology.

Leeds, Anthony. 1974. "Housing—Settlement Types, Arrangements for Living, Proletarianization, and the Social Structure of the City." In *Anthropological Perspectives on Latin American Urbanization,* vol. 4, Wayne A. Cornelius and Felicity M. Trueblood, eds., Beverly Hills: Sage.

Lomnitz, Larissa. 1978. "Mechanisms of Articulation Between Shantytown Settlers and the Urban System: *Urban Anthropology* 7(2):185–205.

Lomnitz, Larissa A. 1977. *Networks and Marginality: Life in a Mexican Shantytown.* New York: Academic Press.

Moore, Joan W. 1978 *Homeboys: Gangs, Drugs, and Prison in the Barrios of Los Angeles.* Philadelphia: Temple University Press.

Romo, Ricardo. 1983. *East Los Angeles: History of a Barrio.* Austin: University of Texas Press.

Shaw, C., and R. McKay. 1942. *Juvenile Delinquency and Urban Areas.* Chicago: University of Chicago Press.

Thrasher, Frederic M. 1963. *The Gang.* (originally published 1927). Chicago: University of Chicago Press.

Valencia, Richard. 1991. *Chicano School Failure and Success: Research on Policy Agendas for the 1990s.* London: The Falmer Press.

Vigil, James Diego. 2001. *A Rainbow of Gangs: Street Cultures in the Mega-City Youth.* Austin: University of Texas Press.

Vigil, James Diego. 1997. *Personas Mexicanas: Chicano High Schoolers in a Changing Los Angeles.* Ft. Worth, TX: Harcourt.

Vigil, James Diego. 1993b. "The Established Gang." In *Gangs: The Origins and Impact of Contemporary Youth Gangs in the United States,* S. Cummings and D. Monti, eds., New York: State University of New York Press, pp. 95–112.

Vigil, James Diego. 1990. "Cholos and Gangs: Culture Change and Street Youth in Los Angeles." In *Gangs in America,* R. Huff, ed., Beverly Hills, CA: Sage, pp. 116–128.

Vigil, James Diego. 1988. *Barrio Gangs.* Austin: University of Texas Press.

Vigil, James Diego, and Steve C. Yun. 1998. "Vietnamese Youth Gangs in the Context of Multiple Marginality and the Los Angeles Youth Gang Phenomenon." In *Gangs and Youth Subcultures: International Explorations*, K. Hazlehurst and C. Hazlehurst, eds., New Brunswick, NJ: Transaction, pp. 117–139.

Vigil, James Diego, and Steve C. Yun. 1996. "Southern California Gangs: Comparative Ethnicity and Social Control." In *Gangs in America*, 2nd ed., R. Huff, ed., Thousand Oaks, CA: Sage, 139–156.

Chapter 5

Gender, Ethnicity, and Race in School and Work Outcomes of Second-Generation Mexican Americans

Robert C. Smith

Why would second-generation Mexican American women in New York City do better in school and at work than their male counterparts? And what can these differences teach us about the construction of ethnicity, race, and gender and their relationship to schooling and work?[1] Although it has recently become true that more women than men attend college in the United States, my observations are intriguing because they contradict cultural expectations for early marriage and childbearing that tend to inhibit school and work success for Mexican American women (Gandara 1995). I hypothesize that second-generation men's and women's divergent fates reflect the construction of gender and "gendered ethnicity" at three strategic sites—at work, in school, and at home/in the community—where these constructions also interact with immigrant incorporation, class, and racial and ethnic processes. In this chapter, I present selected ethnographic, interview, and statistical evidence from a larger, ongoing project for which data are just beginning to be analyzed systematically.

INTRODUCTION

Theoretical Issues

These questions and empirical findings are important theoretically because they suggest previously unconsidered links among gender, race, and ethnicity within the context of second-generation incorporation, adaptation, and assimilation. In particular, this approach complicates and should deepen our understanding of how ethnicity, race, and gender are related and of how this relationship affects school and work. A dominant image in contemporary research on immigration, education, and mobility argues that immigrant ethnicity can facilitate the upward mobility of immigrants and their children, whereas "Americanization" (adaptation to norms and expectations of the native-born, especially those of native minorities) tends to inhibit upward mobility by fostering an oppositional stance toward mainstream institutions, education, and work. This dynamic underlies Ogbu's classic (1974, 1987) analysis of autonomous, voluntary, and involuntary migrants, in anthropology, and Portes and Zhou's (1993) concept of "segmented assimilation," in sociology. It is repeated in various forms by others (Suárez-Orozco 1989; Suárez-Orozco and Suárez-Orozco, 1995; Gibson 1988; Waters 1994; Zhou and Bankston 1998; Rumbaut 1994, 1997). Related work posits that niche formation and maintenance using ethnicity as a marker (Waldinger 1996) or movement into the mainstream economy (Nee, Sanders, and Sernau 1994) is the main mechanism for upward mobility.

This work offers an important alternative to the earlier dominant view that "Americanization" was the only upward path (Warner and Srole 1945). It also draws on solid empirical work to analyze insightfully how minority groups negotiate structural exclusion (Zhou and Bankston 1998; Gibson 1988; Fordham 1996; Portes and MacLeod 1998; Rumbaut 1994, 1997). Moreover, ethnic effects on academic achievement persist even when the study's design controls parents' socioeconomic status, education, and length of residency in the United States; the hours that the child spends on homework; and urban versus suburban location (Zhou 1999, p. 206; Kao and Tienda 1995).

However, none of these analyses takes sufficient account of how gender affects mobility—gender both in its own right and as a lens through which ethnicity is refracted. Portes and Zhou (1993), for example, explain why social organization and the social capital it engenders shape second-generation mobility, but not why this effect would be stronger for women. Matute-Bianchi (1986) analyzes how ethnic identities are related to school performance, but not how or why men and women are differently affected nor how these identities are themselves constructed. Ogbu's analysis does not explain intra-ethnic-group or gender differences well (see Gibson 1997; exceptions in the case of gender are Gibson 1988, Waters 1996, and Zhou and Bankston 1998). Neither Nee, Sanders, and Sernau (1994) nor Waldinger (1996) considers or explains gender's effect on niche formation or movement into the mainstream economy. This chapter attempts to examine the joint effects of gender, ethnicity, and race on the school and work outcomes of second-generation Mexican Americans in New York.

Mexicans in New York and This Study

The New York population of Mexican origin (including both immigrants and the native-born) was approximately 250,000–275,000 in 2000; thus they were the third largest Latino group, after Puerto Ricans and Dominicans. About half of these Mexicans were between the ages of 12 and 24 at the time of the study (Valdes de Montano, Maria, and Smith 1994; Smith 1995). This figure represents an incredible increase from the approximately 35,000–40,000 Mexicans in 1980 and the 100,000 in 1990.[2] Moreover, according to the New York City Department of Health, there was a 232 percent increase in births to Mexican mothers in the city between 1988 and 1996. "Little Mexicos" have sprung up in several places in New York City, in Hudson River valley towns, and on the whole east coast, including Georgia, the mid-Atlantic states, and New England. Moreover, the potential for future growth is tremendous.[3] Census experts estimate that Mexicans will soon become the largest Latino minority on the east coast (Alonso-Zaldivar 1999). In some of the places just mentioned, they already are.

The data analyzed in this chapter come from a larger, ongoing study of the school and work mobility of second-generation Mexicans Americans in New York. This project emerged out of a longitudinal ethnographic study that focused on the first-generation parents of many of these children, analyzing the types and implications of the transnational life that emerged between those in Mexico and in New York. As part of this ethnography, I got to know the children of the first generation, and in 1997 I began interviewing them. Between 1998 and 2000, a team of graduate and undergraduate researchers and I did more than 110 taped interviews, two to six hours in length, as well as extensive ethnographic work in the United States and Mexico, with key informants at home, in school, and at parties and other public places. The informants constitute a purposively stratified sample that is made up of roughly equal numbers of men and women and includes appreciable numbers of people, both those who finished school and who dropped out, both those who engage in transnational and ethnic activities and who do not, and those who are employed in various niches in the economy. We also did focus groups with selected informants, an approach that dovetailed well with the ethnography. These interviews are being coded for statistical analysis, and a variety of other quantitative analyses will eventually be done. This chapter presents some of the ethnographic insights gained and conclusions drawn in the process of doing, transcribing, and coding the interviews and other research.

Gendered Ethnicity at Three Strategic Sites

I propose that a fuller understanding of second-generation Mexican American men's and women's work and educational mobility can be had by examining the construction of gender and ethnicity at three sites: at work, in school, and at home/in the community, where other processes of parents' immigrant adaptation, class, ethnic organization, and racial processes are also important. I hypothesize that gender roles and processes strongly affect how second-generation men and women come to understand their "Mexican" identity and profoundly affect their school and work practices, decisions, and aspirations. Part of the reason why this ethnic identity is so significant is that Mexicans occupy an ambivalent, "in-between" position in New York's racial and ethnic hierarchies. They are not "mainstream American" white, but they are neither in nor completely excluded from the most stigmatized groups, blacks and Puerto Ricans, nor are they completely excluded from the "white ethnic" immigrant groups of Italians, Greeks, and other immigrants and their descendants (see Smith 1995, 1996; Roediger 1991; see also Chapters 1, 2, and 12 in this volume). Moreover, the relationship to this in-between position changes by generation and gender. The second generation has a more complex relationship to this in-between position and can occupy different places on this continuum in different contexts. Women, in general, have an easier time negotiating ethnic spaces and experience different "rules of engagement" with American institutions (Suárez-Orozco 1999, p. 4; Fordham 1996; Zhou and Bankston 1998; Gibson 1988). Finally, the changes in the very nature of migration from Mexico to the United States have important implications for various aspects of incorporation and for Mexicans' negotiation of their "in-between" status.

GENDERED ETHNICITY IN THE LABOR MARKET

Our general findings are that a minority of both men and women in the labor market are upwardly mobile—understood in terms of increasing wages, better working conditions, and occupational prestige—but that the women are more likely than the men to be so and that their niches and mobility paths differ significantly. A cohort analysis (see Myers and Crawford 1997) comparing census figures for Mexican Americans in New York in 1980 and 1990 showed that 19 percent of men and 31 percent of women were upwardly mobile in terms of occupational prestige and income. Moreover, Mexican American women are almost twice as likely (17 percent) as men (9 percent) to work in professional/technical jobs (PUMS, Census 1990). Although our sample had roughly equal numbers of men and women, the men were more than twice as likely to work in immigrant industries and other miscellaneous low-paying jobs than the women (thirty-eight men and fourteen women), and they started to work at a younger age. Women are more likely to start work when they are older and to go into better niches, such as retail and mainstream jobs (secretarial, for example, or preprofessional). Roughly equal numbers of men and women worked in mainstream industry (seven men and eight women), including jobs in publishing, universities, and hospitals, or the retail sector, including the Gap, Banana Republic, and department stores (ten men and ten women). These positions offered some possibility of advancement, as well as benefits and higher wages. Most workers looked for jobs using informal personal references, but only women used formal school or organizational-based connections to look for their jobs. Moreover, the men who went into the retail or mainstream niches did so when they were older, after they had either entered college or secured some other training, such as in the military, whereas women entered these niches younger and usually right after high school or upon completion of a short post-high-school training course. These findings of female "pink collar" mobility and relatively greater male stagnation in immigrant or related economies is consistent with what Myers and Cranston (1997) found in Los Angeles using census data.

How do race, ethnicity, and gender play out in these contexts? There are at least two ways. First, women are more likely to be in jobs and niches where what Moss and Tilly (1996) call "soft skills" matter, and that offer better benefits and pay and greater opportunities for advancement. Second, the meaning of ethnicity is different for men and women in these different niches. Specifically, Mexicanness has a more pluralistic, ethnic meaning for those in the clerical or retail niches, especially the women, and a more racialized, excluded meaning for those in immigrant industries (see also Myers and Crawford 1997; Smith 1998). These points can be briefly illustrated by contrasting the experience of a Mexican American woman who works as a medical secretary with that of a Mexican American man who works in a restaurant with other immigrants. They are roughly the same age. She finished high school, took a training course, and makes nearly $40,000 per year; he dropped out of high school, got his job through his immigrant father's networks, and makes less than $22,000 per year as the only Mexican American working in a restaurant with Mexican immigrant employees. She says that her ethnicity is "not an issue" at work and that she is proud of her job. Her boss says that she is a good employee and offers this about "Lucy's" ethnicity:

> Lucy has an old school work ethic, like me. I've had a lot of problems with employees in the past, but Lucy—she's great, reliable, honest. [Later she adds:] Well, I consider Hispanics like Lucy white. I mean those with light skin. [Later, when asked to give the ethnic breakdown for her department:] Lucy is a lot lighter than the other two [Hispanic, Puerto Rican women]. I don't really consider her Hispanic.

In contrast, the Mexican American man reports that his attempts to get jobs in the retail sector have all been stymied in the interview stage, where, he reports, he does not know how to answer the questions in the way the interviewers want. Instead, he says he is in a job for an "immigrant," for

> [a person] that can't speak English. . . . I'm in a place where I don't wanna be . . . in a restaurant instead of white collar. . . . In blue collar, below blue

collar. . . . I'm in a job still working my butt off. I used to wash dishes—I can't believe it, with knowing English and getting $350 a week (to start) and not twice that in an office.

He lays responsibility for his failures squarely with himself—"It wasn't the school, it was me"—but he also says he did not think he could succeed in school because "you hardly don't see no Mexicans going up."

The meaning of Mexicanness for this second-generation man and woman could not be more different. For the man, his Mexicanness gets conflated with his limited success in the labor market, his lack of education, and his current (and probably future) work in an "immigrant" job, "a place where I don't wanna be." For the woman in the clerical sector, her ethnicity is "not an issue" and seems, indeed, to fade into whiteness in direct proportion to the esteem in which her (white) boss holds for her. The possible personal and theoretical meanings of ethnicity for the men who make their way in the retail sector are intriguing but cannot be pursued here. Yet they suggest, for example, that the niche has important effects on how gender and ethnicity are related. And they raise important questions for theories such as segmented assimilation, which posits that the children of immigrants are subject to stark limitations in mainstream schools and employment. They also raise the question of the impact of what Victoria Malkin, with characteristic wit, has labeled the "Benetton effect": hip urban consumers see a multicultural workforce as a positive selling point (Malkin 2000).

GENDER ROLES OF PARENTS AND CHILDREN AT HOME

These different employment outcomes result at least in part from the different gender roles that second-generation men and women adopt in different "activity settings" (Gallimore, Goldenberg, and Weisner 1993; Reese et al. 1995), a concept akin to "habitus" (Bourdieu 1977), as they focus on daily customs that teach them how to do things and what is normal. Activity settings are both reactions to external conditions and also actions that help create a child's orientation toward the world. Second-generation boys' and girls' activity settings are highly gendered. Nearly all our female informants reported that they were expected to return home directly after school. There they often had to care for siblings and help their parents with housework, while their brothers were allowed to hang out with friends. Our male informants reported largely similar impressions. As a result, despite the fact that the girls had more responsibilities and less free time, they were more likely to spend time studying (see also Kasinitz, Waters, and Mollenkoph 1997; Smith 1998; Fordham 1996). The boys' unstructured time often led to involvement in a variety of activities not conducive to studying, frequently including gangs; this lack of studying among the boys was condemned by parents only when some serious incident occurred. Moreover, parents often do not know what their children, especially boys, are actually doing after school. We have had parents declare confidently that their children were not involved with gangs when the boys had told us that indeed they were gang members, but had kept it a secret from their parents.

The consequences of these gender roles are exacerbated by the actual practices in which the women and men engage, in the activity settings they establish. The men must learn to project a formidable image in the street or in school; the women more often help their parents, and especially their mothers, interact with American institutions such as schools, social services, and others that require English. Valenzuela (1998) notes that girls are more likely than boys to tutor their parents and to help them negotiate contact with these institutions, which probably helps them to develop the "soft skills" required in the service sector in the mainstream economy. The link seems particularly important for the large segment of our female sample that is moving into positions as youth counselors, medical secretaries, and social service employees (Myers and Crawford 1997). Moreover, the kinds of tasks that the women are likely to engage in—not just simple translating, but filling in forms and advocating for their parents—seem particularly suited to educational and pink- or even white-collar success (Lara and Smith 2000). A final dynamic that contributes to the greater educational and work success of women is that the second generation is attuned to the differential changes in power held by their parents. Whereas their mothers often experience an increase in power through working outside of the home, their fathers experience a severe limitation of their prior privileges (Lara 1998; Guerrero-Rippberger 1999; see Hondagneu-Sotelo 1994; Smith, 2000)[4]. Thus second-generation men may believe that the women are "smarter" or "will get jobs ahead of them."

THE DYNAMICS OF GENDERED ETHNICITY AND SCHOOL CHOICE

This section analyzes two other related processes that help produce the differences in outcomes that we have noted between Mexican American men and women in New York. The first is the choosing of a high school, and the second is the different meanings of both Mexicanness and gender (femininity *and* masculinity) within the different school contexts and the evolving friendship groups of the second generation. The boys' experience of their Mexicanness and gender approximates a process of racialization, with the associated difficulties of engagement and entry, whereas the girls' experience approximates a process of ethnicization. Hence the girls benefit from greater ease of engagement and entry than the boys into the respective institutional settings in which they find themselves.

We trace these dynamics by examining a focus group we did with four men and two women during the summer of 1999. The women in the group did better in school than the men. Whereas the women had done well in high school and were all going to four-year colleges with scholarships, three of the men had struggled to complete high school and were currently attempting to make their way through junior colleges, in the hope of going on to four-year schools. One man was hoping to finish high school but has since left school to work.

A key structure here is the process of high school selection for New York City youth. There are formal and informal hierarchies and differences among high schools in New York City, which can be understood to be on a continuum. On one end are the "zone schools" to which everyone who lives within a certain "catchment area" must be admitted; students often regard them as bad and sometimes dangerous schools. On the other end are the elite schools of the system, such as the famous Stuyvesant High School, Bronx Science, and speciality high schools in business or performing arts, for which admission is citywide and highly competitive. Between these two extremes there is a lot of variation, including better zoned schools that also accept out-of-zone students who apply for special programs or in response to the schools' reputations for better teachers or students. But many of the most ill-prepared and poorly behaved students end up in their zone schools by default.

This continuum matters for our analysis. Both of the women in the group had chosen their high schools consciously in order to maximize their chances of school success and to avoid getting put into the local zone school, which they regarded as bad. Both had gotten extensive, explicit help from their older sisters who had gone to college and from school officials. One summarized her experience this way:

> My sister even asked her [high school] teachers about what school [I should] go to. . . . My AP [assistant principal] told me that "I have connections to put you in somewhere else" in case you don't get into a good place. . . . He knew I wanted to go where they will teach me something.

Both girls also ended up with ethnically diverse, academically successful in-school friendship groups, in contrast to the boys. This helped them to stay on track, as we shall see.

The boys, by contrast, simply went to the local zone school. One focus group participant contrasted her painstaking research into which schools to apply to with the lack of concern expressed by many Mexican boys she knows: "Some don't even bother picking [any schools]. They just check the 'Go to my zoned school' box." This process contributes crucially to the gendered importance of Mexicanness within the school. Mexicans who had previously been isolated in elementary and junior high school were brought together in high school, as the following exchange from the focus group illustrates.

> *Carlos:* Every Mexican that I grew up with [was] in Graves High.
>
> *Eunice:* Because everybody gets kicked in there.
>
> *Carlos:* In elementary school, and junior high school. They were—everybody went separate. So we got to Graves High. . . . Everybody. Every Mexican that I knew.
>
> *Eunice:* 'Cause everybody gets zoned around here.
>
> *Carlos:* Yeah. Everybody gets zoned.
>
> *Eunice:* You don't get accepted to a school [you choose], you're going to Graves High.
>
> *Carlos:* You're zoned into Graves High.

Going to Graves High shaped Carlos's educational and social future in important ways. One of the things that happed was that the concentration of a previously dispersed Mexican school population made Mexicans "suddenly" a visible ethnic group. This had two consequences, for the boys especially. It first made them candidates for ethnic conflict with other groups. Puerto Ricans and blacks, and sometimes Dominicans, targeted them, convinced that Mexicans were impinging on their turf. Second, it enabled the Mexicans to defend themselves collectively by forming *pandillas* (crews or gangs). This tendency to form *pandillas* has itself increased greatly with the influx of young, teenage immigrants during the mid-1990s, in part a result of family unification via the 1986 Immigration Reform and Control Act (Smith 2000; see Vigil, in this volume and elsewhere, on the structural causes of *pandillas*). Carlos began "hangin' with" a gang and then started cutting school with them, until it got to the point where "I'd just go in for lunch periods. . . . (and) every Friday we had a hookey jam. . . . Yeah or if not, we'd make it a two-week vacation, and not go to school."

In the end, Carlos was able to graduate after surviving a serious illness and making some insightful choices. His illness removed him from the gang scene for several months. None of the gang members visited him in the hospital, but his family did so daily, and he realized that his family's entreaties that he leave the gang and finish school were good advice. He then requested a transfer out of Graves High, because he knew that staying there would prevent him from achieving his goal. Moreover, he requested a transfer into a school where he would be able to negotiate successfully the racial and ethnic dynamics inside and outside the school. He specified that the school had to have fewer Mexicans but also that it not pose a great danger of black-on-Mexican violence.

> *Carlos:* I was like if I stay here [Graves High] one more year, I'm not gonna do it [graduate]—I'm just gonna waste my time. . . . I'm just gonna keep on cutting, and so I axed them [for a transfer]. They were gonna send me to a school in—.

Gordon: Oooh.

  Elton: Shhhi . . .

   R.S.: Is that worse?

  Carlos: It's not bad. The area's bad. There's people who hang outside, though that don't go to the school, you know. I mean, but the neighborhood's not good though. The, the program, is good. My sister goes there. But for a girl its different, you know.

   R.S.: How's it different for a girl?

  Carlos: Ah, for a girl, I, I don't know. I know it's just different. I don't know.

  Joyce: I think girls–cause they don't get picked on much by gang as guys do.

  Carlos: I was gonna be the only—I mean, not the only Spanish [person], but the majorities there are blacks. . . . And I was like, "I'm gonna be picked on, you know, I'm new in the school. . . ."

In the end, Carlos found a school that did not have too many Mexicans and was also in a neighborhood that did not have a "bad" ethnic balance or the threat of black gangs and violence. He went to night school, made up his failed courses, and graduated. He worked under the table at a construction job—an immigrant job—until asthma forced him to quit, with no benefits. After being unemployed, he found a job through a friend in a department store, and he was recently promoted.

Although space constraints prevent us from analyzing a girl's case with the same kind of ethnographic data cited for Carlos's case, it is useful to review how they differ. First, gender relieved the girls of the need to constantly confront co-ethnic pressures or even violence. Carlos and the other boys always had to consider how they would be pressured to cut school with their Mexican friends, or be confronted or even assaulted by Mexican or other gangs. However, the girls—even in high schools with "bad" ethnic balances or in "bad" neighborhoods—were able to attend largely without fear. Second, the girls went to more selective high schools that had more academically gifted students and in which student ethnicity was dealt with differently. Rather than becoming a constant axis of opposition, it became a secondary dimension of the students' identities that came into relief mainly on ethnic holidays or in the context of class discussions about ethnicity, immigration, or related topics (see especially Miron and Lauria 1998; Smith 2000). Third, these more competitive high schools have higher graduation rates: only one-third of entering freshmen graduate from schools like Graves High, whereas up to two-thirds or more graduate from more selective schools (Fine 1991; Smith 2000). Fourth, the girls formed pan-Latino and panminority friendship groups in school, whereas the boys' friendship groups became almost exclusively Mexican and largely male and gang-focused. The girls' broader friendship networks helped them learn to relate to other groups in institutional settings and also placed their ethnicity within an academically successful context. The boys' ethnicity, by contrast, grew more salient and became a tributary to "doomed resistance" (Willis 1977): being an authentic Mexican American male meant cutting school, not doing homework, and not caring (Valenzuela 1999; Vigil 1997).

CONCLUSION

In this paper and the larger project on which it draws, we have begun to trace a set of social processes that begin in middle school or even grade school and have cumulative consequences for boys' and girls' orientations toward and preparation for school and work, for how they define their ethnicity and race, and for their relationship to work and school. Moreover, we found not simply that "cultural" or "gender" practices by themselves produce these outcomes but also that they interact with an identifiable set of external structures and social contexts. For example, the necessity of choosing a high school and the significant differences in the quality of education that many second-generation boys and girls will receive exacerbates the impact of different gender roles and activity settings.

This analysis has key implications for theories of immigrant and second-generation incorporation, education, and work mobility. For example, the joint construction of race, gender, and ethnicity yields situational identities that are more fluid and institutional contexts that are more variable than what is posited in most theories of incorporation, including some, such as segmented assimilation (Portes and Zhou 1993), that have helped map out the terrain this chapter explores. Mexican boys and girls can adopt either an ethnic incorporational or a racial oppositional stance, depending on their labor market niche, the kind of school they attend, their activity settings, their gender roles and other factors. This underlines the importance of analyzing the profound role that gender plays in defining ethnicity and race and to discover whether these characteristics need be decisive at all in a particular context,—for example, in "non-zone" schools or in office jobs. We must pay attention to how these identity categories themselves are created. Chapters 1 and 2 in this volume also speak to these issues.

These meanings can also be affected by factors largely exogenous to the second generation's school and work environments, such as the influx of adolescent immigrants in the mid-1990s in New York, the changes in power relations experienced by the first-generation parents, and the different gender roles that boys and girls of the second generation play at home. Second-generation Mexican Americans understand that boys and girls have different rules of engagement with these larger processes and institutions, and they adopt different ethnic and racial definitions of Mexicanness.

A final conclusion concerns the implications of these conditions for the use of social capital, which plays a central role in many theories of immigrant adaptation, including segmented assimilation (Stanton-Salazar and Dornbusch 1995). In particular, this analysis points to the gendered construction of social capital: gender helps the women acquire more human capital in school, leads at home to their developing skills as mediators, translators, and surrogate parents, and offers them a gendered and growing labor market niche in the mainstream economy—a niche created by employer preferences and reinforced by the male/female skills gap. Moreover, the consequences of this gendered capital are cumulative. Women stay in school longer or go to better schools, which we hypothesize precludes their attaching a stigmatized meaning to their ethnicity, gives them better skills, and opens up access to more and better ties beyond their immediate networks.

NOTES

The author gratefully acknowledges the support of the following sources and people: National Science Foundation, Sociology Program, for major support of the larger project on second-generation Mexican Americans; the Social Science Research Council, Program on International Migration, for a postdoctoral fellowship during 1999, with funds provided by the Andrew W. Mellon Foundation; the Oral History Research Office at Columbia University, for a postdoctoral grant during 1999–2000, with funds provided by the Rockefeller Foundation; the Spencer Foundation and National Academy of Education, for a postdoctoral grant on gendered ethnicity, during 2000–2002; the Barnard College small-grants program, for seed money for these larger projects. I would also like to thank Sandra Lara and Sara Guerrero-Rippberger for the invaluable research and ruminations they did on and for this project and to acknowledge the able research assistance of Agustin Vecino, Griscelda Perez, Carolina Perez, Lisa Peterson and the rest of the NSF team. Any errors of fact or interpretation remain mine alone. All names used in this paper are pseudonyms.

1. This study includes U.S.-born, second-generation children of immigrants and also "1.5"-generation immigrants who were born abroad but experienced major socialization as children in the United States, arriving by around age ten. I refer to both using the label *second generation* for clarity and because my fieldwork indicates that their socialization and identification overlap significantly. See Rumbaut's thoughtful analysis of the developmental and social bases for these terms (Rumbaut 1997, footnote 2) and Valenzuela's (1999) insightful analysis of the differences that emerge inside schools among 1.0- 1.5- and 2.0- generation Mexicans.

2. These estimates derive from various sources. The Current Population Survey (CPS) of 1998 estimates 306,000 Mexicans in New York City, where the 1999 CPS estimated 194,000. I am averaging the two for a figure of 250,000–275,000 for the year 2000. I thank John Mollenkopf for providing these data and Joseph Salvo of the New York City Planning Department for discussing these data issues and sources with me. The figure of 100,000 for 1990 is an estimate I derived on the basis of the undercount estimate the Census Bureau did, modified for several factors not taken

into account in this estimate. It agrees with New York City Planning Department estimates of the early 1990s.

3. Mexico has a 1998 population of about 95 million, as compared to about 8 million for the Dominican Republic. Mexico will have, for at least the next twenty years, new annual labor market entrants of between 800,000 and 1,000,000, far in excess of its economy's ability to produce jobs. Migration is also likely to increase from nontraditional sending regions in Mexico, thereby initiating new migration streams. And there is a growing tendency for migrants, including first-timers, to stay longer and to settle in the United States (Durand et al. 1999; Cornelius 1991).

4. This insight was pointed out to me by Sandra Lara in an ethnographic discussion in 1998.

REFERENCES

Alonso-Zaldivar, Ricardo. 1999. "Big Apple Takes on a Flavor of Mexico." *Los Angeles Times*, February 19, p.22.

Bourdieu, Pierre. 1977. *Outline of a Theory of Practice.* New York: Cambridge University Press.

Fine, Michelle. 1991. *Framing Dropouts: Notes on the Politics of an Urban High School.* Albany: State University of New York Press.

Fordham, Signithia. 1996. *Blacked Out: Dilemmas of Race, Identity and Success at Capital High.* Chicago: University of Chicago Press.

Gallimore, R., C. Goldenberg, and T. Weisner. 1993. "The Social Construction and Subjective Reality of Activity Settings: Implications for Community Psychology." *American Journal of Community Psychology* 21(4): 537–559.

Gandara, P. 1995. *Over Ivy Walls: Educational Mobility of Low Income Chicanos.* Albany: State University of New York Press

Gibson, Margaret. 1988. *Accommodation Without Assimilation: Sikh Immigrants in an American High School.* Ithaca: Cornell University Press 1988.

———. 1997. "Complicating the Immigrant/Involuntary Immigrant Typology." *Anthropology and Education Quarterly* 28(3): 318–329.

Guerrero-Rippberger, Sara. 1998. "Fieldnotes for NSF project" for project on Second-Generation Mexican Americans in New York City, by Robert Smith.

———. 1999 "But for the Day of Tomorrow: Negotiating Femininity in a New York Mexican Identity." Senior thesis, Sociology and Women's Studies Department, Barnard College.

Hondagneu-Sotelo, Pierrette. 1994. *Gendered Transitions: Mexican Experiences of Migration.* Berkeley: University of California Press.

Kao, Grace, and Marta Tienda. 1995. "Optimism and Achievement: Educational Performance of Immigrant Youth." *Social Science Quarterly* 76(1):1–19.

Kasinitz, Philip, Mary Waters, and John Mollenkopf. 1997. "School to Work Transition in the Second Generation." *Working Paper.* Poughkeepsie, NY: Levy Institute of Economics, Bard College.

Lara, Sandra. 1998. "Observations for Second Generation Project" for project on Second-Generation Mexican Americans in New York City, by Robert Smith.

Lara, Sandra, and Robert Smith 2000. "Concrete Talk and Gendered Educational Outcomes." Paper in preparation.

Lara, Sandra. 2000. "Concrete Talk and Gendered School Outcomes." Presentation at American Psychological Association.

Malkin, Victoria. 2000. Personal communication.

Matute-Bianchi, Maria Eugenia. 1986. "Ethnic Identities and Patterns of School Success and Failure among Mexican-Descent and Japanese American Students in a California High School: An Ethnographic Analysis." *American Journal of Education* 95(1):233–55.

Miron, Luis, and M. Lauria. 1998. "Student Voice as Agency: Resistance and Accommodation in Inner City Schools." *Anthropology and Education Quarterly* 29(2): 189–213.

Moss, Philip, and Chris Tilly. 1996. "'Soft' Skills and Race: An Investigation of Black Men's Employment Problems." *Work and Occupations* 23(3):252–276.

Myers, Dowell, and Cynthia Crawford. 1997. "Temporal Differences in the Occupational Mobility of Immigrant and Native-Born Latina Workers." *American Sociological Review* 63:68–93

Nee, Victor, Jimy Sanders, and Scott Sernau. 1994. "Job Transitions in an Immigrant Metropolis: Ethnic Boundaries and the Mixed Economy." *American Sociological Review* 59:849–872.

Ogbu, John. 1974. *The Next Generation: An Ethnography of an Urban Neighborhood.* New York: Academic Press.

———. 1987. "Variability in Minority School Performance: Problem in Search of an Explanation." *Anthropology and Education Quarterly* 18:312–334.

Portes, Alejandro, and Dag MacLeod. 1996. "Educational Progress of Children of Immigrants: The Roles of Class, Ethnicity and School Context. "*Sociology of Education.* 69(4)255–275.

Portes, Alejandro, and Min Zhou. 1993. "The New Second Generation: Segmented Assimilation and Its Variants." *The Annals of the American Academy of Political and Social Science.* 530:74–93.

Reese, L., R. Gallimore, C. Goldengerg, and S. Balzano. 1995. "The Concept of Educación: Latino Family Values and American Schooling." *International Journal of Education Research.* 23(1):57–81

Roediger, David. 1991. *The Wages of Whiteness.* New York and London: Routledge.

Rumbaut, Rubén. 1994. "The Crucible Within: Ethnic Identity, Self-Esteem, and Segmented Assimilation among Children of Immigrants." *International Migration Review* 28:748–94.

Rumbaut, Rubén. 1997. "Assimilation and Its Discontents: Between Rhetoric and Reality." *International Migration Review* 31, 4 (120): 923–960.

Smith, Robert C. 2000, "Contingent Fates: The Educational and Work Mobility of Mexicans and Mexican Americans in New York City," paper presented at "Conference on Latinos in the 21st Century," Harvard University.

———. 2001a. "Mexicans: Social, Educational, Economic and Political Problems and Prospects in New York" in *New Immigrants in New York,* pp. 275–300. Nancy Foner, ed. New York: Columbia University Press.

———. 2001b. Migration, Settlement, and Transnational Life. Book manuscript.

———. 1999a. "Gender, Strategic Sites, and Soft Skills: Explaining the Divergence in Second-Generation Boys and Girls Work and Educational Success," draft paper.

————. 1999b. "Public Wages, Racial Others and Fictive Co-Ethnicity: Mexicans, African Americans, and Other Immigrants in New York's Doubly Bounded Labor Markets," draft paper.

————. 1998. "The Educational and Work Mobility of Second-Generation Mexican Americans in New York City: Some Preliminary Reflections," paper presented at New School for Social Research

————. 1996. "Mexicans in New York City: Membership and Incorporation of a New Immigrant Group." in *Latinos in New York*, S. Baver and G. Haslip Viera, eds. University of Notre Dame Press.

————. 1995. "Los Ausentes Siempre Presentes: The Imagining, Making and Politics of a Transnational Community Between Ticuani, Puebla, Mexico and New York City." Doctoral Dissertation, Political Science Dept, Columbia University.

Smith, Robert, and Sandra Lara. 1999. "Concrete Talk, Acquired Knowledge and Gendered Pathways: Why and How Second-Generation Mexican American Girls Are Doing Better than their Male Counterparts" paper presented at American Sociological Association Meetings.

Stanton-Salazar, Ricardo, and Sanford Dornbusch. 1995. "Social Capital and the Social Reproduction of Inequality: The Formation of Informational Networks among Mexican-origin High School Students." *Sociology of Education* 68 (2):116–135.

Suárez-Orozco, Carola. 1999. "Conceptual Considerations in Our Understanding of Immigrant Adolescent Girls." Invited address, American Psychological Association, Boston, August 21.

Suárez-Orozco, Carola, and Marcelo Suárez-Orozco. 1995 *Transformations: Migration, Family Life and Achievement Motivation among Latino Adolescents*. Stanford: Stanford University Press.

Suárez-Orozco, Marcelo. 1989. *Central American Refugees and U.S. High Schools: A Psychosocial Study of Motivation and Achievement*. Stanford: Stanford University Press.

Valdes de Montano, Luz Maria, and Robert Smith. 1994. Final Report to the Hewlett Foundation on Mexicans in New York.

Valenzuela, Abel, Jr. 1999. "Gender Roles and Settlement Activities among Children and their Immigrant Families." *American Behavioral Scientist* August. 42:690-720.

Valenzuela, Angela. 1999. *Subtractive Schooling: U.S.–Mexican Youth and the Politics of Caring*. Albany: State University of New York Press.

Vigil, Diego. 1997. *Personas Mexicanas: Chicano High School Students in a Changing Los Angeles*. Fort Worth, TX: Harcourt.

Waldinger, Roger. 1996. *Still the Promised City? New Immigrants and Blacks in Postindustrial New York*. Cambridge MA: Harvard University Press.

Warner, W. Lloyd, and Leo Srole. 1945. *The Social Systems of American Ethnic Groups*. New Haven, CT: Yale University Press.

Waters, Mary C. 1994. "Ethnic and Racial Identities of Second-Generation Black Immigrants in New York City." *International Migration Review* 27(4)975–1020.

————. 1996. "The Intersection of Gender, Race and Ethnicity in Identity Development of Caribbean American Teens." In *Urban Girls*, B. Leadbeater and N. Way, eds. New York: New York University Press.

Willis, Paul. 1977. *Learning to Labor: How Working Class Kids Get Working Class Jobs.* New York: Columbia University Press.

Zhou, Min, and Carl Bankston III. 1998. *Growing Up American: How Vietnamese Children Adapt to Life in the United States.* New York: Russell Sage Foundation.

Zhou, Min. 1999. "Segmented Assimilation: Issues, Controversies, and Recent Research on the New Second Generation." In *Handbook of Immigration: The American Experience,* Charles Hirshman, Josh DeWind and Philip Kasinitz, eds. New York: Russell Sage Foundation, pp. 196–211.

Chapter 6

Unions and Latinos

Mutual Transformation

John Trumpbour and Elaine Bernard

In Los Angeles of the 1930s and early 1940s, Rose Pesotta, vice president of the International Ladies Garment Workers Union (ILGWU), prophesied that someday Latinas "might become the backbone of the union on the West Coast." A Jewish immigrant from Ukraine and the only woman on the general executive board of the ILGWU, she was soon sacked as head of Local 484. According to the *Los Angeles Times* (24 September 2000), Louis Levy, the ILGWU's west coast director, "made little attempt to hide his contempt for both Pesotta and the Latinas she had helped bring into the ILGWU." Many labor leaders could barely tolerate Pesotta's sympathies for anarchism, feminism, and "free love," but her visionary belief that Latinas could someday be in the vanguard of the U.S. labor movement struck them as unusual madness.[1]

At the turn of the new millennium, Los Angeles is suddenly a hotbed of labor activism. The Justice for Janitors campaign, the unionizing of home-care workers, and the victorious strikes of transit workers and the *dry-walleros* of the building trades are among the most stunning labor insurgencies of the past decade. Latinos are playing a critical role in achieving victories in a metropolis legendary for smashing unions and once commonly called "the buckle on the scab belt."

The ferment is not confined to Los Angeles. One out of six new workers in the United States is Latino. Over a million Latino males and over half a million Latinas are in U.S. unions today. In 1999, across the United States there was a net gain of 270,000 union members, with close to half coming from California and a majority of these being women.[2]

Looking back on the last century, it is clear that the labor movement missed great opportunities by so often spurning Latino workers. Samuel Gompers, head of the American Federation of Labor (AFL) for almost the entire period of 1886–1924, openly regarded Mexicans as inferior in productivity and called their expanding presence in U.S. industry "a great evil."[3] In 1903, 800 Japanese and 400 Mexican workers had gone on strike together against the sugar beet growers in Oxnard, California. Gompers told Mexican workers that they could indeed receive an AFL charter and join the ranks of the established labor federation. The charter would be "issued to you [Mexicans] with the express understanding that under no circumstances shall you take into your union any Chinese or Japanese."[4] In a remarkable display of solidarity with their fellow Japanese workers, the Mexicans refused Gompers's offer. Thirty years later, in the depths of the Great Depression, Mexican workers led what were the largest agricultural strikes on the west coast up to that time. Although some AFL trade unionists backed this activity, the national leadership remained largely unmoved. Paul Scharrenberg, secretary of the California Federation of Labor, typified the views of the AFL's leadership of the mid-1930s by declaring that "only fanatics are willing to live in shacks or tents and get their heads broken in the interest of migratory laborers."[5]

The world of work provides some of the experiences that Latinos share, uniting the South and Central American immigrants of today with the Mexicans before them. There is a tendency to regard Latinos as primarily agricultural workers, but this community made a considerable contribution to the building of U.S. railways and in the mining, garment, meatpacking, construction, and automobile industries. Contrary to the rural laborer stereotype, Latinos are much more urbanized than other Americans, with the possible exception of some segments of the Asian diaspora in the United States. The tendency of many rural workers to make the transition to the cities has encouraged the most famous of Latino-led labor organizations, the United Farm Workers (UFW), to implement an urban strategy. The UFW is now trying to organize workers in sectors and industries located in the cities. In the heavily mechanized agribusiness of the United States, only a little over 2 percent of the U.S. workforce is located in the agricultural sector. Agricultural labor struggles will undoubtedly remain significant, but the urban setting is the locale of much work in Latino studies. Some scholars in this field are fascinated with the culture of gangs and the barrio, with emphasis on the "informal economy" of unregulated and "invisible" work" such as homework, contingent labor, and various forms of illegal and illicit labor. The informal economy is important, but Latinos are predominantly in the formal labor market: farming, health care, janitorial services, hospital work, the apparel and laundry services, food processing, and construction. Many of these industries have been the site of labor-organizing struggles, with Latinos playing a pivotal role. Historians in the field of Latino studies have produced valuable reconstructions of the worlds of labor and unions, although they may occasionally need to remind their more postmodern colleagues in the social sciences and literary studies of some sociological realities about Latinos and labor markets.

Meanwhile, there are substantial reasons for Latinos to favor unions and for unions to be targeting members of this community. Back in 1989, Associated Press-Media General conducted a national survey on attitudes toward organized labor. Sixty-two percent of both Hispanics and African Americans answered that they had "favorable" opinions of unions, compared to only 43 percent of whites. Nonunion workers were asked, "Would you join a union at your place of work?" and 56 percent of the African Americans, 46 percent of the Hispanics, and 35 percent of the whites answered "Yes."[6] According to U.S. Department of Labor data compiled for 1998 and released in 1999, union members on average earned 32 percent higher wages than nonunion workers. However, Latinos who are unionized received a remarkable 54.3 percent higher wage than Latinos who lack union representation. To place this union premium in wider perspective, women workers gain an average of 38.6 percent with unions, and African Americans see a 45.2 percent bonus.[7]

Organizers have recognized that the 54.3 percent union advantage in wages is a compelling argument for many Latinos to join unions, but there is a downside. From the employer's point of view, this high premium is a major incentive to resist unionization. Corporations that have bought into the idea that Latino labor is "cheap" will fight unions with extra ferocity in order to preserve this huge discount. From the beginning, corporate opinion makers have been unabashed about their desire to squeeze the most out of Latino labor. Back in 1886, the *Journal of Commerce* expressed it this way: "Men, like cows, are expensive to raise, and a gift of either should be gladly received. And a man can be put to more valuable use than a cow."[8] Approving of the coercion necessary to keep unions at bay, a deputy sheriff testified before the LaFollette Commission of the 1930s that "We protect our farmers here in Kern County. . . . They are our best people. . . . They keep the country going. . . . But the Mexicans are trash. They have no standard of living. We herd them like pigs."[9] Reflecting on the Salinas lettuce strike of 1936, the NLRB reported that "the impression of these events obtained from the record is one of inexcusable police brutality, in many instances bordering on sadism."[10]

In the 1930s, the U.S. government responded to the union militancy of Latino workers by beginning mass deportations of mostly Mexicans. But this campaign was brought to an abrupt—if temporary—halt when the United States again needed massive infusions of Mexican labor during World War II. Washington started the *bracero* program, which from 1942 to 1964 brought laborers to work on farms under strict regulations. Any laborer who sought to leave the farm for industrial employment would be subject to deportation. The *bracero* program worked effectively in tandem with the crudely named Operation Wetback, which deported over three million Mexicans during the 1950s. It became a means of defeating unions by providing access to a pool of replacement workers who could not organize to defend their rights. It served to divide workers, including Latinos—documented and undocumented, *braceros* and immigrants, and migrants and U.S. citizens.

With a sevenfold increase in the number of *braceros* from 67,500 in 1950 to 445,000 in 1956, agribusiness sent the wages of agriculture laborers tumbling downward. In California, the average wage of an agriculture worker went from 65 percent of that of a manufacturing worker in 1948 to 47 percent in 1959.[11] Lee G. Williams, a Department of Labor executive who administered the *bracero* program from 1959 to 1964, later admitted it was "legalized slavery, nothing but a way for big corporate farms to get a cheap labor supply from Mexico under government sponsorship. . . . The *braceros* were hauled around like cattle in Mexico and treated like prisoners in the United States."[12] *Braceros* for the sugar beet industry recall having their bodies and their luggage generously showered with DDT as a precautionary sanitation measure to prevent them from carrying insects across the border.[13] Although the Mexican government sometimes protested abuses that came to light, the Mexican political elite continued to cooperate with the *bracero* program because it was regarded as a response to unemployment and continuing economic distress in Mexico. United States workers and organized labor remained bitterly hostile to immigration, regarding it as a force for stealing jobs from U.S. workers.

In spite of such long-standing rebuffs, Latino sojourners managed to combine the experience of work and labor organizing with family and community. On numerous occasions, Latina women found clever ways to overcome the climate of labor repression in parts of the United States. In 1903, Mexicanas largely from Sonoratown throttled armies of scabs sent in to overcome 700 strikers of the Pacific Electric Railway Company in Los Angeles. A local reporter described them as "more than thirty Amazons" who "approached the workers [scabs] and began seizing the shovels, picks, and tamping irons."[14] Women cannery workers used social networks during the 1930s to outlast union-busting corporations in California. More famously, in the film *Salt of the Earth* (1954), Mexican American women help win a labor struggle, often despite initial resistance from their male partners. The movie is based on a genuine episode in labor history. During the early 1950s, in the midst of a long strike spearheaded by the International Union of Mine, Mill, and Smelter Workers, male miners faced a court injunction denying them the right to picket the site. Thereupon, single women and wives rose up, taking over the picket lines and frustrating the efforts of the authorities to squelch the labor insurgency. The police drove their car at a rapid pace to the picket line in an attempt to intimidate the

Mexican American women. "They'll scatter like quail," the sheriff boasted. But the women don't give way, and perhaps their determination became an inspiration to the Mexican women who resisted the Phelps Dodge Corporation in its efforts to crush the union in 1983. On this occasion, a state trooper declared, "If we could just get rid of those broads, we'd have it made."[15] Only this time, the story had a less happy ending for the insurgent workers. The Reagan-era NLRB ensured victory for the corporation by allowing replacement workers to vote on the union, while denying participation to the strikers. It is only with the recent victories of the late 1990s and 2000 that labor activists are regaining the confidence to avenge the historic defeats of the 1980s.

LATINOS AND LABOR: MOVEMENTS AND THEIR MEANINGS

Work and its organization continue to provide many defining experiences in the lives of Latinos. And their prominent role in the history of U.S. labor struggles is having an impact on the manner in which Latinos transform unions today. In evaluating the interplay of this community and unions in the twenty-first century, it will be helpful to review some of the key movements and their meanings. Latinos are at the forefront of transforming U.S. unions in compelling ways:

1. Social unionism. There is a growing trend in the labor movement to go beyond "pure and simple" unionism, confined to negotiating wages, benefits, and conditions of work, in order to advocate a larger social agenda. Latinos have historically made unions part of a social movement and have been less attracted to the narrow "contracts are us" business unionism that has captured most traditional labor organizations. In the 1990s, under increasing influence from this community, the AFL-CIO has had to rethink its historical hostility to many forms of immigration. The labor federation has come to see the power to be harnessed by organizing immigrants, who are frequently more receptive to unions than large segments of the white U.S. working class. It has also reversed its long-standing position by calling for an amnesty for undocumented workers. By switching to a policy of inclusion, rather than dogged devotion to exclusion, the building trades in Los Angeles have conducted their most successful grassroots organizing drive since the 1930s.
2. Community organizing. Latinos have pioneered new organizing models to deal with the proliferation of contract work and contingent workers. Historically, unions have been institutions that sought to restructure labor markets. The Justice for Janitors campaigns and the efforts to unionize home care workers in the Los Angeles area are thriving because of a devotion to community organizing and a refusal to limit union action to the immediate workplace.

3. Internationalism and North/South solidarity. With direct, familial links to lands to the south, Latino workers have shown how an international labor movement can fortify local struggles. Despite facing rampaging police violence, threats of deportation, and deployment of the RICO (Racketeering Influenced and Corrupt Organizations Act) statutes, the four thousand drywallers in the Los Angeles building trades won by exploiting energetic social networks forged in their native villages, particularly El Maguey in Guanajuato.[16] The Farm Labor Organizing Committee (FLOC) has pioneered a cross-border contract with Campbell Soup, an arrangement considered a historic first. It has come to be recognized that the cities of El Paso and El Juarez, as well as San Diego and Tijuana, share many problems. Latinos in labor unions are in the vanguard of cross-border organizing.

In order to put in context these recent contributions to the revitalization of organized labor, let's take a brief look at the Latino legacy in the movement. Undoubtedly, Cesar Chavez (1927–1993) stands as the most renowned Latino labor leader in U.S. history. Important as a source of power for the Latino community in California, his United Farm Workers (UFW) also played a central role in the 1960s by welding social movements to the labor movement. At the time, the AFL-CIO's leadership appeared to delight in the skull-cracking fury of the Chicago police against antiwar protesters. As George Meany expressed it in 1968, "I know what you would do with this dirty-necked and dirty-mouthed group of kooks."[17] Some of the progressive social movements of the 1960s had become hostile to unions in the face of such brazen provocation, and it was Chavez and his UFW cohort who helped channel activist energies back into labor issues.

Chavez took advantage of a few key loopholes in U.S. labor law to build his movement. Postwar U.S. labor had been severely weakened by the provisions of the Taft-Hartley Act (1948) that forbade secondary strikes and solidarity actions in support of workers in a dispute. The UFW came to realize that agricultural workers were exempted from the National Labor Relations Act (NLRA) and therefore from the solidarity prohibition. (Their exclusion had been a concession to growers who claimed that unionization could threaten both the U.S. food supply and the economic foundations of the farmer, the Jeffersonian bedrock of democracy.) Although he had in the early years of the UFW treated the inhospitable legal framework for farm organizing as an obstacle, Chavez soon seized upon it as an opportunity. He looked for secondary strikes when possible, and he mobilized a national audience through highly publicized boycotts of lettuce and grapes. Nevertheless, Latino workers endured great suffering to achieve this breakthrough. Commenting on the five-year strike and boycott that pushed twenty-nine California grape growers in the Delano-area to sign their first union contracts in July 1970, Chavez himself recalled, "Ninety-five percent of the strikers lost their homes and cars." He then added, "But in losing those worldly possessions, they found themselves."[18]

In spite of these historic confrontations and organizing efforts, the UFW soon sputtered in the 1980s, undoubtedly hurt by the progrower legislative agenda of California Governor George Deukmejian and his ideological twin in Washington, Ronald Wilson Reagan. Heavily larded with funding from agribusiness in his victorious gubernatorial campaign of 1982, Deukmejian expressed revulsion at his opponent Los Angeles mayor Tom Bradley's nominating Cesar Chavez for a Nobel Peace Prize back in 1974. Yet Chavez's leadership was not without critics within the progressive labor community. Some believed that his devotion to lettuce and grape boycotts had for years come at the expense of organizing in the fields. Others pointed out the limitations of the politics of charisma, a style of leadership that relied on saintly feats of sacrifice and spiritual devotion. In writing about the African American community, some scholars have noted the yearning for a "Black Moses," a charismatic leader who would carry the community to the promised land. Similarly, a Mexican American said of Chavez, "He is like Moses in the Bible. He took into his hands a whole nation of farm workers and has tried to lead us out into a better land."[19] Just as Jesse Jackson, the successor to Martin Luther King, Jr., as his community's most likely Moses, has not found a way to transform the Rainbow Coalition into a full-bodied democratic movement, Chavez allowed little space for dissenting ideas and approaches—for those who might be known as the loyal opposition in democratic polities abroad. Through a series of purges pleasing to George Meany and Lane Kirkland at the apex of the AFL-CIO, "the beloved Cesar Chavez . . . willingly sacrificed his most radical and talented cadre," wrote labor historian Paul Buhle, "with the predictable dire results part of the downward spiral of his United Farm Workers."[20] Chavez's exerting pressure on the Carter administration in 1979 to deploy the INS, the hated *migra,* against lettuce-picking scabs angered some Mexicans, who did not buy his explanation that "nonviolent" use of this tool in limited circumstances could be justifiable. Some recalled the INS agent who in 1976 used brass knuckles to beat an undocumented strawberry picker into submission.[21]

Still, the UFW spawned a generation of labor and community organizers, Latino as well as many others. Its ethic of sacrifice became an inspiration to the most dedicated members of the social movements, and its innovative tactics showed how the wider community could be mobilized on behalf of labor struggle.

Although the UFW dropped from a peak of 60,000–100,000 members in the 1970s to 20,000 members in 1994, the union is on the march again. Since 1994, the UFW has won twenty union elections and increased its membership to 27,000 members.[22] Its major drive is to achieve a union breakthrough for 15,000 strawberry pickers in Salinas and Watsonville, workers who have had to endure substandard housing, constant contact with lethal pesticides (such as the soon to be banned methyl bromide), and a dearth of medical benefits. Perhaps in hopes of staving off the union drive, growers have recently delivered the first wage hikes in a decade, and six of the largest growers are now committed to providing medical benefits.[23]

There are other unions in the Watsonville region that have been transformed by the mobilization of Latino workers. Watsonville Canning sought to smash Teamsters Local 912 in the mid-1980s, an action that, had it been successful, would probably have led to a downward process of deunionization throughout the food-processing sector. Supplying half the nation's frozen broccoli, brussels sprouts, cauliflower, and spinach, eight Watsonville plants regarded their neighborhood as "the frozen food capital of the world." The United States had witnessed a leap in frozen vegetable consumption from 2.2 pounds per capita in 1944 to 20 pounds in 1975 to 23 pounds in 1985. Thereafter began a stagnation that in a few years would receive ratification from the broccoli-hating U.S. president, George Herbert Walker Bush.[24] Teamsters Local 912 had been dominated by a white leadership long out of touch with the largely Mexican women who are the social base of the canning industry. Many of their husbands work in the fields picking the vegetables; in the factories, the women do the canning and packaging. In the course of the 18-month strike, *no* strikers crossed the picket line, an incredible achievement in labor solidarity. As former farm worker and labor commentator Frank Bardacke expresses it,

> During the almost two-year Watsonville battle, several other large strikes broke out in northern California, among winery workers, TWA flight attendants, and Kaiser Hospital workers. In each case the strike was defeated after 20 to 50 percent of workers returned to work. Even in the historic Hormel strike 200 to 300 strikers scabbed, allowing management to continue production and providing the UFCW international with a base in Austin and an excuse for disavowing the strike. The Teamster international had no such opening in Watsonville.[25]

He adds that the Mexican social networks were crucial:

> Unlike the winery workers, flight attendants, hospital workers or other big city workers, the frozen food workers all lived and worked in the same community, went to the same churches, played and watched soccer games in the same parks. Large numbers of strikers were actually related to each other, members of the same extended families. . . . Families were able to help one another (even move in with one another) because they already had close relations and were used to a level of cooperation practically forgotten in metropolitan Anglo culture.[26]

The strike made a huge contribution to community empowerment in Watsonville, as the Latino community led a redistricting struggle that went to the 9th U.S. Circuit Court of Appeals in San Francisco in July 1988. After the court ruled that Watsonville must switch from at-large to district elections, which could better represent the 60 percent ethnic majority, Mexican Americans elected for the first time in history a fellow Latino to the city council. Within ten years, Latinos won four of the seven seats on the city council. Nevertheless, saving the union did not avert more frontal assaults from capital: workers had to accept pay cuts, and five of the eight canning firms soon relocated to Mexico.[27]

California was by no means the only site of Latino labor activism in the food and agricultural industry. In the Midwest from the late 1970s to the end of the 1980s, the Farm Labor Organizing Committee (FLOC) modified the UFW's boycott strategy by targeting large organizations, rather than relying too heavily on millions of individuals. The UFW strategy had been to rely on huge numbers of mostly volunteers to staff its efforts to win and keep the loyalty of the general public.

Led by Baldemar Velasquez, a founder of the organization back in 1967 and himself the son of migrant farm workers, FLOC instead wreaked havoc with banks and the largest investors in the food industrial complex. Valasquez appropriated and adapted what has come to be called the corporate campaign approach to labor organizing. FLOC enlisted the cooperation of Roman Catholic bishops and then of the heavily Protestant National Council of Churches to pressure and eventually win concessions from the largest food processors, Campbell Soup and Heinz. FLOC understood that many growers had third-party contracts with food corporate goliaths that specified the very seeds and the conditions for furnishing the crops. The rise of industrial food, featuring the bland, standardized fruits and vegetables of McDonald-ized late capitalism, had transformed agriculture, wresting control away from the individual grower. Traditional campaigns that focused on the individual growers were doomed to failure. By targeting the supercontractors, however, FLOC could bring dozens of growers under its organizing umbrella. Its strategy has not been invincible, and many food processors still shift crops and production to Mexico and those regions of the United States less hospitable to unions. But it has been successful in demonstrating how cross-border solidarity and a corporate campaign can achieve some victories, including a groundbreaking binational contract.

One of the central challenges for the U.S. labor movement in the decades ahead will be the meatpacking industry, which has recruited thousands of workers from Mexico, Central America, and Southeast Asia. The nation's most dangerous industry (over a third of the workforce sustain serious injuries in the course of a year) meatpacking has undergone a halving of wages and a doubling of worker output during the past two decades.[28] Assembly line speedups, deployed against workers who must cut up the carcass with knives, lead to woundings, muscle strains, repetitive-motion disorders, and greater susceptibility to a variety of food-borne illnesses. It has been estimated that a worker on a typical shift (eight and a half hours) makes a slash every three seconds, leading to over ten thousand knife cuts in the course of a day.[29] At Iowa Beef Processors (I.B.P.), owners of the second largest pork factory in the world, a quarter of the plant's employees are Latino, yet these workers apparently made under 5 percent of the workman's compensation claims filed between 1987 and 1995.[30] With the unionization rate for the entire meatpacking sector at half its level of 1963, workers are increasingly vulnerable and disposable.[31]

Con Agra stands as one of the three largest U.S. beef barons. The workers at its giant Montfort plant in Greeley, Colorado, voted in 1992 to be represented by the United Food and Commercial Workers (UFCW). Javier Ramirez, president of the UFCW, Local 990, has been outspoken on the health and safety dangers of the slaughterhouse in the age of the speedup. Six carcasses per minute must be hooked and trimmed by the overwhelmed workers, who maneuver on floors slippery with blood, grease, and gristle. The once dominant Chicago slaughterhouses, home to an earlier wave of immigrants, processed approximately 75 cattle per hour. Montfort, which two decades ago slaughtered 175 cattle per hour, today has a rate closer to 400 per hour. An official at the Montfort-based local estimates that the annual turnover of workers may be as high as 70 percent.[32] Thus the speedup model of production relies on constant replenishment with fresh arrivals of impoverished workers. In a pastoral letter, the Roman Catholic Bishops of the South have condemned sectors of the meatpacking industry for exploiting immigrants, for pursuing the unrelenting speedups, and, more specifically, for remaining complacent as 60 percent of poultry processors appear to be in violation of the Fair Labor Standards Act (FLSA).[33]

In the 1990s, taking their struggles beyond these organizing strongholds in agriculture and food processing, Latinos achieved a series of breakthroughs that are remaking the modern U.S. labor movement. Elected in 1995 on the New Voices slate of John Sweeney, Mexican American Linda Chavez-Thompson is executive vice-president of the AFL-CIO. The first Latina to land such a lofty post in the federation, she is the daughter of cotton sharecroppers from Lubbock, Texas. A former AFSCME (American Foundation of State, County, and Municpial Employees) vice-president, Chavez-Thompson has worked with Sweeney to diversify the AFL-CIO executive council by increasing women and people of color to 30 percent of the executive council. Also joining labor's national leadership body, UFW's Arturo Rodriguez was elected to the AFL-CIO's executive council, overcoming the previous regime's refusal to place Cesar Chavez on the body.[34]

Former president of the Service Employees International Union (SEIU), John Sweeney has watched proudly as Latinos have led this union to labor's most dramatic victories of the decade, particularly the organizing of 74,000 home care workers in the Los Angeles area. This victory represents the largest single organizing certification vote since the 1930s. The SEIU's Justice for Janitors campaign has used new techniques to reach a group of workers sometimes said to be "unorganizable" by combining community organizing with more traditional methods. Led by East Los Angeles native Mike Garcia, whose California state janitors' local claims 22,000 members, the Justice for Janitors campaign sparked a rebellion in the streets and suites of Los Angeles that "many hope will become a labor renaissance," reports Nancy Cleeland of the *Los Angeles Times*.[35] They have won backing and a mass from Los Angeles Catholic Cardinal Roger Mahony, a theological conservative who takes pride in his Spanish fluency and days of marching with Cesar Chavez. Latinos are sometimes skeptical of the Irish Catholic hierarchy's claim of a long-standing green-brown, Celtic-Mexican alliance, but the Roman Catholic Church has played a role in securing concessions from otherwise recalcitrant corporate elites.[36] A coalition of labor activists and those from communities of faith has expanded well beyond California, including new organizations such as the National Interfaith Committee for Worker Justice. Again, Latinos have taken the lead in promoting the combination of labor and communities of faith as a powerful moral and political force committed to the dignity of labor.

Taking their struggle to new frontiers for the labor movement, the janitors had achieved previous victories in the heart of Silicon Valley. Targeting Apple Computer in the early 1990s, Garcia and his local had to endure the agony of watching the Immigration and Naturalization Service audit the computer giant's janitorial contractor, an action that led to the deportation of 200 janitors. Yet, by reaching out to churches and community organizing groups, he triumphed and soon took the struggle to Hewlett-Packard. In Silicon Valley, he adds, "By '94, the industry was 80 percent union."[37]

A future frontier for Latino labor-organizing and social movements is likely to be Silicon Valley's virtual exclusion of Latinos from positions of authority in the industry. Recently released surveys from the Department of Labor indicate that three midsized firms lack a single Latino manager. (The data are zero out of 37 officials/managers at McAfee Associates of Santa Clara, zero out of 68 at Rational Software of Santa Clara, and zero out of 60 at Remedy Corporation of Mountain View. Cara Finn, who runs employee services at the software firm Remedy, denies any discrimination: "It wouldn't matter if you were green with white stripes, if you can code [software] you will get a top job.")[38]

Latinos are under-represented on all rungs of high-tech operations except for outsourced janitorial and cafeteria services. In the Bay Area of northern California, 56 percent of the labor force in all industries is white, 21 percent is Asian, 14 percent is Latino, and 8 percent is black. Yet among the 11,733 employees at Oracle's Redwood Shores headquarters, 73 percent are white, 20 percent Asian, 3 percent Latino, and 3 percent black. Only 1 percent of Oracle's 172 managers/officials are Latino.[39] Many Latinos are undoubtedly locked out of the cyber-economy by poor schools (the national 30 percent Latino dropout rate from high school compares unfavorably to 8 percent for whites and 13 percent for African Americans).[40] Even so, the computer industry has not appeared receptive to Stanford- and Berkeley-educated Latinos. John Templeton of the Coalition for Fair Employment observes, "My experience is that with training, a 14-year-old in East Oakland can be writing code in a year's time."[41] Instead of training workers, U.S. firms prefer to increase the number of H1-B visas from India, and many of these immigrant engineers report a variety of abuses in this high-tech *bracero* program: seven-day work weeks without overtime, fees of $1,450 a month for each of four workers stuffed into a San Jose apartment, and the arbitrary withholding of 25 percent of workers' pay by a company. "After each of us left, none of us received the money," recalls H1-B contract worker Kim Singh of his experience in a high-tech sweatshop that engaged in the 25 percent salary withholding ploy.[42] Although U.S. firms received 115,000 H1-B visas for the year 2000 and 195,000 for 2001, corporate lobbyists at one point sought to expand the limit to 300,000, a generous ceiling that would probably have removed *any* incentive to train Latinos and other workers currently in the United States. Without access to the New Economy in certain regions of the country, Latinos will find it hard to narrow the tenfold difference in average wealth between themselves ($4,700) and the white majority ($45,700).[43]

The Latino labor and union experience is hardly confined to California, and the long history of worker struggle in other regions will need reconstruction. Certain Latino communities suffered considerable economic setbacks with the deindustrialization of many sectors of the U.S. economy in the latter half of the twentieth century. Puerto Ricans, who represented 79 percent of New York's Latino population in 1950, made up 37 percent of the total in 2000 and will within the next decade be surpassed by Dominicans. During the 1990s, the Puerto Rican population of New York dwindled by 11 percent, or nearly one hundred thousand people; over a third of those who left went to Puerto Rico. Forty percent of New York-based Puerto Ricans are poor, a poverty rate that well exceeds the totals for African Americans.[44] Puerto Rican workers arrived in New York in waves during the 1940s and 1950s, many attracted by jobs in the manufacturing sector (apparel, electrical, furniture, mattress assembly, shoes, and toys). Many of these unionized manufacturing firms have given way to deunionized production and to deindustrialization. The deindustrialization of New York and the triumph of the nonunionized FIRE sectors (finance, insurance, and real estate) did not bode well for New York's Puerto Rican community. The guiding lights of FIRE almost made decisions that disrupted community life. Some twenty thousand people, mostly Puerto Ricans, were obliged to move in order to make way for Lincoln Center. When it came to choosing between Puerto Ricans and the symphony, the Rockefellers and their allies easily preferred the ballet dancers and opera singers. "In Lincoln Center alone, in an area not particularly industrial," writes Robert Fitch, "orders were given to demolish over 300 factories."[45]

In 1976 Roger Starr, the head of New York's Housing and Development Administration, gave voice to the idea that with deindustrialization, the Puerto Rican had outlived his or her usefulness to the urban enterprise: "Stop the Puerto Ricans and the rural blacks from living in the city . . . reverse the role of the city . . . it can no longer be the place of opportunity. . . . Our urban system is based on the theory of taking the peasant and turning him into an industrial worker. Now there are no industrial jobs. Why not keep him a peasant?"[46] Although the resulting public outcry led to Starr's resignation, the *New York Times* rewarded him with an opportunity to comment regularly on urban affairs, and foundations and think tanks lavished on him the resources to engage in further musings. Deputy Mayor Herman Badillo would propose in April 1978 a $2.1 billion plan for urban reindustrialization that sought to create jobs for depressed communities in the south Bronx and elsewhere, but opposition from Wall Street caused it to be shelved. Instead, former Harvard dean and Kennedy national security advisor McGeorge Bundy joined with several foundations to promote the greening of the south Bronx: vegetable gardens, parks, and other lush foliage that would lift the spirits of these communities. On the cover of the *New York Times* (5 May 1978) are a bunch of eager workers spreading a substance called "zoo doo," the Bronx Zoo compost that would enable the thousands of blossoms to bloom. Again Fitch reflects, "Open space, windmills, composting, veggie gardens—these were the building blocks of economic development for the south Bronx in the late seventies. . . . But what about jobs? How could the poorest community in urban America survive on "zoo doo"? The fundies [foundations] explicitly opposed broad-scale reindustrialization programs."[47]

In Puerto Rico itself, the economic shocks and global recessions of the 1970s led many U.S. firms to shut down operations there or else relocate to even lower-wage zones of Latin America. Many of the firms that replaced them came with an array of tax incentives and the assumption that they could escape unions. Union density in the manufacturing sector of Puerto Rico shriveled from 30 percent in 1970 to under 5 percent in 1990.[48]

It is feared that the rapidly expanding Dominican community in New York will suffer a fate similar to that of their Puerto Rican predecessors.

Emerging from poor schools, and represented by few with university training, many Dominicans find themselves relegated to fly-by-night construction projects, street vending, and domestic labor.

Although many can see only the economic carnage that may confront these communities, some unions have brought prospects for progress. Thrown out of industrial jobs, Puerto Ricans and other Latinos are organizing themselves in key service sectors. It is estimated that over 25 percent of the health workers in New York City are Latino. Local 1199 is the city's most important health care union, and at 220,000 members nationally, it is today the largest local in SEIU. Led by Dennis Rivera, a liberal arts graduate of the University of Puerto Rico (San Juan) who was elected president in 1989, Local 1199 has been at the heart of John Sweeney's strategy of giving priority to New Voices in the labor movement. Started as a union of mostly Jewish pharmacists in 1932, Local 1199 in 1959 carried out at seven hospitals a forty-six-day strike that mobilized the heavily African American and Puerto Rican base of members. It is a politically connected union and a key player in New York City and state politics.

During the 1990s, this local has emerged as a leader in arts and cultural programs for the labor movement, which includes theater, film, poetry, and photography of special appeal to the Latino, African American, and Asian membership. Besides managing a $5.5-billion pension fund and a $400-million community health plan, the union has its own child care programs and summer camps. Local 1199 helped coordinate the street protest against the police killing of immigrant Amadou Diallo, as a thousand of its rank and file worked as marshals. Risking the umbrage of Cuban Americans, Rivera has been outspoken in calling the embargo against Cuba "immoral"—in particular, the U.S. commitment to denying medical supplies to this quarantined island. He has encouraged the anti-corporate-culture rebellion against franchises such as Starbucks and linked it to a union agenda: "The first thing they [Starbucks] did was get rid of the unions."[49]

Under Rivera, Local 1199 has overcome the shrinkage of union density in the United States, and its membership has more than doubled. The activities of Local 1199 could be regarded as part of the Latino transformation of the U.S. labor movement—the synthesis of social unionism, community organizing, and internationalism.

RESEARCH AGENDAS

A better understanding of the role of labor unions as bridging and assimilation institutions in the United States could prove valuable to the future research agenda of Latino studies. Latino workers, whether because of hostility or indifference from the established labor movement, have developed new forms of organization and innovative tactics. Their success has not been confined to Latinos and their community but, rather, has provided a solid base for forms of cross-community organizing. As Latinos achieve more leadership positions in the U.S. labor movement, some are expressing the tensions between representing the pressing needs of their community and the demands of workers who come from disparate backgrounds. Alex López, the chief negotiator for the steelworkers during the bitter strike against Phelps Dodge of the 1980s, compared his situation with that of Juan Chacón, who played the union leader in the movie *Salt of the Earth*. In real life, Chacón confronted management with charges of rank discrimination. Chacón's attitude, argues López, "was 'I'm Chicano and you're a gringo and you're f***ing the Mexican.' That was his thing. I'm not denying there was once a hell of a lot of discrimination. But it was being resolved."[50] Latinos in labor unions frequently see their wages and working conditions elevated to norms enjoyed by the white majority. There needs to be more study of the role that unions play in the process of assimilation and leadership development. In other cases, it should be asked whether the historical failure of unions such as Dubinsky's ILGWU to promote the considerable Puerto Rican base to leadership positions may have undercut this traditional role of labor organizations.[51]

A second area for study is new Latino communities and traditional ones in new contexts. A large literature exists on Mexicans and Chicanos in California and the Southwest, but this community is the third largest Latino group in New York, and its presence is growing rapidly in southern states such as Alabama, Arkansas, and the Carolinas. Puerto Ricans are well understood in the New York context, but this community has a presence in nine major U.S. cities. Its non–New York component has often achieved faster economic progress and greater integration into the U.S. mainstream. The Dominican transformation of New York is also beginning to capture the attention of researchers. It is sometimes argued that the growing presence of black Dominicans, Brazilians, Cubans, and Puerto Ricans will help provide a bridge to the African American community and alleviate some simmering black-versus-Latino tensions in the United States. This may prove to be a rich area for sociological inquiry.

Whether Latinos arrive as political or economic migrants, the common experience of work has often been a unifying force in the community. But there are significant developments in class stratification that make the picture more complex. The success of certain segments of the community— the development of a Latino middle class of owners (subcontractors, janitorial firms, farm owners, strawberry growers, and construction contractors)— has produced calls for more entrepreneurial verve and less emphasis on social movement *solidarismo*. Advocates of this route point to Cuban Americans, who have achieved levels of affluence close to those of the white majority (see chapter 3). (When *Hispanic Business* listed the seventy-five wealthiest

Latinos in the United States as of 1996, twenty-seven Cuban Americans appeared on the list, compared to 25 Mexican Americans, even though there are over fifteen times more Latinos of Mexican descent than Cubans in the United States![52]) However, later waves of Cuban immigration have added to the members of this community who represent the working class and have been targeted for organizing drives by metalworker unions and others. The entrepreneurial activities of the richest Cubans and this community's domination of Latino media, particularly television ownership, captivate some scholars, who consequently neglect the study of working-class components. Prominent light-skinned Cubans have been prone to condemning black Cubans as part of the (supposedly) criminal class released by Fidel Castro during the escalation of tensions with the U.S. government. Such racialized disparagement has not been conducive to understanding the culture and community of some of the later Cuban diaspora.

These are by no means the only divisions among Latinos. Certain Chicanos and Mexican mestizos have been less receptive to the influx of Zapotecs and Mixtecs, workers from zones of Mexico who retain pride in their Indian cultural heritage and do not regard Spanish as their ancestral tongue. With estimates of their proportion of the California farm labor force as high as 10 percent in the early 1990s, Mixtecs are sometimes scapegoated for declining wages in U.S. agriculture. Unions will have to be more open to recruiting organizers capable of communicating in the languages of these communities and familiar with their traditions.

Finally, in an age of globalization that mixes twenty-first-century technology with nineteenth-century labor standards, it will demand a historiography that is transnational and not simply comparative. Gunther Peck's new study of the padrone system and the building of the North American West is exemplary in this regard. After the exclusion of Chinese workers in 1882, Mexican, Greek, and Italian laborers emerged as part of the workforce for the construction of railways and mines that became foundations of the region's prosperity. "The journeys of Greek, Italian, and Mexican immigrant workers to and from the West were individually unique," he observes, "but they shared common experiences with labor scarcity and mobility, frequent border crossings, padrone exactions at every stage of their sojourns, and remarkably similar personal disappointments and frustrations."[53] Peck's work is the story of how isolated countrysides in distant lands become part of truly international labor markets. Mexicans, Italians, and Greeks did not find themselves warmly greeted by the various Irish, Jewish, and white Protestant leadership of the mainstream labor movement of North America, and they sometimes gravitated to the IWW and anarchist traditions of social dissent.

Today Latinos are transforming unions, and unions are transforming Latinos. The future of the U.S. workforce is increasingly Latino, Asian, and

African American. How the labor movement responds to this historic challenge will set the research agenda for the new century.

NOTES

1. Cecilia Rasmussen, "L.A. Then and Now: Jewish Feminist Drew Latinas to Garment Union," *Los Angeles Times*, 24 September 2000, metro, p. B3. For accounts of how Latinas are leading the contemporary U.S. labor movement, see Ruth Milkman and Kent Wong, *Voices from the Front Lines/Voces desde la lucha* (Los Angeles: Center for Labor Research and Education, UCLA, 2000) for profiles of Cristina Vasquez (vice president of UNITE, the Union of Needletrades, Industrial and Textile Employees, the successor to the ILGWU), Maria Elena Durazo (president of Local 11 of the Hotel Employees and Restaurant Employees and a former ILGWU organizer), and Rocio Saenz (SEIU and Justice for Janitors).

2. Some of these data come from unpublished AFL-CIO sources, but see also the soon-to-be-updated work of Barry T. Hirsch and David A. Macpherson, *The Union Membership and Earnings Data Book* (Washington, D.C.: BNA, 1999).

3. Gompers, quoted by Zaragosa Vargas, *Proletarians of the North: A History of Mexican Industrial Workers in Detroit and the Midwest, 1917–1933* [Berkeley: University of California Press, 1999 (1993)], p. 158. On the AFL leader's belief in Mexican low productivity, see James D. Cockcroft, *Outlaws in the Promised Land: Mexican Immigrants and America's Future* (New York: Grove Press, 1986), p. 39.

4. Gompers, quoted by David Montgomery, *The Fall of the House of Labor: The Workplace, the State, and American Labor Activism, 1865–1925* [New York: Cambridge University Press, 1989 (1987)], p. 86.

5. Scharrenberg, quoted by George P. West, "Communists Tried Under IWW Law," *New York Times*, 20 January, IV, p.1. For the wider context of this quotation, see Camille Guerin-Gonzales, *Mexican Workers and American Dreams: Immigration, Repatriation, and California Farm Labor, 1900–1939* [New Brunswick: Rutgers University Press, 1996 (1994)], p. 124.

6. Manning Marable, "Black Leadership and the Labor Movement," *Working USA*, September/October 1997, p. 46.

7. BLS data available at the website of the International Association of Machinists and Aerospace Workers. See *http://www.iamav.org/departments/organizing/organizing_advantage.htm*

8. Quoted by Cockcroft (see note 3), p. 38.

9. Quoted by Carey McWilliams, *North from Mexico: The Spanish-Speaking People of the United States* [Westport: Praeger, 1990 (1948)], p. 175.

10. Quoted by Guerin-Gonzales, p. 129.

11. Patrick H. Mooney and Theo J. Majka, *Farmers' and Farm Workers' Movements: Social Protest in American Agriculture* (New York: Twayne Publishers, 1995), p. 152. This valuable work also informs much of our analysis below on the rise of the UFW and FLOC.

12. Quoted by Cockcroft, p. 68.

13. See Irving Davis and William H. Metzler, *Sugar Beet Labor in Northern Colorado* (Fort Collins: Colorado State University Experiment Station, Technical Bulletin No.

63, 1958) p. 61. This practice is also cited by Carol Andreas, *Meatpackers and Beef Barons* (Boulder: University Press of Colorado, 1994), p. 15.

14. Reporter quoted by Vicki Ruiz, *From Out of the Shadows: Mexican Women in Twentieth-Century America* (New York: Oxford University Press, 1999), p. 74. Recently named Latina of the Year, Ruiz also wrote the major study of the female cannery workers of the 1930s, *Cannery Women, Cannery Lives: Mexican Women, Unionization, and the California Food Processing Industry, 1930–1950* (Albuquerque: University of New Mexico Press, 1987).

15. Barbara Kingsolver, *Holding the Line: Women in the Great Arizona Mining Strike of 1983* (Ithaca: ILR Press, 1989), p. 17.

16. Mike Davis, *Magical Urbanism: Latinos Reinvent the U.S. Big City* (New York: Verso, 2000), p. 86.

17. Meany, quoted by Paul Buhle, *Taking Care of Business: Samuel Gompers, George Meany, Lane Kirkland, and the Tragedy of American Labor* (New York: Monthly Review Press, 1999), p. 185. On page 184, Buhle writes "Meany applauded the skullcracking."

18. Cesar Chavez, quoted by his son-in-law and current UFW president Arturo Rodriguez, "Remembering Cesar Chavez, Who Helped Farm Workers Alter Their Future," *Raleigh News & Observer*, 29 July 2000. For a sociological account of the reasons for the UFW's earliest successes during its FWA (Farm Workers Association, 1962–1964) and National Farm Workers Association (NFWA, 1964–1966) phases, see Marshall Ganz, "Resources and Resourcefulness: Strategic Capacity in the Unionization of California Agriculture," *American Journal of Sociology*, January 2000, pp. 1003–1062.

19. Quoted by Jacqueline Jones, *A Social History of the Laboring Classes: From Colonial Times to the Present* (Oxford: Blackwell, 1999), p. 216.

20. Buhle, p. 188.

21. Frank Bardacke, "Watsonville: A Mexican Community on Strike," in *Reshaping the U.S. Left: Popular Struggles in the 1980s*, Mike Davis and Michael Sprinker, eds., (vol. III of '*The Year Left*') (London: Verso, 1988), pp. 157–158. "[M]uch of the left. . . argued that the deployment of the *migra* against undocumented scabs was like calling the Ku Klux Klan against black strikebreakers," he elaborates.

22. Data from Rodriguez.

23. Jon Bloom, "Strawberry Fields, Forever Nonunion?" at *www.foodcoop.com/linewaiters/strawberry.html*

24. Bardacke, pp. 152 and 160. Bush put the nation on notice: ". . . [M]y mother made me eat it, and I'm the President of the United States, and I'm not going to eat any more broccoli." He referred to his wife Barbara as "totalitarian" for forcing him to eat it. When a reporter asked if he really thought that, Bush clarified: "She is a total totalitarian—on broccoli only." See "Bush Sticks with Veggie Veto," *San Diego Union–Tribune*, 22 March 1990, p. A3. Trying to quell the rage of vegetable growers, Vice President Dan Quayle soon expressed his love of broccoli, to little avail. Hillary Rodham Clinton caused a similar flap with growers while visiting the set of "Sesame Street." Expected to tell children to eat "green peas," she vetoed the script on the grounds that "Hardly anyone likes peas" (quoted in *Atlanta Journal and Constitution*, 15 October 1993).

25. Bardacke, pp. 168–169.

26. Bardacke, pp. 170–171.

27. See the preface to Frank Bardacke, *Good Liberals and Great Blue Herons: Land, Labor, and Politics in the Pajaro Valley* (Santa Cruz: Center for Political Ecology, 1994), pp. ix–x; John Speyer's introduction to F. Bardacke, "The Workers, United," *El Andar*, October 1995, a tenth-anniversary celebration of the cannery strike; and Margaret Talev, "Santa Paula Not Alone in Latino Voting Issue; Government among 46 Cities in State with a Larger Latino Base," *Los Angeles Times*, 26 September 1999.

28. According to a *U.S. News & World Report* cover story (Stephen J. Hedges and Dana Hawkins, "The New Jungle," 23 September 1996), "Nationally, 36 percent of workers in meatpacking plants sustain serious injuries each year." See also Carol Andreas, *Meatpackers and Beef Barons* (Boulder: University Press of Colorado, 1994), which on page 3 notes a doubling of output and a near halving of wages. Wages continued to fall after she wrote her account.

29. Eric Schlosser, "Fast-Food Nation: Meat and Potatoes," *Rolling Stone*, 3 September 1998. See also Eric Schlosser, *Fast Food Nation* (New York: Houghton Mifflin, 2001).

30. Dana Hawkins, "The Most Dangerous Jobs," *U.S. News & World Report*, 23 September 1996.

31. Marc Cooper, "The Heartland's Raw Deal: How Meatpacking Is Creating an Immigration Underclass," *The Nation*, 3 February 1997. Poultry processing has much lower levels of unionization than beef and pork processing. Under constant threat of plant closures, even unions have frequently surrendered to pay cuts and speedups.

32. See Schlosser for these estimates on kill rate and worker turnover. On page 62 of Andreas, Steve Thomas recalls the kill rate at Montfort, which increased from 120 to 150 in the mid-1970s: "Already in 1975, with a kill of 150 per hour, we were totally maxed out. . . . I was always tired every night when I went home."

33. See "Voices and Choices: A pastoral letter from the Catholic Bishops of the South." They cite a 1997 Department of Labor survey as evidence of the 60 percent FLSA violation rate in poultry processing.

34. For further background on these developments, see Harold Meyerson, "A Second Chance: The New AFL-CIO and the Prospective Revival of American Labor," in *Not Your Father's Union Movement*, Jo-Ann Mort, ed., (New York: Verso, 1998).

35. Nancy Cleeland, "Leader of the Revolutionary Pack: Mike Garcia and his Janitors' Union are breathing new life into the U.S. Labor Movement," *Los Angeles Times Magazine*, 13 August 2000.

36. Jim Newton and Larry B. Stammer, "Mahony's Close Labor Ties Reflected in His Strike Role," *Los Angeles Times*, 13 October 2000. For a more critical look at Mahony's various labor interventions, see Mike Davis, *City of Quartz: Excavating the Future in Los Angeles* (New York: Verso, 1990), chap. 6. On page 336, Davis refers to a famous speech of Mahony's predecessor Cardinal Francis McIntyre, who in 1948 referred to the "Celto-Californian" religious synthesis—the "blend of green and brown, rain and sunshine, a perfect mating of two traditions of faith." Although Davis slams Mahony for opposing the organizing of gravediggers at Catholic cemeteries back in 1985, reporters Newton and Stammer argue that "Since that strike, Mahony's record has been of virtually uninterrupted support for labor and the working poor."

37. Garcia, quoted by Cleeland.

38. Julia Angwin and Laura Castaneda, "The Digital Divide: High-Tech Boom a Bust for Blacks, Latinos," *San Francisco Chronicle*, 4 May 1998.

39. Data from Angwin and Castaneda.

40. Data from Davis, *Magical Urbanism*, p. 111.

41. Templeton, quoted by Benny Evangelista, "Group Asks Tech CEOs to Bridge Racial Gap," *San Francisco Chronicle*, 28 September 1998. In a letter to the *San Francisco Chronicle* (8 May 1998), Templeton denies the Silicon Valley claim that African Americans lack the "ability to do demanding cutting-edge work": "As the Exhibit at the Tech Museum of Innovation reveals, African-American computer pioneers played key roles from the transistor to the disk drive and 3-D graphics, at every stage of Silicon Valley's development. A companion story to today's exclusion is how those black pioneers got forced out from those companies as venture capitalists came on board."

42. David Bacon and Judy Goff, "Law Shouldn't Allow High-Tech Industry to Indenture Immigrants," *San Francisco Chronicle*, 29 September 2000, p. A29.

43. Mike Davis, *Magical Urbanism*, pp. 100–102, 111.

44. Mireya Navarro, "Puerto Rican Presence Wanes in New York," *New York Times*, 28 February 2000.

45. Robert Fitch, *The Assassination of New York* (New York: Verso, 1993), pp. 100–101.

46. Starr, quoted by Fitch, p. viii.

47. Fitch, p. 217.

48. Hector Figueroa, "Puerto Rican Workers: A Profile," *NACLA Report on the Americas*, November/December 1996.

49. Rivera, quoted by David Lefer, "Rivera's Star Rising: Local 1199 Chief Is Emerging as Rights Leader," *New York Daily News*, 18 April 1999, p. 39.

50. López, quoted by Jonathan D. Rosenblum, *Copper Crucible: How the Arizona Miners Strike of 1983 Recast Labor-Management Relations in America* (Ithaca: ILR Press, 1995), p. 170.

51. See Herbert Hill, "Black-Jewish Conflict in the Labor Context: Race, Jobs and Institutional Power," in Noel Ignatiev and John Garvey, eds., *Race Traitor* (New York: Routledge, 1996), pp. 215–246.

52. For a discussion of these data, see Richard L. Zweigenhaft and G. William Domhoff, "The New Power Elite," *Mother Jones*, March/April 1998, p. 47.

53. Gunther Peck, *Reinventing Free Labor: Padrones and Immigrant Workers in the North American West, 1880–1930* (New York: Cambridge University Press, 2000), p. 7.

Commentary

Merilee S. Grindle

How do family and community characteristics affect the life chances of Latinos? What kinds of individual and structural factors mediate the impact of family and community on Latino destinies? These two questions are an important response to a wealth of data on characteristics and achievements of Latinos in the United States. Census, survey, and other kinds of quantitative data regularly indicate that Latinos fall short of many others in terms of income, social mobility, and education, while outpacing many others in terms of the incidence of crime, unemployment, drug and alcohol use, and socially disrupted lives. Not surprisingly, many social scientists have argued that the social and economic contexts within which Latinos live—contexts created by families and communities—are important contributors to their unpromising life chances.

Indeed, it is hard to escape the evidence that families and communities profoundly shape the destinies of individuals. Certainly, there is ample support for believing that family social and economic backgrounds, together with neighborhood ecologies, constrain opportunities for acquiring education, health, work-related skills, and the personal networks and knowledge that mediate between the individual and the real world. For Latinos, this often means that living in poverty and in marginalized neighborhoods significantly limits their opportunities for acquiring a decent education, graduating from high school, speaking "mainstream" English, finding a job, staying employed, and maintaining a set of stable social relationships and living arrangements. At the same time, poverty and marginality open up the opportunities for becoming a member of a gang, having access to drugs, and engaging in criminal or violent activities.

Just as certainly, family and community contexts influence the attitudes that individuals have about their life chances, through the inculcation of cultural norms and social values and by structuring cohort and cross-generational relationships. At the level of attitudes, household and community ecology can increase the chances that Latinos will acquire values that inhibit their chances for "making it" in the broader society—attitudes about the value of attending school, for example, or about the kinds of work that are appropriate for a "real man." Similarly, perceptions of self-worth and experiences with discrimination can shape individual goals and expectations about the future.

As profound as such family and community influences are, however, they do not explain the full range of possibilities that Latinos—or any others—face. The same data that indicate low overall economic and social achievement for Latinos, also demonstrate diversity among them. Qualitative studies shed additional light on the range of individual experiences. Within any given household or community, for example, some adolescent males join gangs and sell drugs, whereas others complete high school and attend college. Within the same household, a young male may hang out with the guys while his sister finds an after-school job working in a department store. Within the same community, organizations such as churches and unions help create social capital among some residents while others remain isolated from such activities or generate alternative kinds of social capital through membership in gangs. Even in spatially, culturally, economically, and socially marginalized neighborhoods, some residents choose incorporation into Anglo American society and adopt its norms of achievement while others ignore or reject such paths toward assimilation.

Explaining this kind of diversity within similar contexts requires us to reconsider the impact of individual experiences or characteristics, such as those related to gender, or broader social and economic opportunity sets, such as the impact of the economy on job availability at a certain time or place. For social scientists, then, what begins as a useful way of understanding marginality, poverty, and individual or group achievement soon becomes a complex calculus of how family and community influences are mediated by individual and structural conditions. This is the task undertaken by Diego Vigil, Robert C. Smith, and John Trumpbour and Elaine Bernard in their contributions to this volume.

Diego Vigil usefully reminds us that the construction of marginality among Latinos—in this case, immigrants from Mexico—is not a new phenomenon. He reviews literature that dates as far back as the 1920s and 1930s to demonstrate how marginal communities develop and how poverty and marginality encourage young males to join gangs and to engage in socially disruptive behavior. Moreover, he argues, the spatial, economic, and social distance between the dominant society and the Mexican communities perpetuates marginality and isolation, factors that increase the likelihood that youths in such communities will not value education, will have access only to inferior education, will not be adequately prepared for the labor force, will not find meaningful or remunerative work, will be victims of discrimination, will have low self-esteem, and will reject the values and norms of the Anglo American society that is responsible for creating such conditions. All of these factors in turn increase the likelihood of the young male's becoming a member of a street gang.

The argument is clear, but the evidence is less so. However persuasive the links among poverty, marginality, and street gangs, Vigil acknowledges that "most barrio youths shun gang activities" and indicates that "most barrio residents are law abiders who have learned to cope with ecological conditions". He further refers to organized efforts by barrio residents to curtail the discrimination their communities face. While focusing on the wide range of factors that propel youths toward socially disruptive behavior, Vigil acknowledges that factors unrelated to community ecology also affect the life chances of Latinos in the United States.

Robert C. Smith, in his chapter on assimilation differences among Mexicans living in New York City, demonstrates how Vigil's community ecology explanation of behavior is mediated by characteristics of individuals and by cultural expectations about individual behavior. Looking at census data, he asks why second-generation Mexican women do better than second-generation men in school and in the labor market? Why, furthermore, do some Mexicans assimilate and others do not? He considers gender differences among individuals and household-level cultural experiences and uses them to explain differential success in escaping from the kind of marginality described by Vigil. His life history interviews with second-generation immigrants and others suggest that women exercise more choice in the schools they attend, that their experiences tend to be affected by gender-related expectations about how they spend their time outside of school, and that their job opportunities are expanded by their own orientations and by employer stereotypes about their skills and characteristics. Even within the context of overall relative downward mobility experienced by Mexicans in New York, then, individual characteristics and social expectations add up to young women doing better than young men in the same community. Indeed, within the community, Smith argues, what it means to be Mexican is mediated by gender and life experiences at school, at work, and within the family.

Smith alludes to larger structural factors that impinge upon the ability of immigrants and their offspring to "make it" in the host economy and society. His focus, however, remains on the individual and cultural factors that enable some Mexican Americans to be more effective than others in negotiating life chances across ethnic and cultural boundaries. His chapter nevertheless encourages us to consider the broader arena of the impact of structural constraints on Latino life chances. If, as Smith argues, fates are gendered and gender is important because of social expectations about individual behavior, to what extent are gendered differences in economic mobility related to conditions in the economy—the number and types of jobs available at any given time, for example? Would a change in the kinds of jobs available in the labor market affect the pattern of success and failure that differentiates females and males in the Mexican American community? These questions remain for analysis that incorporates the census and interview data with economic growth and labor market data.

John Trumpbour and Elaine Barnard also take up the issue of Latino mobility in their chapter on unions. In the twentieth century, Latinos were excluded from many union organizations and labor struggles, but they were centrally important militants in others. As the union movement became revitalized at the close of the century, Latinos had become a major base of support for these organizations. Interestingly, the history of ongoing struggles in agriculture, in the construction and meatpacking industries, and among janitors and home care workers indicates that social marginality has not constrained efforts to unionize or to demand better wages and working conditions. Indeed, with increasing numbers of Latinos as members, some unions have moved to embrace notions of community organizing and cross-border negotiation of working conditions—issues of special concern to this constituency. Latinos have also caused unions to reexamine their policies toward immigration. This chapter, then, demonstrates how historically marginalized communities can alter the organizations that represent them. Trumpbour and Barnard indicate not only the clear rewards that Latinos have reaped from union organizing and membership, but also the impact of Latino communities on the structure and functions of the unions. The fuller incorporation of Latinos into unions has created some tensions, but it is clear that the concerns and experiences of these members will play a significant role in defining the nature of union activities in the future.

The contributions to this volume by Vigil, Smith, and Trumpbour and Barnard are justly concerned with the life chances of Latinos in the United States and with the factors that affect those life chances. For Vigil, the ecology of community is foremost in setting the boundaries within which Latino youths seek their identities and futures. Smith, however, offers evidence that individual characteristics, interpreted through cultural lenses, are at least equally important in determining the opportunities available to Mexican Americans in New York City. Trumpbour and Bernard indicate the importance of structural constraints in the broader society and the ways in which organizations such as labor unions seek to mediate between the group interests of Latinos and those obstacles. There is much to be gained from study of the distinct literatures that these investigators bring to bear on this important question and from the kinds of investigative techniques and interpretive modes that each selects. The debate remains open and the problem of how individual and group destinies are determined will continue to benefit from scholarship that is cross-disciplinary, objective, and rigorous.

Chapter 7

Two Nations under God?

Latino Religious Life in the United States

Peggy Levitt

Although many social scientists are reluctant to admit it, religion is alive and well in the United States. Over half of those questioned in the 1998 General Social Survey (51.7 percent) said they prayed at least once, if not several times, a day. Nearly 50 percent categorized their religious affiliations as "strong" or "somewhat strong" (Lehigh 1999). What Americans believe and how they practice their faith are becoming increasingly complex. Latinos contribute much to this heightened diversity. Researchers predict that by the end of this decade, Latinos will make up more than 50 percent of all Catholics in the United States. By 2010, Latino parishioners are likely to outnumber their Irish and Italian American co-religionists (Cadena 1995). According to Jay Dolan, a historian of U.S. Catholicism (1992, p. 427), "Organized nationally and possessing forceful leaders, Hispanic Catholics will make a major impact on the future of Catholicism in the United States in much the same way the Irish did in the nineteenth century." And it is not just the Catholic Church that Latinos are changing. An estimated one out of every seven Latinos left the Catholic Church in the last twenty-five years. If this trend continues at the same rate, then half of all Latinos will belong to Protestant faiths by the year 2025 (Greeley 1997).

This chapter addresses the ways in which recent Latino immigrants are reshaping religious life in this country and how their social and political incorporation is being transformed in the process. It also explores the relationship between religion and politics within the Latino community. I focus primarily on the Catholic Church, but I draw on examples from the Protestant experience as well. I also include findings from research on Brazilian immigration.

Religious institutions have always helped immigrants integrate into the countries that receive them and enabled them to stay connected to the countries they came from.[1] These groups play a different role for contemporary Latino immigrants. Significant numbers are entering the Catholic Church at a time when its traditional white-ethnic membership is dwindling. Record numbers of Latinos are also rejecting Catholicism in favor of Protestant faiths. To remain strong, and to retain its membership, the Catholic Church has had to make concessions. It has become more linguistically and culturally sensitive, and it allows its members to preserve their ethnic differences if they so choose.

As a result, the Catholic Church today fosters segmented assimilation rather than the complete assimilation it encouraged in the past. It incorporates Latinos into an Anglo-dominated institution while allowing them—and in some cases encouraging them—to remain ethnically apart. It fosters "Americanization" through ethnicization (Gerber, Morawska, and Pozzetta 1992). Segmented assimilation in religious arenas can result in two possible outcomes. Maintaining strong ethnic ties may generate social and cultural capital that foster social and economic advancement, or religious participation may further institutionalize incipient segregation and inequality.

At the same time, religious institutions are extending and expanding their global operations such that migrants can remain active in sending-country religious groups and in the congregations that receive them. Religious participation incorporates migrants into strong transnational institutional networks where they acquire social citizenship and can seek protections, make claims, and articulate their interests, regardless of their political status. It integrates them into a transnational religious civil society that can complement or substitute for partial political membership.

LATINOS AND CONTEMPORARY RELIGIOUS LIFE IN THE UNITED STATES

The national parishes created by the Catholic Church to serve the large numbers of immigrants entering the United States in the early 1900s were intended as stopgap measures. Although migrants were allowed to attend mass conducted in their native tongue and preserve many of their homeland customs during their initial period of adjustment, they were ultimately expected to begin to "pray like Americans." Most national parishes slowly emptied as parishioners advanced economically and moved out to the suburbs. By the time large numbers of Latinos arrived in urban centers following World War II, Catholic leaders recognized that the existing national parish system could not meet the needs of this growing influx.

These pressures forced the Catholic Church to invent new ways to understand and respond to the Latino presence. In 1944, U.S. bishops authorized the formation of a committee to coordinate ministerial activities for migrants at the interdiocesan level. The Bishops' Committee for the Spanish Speaking in the United States, eventually created in 1946, wrote a pastoral plan integrating sacramental activities with social services and religious instruction. These efforts met with limited success, depending on the level of resources made available to the supervising clergy and on how sympathetic they were to new parishioners (Díaz-Stevens and Steven-Arroyo 1998). Latino congregations were often relegated to the basement, and their religious and social activities were often conducted in isolation from Anglo co-parishioners. These arrangements, however, met the needs of the community indirectly by replicating what is for many Latinos a salient distinction between formal and informal religious life. Specifically, their second-class status freed them to bring elements of their informal religious practices to the fore, including a more prominent role for lay leadership and women (Díaz-Stevens 1998).

Another factor that promoted Latino incorporation into the Catholic Church was the introduction of the *Cursillo* movement in 1957. The *Cursillo* movement appealed to Latinos because it was rooted in Spanish Catholicism and because it emphasized the translation of cultural Catholicism into practiced and informed everyday faith. Because the movement was parish-based and -supervised, it produced large numbers of Latino leaders who were intensely committed to their sacramental roots (Díaz-Stevens and Stevens-Arroyo 1998).

The Second Vatican Council of the 1960s created more space for ethnic diversity within the Catholic Church as a whole. The council's constitution repositioned the church as an institution of the people rather than a church controlled by its clergy. It modernized the church, democratized rituals so they were more accessible to followers, and mandated greater tolerance for variations in cultural expressions of faith. Church policy became less focused on "Americanizing" new congregants and more focused on preserving Latino identity.

These reforms coincided with several other social movements that also encouraged the emergence of strong ethnic pride. In the 1960s and 1970s, the civil rights and black power movements and the United Farm Workers' strike all drew national attention to Latino causes. The liberation theology movement, which affirmed the Catholic Church's commitment to the fight for social justice by articulating a theology unique to the Spanish-speaking, was growing stronger throughout Latin America. These factors gave rise to what Stevens-Arroyo (1998) has called a Latino religious resurgence. Latino Catholic leaders redefined their role as restoring and developing a distinct Latino religion that could not be absorbed into the Euro American religious experience. Latino Protestants took their lead from their Catholic colleagues and also initiated changes to preserve Latino uniqueness in their own denominations. This resurgence, Stevens-Arroyo claims, has brought about certain irreversible changes in religion in the United States. Latino religious practices are no longer considered inferior to their Euro

American variants. Permanent institutional spaces have been created for the maintenance of diverse language and cultural expressions. As a result, the Latino community has grown confident and assertive about its unique approach to faith.

Today, Latinos are the largest ethnic group in the Catholic Church. In 1990 they constituted 35 percent of all U.S. Catholics, up from 28 percent in 1980.[2] In Florida, Texas, and New Mexico, Latinos make up over two-thirds of the Catholic population. In 1990 there were twelve archdioceses that had over 50 percent Latino membership and twenty-seven in which 25–50 percent of parishioners were Latino. Whereas the numbers of Euro American Catholics fall annually, the number of Latino Catholics has remained constant or risen, as a result of Latinos' high fertility rates, their young average age, and increased migration (Cadena 1995).

The Latino National Political Survey (LNPS) provides a broad overview of Mexican, Cuban, and Puerto Rican religious practices. It reveals that Latinos tend to be more religious than the population as a whole. One-quarter of all Anglos claimed to have no religious preference; only 13 percent of Latino respondents make this claim (De la Garza et al. 1992). Catholicism is the Latino community's religion of choice. Close to two-thirds or more of all Mexicans (74 percent), Puerto Ricans (65 percent), and Cubans (75 percent) categorized themselves as Catholic compared to 21 percent among Anglos. However, an estimated 10–20 percent of all Latinos said they belonged to Protestant denominations. Protestantism was slightly higher among Puerto Ricans (22 percent), followed by 15 percent among the Mexican respondents and 14 percent among the Cubans (compared to 54 percent among Anglos). According to the 1990 National Survey of Religious Identification, of the 23 percent who said they were Protestants or who belonged to another Christian religious group, Baptists accounted for 7 percent of the respondents, and Pentecostals, Jehovah's Witnesses, and Methodists for about 2 percent each. Four percent of Latinos classified themselves as affiliated with an "other religious group," and 6 percent had no religion (Kosmin and Lachman 1994).

Mexicans, Puerto Ricans, and Cubans often seek guidance from religion (De la Garza et al. 1992).[3] In 1985, 77 percent of Latino Catholics in New York claimed they believed firmly in the existence of God. Eighty-nine percent said they believed that Jesus is the son of God, who died on the cross and was resurrected, and 85 percent believed that the Virgin Mary is the mother of God. Seventy-eight percent claimed they believed strongly in heaven, 61 percent believed in hell, and 36 percent accepted the idea of purgatory.

Many of these beliefs were manifested through popular religious practices that constitute the core of Latino religious life and that are often engaged in outside the formal church. Home altars, pilgrimages, lighting candles in a church, *novenas,* and *promesas* were prominent in every group, although Puerto Ricans (77 percent) and Mexicans (76 percent) were more likely than Cubans to participate in such practices. Afro-Caribbean influences, including Santería or Lucumí, were also prominent among Cubans and Puerto Ricans (Gonzales and La Velle 1985).[4]

Strongly held religious beliefs do not always translate into regular church attendance. Most Latinos attend church services, but they may do so infrequently. Fifty-two percent of the respondents born in Mexico and 41 percent of those of Mexican origin born in the United States attended religious services at least once a month. Among Puerto Ricans, close to 40 percent of those born on the island and on the mainland attended religious services at least once monthly (De la Garza et al. 1992). Latinos went to church more often than their Euro American counterparts, only 30 percent of whom attended church on a monthly basis (Cadena 1995).

Declining recruitment into church offices still plagues the Catholic Church in general and Latino congregations in particular. Fewer than 1,900 of the approximately 54,000 priests working in the late 1980s were Latino, including 200 who were U.S.-born Mexican Americans. Between 1985 and 2000, the number of Latino seminarians declined by 64 percent in the northeast alone; only 4 percent of English-speaking religious leaders were studying Spanish (NCCB/USCC 2000). As a result, lay leaders play a prominent role in church life. Laywomen are particularly important. They continue to be the unofficial ministers of the family-centered traditions that are at the core of Latino religious practices.

These organizational dynamics have encouraged the creation of small communities of fellowship and prayer that are also central to institutional religious life in many Latino congregations. These groups aim to restore a sense of ecclesiastical community to popular Latino religion and to bring spiritual renovation to the church. According to the U.S. Catholic Conference, over 71 percent of the archdioceses in the United States have some sort of Christian-based community activities (Cadena 1995).[5] Because large numbers of Catholics have abandoned the church for Protestant congregations that they feel will be more emotionally and spiritually satisfying, organizing religious practice around small, intimate affinity groups is particularly appealing. The Charismatic Catholic movement, for example, attempts through its more exuberant, close-knit worship style to restore to the Catholic Church the spirituality and passion found in many evangelical congregations.

Catholic Church leaders have tried to be responsive to their new Latino members, although they admit they have not gone far enough. The Bishop's Committee for the Spanish Speaking was elevated to a Secretariat of Hispanic Affairs and now oversees pastoral and social services to Latinos throughout the country. Pastoral encounters in 1972, 1977, and 1985 produced pastoral plans on how to minister in Spanish and in culturally sensitive ways. Services and infrastructure directed at Latinos are on the rise. Between 1990 and 1998, for example, Hispanic Ministry budgets increased by 80 percent, and Hispanic ministries' "presence" at the parish level grew by almost 50 percent (NCCB/USCC 2000).

As a result, alternative ministries and structures that differ ecclesiologically from those used by the Euro American church have become an integral part of Catholic Church practices. Liturgical texts are no longer simply translated from English into Spanish or imported from Latin America but, rather, are customized to speak to the experiences of Latinos in the United States (Díaz-Stevens and Stevens-Arroyo 1998). At the same time, most Latinos continue to worship in "mixed" or "parallel" parish settings. They generally attend their own mass in Spanish, at nonpeak times, and not always in the main sanctuary. They also rarely enjoy the same level of representation in parish governance as non-Hispanics (NCCB/USCC 2000).

In sum, Latinos still constitute a minority of Catholic leadership, but their growing numbers, declining membership among white ethnics, and greater tolerance for religious diversity in the Catholic Church as a whole have enabled them to make their mark. Through their traditions of strong lay leadership, respect for women as carriers of popular faith, and strategy of building faith-based communities that operate independently of priests, they are introducing reforms and practices and fueling changes already set in motion. All too often, however, they still do this in isolation from their Anglo counterparts. They enjoy power and autonomy over their own activities, but this has not translated into a central role in the institution as a whole.

THE CHURCH AS A SITE OF SOCIAL CITIZENSHIP

Despite their declared intention to remain permanently in the United States, many Latinos have not become U.S. citizens. In a 1994 study (Pachón and DeSipio), whereas only 6 percent of all Cubans and 8 percent of all Mexicans planned to return to their country of origin, only 38 percent of the Cubans and 15 percent of the Mexicans in their sample had become naturalized.[6] Verba et al. (1995) found that whereas African Americans and Anglos engaged in fairly similar levels of politicial activism, Latinos were less likely to become involved. Only 52 percent of the Latino citizens in their sample voted, compared to 73 percent of the Anglo Whites and 65 percent of the African Americans. Latinos also displayed lower levels of secular, nonpolitical activities than white Anglo and African American respondents. Thirty-eight percent of Anglo whites and 34 percent of African Americans were active in a nonpolitical organization, compared to 19 percent of Latinos.

At the same time, as we have already seen, Latinos do attend church. Their limited political participation stands in stark contrast to their active religious lives. Much of Latino religious life takes place outside the formal church, but religious institutions are still the primary site of collective membership for many Latinos, although this encounter often reinforces segregation from the larger group.

What does it mean when civic engagement is channeled through religious rather than political channels? If Latinos generally participate less in politics but more at church, what are the consequences for their political and civic incorporation? If Latinos' attempts to democratize the Catholic Church have influenced the church as a whole, in what ways do these changes spill over into political life?

Despite the clear separation of church and state in the United States, religious institutions have always exerted a strong influence on politics. Church leaders take stands on political issues, they endorse candidates, and they can lend their churches to promote debate and mobilization. Even when no explicit political agenda is attached to religious activities, the fund-raising, leadership, and organizing skills that churchgoers acquire through their participation at church are also applicable to politics. These experiences can compensate for the low educational and occupational levels among some groups that might ordinarily lead to their political marginalization. High rates of church attendance are said to promote mobilization, influence the practice of citizenship, and help to even out the political playing field (Verba, Scholzman, and Brady 1995).

But this is truer for some groups than for others. Verba and his colleagues (1995) found that whereas involvement in churches increased resources for African Americans, it did not serve the same compensatory function for Latinos. Although Latinos went to church less often than African Americans, and more often than Anglos, they were the least likely to take part in other kinds of activities at church. Only 23 percent of the Latino sample said they participated in secular church-based activities, compared to 35 percent and 27 percent among the African American and Anglo groups, respectively. Latinos also engaged in fewer skill-building types of activities than their non-Latino counterparts.

These researchers attribute this to the high rates of Catholicism among Latinos. It is not that Catholic churches are apolitical, but the opportunities for skill development to which they expose their members have little demonstrable political content. Across all racial groups, Protestants were three times more likely than Catholics to report a "skill learning opportunity." And although Latino Protestants exercised, on average, fewer skills than their African American or white Anglo counterparts, they still were exposed to far more skill-learning opportunities than were Latino Catholics. The National Council of Catholic Bishops/U.S. Catholic Conference 2000 report supports this view (NCCB/USCC 2000). It found that despite efforts to link faith and social action, pastoral work with Latinos has overemphasized the sacramental dimension. In response to pressures to stop defections to Protestant groups, the subsequent shift toward the creation of small, faith-based communities prompted a move away from social reflection and action and toward a focus on prayer and personal conversions.

These differences in political skill-building opportunities are a function of differences between the Protestant and Catholic churches. Protestant churches are generally smaller, allow for greater participation in the liturgy than their Catholic counterparts, and are organized more democratically. Some Protestant denominations allow women an even greater role in church life than Catholic churches do. Finally, on average, Latino Protestants were less likely than Catholics to attend church services but more likely to engage in church-based activities. Latino Protestants dedicated an average of 2.1 hours to church activities each week, compared to 1 hour among Catholics. In short, Verba and his colleagues conclude (1995, p. 323) that "the Latino disadvantage with respect to opportunities to learn politically salient skills in church seems to derive from the fact that they are disproportionately Catholic."[7]

To date, then, it appears that religious participation has not compensated for the generally low levels of political involvement among Latino Catholics. Latinos enjoy greater power and autonomy with respect to their own church-based activities, but this has not translated into greater power within the institution as a whole or into a more prominent role in the political arena.

THE CHURCH AS A SITE OF TRANSNATIONAL MEMBERSHIP

Increased globalization offers transnational religious institutions, such as the Catholic Church, opportunities to expand, adapt, and act back upon the system that has for so long acted upon it (Casanova 1994). Ever since the mid-1800s, the Catholic Church has worked diligently to create and reinforce its role as a transnational, publicly influential institution. By dispersing religious cadres, mounting missionary campaigns, opening schools, building pilgrimage shrines, and organizing international encounters, the Church created a vast, interconnected network of activities throughout the world.

Vatican II transformed these existing transnational arrangements in somewhat contradictory ways. It reversed a centuries-long trend toward centralization by acknowledging the plurality of national Catholicisms and legitimizing their expression. At the same time, it rehomogenized practice by prompting a theological renewal and instituting a series of liturgical changes throughout the entire Catholic world. In essence, it allowed for national Catholic traditions, with their different cultural and mental worlds, to flourish, but always within the context of a centrally regulated system based in Rome (Hervieu-Léger 1997). These global changes mirrored changes taking place within the Catholic Church in the United States.

The interaction of two trends shapes the new transnational regime of Catholicism (Casanova 1994). The first is a generalized movement toward a "do it yourself" approach to faith and the institutional deregulation of religious beliefs. The second is the proliferation of emotional and spiritual communities and affinity groups that cut across national traditions and make Catholicism even more portable than it was before. Taken together, these changes mean that Latino migrants assert their membership in a powerful, extensive global church, but a church that is grounded locally, by circulating in and out of sending-country and receiving-country parishes and by exiting and entering home-country and host-country religious movement chapters.

Furthermore, these activities are performed under the stewardship of a pope who has positioned himself as a spokesperson for humanity, issuing encyclicals and taking stances on events of concern not only to Catholics but to humankind in general. The pope has become "the high priest of a new universal civil religion of humanity and the first citizen of a global civil society" (Casanova 1994, p. 130). His activities also encourage in church members a sense of belonging in multiple settings, because he articulates a vision of community in which nation-state boundaries recede and a religious transnational civil society takes center stage. He offers an alternative membership that also empowers, protects, and speaks out for its members.

Migrants use these transnational memberships to express different combinations of allegiance to their home and host countries. Cuban exiles used the Catholic Church in Miami to assert their continued membership in their homeland (Tweed 1999). Families brought their newborns to the shrine they created in honor of the Cuban national patron saint to formally transform those born in America into citizens of the imagined Cuban nation. For these Cubans, membership in the Catholic Church eases the pain of waiting to return home. The rituals enacted at the shrine do little to integrate these Cubans into the United States, functioning instead to assert their strong sense of belonging to Cuba.

In the case of Dominicans in Boston, where the majority of immigrants come from the city of Baní, the Catholic Church facilitates simultaneous enduring country membership and integration into the United States. Like all U.S. Catholic churches, the Boston archdiocese needed the new immigrants who came to the city in the late 1950s. To attract them, the church offered a generic, non-nation-specific "Hispanic" religious experience. Many new arrivals continued to practice popular religion outside the church, but the search for social and spiritual comfort, the need to fulfill the sacraments, lifestyle demands, and aspirations to social mobility drew more migrants to the formal church.

Resulting changes in religious ideas and practices in Boston were communicated back to Baní and its environs. These social remittance transfers, in conjunction with the church's stronger presence in the area, altered the nature of island religious life. It became more formal, instrumental, and church-based. Officially sanctioned practices gradually substituted for folk rituals. Relations at the upper echelons of the U.S.–Dominican transnational religious system encouraged these changes at the local level. They became institutionalized as more and more priests and seminarians interacted, money and supplies were donated, and labor-sharing arrangements were formalized. Subsequent migrants arriving in the United States had already been inculcated transnationally in the ways of the U.S. church and hence were integrated more easily into its activities. A happy convergence of supply and demand resulted. New migrants constantly infused the U.S. church with new Dominican blood, although it was more anglicized in tone. These new arrivals helped secure a degree of pluralism in the church. They ensured the preservation of a generic, ethnic space for Latinos, though not a specific space for any particular country-of-origin group (Levitt 1998).

Parish-to-parish connections also encourage dual membership among Brazilian migrants from the city of Governador Valadares who have settled in Massachusetts (Levitt 2000). The Brazilian Apostolate churches in the area follow the same pastoral plans, use the same worship materials, and mount mission campaigns that parallel those undertaken in Brazil. When the National Conference of Brazilian Bishops initiated a year-long campaign against homelessness, Brazilian churches in Massachusetts instituted a campaign for better housing and stronger neighborhoods. Clergy members felt that by engaging in activities similar to those in Brazil, modified to address the needs of Brazilian immigrants, they could simultaneously promote integration and strong homeland ties. Their goal was to encourage religious participation but also to allow parishioners to express their favor transnationally because Valadares still looms so large in their daily lives.

Protestant churches also foster transnational practices among Brazilians. Conversions to Protestantism in Brazil, and particularly in Valadares, are increasing. Some U.S. mainline Protestant denominations, such as the Southern Baptists of America, have long been active in Latin America. Brazilian Baptist priests, who come to the United States to serve Brazilian migrants and to evangelize among Americans, are also building relations with the Southern Baptists' Office of Ethnic Churches. Like the Catholic Church, this increasingly intricate network of national-level connections is reinforced by linkages between church chapters at the local level. Even small, storefront churches in Valadares, which have no national-level affiliations, often have plaques outside their doors referring to their "affiliated chapters" in Massachusetts.

What is particularly interesting about these transnational alliances is that they frequently bring groups with very different political orientations under the same institutional umbrella. For example, the American Baptist Convention of Massachusetts and the Brazilian Baptist Convention have entered into a covenant to serve the burgeoning Brazilian population in New England. This relationship links a particularly liberal U.S. church and a very traditional, conservative Brazilian church. But because American Baptists support ecumenism and because they allow for autonomy at the local level, the match seems to be working.

> I hear the pastor of the Anglo congregation talking and he's saying it's incredible, the energy they have, how they generate things, how they organize things and they're doing this and they're doing that. I mean it cannot go unnoticed. So there is something that is touching there, and this reminds me of a picture, when Jesus said you are the salt of the earth and when you're in touch with salt there's no way to get out not being salty. You know what I am saying? You swim in the ocean and you are going to have salt in your mouth no matter what. You cannot put salt in your food and say well, this part will have salt, because it spreads. It touches everything. So that's what I see, the Brazil theme is permeating now, not penetrating but permeating and everybody's saying wow, these Brazilians (Pastor Josimar, Worcester, Massachusetts).

In sum, globalization transnationalizes religion, and once they are in place, transnational religions contribute to increased globalization. Transnational religious membership incorporates migrants into potentially powerful, politically influential institutional networks that can help them solve problems and voice concerns. It guarantees them certain minimal levels of protection and representation, regardless of their political membership, by giving them access to well-placed institutions that stand for basic human rights and dignity. They may be cut off from their nation of origin or settlement by virtue of their partial political membership, but they are reconnected to the state by virtue of the church-state relationship. The consequences of this reembedding depend on the nature of the church-state settlement, which clearly differs among the United States, Cuba, the Dominican Republic, and Brazil.

The direction and impact of these activities further depends on each pastor's particular vision, how much autonomy a priest grants his followers, how much autonomy he is granted by his superiors, and how these dynamics match up in the sending and receiving countries. Religion has been a source of democratization in opening up totalitarian and authoritarian regimes, in making new democratic demands in established democracies, and in building stronger institutions (Casanova 1994; C. Smith 1996). But clearly there are also many causes in which religious institutions have impeded social change. In their current incarnations, the Boston and Dominican Catholic churches are fairly conservative. What remains to be seen is how religious partnerships, which bring together groups with different politics, will resolve these tensions. Will the Brazilian Baptists conservatize their American counterparts? Or will U.S. Baptists create openings in Brazil? I suspect a little of both.

CONCLUSION

The separation of church and state in the United States is clearly delineated. But as Robert Bellah (1967) has pointed out, Americans observe a civil religion. Religious symbols are publicly and symbolically invoked in the name of nation building and consolidation. Legislative sessions and presidential inaugurations begin with prayers. Religious mottos adorn our coins. Civil religion is the religion of the nation, a nonsectarian faith whose sacred symbols are those of the polity and national history. According to Jay Demereth (1998, p. 30), "The country is irretrievably religious at its roots and its most luxuriant foliage. This is an important part of America's distinctiveness, since few other societies can boast such a natural melding of religion and nationhood."

Many argue that civil religion is at our core and constitutes much of our social glue because it unites us through a shared set of values that foster cultural and social integration. But, as I have argued in this chapter, we live in an increasingly differentiated society. Newcomers arrive with their own versions of Judeo-Christian norms and practices that may challenge the existing value consensus. This chapter suggests that America's civil religious fabric is being irrevocably rewoven in the process of incorporating new Latino immigrants. It also suggests that civil religion no longer stops at our borders but, rather, that increasingly it is a set of values and beliefs that is transnationally defined.

NOTES

1. For a discussion of how the role of churches today differs from their role in the past, see Levitt (2001).

2. According to the United States Catholic Conference, between 67 and 71 percent of the 30 million Latinos in the United States in 1998 were Catholic, and this equals between 30 and 38 percent of all U.S. Catholics (NCCB/USCC 2000).

3. For example, 62 percent of Mexicans and Chicanos reported that religion was a significant source of guidance to them, whereas only 6 percent among both nativity groups sought no guidance from religion. Seventy percent of Puerto Ricans born on the island and 43 percent born on the mainland sought religious guidance, whereas less than 8 percent of both groups never turned to religion. Finally, 63 percent of those born in Cuba and 51 percent of the Cubans born in the United States received high levels of guidance from their faith (De la Garza et al. 1992).

4. Although the findings I present here provide a broad-brushstroke view of Latino religious life, they do not allow for much more. Many present data for all Latinos, which makes it impossible to draw distinctions between different groups (Garcia and Rehfeld 1987; Princeton 1988; Kosmin and Lachman 1994). Most studies do not distinguish between Catholics and Protestants. Finally, some studies are quite dated, but there are no up-to-date surveys with which to replace them.

5. In 2000, the Charismatic Renewal movement was active in 36 percent of the parishes with a significant Hispanic presence. The *Cursillo* movement was active in 31 percent and *Talleres de Oración* in 17 percent.

6. Many factors, including length of time in the country and the relative youth of Latinos in the United States, contribute to these low naturalization and participation rates. Naturalization rates also seem to be increasing, particularly in response to the recent rise in anti-immigration sentiment.

7. This study is one of the few that address the relationship between religion and politics among Latinos nationally, but it still has important limits. Critics claim that the paradox between churchgoing and limited skill acquisition arises because survey respondents are only nominally Catholic and `do not actually attend church on a regular basis. It may also be that the survey fails to capture the skill building that occurs in the context of popular religious practices and through participation in faith-based groups. Finally, the study may not capture regional variations. Catholic churches are likely to be sites of greater learning and springboards to political involvement in places where Latinos are already a majority. Furthermore, since conversions to Protestantism are increasing, the positive impacts of Protestant membership may reverberate among Latinos as a whole. See Jones-Correa and Leal (2000) for an in-depth critique and alternative view.

REFERENCES

Bellah, Robert. "Civil Religion in America." *Daedalus* 96 (Winter):1–21. 1970.

Cadena, Gilbert. "Religious Ethnic Identity: A Socio-Religious Portrait of Latinos and Latinas in the Catholic Church." In Anthony M. Stevens-Arroyo and Gilbert Cadena, eds., *Old Masks, New Faces: Religion and Latino Identities.* New York: Bildner Center for Western Hemisphere Studies. 1995.

Casanova, José. *Public Religions in the Modern World.* Chicago: University of Chicago Press. 1994.

De la Garza, Rodolfo O., Louis DeSipio, F. Chris Garcia, John Garcia, and Angelo Falcon. *Latino Voices: Mexican, Puerto Rican, and Cuban Perspectives on American Politics.* Boulder: Westview. 1992.

Demereth, N.J. "Excepting Exceptionalism: American Religion in Comparative Relief." *Annals AAPSS* 558: (July):28–39. 1998.

Díaz-Stevens, Ana-María. *Oxcart Catholicism on Fifth Avenue.* Notre Dame, IN: University of Notre Dame Press. 1993.

Díaz-Stevens, Ana-María, and Anthony Stevens Arroyo. *Recognizing the Latino Resurgence in the U.S. Religion: The Emmaus Paradigm.* Boulder, CO: Westview. 1998.

Dolan, Jay. *The American Catholic Experience.* Notre Dame, IN: Notre Dame University Press. 1992.

Garcia, F. Chris, and Thomas A. Rehfeld. *A Survey Investigating the Sociopolitical Opinions of Hispanics and Non-Hispanics in the Southwest and the Perceived Influence of the Catholic Church.* Albuquerque, NM: Zia Research Associates. 1987.

Gerber, David A., Ewa Morawska, and George E. Pozzetta. "Response to Comments on the Invention of Ethnicity Paper." *Journal of American Ethnic History* (Fall): 59–63. 1992.

González, Roberto O., and Michael La Velle. *The Hispanic Catholic Church in the United States: A Socio-Cultural and Religious Profile.* New York: Northeast Catholic Pastoral Center for Hispanics. 1985.

Greeley, Andrew. "Detections among Hispanics." *America.* (Sept). 1997.

Hervieu-Léger, Daniéle. "Faces of Catholic Transnationalism: In and Beyond France." In Susanne Hoeber Rudolph and James Piscatori, eds., *Transnational Religion and Fading States.* Boulder: Westview, pp. 104–121. 1997.

Kosmin, Barry A. and Seymour P. Lachman. *One Nation under God.* New York: Harmony Books. 1994.

Lehigh, Scott. "Our Complex Approach to Spirituality." *The Boston Globe.* (December):C2. 1999.

Levitt, Peggy. *The Transnational Villagers.* Berkeley: University of California Press. 2001.

Levitt, Peggy. "They Prayed in Brazil and It Rained in Boston." Paper presented at the Identities, Localities, and Diaspora Conference, University of Hamburg, Hamburg, Germany. 2000.

Levitt, Peggy. "Local-Level Global Religion: The Case of U.S.-Dominican Migration." *Journal for the Scientific Study of Religion* 3:74–89. 1998.

National Council of Catholic Bishops/U.S. Catholic Conference (NCCB/USCC). 2000.

NCCB/USCC Secretariat of Hispanic Affairs. "Input from Dioceses on the Status of the Implementation of the National Pastoral Plan for Hispanic Ministry." Washington, DC: National Catholic Conference of Bishops. 1991.

NCCB/USCC–WWW.NCCBUSCC.org/hispanicaffairs/study.htm: "Hispanic Ministry at the Turn of the New Millennium: A Report of the Bishop's Committee on Hispanic Affairs." 2000.

Pachón, Harry and Louis DeSipio. *New Americans by Choice: Political Perspectives of Latino Immigrants.* Boulder: Westview. 1994.

Princeton Religious Research Center. "The Unchurched American . . . 10 Years Later." Princeton, NJ: Princeton Religious Research Center. 1988.

Smith, Christian. *Disruptive Religion: The Force of Faith in Social Movement Activism.* New York: Routledge. 1996.

Stevens-Arroyo, Anthony. "The Latino Religious Resurgence." *The Annals of the American Academy of Political and Social Science* 558 (July):163–176. 1998.

Stevens-Arroyo, Anthony. "The Emergence of a Social Identity among Latino Catholics: An Appraisal." In Jay P. Dolan and Allan Figueroa Deck, eds., *Hispanic Catholic Culture in the U.S.: Issues and Concerns*. Notre Dame, IN: University of Notre Dame Press. 1999.

Tweed, Thomas. *Our Lady of Exile*. New York: Oxford University Press. 1999.

Verba, Sidney, Kay Scholzman, and Henry Brady. *Voice and Equality*. Cambridge, MA: Harvard University Press. 1995.

Chapter 8

Ambivalent Reception

Mass Public Responses to the "New" Latino Immigration to the United States

Wayne A. Cornelius

This chapter analyzes the sources of public resistance to Latino immigration in the United States in the late twentieth and early twenty-first centuries. It focuses on the complex interplay between economic and ethnocultural factors in determining the attitudes of the general public toward immigrants and immigration policy preferences. A large body of evidence suggests that most Mexican and other post-1970 Latino immigrants to the United States have been fully incorporated into the U.S. economy, mostly filling low-wage, low-skill jobs that native-born Americans typically avoid. To many native-born residents, however, the economic benefits of a large, flexible, relatively low-cost supply of immigrant labor are offset by the *noneconomic* costs of a rapidly expanding and increasingly settled immigrant presence.

Thus, despite an increasingly tight domestic labor market in the United States, public concern about "excessive" Latino immigration has persisted. A broadly based, anti-immigrant backlash has not yet developed because of the low salience of immigration as a policy issue among the general public, a sharp decline in immigrant bashing by politicians (in recent years, both the Republican and Democratic parties have actively courted the immigrant vote and avoided anti-immigration rhetoric) and (until recently) the robustness of the national economy. Furthermore, a growing number of U.S. labor unions have recognized that they have more to gain by organizing immigrants—even the undocumented—in workplaces where they now predominate in the labor force than by opposing their employment.[1]

I argue that an ethnocultural objection to the most recent wave of Latino immigration underlies persistent U.S. public concern about immigration levels, regardless of the state of the macroeconomy. Native-born residents of states and local communities affected by heavy immigration are increasingly concerned about the potential of migrants from Latin American and the Caribbean to shift the ethnic, cultural, and linguistic balance within their communities. Just as it has been since the mid-eighteenth century, ethnicity remains a powerful determinant of the U.S. public's attitudes toward immigration and its consequences, as well as of their voting behavior on immigration-related issues.

In the public-policy arena, the ambivalence of public opinion on this issue—recognition of the economic utility of Latino immigrants coupled with anxiety about their sociocultural impact—translates into a reluctance among legislators to raise permanent legal immigration ceilings or to approve a general amnesty for undocumented immigrants (measures that would largely benefit low-skilled Latino immigrants with family ties to the United States), even as they open the door more widely for highly skilled, mostly *non*-Latino immigrants (Cornelius, Espenshade, and Salehyan 2001).

PATTERNS OF ECONOMIC INCORPORATION

Labor-force participation rates among the recent Latino immigrants to the United States—men and women, legals and illegals—are high. The vast majority are fully employed, many of them working two or even three different jobs. In southern California, for example, only the recent arrivals from Mexico and Central America who seek work as day laborers in street-corner labor markets are not fully employed, and field research shows that even they typically can find employment for at least 2 or 3 days per week (Cornelius and Kuwahara 1998; Valenzuela 2000). Advocacy groups and individual scholars who favor reduced immigration levels and/or a more skill-based U.S. immigrant policy commonly argue that employment opportunities for low-skilled immigrant laborers are rapidly disappearing in the knowledge-intensive, postindustrial U.S. economy.[2] But this has not stopped millions of Latino immigrants arriving in the 1980s and 1990s from finding work, notwithstanding their limited job skills, formal education, and competence in English. In Los Angeles, for example, 85 percent of Mexican men with no formal education whatsoever were fully employed in 1990, and employment rates rose from there, commensurate with educational attainment (Waldinger and Bozorgmehr 1996).

As the economic expansion of the 1990s rolled on, it became clear that the U.S. economy was generating large numbers of jobs at both the top and the bottom of the skill hierarchy that could be filled by immigrants. And Latino immigrants are not just being incorporated into declining, slow-growth, technologically backward industries. In fact, the evidence for California shows that Latino workers are concentrated in *rapidly growing* industries: 60 percent of Latinos in California were employed in fast-growth industries in 1999, according to the U.S. Census Bureau's Current Population Survey (Pastor and Marcelli 2000).

Debate continues over what proportion of the low-skilled jobs held by Latino immigrants are minimum-wage "mobility traps" (most of these jobs provide no real career ladder, but they do have a wage hierarchy). However, there is no question that U.S. employers have learned to use low-skilled Latino immigrant labor extensively and productively to fill the kinds of jobs that are shunned by most native-born workers, especially the young. The following description of the Los Angeles economy could be generalized to every major U.S. city (and to many smaller ones) where immigrants are now a substantial segment of the labor force:

> There can be little question that L.A. needs the large Mexican and Central American population that it has acquired over the past few decades. It is not just anecdotal evidence that suggests that there would be no gardeners, no baby-sitters, no garment workers, no hotel housekeepers without the Mexican and Central American newcomers. The census data tell the same story; the bottom tier of L.A.'s manufacturing and service sectors rests on a labor force that disproportionately comes from Latino immigrant ranks. Thus, while some segments of the region's population may dream of "sending them home," the reality is that L.A.'s Mexican and Central American immigrants are here to stay, largely because the economy has learned to make good use of them. (Waldinger 1996b. p. 457; see also Marcelli 1999, 2002)

Indeed, the demand for Latino immigrant labor has become so deeply embedded in the U.S. economy and society that it is now largely decoupled from the business cycle; the number of immigrant workers employed in firms that make substantial use of this labor source does not drop appreciably during a recession, and many businesses even add immigrants to their payrolls during economic contractions. Moreover, employer demand for this type of labor is largely insensitive to changes in immigration laws and law enforcement levels. Not even military-style "concentrated border enforcement operations" carried out by the Border Patrol since the mid-1990s in the principal corridors for illegal entry in California, Arizona, and Texas have reduced the supply of migrant labor available to employers in U.S. cities (Cornelius 2000). In short, the demand for Latino immigrant labor in the United States has become *structural* in character.[3]

Immigrant-dominated labor markets in the United States are highly institutionalized and operate with remarkable efficiency and flexibility. Mature, transborder immigrant social networks linking places of origin in Mexico and Central America with destination cities (and usually with specific employers in those cities) now provide a continuous and easily accessed supply of labor for small and medium-sized businesses (Waldinger 1997; Cornelius 1998; Singer and Massey 1998). In addition, new niches for Latino immigrants are being created by immigrants who start their own businesses. Immigrant-owned businesses have proliferated rapidly in the cities and towns where immigrants cluster, and they hire preferentially within their own ethnic group and social network (see, for example, Guarnizo 1997).

The demand for Latino immigrant labor has also become more dispersed sectorally and spatially. Today's Latino immigrant-absorbing industries are not just sectors that have traditionally employed newly arriving migrants (such as agriculture and restaurants) but a wide variety of service and manufacturing industries, including high-tech manufacturing (see Cornelius and Kuwahara 1998; Zlolniski 1998, 2001).

The process of spatial dispersion has been under way since the 1970s, but U.S. Census Bureau estimates indicate that it accelerated sharply in the 1990s. In 1998, 58 percent of the U.S. Latino population was living in ten metropolitan areas, all of which had large Latin American populations at the beginning of the decade. The greater Los Angeles area alone accounted for one-fifth of all Latinos in the United States (Frey and DeVol 2000, p. 22). But in the 1990s, as labor markets in Los Angeles and other major California cities became saturated, Mexican and Central American migrants ventured east and north, filling occupational niches in the Pacific Northwest, the South, the Midwest, and the mid-Atlantic states (Durand and Massey 1998; Smith 1996). The southern states have experienced particularly rapid growth of the Latino immigrant population in recent years. For example, North Carolina's Latino population grew by 110 percent from 1990–1998, Georgia's by 102 percent, Tennessee's by 90 percent, and South Carolina's by 63 percent. During the same period, there was a surge in Latino immigration to "second-tier" cities in other regions, including the Pacific Northwest, the Midwest, and the Rocky Mountain states. In all of these cases, the explosion of the Latino immigrant population has been driven by the rapid creation of hard-to-fill jobs in industries that require large amounts of manual labor, such as meatpacking, egg processing, construction, landscaping, restaurants, warehousing, foundries, and carpet manufacturing.

Barring a complete collapse of demand as the result of a prolonged and deep recession, it is difficult to envision a realistic scenario for reversing the incorporation of Latino immigrant labor into the U.S. economy. The ratio of low-skilled jobs to total new jobs being created in California and other high-growth states *has* declined significantly since 1980 (McCarthy and Vernez 1997), but in absolute terms, we can expect the demand for low-skilled Latino immigrant workers in these states to remain robust well into the twenty-first century. Even firms that use highly advanced technologies continue to require substantial numbers of low-skilled workers for production, packaging, and maintenance work.

Finally, it is highly unlikely that the U.S. government will intervene so aggressively and massively in labor markets now dominated by Latino immigrants—especially undocumented immigrants—that employer demand for them will be seriously eroded in the foreseeable future. The U.S. Congress, always mindful of the interests of its business constituents and contributors, has been extremely reluctant to strengthen enforcement of immigration laws in the workplace. Even as it poured unprecedented sums into border enforcement, Congress actually cut the budget requests of the U.S. Immigration and Naturalization Service for worksite enforcement in recent years. In Fiscal Year 1998, only 2 percent of the INS's total enforcement effort was devoted to enforcing immigration laws in the workplace (U.S. General Accounting Office 1999, p. 4). Since 1998, worksite enforcement has virtually ceased. Thus, once past the border area, undocumented immigrants run an extremely low risk of apprehension, estimated at 1–2 percent in any given year (Espenshade 1994, p. 872).

With key opinion leaders such as U.S. Federal Reserve chairman Alan Greenspan advocating more immigration to relieve the inflationary pressures of an excessively tight labor market, and with both business elites and organized labor pressing for congressional action to liberalize U.S. immigration policy in various ways, there is no evident political will to uproot and expel the millions of clandestine entrants and visa overstayers now employed in the United States. Consequently, the economic incorporation of Latino immigrants, regardless of their legal status, will continue apace.

THE GENERAL PUBLIC'S RESPONSE TO LATINO IMMIGRATION

Public-opinion surveys show that the average native-born American is at least vaguely aware of the macroeconomic benefits the nation reaps from the presence of Latino immigrants. Majorities of respondents in most polls conducted since the mid-1990s have expressed the view that immigrants to the United States mostly take jobs that native-born Americans do not want (see Table 8.1). Most Americans—especially the more highly skilled—do not view immigrants as their direct competitors in the labor market. Significantly, respondents who identified themselves as Latinos or Hispanics in these surveys were *less* likely than other respondents to perceive labor market competition from immigrants. Although these positive perceptions may reflect cultural affinity with Latino immigrants, they may also be explained by real-life labor market experience—that is, the relative infrequency of direct competition for jobs between native-born Latinos and recently arrived, first-generation immigrants, who tend to be channeled into different segments of the labor market.[4]

TABLE 8.1. U.S. Public's Perceptions of Immigrants
as Labor Market Complements or Competitors

Survey question: *"Do you think immigrants coming to this country today mostly take jobs away from American citizens, or do they mostly take jobs Americans don't want?"*

	Survey		
	New York Times (December 1995)	CBS/ New York Times (February 1996)	Princeton Survey Research Associates (March 1996)
Immigrants take jobs from American citizens	36%	39%	21%
Immigrants take jobs Americans don't want	54	51	65
Both	—	7	—
Don't know	10	3	14

SOURCE: Espenshade and Belanger (1998), Appendix Table 12.1.

Even in California, the hotbed of anti-immigrant sentiment in the early 1990s, a plurality of interviewees in a 1998 statewide survey agreed with the statement that "immigrants today are a benefit to California because of their hard work and job skills" (see Table 8.2). When asked specifically about *Mexican* immigrants, a majority (52 percent) of respondents in another statewide California survey in 1998 said that they consider Mexican immigrants to be a net benefit to the state (Baldassare 2000, p. 105).

There is some evidence that anti-immigrant sentiment may have peaked in 1994, the year in which 59 percent of California voters approved an explicitly anti-immigrant ballot initiative, Proposition 187. Had its implementation not been blocked in the federal courts, this Draconian measure would have virtually ended the access of undocumented immigrants to most public services, including education for their children. In sharp contrast, a 1998 statewide poll in California found that only one out of five residents (22 percent) still favored preventing undocumented immigrant children from attending public schools (Public Policy Institute of California 1999).

A national survey done in July-August 1997 found that less than half (46 percent) of Americans wanted immigration levels to be *lowered*— the smallest such percentage recorded by a national public-opinion poll since 1977 (Princeton Survey Research Associates 1997a). Similarly, a 1999

TABLE 8.2. Californians' Perceptions of Immigrants
as an Economic Benefit or Burden

Survey question: *"Which of these views is closest to yours? (a) Immigrants today are a benefit to California because of their hard work and job skills; (b) Immigrants today are a burden to California because they use public services."*

	All Adults	Latinos	Asians	Blacks	Whites
Benefit	46%	66%	68%	45%	37%
Burden	42	25	23	45	49
Don't know	12	9	9	10	14

SOURCE: Public Policy Institute of California Statewide Survey, April 1998. N = 2,002 (California adult residents). Sampling error for the total sample is plus or minus two percentage points at the 95% confidence level. As reported in Baldassare (2000), Table 4-2, p. 105.

Gallup poll found that 44 percent of the U.S. public wanted to reduce immigration, compared with 65 percent in a 1995 Gallup poll (*Migration News*, 2000). A 2001 Gallup poll, taken after the U.S. economy had begun to contract, found some hardening of public opinion toward immigration but continued recognition of its macroeconomic benefits (Jones 2001).

Nevertheless, in virtually all surveys, large majorities of respondents oppose *increasing* the number of immigrants who can be legally admitted to the United States. In a December 1998 national survey conducted by the *Wall Street Journal* and NBC News, 72 percent expressed opposition to raising the immigration ceiling (*Wall Street Journal* 1998). These results are consistent with many other samplings of U.S. public preferences on immigration levels since the 1940s. Only once—in 1953—did more than 10 percent of the U.S. public favor *increasing* the number of immigrants permitted to enter the country legally. Throughout the period from 1946 to 1990, at least three times as many Americans supported *reducing* the number of immigrant admissions (Simon 1993, p. 63).

EXPLAINING THE PUBLIC RESPONSE

The most plausible explanation for the drop in anti-immigrant sentiment since the mid-1990s is that more Americans are satisfied with the condition of the economy. Since the mid-nineteenth century, pressures to restrict immigration usually have been associated with sharp economic downturns and high levels of economic uncertainty (see Higham 1994). In good times, the U.S. public has virtually ignored immigration (Espenshade and Belanger 1998, pp. 378–79). Every public-opinion survey conducted since the early 1980s that has dealt with immigration has shown that the more optimistic one's assessment of the nation's current economic situation, the more tolerant one's attitudes concerning the appropriate level of immigration. Over the fifty-year period from 1945–1995, the national unemployment rate and the percentage of Americans wanting fewer immigrants to be admitted "track" together well, except for a few years in the late 1950s and early 1960s for which there are no national survey data on preferred immigration levels (Espenshade and Belanger 1998, p. 367).

What happens when the economy is robust—characterized by rapid job creation, low inflation, rising stock prices, and strong consumer confidence? The zero-sum mentality of recessionary times gives way to an expectation of general improvement in living standards. Government deficits shrink, welfare caseloads fall, and the fiscal burden of providing services to immigrants becomes more tolerable to taxpayers. Scapegoats for all types of problems become less necessary. Equally important, labor shortages become more generalized and visible. In the late 1990s, with unemployment rates hovering in the range of 3 to 4 percent in many parts of the country, and with employers from small retailers and service providers to "Fortune 500" companies making increasingly desperate attempts to recruit new workers, the need for a large pool of immigrant labor was rarely so self-evident.

Why, then, have so many Americans—roughly 50 to 70 percent, depending on the poll and the question asked—remained "negative" about immigration? Even in California, where the economy has outperformed the national economy in recent years, many white Californians continue to hold negative views about immigration (Baldassare 2000, p. 106). One plausible explanation is that the benefits of the unprecedented period of economic growth that followed the recession of the early 1990s have been unevenly distributed among the native-born population. Indeed, the 1990s were a decade of growing inequality in the U.S. distribution of wealth. People who have less than a college education, people who hold low-wage jobs, and certain racial minorities have not seen much improvement in their real incomes. Thus, whereas managers and professional people think immigration is good for the economy, blue-collar workers with stagnant earnings are more inclined to see the downside. The evidence from various national surveys of public opinion clearly indicates that less-skilled persons prefer more restrictive immigration policies (Scheve and Slaughter 2001; Kessler 2001). Education has the same effect: higher levels of education are generally associated with greater tolerance for immigration (see Espenshade and Calhoun 1993; Espenshade and Hempstead 1996). In short, people at the lower end of the socioeconomic hierarchy are likely to feel more threatened by immigrants, even if they have had virtually no personal interaction with them and have never had to compete against them in the job market (Muller 1997, pp. 108–09). Their concerns, especially about wage depression resulting from immigration, appear to be rooted in general labor supply and demand considerations.

However, multivariate analyses of anti-immigrant sentiment in the United States and other industrialized Western democracies provide mixed support for the economic self-interest mode of explanation. In a cross-national study based on U.S., French, and German public-opinion survey data gathered in the 1986–1995 period, being unemployed, perceiving a recent deterioration in one's personal finances, and working as a manual laborer had no statistically significant effect on anti-immigrant attitudes in any of the three countries (Fetzer 2000a, 2000b).[5] Several other multivariate analyses have also found that *personal* economic circumstances (as distinct from one's assessment of the health of the national economy) play little role in determining U.S. public attitudes toward immigrants and immigration policy options (Espenshade and Calhoun 1993; Vidanage and Sears 1995; Espenshade and Hempstead 1996; Citrin et al. 1997; Soule 1997; Burns and Gimpel 2000). Less-skilled American workers appear to make a connection between immigration and labor market pressures that may adversely affect them, now or in the future (Hanson, et al. 2002), but such concerns are not shared by the U.S. public in general.

If most Americans today do not see immigration as a threat to their personal economic interests, why do they oppose raising legal immigration ceilings, and why do large majorities in national opinion surveys favor tightening border enforcement and imposing stiffer penalties on employers who hire undocumented immigrants (Espenshade and Belanger 1997)? Granted, all available U.S. public-opinion data reveal much less tolerance for *illegal* immigration than for the legal kind (Baldassare 2000, pp. 105–6; Cain, Citrin, and Wong 2000, p. 17; Espenshade and Belanger 1998, pp. 375–76; Soule 1997, pp. 3–4). Therefore, evidence that the flow of illegal entrants—especially from Mexico—continues undiminished despite the post-1993 buildup of border enforcement resources may feed public concern about immigration levels in general. This is precisely why anti-immigration advocacy groups have labored in recent years to draw a sharp distinction between legal and illegal immigration (Fry 2001, p. 210). But many Americans lump legal and illegal immigration together and do not see significantly different consequences flowing from each.

An alternative way of explaining the persistence of anti-immigrant sentiment in the contemporary United States emphasizes the influence of *noneconomic* factors, especially ethnicity, language, and culture. For example, national survey respondents who have a negative perception of Latinos as an *ethnic group*, not just as immigrants, are more likely to prefer a restrictive immigration policy (Citrin et al. 1997). Similarly, white respondents in a 1994 survey of Los Angeles County residents who saw Latinos as "too demanding" in pushing for equal rights or in seeking assistance from government were more likely to have negative feelings about immigration. Whites in this survey had a more positive perception of Asians, believing the impact of Asian immigration to be less deleterious than that of Latino immigration. The researchers conclude that "whites' attitudes toward the impact of immigration in general are more closely aligned with their perceptions of Hispanics [vs. Asians], suggesting that their anti-*immigrant* feeling may be largely anti-*Hispanic* feeling" (Vidanage and Sears 1995, p. 13).

Specifically, what is it about Latinos as an ethnic category that may feed anti-immigration sentiment? Culture and language appear to be important irritants. Although a "culture of multiculturalism" has taken root in the United States (Suárez-Orozco and Suárez-Orozco 2001, pp. 62–64) to a greater extent than in most West European countries today, the celebration of multiculturalism is by no means universal. A statewide survey of Texas college students found that Anglos who oppose multiculturalism in various forms are more likely to have a negative view of immigration (Martínez-Ebers and Deng 1996). Among the general U.S. population, those who disapprove of bilingual education or bilingual ballots and who view immigrants as making little effort to learn English are among the most likely to view immigration and its consequences negatively (Espenshade and Calhoun 1993). In California, a county-by-county comparison of the vote for Proposition 63—a 1986 state ballot initiative declaring English to be the only language in which the state government can conduct business—and the vote for Proposition 187 revealed a heavy overlap of supporters. When different economic and policy conditions in the counties were controlled for, there was almost a one-to-one correspondence between county support levels for Propositions 63 and 187 (MacDonald and Cain 1998, pp. 296–97).

Language is not the only lightning rod. For example, the fact that Latino immigrants tend to have larger families and to live in multigenerational households, often crowded into small apartments, clashes with Anglo European concepts of family/household organization. Because of the larger number of income earners in each household unit, many more cars and trucks tend to be parked in driveways and along the streets in neighborhoods where Latino immigrants cluster than in predominantly Anglo neighborhoods. The fact that many recent Latino immigrants are "illegals" lends to the expectation that they will commit other types of crimes (Wolf 1988; Espenshade and Belanger 1997). Groups of Latino migrant day laborers waiting on street corners or in shopping centers for contractors to pick them up arouse anxiety and irritation (Eisenstadt and Thorup 1994). In sum, a fairly wide range of negative cultural stereotypes and misunderstandings contribute to a less than sympathetic welcome for Latino newcomers. The line between anti-immigrant and anti-Latino sentiment is often blurred, but it is clear from the empirical evidence

TABLE 8.3. Immigration Perceived as a Cultural Threat

Survey question: "Does the increasing diversity that immigrants bring to this country mostly improve American culture or mostly threaten American culture, or does it not affect American culture?"

Improve	30%
Threaten	42
Has no effect	18
Depends on the group of immigrants	4
Don't know	6

SOURCE: Nationwide survey conducted by the *Los Angeles Times*, August 1996.

that the latter contributes significantly to the general public's hostility toward immigration.[6]

Multivariate analysis of data from the National Opinion Research Center's 1994 General Social Survey shows that the belief that immigration makes it "harder to keep the country united" (a belief that three-quarters of Americans hold) is a highly significant predictor of anti-immigration policy preferences, independent of other attitudes or personal attributes (Soule 1997, pp. 13, 25). The perception of immigration as a source of cultural fragmentation is widely distributed among the U.S. public. A 1996 national survey conducted by the *Los Angeles Times* found that a plurality of respondents viewed the increased diversity brought about by immigration as a threat to American culture (see Table 8.3).

Principled fiscal conservatives can see immigrants as contributing to budget deficits and higher taxes. Holding other attitudes and attributes constant reveals that those who think they pay too much in federal taxes are significantly more likely to prefer reduced immigration (Soule 1997, p. 27). But the concern about immigrants' use of costly public services that respondents express in public-opinion surveys may also be a smoke screen, used to rationalize policy preferences that are actually driven by more deeply felt concerns about national identity, language diversity, and the shifting ethnic and racial composition of the population. For example, MacDonald and Cain's (1998) analysis of the vote in California for Proposition 187—which is *not* based on opinion survey data—suggests that concerns about the fiscal impact of immigration on state and local government could explain the especially strong "yes" vote in California's small, rural counties, whose public finances were particularly fragile in 1994. But "pragmatic" fiscal concerns can be triggered or amplified by negative stereotypes of particular ethnic groups and nationalities. According to polling data analyzed by Espenshade and Belanger (1997), the U.S. public believes that Mexicans and other Latin American immigrants are much more likely than

TABLE 8.4. U.S. Public's Evaluations of Recent Immigrants
by Region or Country of Origin (1997)

Survey question: *"I'm going to read you some different groups of recent immigrants. (Recent immigrants means people who have come to live in the United States since 1980.) Please give me your opinion of each group on a 10-point scale, where '10' means you have a very favorable opinion of them and '1' means you have a very unfavorable opinion. You can name any number between 1 and 10— the higher the number, the more favorable your opinion."*

Region or Country of Origin	Respondents Expressing Unfavorable Opinion of Recent Immigrants from This Region or Country
Africa	18%
Europe	12
Middle East	30
Mexico	**34**
Central/South America	**23**
Cuba	**35**
Other Caribbean (Haiti, Dominican Republic, Jamaica, etc.)	**29**
India	21
China	19
Japan	18
Philippines	19
Other Asian (Korea, Vietnam, etc.)	25

SOURCE: Princeton Survey Research Associates, for Knight-Ridder Newspapers, "Attitudes toward Immigrants Survey," May 2–26, 1997.

Asians and other immigrant groups to end up on welfare. Such beliefs are statistically significant predictors of anti-immigration views.

The perception that immigration to the United States has come to be dominated by a single "problem" nationality, the Mexicans, is also widespread. Since 1965, surveys have shown that Latin America—Mexico in particular—ranks near the bottom in terms of public preferences among sources of U.S. immigration. Europeans immigrants are most favored, and Asians are somewhere in the middle (see Table 8.4; see also Cornelius 1983; Espenshade and Belanger 1997; Soule 1997; Hanson et al. 2002). When a national sample of the U.S. public was asked in 1997 whether there was "any *one* nationality group of recent immigrants you think has done the most to create problems for the United States," Mexicans were the most frequently mentioned (20 percent), followed by Cubans (10 percent) whose image has been tarnished by the Mariel boatlift and its aftermath (Princeton Survey Research Associates, 1997b).

TABLE 8.5. Mexican Immigration to the United States Fiscal Year 1996

Total Immigrants to the United States Entering Legally and Illegally*	Total Mexican Immigrants to the United States Entering Legally and Illegally[†]	Mexican Immigrants as Percent of Total Immigrants
1,190,900	315,000	26.5%

*Includes 915,900 legally admitted immigrants and 275,000 illegally entering immigrants (estimate by INS) of all nationalities, who settled in the United States in fiscal year 1996.

†Estimate by the Binational Study of Migration Between Mexico and the United States (August 1997), p. iii. It represents the number of Mexicans, entering both legally and illegally, who established permanent residence in the United States in fiscal year 1996 (total Mexican migrants entering the United States minus those who returned to Mexico in the same year).

During the 1980s and 1990s, Mexico was the single most important source country for immigrants entering the United States, both legally and illegally. In 1996, for example, Mexicans accounted for 17.9 percent of all legally admitted immigrants. If a reasonable estimate of undocumented Mexican migrants is added (see Table 8.5), then the proportion of Mexicans rises to slightly more than a quarter of all immigrants—far less than the Irish-dominated U.S. immigration in the mid-nineteenth century.[7]

However, that degree of numerical dominance has been enough to provoke anger and anxiety in many Americans today, especially in California, the primary destination for Mexican migrants to the United States. The dense concentration of Mexican immigrants in southern California helps to explain why that region became the nation's principal hotbed of anti-immigrant activism in the early 1990s. By contrast, residents of New Jersey appear more tolerant of immigration than people in the rest of the country, possibly because the state's immigrant population is more diverse than that in other major immigrant-receiving states (Espenshade 1997). In New Jersey, European-origin immigrants (especially Italians) still outnumber immigrants from Third World countries, and there is no single numerically dominant nationality.[8]

For more than 200 years, new waves of immigrants to the United States have been viewed as a source of disunity or cultural fragmentation. (*Balkanization* is the currently fashionable term—see Lee 1998, p.154.) It has been assumed that the cultural baggage carried by the most recently arrived immigrants will cause them to resist assimilation or to assimilate incompletely (Reimers 1998, pp. 109–29; Simon 1985). Today, Mexicans provoke particular concern because their cultural traditions and Spanish-language use are constantly being reinforced through continuing, large-scale immigration from Mexico, making them prime candidates for ethnic separatist movements. The specter of a "Chicano Québec in the Southwest" is raised even by mainstream U.S. historians (see, for example, Kennedy 1996).

The overarching concern here is that contemporary Latino immigration is upsetting the country's ethnocultural balance, potentially leading to a crisis of national identity. Some demographers warn that the combination of very low fertility rates among the native-born population with high levels of immigration from high-fertility source countries makes such a crisis virtually unavoidable (see, for example, Teitelbaum and Winter 1998). Geographers point out that "balkanization" can also take the form of growing spatial inequality (increasing differences between poor inner-city neighborhoods flooded with newly arrived immigrants and affluent suburbs populated by the native-born and the minority of immigrants who have achieved economic mobility) and resegregation (out-migration by natives from areas heavily affected by immigration to less heavily affected areas) (Clark 1998; Frey 1996; Gimpel 1999).

In contrast to the "classic"American nativism of the 1850–1929 period—a witches' brew of simple racism, xenophobia, and religious intolerance—today's anti-immigration rhetoric stressing issues of ethnocultural balance rarely takes an explicitly racial or xenophobic tack (a conspicuous exception is Brimelow 1995). The basic claim is that the United States is experiencing an immigrant integration crisis, because the latest wave of immigrants—especially Mexicans and people from other Spanish-speaking countries—are clinging stubbornly to their home countries' language and culture, and they are now numerous enough to change or dilute America's "core culture." In 1997, for example, the national media made a great fuss over the revelation that in the preceding year, for the first time, there was more salsa sold in the United States than ketchup!

Language issues, in particular, have often been a lightning rod for anti-immigrant sentiment in the United States in recent decades. Attempts by state and local governments to impose "English-only" laws, to provide bilingual ballots, and to implement or dismantle bilingual education programs in the public schools have generated considerable tension between immigrants and natives (Citrin et al. 1990; Crawford 1992). Latino immigrants tend to be viewed by many Anglo Americans as a "problem minority" because they do not appear to be assimilating fast enough into the dominant culture, and continued use of Spanish is, for most native-born Americans, the most conspicuous indicator of a failure to assimilate.

The empirical evidence indicates that most Latino immigrants eventually learn some English, and "virtually all second- and third-generation descendants have good English language skills" (Smith and Edmonston 1997, p. 378). Less than half of second-generation (U.S.-born) eighth- and ninth-grade Latino students in the Miami and San Diego areas were found

TABLE 8.6. The "Yes" Vote on California's
Propositions 187 and 227, by Race/Ethnicity

Racial/Ethnic Group	Voted "Yes" on Proposition 187	Voted "Yes" on Proposition 227
Non-Hispanic whites	63%	67%
Asian Americans	47	57
Blacks	47	48
Latinos	23	37

SOURCE: *Los Angeles Times* exit polls for the 1994 and 1998 California state elections.

to be fluent bilinguals (Portes and Hao 1998). Mexicans are more likely than other contemporary immigrant groups to retain some proficiency in the first generation's language into the second and third generations, but U.S. Census Bureau data show that Mexican-origin persons who were born more recently are much more likely to be monolingual English speakers (Smith 1998, pp. 25–26). Nevertheless, the general U.S. public tends to focus on the Spanish-dominant first-generation immigrants in their midst, and they see linguistic diversity attributable to Latino immigration as a growing threat to cultural cohesion.

This mind-set is considerably more complex than simple racism. Usually it is not grounded in perceptions of the newest immigrants as racially inferior, a recurrent theme in American nativism of the nineteenth and early twentieth centuries. Even the California electorate's approval of ostensibly anti-immigrant ballot initiatives such as Propositions 187 and 227 (the anti-bilingual-education measure approved by 61 percent of California voters in June 1998) cannot be categorized as purely racist responses to Latino immigration, if only because substantial minorities of Latino voters supported both of these measures. Forty-three percent of the voters in Latino-majority neighborhoods of Los Angeles County supported Proposition 187 (Clark 1998, pp. 176–77), and 37 percent of Latino voters, statewide, supported Proposition 227. Nevertheless, the nearly complete overlap of the vote for Proposition 187 and the vote for the "English-only" Proposition 63 in 1986 "suggests that there was a strong element of cultural nativism in the Prop. 187 vote" (MacDonald and Cain 1998, p. 301). And the sharp ethnic/racial divisions in the votes on Propositions 187 and 227 (see Table 8.6) suggest that there was some racially grounded nativism as well (see also Hollifield and Martin 1996).

The cultural-nativist component of the vote on Proposition 227 was significant: 40.1 percent of exit poll respondents—a plurality—explained their "yes" vote on Proposition 227 by agreeing with the statement "Americans should speak English." The belief that bilingual education is pedagogically ineffective ("doesn't work") was far behind as a motivating factor; only 12.4 percent of exit poll respondents cited it as the reason for their "yes" vote (Alvarez 2002). Latinos were relatively opposed to Proposition 227, whereas the white and Asian communities strongly supported it. Similarly, polling data from California reveal huge differences between Latinos and people of other ethnicities in their perceptions of the benefits accruing from immigration. In one recent survey, only 37 percent of non-Latino whites perceived immigrants as a benefit to California, compared with 66 percent of Latinos (see Table 8.2).

These data are generally consistent with the argument advanced at the outset of this chapter: that *noneconomic* factors (especially ethnicity, language, and culture) are highly influential in shaping Americans' response to the "new" Latino immigration. A recent, survey-based analysis of the mass politics of immigration in the United States, France, and Germany concluded,

> Opposition to immigration in these three countries has as much to do with symbolically delegitimating the values and cultures of immigrant minorities as with preventing foreigners from "taking natives' jobs" or even "bankrupting the country." Possibly sensing a challenge to their hegemony from "new immigrants," the dominant cultural "insiders" (e.g., French Catholics, white American Protestants) appear to be lashing out at the cultural "interlopers" (e.g., North-African or Turkish Muslims, Latin-American Catholics) in their midst." (Fetzer 2000a, pp. 17–18)

Revisionist historians of American nativism argue that earlier conceptualizations of anti-immigrant sentiment as a special kind of nationalistic fervor (Higham 1994) have led us to underestimate the connections between anti-Mexican and anti-Asian racism and the resurgence of nativism at various points in U.S. history. The 1880s movement to restrict Chinese immigration "was led by skilled workers who had relatively little to fear from competition from coolie labor; but in a broader sense [these] white workers saw Chinese immigration as endangering their families. The threat of Chinese laborers was viewed in sexual as well as economic terms" (Kusmer 1999, p. 7). Even among immigrants of European origin, such negative ethnocultural stereotypes were by no means absent. In the early twentieth century, for example, German American and Irish American dock workers refused to recognize their Italian immigrant counterparts as "white men." The newest European immigrants were "'in-between people,' whose racial acceptability, to native-born white Americans, was at best uncertain" (Kusmer 1999, p. 6).

Again, the U.S. public's uneasiness about the current wave of Latino immigrants seems considerably more complex than the strictly racial or cultural nativism of earlier eras. Both economic and noneconomic factors are shaping public opinion toward the latest generation of Latino immigrants. We find a fluid mixture of uncertainty about future job and wage prospects (if one is less-skilled) and stereotypical beliefs about the welfare use, cultural assimilability, and propensity to commit crimes of Latino immigrants (especially Mexicans). Most analysts have concluded that determining the relative weight of these economic and noneconomic factors is virtually impossible within the confines of extant data sets (see, for example, Hanson et al. 2002). However, it would be naïve to ignore the strength and persistence of the ethnocultural objection to Latino immigration. Indeed, continuing large-scale immigration from Latin America may be nudging the United States toward what some public-opinion analysts have termed a more restrictive or ethnocultural version of American nationality (Citrin, Reingold, and Green 1990). Moreover, latent, ethnoculturally grounded anti-immigrant sentiment can still be exploited by entrepreneurial politicians, especially if a prolonged recession raises the perceived economic threat posed by immigration.

The countervailing force is the twenty-first century U.S. labor market. The employers that depend most heavily on Latino immigrant labor have few attractive and realistic alternatives to its continued use (see Cornelius 1998). Small cities with shrinking native-born labor pools face a stark choice: either accept and adjust to large numbers of culturally distinct immigrant workers or forego the economic benefits of a major new industry. With the local labor market very tight, unskilled native-born workers can find better-paying, "cleaner" work elsewhere (Horowitz and Miller 1997, p. 13). In big cities such as Los Angeles,

> it was not simply that the region's economy had learned [during the economic boom of the 1980s] to accommodate to the immigrant presence; more importantly, its adaptation to immigration was so deep and pervasive that any change in the abundant flow of newcomers would come at a fairly stiff price. One could reduce the supply of immigrant cooks and maids, but hotel and restaurant prices would then go up, with less than salutary effects on the region's crucial tourist trades. One could curb the inflow of foreign-born garment workers, but that would simply transform what had been a growth industry into another of the region's declining sectors. And one could encourage the legions of foreign-born laborers and construction workers to go home, but their departure would not help the region's hard-pressed builders nor do anything to contain home prices that were already too high. (Waldinger 1996b, p. 469)

In short, the rapidly accumulating ethnocultural residue of the "new" Latino immigration is the inevitable consequence of the apparently insatiable U.S. demand for workers willing to do its dirty jobs at relatively low wages. There is a growing recognition among the general public that both low-skilled and high-skilled immigrant labor is beneficial in today's tight labor markets and may even be essential to the economy's health. But this awareness is coupled with a persistent reluctance to pay the social, cultural, and human services costs of a rapidly expanding, increasingly permanent population of Latino immigrants and their dependents.[9]

A FUTURE DIRECTION FOR LATINO IMMIGRATION RESEARCH

Are Americans prepared to accept the ways in which large-scale Latino immigration will inevitably change certain aspects of their society and culture—from condiments to mass entertainment to religion to political life? The answer might be pursued effectively through comparative research on the numerous small towns and cities outside of the principal immigrant-receiving states that experienced a rapid influx of migrant workers from Mexico and Central America during the 1990s. Usually the migrants were attracted by the start-up or expansion of a labor-intensive industry offering low-skill, low-status jobs shunned by native-born workers in the area. They arrived in towns that until recently had no discernible foreign-born population. The cultural gap between new Latino immigrants and natives is much greater in these small, predominantly European American communities than in major gateway cities such as Los Angeles, San Diego, Chicago, Miami, and New York. They are a microcosm of the growing racial-ethnic-cultural diversity that the "new" Latino immigration has brought.

A case in point: the city of Georgetown, Delaware (4,500), which in less than five years experienced an influx of 1,200-1,500 Mexican, Guatemalan, and other Central American immigrants, attracted by new poultry-processing plants in the surrounding area. A Spanish-language newspaper and radio station, along with retail stores catering to the immigrant population, sprang up virtually overnight. "Established residents became fearful of their new neighbors, both because of tangible worries about property values and more abstract concerns about these people who seemed so different" (Horowitz and Miller 1997, p. 1). Eventually, tensions were defused through a series of public meetings and interventions by public officials and nongovernmental organizations, but the cultural gap between immigrants and native-born residents reportedly remains wide.

A similar case of precipitous change in the ethnocultural balance as a result of recent Latino immigration has been documented through ethnographic research in a town in southwestern Iowa (population about 1,250) where the expansion of a food-processing plant had quickly exhausted the local labor supply:

> Initial research in the early 1990s found only reluctant attempts to deal with the perceived differences [between native-born residents and newly arrived Latino migrants]. Many white European-American residents contrasted the ideal-typical traditional resident with the newcomers. And, of course, the

Latinos were viewed as not measuring up for a variety of reasons. The racism implicit in many comments about the Mexicans was couched in discussions of the white residents' fear of increased crime, a growing underclass, and a rise in the cost of education and social services. By the end of the 1990s, a number of significant shifts had taken place. Since a growing proportion of Latinos were remaining for longer periods than in the early 1990s, their presence was now viewed as a permanent feature of the community. Furthermore, as Latino children entered the schools, they formed friendships with Anglo children, thus breaking down divisions between residents of different racial-ethnic backgrounds. (Naples 2000)

Siler City, North Carolina (population 5,500) also went through a period of denial in regard to its rapid transformation into what some long-time residents derisively call "Little Mexico." As recounted by the director of a local nongovernmental organization that assists the workers attracted from Mexico, Nicaragua, and other countries during the past five years by two poultry-processing plants, "the feeling I got from local officials at first was that the Latinos were going to come and go. They were seen as migrants. It took a while for people here to realize they were not going to leave; they were going to stay. Everyone has to adapt to what the city looks like now, and it's a different city from what the older residents grew up in. And these new people are not white Anglo-Saxons, which makes it harder, because after all, this is still the South" (Pressley 2000).

Like other small towns and "second-tier" cities in nontraditional receiving areas for Latino immigrants, Siler has had to deal with a wide range of immigration impacts: a housing shortage, inadequate medical services, overcrowding in the schools, the newcomers' lack of driver's licenses, and communication problems between the immigrants and local police and government officials. Studying the ways in which such problems have been addressed, and the sociocultural adjustments that have and have not been made by native-born residents as well as newcomers, provides an intriguing and important optic for viewing the larger U.S. political response to the "new" Latino immigration.

NOTES

1. In February 2000, the national AFL-CIO leadership called for elimination of sanctions against employers who "knowingly" hire undocumented workers (penalties that it had staunchly advocated since the 1970s and had helped write into federal law in 1986) as well as a general amnesty for five million or more undocumented immigrants thought to be living in the United States.

2. For example, economist Barry R. Chiswick: "The nature of the [U.S.] economy has changed. Jobs for low-skilled workers have been drying up, and the opportunities for those who are higher-skilled have been growing rapidly" (quoted in D. W. Miller, "Scholars of Immigration Focus on the Children," *The Chronicle of*

Higher Education, 5 February 1999, p. A19). The hypothesized mismatch between low-skilled immigrants and the highly skilled jobs being created in the contemporary U.S. economy is also the central argument of a widely cited analysis of immigration impacts in California (McCarthy and Vernez 1997).

3. For empirical evidence of the structural embeddedness of demand in San Diego and New York City, see Cornelius 1998; Cornelius and Kuwahara 1998; Smith 1996; Waldinger 1996a.

4. The empirical evidence on the extent and nature of labor market competition between Latino immigrants and native-born workers is mixed, but large-scale substitution of immigrants for native workers appears to be limited to a relatively few occupational niches in specific localities (such as janitors and maids in Los Angeles). For a review of the evidence from three U.S. cities, see Rosenfeld and Tienda (1999). See also Hanson, Scheve, Slaughter, and Spilimbergo (2002).

5. Similarly, a cross-national analysis of attitudes toward immigration in twelve OECD countries finds that being unemployed does not affect natives' perceptions of the impact of immigrants on the economy or the opinions about whether immigration should be reduced (Bauer, Lofstrom, and Zimmermann 2000, p. 20). Marques (1999) concludes that among Portuguese workers, the perception that immigrants are an economic threat is a consequence of generalized lack of confidence in the opportunity structure of Portugal.

6. Similarly, racial prejudice toward immigrants from the West Indies and Asia has been found to be by far the most important predictor of negative attitudes toward immigration among white Britons (Dustmann and Preston 2000).

7. In 1851, for example, 58 percent of all immigrants entering the United States were Irish.

8. The empirical evidence of a geographic-concentration effect of immigrants *in general* on public attitudes toward immigration is weak. For example, an analysis of data from a nationwide survey conducted in 1998 reveals that simply living in a metropolitan area in a state with a high rate of immigration has no effect on attitudes toward immigration. However, personal familiarity with immigrants (as coworkers and friends) was a significant predictor of favorable attitudes toward immigration (Moore, Pelletier, and Harrison, 1999). Similarly, Scheve and Slaughter (2001) find that low-skilled workers living in high-immigration areas do not hold more restrictionist preferences for immigration policy than less-skilled workers in low-immigration communities.

9. On the trend toward a higher incidence of permanent settlement among Mexican migrants to the United States, see Cornelius (1998, pp. 136–139) and Marcelli and Cornelius (2001). Compare Durand, Massey, and Zenteno (2001).

REFERENCES

Alvarez, R. Michael (2002) "Why Did Proposition 227 Pass?" In Wayne A. Cornelius and Idean Salehyan, eds., *Educating California's Immigrant Children: Origins, Implementation, and Short-term Consequences of Proposition 227*, Anthology Series, No. 2. La Jolla: Center for Comparative Immigration Studies, University of California–San Diego.

Baldassare, Mark (2000) *California in the New Millennium: The Changing Social and Political Landscape.* Berkeley: University of California Press.

Bauer, Thomas K., Magnus Lofstrom, and Klaus F. Zimmermann (2000) "Immigration Policy, Assimilation of Immigrants, and Natives' Sentiments towards Immigrants: Evidence from 12 OECD Countries," Discussion Paper No. 187. Bonn, Germany: Institute for the Study of Labor (IZA), iza@iza.org.

Brimelow, Peter (1995) *Alien Nation: Common Sense about America's Immigration Disaster.* New York: Random House.

Burns, Peter, and James G. Gimpel (2000) "Economic Insecurity, Prejudical Stereotypes, and Public Opinion on Immigration Policy," *Political Science Quarterly* 115:201–25.

Cain, Bruce, Jack Citrin, and Cara Wong (2000) *Ethnic Context, Race Relations, and California Politics.* San Francisco: Public Policy Institute of California.

Citrin, Jack, Beth Reingold, Evelyn Walters, and Donald P. Green (1990) "The 'Official English' Movement and the Symbolic Politics of Language in the United States," *Western Political Quarterly* 43:535–59.

Citrin, Jack, Beth Reingold, and Donald P. Green (1990) "American Identity and the Politics of Ethnic Change," *Journal of Politics* 52(4):1124–1154.

Citrin, Jack, Donald P. Green, Christopher Muste, and Cara Wong (1997) "Public Opinion toward Immigration Reform: The Role of Economic Motivations," *Journal of Politics* 59:858–81.

Clark, William (1998) *The California Cauldron: Immigration and the Fortunes of Local Communities.* New York: Guilford Press.

Cornelius, Wayne A. (1983) "America in the Era of Limits: Migrants, Nativists, and the Future of U.S.–Mexican Relations." In Carlos Vásquez and Manuel García y Griego, eds., *Mexican–U.S. Relations: Conflict and Convergence.* Los Angeles: UCLA Chicano Studies Research Center.

Cornelius, Wayne A. (1998) "The Structural Embeddedness of Demand for Mexican Immigrant Labor: New Evidence from California." In Marcelo Suárez-Orozco, ed., *Crossings: Mexican Immigration in Interdisciplinary Perspective.* Cambridge, MA: Harvard University Press.

Cornelius, Wayne A. (2001) "The Efficacy and Unintended Consequences of U.S. Immigration Control Policy, 1993–2000," *Population and Development Review* 27(4).

Cornelius, Wayne A., with Yasuo Kuwahara (1998) *The Role of Immigrant Labor in the U.S. and Japanese Economies: A Comparative Study of San Diego and Hamamatsu, Japan.* La Jolla: Center for U.S.–Mexican Studies, University of California–San Diego.

Cornelius, Wayne A., Thomas J. Espenshade, and Idean Salehyan, eds. (2001) *The International Migration of the Highly Skilled: Demand, Supply, and Development Consequences for Receiving and Sending Countries.* La Jolla: Center for Comparative Immigration Studies, University of California–San Diego.

Crawford, James (1992) *Hold Your Tongue: Bilingualism and the Politics of "English Only."* Reading, MA: Addison-Wesley.

Durand, Jorge, and Douglas S. Massey (1998) "Historical Dynamics of Mexican Migrant Destinations, 1920–1996." Paper presented at the XXI International Congress of the Latin American Studies Association, Chicago, September 24–26.

Durand, Jorge, Douglas S. Massey, and René M. Zenteno (2001) "Mexican Immigration to the United States: Continuities and Change," *Latin American Research Review,* 36(1):107–27.

Dustmann, Christian, and Ian Preston (2000) "Racial and Economic Factors in Attitudes to Immigration," Discussion Paper No. 190. Bonn, Germany: Institute for the Study of Labor (IZA).

Eisenstadt, Todd A., and Cathryn L. Thorup (1994) *Caring Capacity versus Carrying Capacity: Community Responses to Mexican Immigration in San Diego's North County.* La Jolla: Center for U.S.–Mexican Studies, University of California–San Diego.

Espenshade, Thomas J. (1994) "Does the Threat of Border Apprehension Deter Undocumented U.S. Immigration?" *Population and Development Review,* 2 (4): 871–892.

Espenshade, Thomas J. (1997) "Taking the Pulse of Public Opinion toward Immigrants." In T. J. Espenshade, ed., *Keys to Successful Immigration: Implications of the New Jersey Experience.* Washington, DC: Urban Institute Press.

Espenshade, Thomas J., and Maryann Belanger (1997) "U.S. Public Perceptions and Reactions to Mexican Migration." In Frank D. Bean, Rodolfo O. de la Garza, Bryan R. Roberts, and Sidney Weintraub, eds., *At the Crossroads: Mexican Migration and U.S. Policy.* New York: Rowman and Littlefield.

Espenshade, Thomas J., and Maryann Belanger (1998) "Immigration and Public Opinion." In Marcelo Suárez-Orozco, ed., *Crossings: Mexican Immigration in Interdisciplinary Perspective.* Cambridge, MA: Harvard University Press.

Espenshade, Thomas J., and Charles A. Calhoun (1993) "An Analysis of Public Opinion toward Undocumented Immigration," *Population Research and Policy Review,* 12:189–224.

Espenshade, Thomas J., and Katherine Hempstead (1996) "Contemporary American Attitudes toward U.S. Immigration," *International Migration Review* 30(2):535–70.

Fetzer, Joel S. (2000a) "Economic Self-Interest or Cultural Marginality? Anti-Immigrant Sentiment and Nativist Political Movements in France, Germany, and the USA," *Journal of Ethnic and Migration Studies* 26(1):5–23.

Fetzer, Joel S. (2000b) *Public Attitudes toward Immigration in the United States, France, and Germany.* Cambridge, U.K.: Cambridge University Press.

Frey, William H. (1996) "Immigration, Domestic Migration, and Demographic Balkanization in America: New Evidence for the 1990s," *Population and Development Review,* 22:741–63.

Frey, William H., and Ross C. DeVol (2000) *America's Demography in the New Century: Aging Baby Boomers and New Immigrants as Major Players.* Policy Brief No. 9. Santa Monica: Milken Institute.

Fry, Brian N. (2001) *Responding to Immigration: Perceptions of Promise and Threat.* New York: LFB Scholarly Publishing.

Gimpel, James G. (1999) *Separate Destinations: Migration, Immigration, and the Politics of Places.* Ann Arbor: University of Michigan Press.

Guarnizo, Luis E. (1997) "De migrantes asalariados a empresarios transnacionales: la economía étnica mexicana en Los Angeles y la transnacionalización de la migración," *Revista de Ciencias Sociales* (Universidad de Puerto Rico–Río Piedras).

Hanson, Gordon H., Keneth F. Scheve, Matthew J. Slaugher, and Antonino Spilimbergo (2002) *Immigration and the U.S. Economy.* New York and Oxford, U.K.: Oxford University Press.

Higham, John (1994) *Strangers in the Land: Patterns of American Nativism, 1860–1925.* New Brunswick: Rutgers University Press.

Hollifield, James F., and David L. Martin (1996) "Strange Bedfellows? Immigration and Class Voting on Proposition 187 in California." Paper presented at the Annual Meeting of the American Political Science Association, San Francisco, August 29–September 1.

Horowitz, Roger, and Mark J. Miller (1997) "Immigrants in the Delmarva Poultry Processing Industry: The Changing Face of Georgetown, Delaware and Environs." Paper presented at the "Changing Face of Delmarva" conference, University of Delaware, September 11–13.

Jones, Jeffrey M. (2001) "Americans Have Mixed Opinions About Immigration," *Gallup News Service*, July 18, www.gallup.com/poll/releases/pr010718.asp.

Kennedy, David M. (1996) "Can We Still Afford to Be a Nation of Immigrants?" *Atlantic Monthly*, 278(5):52–68.

Kessler, Alan E. (2001) "Immigration, Economic Insecurity, and the 'Ambivalent' American Public," Working Paper No. 41, Center for Comparative Immigration Studies, University of California–San Diego, www.ccis-vcsd.org.

Kusmer, Kenneth L. (1999) "Strangers in the Land and American Nativism: A Reconsideration." Paper presented at the Balch Faculty Forum, Balch Institute for Ethnic Studies, Philadelphia, February 19.

Lee, Kenneth K. (1998) *Huddled Masses, Muddled Laws: Why Contemporary Immigration Policy Fails to Reflect Public Opinion*. Westport, CT: Praeger.

McCarthy, Kevin F., and Georges Vernez (1997) *Immigration in a Changing Economy: California's Experience*. Santa Monica: RAND Corporation.

MacDonald, Karin, and Bruce E. Cain (1998) "Nativism, Partisanship, and Immigration: An Analysis of Prop. 187." In Michael B. Preston, Bruce E. Cain, and Sandra Bass, eds., *Racial and Ethnic Politics in California*, Vol. 2. Berkeley: Institute of Governmental Studies Press, University of California–Berkeley.

Marcelli, Enrico (1999) "Undocumented Latino Immigrant Workers: The Los Angeles Experience." In David W. Haines and Karen E. Rosenblum, eds., *Illegal Immigration in America: A Reference Handbook*. Westport, CT: Greenwood Press.

Marcelli, Enrico (2002) *California in Denial: A Political Economy of Unauthorized Mexican Immigration*. Boulder: Westview Press.

Marcelli, Enrico, and Wayne A. Cornelius (2001) "The Changing Profile of Mexican Migrants to the United States: New Evidence from California and Mexico," *Latin American Research Review*, 36(3):105–31.

Marques, M. Margarida (1999) "Attitudes and Threat Perception: Unemployment and Immigration in Portugal," *South European Society and Politics*, 4(3):184–205.

Martínez-Ebers, Valerie, and Zixian Deng (1996) "Americans' Cultural Perspectives and Immigration Attitudes: A Structural Model." Paper presented at the Annual Meeting of the American Political Science Association, San Francisco, August 29–September 1.

Migration News (2000) May.

Moore, Kathleen, Stephen Pelletier, and Chase Harrison (1999) "American Public Opinion and Immigration in the 1990s: A Familiarity Index." Unpublished paper, Dept. of Political Science and Center for Survey Research and Analysis, University of Connecticut, Storrs.

Muller, Thomas (1997) "Nativism in the Mid-1990s: Why Now?" In Juan F. Perea, ed., *Immigrants Out! The New Nativism and the Anti-Immigrant Impulse in the United States*. New York: New York University Press.

Naples, Nancy A. (2000) "Economic Restructuring and Racialization: Incorporation of Mexicans and Mexican Americans in the Rural Midwest." Working Paper No. 7. La Jolla: Center for Comparative Immigration Studies, University of California-San Diego, www.ccis-ucsd.org.

Pastor, Manuel, Jr., and Enrico A. Marcelli (2000) "Social, Spatial, and Skill Mismatch Among Immigrants and Native-born Workers in Los Angeles," Working Paper No. 1. La Jolla: Center for Comparative Immigration Studies, University of California–San Diego, www.ccis-ucsd.org.

Portes, Alejandro, and Lingxin Hao (1998) "E Pluribus Unum: Bilingualism and Loss of Language in the Second Generation," *Sociology of Education,* 71 (October):269–94.

Pressley, Sue Anne (2000) "Hispanic Immigration Boom Rattles South: Rapid Influx to Some Areas Raises Tensions," *Washington Post,* March 6, p. A03.

Princeton Survey Research Associates (1997a) "Attitudes toward Immigrants Survey," for Knight-Ridder Newspapers, May 2–26. Princeton: Princeton Survey Research Associates.

Princeton Survey Research Associates (1997b) "Survey of U.S. Public Opinion," for National Public Radio, July 31–August 17. Princeton: Princeton Survey Research Associates.

Public Policy Institute of California (1999) "PPIC Statewide Survey: Social and Economic Trends," December 4–13, 1998. San Francisco.

Reimers, David M. (1998) *Unwelcome Strangers: American Identity and the Turn Against Immigration*. New York: Columbia University Press.

Rosenfeld, Michael J., and Marta Tienda (1999) "Mexican Immigration, Occupational Niches, and Labor-Market Competition: Evidence from Los Angeles, Chicago, and Atlanta, 1970–1990." In Frank D. Bean and Stephanie Bell-Rose, eds., *Immigration and Opportunity: Race, Ethnicity, and Employment in the United States*. New York: Russell Sage Foundation.

Scheve, Kenneth F., and Matthew J. Slaughter (2001) "Labor Market Competition and Individual Preferences over Immigration Policy," *Review of Economics and Statistics,* 83(1):133–145.

Simon, Rita J. (1985) *Public Opinion and the Immigrant: Print Media Coverage, 1880–1980*. Lexington, MA: Heath-Lexington Books.

Simon, Rita J. (1993) "Old Minorities, New Immigrants: Aspirations, Hopes, and Fears," *The Annals of the American Academy of Political and Social Science,* 530 (November):61–73.

Singer, Audrey, and Douglas S. Massey (1998) "The Social Process of Undocumented Border Crossing among Mexican Migrants," *International Migration Review* 32 (3):561–92.

Smith, James P. (1998) "Progress across the Generations." Paper presented at the Annual Meeting of the American Economic Association, Chicago, January.

Smith, James P., and Barry Edmonston, eds. (1997) *The New Americans: Economic, Demographic, and Fiscal Effects of Immigration*. Washington, DC: National Academy Press.

Smith, Robert C. (1996) "Mexicans in New York: Membership and Incorporation of a New Immigrant Group." In S. Baver and G. Haslip Viera, eds., *Latinos in New York*. Notre Dame: University of Notre Dame Press.

Soule, Suzanne R. (1997) "Affect or the Economy? U.S. Public Opinion and Anti-Immigrant Sentiment." Paper presented at the Fall Workshop of the University of California Comparative Immigration and Integration Research Program, Davis, October 10–11.

Suárez-Orozco, Carola, and Marcelo M. Suárez-Orozco (2001) *Children of Immigration*. Cambridge, MA: Harvard University Press.

Teitelbaum, Michael S., and Jay Winter (1998) *A Question of Numbers: High Migration, Low Fertility, and the Politics of National Identity*. New York: Hill & Wang.

U.S. General Accounting Office (1999). *Illegal Aliens: Significant Obstacles to Reducing Unauthorized Alien Employment Exist*. Washington, DC: GAO, Report GAO/T-GGD-99-105 (July).

Valenzuela, Abel (2000) "Working on the Margins: Immigrant Day Labor Characteristics and Prospects for Employment," Working Paper No. 22. La Jolla: Center for Comparative Immigration Studies, University of California–San Diego, www.ccis-ucsd.org.

Vidanage, Sharmaine, and David O. Sears (1995) "The Foundations of Public Opinion Toward Immigration Policy: Group Conflict or Symbolic Politics?" Paper presented at the Annual Meeting of the Midwest Political Science Association, Chicago, April 6–8.

Waldinger, Roger (1996a) *Still the Promised City? Blacks and Immigrants in Post-Industrial New York*. Cambridge, MA: Harvard University Press.

Waldinger, Roger (1996b) "Ethnicity and Opportunity in the Plural City." In R. Waldinger and Mehdi Bozorgmehr, eds., *Ethnic Los Angeles*. New York: Russell Sage Foundation.

Waldinger, Roger (1997) "Social Capital or Social Closure? Immigrant Networks in the Labor Market." Working paper Series, No. 26. Los Angeles: Lewis Center for Regional Policy Studies, UCLA.

Waldinger, Roger, and Mehdi Bozorgmehr, eds. (1996) *Ethnic Los Angeles*. New York: Russell Sage Foundation.

Wall Street Journal (1998) "The Wall Street Journal/NBC News Poll," Hart-Teeter Study 4098, December 3–6, *Wall Street Journal Interactive Edition*.

Wolf, Daniel (1988) *Undocumented Aliens and Crime: The Case of San Diego County*. Monograph Series, No. 29. La Jolla: Center for U.S.–Mexican Studies, University of California-San Diego.

Zlolniski, Christian (1998) "In the Shadow of the Silicon Valley: Mexican Immigrant Workers in a Low-Income Barrio in San Jose." Ph.D. diss. University of California–Santa Barbara.

Zlolniski, Christian (2001) "Unskilled Immigrant Labor in High-Tech Companies: The Case of Mexican Janitors in Silicon Valley." In Wayne A. Cornelius, Thomas J. Espenshade, and Idean Salehyan, eds., *The International Migration of the Highly Skilled: Demand, Supply, and Developmental Consequences*. Anthology Series, No. 1. La Jolla: Center for Comparative Immigration Studies, University of California–San Diego.

Chapter 9

Resurrecting Exclusion

The Effects of 1996 U.S. Immigration Reform on Communities and Families in Texas, El Salvador, and Mexico

Jacqueline Hagan and Nestor Rodriguez

The Personal Responsibility and Work Opportunity Act (PRWOA) and the Illegal Immigrant Reform and Immigrant Responsibility Act (IIRIRA) of 1996 create a significant departure from the immigrant and immigration policies of the past several decades. Since the enactment of the Immigration and Nationality Act Amendments of 1965, U.S. immigration laws have increasingly granted rights and privileges to immigrants. However, PRWOA and IIRIRA together represent an exclusionary shift in post–World War II U.S. immigration policy. Collectively, these two laws restrict public services for immigrants, limit immigrant sponsors, and significantly expand border and criminal alien enforcement activities (Hagan, Rodriguez, and Capps 1999; Fix and Zimmermann 1997).

Binational working-class families, and the poverty-stricken communities in which they reside in Texas, Mexico, and Central America, have been hit especially hard by the concurrent effects of these exclusionary laws. The impacts are particularly severe in Texas border counties, where even during the national economic boom of the late 1990s, unemployment rates reached double-digit figures (Texas Workforce Commission 1999). In these border communities, immigrants have historically relied heavily on public benefits and thus were at risk of losing them as a result of welfare reform. Similarly, because of IIRIRA provisions, which have heightened immigration enforcement along the border and boosted criminal-alien removals of Mexican and Central American males, families are at greater risk of hardship, as are the often impoverished communities of origin to which they return.

This chapter reports selected findings from an ongoing study of the implementation and effects of the immigration and welfare reform laws passed by the U.S. Congress in the summer of 1996 (Hagan, Rodriguez, and Capps 1999). In this chapter, we specifically restrict our focus to the effects of the 1996 immigration reform law on immigrant families and on the communities in which they live and work in Texas, Mexico, and El Salvador.

RESEARCH DESIGN

The study was initiated in the spring of 1997 in two Texas interior cities (Houston and Fort Worth), three Texas border cities (El Paso, Laredo, and Hidalgo), and their sister Mexican border cities (Juárez, Nuevo Laredo, and Reynosa). During this first stage of fieldwork, research teams in each of the five Texas sites interviewed governmental agency officials charged with implementing the new laws (such as the Immigration and Naturalization Service and the Texas Department of Health and Human Services). In cities on the Mexican side of the border, interviews were conducted with local government officials and administrators of social service agencies that provide assistance to returning deported migrants. Many of these officials and community leaders were interviewed again in the spring of 1998, which brought the total number of agency and community leader interviews conducted on both sides of the border to one hundred.

The initial phase of the project on the U.S. side also involved selecting neighborhoods in which to conduct household interviews. Criteria for selecting neighborhoods included the presence of a sizable portion of low-income households and Hispanic-origin and immigrant residents, especially legal permanent residents. One hundred households were recruited at each of the five Texas sites. Household recruitment varied by site; some household respondents were obtained through snowball sampling, others were obtained by interviewers going door to door, and in one study site, the researcher obtained interviews by teaching English at an apartment complex from which her households were recruited for the sample. A total of 510 household interviews were conducted in the summer and fall of 1997.

The large majority of the household respondents were either U.S. citizens (38 percent) or legal permanent residents (39 percent), less than one-fifth (16 percent) were undocumented, and the remaining 7 percent were tourists or foreign students. Of the 452 respondents who gave their country of origin, 62 percent were from Mexico, 28 percent from the United States, 6 percent from El Salvador, 3 percent from Guatemala, and 1 percent from other countries.

A nonrandom sample of migrant household members was also interviewed in the Mexican border cities of Nuevo Laredo, Reynosa, and Ciudad Juárez. Household members were invited to participate in the study if they crossed the border at least once a month. A total of 68 border residents were interviewed in Mexico in this first phase of household interviews during the fall of 1997 and the summer of 1998.

The idea for a second phase of research emerged from our initial findings. Preliminary findings from the household interviews highlighted a pattern of family separation resulting from the deportation of a family member. Thus a second phase of interviewing was launched in the fall of 1998 to investigate how deportations affected family households and what were the conditions of Mexican and Salvadoran deportees during and after the deportation process. With the assistance of Mexican and Salvadoran researchers, a Salvadoran nongovernmental organization (NGO) that assists returning deportees, and the families of deportees, we conducted 178 interviews in Mexico, El Salvador, and Texas. Eighty-five interviews were conducted with deportees (14 of whom were going through deportation proceedings) and 93 with families of deportees. Because family members of deportees could not or would not answer some of the survey questions, our findings will sometimes be drawn from the smaller sample of the 85 deportees themselves.

Not surprisingly, and as is consistent with national profiles of U.S. deportees provided by the Immigration and Naturalization Service (INS), most of the 178 deportees in the larger sample were male (92 percent), between the ages of 17 and 30 (58 percent), and undocumented (87 percent). Almost three-quarters of the deportees were Salvadoran, the remainder being primarily Mexican. Noteworthy, however, are the deportees' work and residential histories in the United States. Forty-three percent of the deportees had lived in the United States for more than three years before apprehension, and 14 percent had lived in the United States for more than ten years. In addition, almost three-quarters (71 percent) of the deportees in our study were working at the time of apprehension.

We now turn to our thematic findings from which we conclude that changes in three areas of immigration law and procedure have had especially strong adverse effects on families and communities. These effects include (1) an increase in INS and other official policing of immigrant neighborhoods in particular and of Latino border communities more generally, (2) an expansion in definitional scope and thus an increase in INS removals (formerly called "deportations"), and (3) elevated and binding income requirements for sponsors of legal immigrants.

PLACING NEIGHBORHOODS UNDER SUSPICION

U.S. border enforcement efforts were dramatically enhanced and restructured in the years between 1993 and 1999, during which time the INS budget nearly tripled from $1.5 to $4.2 billion. The lion's share of this increase has been directed toward policing the United States–Mexico border. From 1994 to 1998, the number of U.S. Border Patrol agents policing the southwest border more than doubled from 3,389 to 8,200 (Andreas 2000).

Given the concentration of U.S. Border Patrol agents along the border, it is not surprising that their presence would be most acutely felt in border neighborhoods and communities. Of the 510 Texas household respondents interviewed in the study's first phase, almost a fifth (84) reported that officials had stopped them or members of their households and questioned them about their immigration status. More than a third (39) of those stopped were apprehended for unauthorized entry, but about half (45) were questioned in general about their residential status despite the fact that they were legal residents of the United States. In a fifth of these 84 cases, the encounter appeared intrusive because it occurred in the conduct of normal community life, while people were walking to a store, park, or work; waiting for a taxi or bus; or picking up children at school. Almost two-thirds of the cases that involved questioning about residential status occurred in the border cities of Hidalgo, Laredo, and El Paso, and all but one of the apparently intrusive cases occurred along the border as well.

Respondents also commented on the intrusive impact that Border Patrol and other official policing has had on neighborhood life. In all the research sites, a substantial number of respondents reported a visible increase in the number of local police and INS officials in their neighborhoods. For example, over half of the 100 people we interviewed in Houston reported an increase in INS agents in their neighborhoods. The fear of being deported is so great among undocumented families in these neighborhoods that they develop heart-wrenching strategies to overcome official detection. In one Houston case, a husband and wife reported that they never traveled together for fear of being arrested, deported, and hence separated from their child. As the wife stated, "we feel as though we are constantly on the run."

Although the Houston Police Department denies having anything to do with the implementation of immigration laws in the city, respondents also reported police harassment. One respondent seeking emergency care at a neighborhood hospital was approached by a Houston police officer who told her, "No English, no attention." The respondent was shocked by the officer's comment but felt helpless to do anything about it. In another Houston case, a respondent and her husband were pulled over by police officers who told the respondent that they were being stopped and that their car was being searched because they were "Hispanic." In low-income Latino neighborhoods across the state, but especially in those along the border, there has been a long history of law enforcement harassment (United Commission on Civil Rights 1970). It seems that IIRIRA has declared open season on Hispanics.

DEPORTATION: CRIMINALIZING THE MIGRANT

As we have said, IIRIRA has shifted substantial resources to the U.S.–Mexico border to intensify border enforcement, immigrant detention, and "removal" operations. IIRIRA changed the term *deportation* to *removal*, which now includes people formally excluded at the border as well as people deported from the interior of the United States. IIRIRA also substantially expanded the definition of *criminal aliens* and the crimes for which they can be deported. The basis for the removal of criminal aliens is "aggravated felonies," which, under immigration law, includes twenty-eight separate offenses (Aleinikoff, Martin, and Motomura 1998). The majority of criminal aliens are deported for drug convictions and immigration violations. However, since 1997, INS has conducted "surveys" (raids) to apprehend legal permanent residents who have previously been convicted of crimes now listed in IIRIRA as aggravated felonies. In September 1998, the INS conducted a Texas crackdown on legal immigrants with three or more convictions for drunk driving, which is considered an aggravated felony under IIRIRA. In Texas this crackdown, known as "Operation Last Call," placed 533 immigrants with three drunk-driving convictions in deportation proceedings during its first month (Koppel 1998). In October 1998, INS headquarters in Washington, DC, agreed to review the deportations of these immigrants on a case-by-case basis, but IIRIRA gives aggravated felons few exceptions to deportation, and INS has not been willing to drop the charges against them (Hagan, Rodriguez, and Capps 1999).

A net result of these policy and procedural changes is that more and more people are being deported. Fiscal year 1998 (FY98) saw 50 percent more removals than did FY97 (INS 1998). In fact, the INS set a goal of removing 123,000 undocumented immigrants during FY98 (from October 1, 1997, to September 30, 1998); it exceeded this goal by 39 percent, effecting 171,154 removals in FY98 (INS 1999a). Furthermore, the INS reported that in FY99 it set a removals record, deporting 176,990 people (INS 1999b).

Most of these removals occur at ports of entry along the U.S.-Mexico border. The two biggest southwestern metropolitan areas on the border, San Diego and El Paso, experienced the largest number of removals during FY99—65,540 and 16,769, respectively. Data on FY1999 removals show a disproportionate impact on immigrants of Mexican and Central American origin, who together accounted for 89 percent of all immigrant removals. Immigrants from Mexico accounted for 83 percent of all deportees, and immigrants from El Salvador, Guatemala, and Honduras accounted for another six percent (INS 1999b).

This dramatic increase in removals is largely due to the expedited removal process, which was designed to remove aliens without proper documents at ports of entry. Expedited removals are enforced with no rights to appeal and without any formal procedures. In FY99, 89,035 illegal aliens were deported by expedited removal (up approximately 16 percent from FY98), and those deportations constituted about 50 percent of all FY99 removals (INS 1999b). However, the increase in removals is also due to criminal-alien removals, which rose by 12 percent from FY98, reaching a total of 62,359, and represented almost a third of all removals in FY99. The INS is removing more than 1,199 criminal aliens each week. Drug convictions occasion 47 percent of these removals, immigration violations 13 percent, assault convictions 6 percent, and burglary convictions 5 percent (INS 1999b).

Our respondents likewise varied in the reasons for their deportation. Of the 155 respondents in the larger sample who reported a reason for their deportation, approximately 69 percent were deported because of their undocumented status (approximately 46 percent under the expedited-removal process), 2 percent were removed as a result of immigration violations (such as the use of fraudulent documents), and 29 percent were removed because of criminal activity (such as DWI convictions, theft, or rape). Given that many of our interviews were conducted along the Mexican border, it is not surprising that nearly all of the Mexican deportees in our study (95 percent) were arrested at the border by Border Patrol or INS agents and deported by expedited removal. In contrast, most Salvadoran deportees were picked up in the interior of the United States, and many reported being picked up by both the police and the INS.

EFFECTS ON MEXICAN AND SALVADORAN COMMUNITIES OF ORIGIN

The INS enforcement strategies that we have described have dire consequences for the communities abroad to which immigrants are deported, as well as for the families the deportees leave behind in the United States. Our study's investigation of selected Mexican border municipalities found a growing presence of migrants who were dumped in these sites by INS-expedited removal. Also, U.S.-bound migrants along the Mexico border, preparing to move north into the United States, are spending more time in Mexican border communities before crossing as a consequence of heightened and sophisticated border enforcement and higher smugglers' fees. In our study's Mexican research sites of Reynosa, Nuevo Laredo, and Ciudad Juárez, municipal officials and segments of the general public increasingly view the accumulating, unemployed migrants as "criminals." Officials and the public alike blame the migrants for urban crime and see them as a threat to public safety. The head of Nuevo Laredo's police department blames migrants for about half of the crime that occurs in that city. The migrants are also blamed for taking jobs away from local residents and increasing the demands on city services. Unwanted in the United States, the deported Mexican migrants now also become unwanted in the northern regions of their homeland.

Some Mexican municipal governments on the border have begun returning deported migrants to their communities of origin, providing them with one-way bus or train tickets. Many deported migrants who refused the offer became targets of police raids in public areas where they congregated. The migrants were rounded up, detained in jail, made to work for a day, and then sent to their communities of origin in buses leased by the city.

In the first phase of the study in 1997, only a few agency personnel in our Mexican research sites saw an increase in the number of migrants asking for assistance, but by the second phase of our study in 1998, most agency personnel whom we interviewed did. In the Mexican research sites, accumulating population of migrants exerted great stress on the community agencies assisting them, including shelters run by religious and civic organizations, nongovernmental human rights organizations, municipal governments, border police in Matamoros, shelters for deported minors, and community soup kitchens.

Some directors of Mexican agencies reported problems meeting the growing demand for food and shelter occasioned by migrants. A shelter director, for instance, saw a doubling of his agency's work in just a few months as more migrants arrived and stayed longer in the city. In Nuevo Laredo, the director of a soup kitchen made a similar claim, stating that the number of migrants asking for a daily meal had doubled from 1997 to 1998. Some Mexican agency personnel also described increased demand for assistance by new migrants from the politically troubled southern states of Chiapas, Guerrero, and Oaxaca.

Although we have yet to interview officials and social service agency staff in the Salvadoran communities, an initial examination of the interviews with family members of deportees in El Salvador suggests that deportees also place substantial strains on their local communities. The deportees are returning to poor Salvadoran communities that offer very few opportunities for work. Indeed, less than 10 percent of the deported Salvadorans in our study who were deported in 1997 and 1998 have found work back home in El Salvador. The large majority of them hang out in the streets, becoming a burden to their families and communities.

MORE BORDER AND CRIMINAL-ALIEN ENFORCEMENT EQUALS MORE FAMILY HARDSHIP

Most of the deportees interviewed in our study had established lives in the United States before deportation. Of the 178 deportees in the larger sample study, 43 percent reported living in the United States for at least three years prior to apprehension, which indicates that a great many had been well established in the United States before being sent back to their home countries or entering deportation proceedings. Indeed, over a fourth (27 percent) of the sample had been in the United States for more than five years, and 14 percent had been in the United States for over ten years.

Although 127 of our larger deportee sample reported being employed at the time of apprehension, only 57 percent (75) of those reported a household income in the United States. Many of the U.S. household incomes reported are comparable to those of larger and more established Hispanic populations in the United States. The median yearly income for Hispanic-origin households in 1998 was $28,330 (U.S. Bureau of the Census 1999), which is actually below the median income (approximately $31,200) of those subjects in our sample who reported their household incomes. In short, a substantial number of deportee respondents, although undocumented, had made lives for themselves in the United States that were not unlike those of long-term residents with legal status or citizenship. Many of the deportees have contributed to the U.S. economy for many years with their labor and buying power.

Many of the deportees in our study had sent cash remittances on a regular basis to their families back home. Indeed, over two-thirds (67 percent) of the eighty-five deportees interviewed helped support their families abroad, sending remittances of $50 to $1,000 per month—a significant amount of money for families in Mexico and El Salvador, many of whom depend on the extra income to survive. These remittances did not come only from the more established immigrants who had lived in the United States for over three years. In fact, among the eighty-five deportees interviewed who had lived in the United States for less than three years, almost 48 percent reported having sent money to family households back home. The ninety-three family members interviewed were less likely to talk about remittances, but of those fifty-one who did, more than half (twenty-eight) reported having received help from their deportee relative.

Once the U.S. breadwinners are deported and no longer able to continue sending money home, some families abroad suffer from financial shock. One example of such hardship involves a family in El Salvador who experienced what the respondent described as "a very hard time" since the respondent's deportation. "My son [still in the United States] works and earns a little regularly and helps us. If it were not for him, we would be going hungry." Another case involves a deportee whose family "went hungry at first"; they had to find ways of adjusting to having their financial lifeline cut. Another Salvadoran respondent reported that his deportation resulted in his wife and parents "having many limitations and hunger" as a result of his not being able to send money to them from the United States, and yet another stated that his income "is greatly missed. . . . Here, they are almost going hungry."

Not only do families abroad experience financial hardship, in many cases deportees are forced to leave dependent family members in the United States, including spouses and children. Indeed, 75 percent of the eighty-five deportees we interviewed left a family member in their U.S. household. Thirty-nine percent reported leaving a spouse, 27 percent of whom were U.S. citizens. Altogether, 45 percent of the deportees in our sample left children in their U.S. household, 38 percent of whom were U.S. citizens. Clearly, immigration reform does not take into account the effects of its practices on mixed-status families.

These U.S. family members, some of whom are U.S. citizens or permanent legal residents, suffer hardship because they can no longer benefit from the income of their deported breadwinner. One deportee whom we interviewed in Mexico had left a wife in the United States with no means of paying rent or utilities. Another had left behind a wife and three children, none of whom had any other source of income besides the deportee's support. His wife was forced to seek public assistance and to then work to support the three children she was raising alone. Deportees from El Salvador have reported similar hardships. One stated that since his deportation, his wife in the United States has had to work as a domestic to support their two children and that she was having difficulty raising a family without his help. Another respondent stated that his wife and children in the United States eat poorly and that his wife does the best she can to "make a go of it with the children." Yet another, speaking also of his wife in the United States, stated that his deportation "is hitting the poor wife hard now that she has to work double."

But harm does not come only from lack of financial support. Deportation can have painful psychological and emotional ramifications. Almost 11 percent of the eighty-five deportees and 11 percent of the ninety-three deportee families whom we interviewed reported some sort of emotional hardship. These respondents described suffering emotional hardship even though such information was not elicited from them, so it may be that the emotional impact of deportation is even greater than the financial. Many respondents stated that family separation was the specific cause of their emotional suffering.

One example of such emotional hardship involves the family of a thirty-eight-year-old male legal resident picked up at home in 1998 for three prior DWIs, the last one in 1994. This respondent has lived in the United States for twelve years, has a U.S.-citizen wife, and has four U.S.-born children all of whom are under 18 years old. He is the sole provider for the family. In describing the adverse affect of his pending deportation on his family, he stated that although his older children can comprehend the reasons for losing their father, his younger children are constantly worried. If they don't see their father as soon as they get home from school, they begin asking whether he has left for Mexico. They insist on not being torn from their father, but the separation is inevitable. The deportee knows that if he is returned to Mexico, he will not take his family. He says, "Why take them? So they can suffer alongside of me?" Recent surveys that immigrant advocacy and civil rights organizations have conducted of long-established

Mexican nationals, rounded up under Operation Last Call, also found a pattern of long-established residents and breadwinners separated from their wives and U.S.-citizen children (Ortíz Rocha 1998; Operación Unidad Familiar, Las Américas Immigrant Advocacy Center, Texas Lawyers Committee for Civil Rights and Immigration Law Enforcement Monitoring Project 1999).

Regarding the children of deportees left behind in the United States, our sample revealed that in most cases, family members in the United States were available to care for the children. But this is not always true. In one especially tragic case, a husband and wife were picked up at work during an INS raid while their child was at day care. Immigration agents arrived and surrounded their place of work, questioning people about whether they had papers. Neither the respondent nor her husband had papers, so they were handcuffed and taken to a detention center. They were subsequently deported and forced to leave their child behind. One immigration official, aware that the couple had left their child at day care, told the wife to come back later and get her child or to start her life over. The official told her not to tell anyone he had said this. In cases like this, parents facing deportation are now forced to make the tough choice of either leaving their children in the United States, under the care of the state, or taking their children, many of whom are U.S. citizens, with them to home countries with diminishing opportunities.

FAMILY SPONSORSHIP: UNIFICATION OR SEPARATION?

An additional family hardship emerged from our interviews with 510 households in the first phase of the project. A number of the household respondents were motivated to apply for naturalization so that they could expedite the immigration of family members to the United States. Unfortunately, and unbeknownst to many in the sample, most households will be unable to sponsor family members to come to the United States because IIRIRA imposes new sponsorship requirements. Prior to IIRIRA, the federal poverty level was one of several means of determining a sponsor's ability to support an immigrant. For example, in lieu of an affidavit of support, the applicant could present a credible job offer. However, IIRIRA elevated the family income requirements of the petitioner to 125 percent of the poverty level and made affidavits of support legally binding. Under these new earning requirements, about 68 percent of the households in our original household sample of 510 do not qualify to sponsor the immigration of a family member. Especially hard hit by this new requirement are long-established poor Mexican and Mexican American families along the border, many of whom were sponsored by their own family when they arrived years ago. One ironic result of these new sponsorship requirements is that poor families are now prevented from sponsoring members who might, through their own employment, improve the families' financial situations.

The binding affidavit of support appears to affect poor Mexican-origin immigrant applicants disproportionately. One respondent went as far as describing the new immigration law as "The Mexican Exclusionary Act of 1996." As reported by the Urban Institute, 26 percent of U.S. families with native-born household heads would be unable to sponsor immigrants under the new affidavit-of-support requirements. Among all families with foreign-born heads of household, this share was 41 percent, but among families with heads of household born in Mexico or Central America, the percentage was 57 percent (Fix and Zimmermann 1997). Recall that in our sample of 510 households, the proportion of household heads unable to sponsor their family members is even higher (roughly two-thirds), reflecting the disproportionate number of poor Mexican-origin households along the border.

The 1965 amendments to the Immigration and Nationality Act ended decades of discriminatory principles in U.S. immigration law by repealing the national-origins quota system, replacing it with uniform limits for all countries, and emphasizing immigration through family reunification. The 1996 law repeals the egalitarian intent of the 1965 amendments by introducing new income requirements, which now disproportionately prevent the reunification of low-income families. With such a high share of legal immigration cut off through side-door sponsorship provisions by the 1996 law, it should not be surprising if more people resort to unauthorized entry through the back door.

CONCLUSION

The findings of our study indicate that the implementation of IIRIRA is having a harsh impact on immigrant families and on the communities in which they live and work. Immigrants know that times have gotten tougher for them, that life is riskier, and that they have to make fewer demands and tolerate more hardship if they are to survive. Even permanent legal residents know that life is no longer as secure for them as it was before enactment of the new immigration law. They know this especially when they see their relatives deported for crimes committed (and sentences served) decades ago in some cases. That some deportees interviewed in our study had already returned to the United States, and that others in Mexico and El Salvador were planning to return, indicate that IIRIRA, with all its restrictive measures, is not stopping undocumented immigration. For many deported immigrants, the risk of long-term imprisonment, if they are apprehended again in the United States, must pale in comparison to the payoffs of returning to their loved ones and livelihoods in the United

States. For many of these immigrants and their families and communities, IIRIRA will not end their transnational system of survival; it will just make it harder to live in it.

NOTES

We would like to thank the Ford Foundation for their project support. We would also like to thank Nika Kabiri for her invaluable research assistance.

REFERENCES

Aleinikoff, T. Alexander, David A. Martin, and Hiroshi Motomura. 1998. *Immigration and Nationality Laws of the United States: Selected Statutes, Regulations, and Forms.* St. Paul: West Group.

Andreas, Peter. 2000. *Border Games.* Ithaca: Cornell University Press.

Fix, Michael E., and Wendy Zimmermann. 1997. *Welfare Reform: A New Immigrant Policy for the United States.* Washington, DC: The Urban Institute.

Hagan, Jacqueline, Nestor Rodriguez, and Randy Capps. 1999. "The Effects of the 1996 Welfare and Immigration Reform Acts on Low-Income Immigrant Communities in Texas." Preliminary report prepared for the Ford Foundation, New York.

Immigration and Naturalization Service. 1998. "INS Deploys $3.8 Billion in FY 1998 Resources." Press release, March 10. *http://www.ins.usdoj.gov*

Immigration and Naturalization Service. 1999a. "INS Breaks Previous Removals Record; Fiscal Year 1998 Removals Reach 171,154." Press release, January 8. *http://www.ins.usdoj.gov*

Immigration and Naturalization Service. 1999b. "INS Sets New Removals Record: Fiscal Year 1999 Removals Reach 176,990." Press release, November 12. *http://www.ins.usdoj.gov*

Koppel, Nathan. 1998. "Immigration Lawyers Irate Over Operation Last Call: A New INS Roundup of Immigrants Convicted of Multiple DWIs Brings Complaints." *Texas Lawyer,* October 5.

Operación Unidad Familiar, Las Américas Immigrant Advocacy Center, Texas Lawyers Committee for Civil Rights and Immigration Law Enforcement Monitoring Project. March 1999. "Families in Crisis: The Human Consequences of the Denial of the Right to Permanent Residence." Unpublished report. El Paso, Texas.

Ortíz Rocha, Armando. 1998. "Mexican Consul Urges Review of 'Last Call.'" *El Paso Times,* September 14.

Texas Workforce Commission. 1999. *Texas Labor Market Review.* December. Austin, Texas.

United Commission on Civil Rights. 1970. "Mexican Americans and the Administration of Justice in the Southwest." March. Washington, DC: U.S. Government Printing Office.

U.S. Bureau of the Census. 1999. "Household Income at Record High; Poverty Declines in 1998, Census Bureau Reports." Press release. September 30. *http://www.census.gov/Press-Release/www/1999/cb99-188.html*

Commentary

Mary Waters

In the past forty years the largest immigration flow in the nation's history has profoundly transformed U.S. society. For some, this influx of predominantly "nonwhite" immigrants is nothing short of a social, economic, and cultural disaster, displacing native workers, swelling the largely minority "underclass," and exacerbating racial and ethnic conflict (Brimelow 1995; Bouvier 1991). For others, the new immigrants strengthen and reinforce the best in American traditions, revitalizing decaying neighborhoods and stagnant industries and adding new talents and energies to the U.S. civic culture (Binder and Reimers 1995; Muller 1993).

Many Americans find particular cause for concern in the changing sources of the post-1965 immigration, compared to earlier waves of European immigrants. Since the 1960s, immigrants have increasingly come from Asia, Latin America, and the Caribbean. The predominance of Latinos in this flow concentrates public attention on them as a group, as we learn from Cornelius and from Hagan and Rodriguez in their chapters, and their sheer numbers affect American institutions in very visible ways, as Levitt shows in her analysis of how Latinos are transforming religious institutions.

Americans exhibit a fundamental ambivalence about immigration and immigrants. We are a nation of immigrants, and yet racism is a constitutive part of our national psyche. We tend to have warm feelings about immigrants when we think of our ancestors, and yet the immigrant is often seen as "the other." The United States has a long history of trying to restrict immigration, and that history is currently being reviewed in the debate over present-day immigration. Because few people are willing to argue that past immigration was bad for America, the debate about immigration restrictions in our own time hinges on the question of how immigration today differs from earlier periods of immigration. Are today's immigrants fundamentally different from the immigrants who arrived during the nineteenth and early twentieth centuries? Are historical conditions fundamentally different now than they were before?

These chapters highlight important themes that underlie such historical comparisons. Cornelius directs our attention to the specific antipathies and fears with which Anglo Americans regard Latinos as a group. Some Americans, he argues, believe that Latinos find it particularly difficult to integrate into U.S. society because of their strong linguistic and cultural distinctness. In terms of the implicit historical comparison undergirding America's immigration debate, Cornelius suggests that many Americans believe that even though earlier waves of European immigrants were successfully assimilated, the concentration and numbers of current Latino immigrants, along with the proximity of the border, make it possible that the United States will fail to integrate Latino immigrants. And ironically, the very anti-immigration policies discussed by Hagan and Rodriguez are quite likely to hinder their integration into American society.

Levitt's chapter speaks to another theme that often surfaces in immigration debates. She argues that the Catholic Church allows Latino immigrants to engage in transnational practices that link sending and receiving countries in a process of globalization. Instead of the Catholic Church assimilating new immigrants, as it did European immigrants at the turn of the twentieth century, the Church itself is being transformed as Latinos move toward a majority demographically and as the Church reinforces links between sending and receiving societies through its transnational ties. There is a tension inherent in the current situation. As the main point of contact that immigrants have with a nonethnic, noneconomic institution in the United States, the Catholic Church has a powerful role as an assimilating institution. Yet the Church has been transformed in recent decades from an assimilator into a preserver of diversity and multiculturalism, allowing services in Spanish and instituting special parishes to serve the Latino community. The importance of transnational ties and practices is clear in scholarship on contemporary Latino immigrants. But are these transnational ties new? And do they portend a less than complete integration of today's immigrants, compared to previous generations?

Two themes are key issues in the political debates over immigration: (1) the ethnic/cultural distinctness of current immigrants and the difficulties they are thus presumed to have with assimilation and (2) the increasing role of transnationalism in current immigrant experiences. These themes are relevant to all current immigrant groups. Yet Latinos, by their sheer numbers and by their origins in America's closest neighbors—Mexico, the Caribbean, and Central and South America—bring these themes into stark relief. Social science theories and models of immigration were developed in the twentieth century largely to illuminate the experiences of the great wave of immigrants from Europe, and most did not deal with Latinos, even though Latinos were also immigrating to the United States at that time. These theories of immigrant assimilation focused on changes between generations. But those generational changes were strongly affected by the historical fact that immigration from Europe was radically reduced or eliminated from the late 1920s onward. The immigration restrictions of the 1920s meant that for three generations, the flow of immigrants from Europe essentially stopped. The cutting off of immigration from Europe eliminated the supply of "raw material" for ethnicity, so what it means to be Jewish or Italian or Polish in the United States reflects what happened in the United States over those 50 to 60 years. Without new immigrants arriving in any appreciable numbers, successive generations dominated the population. Thus, by the 1980s and 1990s the overwhelming majority of Italian Americans and Polish Americans were second-, third-, and fourth-generation U.S. residents. The incorporation of these later-generation European Americans was very visible. As they became less occupationally and residentially segregated, as they intermarried more, and as their ethnic identities became more symbolic and more a matter of choice, few if any "more ethnic" new immigrants arrived to take their place.

New immigrants from Latin America and Asia face different incorporation experiences. Because there is a continuous supply of new immigrants, these ethnic populations are therefore heterogeneous on measures of assimilation. Individuals may undergo marked assimilation, but new arrivals keep the ethnic group "fresh." Ethnic neighborhoods such as East Los Angeles and Spanish Harlem will not shrink like Little Italy did, becoming quaint shrines to an earlier way of life. Rather they will remain vibrant new neighborhoods. But that does not mean that the same people will stay in them. A third-generation Mexican American might intermarry, move to the suburbs, achieve marked social mobility, and develop a "symbolic" identity as Latino American. Yet he or she will be replaced with a first-generation Mexican American who will live in a Mexican neighborhood, speak little English, and live a richly and very visibly ethnic Mexican lifestyle.

This demographic replenishment and the resulting heterogeneity of what it means to be "Latino" clearly affect American public opinion on immigration policy, as Cornelius so ably shows. Because ongoing immigration means there will always be a fresh, new first generation of immigrants, it will appear to the average American that the new immigrants are not assimilating in the same way that European immigrants did in earlier times. This is because the most visible aspects of ethnicity—speaking a language other than English, occupational specialization, and residential concentration—will not be diluted even when a great deal of assimilation is taking place among the second and third generations.

Hence the demographic patterns of current Caribbean, Latin American, and Asian immigrants will be more complex than those of earlier immigrants. Some intermarriage and identity changes are already occurring among the descendants of these immigrants. Yet the fact that immigration is ongoing means that there may be two stories to tell—one story of new arrivals and the replenishment of an ethnic culture and another story of the quiet assimilation of individuals into a much more integrated and blended culture. The danger is that the ongoing assimilation of the new immigrants and their children and grandchildren will be obscured by the replenishment of the immigrant generation. In that case, public support for restricting immigration may increase because people are not aware of the sometimes hidden assimilation that is occurring.

This distinction between immigration patterns may account for public attitudes of the type Cornelius describes toward different Latino groups. Mexican Americans exhibit the most generational diversity: some come from families that have been present in the United States for many, many generations, but a large number are foreign-born. Accordingly, they might serve as a lightning rod for the type of cultural anxieties Cornelius describes. Cuban Americans, by contrast, because of the paucity of current immigration from Cuba, are aging generationally in a way reminiscent of the European immigrants. (Of course, this could change dramatically when Cuba experiences a change in its current government, possibly allowing more immigration.)

Yet regardless of the variation among groups, Latino Americans as a whole will be integrating into American society within a context of constant immigration and replenishment of the first generation. This means that the assimilation that does occur among individuals—especially later-generation individuals—will be obscured, and the kinds of cultural anxieties Cornelius outlines will probably persist. In this sense, Latinos are models for other groups, such as Asian Americans and immigrant African Americans. Their economic, cultural, and political incorporation into American society proceeds apace, but the constant supply of new immigrants may make much of that assimilation invisible to the broader public.

This recency and continual nature of immigration among Latino Americans may also explain some of the high levels of transnationalism that Levitt points out in religious practices. The Church may link sending and receiving communities in the first generation, but it may play a very different role for more established, later-generation Latinos. One of the most often cited models developed to explain European immigrant assimilation was the triple melting pot. It was assumed that immigrants would become American by melting into the three major religious groups as Protestants, Catholics, and Jews. The tremendous religious diversity characterizing the current wave of immigration shows how outdated such a theory has become. Yet Levitt's chapter refocuses our attention on one historical continuity—the enormous role religion plays in the lives of immigrants, and the complex ways in which immigrants shape religious institutions and are shaped and incorporated by them.

REFERENCES

Binder, Frederick and David Reimers. 1995. *All the Nations under Heaven.* New York: Columbia University Press.

Bouvier, Leon. 1991. *Peaceful Invasions: Immigration and Changing America.* Lanham, MD: University Press of America.

Brimelow, Peter. 1995. *Alien Nation: Common Sense about America's Immigration Disaster.* New York: Random House.

Muller, Thomas 1993. *Immigrants and the American City.* New York: New York University Press.

PART TWO

Health, Families, Languages, Education, and Politics

T
he second section of this book is devoted to conceptual, theoretical, and empirical work on a host of social formations that are central to understanding the Latino experience in the United States—the study of health, families, languages, education, and politics. The first chapter, by medical scholar David Hayes-Bautista, presents a broad overview of the health profile of Latinos in the United States. At the heart of Latino health is a great paradox. Although Latinos tend to be poor, to derive from immigrant backgrounds, and to have lower levels of education, their health in general is much better than that of non-Hispanic whites. This is the so-called Latino "epidemiological paradox." Hayes-Bautista analyzes this phenomenon by reviewing what is known about a host of health indicators among Latinos. He identifies and discusses three general goals for scientific research: (1) the need to approach Latino health as a unique phenomenon in its own right, (2) the need to develop Latino-based norms of diseases and behaviors, and (3) the need to develop robust theoretical models examining the relationships between health and culture. As Dr. Hayes-Bautista suggests, the task facing scholars in the health sciences is quite formidable because Latinos "exhibit patterns that are not predicted by the use of conventional metrics and models." In addition to the need for better theoretical and scientific work in the area of Latino health, there is also an urgent need to examine the problem of Latino access to the health care system.

Access to health care services is critical to the healthy development of families, children, and the elderly alike. Health policy researchers Richard Brown and Hongjian Yu present a detailed and troubling overview of Latino access to the health care system. Brown and Yu report that more than one in three Latinos has no public or private health insurance. This stunningly high rate of lack of insurance among Latinos is chilling because lack of health insurance creates significant barriers to obtaining vital services. Although the Latino "epidemiological paradox" suggests that Latino immigrants overall are healthier than other populations, the systemic lack of access to health care services augurs troubling developments for the Latino community in the future. Improving Latino access to needed health services must be a fundamental policy priority, especially in the context of the extraordinary rate of growth in the Latino population.

The next three chapters present a broad overview of the major issues currently dominating scholarship in the study of Latino families. Sociologist Pierrette Hondagneu-Sotelo approaches the topic of Latino families along a gendered and transnational framework. She discusses how the emergence of a new pattern of "social reproduction"—the "activities that are necessary to maintain human life daily and intergenerationally"—has led to a voracious appetite for immigrant Latina workers in Southern California and beyond. Drawn to plentiful work as live-in domestics, housekeepers, and child care workers, these new braceras are forced to leave behind their own children and other family members. Bringing to bear a compelling combination of gender and transnational lenses, Hodagneu-Sotelo examines how gendered and racialized occupational niches are generating new transnational family forms and dynamics among large numbers of Latinas.

Psychologist Celia Falicov approaches the study of Latino families from a highly original conceptual framework. She borrows freely from family systems theory, race and ethnicity theory, and acculturation theory. She introduces a series of conceptual tools, including the ideas of "ambiguous loss" and "relational resilience," to explore the psychosocial processes of family upheaval and change over time and across generations. She claims that Latinos are no longer displaying an "either/or" acculturative strategy of "abandoning one culture to embrace another" (Falicov, this volume) but, rather, favor a "both/and" style of adaptation, wherein one manages what might be called "a dual embrace." This observation opens up important new areas for further conceptual and empirical work on the varieties of acculturation styles.

Psychoanalyst Ricardo Ainslie extends the conversation on Latino families by examining broad sociocultural formations—immigration and acculturation—from a psychodynamic perspective. Ainslie's ideas of "cultural engagement" and "cultural plasticity" vitalize our understanding of transculturation processes. He examines cultural transformations in terms of interpersonal as well as intrapsychic conscious and unconscious processes. Ainslie's innovative conceptual approach underscores the extraordinary complexities involved in the study of families, immigration, and cultural change.

The next three chapters are devoted to the study of language. Language is the marker that defines much of the Latino experience in the United States. Regardless of their various language preferences and proficiencies, Latinos are a linguistically marked minority. Indeed, Spanish is at the forefront of nearly all major social, political, and educational debates involving Latinos in the United States. These three chapters touch upon various domains in the study of language—psycholinguistic, sociolinguistic, and language policy. Barbara Zurer Pearson, a psycholinguist with developmental interests, addresses three questions related to the linguistic characteristics of Latino children in the United States. First, she addresses a theoretical question: When does bilingual development begin? Second, she explores whether bilingual children are slower to develop in their two languages than monolinguals are in one. Finally, at the practical level, Pearson discusses various paths to successful bilingual development. Sociolinguist Ana Celia Zentella examines the use of varieties of Spanish (and *Spanglish*) in the United States and its implications for an understanding of Latino identities. Her analysis emphasizes the complex varieties of linguistic use among different Latino subgroups and makes an articulate case for the study of language that is rooted in broader community, economic, political, and social forces that affect Latinos. Finally, educational researcher Patricia Gándara provides a thorough overview of the current politics and policies that shape the education of Latino youth in California. She provides a historical perspective and reviews the context, implementation, and effects of new policy initiatives that are dismantling bilingual education in California schools. Gándara concludes with an incisive reflection of the role of research in the controversial area of bilingual education. Rather than continue to focus narrowly on research efforts that seem to feed politicized interventions, Gándara argues that the new research agenda ought to consider multilingualism as a realistic possible outcome for all English learners.

The next two chapters in this section are devoted to the crucial issues that frame the education of Latinos in the United States. The twin forces of globalization and the emergence of knowledge-intensive economies have given schooling and education a more important role than ever in determining opportunities and well-being. Because Latinos are such a youthful population (over a third of them are under age 18), education is even more important for them, as a group, than for other major demographic groups. The future fortunes of Latinos in the United States will in no small measure be determined by the schooling experiences, opportunities, and outcomes of Latino youngsters today. The data paint an alarming picture. Latino children are attending highly segregated, impoverished schools at a higher rate than any other group in the United States. Large numbers of Latino children are enrolled in substandard schools that fail to impart even basic skills. Indeed, unacceptable numbers of Latino youngsters are either dropping out of school or graduating from school without the skills and competencies that are required to navigate in the new opportunity structure. Many Latino children are doing brilliantly in school, but too many others are failing to thrive.

With this general background in mind, the chapter by educational researchers Luis Moll and Richard Ruiz places the schooling of Latino youngsters in historical and social context. They develop a case study around the Los Angeles Unified School District, the nation's second largest, where 70 percent of the students are Latinos. The authors present an overview of various indicators in the schooling experiences and outcomes of Latino youngsters. They identify a host of reductionistic policies and pedagogies—especially around bilingualism and language instruction—that seem to be putting large numbers of Latino youths at risk of failure. Astonishingly, broad and far-reaching policies have been implemented in the state of California without any systematic research to assess their probable long-term consequences. To counteract such reactionary policies, Moll and Ruiz propose the concept of "educational sovereignty."

Demographer Jorge Chapa examines the new conditions facing Latinos in higher education in the post-affirmative-action environment of California, Texas, and elsewhere. He argues that affirmative action for Latinos is justified because they have been "relegated to separate, unequal and inferior public educational facilities." Chapa considers the prospects for increasing Latino participation in higher education and presents a thorough assessment of current initiatives, such as the Texas "top 10 percent" plan—a law (similar to California's "top 4 percent plan") that requires public institutions of higher education in that state to admit all students who graduate in the top 10 percent of their class. The issues at stake in Latino higher education are monumental. Census data reveal that only 7.8 percent of all Latinos age twenty-five years or older have a Bachelor's degree and only 3.1 percent have an advanced degree—compared to 17 and 8.2 percent in the total U.S. population. Increasing Latino participation in higher education is an absolute priority. Tertiary education imparts the higher-order skills and credentials that are increasingly demanded by the global economy. Whereas all other workers have lost ground in terms of real wages, workers with advanced skills have seen their fortunes improve significantly in the new economy.

Politics has played a critical role in the experience of previous waves of immigrants to the United States. To paraphrase Harvard historian Oscar Handlin, the history of ethnic politics in American cities—Boston, New York, Chicago—is in an important way a history of American politics. Citizenship and politics determine the opportunities that Latinos can access, their ability to voice their concerns, and their capacity to influence developments in the here and now. But political processes are also critical in forecasting the influence and power of a community in the future. This is especially true for Latinos, given their stunning growth in numbers in such a short period of time. Latino demographic growth today will translate into Latino political power tomorrow. The last two chapters in this book are devoted to new scholarship on Latino citizenship and politics. Political scientists Louis DeSipio and Rodolfo O. de la Garza present an overview of recent patterns of Latino participation in national elections. They ponder what is "new" in the Latino electorate and examine a variety of factors shaping the nature of Latino electoral participation. They discuss demographic factors, issues pertinent to naturalized Latino citizens and non-naturalized immigrants alike. They examine partisanship among Latinos as well as their concentration in key electoral sites. They analyze the role of elites and institutions in reshaping the political process for Latinos. They claim that over the years and across generations, Latinos will gradually gain a more important voice in American politics. Political scientist Lisa Montoya examines the determinants of Latino participation in American politics. She focuses on gender and citizenship, and on the role of institutions, as important vectors structuring and mobilizing Latino political participation. Her empirical findings suggest that patterns of political participation differ by gender but tend to be similar among Latino citizens and noncitizens. She concludes that institutions play a critical role in mobilizing Latinos and makes a plea for the development of better data and conceptual work on the ways political elites, schools, and voluntary associations generate Latino political involvement.

In the epilogue, cultural theorist Silvio Torres-Saillant offers some reflections that will help guide future research on Latino studies. He reiterates the importance of acknowledging Latino heterogeneity and reflects on the internal borders separating Latinos from each other as a function of race, color, culture, and country of origin. In his sober assessment of the internal fragmentation of the Latino diaspora in the United States, Torres-Saillant cautions us to proceed carefully lest we make facile assumptions about Latino homogeneity and internal unity. Latinos, he claims, import with them the structures and habits of racial privilege, including deep-rooted Negrophobia and anti-*Indio* sentiment. He reminds us that the fortunes of lighter (and—no surprise—wealthier Latinos) are quite distinct from those of darker and poorer Latinos (see also Mirta Ojito, "Best of Friends, Worlds Apart," *New York Times,* 5 June 2000 pp. 1–17). He also warns us against rashly framing the Latino experience as a hemispheric and transnational phenomenon. Torres-Saillant claims that the borders that separate Latinos in the United States from their brothers and sisters in Latin America need to be taken seriously; these distinct realities are in some ways incommensurable. For the average Latin American, the average Latino in the United States is wealthy beyond measure. Therefore, those interested in developing hemispheric analyses linking Latinos in the United States to Latin Americans must proceed with caution.

Chapter 10

The Latino Health Research Agenda for the Twenty-first Century

David E. Hayes-Bautista

INTRODUCTION

Until recently, medical research has been conducted overwhelmingly on non-Hispanic white male populations, with the result that baseline patterns of illnesses, behaviors, knowledge, and attitudes reflected the patterns of that population group. Under the prodding of the *Report of the Secretary's Task Force on Black and Minority Health* (USHHS 1987), gentle pressure has been exerted on investigators to include women and minorities in study populations. Current research guidelines now require that a principal investigator justify any exclusion of women and minorities from a research sample, and slowly these groups are becoming part of the nation's research focus. However, this prodding has been too little and too late for large states such as California, which have experienced rapid "minority" population growth in the years since the *Report of the Secretary's Task Force.*

In 1999 the non-Hispanic white population in the state of California became a minority population (49.7 percent), with Latinos making up the next largest group (31.3 percent), followed by Asian/Pacific Islanders (11.8 percent), African Americans (6.7 percent), and American Indians (0.6 percent). Among children, the changes are even more impressive. In 1998 nearly half of all the state's newborns (47.5 percent) were Latino, with non-Hispanic whites constituting barely a third (33.9 percent), Asian/ Pacific Islanders 10.7 percent, and African American 6.8 percent of the state's births.

In spite of these dramatic population changes, health and medical research in California is still largely "normed" on the non-Hispanic white population, as it is in the rest of the country. But when theoretical models that explain patterns and variations of illnesses and disease are developed on the basis of non-Hispanic white populations and then applied to Latino populations, the results are confusing, seemingly paradoxical, and of little use in creating policies and programs aimed at the Latino population. In essence, non-Hispanic white metrics have been used to craft health policies and programs in a state in which barely a third of the state's children are non-Hispanic white. This approach is no longer suitable.

The Socioeconomic Status (SES) Model

The socioeconomic status model, which undergirds much thinking on health in general and minority health in particular, is one example of how a non-Hispanic white metric has been used for health policy. This model was developed from analysis of health patterns in different economic segments of the non-Hispanic white population. In this population, low socioeconomic status (SES) leads to poor health outcomes, whereas higher SES leads to good health outcomes. In other words, "wealth equals health."

When this model is applied to minority populations, who are generally poorer than non-Hispanic whites, even poorer health outcomes may be predicted. Minority health thus may be characterized as consisting of "health disparities" with indicators consistently worse than those of non-Hispanic whites. Here, for example, is a statement from the National Center for Health Statistics: "This chartbook documents the strong relationship between race, ethnicity and various measures of socioeconomic status: income, poverty status, level of education. . . . Racial and ethnic minorities are disproportionately represented among the poor . . . only the higher socioeconomic groups have achieved the target, while lower socioeconomic groups lag farther behind." (NCHS 1998, pp. 23–25)

So consistently has the association among race, low socioeconomic status and poor health outcomes been assumed that this model serves as the justification for national health policy, such as Healthy People 2010, which sets as its goal to reduce "health disparities among racial and ethnic subgroups of the population." (NCHS 1998, p. 23)

Naturally, the SES model has been applied to Latino populations, often without the support of good data. There is a consistent bias toward assuming that because Latinos are of low SES, their health must show adverse indicators. However, as this chapter will demonstrate, Latinos, nationally as well as in California, do not exhibit these adverse indicators; Latinos exhibit patterns that are not predicted by use of conventional metrics and models. With the growth in the Latino population, this paper argues, the development of Latino-based metrics and models is crucial for the formulating of sound health policies that accurately address Latino health dynamics.

Population Metrics and Modern Medicine

Population-Based Medicine.   A major shift in medical research has been away from a nearly exclusive focus on the individual (and the constituent organs and systems) to a focus on larger groups of individuals. As providers become responsible for the care of large, enrolled populations, they need to understand better the patterns of health and disease in the groups for which they are responsible so that they can be prepared to deliver the appropriate levels of care in a timely fashion. It is no longer enough to implement heroic measures after a heart attack. It is now prudent medicine to understand how, when, and why heart attacks occur, and to whom, and to work with patients to minimize their occurrence. While expanding the research focus from the individual to the group, it is important to acknowledge that not all groups exhibit the same profiles. Latinos, for example, are sufficiently distinct in health issues from non-Latinos (non-Hispanic whites and African Americans) that their health patterns warrant understanding.

Evidence-Based Medicine.   Over the years, medicine has developed a number of protocols for treating specific diseases and conditions. Evidence-based medicine requires that treatment protocols be measured against actual results, rather than used on the assumption that if they function in one population of patients, they will function equally well in another. Such protocols were almost never developed on Latino patient populations, although they have been applied to those populations. Do results justify their use?

To answer this question, the Center for the Study of Latino Health & Culture of the School of Medicine, UCLA, has been studying the relationship between health and culture, with an eye to improving medical care research and practice. Among its goals are to

· Provide data on the dynamics of Latino health.
· Provide a conceptual model of Latino risk factors so that interventions can be developed.
· Develop educational curricula to train providers.
· Create policy models to better serve the needs of the Latino communities.
· Facilitate improvements in the delivery of services.

This may appear to be an ambitious research agenda. However, the need to manage the health of Latino communities effectively requires no less than this level of effort. Furthermore, as this research is slowly implemented, its findings may well make some key intellectual contributions to the scientific basis for the existence of Latino studies.

STATISTICAL BASIS FOR LATINO METRICS

Large populations make possible the development of the statistical norms (Buttner 1996) on which policy prioritization and program setting are based. With Latinos becoming a large population, it is time now to consider developing Latino norms. Not only are there large Latino populations in many states, but these populations also present a health profile that is not consistent with the current thinking about "race/ethnic disparities" in program and policy development.

A brief overview of the Latino health profile will illustrate

- The need to understand Latino health *sui generis*—as constituting a unique phenomenon in its own right.
- The need for Latino-based norms of diseases and behaviors.
- The need for conceptual models that delineate the relationship between health and culture.

Latino Birth Outcomes

The "unpredictability" of Latino health norms is seen most comprehensively in birth outcomes. When we examine data from the National Center for Health Statistics (1998), extracted from birth certificates, the unusual contours of the Latino-based norms become clear.

Low Education. The Latinas who gave birth in 1996 were far less educated than non-Hispanic white, African American, and Asian/Pacific Islander mothers. Over half of Latina mothers (51.4 percent) had not completed high school at time of giving birth, whereas only 21.6 percent of non-Hispanic white mothers, 28.2 percent of African American mothers, and 15.0 percent of Asian/Pacific Islander mothers had not completed high school. See Figure 10.1. A far lower percentage of Latina mothers were college graduates (6.4 percent) than were non-Hispanic white (23.9 percent), African American (10.0 percent), and Asian/Pacific Islander mothers (36.2 percent).

Low Access to Care. Numerous studies have pointed to the lower percentage of Latinos who have health insurance (see Brown and Yu, this volume). This is reflected, in part, in the lower access to first-trimester prenatal care: 72.2 percent of Latina mothers received care in the first trimester of pregnancy, compared to 84.0 percent of non-Hispanic white and 81.2 percent of Asians/Pacific Islanders. Only African American mothers received less first-trimester care (71.4 percent). See Figure 10.2.

Low Income. Income data are not captured on the birth certificate, but data from the 1998 Current Population Survey indicate that Latinas

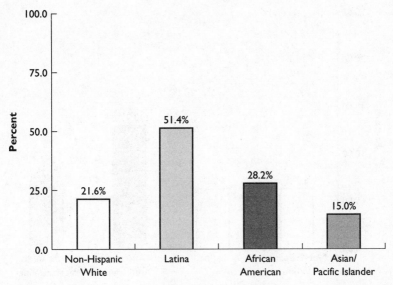

Figure 10.1. Maternal Education Less than Twelve Years, U.S.A. 1996

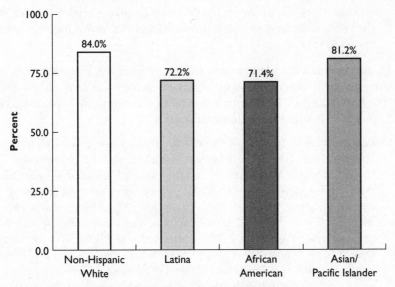

Figure 10.2. First-Trimester Prenatal Care, U.S.A. 1996

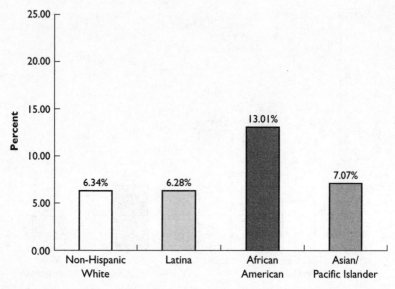

Figure 10.3. Low Birthweight (Percent of Live Births), U.S.A. 1996

have the highest poverty rates, and the lowest income levels, of all groups. Thus it is indisputable that Latinas giving birth have one of the worst risk-factor profiles: lowest education, lowest income, low access to care.

In the conventional wisdom, this combination of risk factors should lead to adverse birth outcomes—specifically, to a high percent of low birth-weight babies and elevated infant mortality. However, the birth outcomes of Latina mothers do not fit this expectation.

Little Low Birthweight. In spite of the risk factors, Latinas give birth to comparatively few low-birthweight babies. Only 6.28 percent of Latino babies born nationally in 1996 were of low birthweight (less than 2,500 grams). This is a lower percentage than that achieved by non-Hispanic white mothers (6.34 percent), African American mothers (13.01 percent) and Asian/Pacific Islander mothers (7.07 percent). See Figure 10.3. This pattern also holds for very-low-birth-weight babies (less than 1,500 grams), where Latinas had a percent-age (1.12 percent) less than half that of African Americans (3.02 percent) and only slightly higher than non-Hispanic white (1.08 percent) and Asians/Pacific Islanders (0.99 percent).

Low Infant Mortality. Contrary to expectations, the Latina mothers, in spite of the high risk factors, have relatively low infant mortality.

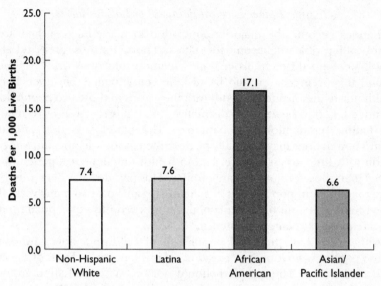

Figure 10.4. Infant Mortality, U.S.A. 1989–1991

At 7.6 deaths per 1,000 live births, Latina infant mortality is less than half that of African Americans, at 17.1 deaths per 1,000 live births. Non-Hispanic white infant mortality is slightly lower than Latina, at 7.4. However, non-Hispanic white mothers have far more education, higher incomes, and better access to care. Asian/Pacific Islander mothers have the lowest infant mortality at 6.6 deaths per 1,000 live births. See Figure 10.4.

This paradoxical pattern recurs in neonatal mortality (0 to 30 days after birth), where the Latino rate of 4.8 deaths per 1,000 live births is half that of the African American rate of 11.1 and only slightly higher than the non-Hispanic white rate of 4.6 and the Asian/Pacific Islander rate of 3.9. Likewise, in postneonatal mortality (31 to 365 days after birth), the Latino rate of 2.7 is half the African American rate of 6.1, equal to the non-Hispanic white rate of 2.7, and only slightly higher than the Asian/Pacific Islander rate of 2.6 deaths per 1,000 live births.

In birth outcomes alone, the need for Latino-based norms and models is obvious. In spite of the high risk factors, Latina birth outcomes more closely resemble those of the non-Hispanic white and Asian/Pacific Islander populations, which had higher income, more education, and better access to first-trimester care. None of this would be expected from the standard norms and models.

Latino "Epidemiological Paradox" or Latino Norm?

As Latinos become the majority population in many major urban areas, their health profile will become the statistical norm for those areas. If Latino health were no different from non-Hispanic white or African American health, this occurrence would be of little consequence. However, Latino health norms are distinctly at odds with the norms of those two populations.

Indeed, Latino health is so distinctive that it has received its own label: the Latino "epidemiological paradox." The paradox is this: although Latino populations may generally be described as low-income and low-education with little access to care, Latino health outcomes are generally far better than those of non-Hispanic whites. This paradox has been observed in so many Latino populations in so many regions over so many years that its existence cries out to be explained. Yet no currently conceptual models can adequately explain its existence.

With nearly half the child population of California now Latino, the Latino pattern is no longer a "paradox"; it is the norm for most of the children in the state. The question should not be "Why are Latino children doing so well in spite of high risk factors?" but instead "Why are non-Hispanic white children doing so poorly in spite of all their advantages?"

Latino health patterns become more understandable if they are analyzed, not from the perspective of "white versus minority" metrics, but from the perspective of Latino-based metrics. Once Latino-based norms are understood, variations from the Latino norms can be understood, and Latino health can be understood on its own merits.

Latino Mortality Patterns: Diseases and Norms

Mortality data from the National Center for Health Statistics for 1996 (and, occasionally, other aggregated years) provide an illustration of the need for a Latino-based norm (NCHS 1998).

The Latino "epidemiological paradox" can also be seen at the opposite end of the life spectrum, in causes of death. Latino crude death rates are around 80 percent lower than non-Hispanic white rates, but because the Latino population is so much younger than the non-Hispanic white, the age-adjusted rates provide a more meaningful comparison. In order to age-adjust rates, the Latino population is artificially "aged" and the non-Hispanic white population artificially "youthened" so that they have (artificially) the same age structure. This way, the effects of age are removed, and the death rates can be compared on a similar basis.

For all causes of death, the 1994–1996 Latino age-adjusted death rate of 376.1 deaths per 100,000 population is 20.5 percent lower than the non-Hispanic white rate of 473.6 deaths per 100,000 population. The Latino age-adjusted death rate is half (50.4 percent) that of the African

American population, whose death rate is 758.7 deaths per 100,000 population. Only the Asian/Pacific Islander population rate of 282.8 deaths per 100,000 population is lower than the Latino rate, and this population has substantially higher income, more education and greater access to care. See Figure 10.5.

In the aggregate, the lower Latino death rate in the face of higher risk factors appears paradoxical. This holds true generally for most causes of death. In fact, of the top eleven causes of death in the United States, Latinos have age-adjusted rates equal to or lower than those of non-Hispanic white for seven, including the top three causes of death: heart disease, cancer, and stroke. Again, given rapid Latino population growth, these patterns in many areas should be considered not a paradox but the new norm.

Latino Death Rates Equal to or Lower Than

Heart Disease. The number-one cause of death in the United States is heart disease. The Latino age-adjusted death rate of 88.6 per 100,000 population is 32.4 percent lower than the non-Hispanic white rate of 131.0 and 53.7 percent lower than the African American rate of 191.5. Only the Asian/Pacific Islander rate of 71.7 is lower than the Latino rate. See Figure 10.6.

Cancer. The number-two cause of death in the United States is cancer. The Latino age-adjusted death rate of 77.8 deaths per 100,000 population is 39 percent lower than the non-Hispanic white rate of 127.6 and 53.6 percent lower than the African American rate of 167.8. The Asian/Pacific Islander rate of 76.3 is slightly below the Latino rate. See Figure 10.6. This lower Latino cancer mortality rate holds for most major sites.

    For *lung (respiratory system) cancer,* the Latino rate of 15.4 is less than half the non-Hispanic white rate of 40.2 and is well under half the African American rate of 48.9. It is slightly lower than the Asian/Pacific Islander rate of 17.4. For *breast cancer,* the Latino rate of 12.8 is nearly one-third lower than the non-Hispanic white rate of 20.1 and is half that of the African American rate of 26.5. The Asian/Pacific Islander rate of 8.9 is somewhat lower than the Latino rate. For *prostate cancer,* the Latino rate of 9.9 is about one-third lower than the non-Hispanic white rate of 13.6. The African American rate of 33.8 is three times higher than the Latino rate. For *colorectal cancer,* the Latino rate of 7.3 deaths per 100,000 is lower than the non-Hispanic white rate of 12.1 and the African American rate of 16.8. It is also slightly lower than the Asian/Pacific Islander rate of 7.7.

Stroke. The number-three cause of death in the United States is cerebrovascular diseases. The Latino age-adjusted death rate of 19.5 deaths

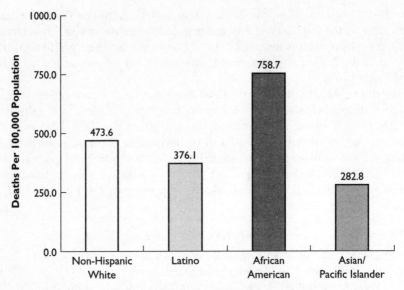

Figure 10.5. Age-Adjusted Death Rates, U.S.A. 1994–96

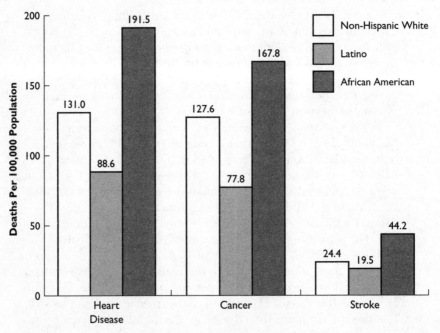

Figure 10.6. Heart Disease, Cancer, and Stroke, Age-Adjusted Death Rates, U.S.A. 1996

per 100,000 population is lower than the non-Hispanic white rate
of 24.4, the African American rate of 44.2, and the Asian/Pacific
Islander rate of 23.9. See Figure 10.6.

Other Causes of Death. The number-four cause of death in the United States
is chronic obstructive pulmonary disease. The Latino age-adjusted
death rate of 8.9 per 100,000 population is 59.7 percent lower than
the non-Hispanic white rate of 22.1, and is 50 percent lower than
the African American rate of 17.8. The Asian/Pacific Islander death
rate of 8.6 is slightly below the Latino rate. The Latino age-adjusted
death rate of 9.7 for pneumonia and influenza is 20.4 percent lower
than the non-Hispanic white rate of 12.2 and is 45.5 percent lower
than the African American rate of 17.8. The Latino rate is also
slightly lower than the Asian/Pacific Islander rate of 9.9. The Latino
death rate for suicide of 6.7 deaths per 100,000 population is 44.2
percent lower than the non-Hispanic white rate of 12.0. The African
American rate of 6.6 and the Asian/Pacific Islander rate of 6.0 are
slightly lower than the Latino rate.

Motor Vehicle accidents are one cause of death for which the Latino
rate of 16.1 is virtually identical to the non-Hispanic white rate of
16.0 and to the African American rate of 16.7. The Asian/Pacific
islander rate of 9.5 was lower than the rates for the other three
groups.

Higher Latino Death Rates

There are four causes of death for which the Latino rate is higher than the
rate for non-Hispanic white rate.

Diabetes. The Latino age-adjusted death rate of 18.8 per 100,000 population is 63.5 percent higher than the non-Hispanic white rate of 11.5.
For some time, diabetes has been depicted as the "Latino disease"
However, the African American rate of 28.8 is 53.2 percent higher
than the Latino rate. The Asian/Pacific Islander rate of 8.8 is the
lowest of all the groups. See Figure 10.7.

HIV/AIDS. Nationally, the Latino death rate due to HIV/AIDS is 16.3,
over twice the non-Hispanic white rate of 6.0. There are sharp
regional variations, however, such that in the southwestern states,
the Latino death rate due to HIV/AIDS is about half the rate for
non-Hispanic whites. The African American death rate of 41.4
deaths per 100,000 population is more than twice the Latino rate.
The Asian/Pacific Islander rate of 2.2 is the lowest of all four groups.
See Figure 10.7.

Homicide and Legal Intervention. The Latino age-adjusted death rate of
12.4 is over three times the non-Hispanic white death rate of 3.5.

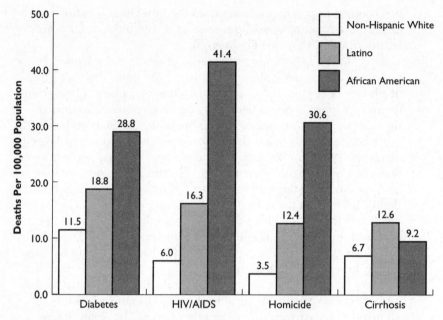

Figure 10.7. Diabetes, HIV/Aids, Homicide, and Cirrhosis Age-Adjusted Death Rates, U.S.A. 1996

This finding is gender-linked, as will be discussed below. The African American rate of 30.6 is two and one-half times higher than the Latino rate. The Asian/Pacific Islander rate of 4.6 is slightly higher than the non-Hispanic white rate. See Figure 10.7.

Chronic Liver Disease and Cirrhosis. This cause of death is the only one for which the Latino rate is simply the highest of all groups. The Latino death rate of 12.6 is nearly twice the non-Hispanic white rate of 6.7 and is 3.4 higher than the African American rate of 9.2. As will be discussed, this is due largely to male drinking patterns. See Figure 10.7.

Illustrations could also be drawn from other data sets tracking other areas of Latino health: the hospital discharge summary, the National Health and Nutrition Evaluation Survey, the Behavioral Risk Factor Surveillance Survey, and similar population-based samples. The need for Latino-based norms is apparent in most large-scale studies; in spite of high risk factors, Latino health generally can be described as quite good.

This observation is so persistent, and so consistent, that it should no longer be viewed as a paradox, or as an interesting exception to a larger pattern. Instead, it should be considered a pattern in its own right—a pattern

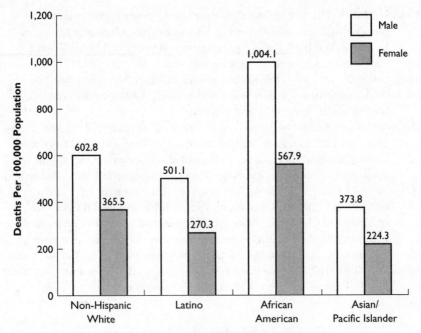

Figure 10.8. All Causes, Age-Adjusted Death Rates, Male and Female,
U.S.A. 1994–96

that is rapidly becoming the norm for large states such as California and
Texas.

THE LATINO HEALTH RESEARCH AGENDA:
DEVELOPING LATINO METRICS

Identifying and Documenting Latino Norms

For too long, Latino health research has been an afterthought, given attention only after the health of the non-Hispanic white and African American
populations were studied. At one point, when Latinos were a small minority, this oversight might have been understandable. However, Latino births
currently account for nearly half of all births in California, Texas, Arizona,
and New Mexico, and their outcome profile is quickly becoming the
"norm" for all births. Yet Latino norms have not been clearly established.
Indeed, the fact of the Latino "epidemiological paradox" is still surprising
to many health services, researchers, and providers.

The basic epidemiological work of documenting Latino norms needs to
occur in a number of areas:

Causes of Death. The preceding data on causes of death give only a
glimpse into the uniqueness of Latino norms. These norms need
to be tracked backwards for a number of years and established for
states, counties, metropolitan areas, cities, and zip codes.

Birth Outcomes. Likewise, the Latino norms in birth outcomes need to
be documented for past years and broken down by state, county,
metropolitan area, city, and zip code.

Behavior. Latino behavioral patterns in smoking, drinking, drug use, exercise, seat belt use, and the like are not well established. There are
contradictory data from a number of small-area studies. Norms for
these and related behaviors need to be documented and established.

Access to and Utilization of Health Services. Very few data exist on Latino
utilization of health services, including inpatient and outpatient
services and physician office visits. Some data are available from the
Current Population Survey on insurance coverage, but not enough to
support a detailed analysis of patterns of coverage. The private insurance and HMO worlds have very little Latino data, because they have
not had any place to indicate Latino ethnicity on their records.

Identifying Variations from Latino Norms

Once the norms for Latino populations are established, the variations
from the norms can be identified, and then the risk factors that cause these
variations can be sought. Several important variations need to be understood. They include variations that involve gender, geography, and Latino
subgroup.

Gender. Generally, females of any ethnic group have a lower death rate
than males. Latina females have a death rate that is 46% lower than
that of Latino males. See Figure 10.8. However, for specific causes
of death, this can vary. Nationally, the Latino male rate for firearm-
related deaths is nearly ten times as high as the Latina rate. See
Figure 10.9. However, for diabetes among adults in California, the
female death rate does not follow the 40 percent lower pattern we
would expect but, rather, is virtually identical to the Latino male rate.
See Figure 10.9. We need to understand such gender variations.

Geography. In the Southwest, the norm is for Latino mortality to be
lower than non-Hispanic white mortality, but this pattern is not
observed in New Mexico and Colorado (NCHS 1998). See Figure
10.10. Another variation involves HIV/AIDS. Although nationally,
the Latino incidence rate is higher than the non-Hispanic white
incidence, there is great regional variation. In fact, in California
and Texas, the Latino rate is consistently lower than the non-Hispanic

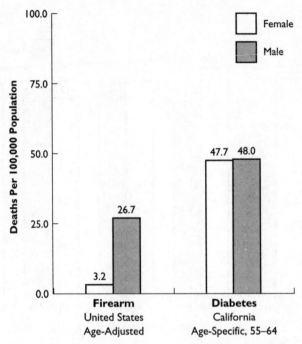

Figure 10.9. Latino Gender Variations: Homicide and Diabetes, 1996

white rate and is nearly one-fifth the rate observed among Latinos in New York and Connecticut (CDC 1993). See Figure 10.11. Additionally, the major mode of transmission in the Southwest for Latinos, non-Hispanic whites, and African Americans is male-male sex, with injection drug use being relatively minor, whereas in the Northeast, the major mode of transmission is injection drug use among Latinos, non-Hispanic whites, and African Americans, with male-male sex being relatively minor. See Figure 10.12.

Latino Subgroup. We need to understand the differences between different Latino subgroups. In terms of birth outcomes, when we compare Mexican, Puerto Rican, Cuban, and Central/South American mothers, it is clear that mothers of Mexican origin have far lower educational levels and receive far less first-trimester prenatal care. Yet Mexican-origin Latinas also give birth to the lowest percentage of low-birthweight babies and have infant mortality 30.7 percent lower than that of mothers of Puerto Rican origin (NCHS 1998). See Figure 10.13.

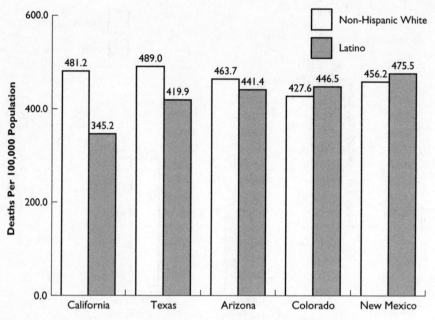

Figure 10.10. Geographic Variations, Latino and Non-Hispanic White Age-Adjusted Mortality, 1996

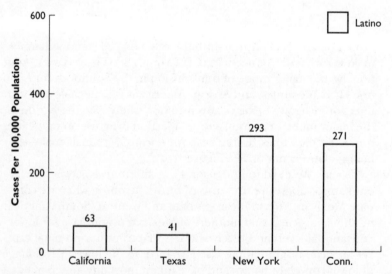

Figure 10.11. Geographic Variations, in Incidence of HIV Among Latinos, 1993

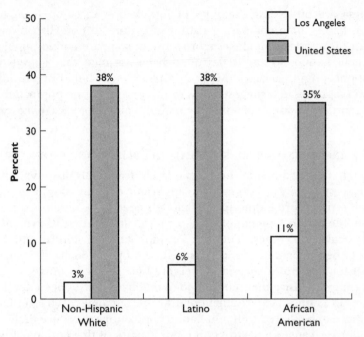

Figure 10.12. Geographic Variations in HIV Transmission via Intravenous Drug Use, 1996

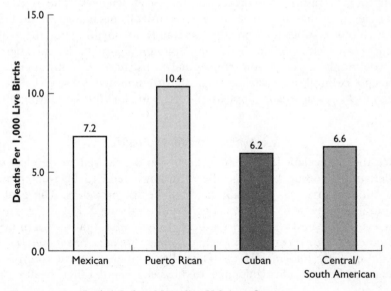

Figure 10.13. Latino Infant Mortality, U.S.A. 1989–1991

These are but a few examples of intra-Latino variation from Latino norms. Rather than comparing Latino subgroups to non-Hispanic whites or African Americans, it makes more sense to compare Latino populations to overall Latino norms. It has often been assumed that Latinos come in national-origin packages (Mexican, Cuban, etc.), but efforts to identify Latino subgroups may suggest new ways to segment Latino populations that will go further toward explaining the Latino "epidemiological paradox."

USING LATINO METRICS FOR LATINO POLICIES AND PROGRAMS

Although investigators in health research frequently assume that the socioeconomic status (SES) model is applicable to Latino populations, generally it is not. More Latino-specific models need to be developed that can explain the Latino "epidemiological paradox" and harness its dynamics for better health outcomes. The relationship between culture and health needs to be understood, conceptualized, and operationalized. It may well be that the current SES-based models are but specific examples of larger, more comprehensive theoretical models that have not yet been developed.

How do Latinos achieve such good health outcomes? What do Latinos have that can be shared with non-Latino populations to reduce their risk of heart disease, cancer, and stroke? It is our hypothesis that Latino culture, in some unknown way, plays a major role in the existence of the Latino "epidemiological paradox."

The study of Latino culture has largely been the province of researchers in history, literature, the arts, and the social sciences. The university resources provided for such study have usually been meager and the research results spotty and tentative—certainly not anything that the health sciences can use to explain the Latino "epidemiological paradox." There is no commonly agreed-upon conceptual construct for Latino culture, although cultural-sensitivity curricula have attempted to reduce it to a dozen or so characteristics applied uniformly to all Latinos everywhere.

Developing Educational Models

Once the basic data have been collected and analyzed to develop the underlying theoretical models, these findings need to be worked into educational curricula, especially those of health providers. The goal of "cultural competency" has often been held as an ideal, but there is very little evidence-based research to indicate exactly what that means in medical practice. Our recent book *Healing Latinos: Realidad y Fantasía: The Art of Cultural Competence in Medicine* (Hayes-Bautista and Chiprut 1999) is an initial attempt to offer guidance to physicians and other health care providers.

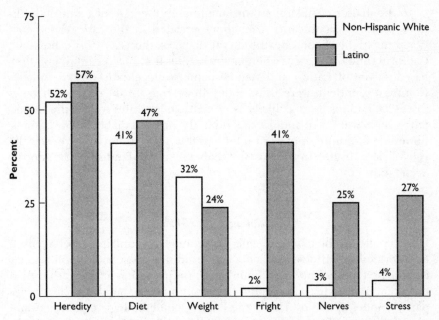

Figure 10.14. Causes of Diabetes Among Latino and Non-Hispanic Whites, Los Angeles County, 1997

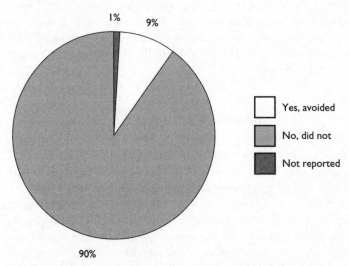

Figure 10.15. Field Institute: "Avoided getting medical care for selves or someone close because of immigration status concerns." California, 2000

In the matter of health, culture matters. In the case of Latino populations, culture's significance can be appreciated in the case of diabetes.
Given the higher Latino death rate for diabetes, this is a priority disease in
California and other areas where many Latinos live. In a recent population-
based survey of Latino and non-Hispanic white elderly in Los Angeles
County, respondents were asked about the reasons for the onset of diabetes
in adults. Latinos were as likely as non-Hispanic whites to cite the importance of heredity, diet, and overweight in the onset of diabetes. For Latinos,
however, even more important than heredity, diet, and overweight was the
role of *susto* (fright) in the onset of diabetes (Hayes-Bautista et al. 2000a).
See Figure 10.14.

Developing Policy Models

Health policy at the national, state, and county or municipal level needs to
be informed by Latino-specific data and findings. Most health policy today
is still based on assumptions about Latino norms and behavior, rather than
on actual data. One such common assumption is the "minority health disparity" model, which overlooks the Latino "epidemiological paradox" and
its implications for improving the health of non-Latino populations.
Another common assumption is that low levels of Latino enrollment in
Medicaid and other programs is due to fear of the I.N.S. However, a recent
survey by the Field Institute showed that less than 9 percent of Latino
respondents reported that they or any member of their family had avoided
seeking services because of concerns about their immigration status. See
Figure 10.15. Far more important as barriers are the costs of care, lack of
insurance coverage, and limited availability of services (California Healthcare Foundation 2000).

Designing the Delivery of Services

The design of delivery systems needs to reflect an understanding of Latino
wants, needs, and desires. One major factor cited by Latino patients, especially immigrants, is the need for providers who speak Spanish. Recent
work by our Center has confirmed this need. The shortage of Latino physicians, at least in California, is of nearly disastrous proportions. Latinos
make up 30.4 percent of the state's population, but only 4.8 percent of
California physicians are Latino. To express this another way, in non-Latino
California, for every non-Latino physician there are 335 non-Latino Californians. In Latino California, for every Latino physician there are 2,893
Latino Californians (Hayes-Bautista et al. 2000b). This dismal ratio will get
worse, in part because of declining first-year Latino matriculations.

CONCLUSIONS

The guiding maxim in health sciences research is that when the science is good, then all else follows. Latino health research is good science that can contribute in many areas: to the increased well-being of our nation's burgeoning Latino population, to the well-being of non-Latinos who can learn from the anomalies in Latino health that defy the dominant socioeconomic explanations of health, and to the scientific and intellectual foundations of Latino studies. Not only must Latinos be researched (and hence identified in records and samples) but research in Latino culture, in all its heterogeneity, must be understood, taught, and valued. Such a course might well lead to a reduction of deaths due to heart disease, cancer, and stroke in the entire population.

Latino studies does not exist just to make Latino undergraduate students feel good. Its findings are needed by all Americans.

REFERENCES

Buttner, J. 1996. Biological variation and quantification of health: The emergence of the concept of normality. *Clinical Chemistry and Laboratory Medicine*, 36 (1):69–73.

California Healthcare Foundation 2000. *A Political Profile of California Latinos and Their Views on Health Issues in the 2000 Primary Elections*. Oakland: Centers for Disease Control (1993). HIV/AIDS Surveillance Report. May: 5(1).

Hayes-Bautista, D., E. and R. Chiprut. 1999. *Healing Latinos: Realidad y Fantasiá: The Art of Cultural Competence in Medicine*. Los Angeles: Cedars-Sinai Health System.

Hayes-Bautista, D., E. P. Hsu, M. Hayes-Bautista, D. Iniguez, and D. Rose 2000a. *Latino elderly diabetes knowledge, attitudes and behavior in Los Angeles County* (in preparation).

Hayes-Bautista, D., E. P. Hsu, P. Dowling, R. Stein, R. Beltran, and J. Villagomez. 2001b. "Latino physician patterns in California: Sources, locations and projections." *Academic Medicine.* 75(7):727–736.

National Center for Health Statistics 1998. *Health, United States, 1998, with Socioeconomic Status and Health Chartbook*. U.S. Department of Health and Human Services. DHHS Publication number (PHS) 98-1232.

USHHS 1987. *Report of the Secretary's Task Force on Black and Minority Health*. Washington, DC: USDHHS.

Chapter 11

Latinos' Access to Employment-based Health Insurance

E. Richard Brown and Hongjian Yu

INTRODUCTION

More than one in every three Latinos (37 percent) in the United States is without any public or private health insurance; this is more than two and one-half times the uninsured rate of 14 percent among non-Latino whites (Brown et al. 2000). Lack of health insurance creates significant barriers to obtaining needed health services, exacerbating disparities in access and health status between Latinos and non-Latino whites.

Latinos' Health Status and Access to Health Care

Many Latino immigrants come to the United States with a more favorable health status than would be expected given their economic circumstances—the now well-documented "epidemiologic paradox"—but residency in their new country is associated with increasingly adverse risk factors and poorer health status (Vega and Amaro 1994; Fuentes-Afflick and Lurie 1997; Abraaido-Lanza et al. 1999; Hayes-Bautista, this volume). This decline is particularly notable among those who have lived longer in the United States and among second- and third-plus-generation, compared with first-generation, immigrants (Hernandez and Charney 1998).

The epidemiologic paradox characterizes only one perspective on Latinos' health. Other studies have found that Latino immigrants are at higher risk for tuberculosis and other infectious diseases, and some studies have found that Latino immigrants engage in more behaviors that put their current and future health at risk (Pong et al. 1998; Brindis et al. 1995; Guendelman, English, and Chavez 1995).

Perhaps as a result of lower incomes and less wealth, more hazardous social and physical environments in which they live and work, and acculturation into American culture linked to social class, Latinos overall are more likely than non-Latino whites of the same age group to report being in fair or poor health (Hajat, Lucas, and Kington 2000)—a robust indicator of the need for health services. This finding applies to the major Latino ethnic subgroups as well, although Puerto Ricans stand out as having particularly poor health status.

Although health status indicators demonstrate health care needs among Latinos that are at least equal to those of non-Latino whites, their use of health services demonstrates significant disparities. Among young children (aged 0 to 5 years), 8 percent of Latinos did not have a physician visit during the past year, compared to 5 percent of non-Latino whites; and among children aged 6 to 17, 16 percent of Latinos have not seen a physician in the past two years, compared to 7 percent of non-Latino whites.[1] Among women who report being in fair or poor health, 13 percent of Latinas did not have a doctor visit in the past year—twice the rate of 6 percent for their non-Latino white counterparts (Brown et al. 2000).

Health insurance provides both children and adults an important degree of financial access to health services for acute and chronic conditions, as well as for preventive care (Freeman et al. 1990; Newacheck, Hughes, and Stoddard 1996; Halfon et al. 1997). Latinos' high uninsured rates thus adversely affect their access to health care. Uninsured Latino children aged 0 to 5 are two and one-half times as likely as those with any public or private health insurance not to have had even one doctor visit in the past year: 16 percent of uninsured children versus 6 percent of children with any coverage. Uninsured Latino children aged 6 to 17 are two to three times as likely as those with any private insurance or Medicaid not to have visited a doctor during the previous two years: 29 percent of the uninsured versus 12 percent of those with private insurance and 9 percent of those with Medicaid (Brown et al. 2000). Without physician visits, at these minimum frequencies, children cannot receive recommended monitoring of growth and development and essential preventive services. And this minimum standard does not take into account any additional health care needs for acute and chronic conditions.

Among uninsured adult Latinas in fair to poor health, one in four (24 percent) did not see a physician in a twelve-month period despite their health problems. This proportion is at least three times the rates of 7 percent and 8 percent, for those with private insurance and those with Medicaid, respectively, demonstrating the severe impact of not having insurance or access to health services. Among uninsured Latino men in fair or poor health, 40 percent did not have a doctor visit in the past year, twice the rate for those with coverage (19 percent).

The access barriers created by not having health insurance coverage undoubtedly contribute to the overall disparities in health status between

Latinos and non-Latino whites. Health insurance coverage and access to medical care can ameliorate and improve Latinos' health problems and reduce disparities even if they cannot compensate fully for the powerful effects on health status of adverse economic and social factors (Brown et al. 2000). For persons in all ethnic groups, lack of health insurance coverage results in weak connections to the health care system and poor access to health services. Because insured persons in fair or poor health visit physicians more often than their uninsured counterparts, they are more likely to receive the care they need to manage their chronic conditions, such as diabetes or high blood pressure. Insured children and adults, whether in good or poor health, are more likely to receive preventive health services and care for acute conditions.

Latinos' Low Rates of Employment-based Health Insurance

Latinos' high rates of uninsurance are due to their low rates of employment-based health insurance, the primary source of health insurance for the nonelderly population. Access to employment-based health insurance (EBHI) is much lower among Latino workers than among other ethnic groups and has declined during the past decade (Valdez et al. 1993; Berk, Albers, and Schur 1996; Brown et al. 2000; Seccombe, Clarke, and Coward 1994; Fronstin, Goldberg, and Robins 1997; Freeman et al. 1990; Cooper and Schone 1997).

In the United States, employment is the most important source of health insurance coverage for the nonelderly population; 81 percent of those with any coverage receive it through their own or a family member's employment. Employers' payments for health benefits are the principal source of funding that helps make private health insurance affordable to many working families and individuals; employer contributions account for about three-fourths of all nongovernmental expenditures for private health insurance (U.S. Congressional Budget Office 1997). In the absence of employer contributions and group purchasing, health insurance coverage is less affordable for workers and their families, which diminishes their access to health services if other sources of coverage or services are not available.

Several studies have focused on factors that account for differential rates of EBHI between Latinos and non-Latino whites and among Latino subgroups. These studies have found that differences in employment and demographic characteristics explain some of the differences between Hispanic employees' and non-Hispanic white employees' receipt of EBHI in their own name and for some of the differences among Hispanic groups (Berk, Albers, and Schur 1996; Seccombe, Clarke, and Coward 1994). None of these studies, however, takes into account either citizenship status or immigration status among Latinos.

This paper examines the effects of demographic characteristics, employment factors, and citizenship status and immigration status on access to EBHI of Latino nonelderly adult employees, both in comparison with non-Latino whites and among subgroups of Latinos. The analysis helps explain why employed Latino adults are so much less likely to have EBHI than their non-Latino white counterparts and identifies public policies that might improve their coverage.

STUDY METHODS

We focus on nonelderly adult employees aged eighteen to sixty-four, comparing the access to EBHI of Latinos with that of non-Latino whites and, among Latinos, exploring differences by ethnic subgroup. We also examine the role that citizenship status and immigration status play in access to EBHI among Latinos of Mexican origin or ancestry (whom we will refer to as "Mexican-origin"). We distinguish four citizenship and immigration groups: U.S.-born citizens, naturalized citizens, noncitizens who are residing legally in the United States, and noncitizens who are undocumented.

The study uses data from two sources. We relied on the March 1998 Current Population Survey (CPS) to estimate health insurance coverage from all sources as well as demographic and employment characteristics of the study population. The CPS is a national cross-sectional survey, administered in person and by telephone, with a sample of approximately 50,000 households; information is obtained on a sample of 136,000 persons. The CPS is conducted monthly by the U.S. Bureau of the Census to obtain information on employment, unemployment, and earnings of the noninstitutionalized U.S. civilian population. The March CPS contains extensive information on health insurance coverage, employment, and income during the previous calendar year, as well as on ethnicity, immigration and citizenship status, nativity, and other demographic characteristics of each household member. For this paper, we analyzed the CPS for March 1998, which reflects health insurance coverage in 1997.

In addition, we use data from the February 1997 CPS, which asks employed adults whether their employer offers health insurance to anyone who works in the firm, whether the employee is eligible, and whether the employee accepts the coverage. The percentage of employees whose employers offer EBHI is called the "offer" rate, and the percentage who accept EBHI offered by their employers when they are eligible for it is called the "take-up" rate. This supplement, which collects information on a smaller number of persons than the March supplement, asks about current coverage and access to it. Thus it reflects coverage in February 1997.

The CPS includes information about race and ethnicity. In our analyses, non-Latino whites are persons who are identified as "white" and who said they were not of Hispanic origin. We selected non-Latino whites as a comparison group because they have the most favorable health insurance coverage rates of all races and ethnic groups.

The CPS provides a breakout of Hispanic national subgroups, which we used to classify Latinos into the following ethnic subgroups: Mexican-origin (which includes persons who said they were Mexican-American, Chicano, Mexican, or Mexicano), Puerto Rican, Cuban, and Central and South American.

Using CPS information on citizenship status and country of birth, we classified respondents as noncitizens, naturalized citizens, or U.S.-born citizens. In addition, we imputed immigration status for noncitizens. Using data from a survey of Mexican immigrants in Los Angeles (Marcelli and Heer 1998), we modeled legal status and classified noncitizen CPS respondents as either "documented" (immigrants who are residing legally in the United States) or "undocumented."[2]

FINDINGS

Compared to non-Latino white employees, Latinos—both overall and all subgroups—are far less likely to have employment-based health insurance (EBHI) and thus far more likely to be uninsured. Eight in ten (80.2 percent) non-Latino white employees receive EBHI through their own or a family member's employment, compared to just over half of Latinos (53.7 percent; Table 11.1). Among Latino subgroups, employees of Mexican and of Central and South American origin have the lowest rates of EBHI (52.3 percent and 51.0 percent, respectively), whereas Puerto Rican and Cuban-origin employees fare somewhat better (63.9 percent and 64.0 percent, respectively) but are still well below the rate for non-Latino whites.

Latino employees' lower EBHI rates result in an uninsured rate three times as high as that of non-Latino whites: 39.3 percent versus 13.3 percent. Because of their low EBHI rates, employees of Mexican origin and of Central and South American origin have the highest uninsured rates: 41.5 percent and 43.2 percent, respectively.

Employment is the most important source of private health insurance because the employer contribution and its tax exemption make health insurance more affordable for individuals and their families. However, an employee can access job-based insurance only through an employer or a union. Thus employees who work for an employer that does not offer health benefits at all, as well as those who are not eligible for the benefits that are offered, have no access to job-based insurance.

Not surprisingly, then, the ethnic-group disparity found in EBHI coverage is also found in "offer" rates. Three in ten Latino employees (30.5 percent) work for an employer that does not offer health benefits to any

TABLE 11.1. Health Insurance Coverage of Non-Latino
White and Latino Employees, Aged 18–64, U.S.A. 1997

	Non-Latino White	All Latinos	Mexican-Origin	Central and South American	Puerto Rican	Cuban-Origin
Total Employees Aged 18–64	92,920,000 100%	12,240,000 100%	8,262,000 100%	2,240,000 100%	1,179,000 100%	564,000 100%
Uninsured	13.3%	39.3%	41.5%	43.2%	25.4%	21.4%
Employment-Based Health Insurance	80.2%	53.7%	52.3%	51.0%	63.9%	64.0%
Privately Purchased Insurance	3.7%	2.1%	1.4%	2.7%	2.0%	10.4%
Medicaid	1.8%	4.0%	4.1%	2.6%	6.3%	3.9%
Other Government Coverage	1.1%	0.8%	0.7%	0.5%	2.4%	0.4%

SOURCE: March 1998 Current Population Survey

worker; this is twice the proportion of non-Latino white employees (13.6 percent; Table 11.2). To put it another way, only 69.5 percent of Latino employees work for an employer that offers health benefits, compared to 86.4 percent of non-Latino white employees. Again, employees of Central and South American origin (61.0 percent) and of Mexican origin (69.7 percent) are the most severely disadvantaged among Latinos, whereas Puerto Rican employees (83.4 percent) have an offer rate that approximates that of non-Latino whites. Thus Latino employees overall have less access to health insurance coverage through their employment, the primary way in which Americans get such coverage.

Overall, only about half (52.4 percent) of Latino employees, compared to two-thirds (66.3 percent) of non-Latino white employees, work for an employer that offers EBHI, are eligible for benefits, and accept them (Table 11.2). Employees of Central and South American orgin and of Mexican origin are less likely than employees of Puerto Rican or Cuban origin to be in this advantageous situation.

Differences in eligibility for benefits do not explain disparities in EBHI coverage between Latinos and non-Latino whites. Compared with non-Latino whites, a smaller proportion of Latino employees work for an employer that offers health benefits but are not eligible for the benefits because they work too few hours per week, because they have not been employed long enough, or for other reasons. However, among employees whose employer does offer health benefits, statistically similar proportions of Latinos and non-Latino whites are eligible (data not shown).

If differences in eligibility do not explain disparities in EBHI, then perhaps acceptance, or "take-up," rates do. When offered and eligible for EBHI, however, Latinos and non-Latino whites are about equally likely to accept the offer. More than 80 percent of non-Latino white and Latino employees, as well as of all Latino subgroups, accept job-based insurance when it is offered and when they are eligible (Table 11.3).

Furthermore, those who are eligible but don't take up the offer report a number of reasons why they don't. The reason given more than any other is that they are covered by another family member, although non-Latino whites have more access to such coverage than do Latinos (65.0 percent versus 43.0 percent, data not shown). The second most common reason for not taking up an employer's offer is that the premiums are too high: this reason is given by 28.9 percent of Latinos and 18.3 percent of non-Latino whites. Only 3.0 percent of Latinos and 1.3 percent of non-Latino whites say they don't need or don't want health insurance. Contrary to the views of some observers, then, cultural differences play little if any role in determining whether an eligible employee will accept health insurance coverage when it is offered.

TABLE 11.2. Employer Offer and Employee Acceptance of Health Benefits, Non-Latino White and Latino Employees, Aged 18–64, U.S.A. 1997

		Non-Latino White	All Latinos	Mexican-Origin	Central and South American	Puerto Rican	Cuban-Origin
Employer Does Not Offer EBHI		13.6%	30.5%	30.3%	39.0%	16.6%	29.7%
Employer Offers EBHI		86.4%	69.5%	69.7%	61.0%	83.4%	70.3%
Employer Offers EBHI	Employee Eligible and Accepts EBHI	66.3%	52.4%	51.3%	47.8%	65.1%	59.6%
	Employee Eligible but Does Not Accept EBHI	11.9%	10.9%	11.8%	9.9%	9.1%	5.8%
	Employee Not Eligible for EBHI	8.2%	6.2%	6.6%	3.4%	9.3%	4.9%

SOURCE: February 1997 Current Population Survey

NOTE: EBHI = employment-based health insurance

Thus differences in offer rates—not differences in eligibility or take-up rates—explain much of the disparity in uninsured rates between Latino and non-Latino white employees. Among employees whose employers do not offer EBHI, uninsured rates for both Latinos and non-Latino whites are very high (85.1 percent and 46.7 percent, respectively, Table 11.4)— more than ten times as high as the uninsured rates among those whose employers do offer EBHI. This finding underscores the importance of an employer's decision whether to offer health benefits, but it also suggests that non-Latino whites have more options for coverage when their employers do not offer it.

Latinos face many barriers to obtaining EBHI. Compared with non-Latino whites, Latino employees are more likely to be younger, to have lower educational attainment, to work full-time but for less than the full year, to work in a small firm, to work low-coverage industries and occupations, and to earn less and have lower family incomes (Table 11.5)—all characteristics that are associated with lower levels of EBHI. These disadvantages are more characteristic of employees of Central and South American orgin and of Mexican origin, who together make up about 86 percent of all Latino employees in the United States, than they are of Puerto Rican or Cuban-origin employees.

Compounding the greater likelihood of their having characteristics associated with low rates of EBHI for all ethnic groups, Latinos within each characteristic grouping are more likely than non-Latino whites to work for an employer that does not offer coverage at all (Table 11.6). This disadvantage appears to be greater, in general, for employees of Central and South American and of Mexican origin than for other Latino ethnic subgroups, but the small samples sizes for Cuban-origin and Puerto Rican employees make these estimates very imprecise.

Finally, among non-Latino white and Mexican-origin employees, both citizenship status and immigration status strongly affect the probability of working for an employer that does not offer health benefits to any employees (Table 11.7). Among non-Latino whites, those who are U.S.-born are, in general, less likely than naturalized citizens or noncitizens to have an employer that provides no access to EBHI, and noncitizens, very few of whom are undocumented, are even more disadvantaged in their access to EBHI than naturalized citizens.

For Mexican-origin employees, however, the pattern is somewhat different. Those who are U.S.-born citizens are, in some cases, more disadvantaged in their access to EBHI than those who are naturalized citizens. But noncitizens who are legal residents of the United States are generally about twice as likely as citizens, and three times as likely as U.S.-born white citizens, not to have any access to job-based insurance through their employment. Undocumented immigrants, who constitute about 19 percent

TABLE 11.3. Employee Acceptance among Employees Offered and Eligible for Health Benefits, Non-Latino White and Latino Employees, Aged 18–64, U.S.A. 1997

	Non-Latino White	All Latinos	Mexican-Origin	Central and South American	Puerto Rican	Cuban-Origin
Employee Accepts EBHI	84.7%	82.8%	81.3%	82.8%	87.7%	91.1%
Employee Does Not Accept EBHI	15.3%	17.2%	18.7%	17.2%	12.3%	8.9%

SOURCE: February 1997 Current Population Survey

NOTE: EBHI = employment-based health insurance

TABLE 11.4. Percent Uninsured by Employer Offer and Employee Eligibility for and Acceptance of Health Benefits, Non-Latino White and Latino Employees, Aged 18–64, U.S.A. 1997

	Non-Latino White	All Latinos	Mexican-Origin	Central and South American	Puerto Rican	Cuban-Origin
Employer Offers, Employee Eligible for EBHI	3.1%	8.1%	9.2%	6.4%	5.5%	1.0%
Employer Offers, Employee Not Eligible for EBHI	32.9%	61.0%	60.5%	NSD	48.1%	68.2%
Employer Does Not Offer EBHI	46.7%	85.1%	88.5%	83.8%	82.6%	56.6%

SOURCE: February 1997 Current Population Survey

NOTE: EBHI = employment-based health insurance

NSD: Not sufficient data

	Non-Latino White	All Latinos	Mexican-Origin	Central and South American	Puerto Rican	Cuban-Origin
Ages (years)						
18–29	26.8%	36.6%	39.0%	33.1%	34.0%	19.8%
30–44	40.2%	42.1%	41.2%	43.7%	41.9%	49.8%
45–54	22.1%	14.9%	14.3%	15.9%	16.1%	16.8%
55–64	11.0%	6.4%	5.5%	7.3%	8.0%	13.6%
Immigration and Citizenship Status						
U.S.-born citizen	96.2%	47.3%	50.1%	15.4%	97.9%	26.1%
Naturalized citizen	1.8%	13.2%	9.7%	25.6%	2.1%	37.9%
Noncitizen, legal resident	1.7%	21.0%	21.6%	27.8%	N/A	29.2%
Noncitizen, undocumented	0.3%	18.6%	18.6%	31.2%	N/A	6.8%
Educational Attainment						
Less than 9 years	1.2%	21.2%	25.3%	18.4%	5.4%	6.8%
9–12 years	39.8%	46.4%	47.2%	42.7%	51.8%	37.8%
Some college	30.5%	21.7%	19.9%	23.0%	29.1%	26.9%
College graduate	28.6%	10.7%	7.7%	16.0%	13.6%	28.5%
Job Tenure						
Full-time full-year employee	67.8%	65.6%	65.0%	67.4%	63.9%	70.5%
Full-time part-year employee	14.5%	18.6%	19.5%	16.8%	17.1%	14.4%
Part-time employee	17.8%	15.9%	15.5%	15.9%	19.0%	15.0%
Size of Firm (number of workers)						
Fewer than 10	14.5%	17.9%	17.7%	21.4%	11.7%	18.9%
10–24 workers	9.6%	12.0%	12.1%	12.5%	9.6%	12.5%
25–99 workers	13.9%	16.9%	17.5%	16.6%	14.1%	14.2%
100–499 workers	14.5%	14.2%	14.0%	15.0%	14.8%	12.6%
More than 500 workers	47.6%	39.2%	38.7%	34.5%	49.8%	41.8%
Industry*						
Low-coverage	35.8%	47.9%	49.6%	49.9%	36.6%	38.0%
High-coverage	64.2%	52.1%	50.4%	50.1%	63.4%	62.0%
Occupation†						
Low-coverage	14.9%	32.2%	33.7%	34.6%	24.5%	17.0%
High-coverage	85.1%	67.8%	66.3%	65.4%	75.5%	83.0%
Individual Annual Earnings						
<$10,000	22.0%	30.2%	31.8%	27.6%	26.6%	24.3%
$10,000–$19,999	19.7%	33.4%	33.9%	37.5%	27.3%	23.4%
$20,000–$29,999	18.9%	17.3%	17.1%	16.1%	21.0%	17.9%
$30,000–$39,999	14.8%	9.3%	8.7%	9.0%	11.3%	14.6%
$40,000–$49,999	9.1%	4.3%	3.9%	4.0%	6.2%	7.7%
$50,000+	15.7%	5.5%	4.7%	5.9%	7.6%	12.1%
Family Income						
Below poverty	4.4%	13.8%	15.2%	10.6%	11.6%	10.1%
100%–199%	11.1%	29.8%	32.1%	27.5%	23.7%	17.3%
200%–299%	16.3%	21.7%	22.3%	21.5%	20.6%	16.6%
300%+	68.2%	34.7%	30.4%	40.5%	44.1%	56.0%

SOURCE: March 1998 Current Population Survey

*Low-coverage industries include agriculture, forestry, and fisheries; construction; retail trade; business and repair services; personal services; mining; and entertainment and recreation services. High-coverage industries include manufacturing; transportation, communication, and utilities; wholesale trade; financial services; professional services; and public administration.

†Low-coverage occupations include sales; private household; services; farming, forestry, and fishing; precision production; laborers; and armed forces civilians. High-coverage occupations include executive, administrative, and managerial; professional specialty; technicians; administrative support; protective services; transportation; and machine operators.

NSD: Not sufficient data; population estimate less than 75,000.

TABLE 11.6. Percent Whose Employer Does Not Offer
Health Benefits by Ethnicity and Selected Demographic
and Employment Characteristics, Latino and Non-Latino
White Employees, Aged 18–64, U.S.A. 1997

	Non-Latino White	All Latinos	Mexican-Origin	Central and South American	Puerto Rican	Cuban-Origin
All Ages	13.6%	30.5%	30.3%	39.0%	16.6%	29.7%
Ages						
18–29	19.2%	37.0%	39.0%	33.1%	34.0%	19.8%
30–44	12.0%	26.5%	41.2%	43.7%	41.9%	49.9%
45–54	10.5%	27.8%	14.3%	15.9%	16.1%	16.8%
55–64	13.5%	27.9%	5.5%	7.3%	8.0%	13.6%
Education						
Less than high school	29.2%	43.2%	42.5%	54.0%	23.4%	NSD
High school graduate	17.1%	28.1%	26.9%	38.3%	15.5%	34.0%
At least some college	9.9%	19.0%	17.4%	25.8%	14.8%	25.5%
Work Status						
Full-time	10.1%	26.8%	27.2%	33.0%	13.8%	24.7%
Part-time	36.8%	46.0%	38.7%	79.5%	54.5%	56.0%
Industry*						
Low-coverage	27.9%	46.6%	44.7%	58.8%	35.1%	51.7%
High-coverage	7.2%	18.4%	18.1%	25.7%	9.3%	17.7%
Occupation						
Management, technical, sales	9.8%	16.2%	17.4%	20.1%	6.92%	13.2%
Production, craft, repair occupations	15.0%	32.3%	31.3%	40.4%	19.2%	44.5%
Service occupations	29.7%	49.5%	47.1%	57.4%	36.9%	69.6%
Farm, forestry, fishing occupations	51.9%	54.8%	52.6%	NSD	NSD	NSD
Earnings						
Less than $190/wk	38.3%	63.5%	64.9%	68.7%	34.2%	NSD
$190–$380/wk	21.6%	37.6%	34.7%	48.3%	32.4%	NSD
$380–$570/wk	9.9%	20.7%	21.3%	23.5%	13.8%	NSD
$570–$760/wk	5.3%	6.5%	5.4%	20.1%	NSD	NSD
$760 or more /wk	2.8%	9.9%	8.0%	5.3%	8.4%	NSD

SOURCE: February 1997 Current Population Survey

NSD: Not sufficient data; population estimate less than 75,000

*Low-coverage industries include agriculture, forestry, and fisheries; construction; retail trade; business and repair services; personal services; mining; and entertainment and recreation services. High-coverage industries include manufacturing; transportation, communication, and utilities; wholesale trade; financial services; professional services; and public administration.

TABLE 11.7. Percent Whose Employer Does Not Offer Health Benefits by Citizenship and Immigration Status and Selected Characteristics, Non-Latino White and Mexican-Origin Employees, Aged 18–64, U.S.A. 1997

	Non-Latino White				Mexican-Origin			
	U.S.-Born Citizen	Naturalized Citizen	Legal Resident	Undocu-mented	U.S.-Born Citizen	Naturalized Citizen	Legal Resident	Undocu-mented
All Ages	13.4%	16.5%	20.2%	27.7%	20.0%	21.7%	39.0%	55.6%
Ages								
18–29	19.2%	16.2%	16.9%	NSD	23.0%	18.9%	50.0%	58.8%
30–44	11.8%	13.5%	22.2%	NSD	18.0%	21.0%	35.5%	47.6%
45–54	10.2%	18.0%	17.1%	NSD	17.8%	32.8%	35.7%	62.2%
55–64	13.1%	19.1%	24.2%	NSD	19.8%	10.4%	38.6%	NSD
Education								
Less than high school	28.3%	36.5%	42.6%	NSD	33.2%	30.8%	39.7%	57.9%
High school graduate	16.9%	20.6%	29.8%	NSD	20.7%	17.2%	39.9%	59.4%
At least some college	9.8%	13.0%	12.1%	NSD	13.5%	11.1%	35.0%	38.3%
Work Status								
Full-time	9.9%	14.4%	19.0%	NSD	16.7%	19.0%	35.9%	52.6%
Part-time	36.3%	48.3%	48.3%	NSD	29.5%	44.4%	64.9%	48.6%
Industry*								
Low-coverage	27.6%	31.5%	36.7%	48.6%	32.8%	38.9%	48.7%	64.7%
High-coverage	7.1%	11.1%	11.4%	13.7%	12.0%	10.6%	27.5%	40.8%
Occupation								
Management, Tech, Sales	9.7%	12.9%	14.7%	NSD	13.2%	17.0%	40.2%	34.1%
Production, Craft, Repair	14.8%	20.6%	24.4%	NSD	22.8%	16.3%	30.8%	56.6%
Service Occupations	29.4%	31.9%	32.4%	NSD	35.7%	39.3%	55.0%	62.5%
Farm, Forestry, Fishing	51.3%	33.6%	77.3%	NSD	43.3%	59.6%	49.4%	60.3%
Earnings								
Less than $190/wk	37.9%	55.9%	48.6%	NSD	42.4%	NSD	75.5%	87.9%
$190–$380/wk	21.4%	34.2%	26.7%	NSD	21.9%	NSD	38.3%	56.2%
$380–$570/wk	9.7%	17.0%	18.5%	NSD	14.5%	NSD	17.5%	73.1%
$570–$760/wk	5.2%	6.3%	9.0%	NSD	3.6%	NSD	NSD	NSD
More than $760/wk	2.8%	2.7%	1.3%	NSD	6.7%	NSD	NSD	NSD

SOURCE: February 1997 Current Population Survey

NSD: Not Sufficient Data; population estimate less than 75,000.

*Low-coverage industries include agriculture, forestry, and fisheries; construction; retail trade; business and repair services; personal services; mining; and entertainment and recreation services. High-coverage industries include manufacturing; transportation, communication, and utilities; wholesale trade; financial services; professional services; and public administration.

of Mexican-origin employees, are severely disadvantaged: more than half (55.6 percent) work for an employer that does not offer health benefits at all.

Nevertheless, noncitizen status, whether documented or not, in many cases confers the same magnitude of risk on employees. One-third of Mexican-origin employees who have had at least some college have no access to EBHI through their employment, regardless of whether they are legally residing in the United States (35.0 percent) or are undocumented (38.3 percent).

CONCLUSION

Latinos' low rates of EBHI and their resulting high uninsured rates are due in large part to the low proportion of Latino employees whose employers offer job-based insurance. This disparity between Latinos and non-Latino whites prevails across most demographic, labor force, and income groups. Latinos, in general, experience lower "offer" rates than do non-Latino whites, regardless of whether they have less than a high school education or are college educated, whether they work full-time or part-time, whether they work in low-coverage or high-coverage industries and occupations, and whether they are low-wage or higher-wage employees. The problem is especially acute for employees of Mexican and Central and South American origin. Mexican-origin employees who are noncitizens are especially likely not to be offered EBHI, and more than half of those who are undocumented suffer this disadvantage.

This low proportion of Latino employees who work for an employer that offers health benefits suggests that Latinos experience a systematic disadvantage in the labor market—an apparent form of labor market inequity or abuse. A study of health insurance coverage in the nation's 85 largest urban areas provides further evidence of this inequity (Brown, Wyn, and Teleki 2000).

The inequities in health insurance coverage of Latinos have both ethical and public-policy importance. Inequities in access to health services suffered by any group raise social justice concerns. In addition, diminished access to health insurance for any large group can have significant consequences for the nation, potentially increasing the amount of uncompensated care rendered by health care providers, decreasing the group's contributions to the economy, and boosting social tensions. Latinos are a large and growing population that represented 11.8 percent of the U.S. population in 2000 and is projected to reach 17.0 percent by 2020 (U.S. Bureau of the Census 2000); they represent an even larger share of the working-age population. Their health and access to health services is an important concern of the nation.

Public policy could reduce the disparities in health insurance coverage experienced by Latinos. For the majority of uninsured persons of all ethnic groups, low incomes make insurance coverage unaffordable without substantial financial assistance. A national health care system that covered the entire population, or even a mandate that all employers cover those who work for them and those workers' dependents, would address the health insurance needs of this population. However, given the voluntary employment-based health insurance system that prevails in the United States, and given the limited prospects for a mandate that employers cover their employees, subsidies from government are the only feasible option.

In the absence of universal coverage, however, Medicaid or an alternative public program could provide more generous opportunities for working families and individuals to obtain subsidies for health insurance coverage. States now have the opportunity to cover working families with children to a greater extent than ever before, with generous matching federal financial support. The family coverage option of Section 1931 of the Social Security Act allows states considerable flexibility in setting income eligibility for Medicaid to working families with children, including their parents, well above the federal poverty level (Guyer and Mann 1998). In addition, Section 1115 allows states to obtain federal waivers in order to restructure their Medicaid programs and enable uninsured adults without children, as well as families above the current income eligibility limits, to buy into the program on a sliding scale (Riley and Pernice 1998). These options, which could cover all low- and moderate-income workers and their families, would address the needs of many Latino employees.

Expansions of federally funded programs, however, would not benefit undocumented immigrants or even legal residents who arrived in the United States after August 22, 1996.[3] Opportunities for cross-border coverage could benefit Mexican immigrants who frequently cross the border for work or who alternate between living in Mexico and living in the United States. Such a transnational solution would be difficult to implement and would probably benefit relatively few workers.

Greater benefits would accrue from broader policy changes. Entitlement for legal immigrants could be restored by Congress, as now-former President Clinton proposed for at least some new immigrants. In addition, many of the estimated 9 million undocumented immigrants currently in the United States could gain entitlement if Congress enacted a new amnesty program, as the AFL-CIO and a growing number of business organizations have advocated. A new amnesty would enable many of these immigrants to assert themselves more effectively in the labor market by joining unions and bargaining with employers. It might also reduce the transnational movement of many Latino immigrants, facilitating more stable opportunities for obtaining and keeping health insurance coverage and for accessing health services.

It is not hyperbole to suggest that the future of the nation and its economy depend on the well-being of Latinos. Effective public policies are needed and available to expand health insurance coverage and improve access to care for all population groups.

Policy changes result from political processes, but scholarship can inform and stimulate policy debates. One line of scholarship that deserves special attention is the trajectory of immigrants' health status. To what extent does the "epidemiologic paradox" characterize Latino immigrant populations? Are immigrants healthier than their U.S.-born counterparts in spite of experiencing more adverse social and economic conditions? If so, what factors are protective? Controversies related to the "epidemiologic paradox" can best be resolved by longitudinal studies.

Whether or not the "epidemiologic paradox" is an accurate construct to describe Latinos' health status, it is clear that in the absence of health insurance coverage, Latinos—like other ethnic groups—have greatly diminished access to health care. Reduced access to care has real consequences for Latino health in the face of higher rates of some chronic conditions, such as diabetes, and some acute conditions. Latinos' low rates of EBHI underscore the weaknesses of the American system of relying on the voluntary actions of employers to provide affordable health insurance to the majority of the population. The inequities that many Latinos face in the labor market raise fundamental questions about the viability of the current voluntary system of employment-based health insurance.

NOTES

1. The American Academy of Pediatrics (1995) recommends annual visits for children and adolescents aged 24 months through age 17 years (except for children aged 7 and 9) and more frequent visits for children under 24 months of age.

2. The Current Population Survey and other surveys of the general population do not directly ask noncitizens whether they are legal or undocumented residents. However, we were able to estimate undocumented status among Mexican noncitizens on the basis of information from a household survey of Mexican immigrants in Los Angeles that did ask about immigration status and verified the information provided. We modeled undocumented status among that survey sample and then applied that model to predict undocumented status among respondents to the Current Population Survey.

3. That was the date on which federal welfare reform legislation was enacted, excluding from Medicaid entitlement most immigrants who arrived after that date.

REFERENCES

Abraaido-Lanza, A. F., B. P. Dohrenwend, D. S. Ng-Mak, and J. B. Turner. "The Latino Mortality Paradox: A Test of the 'Salmon Bias' and Healthy Migrant Hypotheses," *American Journal of Public Health*, 1999; 89(10):1543–48.

American Academy of Pediatrics, "Recommendations for Preventive Pediatric Health Care," *Pediatrics* 1995; 96:712.

Berk, M. L., L. A. Albers, and C. L. Schur. "The Growth in the U.S. Uninsured Population: Trends in Hispanic Subgroups, 1977 to 1992," *American Journal of Public Health* 1996; 86:572–576.

Brindis, C., A. L. Wolfe, V. McCarter, S. Ball, and S. Starbuck-Morales. "The Associations between Immigrant Status and Risk-Behavior Patterns in Latino Adolescents," *Journal of Adolescent Health*, 1995; 17:99–105.

Brown, E. R., V. Ojeda, R. Wyn, and R. Levan. *Racial and Ethnic Disparities in Access to Health Insurance and Health Care*, Los Angeles and Menlo Park, CA: UCLA Center for Health Policy Research and Henry J. Kaiser Family Foundation, April 2000.

Brown, E. R., R. Wyn, and S. Teleki. *Disparities in Health Insurance and Access to Care for Residents across American Cities*, New York and Los Angeles: The Commonwealth Fund and the UCLA Center for Health Policy Research, August 2000.

Cooper, P., and B. Schone. "More Offers, Fewer Takers for Employment-based Health Insurance: 1987 and 1996," *Health Affairs* 1997; 16(6):142–149.

Freeman, H. E., L. H. Aiken, R. J. Blendon, and C. R. Corey. "Uninsured Working-Age Adults: Characteristics and Consequences," *Health Services Research* 1990; 24: 811–823.

Fronstin, P., L. G. Goldberg, and P. K. Robins. "Differences in Private Health Insurance Coverage for Working Male Hispanics," *Inquiry* 1997; 34:171–180.

Fuentes-Afflick, E., and P. Lurie. "Low Birth Weight and Latino Ethnicity: Examining the Epidemiologic Paradox," *Archives of Pediatrics and Adolescent Medicine*, 1997; 151(7):665–74.

Guendelman, S., P. English, and G. Chavez. "Infants of Mexican Immigrants. Health Status of an Emerging Population," *Medical Care* 1995; 33:41–52.

Guyer, J., and C. Mann. *Taking the Next Step: States Can Now Take Advantage of Federal Medicaid Matching Funds to Expand Health Care Coverage to Low-Income Working Parents*, Washington, DC: Center on Budget and Policy Priorities, August 1998.

Hajat, A., J. B. Lucas, and R. Kington. *Health Outcomes among Hispanic Subgroups: Data from the National Health Interview Survey, 199–95*, Advance Data from Vital and Health Statistics; no. 310. Hyattsville, MD: National Center for Health Statistics, 2000.

Halfon, N., D. L. Wood, R. B. Valdez, M. Pereyra, and N. Duan. "Medicaid Enrollment and Health Services Access by Latino Children in Inner-City Los Angeles," *Journal of American Medical Association* 1997; 277:636–41.

Hernandez. D. J., and E. Charney (eds.) and Committee on the Health and Adjustment of Immigrant Children and Families. *From Generation to Generation: Health and Well-Being of Children in Immigrant Families*, Washington, DC: National Academy Press, 1998.

Marcelli, E. A., and D. M. Heer. "The Unauthorized Mexican Immigrant Population and Welfare in Los Angeles County: A Comparative Statistics Analysis," *Sociological Perspectives* 1998; 41:279–303.

Newacheck, P. W., D. C. Hughes, and J. J. Stoddard. "Children's Access to Primary Care: Differences by Race, Income, and Insurance Status," *Pediatrics*. January 1996; 7(1)26–32.

Pong, A. L., B. J. Anders, K. S. Moser, M. Starkey, A. Gassmann, and R. E. Besser. "Tuberculosis Screening at Two San Diego High Schools with High-Risk Populations," *Archives of Pediatrics and Adolescent Medicine*, 1998; 152:646–650.

Riley, T., and C. Pernice. *How Are States Implementing Children's Health Insurance Plans?* Second edition. Portland, ME: National Academy for State Health Policy, September 1998.

Seccombe, K., L. L. Clarke, and R. T. Coward. "Discrepancies in Employment-Sponsored Health Insurance among Hispanics, Blacks, and Whites: The Effects of Sociodemographic and Employment Factors," *Inquiry* 1994; 31:221–229.

U.S. Bureau of the Census, Population Division, Population Projections Branch, "Projections of the Resident Population by Race, Hispanic Origin, and Nativity: Middle Series, 1999 to 2100," Washington, DC: U.S. Census Bureau, January 13, 2000.

U.S. Congressional Budget Office, *Trends in Health Care Spending by the Private Sector*, Washington, DC: U.S. Congressional Budget Office, April 1997.

Valdez, R. B., H. Morgenstern, E. R. Brown, R. Wyn, C. Wang, and W. Cumberland. "Insuring Latinos Against the Costs of Illness," *Journal of American Medical Association* 1993; 269:889–94.

Vega, W. A., and H. Amaro. "Latino Outlook: Good Health, Uncertain Prognosis," *Annual Review of Public Health*, 1994; 15:39–67.

Commentary

Paul Farmer

As a physician-anthropologist with no expertise in the field of Latino studies, I initially demurred when asked to participate in this project. But in truth, I work in a Latin American country that sits between the Dominican Republic and Cuba. Haiti, which paradoxically is often forgotten in Latin American studies, is in many ways the most representatively Latin American of Latin American countries. I have also worked—as a physician if not as an anthropologist—in slums in Lima, Peru, and the Mexican state of Chiapas. Thus, although I have had no research experience with Latino populations, my commentary is that of someone who has worked extensively in Latin America, the place of origin of the majority of Latinos in the United States.

In the 1980s, there was evidence that if socioeconomic status (income and education) alone were to determine health outcomes, then Latino health outcomes would be far worse than they are. In the chapter that he contributed to this volume, David Hayes-Bautista cogently reminds us that we do not have adequate research models even now, over a decade after this discrepancy between prediction and reported outcomes was first discovered. As Dr. Hayes-Bautista suggests, we still do not have a research model to illuminate the factors that might explain the so-called Latino "epidemiological paradox." This becomes even more complicated when we look at different disease categories and at different Latino populations over time and across generations. Dr. Hayes-Bautista begins the arduous task of picking apart a great number of factors that doubtless contribute to some of these divergent outcomes and then assigning different weights to these factors.

As Dr. Hayes-Bautista points out, the models that we have are no longer adequate (if ever they were); they are usually crude and unidirectional, when in fact patterns of Latino health are quite complicated. What, then, accounts for paradoxical outcomes? In order to find out, we need to understand the daily lived experience of the populations in question. This underlines the need for a robust biosocial model that reflects the fact that with different diseases, radically different mechanisms are in play and bring about different outcomes. Consider, for example, diabetes versus HIV. Differential access to insulin and careful monitoring of serum glucose may reflect the type of insurance one has, and insurance status is of course tightly linked, among U.S. Latinos, to income, immigration status, and state of residence (see Brown, this volume). HIV transmission by contrast, is more tightly linked to gender inequality than to insurance status, even though access to HIV care determines outcomes once the individual is infected. Only a robust biosocial model can hope to reveal how social inequalities of various sorts come to be embodied as differential health outcomes.

Dr. Hayes-Bautista's work also sets the stage for a discussion of what is meant by "Latino" or "Hispanic." As Suárez-Orozco and Páez (this volume) suggest, the category itself is problematic. There are very significant differences between the experience in the United States of a Guatemalan peasant and that of a member of the Argentinean elite, not to mention the different life courses of Puerto Rican residents of Manhattan and dwellers in Texas border towns, even though we know that in many surveys there is a lot of "lumping" of all the individuals. This occurs not only in census surveys but also in academic research. Robust and detailed explanatory hypotheses will demand a great deal more "splitting," even though certain concepts used in the anthropological and sociological literature do seem to occur across subgroups and, therefore, may justify some generalizations about the "Latino experience" as a whole.

Richard Brown and Hongjian Yu's chapter teaches us that health services research can also shed light on a number of these issues. Such research can subject the received wisdom to informed scrutiny. Noting that living in the United States is dangerous, health scholars choose as examples a number of pathologies related to substance abuse, smoking, alcohol, HIV, and violence. These are disorders that are tightly linked to social inequalities in nearly every region of the world. The steeper the grade of social inequalities, the greater the difference between the top tier and the bottom tier of the social structure, and the fewer the opportunities for bettering one's condition. It is for these reasons that I have referred to this form of social inequality as "structural violence."

Understanding the complexities of social causation demands more complex models. Although the correlations between inequality and poor health outcomes are, to my mind, indisputable, we need to refine the nature of this causation and the mechanisms by which factors take on greater or lesser importance in this or that community, at this or that moment of history. As health scholars have pointed out, the risks are changing over time, just as they are changing with movement between countries. The resident of a village in Chiapas has a far higher risk of contracting typhoid or tuberculosis than the resident of a Los Angeles barrio, where the risk of death associated with substance abuse is greater. But in both settings we observe a very high risk of death associated with violence, although the kinds of violence are clearly different. In both instances, the violence is linked to structural inequality. In Chiapas there is a great deal of officially sanctioned brutality against poor populations, whereas in Los Angeles a different kind of official sanction breeds a different kind of violence. Although the specter of federal troops arriving on the scene to maintain order and enforce curfews is rather rare, there is nonetheless violence involved in denying medical or educational benefits to a great many working residents, violence in the treatment of sweatshop workers, violence among those urban entrepreneurs we call gangs, and the like. In the case of Latinos living in the United States, such as Mexican immigrants in Los Angeles, we need to acknowledge the interconnectedness and continuities between these two places and to understand the relationship among the forms of violence that affect Latinos in these different circumstances.

Bringing these linkages into relief is going to be a major research and policy challenge for scholars interested in Latino health. One of the main lessons in Brown and Yu's chapter is the danger in circulating ideas not underpinned with sound empirical data. For example, the authors show that the "lack of experience with health insurance" so often invoked by employers actually has little bearing on why so many Latinos in the United States do not have employment-based insurance. If job-based insurance is not available, Latinos on a tight budget are not going to shop for it elsewhere. But this problem is a structural feature of American employment and health insurance, rather than a cognitive or psychological or cultural feature of the workers in question. Such confusion conveniently shifts the focus from the powerful to the disempowered—from "Why won't employers give an opportunity to purchase insurance?" to "Why don't these people have the modern urban middle-class common sense to take out health insurance?" Such smoke screens are one of the means by which structural violence is perpetuated.

Above all, our explanatory mechanisms need to be framed in an international and world-systemic context. The elephant in the room is the extraordinary steep grades of inequality in many of the places from which U.S. Latinos hail (see Suárez-Orozco and Páez, this volume). Furthermore, we need a better conceptual model to explain what happens when large numbers of people move from poor places and settle in a highly affluent but deeply inequitable society such as the United States. I think that if researchers want to illuminate the mechanisms of differential outcomes, we are going to have to be transnational and very ambitious and to look at migration in a much more dynamic and systematic fashion. We must look at the nations from which people come, and also at the paths that link them to the places where people end up. There is an enormous difference between the New York–Dominican nexus and the Mexico–California nexus, and yet national studies of Latinos' access to health insurance will obscure these and other salient differences unless they adopt a more fine-grained approach. Once more I claim that it is better now to be a splitter than to be a lumper. Looking at the data Brown and Yu present, we see the need for a better understanding of U.S. Latinos in general, but also of the differences in experiences between and among those hailing from Central America, from Cuba, from Puerto Rico, and from the Dominican Republic. The differences that are revealed will help to explain divergences not only in health-seeking behavior but also in employment opportunities in this country and in access to health insurance through that mechanism.

Brown and Yu close their argument with some policy recommendations about reducing the demand for undocumented workers. This sounds laudatory, but of course immigration involves both "pushes" and "pulls." Extreme poverty, violence, and growing inequality in South America, Central America, and parts of the Caribbean push people out of these regions into that part of an international social and economic system that is based more in the United States than in any other single nation.

I would like to close by looking at some themes that run through all of these papers. These themes have obvious relevance for setting future research agendas.

First, significant local variations need to be taken into account. These variations clearly include country of origin, also region of origin, continents, groups of nations, and various interdependencies; none of these are articulated in a blanket category such as "Latino." We need to see Central America, South America, and the Caribbean as radically different cases; we need to refuse to let our investigations be constrained by categories that we did not choose. Census data and large-scale surveys have their value, but they often conceal as much as they reveal. Remember that the individual is never a "Latino" or "Latina" per se. Rather, he or she is a specific person from a specific region with particular genetic, economic, linguistic, educational, and conceptual inheritances, living in a specific place and facing specific constraints and opportunities. Within the Latino population—and within each subgroup, country of origin, or region of origin—we cannot fail to observe significant gender differences and also differences based on socially constructed categories such as race. I come from Florida, and everybody in Florida learns very early to recognize a hierarchy of Latinos, as you can discover in even a brief visit to Miami (see Stepick and Stepick, this volume). That hierarchy is manifest in political influence and in access to education, wealth, and medical care. It also perpetuates itself, as the higher placed exploit their present status in seeking further enhancements. The amount of time one's group has spent in the United States certainly helps shape the health outcomes we are hearing about, as do geographic location in the United States, employment history, language of expression, and a host of other factors. These factors bear a very significant relation to adverse outcomes: they put people on the path to encountering certain pathologies and not others, to overcoming certain diseases or challenges and succumbing to others.

Second, there is the issue of the disease categories. It is probably a mistake to talk about the Latino "epidemiological paradox" and then to group heart disease, birth rate, low birthweight, violence, and HIV together as though what is true for one pathology held for all of them. Just as "Latino" is a category in need of careful splitting, so the various "Latino"-associated categories of health and disease need to be scrutinized one by one.

Third, in addition to social and biological variations, we need research that can capture the complexity of the problems studied. Such research will necessarily include both population-based, quantitative research and qualitative research. Ethnography and participant-observation studies, as well as in-depth case studies (in both medicine and the social sciences) are becoming increasingly important. I think that these sorts of exercises are going to be very illuminating when we take larger studies such as those presented in this volume and attempt to work out the important variables and then weight them properly.

Fourth and finally, the pathogenic world of social inequality was not the explicit focus of any of the contributions, but each study suggests that social inequality of one form or another has its own logic and its own cost in terms of poor outcomes. This is related again to the vast difference between places such as highland Guatemala, Chiapas, and Los Angeles. The fact that the same people are moving in these various social spaces, sending back remittances to their home communities, and leading transnational lives over several generations represents a social complexity that health researchers are only just beginning to acknowledge. This volume is an important step toward bringing these complexities into relief.

Chapter 12

Families on the Frontier

From Braceros in the Fields to Braceras in the Home

Pierrette Hondagneu-Sotelo

Why are thousands of Central American and Mexican immigrant women living and working in California and other parts of the United States while their children and other family members remain in their countries of origin? In this chapter, I argue that U.S. labor demand, immigration restrictions, and cultural transformations have encouraged the emergence of new transnational family forms among Central American and Mexican immigrant women. Postindustrial economies bring with them a labor demand for immigrant workers that is differently gendered from that typical of industrial or industrializing societies. In all postindustrial nations, we see an increase in demand for jobs dedicated to social reproduction, jobs typically coded as "women's jobs." In many of these countries, such jobs are filled by immigrant women from developing nations. Many of these women, because of occupational constraints—and, in some cases, specific restrictionist contract labor policies—must live and work apart from their families.

My discussion focuses on private paid domestic work, a job that in California is nearly always performed by Central American and Mexican immigrant women. Not formally negotiated labor contracts, but rather informal occupational constraints, as well as legal status, mandate the long-term spatial and temporal separation of these women from their families and children. For many Central American and Mexican women who work in the United States, new international divisions of social reproductive labor have brought about transnational family forms and new meanings of family and motherhood. In this respect, the United States has entered a new era of dependency on braceras. Consequently, many Mexican, Salvadoran, and Guatemalan immigrant families look quite different from the images suggested by Latino familism.

This chapter is informed by an occupational study I conducted of over two hundred Mexican and Central American women who do paid domestic work in private homes in Los Angeles (Hondagneu-Sotelo 2001). Here, I focus not on the work but on the migration and family arrangements conditioned by the way paid domestic work is organized today in the United States. I begin by noting the ways in which demand for Mexican—and increasingly Central American—immigrant labor shifted in the twentieth century from a gendered labor demand favoring men to one characterized by robust labor demand for women in a diversity of jobs, including those devoted to commodified social reproduction. Commodified social reproduction refers to the purchase of all kinds of services needed for daily human upkeep, such as cleaning and caring work. The way these jobs are organized often mandates transnational family forms, and in the subsequent section, I (1) draw on a modest-size survey to suggest the prevalence of this pattern and (2) sketch trajectories leading to these outcomes.

I then note the parallels between family migration patterns prompted by the Bracero Program and long-term male sojourning, when many women sought to follow their husbands to the United States, and the situation today, when many children and youths are apparently traveling north unaccompanied by adults, in hopes of being reunited with their mothers. In the earlier era, men were recruited and wives struggled to migrate; in a minority of cases, Mexican immigrant husbands working in the United States brought their wives against the latters' will. Today, women are recruited for work, and increasingly, their children migrate north some ten to fifteen years after their mothers. Just as Mexican immigrant husbands and wives did not necessarily agree on migration strategies in the earlier era, we see conflicts among today's immigrant mothers in the United States and the children with whom they are being reunited. In this regard, we might suggest that the contention of family power in migration has shifted from gender to generation. I conclude with some questions for a twenty-first-century research agenda.

GENDERED LABOR DEMAND AND SOCIAL REPRODUCTION

Throughout the United States, a plethora of occupations today increasingly rely on the work performed by Latina and Asian immigrant women. Among these are jobs in downgraded manufacturing, jobs in retail, and a broad spectrum of service jobs in hotels, restaurants, hospitals, convalescent homes, office buildings, and private residences. In some cases, such as in the janitorial industry and in light manufacturing, jobs have been re-gendered and re-racialized so that jobs previously held by U.S.-born white or black men are now increasingly held by Latina immigrant women (Cranford, forthcoming). Jobs in nursing and paid domestic work have long been regarded as "women's jobs," seen as natural outgrowths of essential notions of women as care providers. In the late twentieth-century United States, however, these jobs have entered the global marketplace, and immigrant women from developing nations around the globe are increasingly represented in them. In major metropolitan centers around the country, Filipina and Indian immigrant women make up a sizable proportion of HMO nursing staffs—a result due in no small part to deliberate recruitment efforts. Caribbean, Mexican, and Central American women increasingly predominate in low-wage service jobs, including paid domestic work.

This diverse gendered labor demand is quite a departure from patterns that prevailed in the western region of the United States only a few decades ago. The relatively dramatic transition from the explicit demand for Mexican and Asian immigrant *male* workers to demand that today includes women has its roots in a changing political economy. From the late nineteenth century until 1964, the period during which various contract labor programs were in place, the economies of the Southwest and the West relied on primary extractive industries. As is well known, Mexican, Chinese, Japanese, and Filipino immigrant workers, primarily men, were recruited for jobs in agriculture, mining, and railroads. These migrant workers were recruited and incorporated in ways that mandated their long-term separation from their families of origin.

As the twentieth century turned into the twenty-first, the United States was once again a nation of immigration. This time, however, immigrant labor is not involved in primary, extractive industry. Agribusiness continues to be a financial leader in the state of California, relying primarily on Mexican immigrant labor and increasingly on indigenous workers from Mexico, but only a fraction of Mexican immigrant workers are employed in agriculture. Labor demand is now extremely heterogeneous and is structurally embedded in the economy of California (Cornelius 1998). In the current period, which some commentators have termed "postindustrial," business and financial services, computer and other high-technology firms, and trade and retail prevail alongside manufacturing, construction, hotels, restaurants, and agriculture as the principal sources of demand for immigrant labor in the western region of the United States.

As the demand for immigrant women's labor has increased, more and more Mexican and (especially) Central American women have left their families and young children behind to seek employment in the United States. Women who work in the United States in order to maintain their families in their countries of origin constitute members of new transnational families, and because these arrangements are choices that the women make in the context of very limited options, they resemble apartheid-like exclusions. These women work in one nation-state but raise their children in another. Strikingly, no formalized temporary contract labor program mandates these separations. Rather, this pattern is related to the contemporary arrangements of social reproduction in the United States.

WHY THE EXPANSION IN PAID DOMESTIC WORK?

Who could have foreseen that as the twentieth century turned into the twenty-first, paid domestic work would become a growth occupation? Only a few decades ago, observers confidently predicted that this job would soon become obsolete, replaced by such labor-saving household devices as automatic dishwashers, disposable diapers, and microwave ovens and by consumer goods and services purchased outside the home, such as fast food and dry cleaning (Coser 1974). Instead, paid domestic work has expanded. Why?

The exponential growth in paid domestic work is due in large part to the increased employment of women, especially married women with children, to the underdeveloped nature of child care centers in the United States, and to patterns of U.S. income inequality and global inequalities. National and global trends have fueled this growing demand for paid domestic services. Increasing global competition and new communications technologies have led to work speedups in all sorts of jobs, and the much bemoaned "time bind" has hit professionals and managers particularly hard (Hochschild 1997). Meanwhile, normative middle-class ideals of child rearing have been elaborated (consider the proliferation of soccer, music lessons, and tutors). At the other end of the age spectrum, greater longevity among the elderly has prompted new demands for care work.

Several commentators, most notably Saskia Sassen, have commented on the expansion of jobs in personal services in the late twentieth century. Sassen located this trend in the rise of new "global cities," cities that serve as business and managerial command points in a new system of intricately connected nodes of global corporations. Unlike New York City, Los Angeles is not home to a slew of Fortune 500 companies, but in the 1990s it exhibited remarkable economic dynamism. Entrepreneurial endeavors proliferated and continued to drive the creation of jobs in business services, such as insurance, real estate, public relations, and so on. These industries, together with the high-tech and entertainment industries in Los Angeles, spawned many high-income managerial and professional jobs, and the occupants of these high-income positions require many personal services that are performed by low-wage immigrant workers. Sassen provides the quintessentially "New York" examples of dog walkers and cooks who prepare gourmet take-out food for penthouse dwellers. The Los Angeles counterparts might include gardeners and car valets, jobs filled primarily by Mexican and Central American immigrant men, and nannies and house cleaners, jobs filled by Mexican and Central American immigrant women. In fact, the numbers of domestic workers in private homes counted by the Bureau of the Census doubled from 1980 to 1990 (Waldinger 1996).

I favor an analysis that does not speak in terms of "personal services," which seems to imply services that are somehow private, individual rather than social, and are superfluous to the way society is organized. A feminist concept that was originally introduced to valorize the nonremunerated household work of women, *social reproduction* or alternately, *reproductive labor*, might be more usefully employed. Replacing *personal services* with *social reproduction* shifts the focus by underlining the objective of the work, the societal functions, and the impact on immigrant workers and their own families.

Social reproduction consists of those activities that are necessary to maintain human life, daily and intergenerationally. This includes how we take care of ourselves, our children and elderly, and our homes. Social reproduction encompasses the purchasing and preparation of food, shelter, and clothing; the routine daily upkeep of these, such as cooking, cleaning and laundering; the emotional care and support of children and adults; and the maintenance of family and community ties. The way a society organizes social reproduction has far-reaching consequences not only for individuals and families but also for macrohistorical processes (Laslett and Brenner 1989).

Many components of social reproduction have become commodified and outsourced in all kinds of new ways. Today, for example, not only can you purchase fast-food meals, but you can also purchase, through the Internet, the home delivery of customized lists of grocery items. Whereas mothers were once available to buy and wrap Christmas presents, pick up dry cleaning, shop for groceries and wait around for the plumber, today new businesses have sprung up to meet these demands—for a fee.

In this new milieu, private paid domestic work is just one example of the commodification of social reproduction. Of course, domestic workers and servants of all kinds have been cleaning and cooking for others and caring for other people's children for centuries, but there is today an increasing proliferation of these services among various class sectors and a new flexibility in how these services are purchased.

GLOBAL TRENDS IN PAID DOMESTIC WORK

Just as paid domestic work has expanded in the United States, so too it appears to have grown in many other postindustrial societies, in the "newly industrialized countries" (NICs) of Asia, in the oil-rich nations of the

Middle East, in Canada, and in parts of Europe. In paid domestic work around the globe, Caribbean, Mexican, Central American, Peruvian, Sri Lankan, Indonesian, Eastern European, and Filipina women—the latter in disproportionately large numbers—predominate. Worldwide, paid domestic work continues its long legacy as a racialized and gendered occupation, but today, divisions of nation and citizenship are increasingly salient.

The inequality of nations is a key factor in the globalization of contemporary paid domestic work. This has led to three outcomes: (1) Around the globe, paid domestic work is increasingly performed by women who leave their own nations, their communities, and often their families of origin to do the work. (2) The occupation draws not only women from the poor socioeconomic classes, but also women who hail from nations that colonialism has made much poorer than those countries where they go to do domestic work. This explains why it is not unusual to find college-educated women from the middle class working in other countries as private domestic workers. (3) Largely because of the long, uninterrupted schedules of service required, domestic workers are not allowed to migrate as members of families.

Nations that "import" domestic workers from other countries do so using vastly different methods. Some countries have developed highly regulated, government-operated, contract labor programs that have institutionalized both the recruitment and the bonded servitude of migrant domestic workers. Canada and Hong Kong provide paradigmatic examples of this approach. Since 1981 the Canadian federal government has formally recruited thousands of women to work as live-in nannies/housekeepers for Canadian families. Most of these women came from Third World countries in the 1990s (the majority came from the Philippines, in the 1980s from the Caribbean), and once in Canada, they must remain in live-in domestic service for two years, until they obtain their landed immigrant status, the equivalent of the U.S. "green card." This reflects, as Bakan and Stasiulis (1997) have noted, a type of indentured servitude and a decline in the citizenship rights of foreign domestic workers, one that coincides with the racialization of the occupation. When Canadians recruited white British women for domestic work in the 1940s, they did so under far less controlling mechanisms than those applied to Caribbean and Filipina domestic workers. Today, foreign domestic workers in Canada may not quit their jobs or collectively organize to improve the conditions under which they work.

Similarly, since 1973 Hong Kong has relied on the formal recruitment of domestic workers, mostly Filipinas, to work on a full-time, live-in basis for Chinese families. Of the 150,000 foreign domestic workers in Hong Kong in 1995, 130,000 hailed from the Philippines, and smaller numbers were drawn from from Thailand, Indonesia, India, Sri Lanka, and Nepal

(Constable 1997, p. 3). Just as it is now rare to find African American women employed in private domestic work in Los Angeles, so too have Chinese women vanished from the occupation in Hong Kong. As Nicole Constable reveals in her detailed study, Filipina domestic workers in Hong Kong are controlled and disciplined by official employment agencies, employers, and strict government policies. Filipinas and other foreign domestic workers recruited to Hong Kong find themselves working primarily in live-in jobs and bound by two-year contracts that stipulate lists of job rules, regulations for bodily display and discipline (no lipstick, nail polish, or long hair, submission to pregnancy tests, etc.), task timetables, and the policing of personal privacy. Taiwan has adopted a similarly formal and restrictive government policy to regulate the incorporation of Filipina domestic workers (Lan 2000).

In this global context, the United States remains distinctive, because it takes more of a laissez-faire approach to the incorporation of immigrant women into paid domestic work. No formal government system or policy exists to legally contract foreign domestic workers in the United States. Although in the past, private employers in the United States were able to "sponsor" individual immigrant women who were working as domestics for their "green cards" using labor certification (sometimes these employers personally recruited them while vacationing or working in foreign countries), this route is unusual in Los Angeles today. Obtaining legal status through labor certification requires documentation that there is a shortage of labor to perform a particular, specialized occupation. In Los Angeles and in many parts of the country today, a shortage of domestic workers is increasingly difficult to prove. And it is apparently unnecessary, because the significant demand for domestic workers in the United States is largely filled not through formal channels of foreign recruitment but through informal recruitment from the growing number of Caribbean and Latina immigrant women who are *already* legally or illegally living in the United States. The Immigration and Naturalization Service, the federal agency charged with enforcement of illegal-migration laws, has historically served the interests of domestic employers and winked at the employment of undocumented immigrant women in private homes.

As we compare the hyperregulated employment systems in Hong Kong and Canada with the more laissez-faire system for domestic work in the United States, we find that although the methods of recruitment and hiring and the roles of the state in these processes are quite different, the consequences are similar. Both systems require the incorporation as workers of migrant women who can be separated from their families.

The requirements of live-in domestic jobs, in particular, virtually mandate this. Many immigrant women who work in live-in jobs find that they must be "on call" during all waking hours and often throughout the night, so there is no clear line between working and nonworking hours. The line between job space and private space is similarly blurred, and rules and regulations may extend around the clock. Some employers restrict the ability of their live-in employees to receive phone calls, entertain friends, attend evening ESL classes, or see boyfriends during the workweek. Other employers do not impose these sorts of restrictions, but because their homes are located in remote hillsides, suburban enclaves, or gated communities, live-in nannies/housekeepers are effectively restricted from participating in anything resembling social life, family life of their own, or public culture.

These domestic workers—the Filipinas working in Hong Kong or Taiwan, the Caribbean women working on the East Coast, and the Central American and Mexican immigrant women working in California constitute the new "braceras." They are literally "pairs of arms," disembodied and dislocated from their families and communities of origin, and yet they are not temporary sojourners. In the section that follows, I suggest some of the dimensions of this phenomenon and present several illustrative career trajectories.

THE NEW BRACERAS AND TRANSNATIONAL MOTHERHOOD

What are the dimensions of this phenomeon which I refer to as the new braceras and the new forms of transnational motherhood? Precise figures are not available; no one has counted the universe of everyone working in private paid domestic work, which continues to be an informal sector—an "under the table" occupation—and accurately estimating the numbers in immigrant groups that include those who are poor and lack legal work authorization is always difficult. Several indicators, however, suggest that the dimensions are quite significant. My nonrandom survey of 153 Latina immigrant domestic workers, which I conducted at bus stops, at ESL evening classes, and in public parks where Latina nannies take their young charges, revealed the following. Approximately 75 percent of the Latina domestic workers had children of their own, and a startling 40 percent of the women with children had at least one of their children "back home" in their country of origin.

The survey finding that 40 percent of Latina domestic workers with children of their own had at least one child living in their country of origin is substantiated by other anectodal indicators. In a study of immigrant children in the Pico-Union area of Los Angeles, a largely Central American and Mexican immigrant neighborhood, sociologists Barrie Thorne and Marjorie Faulstich-Orellana found that half of the children in a first-grade class had siblings in El Salvador. Investigative journalist Sonia Nazarrio (personal communication), who has researched immigration in Mexico, in El Salvador, and in newcomer schools in Los Angeles, reports that a high percentage of Central American children remain "back home" for lengthy periods while their parents are working in the United States. Similarly, sociologist Cecilia Menjívar (2000), in her study of Salvadorans in San Francisco, finds that many Salvadoran immigrant workers are supporting their children in El Salvador.

Given these various indicators, an estimated 40 to 50 percent of Central American and Mexican women leave their children in their countries of origin when they migrate to the United States. They believe the separation from their children will be temporary, but physical separation may endure for long, and sometimes undetermined, periods of time. Job constraints, legal-status barriers, and perceptions of the United States as a dangerous place to raise children explain these long-term separations. In the remainder of this section, I discuss how job constraints in live-in paid domestic work encourage this pattern, but first, I briefly discuss how legal status and perceptions of the United States play a role.

Private domestic workers who hail primarily from Mexico, Central America, and the Caribbean hold various legal statuses. Some, for example, are legal permanent residents or naturalized U.S. citizens, many of them beneficiaries of the Immigration Reform and Control Act's amnesty-legalization program, enacted in 1986. Most Central American women, who prevail in the occupation, entered the United States after the 1982 cutoff date for amnesty-legalization, so they did not qualify for legalization. Throughout the 1990s, a substantial proportion of Central Americans either remained undocumented or held a series of temporary work permits, granted to delay their return to war-ravaged countries.

Their precarious legal status as an "illegal" or "undocumented immigrant" discouraged many immigrant mothers from migrating with their children or bringing them to the United States. The ability of undocumented immigrant parents to bring children north was also complicated in the late 1990s by the militarization of the U.S.–Mexico border through the implementation of various border control programs (Operation Gatekeeper, etc). As Jacqueline Hagan and Nestor Rodriguez's chapter in this volume compellingly shows, the U.S.–Mexico border has become a zone of danger, violence, and death. This not only made it difficult to migrate with children, it also made it difficult to travel back and forth to visit family members "back home." Bound by precarious legal status in the United States, which might expose them to the risk of deportation and denial of all kinds of benefits, and by the greater danger and expense in bringing children to the United States, many immigrant mothers opted not to travel with their children or send for them. Instead, they endure long separations.

Many immigrant parents of various nationalities also view the United States as a highly undesirable place to raise children. Immigrant parents fear the dangers of gangs, violence, drugs, and second-rate schools to which their children are likely to be exposed in poor, inner-city neighbor-hoods. They are also appalled by the way immigration often weakens generational authority. As one Salvadoran youth put it, "Here I do what I please, and no one can control me" (Menjivar 2000, p. 213).

Even mothers who enjoyed legal status and had successfully raised and educated their children through adolescence hesitated to bring them to this country. They saw the United States as a place where their children would suffer job discrimination and economic marginalization. As one Sal-vadoran domestic worker, who had raised her children on earnings predi-cated on her separation from them exclaimed when I spoke with her at an employment agency, "I've been here for 19 years. I've got my legal papers and everything, but I'd have to be crazy to bring my children here. All of them have studied for a career, so why would I bring them here? To bus tables and earn minimum wage? So they won't have enough money for bus fare or food?" (Hondagneu-Sotelo and Avial 1997).

Although precarious legal status and perceptions of the United States as an undesirable place in which to raise children are important in shaping transnational family forms, the constraints of paid domestic work, par-ticularly those that are typical in live-in work, virtually mandate family separations.

Live-in jobs serve as a port of entry for many Latina immigrant women, especially for those who lack access to rich social networks. According to the survey I conducted in Los Angeles, live-in domestic workers work, on aver-age of sixty-four hours per week. Work schedules typically consist of six very long workdays and may include overnight responsibilities with sleepless or sick children. This makes it virtually impossible for live-in workers to sustain daily contact with their own family members. As a consequence of the sub-minimum wages typical of live-in work, and the blurred line around hourly parameters in their jobs, some women remain separated from their families and chilren while working as "braceras" for more years than they had origi-nally anticipated. Two cases will illustrate some of these trajectories.

When I met her, Carmen Velasquez, a thirty-nine year-old Mexicana, was working as a live-in nanny-housekeeper, in charge of general housekeeping and the daily care of one toddler, in the hillside suburban home of an attor-ney and schoolteacher. Carmen, a single mother, had migrated to Califor-nia alone ten years before, leaving behind her three children, when they were four, five, and seven years old. Since then, she had seen them only in photographs. The children were now in their teens. She regularly sent money to the children and communicated by letters and phone calls with them and her three *comadres* (co-godmothers), who cared for one of the children each in Mexico.

Carmen had initially thought that it would be possible for her to main-tain these arrangements for only a short while. She knew she could work hard and thought that working as a live-in domestic worker would enable her to save her earnings by not paying rent or room and board. But, as she somberly noted, "Sometimes your desires just aren't possible."

A series of traumatic events that included incest and domestic violence prompted her migration and had left her completely estranged from the father of her children, from her parents, and from her siblings. With the support only of her female comadres in Mexico, and assisted by the friend of a friend, she had come north "without papers," determined to pioneer a new life for herself and her children.

Her first two live-in jobs, in which she stayed for a total of seven years, included some of the worst arrangements I have had described to me. In both cases, she worked round-the-clock schedules in the homes of Mexican immigrant families, slept on living room couches or in hallways, and earned only $50 a week. Isolated, discouraged, and depressed, she stayed in those jobs out of desperation and lack of opportunity.

By comparison with what she had endured, she expressed relative satisfaction with her current live-in job. Her employers treated her with respect, paid $170 a week, gave her a separate bedroom and bathroom, and were not, she said, too demanding in terms of what they expected of her. Unlike the workdays of many other live-in nannies/housekeepers, her workday ended when the *señora* arrived home at 5 P.M. Still, when I asked whether she now had plans to bring her children to Los Angeles, she equivocated.

She remained vexed by the problem of how she could raise her children in Los Angeles and maintain a job at the same time. "The *señora* is kind and understanding," she said, "but she needs me here with the baby. And then how could I pay the rent, the bus fare to transport myself? And my children [voice quivering] are so big now. They can't have the same affection they once had, because they no longer know me. . . ." As psychologist Celia Falacov (this volume) underscores, there are many losses incurred with migration and family reunification. Women such as Carmen sacrifice to provide a better life for their children, but in the process, they may lose family life with their children.

Some women *do* successfully bring and reintegrate their children with them in the United States, but there are often unforeseen costs and risks associated with this strategy. Erlinda Castro, a Guatemalan mother of five children, came to the United States in 1992. She left all five children behind in Guatemala, under the care of the eldest, supervised by a close neighbor, and joined her husband in Los Angeles. She initially endured live-in domestic jobs. These jobs were easy to acquire quickly, and they enabled her to save on rent. After two years, she moved into an apartment with her husband and her sister, and she moved out of live-in domestic work into house cleaning. By cleaning different houses on different days, she gained a more flexible work schedule, earning more with fewer hours of work. Eventually, she was able to send money for two of the children to come north.

The key to Erlinda's ability to bring two of her children to the United States was her shift in domestic employment from live-in work to house cleaning. According to my survey results, Latina immigrant mothers who work in live-in nanny/housekeeping jobs are the most likely to have their children back home (82 percent) than are women who work cleaning houses. And mothers who clean different houses on different days are the least likely to have their children in their countries of origin (24 percent).

Bringing children north after long periods of separation may entail unforeseen "costs of transnationalism," as Susan Gonzalez-Baker suggests. Just as migration often rearranges gender relations between spouses, so too, does migration prompt challenges to familiar generational relations between parents and offspring. In the following section, I draw some parallels between these rebellions of gender and generation.

BRACEROS AND THEIR WIVES, BRACERAS AND THEIR CHILDREN: REBELLIONS OF GENDER AND GENERATION

The Bracero Program, the institutionalized contract labor program that authorized the granting of five million contracts to Mexican agricultural workers, most of them men, remained in place from 1942 to 1964. This program, like earlier contract labor programs that recruited Mexican, Filipino, and Chinese men to work in the western and southwestern regions of the United States, incorporated men as pure workers, not as human beings enmeshed in family relationships. Mandated by formal regulations, but made possible by patriarchal family culture and male-dominated social networks, this pattern of male-selective migration remained in place for many years following the end of the Bracero Program (Hondagneu-Sotelo 1994). This pattern is still not uncommon.

In many families, however, this migration pattern prompted gender rebellion among the wives of braceros. Many wives of braceros and other Mexican immigrant men working in the United States after the end of the program sought to migrate to the United States, and many of them did so in the face of resistance from their husbands. Elsewhere, I have detailed some of these processes and have referred to this pattern as "family stage migration" (Hondagneu-Sotelo 1994). In many instances, Mexican women worked hard to persuade their husbands to help them migrate to the United States, and when this failed, many of them turned to their own social-network resources to accomplish migration. Although patriarchal practices and rules in families and social networks have persisted, labor demand has changed in ways previously outlined in this chapter, and now both women and men creatively reinterpret normative standards and creatively manipulate the rules of gender. As they do, understandings about proper gendered behavior are reformulated, and new paths to migration are created.

Just as wives have followed their husbands north, so too are children today following their mothers to California and other states. According to the *Los Angeles Times* investigative journalist Sonia Nazarrio (personal communication), every year the I.N.S. captures approximately 5,000 unaccompained minors traveling illegally across the U.S.–Mexico border. Because this figure does not include those who are apprehended and choose voluntary deportation within 72 hours, and those who are never apprehended, Nazarrio believes that the number of unaccompanied minors migrating to the United States from Central America and Mexico each year may be as high as forty to fifty thousand—and she estimates that about half are coming to be reunited with their mothers.

In some cases, these are the children of mothers who, after having established themselves financially and occupationally, have sent money for the children's migration. These children and youths enter either accompanied by smugglers or through authorized legal entry. In other cases, these are children who have run away from their grandmothers, paid caregivers, or fathers. In both cases, the children and youths face tremendous dangers, and fatalities are not unheard of. Nazarrio reports that many of them travel north by hopping moving trains, risking life and limb as they embark and disembark, and that they are victimized, robbed, and raped by roving bandits and thugs and by delinquent gang members who are returning north after having been deported. After the 1996 immigration law imposed new restrictions on criminal aliens—even on legal immigrants falsely convicted of crimes (a common practice in Los Angeles, which was victimized by a corrupt police force in the 1990s)—many immigrants were deported. Members of tough Los Angeles street gangs, such as Mara Salvatrucha or the 18th Street gang, have been deported to El Salvador, Guatemala, and Mexico, and they too are traveling on these northbound trains back to California. Meanwhile, children and other minors are trekking northward for the first time, in hopes of being reunited with their mothers and other family members.

What happens once these children are reunited with their mothers? A short honeymoon may occur upon reunification, but long periods of discord typically follow. Once in the United States, the children are apt to blame their mothers for the economic deprivation and the emotional uncertainty and turmoil they have experienced. They may express contempt and disrespect for their mothers. The emotional joy of reunification that they may have anticipated quickly sours when they realize their mothers are off working for hours, and they may feel betrayed when they discover that their mothers have new husbands and children. Competition with new half-siblings forms part of the backdrop through which they reintegrate. And finally, their mothers' long workdays leave them on their own for a good portion of their waking hours. In one case reported by Menjivar (2000, p. 209), a Salvadoran mother brought her daughter to San Francisco, only to have Child Protective Services take her daughter and deem her an unfit mother for working seventy hours a week. Many of the children and youths miss their grandmothers, or whoever was their primary caregiver during their formative years, and feel neglected and rejected by family in the United States. Many, indeed, wish to return to their homeland.

CONCLUSION

What do these developments mean for a twenty-first-century research agenda on Latino families? Clearly, they force us to rethink monolithic understandings of Latino families, familism, and sentimentalized notions of motherhood. There are also many remaining empirical questions about the impact of these transnational processes on children and youth. How does the length of separation affect processes of adaptation? How does the age at which the children are reunited with their "bracera" mothers affect family social relations? How do these migration processes affect adolescent identity and school performance? Answering questions such as these will require incorporating children and youths into research as active agents in migration.

The trajectories described here pose an enormous challenge to those who would celebrate any and all instances of transnationalism. These migration patterns alert us to the fact that the continued privatization of social reproduction among the American professional and managerial class has broad repercussions for the social relations among new Latina immigrants and their families. Similarly, strong emotional ties between mothers and children, which we might dismiss as personal subjectivities, are fueling massive remittances to countries such as El Salvador and the Philippines. Our most fundamental question remains unanswered: Who will continue to pick up the cost of raising the next generation? Surely, we can hope for a society wherein Latina immigrant women and children are not the first to bear those costs.

REFERENCES

Bakan, Abigail B., and Daiva Stasiulis. 1997. "Foreign Domestic Worker Policy in Canada and the Social Boundaries of Modern Citizenship," In Abigail B. Bakan and Daiva Stasiulis (eds.), *Not One of the Family: Foreign Domestic Workers in Canada*, Toronto: University of Toronto Press, pp. 29–52.

Constable, Nicole. 1997. *Maid to Order in Hong Kong: Stories of Filipina Workers.* Ithaca and London: Cornell University Press.

Cornelius, Wayne. 1998. "The Structural Embeddedness of Demand for Mexican Immigrant Labor: New Evidence from California." In Marcelo M. Suárez-Orozco (ed.), *Crossings: Mexican Immigration in Interdisciplinary Perspectives.* Cambridge, MA: Harvard University, David Rockefeller Center for Latin American Studies, pp. 113–44.

Coser, Lewis. 1974. "Servants: The Obsolescence of an Occupational Role." *Social Forces* 52:31–40.

Hochschild, Arlie. 1997. *The Time Bind: When Work Becomes Home and Home Becomes Work.* New York: Metropolitan Books, Henry Holt.

Hondagneu-Sotelo, Pierrette. 1994. *Gendered Transitions: Mexican Experiences of Immigration.* Berkeley: University of California Press.

Hondagneu-Sotelo, Pierrette. 2001. *Domestica: Immigrant Workers and Their Employers.* Berkeley: University of California Press.

Hondagneu-Sotelo, Pierrette, and Ernestine Avila. 1997. "'I'm Here, But I'm There': The Meanings of Latina Transnational Motherhood," *Gender & Society,* 11:548–571.

Lan, Pei-chia. 2000. "Global Divisions, Local Identities: Filipina Migrant Domestic Workers and Taiwanese Employers." Dissertation, Northwestern University.

Laslett, Barbara, and Johanna Brenner. 1989. "Gender and Social Reproduction: Historical Perspectives," *Annual Review of Sociology* 15:381–404.

Menjivar, Cecilia. 2000. *Fragmented Ties: Salvadoran Immigrant Networks in America.* Berkeley: University of California Press.

Waldinger, Roger, and Mehdi Bozorgmehr. 1996. "The Making of a Multicultural Metropolis." In Roger Waldinger and Mehdi Bozorgmehr, (eds.), *Ethnic Los Angeles.* New York: Russell Sage Foundation, pp. 3–37.

Chapter 13

Ambiguous Loss

Risk and Resilience in Latino Immigrant Families

Celia Jaes Falicov

I wanted to bind Texas and Mexico together like a raft strong enough to float out onto the ocean of time, with our past trailing in the wake behind us like a comet trail of memories.

JOHN PHILLIP SANTOS, *Places. . . , 1999, p. 5*

Latino immigrants, like many other immigrants, experience some degree of loss, grief and mourning. These experiences have been compared with the processes of grief and mourning precipitated by the death of loved ones (Shuval 1982; Warheit et al. 1985; Grinberg and Grinberg 1989; Volkan and Zintl 1993). Here I will argue, however, that migration loss has special characteristics that distinguish it from other kinds of losses. Compared with the clear-cut, inescapable fact of death, migration loss is both larger and smaller. It is larger because migration brings with it losses of all kinds. Gone are family members and friends who stay behind, gone is the native language, the customs, and rituals, and gone is the land itself. The ripples of these losses touch the extended kin back home and reach into the future generations born in the new land.

Yet migration loss is also smaller than death, because despite the grief and mourning occasioned by physical, cultural, and social separation, the losses are not absolutely clear, complete, and irretrievable. Everything is still alive but is just not immediately reachable or present. Unlike the finality of death, after migration it is always possible to fantasize the eventual return or a forthcoming reunion. Furthermore, immigrants seldom migrate toward a social vacuum. A relative, friend, or acquaintance usually waits on the other side to help with work and housing and to provide guidelines for the new life. A social community and ethnic neighborhood reproduce in pockets of remembrance, the sights, sounds, smells, and tastes of one's country. All of these elements create a mix of emotions—sadness and elation, loss and restitution, absence and presence—that makes grieving incomplete, postponed, ambiguous.

In this paper, I attempt to integrate concepts from family systems theory (ambiguous loss, boundary ambiguity, relational resilience) with concepts drawn from studies on migration, race, and ethnicity (familism, bicultural-ism, double consciousness) to deepen our understanding of the risks and resiliences that accompany migration loss for Latinos. I propose that an inclusive, "both/and" approach rather than an "either/or" approach, to the dilemmas of cultural and family continuity and change increases family resilience in the face of multiple migration losses. As we will see, however, risks arise when the experience of ambiguous loss becomes unbearable and thwarts attempts at integrating continuity with change.

Although Latinos share many similarities in the aspects of family coping with loss that are addressed in this paper, each family has a particular "eco-logical niche" created by combinations of nationality, ethnicity, class, edu-cation, religion, and occupation and by its individual history. Other vari-ables that mediate the experience of migration are the degree of choice (voluntary or forced migration), proximity and accessibility to the country of origin, gender, age and generation, family form, and the degree and level of social acceptance encountered in the new environment (Falicov 1995, 1998).

AMBIGUOUS LOSS AND MIGRATION

The concept of ambiguous loss proposed by Pauline Boss (1991, 1999) describes situations in which loss is unclear, incomplete, or partial. Basing her thesis on stress theory, Boss describes two types of ambiguous loss. In one, people are physically absent but psychologically present (the family with a soldier missing in action, the noncustodial parent in divorce, the migrating relative). In the second, family members are physically present but psychologically absent (the family living with an Alzheimer's victim, the parent or spouse who is emotionally unavailable because of stress or depression).

Migration represents what Boss (1999) calls a "crossover" in that it has elements of both types of ambiguous loss. Beloved people and places are left behind, but they remain keenly present in the psyche of the immigrant. At the same time, homesickness and the stresses of adaptation may leave some family members emotionally unavailable to others. The very decision to migrate has at its core two ambiguous poles. Intense frustration with eco-nomic or political conditions compels the immigrant to move, but love of family and surroundings pull in another direction.

Dealing with Ambiguous Loss

Many internal conflicts, moods, and behaviors of immigrants can be more easily understood when seen through the lens of "ambiguous loss."

Visits to the country of origin close the gap between the immigrant and that
  which is psychologically present but physically absent. Phone calls,
  money remittances, gifts, messages, and trips back home contribute
  to transnational lifestyles (Rouse 1992)—and to a psychologically
  complex experience of presence and absence.

Leaving family members behind has pragmatic and economic justifications,
  but it may also ensure a powerful psychological link. It may symbolize that migration is provisional and experimental rather than permanent. Leaving a young child with the immigrant's own parents
  may also assuage the immigrant's guilt about leaving and offer
  an emotional exchange for the help of shared parenting.

Encouraging relatives and friends to migrate eases the wrenching homesickness of migration. It is a way of saying "hello again" to some
  of the many to whom one has bid good-byes. It also means that
  social networks dismantled by migration may stand a chance of
  being partially reconstructed in the host country.

  Latino immigrants also reconstruct urban landscapes of open
  markets and ethnic neighborhoods that provide experiences with
  familiar foods, music, and language. *Recreating cultural spaces* in
  this manner reestablishes links with the lost land, while helping
  to transform the receiving cultures into more syntonic spaces
  (Ainslie 1998).

The long-lasting dream of returning home reinforces the gap between physical absence and psychological presence. A family may remain in
  a provisional limbo, unable to make settlement decisions or take
  full advantage of existing opportunities, paralyzed by a sort of
  frozen grief.

Family polarizations ensue when ambiguities overwhelm, as it were, the
  immigrant family's psyche. Spouses may come to represent each side
  of the conflict between leaving and staying, one idealizing and the
  other denigrating the country of origin or the "new" culture (Sluzki
  1979). When such polarizations exist, they hint powerfully at denied
  or suppressed grief that may result in symptoms: depression or other
  emotional blocks to adaptation in adults, psychosomatic illness and
  selective mutism in children (Sluzki 1979, 1983; Grinberg and Grinberg 1989; Falicov 1998).

Generational legacies evolve when immigrant parents pass on their doubts,
  nostalgia, and sense of ambiguities to their children, who are sometimes recruited to one side or the other of the polarizations. Immigrant children may experience ambiguous loss themselves, but exposure to their parents' mixed emotions may significantly increase
  their stress.

The migration story itself can provide meaning and narrative coherence (Cohler 1991) to all life events. Experiences of success or of failure, the wife's new-found assertiveness, the ungrateful adult child—all can be readily explained: "It is because we came here." The question that will remain perennially unanswered is "How much is it migration, or is it just life challenges that would have appeared anywhere?" (Troya and Rosenberg 1999).

The construction of bicultural identities may result. The flow of people and information in a two-home, two-country lifestyle may give rise to a sense of "fitting in" in more than one place. Equally possible is the sense of not belonging in either place.

These behaviors of immigrants demonstrate the ambiguous, conflictual nature of migration losses. Yet they carry with them certain dynamic responses or "solutions" that demonstrate that people can learn to live with the ambiguity of never putting final closure to their loss. The adaptation depends on the contextual stresses that families encounter. Some are so excruciatingly oppressive that they prompt the family to repatriate. Under better circumstances, mixed feelings may be counteracted in part by building on family ties, social supports, and cultural strengths. Concepts from family systems theory and from acculturation studies can help us understand how ambiguous losses come to be tolerated and integrated in ways that strengthen families' resilience and empower their activism against social marginalization and injustice.

Dual Visions of Continuity and Change

From a family systems viewpoint, for a family to be succesful in coping with family transitions, flexible attitudes toward change and flexible efforts to preserve continuity need to coexist (Hansen and Johnson 1979; Melitto 1985; Falicov 1993). Most immigrant families manage to maintain contacts with their culture of origin and to reinvent old family themes while carving out new lives. New acculturation theories reflect this dynamic balance of continuity and change, rather than the traditional "either/or" linear theory of abandoning one culture to embrace the other. Terms such as *binationalism, bilingualism, biculturalism,* and *cultural bifocality* (see Levitt, this volume) describe dual visions, ways of maintaining familiar cultural practices while making new spaces manageable, and ways of alternating language or cultural codes according to the requirements of the social context at hand (LaFramboise, Coleman, and Gerton 1993; Rouse 1992). Although there are compelling adaptational reasons for acquiring new language and cultural practices, there are equally compelling reasons for retaining cultural themes in the face of change, among them the attempt to preserve a sense of family coherence.

RELATIONAL RESILIENCE IN THE FACE OF LOSS

The concept of a "family sense of coherence" developed by Antonovsky and Sourani, (1988) refers to the human struggle to perceive life as comprehensible, manageable, and meaningful. This striving for a sense of coherence (and hopefulness) is one of the key ingredients of *relational resilience*, those processes by which families cope and attempt to surmount persistent stress (Walsh 1998).

In this section, I explore immigrant families' attempts to restore meaning and purpose in life in the midst of multiple ambiguous losses. The aspects of relational resilience addressed in this discussion are family connectedness, family rituals, awareness of social marginalization, and belief or spiritual systems.

Family Connectedness

Latinos' ethnic narratives almost invariably stress familism: inclusiveness and interdependence. In family systems terms, family connectedness—the obligation to care and support one another—is a defining feature of extended family life. This cultural tendency toward family connectedness seems to withstand migration and to persist in some form for at least one or two or more generations (Suárez-Orozco and Suárez-Orozco 1995; Sabogal et al. 1987). For immigrant families, familism may be manifest in the persistence of long-distance attachments and loyalties in the face of arduous social or economic conditions, in attempts to migrate as a unit and live close to one another, and in the desire to reunify when individuals have taken up the journey alone. The family members and the ideologies of these richly joined systems make their presence felt at a psychological and a physical level.

The Psychological Presence of Extended Familism.   When extended family members are far away, *la familia* may become the emotional container that holds both dreams not yet realized and lost meanings that are no longer recoverable. At the most concrete level, immigrants send remittances back home in exchange for collective caretaking of remaining family members (children and/or elders), thus reinforcing a traditional system of emotional and economic interdependence. At a more abstract level, the idea itself of three-generational family can trigger other large existential meanings, such as one's lost national identity. A study of young adults (Troya and Rosenberg 1999) who had migrated to Mexico as children with parents seeking political refuge from South America demonstrates the powerful psychological presence of absent relatives. When asked for their spontaneous images formed in response to the words *patria* ("fatherland") and *tierra* ("land"), they associated these with the street or house where the grandmother or the aunt lived, reflecting (or perhaps creating anew) deep intergenerational bonds between country and family—a psychological familism.

Other studies show that as families acculturate (Rueschenberg and Buriel 1989; Sabogal et al. 1987; Suárez-Orozco and Suárez-Orozco 1995) they learn how to behave externally in a dominant culture that values assertiveness, independence, and achievement. Yet they do not abandon internally the connectedness and interpersonal controls of many collectivistic family systems.

The Physical Presence of Extended Family.   When extended family members are physically present, they play a significant role in shoring up the immigrant family. Their familism drives a concern for one another's lives, a pulling together to weather crises, a sociocentric child rearing (Harwood, Miller, and Irizarry 1995), and a closeness among adult siblings (Chavez 1985).

Multigenerational dwellings, particularly the presence of grandmothers, can be influential in terms of transfers of knowledge, cultural exposures, nurturance, and instrumental help embedded in established sociocultural practices (Garcia-Coll, et al. 1996) or even as a buffer against parental neglect or abuse (Gomez 1999). However, family life is not always as rosy as it seems. The description of Latino family connectedness is sometimes taken to such extremes that stereotypical images of picturesque family life dominate while tensions and disconnectedness among extended family members simmer below, ignored or discounted. Perhaps what matters, regardless of the particular positive or negative tone of the interactions, is the sense of being part of a family group, and that in itself affords a sense of continuity in the face of ruptured attachments and the disruptions of relocation.

Cultural Family Rituals

Another interesting avenue to study family resilience in the face of ambiguous losses is through the transmission of family rituals that reaffirm family and cultural identity. Family systems theorists have long known about the power of rituals to restore continuity with a family's heritage while reinforcing family bonds and community pride (Bennett, Wolin and McAvity 1988; Imber-Black, Roberts and Whiting 1988). A good example is a clinical case of mine.

A poor, working-class, Mexican-immigrant mother was very distressed over her daughter's refusal to have a *quinceañera* party. The intensity of the mother's emotion surprised me, because the party's ritual affirmation of the girl's virginity and future availability for dating hardly applied—everybody knew the girl was sexually involved with an older boyfriend. But for the mother, the *quinceañera* was the most unforgettable (*"inolvidable,"* she said) event in a woman's life and a memory that all parents dream of bestowing upon a daughter ever since the time of her birth. To abandon this valued ritual that lends coherence to a woman's life—even when its original contents had shifted or faded—represented too much cultural discontinuity for this mother.

The enactment of life cycle rituals in the midst of cultural transformation can be construed as reflecting dual lifestyles, as being both ethnic and modern at the same time. Studies of immigrant families should include a close look at the persistence and the evolving new shapes of traditional family rituals—from routine family interactions (dinners or prayers) to celebrations of birthdays, holidays, and rites of passage or any gathering where a sense of family and national belonging is reaffirmed. Such study could help us understand not only the stable and shifting meanings of rituals but also their functions as metaphors for continuity and change.

Awareness of Social Marginalization

Although the notion of "dual vision" characterizes the incorporation of culture in the inner workings of many immigrant families, it also captures the nature of their interaction with larger external and institutional systems of the host country. The concept of "double consciousness," first described by Du Bois (1903) for African Americans, is useful here because it encompasses a perception of who one really is as a person within one's own group *and* a perception of who one is in the attributions of the larger society's story regarding the same group. Racial, ethnic, and class discriminations plague the individual stories of many Latino and Latina immigrant adults and children. One case of mine illustrates the painful awareness a Mexican family had of the gross, racist preconceptions of Latino immigrants by whites.

This family, a married couple with six children who had arrived from Oaxaca seven years ago, consulted me because a white, upper-class neighbor had accused their nine-year-old son of "molesting" her four-year-old daughter. As the Mexican boy's story unfolded, I learned that several children had been playing together in the fields when the little girl said she needed to urinate. The boy quickly pulled her panties down and held her in the upright position, but the girl ran crying home. Racism was undoubtedly part of the reaction to the boy's behavior. I recounted to the parents the alternative explanation to the "molestation," but the father responded, "I thank you but we want you to tell [the white family that you think] our son is cured and this will never happen again." When asked why should I do this, he said, "Because, when they look at us, they think 'These Mexicans are good people, *le hacen la lucha* [they struggle hard],' but if something goes wrong they suddenly see in us the faces of rapists and abusers. I promise you I will keep an eye on this boy, but please do not question their story. *No vale la pena* [It is not worth it]. It could cost us everything we worked for."

Here again is the ambiguity of gains, losses, and dual visions of immigrants. Striving for the dream of stability in a new land is riddled with pressures to subscribe to the dominant culture's story, which negatively judges dark-skinned, poor immigrants and deprives them of legal resources to fight unfair accusations. The social climate of structural exclusion and psychological violence suffered by immigrants and their children is not only detrimental to their participation in the opportunity structure but it also affects the immigrant children's sense of self, through a process of what Carola Suárez-Orozco (2000) aptly calls "social mirroring."

Indeed, most immigrants and their children are aware of the hostilities and prejudice with which they are regarded. From a psychological viewpoint, this awareness may be debilitating when internalized or denied, but it may be empowering when it helps stimulate strategic activism for social justice. Educators who stress the need for minority families' democratic participation in schools emphasize that awareness of one's own marginal status is the first step toward empowerment (Trueba 1999). Thus awareness of social injustices may create a measure of family resilience against assaults on identity.

Long-held Beliefs and Spiritual Systems

People's *belief system*, or the meaning they make of their lives and experience, is a narrative construct that helps us understand a family's ability to deal with adversity (Walsh 1998; Wright, Watson, and Bell 1996). A family's tolerance for loss and ambiguity is related to its culture's tolerance for ambiguity; fatalistic and optimistic stances are likewise embedded in culturally based systems of meaning (Boss 1999).

Some Latino cultural narratives and spiritual beliefs promote acceptance of life's adversities, tempering the need to find answers and definitive solutions to losses (Falicov 1998). Roman Catholic beliefs value acceptance of suffering, destiny, and God's will. A belief that little in life is under one's control is also related to conditions of poverty and decreased agency (Garza and Ames 1972; Comas-Díaz 1989). These beliefs should not be misconstrued as passivity, however, but as a way of marshaling one's initiative to solve what can be solved while accepting what cannot be changed—a sort of mastery of the possible.

Like other cultural and ritual practices, the old religion often takes new forms and functions in the new land. Church participation may actually help inscribe various Latino groups in dual, evolving transnational spaces. As Peggy Levitt so cogently describes in this volume, immigrants' church attendance can allow a double membership that crosses border arenas in the homeland while it grounds them locally through host country participation and even civic engagement. This balance of continuity and change may be at the core of resilient adaptations to ambiguous loss. Yet these dual visions are not always obtainable, nor is it always possible to make positive meaning out of the experience of migration. In the next sections, I describe situations where attempts to restore a sense of family coherence fail in the face of intense loss and irreparable ambiguity.

WHEN AMBIGUOUS LOSS BECOMES UNBEARABLE

Many circumstances surrounding migration can lead to overwhelmingly problematic physical and emotional disconnections among family members. Two of these circumstances are addressed here: (1) the overlap of the consequences of migration with the impact of other life cycle transitions at any point in the life of an immigrant and (2) the short- and long-term effects of migration separations and reunifications among all family members. Both situations can be understood better by utilizing the concept of boundary ambiguity.

Boundary Ambiguity

Ambiguous loss may become problematic when it generates confusion about who is in and who is out of the family. Boss (1991) labeled this phenomenon "boundary ambiguity," a concept that is increasingly being used in family research to describe effects of family membership loss over time (Boss, Greenberg, and Pearce-McCall 1990) and that may be very helpful in illuminating migration losses. This construct encompasses the rules and definitions of family subsystems (parental, marital, sibling and other subgroups) and how they are perceived by each family group.

When Ambiguous Loss Is Compounded by Life Cycle Transitions

When nonambiguous, irretrievable losses—such as the death of a relative back home—occur in the life of an immigrant family the uncertain, provisional, and ambiguous quality of the old good-byes accentuates that loss and creates confusion about where one belongs and exactly who constitutes one's family.

A thirty-six-year-old woman consulted me for depression after her father died suddenly in Argentina. Overwhelmed by sadness and guilt at not having made the effort to see him more often and by the unbearable loneliness of not being able to participate in communal grieving, this woman asked to have a separation from her Anglo-American husband. He was the one who had brought her to this country, and she felt him to be a much less loving man than her father. Asked about her adoring father's reaction to her leaving her country twelve years ago to get married, she promptly said, "Everybody told me that for him that day was like *el velorio del angelito* [the wake of his little angel]." Now she was experiencing a great deal of confusion about where she belonged. Her husband and children, who hardly knew her father, provided little comfort. She needed the support of her family of origin, but her own shared history with them had been truncated long ago. This case illustrates the rippling effects of ambiguous loss for the immigrant, for their children, and for the family of origin left behind. This woman's eight-year-old daughter was having behavior and school difficulties that paralleled the mother's depression.

Calling Two Women "Mami"

In addition to separations between extended and nuclear family, Latino immigrants increasingly experience separations between parents and children. A father or a mother frequently migrates first, leaving children behind and planing for later reunification. Such separations complicate experiences of loss, raise issues of inclusion/exclusion, and set the stage for boundary ambiguity.

When a father or a mother migrates first, leaving the family to be reunited later, the confusion may be mild and temporary or intense and prolonged. If sufficient time passes, a family in which the father migrated first may reorganize into a single-parent household, with mother as head and substitutes performing the parental functions of the absent parent. Subsequent reunification is often stressful because family boundaries need to change yet again to allow for reentry of the absent member.

Increasingly today, mothers recruited for work make the journey north alone, leaving the children with other women in the family or social network. It is only after several years that these mothers are joined by their children, who often travel unaccompanied. Sociologist Pierrette Hondagneu-Sotelo's incisive analysis (this volume) of the changing labor demands driving these emergent transnational family forms, and of the possible new meanings of family and motherhood, provides a historical, economic, and social context for these complex and often traumatic separations and equally traumatic reunifications between mothers and children. Children are left behind with grandparents or other relatives so that an immigrant parent can face the dangers of illegal passage and the economic hardships of getting established in the new country without the added worry of having youngsters under their wing. Over time, the costs of these arrangements are significant.

The adjustments to parting and the adjustments at the time of a subsequent reunion place not only mother and child but also all the subsystems of a three-generational family (including siblings who stayed in the sending culture and those born in the receiving country) at risk for developing boundary ambiguities and concomitant individual and relational problems. Psychotherapists and social workers often encounter an immigrant child who calls two women "Mami." We know very little about the meaning of this behavior. Does it point to an attempt to deal with ambiguous loss by accepting two mothers, one here and one there? Could it represent a fluid definition of family that reflects multiple attachments and wherein "Mami" is just a generic term for significant others? Of more concern, does it signify boundary ambiguity, the beginning of divided loyalties, and confusion about who is the real mother? What makes for a successful separation and reunion? What are the consequences of separation at different ages and for various lengths of time? What transforms ambiguous loss into conflict-laden boundary ambiguity?

A recent international furor over the fate of one young Cuban immigrant highlights an extreme case of boundary ambiguity. Custody of Elián González, a six-year-old Cuban shipwreck survivor was fiercely contested by his deceased mother's relatives in Miami and by his father and grandmothers in Cuba, each side of the family (the immigrants and the nonimmigrants) claiming the right to decide where Elián belonged (Cooper Ramo 2000). At the political level, the boundary ambiguity could not be resolved because it represented the long-standing tensions between Little Havana in Miami and Havana in Cuba. Yet the symbolism of belonging goes beyond the political. At the level of migration loss, the dispute struck deep in the hearts of immigrants who have remained in perpetual mourning for the total loss of the Cuba they once knew. It is tempting to speculate that it is precisely the prohibition to visit that makes it impossible for these immigrants to lead satisfactory dual lives, recharging their emotional batteries and becoming binational or bicultural. Their ambiguous losses instead solidify into a rigid migration narrative confined to an idealization of the island's past, recreated exclusively in the space of Little Havana. The conflict over Elián González's future was magnified by these historical factors, but it illustrates what may happen in families that polarize over their efforts to keep a child close to both sides of their existential predicament.

Clinicians encounter many families from Mexico, Central America, and the Caribbean who have undergone separation and reunion with children of all ages. After a period of time following reunification, mothers often request professional help with behavior problems and defiance of their authority. Many social and psychological factors contribute to mother-child disconnections and to the development of conflict. From a family systems viewpoint, we can speculate on the family interactions that may contribute to—or help prevent—pernicious family boundary ambiguities. One factor seems to be each family member's positive or negative perceptions of the decision to migrate—that is, how much approval or dissaproval there is among the adults (the biological mother and the caretaker, for example) about the decision to separate temporarily. A related outcome is the quality of the relationship between the migrating parent(s) and the temporary caretakers and whether they all try to be cooperative and inclusive at long distance.

Ongoing studies will help us learn more about how to help families strengthen their resilience in the face of the many individual and relational risks inherent in these separations, yet the separations themselves, especially if prolonged, may pose nearly insurmountable obstacles to family cohesion. Studies of the nature of the ruptured attachments among family members, the loss of shared histories, and the effects of persistent economic stress on family life may yield greater understanding of the problematic "costs of transnationalism" for immigrant families.

DIRECTIONS FOR RESEARCH

Family systems theorists and family therapists have become increasingly aware of the need to incorporate findings from studies of migration, race, and ethnicity in their efforts to develop culturally and socially responsible family systems frameworks and approaches. Likewise, researchers investigating issues in migration, race, and ethnicity would enhance their work by expanding their studies of individuals to encompass three-generational immigrant family units as social systems in cultural transition.

The constructs of *ambiguous loss* and *boundary ambiguity* can be applied to studies of migration and to its intersection with life cycle transitions, including the separations and reunions among all the generations and subsystems of immigrant families. Integrating these concepts may contribute to a better theoretical understanding of risks and resilience for different families in the trajectory of migration. Likewise, exploring *family resilience* helps identify key relational processes that enable families to succeed and make some order and meaning out of the many stresses they encounter.

Narrative approaches and concepts, such as belief systems, incorporate a meaning-making lens that enables people to tell their stories and express their own insights into their unique experiences of loss, hardship and resilience. It is difficult to capture the rich texture of migration through quantitative work alone. The addition of other approaches—qualitative interviews, ethnographic texts, diaries and case studies—may tap the nuances of multiple and unique outcomes. Small-scale comparative and longitudinal qualitative studies, such as following a small group of nuclear families who have undergone separations and reunifications and a similar group of families who have migrated as a nuclear unit, may greatly enrich our understanding of the many dimensions involved in these experiences.

Concepts that belong to the domain of family systems studies have much potential to enhance the themes and findings generated in the domains of immigration research. Integrating the two streams of work would be mutually invigorating and would lead to greater understanding of the impact of migration on Latino families.

REFERENCES

Ainslie, R. C. 1998. Cultural mourning, immigration, and engagement: vignettes from the Mexican experience. In M. M. Suárez-Orozco (ed.), *Crossings* Cambridge, MA: Harvard University Press, pp. 285–305.

Antonovsky, A., and Sourani, T. 1988. Family sense of coherence and family adaptation. *Journal of Marriage and the Family,* 50:79–92.

Bennett, L. A., Wolin, S. J., and McAvity, K. J. 1988. Family identity, ritual, and myth: a cultural perspective on life cycle transitions. In C. J. Falicov (ed.), *Family transitions: Continuity and change over the life cycle.* New York: Guilford Press.

Boss, P. 1991. Ambiguous loss. In F. Walsh and M. McGoldrick (eds.), *Living Beyond Loss: Death in the family.* New York: Norton.

Boss, P. 1999. *Ambiguous Loss: Learning to live with unresolved grief.* Cambridge, MA: Harvard University Press.

Boss, P., Greenberg, J. R., and Pearce-McCall, D. 1990. Measurement of boundary ambiguity in families. *Minnesota Agricultural Experiment Station Bulletin* 593-1990:1–25.

Chavez, L. R. 1985. Households, migration, and labor market participation: The adaptation of Mexicans to life in the United States. *Urban Anthropology* 14: 301–346.

Cohler, B. 1991. The life story and the study of resilience and response to adversity. *Journal of Narrative and Life History* 1:169–200.

Comas-Díaz, L. 1989. Culturally relevant issues and treatment implications for Hispanics. In D. R. Koslow and E. Salett (eds.), *Crossing cultures in mental health.* Washington, DC: Society for International Education, Training, and Research.

Cooper Ramo, J. 2000. A big battle over a little boy. *Time,* January 17.

Du Bois, W. E. B. 1903. *The souls of black folk.* Chicago: McClurg.

Falicov, C. J. 1993. Continuity and change: Lessons from immigrant families. *American Family Therapy Association Newsletter,* Spring:30–36.

Falicov, C. J. 1995. Training to think culturally: A multidimensional comparative framework. *Family Process,* 34:373–388.

Falicov, C. J. 1998. *Latino families in therapy: A guide to multicultural practice.* New York: Guilford Press.

Hansen, D., and Johnson, V. 1979. Rethinking family stress theory: Definitional aspects. In W. Burr, R. Hill, F. Nye, and I. Reiss (eds.), *Contemporary theories about the family. Vol. I: Research-based theories.* New York: The Free Press.

García-Coll, C., Lamberty, G., Jenkins, R., McAdoo, H. P., Crnic, K., Wasik, B. H., and Vásquez García, H. 1996. An integrative model for the study of developmental competencies in minority children. *Child Development* 67:1891–1914.

Garza, R. T., and Ames, R. E. 1972. A comparison of Anglo and Mexican-American college students on locus of control. *Journal of Consulting and Clinical Psychology*, 42:919–922.

Gomez, M. Y. 1999. The grandmother as an enlightened witness in the Hispanic culture. *Psycheline* 3(2):15–22.

Grinberg, L., and Grinberg, R. 1989. *Psychoanalytic perspectives on migration and exile.* New Haven, CT: Yale University Press.

Harwood, R. L., Miller, J. G., and Irizarry, N. L. 1995. *Culture and attachment: Perceptions of the child in context.* New York: Guilford Press.

Imber-Black, E., Roberts, J., and Whiting, R. (eds.). 1988. *Rituals in families and family therapy.* New York: Norton.

LaFramboise, T., Coleman, H. L., and Gerton, J. 1993. Psychological impact of biculturalism: Evidence and theory. *Psychological Bulletin* 114(3):395–412.

Melitto, R. 1985. Adaptation in family systems: A developmental perspective. *Family Process* 24(1):89–100.

Rouse, R. 1992. Making sense of settlement: Class transformation, cultural struggle and transnationalism among Mexican immigrants in the United States. In N. G. Schiller, L., Basch and C. Blanc-Szanton (eds.), *Towards a transnational perspective on migration.* New York: New York Academy of Sciences.

Rueschenberg, E. and Buriel, R. 1989. Mexican American family functioning and acculturation: A family systems perspective. *Hispanic Journal of Behavioral Sciences* 11(3):232–244.

Sabogal, F., Marín, G., Otero-Sabogal, R., Marín, B. V., and Perez-Stable, P. 1987. Hispanic familism and acculturation: What changes and what doesn't. *Hispanic Journal of Behavioral Sciences* 9(4):397–412.

Santos, J. P. 1999. *Places Left Unfinished at the Time of Creation.* New York: Viking.

Shuval, J. T. 1982. Migration and stress. In L. Goldberger and S. Breznitz (eds.), *Handbook of stress: Theoretical and clinical aspects,* 2nd ed. New York: Free Press, pp. 641–657.

Sluzki, C. E. 1979. Migration and family conflict. *Family Process* 18(1):79–92.

Sluzki, C. E. 1983. The sounds of silence. In C. J. Falicov (ed.), *Cultural perspectives in family therapy.* Rockville, MD: Aspen, pp. 68–77.

Suárez-Orozco, C. E. 2000. Identities under siege: Immigration stress and social mirroring among the children of immigrants. In A. Robben and M. Suárez-Orozco (eds.). *Cultures under siege: Violence and trauma in interdisciplinary perspective.* Cambridge: Cambridge University Press.

Suárez-Orozco, M. M., and Suárez-Orozco, C. E. 1995. *Transformations: Immigration, family life and achievement motivation among Latino adolescents.* Stanford, CA: Stanford University Press.

Troya, E., and Rosenberg, F. 1999. "Nos fueron a México: ¿Qué nos paso a los jóvenes exiliados consureños?" *Sistemas Familiares* 15(3):79–92.

Trueba, E. T. 1999. *Latinos Unidos: From cultural diversity to the politics of solidarity.* Lanham, MD: Rowman & Littlefield.

Volkan, V. D. and Zintl, E. 1993. *Living beyond loss: The lessons of grief.* New York: Charles Scribner's Sons.

Walsh, F. 1998. *Strengthening family resilience.* New York: Guilford Press.

Warheit, G., Vega, W., Auth, J., and Meinhardt, K. 1985. Mexican-American immigration and mental health: A comparative analysis of psychosocial stress and dysfunction. In W. Vega and M. Miranda (eds.), *Stress and Hispanic mental health.* Rockville, MD: National Institutes of Health, pp.76–109.

Wright, L. M., Watson, W. L., and Bell, J. M. 1996. *Beliefs: The heart of healing in families and illness.* New York: Basic Books.

Chapter 14

The Plasticity of Culture and Psychodynamic and Psychosocial Processes in Latino Immigrant Families

Ricardo C. Ainslie

In this chapter I wish to delineate some aspects of an intrapsychic or psychodynamic perspective on how acculturative processes work and how they come into play in the lives of Latino immigrants and their families. The degree to which immigrant families are influenced by mainstream American culture varies as a function of myriad factors, such as the location and character of the community within which a family lives and whether the immigrants have come alone, with friends, or with an extended family (see Gutiérrez 1998; Sanchez 1998, and Falicov, this volume). Language variables also affect the way acculturative processes shape experience (Ekstrand 1978; also see Zentella, this volume). These variables have effects that come to reside within us as psychological realities. The mere *fact* of living in America begins to alter one's understanding of oneself and of others almost immediately upon one's arrival. My presenting and illustrating psychodynamic contributions to these processes should be viewed as complementary to the theorizing on acculturation and ethnic identity that takes place in such disciplines as anthropology, psychology, and sociology. However, in exploring these processes, a psychoanalytic perspective has the virtue of yielding a closer reading of their phenomenology as well as of the psychological mechanisms operating within them. I will draw from clinical material (that is, the psychoanalytic situation viewed as an extended dialogue that is particularly suited to exploring the nuances of lived experience), as well as from literature and ethnographic observations.

PSYCHOANALYSIS AND IMMIGRATION

The first comprehensive psychoanalytic treatment of the psychological elements that form the core of the immigration experience is by Grinberg and

Grinberg (1989), psychoanalysts whose work with largely middle-class individuals prior and subsequent to their immigration experiences forms the basis for their observations. Notwithstanding this "sampling" limitation, Grinberg and Grinberg offer important insights into both the psychodynamics of the immigration experience and the factors that mediate them: "Each migration, together with its 'why' and 'wherefore' is inscribed in the history of the family and the individual" (p. ix). They liken the immigration experience to a form of "cumulative" or "tension" trauma (Moses 1978) because of the character of the psychological stresses that are brought to bear. However, one's personal psychological traits and capacities, in combination with the circumstances surrounding the act of immigration (including one's reception by the host country), determine one's adjustment to those stresses.

Psychoanalytic accounts of the psychological impact of immigration typically stand on these two propositions. That is, the psychological resources available to the immigrant, and, in particular, the quality of the immigrant's object relations (the meaning of developmentally defining emotional ties and how these exert a continuing influence on our capacity for engagement with others and with the cultural milieu), are viewed as crucial. Even though immigrants' families may not be physically present, such ties are part of the internalized emotional history that they carry in conscious and unconscious ways. Second, the intensity of the stresses that are brought to bear upon the immigrant by "reality" during the course of the immigration experience are obviously a powerful factor in determining the character of the immigrant's engagement. This is true not only in reference to the initial encounter with the new country, but also in reference to the more enduring, though perhaps more subtle and latent, consequences of the immigration experience (Grinberg and Grinberg 1989).

Prominently featured among the stresses that immigrants encounter are a new culture, a new language, and the threats to one's sense of identity brought about by a profound dislocation (Volkan 1993; Akhtar 1995). The very elements that one takes for granted in day-to-day living in one's country of origin are severely challenged or undermined by the immigration experience. A key additional variable that taxes the immigrant is the emotional implication of losing one's homeland and loved ones and the impact of being separated from these. This loss engenders a process of mourning which, although it varies in intensity, is viewed by psychoanalytic theorists as a universal component of the immigration experience (Garza-Guerrero 1974; Grinberg and Grinberg 1989; Modell 1991; Apprey 1993; Volkan 1993; Akhtar 1995; Ainslie 1998).

ACCULTURATION'S ELUSIVE CONSTRUCTS

Most of the social science research on acculturation and ethnic identity processes fails to look closely at how these stresses are manifested at an individual level or at how cultural variables come into play as part of individual and familial psychodynamics. The construct of acculturation is the primary explanatory tool that researchers use to understand changes in cultural attitudes, values, and behaviors that result from immigration experiences. Researchers initially viewed acculturation as a linear process. It was assumed that immigrants arrived in this country with identities defined in terms of the culture they had left behind and that they gradually relinquished those ties as they became increasingly assimilated (Gordon 1964, 1978). These researchers attempted to track the trajectory of assimilation by assessing immigrants' identification and involvement with the two cultures in question under the assumption that individual immigrants would occupy a position along an assimilative continuum. The implicit goal, at least in early studies, was acceptance by the host culture (Ruiz 1981). This research, like most of the acculturation studies, has produced inconsistent findings (Phinney 1990).

Acculturation researchers also assumed that immigrants who remained caught between cultures—that is, those who lacked the support of their culture of origin and yet were not fully accepted by the host country—would suffer higher levels of stress and alienation (LaFromboise, et al. 1993). Of course, being forced by external pressures as well as changed circumstances to relinquish or weaken the links to one's native culture is itself a source of considerable stress (see Salgado de Snyder 1987, and Fordham 1988). Acculturation researchers have examined a variety of factors or variables assumed to play a role in the effectiveness with which individuals manage the transition from one culture to another. Not unlike psychoanalytic observers, these researchers emphasize both premigration and situational characteristics within the host society (Pierce, Clark, and Kaufman 1978), as well as communicative contexts and abilities (Kim 1979), behavior and values (Szapocznik et al. 1978), and cultural awareness and loyalty (Padilla 1980).

It is likely that the complexity of immigration-related phenomena is due to their rich, fluid, and dynamic character. This makes reliable assessment and conceptual clarity elusive. Take, for example, the following vignette. It might be thought of as a moment in time that captures a multiplicity of cultural factors and experiences in a context that is designed (for economic as much as cultural reasons) to be responsive to a broad range of positions on the Latino-Anglo cultural spectrum.

The Fiesta Market in Austin, Texas, lies just east of the highway that separates predominantly Anglo West Austin from predominantly African American and Latino East Austin. Any day of the week, a spectrum of acculturation is reflected in the market's clientele. For example, there are clusters of men dressed in rural Mexican attire—hats, elaborate leather belts, western shirts and boots—all obviously recent arrivals from Mexico's impoverished rural communities. There are also, shopping individually or in family groups, significant numbers of Latino men and women who are American-born and clearly much more acculturated than the individuals just described. They may be bilingual, or they may not speak any Spanish whatsoever.

An "unobtrusive measures" approach (Webb et al.1966) to the clientele at the Fiesta Market would yield a fairly reliable index of how long each customer has been in the United States. One would simply need to examine the contents of the shopping carts at the checkout counters. For recent arrivals, the Fiesta Market is the closest thing to being home in Mexico. Many of the products that these shoppers would have sought out in their home communities are available on the Fiesta shelves: *Knorr Suiza Caldo en Cubos, Jumex* juices, Mexican brands of canned chiles and salsas and *moles*. The produce section similarly carries everything from *nopales* to *epazote*. More acculturated Latinos are likely to include more traditional American goods in their selections. There are also a number of Anglo Americans in the store buying freshly made tortilla and *mole* or watching the television set that sits above a display of *masa* and dried corn husks where, alternating between English and Spanish, a woman demonstrates the proper technique for making tamales. The more recent the immigrants, the more indistinguishable their baskets from those of their counterparts in any Mexican grocery store. Conversely, the longer one has been in the United States, the greater the likelihood that one's market basket will contain Eggo waffles, frozen French fries, and other typically American foods.

Linguistically, too, one readily sees—or hears—the whole spectrum of acculturation processes. The newer immigrants speak only Spanish to one another and to the market's personnel, who are all bilingual. Other Latinos, however, make their inquiries in English. It is in this linguistic terrain that one begins to fathom the enormous complexity of acculturative processes and the subtle manner in which they come to reside within the lives of individuals and families. Consider the following observation:

A Latino family—a mother, father, son, and daughter—walk into Fiesta, having come directly from church. The ten-year-old daughter spots the watermelons stacked at the entry and implores her father, in English, to buy one. The girl's father answers in Spanish that they do not have time to examine the watermelons (her mother has already headed for the bakery). Ignoring her father, the girl proceeds to pick one up, at which point her nine-year-old brother pushes it out of her hand. In response to that provocation, the girl punches him in the arm, leading the brother to protest loudly to their father, again in English, that she should be punished. Exasperated, the father threatens: "*Les voy a dar una nalgada si no me obedecen*," ("I'm going to give you both a spanking if you don't obey me"). The children get the message, running off to join mother, who is buying *bolillos*.

This family had been in the United States for only six years, they later informed me. The parents spoke little English. Their children, on the other hand, were already immersed in a bicultural world, although linguistically they preferred to speak English (to which their parents did not object). Within this family milieu, there was an obvious, easy cultural fluidity. One can imagine this family's cultural world continuously evolving as each member brings to it cultural contributions from which they collectively fashion their own unique, familial cultural "holding environment" (Modell 1976) that is related to both American and Mexican cultural elements but is simultaneously distinct from them. In fact, although the Fiesta illustration lends itself to the kind of linear acculturation thinking characteristic of earlier assimilation models (Spanish-less, french-fry eating shoppers at one end, English-less, rural Mexican laborers at the other), the experience of the setting is much more culturally dynamic. The family that I have described might also be thought of in those terms, but the subjective experience of its members is certainly more layered and complex than a linear assimilation model permits. The exchanges between father and children, in spite of alternating between English and Spanish, were spontaneous and facile. It was as if this family had developed its own (evolving) hybridized cultural space, drawing from both mainstream American and Mexican elements.

Dissatisfaction with the assumption that individuals must relinquish their cultural or ethnic identities in favor of mainstream cultural identifications has fostered the development of models of acculturation that focus on the characteristics of acquiring a second culture. These models emphasize the idea that individuals can be competent in more than one cultural setting and in different cultural contexts without necessarily developing the values of the majority group (LaFromboise et al. 1993). These more recent bicultural and multicultural models acknowledge that immigrants, like other minority groups, must engage the majority culture; however, they emphasize that it is not necessary to relinquish cultural identities in order to effect that engagement successfully. These models clearly are part of an effort to take into account the complexity of the experience of individuals whose lives require engagement with more than one culture. They also attempt to factor in the marginalizing effects of racism and social devaluation and the way these potent forces problematize the constructs of acculturation and ethnic identity (Phinney 1990).

Although they are useful as conceptual tools that represent a more realistic picture of the complexities of cultural conflicts and how they come to play a role in the lives of immigrants (and other minorities), the various bicultural and multicultural models are nevertheless limited in at least one important way. They lack a nuanced, ideographic understanding of the powerful ways in which individuals utilize cultural elements, psychologically, as part of their engagement with the world around them, including the people who are most important to them. It is here that psychoanalysis and psycho-dynamic ideas can make a contribution that complements the social science literature, while perhaps also illustrating why these concepts can be illusory and can yield inconsistent or contradictory results.

THE PLASTICITY OF CULTURE

From a psychoanalytic perspective, the first experience of culture is created within the familial realities that govern children's lives, especially as reflected in the parent-child relationship (Winnicott 1967). It is within this relational matrix that every child begins to *feel* the character of the kinds of experiences that we term cultural, although it will be years before a child has an awareness of those experiences as *specifically* cultural. To the developing child, what we term cultural is simply that which is in the realm of the familiar—the assumed and received reality that is accepted without reflection or awareness. Psychologically, those elements live within children without the conceptual delineations that eventually suggest to them that there are others whose lives are organized differently.

Children do not begin to understand the construct of cultural experience until they are well into the elementary school years, and not until adolescence do they establish a distinct sense of ethnic identity (Erikson 1950). For example, in a study conducted by Phinney and Taver (1988) only about a third of black and white eighth-graders showed evidence of what the investigators termed "ethnic identity search," as compared to about 50 percent of tenth-graders (Phinney 1990). In other words, a child only gradually realizes that significant elements of the experience that he or she has taken for granted are, in fact, unique to that child's family, neighborhood, or ethnic group.

If we look closely at the ways in which individuals construe and use cultural terms, we see immediately the richness of these processes. From the beginning of life, parents embody and certify a certain version of the cultural universe that exists beyond the child's capacity to perceive or know (Ainslie 1995). We construct an understanding of cultural terms and what they mean or represent through the people around us. However, even families that share a common cultural world with others in their community (such as language, social class, and aesthetic, culinary, and other cultural practices and conventions) often differ from one another in substantive ways when it comes to invoking or defining the components of this shared cultural milieu. Each household activates these components in unique ways, so there may be significant variations among and within families that are assumed to share cultural assumptions. These differences have implications, at the individual and familial levels, for the way elements of acculturation and ethnic identity are understood and engaged.

The Individuality of Acculturation and Ethnic Identity

Take, for example, the family of Carlos (eighteen years old) and his sister Lydia (twenty years old). Their family spent most of the siblings' childhood years in Mexico, where Carlos and his mother were born, although Lydia was born in the United States. Their father is Anglo and was raised in the United States. In this family, patterns of language use reflect the parents' respective backgrounds as well as the respective alliances and identifications that the children have constructed with them. For example, although all four family members speak Spanish, Carlos and his sister speak to their father exclusively in English and to their mother almost exclusively in Spanish. The siblings switch off between the two languages when speaking to one another. When the family is together, however, they speak in English. Such linguistic practices have implications for how each member of the family construes his or her sense of identity and its relationship to ethnic elements (see Zentella, this volume).

In this family, each sibling's relationship to his or her parents plays an important role in defining his or her psychology and has implications for each child's experience of ethnic identity. For example, Carlos is seen as being more like his mother and therefore more Mexican. "I'm more laid back," Carlos told me, indicating that he views this as a Mexican trait. "My sister is more argumentative and impatient, like my father": these are characteristics that the family views as typically Anglo American. Lydia and her father prefer American cuisine, whereas Carlos and his mother prefer spicy, more traditional Mexican food. Carlos believes he has a special alliance with his mother because the two of them were born in Mexico and, to a lesser extent, because they both have darker complexions than his sister and father.

Thus, within this family, differing alliances between the parents and children have translated into enduring family myths about the psychology of each of the children. These alliances are accounted for partly in terms of the geographic circumstances of each member's birth. Similarly, it is a common (though by no means universal) phenomenon in families that older siblings are more identified with fathers and younger ones with mothers. It is unlikely, however, that birth order is the only variable at work in setting these alliances and identifications. What is important in terms of the present argument is the fact that even within the same family, different characteristics readily become infused with cultural and ethnic meanings. In every family, the psychodynamics of family interactions are nearly always affected by the family's response to these cultural meanings. Their intensity, and the way they are managed within the family, may vary widely. For example, in Carlos and Lydia's family there was considerable good-humored banter about these issues; they were playfully engaged as part of the day-to-day family teasing and myth making about each member's dispositions and qualities (see Falicov, this volume, for a related description of culture and family rituals). In other families they may be unspoken or even unconscious. Either way, these cultural terms come to reside as elements of each family member's psychology and therefore inform and influence the character of acculturative processes and the experience of ethnic identity of the different family members.

How Individuals Engage Their Cultural Context

In the family just described, cultural elements operate in highly complex ways, and neither current acculturation models nor current ethnic identity models do them justice. Contributing to this complexity is the plasticity of cultural terms and the ease with which they are appropriated and put to use, psychologically, in day-to-day life. Cultural terms are infinitely malleable, and they adhere readily to a variety of ideas, objects, and actions. In other words, we appropriate cultural terms and utilize them as psychological tools as we engage others around us. In what follows, I want to illustrate this plasticity by showing two very different ways in which individuals engage their cultural context.

We know that children are active participants in the construction of the social realities within their families and, by extension, in the construction of the cultural realities as well (Winnicott 1967). This fact alerts us to the idea that cultural elements can be used in the service of psychological issues or purposes. Cultural terms are thoroughly embedded within the relational universe of those fundamental relationships that define subjective experience from the earliest years (Ainslie 1995). This is what makes culture itself readily conceivable as a medium for the enactment of intrapsychic conflicts and needs. In other words, culture not only shapes and defines us; it also represents a social artifact to be appropriated, manipulated, and engaged in ways that tap the central elements of our psychological experience.

As cultural categories take on increasing significance, especially in adolescence and adulthood, cultural elements become a psychological medium. For example, individuals may use cultural elements as a source of emotional refueling or, alternatively, as a tool for enacting ambivalent feelings against others, depending on the individual's familial history and the character of the psychological issues that are defining her or his life. This brings infinite complexity to our reading or understanding of overt cultural practices and behaviors.

The following illustrations reflect two distinct uses of cultural elements in the management of psychological issues and tensions. In the first, I draw from a novelized autobiography in which the salient feature is the secret holding on to one's culture of origin—and the psychological need answered by doing so.

In Julia Alvarez's *How the García Girls Lost Their Accents* (1991) one of the main protagonists, Yolanda, gives us an unusually vivid illustration of how cultural elements work for us, psychologically speaking. This Latina is away at an Ivy League college and is faced with the sexual expectations of a boyfriend whose advances she is not prepared to accept. "By the time I went to college, it was the late Sixties, and everyone was sleeping around as a matter of principle. By then, I was a lapsed Catholic; my sisters and I had been pretty well Americanized since our arrival in this country a decade before, so really, I didn't have an excuse." (p. 87)

Yolanda feels she has lost a certain protective function afforded by her Latino culture. Having become Americanized, she tells us, she is now vulnerable. In Alvarez's depiction, Catholicism is intimately associated with her pre-Americanized identity. To be Latina and to be Catholic were inseparable. Now, post-Americanization, she must search for other tools to engage her predicament, but our young protagonist is at a loss. She apparently feels that she has given up something essential to who she is or who she wants to be.

Later in this same chapter, Alvarez describes Yolanda's deep disappointment when her boyfriend leaves her.

> Had I been raised with the tradition of stuffed animals, I would have hugged my bear or stuffed dog or rabbit, salting the ragged fur with my tears all night. Instead, I did something that even as a lapsed Catholic I still did for good luck on nights before exams. I opened my drawer and took out the crucifix hidden under my clothes, and I put it under my pillow for the night. This large crucifix had been a 'security blanket' I took to bed with me for years after coming to this country. I had slept with it so many nights that finally Jesus had come unglued, and I had to fasten him back on his cross with a rubber band. (p. 100)

In this instance, her former religious beliefs function as "transitional" activities (Winnicott 1971). That is, they provide her with a culturally prescribed mechanism for restoring emotional equilibrium in the face of stress and dislocation. Under stress, the story's protagonist reinvokes aspects of her pre-Americanized self, rediscovering or reengaging a Dominican Catholic self that had seemingly been buried. In fact, it has simply been latent, acting as an unconscious resource, still available for her in times of stress, need, and regression. It remains a rich resource for a young, "Americanized" Latina college student reeling from the dislocation of a romantic disappointment. The crucifix, a cultural object dense with emotional significance, helps her absorb a significant disappointment.

Alvarez's protagonist illustrates a psychoanalytic reading of one aspect of the complexity of culture and how it works for us. This is the "holding function" (Modell 1976) of culture, and it is the element that is most clearly at work in what I have termed the cultural mourning of the immigrant (Ainslie 1998). In cultural mourning, part of what immigrants must do is come to terms with the dilution or loss of their culture of origin.

The next example illustrates a very different psychological use to which cultural elements can be put. In this case, a young Latina woman whom I will call Laura turns away from her cultural origins for psychodynamic reasons. That is, there is a motivated pushing away, or disidentification, from her cultural roots.

Laura's father had died when she was a preschooler. Prior to her adolescence, Laura, her mother, and her maternal grandmother immigrated to the United States. For most of her life, Laura had had a very close relationship with her grandmother. In contrast, Laura reported having felt significantly estranged from her mother all of her life.

During her initial years in this country, Laura became fluent in English. She was an excellent student. Shortly after Laura's fifteenth birthday, her grandmother suffered a stroke and abruptly died, leaving Laura alone with her mother. Up until the death of her grandmother, Laura had maintained a strong attachment to her Mexican culture. She and her grandmother spoke Spanish almost exclusively, for example. Although the three women all spoke Spanish at home, it was her grandmother, rather than her mother, with whom Laura spent many hours in conversation after school, sometimes helping her grandmother prepare the traditional dishes of Puebla, the region in Mexico from which they had come.

Laura's mother worked long hours away from home and also spent considerable time with a boyfriend, a Latino man who was also from Mexico. Following the death of her grandmother, this boyfriend moved into the home. Laura was sixteen then, and her resentment toward her mother was compounded by the death of her grandmother and the new living arrangements. She started "acting out" significantly, and she became unmanageable at home. For example, she started dressing provocatively—in a style she had always associated with the Anglo girls at school—and she became sexually active. In one of their altercations, when Laura came home at sunrise one morning, Laura's mother told her she was acting like *"una de esas putas gringas"* ("one of those 'gringa' whores") in a shouting match that could be heard by the neighbors. This was, perhaps, the mother's way of situating her struggles with her daughter on a cultural plane. Laura also commented that during that time, when spoken to by her mother she had increasingly taken to responding to her in English, which made her mother angry.

With the death of her grandmother, Laura appeared to have lost not only someone she deeply loved but also a cultural mooring. No doubt there were other forces at work, such as the separation-individuation conflicts of adolescence (Blos 1967) that made Laura receptive to, or vulnerable to, an infusion of Americanizing cultural forces. However, several years later, when she came to see me as a college student, the disidentification aspects of these exchanges were salient: Laura would recount feeling a measure of satisfaction knowing that her mother felt intensely irritated by Laura's increasing Americanization. Laura remembered purposefully inciting her mother by talking to her in English, taking on the trappings of American adolescents, and in other ways actively dissociating herself from her mother. Her mother found these behaviors profoundly disturbing, and they became the focus of constant battles within the household.

CONCLUSION

The ways in which individuals put cultural terms to work in the service of intrapsychic needs and conflicts are always complex. In the first example, Carlos and Lydia come to experience their different relationships with their parents as strongly linked to cultural elements. However, despite the culturally linked banter that was typical of this family, cultural terms appeared to be playfully engaged rather than tension-laden.

In the latter two illustrations, we see a more clearly motivated and perhaps conflictual component in the utilization of cultural characteristics. This difference in tone is probably a function of the affective intensity associated with the circumstances described. Alvarez's character illustrates a reappropriation of cultural terms in the face of emotional stress. Beneath Yolanda's apparent "Americanization" lay strong, enduring attachments and identifications with her Latino cultural roots that continued to function as important psychological resources, even though these were to some extent unconscious.

Laura, on the other hand, utilized what appeared to be a more assimilated posture to distance herself from her mother. She also used this posture as a psychological weapon with which to punish her mother for ignoring Laura when she was growing up. Laura was angry because her mother was not the kind of loving presence in her life that her grandmother had been. To be sure, these psychological elements do not necessarily account for all of the behavior and qualities that Laura evinced at this time in her life. She also had lost her father as a young girl, had lost her grandmother as an adolescent, and had been confronted with the task of mastering a new cultural context on the cusp of adolescence—all significant developmental challenges. Nevertheless, with Laura we can see the manner in which cultural elements are utilized in acting out family dynamics. Laura spent a good part of her adolescence apparently disidentifying from Latino culture, adopting an assimilated stance as part of an unconscious strategy for working out a variety of family conflicts.

The complexity reflected in these illustrations is in part a function of the plasticity of cultural terms. They reveal why it is so difficult to operationalize satisfactorily such concepts as acculturation and ethnic identity. There are nearly always subtle yet powerful undercurrents at work in our construction of cultural terms. This is because cultural elements are inextricably linked to the relationships that have formed us, psychologically speaking. For this reason, cultural terms are ready-made tools, infused with personal meaning and readily pressed into service in our ongoing engagements with the world around us.

REFERENCES

Ainslie, R. C. 1995. *No Dancin' in Anson: An American Story of Race and Social Change.* Northvale, NJ: Jason Aronson.

Ainslie, R. C. 1998. Cultural mourning, immigration, and engagement: Vignettes from the Mexican experience. In: *Crossings: Mexican Immigration in Interdisciplinary Perspectives,* ed. M. Suárez-Orozco. Cambridge, MA: Harvard University Press, pp. 283–300.

Akhtar, S. 1995. A third individuation: Immigration, identity, and the psychoanalytic process. *Journal of the American Psychoanalytic Association,* 43(4):1051–84.

Alvarez, J. 1991. *How the Garcia Girls Lost Their Accents.* New York: Penguin.

Apprey, M. 1993. The African-American experience: Forced immigration and the transgenerational trauma. *Mind and Human Interaction,* 4:70–75.

Blos, P. 1967. The second individuation process of adolescence. *Psychoanalytic Study of the Child,* 22:162–86.

Ekstrand, L. 1978. Bilingual and bicultural adaptation. In *Educational and psychological Interactions.* Malmo, Sweden: School of Education, pp. 1–72.

Erickson, E. 1950. *Childhood and Society.* New York: Norton.

Fordham, S. 1988. Racelessness as a factor in black students' school success: Pragmatic strategy or pyrrhic victory? *Harvard Educational Review,* 58:54–84.

Garza-Guerrero, A. C. 1974. Culture shock: Its mourning and the vicissitudes of identity. *Journal of the American Psychoanaytic Association,* 22:408–29.

Gordon, M. 1964. *Assimilation in American Life.* New York: Oxford University Press.

Gordon, M. 1978. *Human nature, Class, and Ethnicity.* New York: Oxford University Press.

Grinberg, L., and Grinberg, R. 1989. *Psychoanalytic Perspectives on Migration and Exile,* trans. N. Festinger. New Haven, CT: Yale Univerity Press.

Gutiérrez, D. G. 1998. Ethnic Mexicans and the transformation of "American" social space: Reflections on recent history. In *Crossings: Mexican Immigration in Interdisciplinary Perspectives,* ed M. Suárez-Orozco Cambridge, MA: Harvard University Press, pp. 307–35.

Kim, Y. Y. 1979. Toward an interactive theory of communication-acculturation. In D. Nimmo (ed.), *Communication Yearbook 3.* New Brunswick, NY: Transaction Books, pp. 435–53.

LaFromboise, T., Coleman, H. L. K., and Gerton, J. 1993. Psychological impact of biculturalism: Evidence and theory. *Psychological Bulletin.* 114(3):395–412.

Modell, A. 1976. "The holding environment" and the therapeutic action of psychoanalysis. *Journal of the American Psychoanalytic Association,* 24:285–307.

Modell, A. 1991. A confusion of tongues, or, whose reality is it? *Psychoanalytic Quarterly,* 60:227–44.

Moses, R. 1978. Adult psychic trauma: The question of early predispositions and some detailed mechanisms. *International Journal of Psycho-Analysis,* 59:2–3.

Padilla, A. M. 1980. *Acculturation: Theory, models and some new findings.* Boulder, CO: Westview Press.

Phinney, J. S. 1989. Stages of ethnic identity in minority group adolescents. *Journal of Early Adolescence,* 9:34–49.

Phinney, J. S. 1990. Ethnic Identity in adolescents and adults: Review of research. *Psychological Bulletin* 108(3):499–514.

Phinney, J. S., and Taver, S. 1988. Ethnic identity search and commitment in black and white eighth-graders. *Journal of Early Adolescence,* 8:265–77.

Pierce, R. C., Clark, M., and Kaufman, S. 1978. Generation and ethnic identity: A typological analysis. *International Journal of Aging and Human Development* 9:19–29.

Ruiz, R. 1981. Cultural and historical perspectives in counseling Hispanics. In *Counseling the Culturally Different,* ed. D. Sue. New York: Wiley, pp. 186–215.

Salgado de Snyder, V. (1987). Factors associated with acculturative stress and depressive symptomatology among married Mexican immigrant women. *Psychology of Women Quarterly,* 11:475–88.

Szapocznik, J., Scopetta, M. A., Kurtines, W., and Arandale, M. A. 1978. Theory and measurement of acculturation. *Interamerican Journal of Psychology,* 12:113–20.

Volkan, V. D. 1993. Immigrants and refugees: A psychodynamic perspective. *Mind and Human Interaction,* 4(2):63–9.

Webb, E. J., Campbell, D. T., Schwartz, R. D., and Sechrest, L. 1966. *Unobtrusive Measures: Nonreactive research in the Social Sciences.* Chicago: Rand McNally.

Winnicott, D. W. 1951. Transitional objects and transitional phenomena. In *Playing and Reality,* New York: Basic Books, pp. 1–25.

Winnicott, D. W. 1967. The location of cultural experience. In *Playing and Reality,* New York: Basic Books, pp. 95–103.

Commentary

Carola Suárez-Orozco

The chapters in this section represent the work of some of the leading scholars in the field of Latino families. Coming from a variety of disciplines, they have expressed thoughtful insights into the experience of these families. Pierrette Hondagneu-Sotelo brings us a sociological perspective on the growing role of immigrant women in the social reproduction service sector. She describes the concomitant long-term family separations and our consequent need to rethink and expand our definitions of family and motherhood. Family therapist Celia Falicov's many years of experience with Latino families, along with her exhaustive reading of the research literature, leads to her deeply textured theoretical formulation of immigrant families' experiential realties and challenges. She demonstrates the crucial function of preserving cultural practices and what she terms "dual visions" within the family. These practices are essential to maintaining family coherence and to increasing familial resilience in the face of the many ambiguous losses and assaults on identity that come with racial and minority status. Psychologist Ricardo Ainslie offers a psychodynamic perspective on how acculturative processes function in the lives of Latino immigrants and their families. He illustrates how the familial relational matrix is the foundation of a sense of embedded cultural identity and describes the "profoundly transformational" experience of the contacts between the old and new cultures. He demonstrates the psychological function of cultural symbols in the face of dislocation with implications for identity formation. Although these chapters are written from very different vantage points, they show a remarkable convergence of themes.

The papers eloquently articulate the inevitable losses (as well as the gains) that accompany migration. Nearly 40 percent of Latinos in the United States are foreign-born. But immigration does not affect only the first generation.

The rippling effect of migration shapes generations well beyond that initial journey. The process of migration inexorably changes the family. As researchers and service providers, we must understand the effects of migration. How do families typically respond? What are the characteristics that enable them to face the process resiliently? What are the factors that place them at risk? How can we build upon their many strengths?

These papers underscore the centrality of *la familia* for Latinos. The authors also urge us to expand our understanding of just what *la familia* is. Certainly, because much of the research has focused on families of Mexican origin, our deepest understanding is of this group. We now need to move to more nuanced understandings of other Latino families. For each of the major sending areas, what are the characteristics of the "typical family" in the country of origin? "Typical" Caribbean family patterns are quite different from "typical" South American patterns, for example. Once immigrants are in the new setting, which elements of traditional family practices are maintained, which are amplified, and which are discarded?

It is important always to be mindful of socioeconomic status (both before migration and after), urban or rural origins and destinations, and the role of race and color. We cannot expect the same dynamics to be operating in an upper-middle class Uruguayan family from Montevideo as in a poor family from a sugarcane plantation in the Dominican Republic.

We must also ask ourselves just who falls under the rubric of family? Clearly, the mother-father-children definition does not do justice to the significant role of *abuelitas y abuelos* (grandmothers and grandfathers), *madrinas y padrinos* (godmothers and godparents), *tíos y tías* (uncles and aunts), older siblings, and multiple caregivers. How do these more broadly defined families immunize their children against the shocks and stress they may encounter as all too many settle in poverty-stricken, highly segregated neighborhoods where schools are inferior and where violence and discrimination regularly punctuate their lives? As Gary Orfield has found, Latino children today are more likely than any other group of children to enroll in highly segregated, deeply impoverished schools (Orfield and Yun 1999).

How too do families negotiate and process the separations that occur so frequently following immigration? In our ongoing study of immigrant children and families, fully 85 percent of the children in our sample underwent separations of anywhere from a few months to many years (Suárez-Orozco and Suárez-Orozco 2001). How do the families metabolize the temporary as well as the permanent separations that occur? How do family members maintain a psychological presence in the periods of absence?

Two other threads run through these chapters: that of selective assimilation and identity formation. How do families maintain a sense of family coherence in the face of contact with a seductive new cultural context? What characteristics quickly dissipate as a result of contact with the new culture? What others leave their indelible mark, preserving comforting traditions and strengthening affective ties?

Clearly, the goal of all Latino parents is to have their children develop instrumental competencies that will enable them to be successful in the new land. At the same time, they want their children to honor their heritage, to continue to know their language, and to preserve dearly held values: *respeto* (respect), the centrality of the family, the worth of *educación* (education), and traditions of mutuality and collective responsibility. They worry about the toxic elements of American youth culture and the damaging results of discrimination and negative social mirroring. They understand the value of family traditions, of shared language, of freely exchanged *cariños* (words of affection) (Suárez-Orozco and Suárez-Orozco 2001).

Old models of straight-line assimilation assumed that the goal was for immigrants to disappear into the mainstream within a couple of generations. In an earlier era, when most immigrants came from Europe, such a pathway was possible via name changes and loss of accents. But in this race-conscious society, straight-line assimilation is simply not an option for many Latino and Caribbean immigrants. The task at hand, then, is to assimilate, selectively developing the instrumental competencies of the new culture while maintaining many of the instrumental and expressive elements of the old. Helping family members forge these bicultural identities and competencies is a critical role of the family.

This process need not lead to cultural alienation and a feeling of belonging to neither culture. The choice need not be *either* this culture *or* that one. Increasingly, there is recognition that this process can be additive—"both/and." Bicultural individuals can effectively code-switch between cultural contexts, remaining comfortable and competent in both. They may even enter a third space—a "culture of biculturality" that they share with others (from a variety of backgrounds) who have embraced biculturalism. We need a more precise conceptual understanding of the processes involved in the emergence and maintenance of such bicultural identities. The work of our colleagues in the study of bilingualisim might be a useful point of departure from which to develop a more refined understanding of the dynamics of bicultural identity.

As we enter the twenty-first century, social scientists must continue to grapple with the complex issues that Latino families face by using a variety of methodologies. There is an urgent need for interdisciplinary collaborations. Each academic discipline provides some insights into the phenomenon, and each is enriched by perspectives from other disciplines. To date, much of the research on Latino families has been heavily discipline-based. Cross-fertilization of insights, along with collaborative research, is essential for a deeper understanding of the complexities of the Latino family experience. We need continued and sustained conversations like the one exemplified in these chapters.

Although conducting research with this population is challenging, it is a challenge we must embrace. Latino families face many hurdles as they navigate entry into this society and establish a place within it. We must continue to deepen our understanding so that we can, in turn, develop informed interventions to help them thrive. How Latino families and their children fare is critical to this nation's well-being as well as to them.

REFERENCES

Orfield, G., and Yun, J. T. 1999. *Resegregation in American Schools.* Cambridge, MA: The Civil Rights Project, Harvard University.
Suárez-Orozco, C., and Suárez-Orozco, M. 2001. *Children of Immigration.* Cambridge, MA: Harvard University Press.

Chapter 15

Bilingual Infants

Mapping the Research Agenda

Barbara Zurer Pearson

The most important linguistic characteristic of Latino infants in the United States setting is their potential for becoming bilingual. With two languages as their "first language," Latino infants may participate as insiders in two language communities—and even perhaps in a third, the community of bilinguals. But babies don't decide to be or not to be bilingual: their parents (and educational institutions) make these decisions for them. If economic, cultural, and political circumstances warrant the coexistence of multiple languages, then children will learn them. Without compelling reasons to use two languages, children will not learn both. How does bilingual development unfold? When does it happen? And when does it not happen? There begins our research agenda.

The work I will describe was done collaboratively by the Bilingualism Study Group (BSG) at the University of Miami from 1988 to 1997 with co-authors D. K. Oller, V. Umbel, M. Fernández, V. Gathercole, and A. Cobo-Lewis and a cadre of students. We explored a number of topics with bilingual subjects at several ages and in several domains, beginning with a longitudinal study of twenty-four Spanish- and English-learning babies from three months to three years of age, focusing on early vocalizations. Our last project was a large cross-sectional study involving a thousand school-age children. I cannot report on everything our small group covered, much less do justice to the dynamic and expanding field of early bilingual studies. Instead, this chapter focuses on three questions we investigated about bilingual babies—questions that I think are of interest to a more general audience and where we have something new to say. The first question is theoretical, the second normative, and the third practical.

1. Are infants bilingual? Does bilingual development begin with babbling?
2. Are bilingual infants slower in developing their two languages than monolingual infants are in developing one?
3. Is infant bilingualism desirable? Is it more or less desirable than other types of bilingualism?

Before turning to our findings, let us begin with two crucial definitions, those of *Latino* and *infant*. First we can note that an infant is one who, according to the origin that the dictionary gives the word, "does not speak" [*in* (not) + *fare* (speak)]. Because most children begin producing their first words at around one year of age and their first sentences near their second birthday, technically we will be focusing our attention here on linguistic issues for children under the age of two, although infant research often goes to age three, as did ours.

Next, who will be defined as "Latino"? Increasingly, there are large Latino communities in the United States. To what extent those communities differ if they came originally from Cuba or Mexico or Puerto Rico or "other" is not solely, or even most crucially, a language question, so we will not pretend to answer that. The populations in our studies were generally just over half Cuban, about one-quarter other Central American (Dominican, Nicaraguan, Salvadoran), and the rest mixed. There were very few Puerto Ricans and almost no Mexicans. We always carefully recorded the country of origin of the families in our studies and, when possible, tested them for group differences. Within our Miami samples, we never found any group differences favoring one national origin or another. We learned what is reported here largely from Cubans, but we hope to extract more general themes that are applicable to other national origins and even other language groups.

METHOD

Participants were twenty-four Spanish- and English-learning babies, whom we followed from ages three months to thirty-six months. The children were from families of both high and low socioeconomic status (SES), so we were able to study the effects of bilingual upbringing independent of the effects of low SES. In addition, the children were seen in the context of a larger study of mostly children, learning only English and some learning only Spanish, who served as controls. (There were also groups of Down syndrome, deaf, and premature-birth children at comparable ages.) The bilinguals' parents and caregivers brought them to our lab at the Mailman Center of the University of Miami Medical School twice monthly for the first year of life, monthly for the second year, and quarterly for the third. At each observation point, we took two language samples, one in each language environment, and periodically we gave standardized tests or updated diaries that the parents helped us keep for the children.

The BSG made important progress on both the theoretical question and the normative question. We did one of the first longitudinal studies of a *group* of babies, whereas most infant bilingual research had been case studies of linguists' children. But our results are certainly far from the last word on any of these questions, so they remain a valuable basis for our (bilingual) research agenda (of the future).

Question 1: When Does Bilingual Development Begin?

The predominant question in early-bilingualism research is often abbreviated as "One language or two?" Do children start with Language A clearly differentiated from Language B, or is their first language a composite code with elements of A and B mixed together? Given our definition of *infancy* as synonymous with *prelinguistic*, we reinterpreted this question to ask whether bilingual babies' prelinguistic vocalization, or babble, is in two languages. That is, children are first bilingual by virtue of the environment provided to them. When would our subjects *themselves* begin to exhibit language behavior that could distinguish them from monolingual-learning babies? If they did so in the babbling stage, were the two languages developing separately, like "two monolinguals in one person," or were these infants developing a composite code with elements of both languages?

In fact, the earliest utterances of our subjects exhibited specific elements of *neither* language. Their words, taken from both languages being learned, were formed with phonetic elements common to all languages—from the core of universal syllables that babies learning any language are observed to use (Locke 1983). Our subjects' babbles and even their early words could as easily have been Spanish or English. What assigned them to one or the other language was the context and the interpretations of the listeners. Although many phonetic features distinguish adult English from adult Spanish—the r's, the vowel quality, the way the p's, k's, and t's are articulated, for example—the babies had not yet learned to produce them reliably in different ways for the two languages. This was true for the monolingual-learning babies as well as for the bilingual-learning babies, so in infancy there was no basis for concluding either that the bilingual babies were differentiating the languages phonetically or that they were mixing them.

A widely cited study by de Boysson-Bardies and Vihman (1991), comparing five each monolingual English-, French-, Swedish-, and Japanese-learning children between ten and nineteen months, showed "corpus" differences between the language groups at the earliest comparisons. These differences mirrored differences in the adult languages, supporting the authors' claims of early ambient-language effects. These researchers found only differences that could be spotted by intensive examination of a large number of utterances pooled across children, not differences that could be discovered in a single sample. By contrast, our goal was to find ways to distinguish the language background of a child from single samples. Our research design, with a monolingual control group for each language, enabled us to investigate the milestones of phonetic development with monolingual children first. In this way, we could make a prediction of when and where bilingual children would begin to show differentiation of their two language codes. (The details of this work can be found in Navarro et al. 1995 and Navarro 1998.)

The broad conclusion drawn from these experiments was that bilingual development begins to manifest itself not in babbling but in early words. These words, however, do not exhibit distinct phonetic characteristics of English or Spanish segments until toward the beginning of the third year— and even then, they did so only in some utterances, not in all. Furthermore, four of ten children in both monolingual groups showed no recognizable phonetic differentiation at all, nor did a similar proportion among the bilinguals. We propose, therefore, that the effects of bilingual input may not be clearly manifested in the period of infancy. Even so, this does not diminish the importance of nurturing two languages and two cultures in the emerging bilingual of this age, as we shall see when we explore question 3.

Question 2: Are Bilinguals Slower in Developing Their Two Languages Than Monolinguals Are in Developing One?

It is an amazing fact that in the United States, bilingual ability is rarely seen as an asset but more often as a handicapping condition. Mainstream schools spend millions of dollars and thousands of hours of nearly fruitless effort unsuccessfully teaching a second language to high schoolers; the same school systems suppress second-language abilities in preschool and elementary schoolchildren in the name of hastening their acquisition of English. In study after study of language proficiency (chronicled in Hakuta 1986), monolingual children consistently outperform bilingual children— on monolingual measures. Even in the folk psychology of language learning, among bilinguals themselves bilingualism has a reputation for making children slower at learning. Often one hears, "Oh, he's slow, but of course that's because he's bilingual."

We examined this prejudice against bilingualism by doing careful comparisons with adequate scientific controls of bilingual and monolingual language learning at several levels and in various domains. Our studies with infants looked at ways to make appropriate comparisons, even using tools that are inappropriate for the bilingual group. In the process, we developed some comparison techniques that are applicable to similar monolingual/bilingual comparisons at any age.

Our studies of infants showed *no* statistical difference between monolingual and bilingual groups when the comparison groups were adequately matched and when appropriate controls for a monolingual bias in measurement were imposed. But such safeguards are nearly impossible to achieve. There are, to our knowledge, no language measures in common use that are free of a monolingual bias. That is, standardized measures are all referenced to performance of groups of monolingual children, whose total language knowledge is in one language. For bilinguals, such comparisons fail to credit the portion of their knowledge that is known in their other language. Fortunately, in the future, new techniques of early assessment of nonverbal symbolic behavior may be independent of any specific language and of the number of languages being learned (Wetherby and Goldstein 1999), so there is hope that negative assessments of bilingual children will not continue to be made on the basis of faulty measures. But until new measures and/or new norms are available, assessments of bilinguals with monolingual instruments will remain highly suspect.

On the basis of what data do we make claims of bilingual/monolingual equivalence?

The first linguistic milestone in language production is the onset of canonical babbling (CB), or the development of mature syllables (such as "bababa" or "dadada"). In a comparison of forty-four monolinguals and twenty-nine bilinguals, the average age of CB onset was four days apart, in favor of the bilinguals. In further quantitative measures of the proportions of usage of well-formed syllables, no significant differences were found between bilingual and monolingual infants (Oller et al. 1997).

Continuing with phonological development, we saw no difference in groups at age two or at age three on a number of phonological indices. (With a finding of "no difference," it is hard to know whether the children really are the same or our measure is just too poor to show a difference, so we always report other comparisons with the same measures where we did find a difference.) In the case of Navarro et al. (1995), using the measures of correctly produced segments, consonants and vowels, three-year-olds were significantly different from themselves a year later, but the monolingual and bilingual groups were not different from each other at either time point. Not only were they not different, but the means for both were within the 95 percent confidence intervals for the other group.

A comparison of the phonetic skill of the children at twenty-six months (Navarro 1998) at first appeared to favor the monolinguals, but careful examination of the results showed the bilinguals to be keeping pace with their monolingual peers. The group mean for the monolinguals was higher

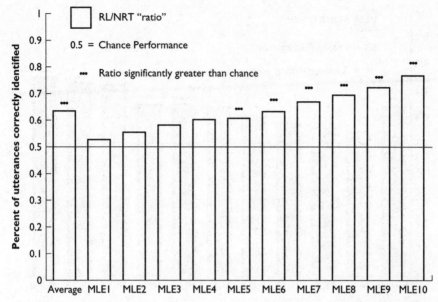

Figure 15.1. "Right Language Given No Right Target" Ratio, Monolingual English

than that for the bilinguals—significantly higher in Spanish and nearly so in English. One might conclude from these figures that bilinguals did not learn language-specific phonology as quickly as monolinguals. But looking carefully at the individual results reveals that the group difference is misleading.

Note in Figures 15.1 and 15.2 that there were six monolingual English-learning children whose performance on this task was better than chance and six monolingual Spanish-learning children with performance above chance. Among the bilinguals, there were *seven* children who did better than chance: three in English only, three in Spanish only, and one in both (Figure 15.3). Thus the bilingual children *were* learning language-specific phonology as fast and as well as monolinguals, but not *twice* as fast.

When we then averaged the "higher language" of each child, the bilinguals' mean was the same as the monolinguals'. By contrast, in the aggregated mean, children who heard English as little as 20 percent of the time contributed to the English score, pulling down that average. At the same time, their higher Spanish scores were being averaged with those of some children who heard hardly any Spanish, so neither the Spanish average nor the English average represented the best performances of all the bilinguals. By contrast, the monolingual scores all represented the best (and only) performance for the children. Hence the necessity to clarify the

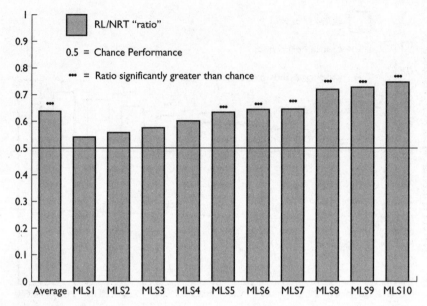

Figure 15.2. "Right Language Given No Right Target" Ratio, Monolingual Spanish

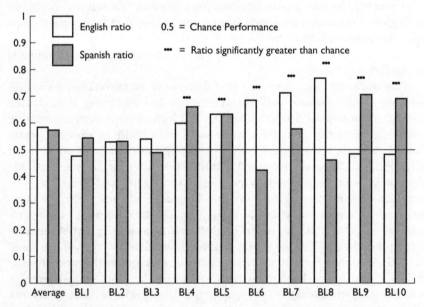

Figure 15.3. "Right Language Given No Right Target" Ratio, Bilingual English and Spanish

basis of the comparison being made and avoid the bias of simple means is clearly shown.

A study of early lexical development also shows equivalent development, while illustrating the problems of monolingual bias in language measures. We used the MacArthur CDI, Communicative Development Inventory, based on early work by Bates and her colleagues (Fenson et al. 1991) and a version by Jackson-Maldonado and Bates in Spanish (1988), which we adapted to reflect terms used in Miami, especially names for games and foods. Although the name of the CDI includes the word "inventory," the instrument does not give an exhaustive list of words that children understand and produce but, rather, it establishes a fixed set of words as a basis, and the standardization helps make the comparison to how other children perform with these same words. All children, including those in the standardization sample, know additional words not on the list, so for everyone the CDI words are only a basis for extrapolation to the whole vocabulary.

We gave our twenty-four sets of parents and caregivers the forms in both languages every two months. Four parents filled out six to ten forms over the course of the study; nine gave us three or four and for the others we have one or two observation points per child. From one of the four papers that came out of this study from 1993 to 1997, we reproduce here the graphs of the groups' productive vocabulary measures averaged across all ages (Pearson, Fernández, and Oller, 1993, p. 106).

Figure 15.4 compares the English and Spanish scores (percentiles averaged across ages) of thirty-three monolingual children's scores (from the parent study). The Spanish and English scores are about the same, and both are substantially lower than the monolingual English scores. Figure 15.5, shows that the differences are less dramatic when only the bilinguals' stronger language is entered into the comparison. But there is more to the story. We had made a mapping of translation equivalents from the Spanish and English forms, and we tracked not just the number of words but also whether a word was known in only one language (a "singlet") or in both (a "doublet") and, further, whether new words learned were already known in the other language. Thus for each child, we had the number of doublets and the number of singlets in each language. With those, we also made two composite scores, Total Vocabulary and Total Conceptual Vocabulary (TCV). Total Vocabulary was found by just adding all the Spanish and all the English, but subtracting when the child used the same word shape in both languages (for example, [wawa] for "agua" and for "water" would be one, whereas "mama" and "mommy" would be two because they were pronounced differently). For TCV, a word was counted only once whether it was known in one or both languages. That gave us the total number of concepts for which the child had a lexical representation (basically, all the words in one language plus the singlets in the other). Note in both charts

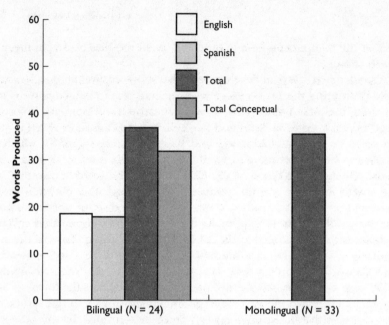

Figure 15.4. Comparison of Monolingual and Bilingual Toddlers'
Productive Vocabulary in English and Spanish, Percentile Rankings
SOURCE: Pearson, Fernández, and Oller 1993, pp. 106–107

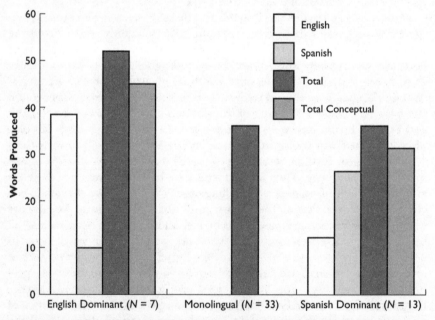

Figure 15.5. Comparison of Monolingual and Bilingual Toddlers' Productive Vocabulary in English and Spanish, English-Dominant and Spanish-Dominant Groups
SOURCE: Pearson, Fernández, and Oller 1993, pp. 106–107

that these totals are the same for bilinguals as for monolinguals. Thus, in expressive vocabulary, as in phonology, when it came to the ability to learn words, the bilinguals did as well as the monolinguals.

However, the fact is that their vocabulary knowledge was distributed in the two languages. They did *not* have primarily doublets. (The infants had about 30 percent doublets. A subsequent analysis estimated doublets at 60 percent at six years, 70 percent at ten, and 90 percent for college students (Pearson et al. 1999). The bilinguals tended to have fewer words in each language than monolingual children of comparable ability had in their single language. By late adolescence, we expect that individuals will know most of their words in two languages (with a few domains reserved for one language or the other), but as children are growing they do not automatically transfer vocabulary knowledge from one language to the other. (We have evidence that they transfer general literacy skills between languages, but vocabulary is more bound to the language in which it is learned.)

In the present assessment climate, bilinguals nearly always look a little behind where they would be if they were monolingual. This is in part because they are being held up to a monolingual standard. "A child should know this many English words (or this many Spanish words) by this age," that number being determined by averages for monolinguals. With monolinguals, however, that number represents the sum total of their knowledge, whereas for the bilingual, it is only a portion of the child's knowledge. (See Pearson 1998 for a fuller explanation.)

I am pleased to report that a language assessment test for bilingual five-year-olds is being developed with funding from the National Institutes of Health. It is being designed *for* bilinguals and will be normed on bilinguals (Iglesias et al. 1999). It should be ready by about 2004. But even with such norms, it will still be hard to know where a particular child should be at a given age. Indeed, when there are so many paths to becoming bilingual, which is the proper reference group for bilinguals? Is the infant bilingual the "true" bilingual? Or should the reference be to the more common pattern where the child begins learning the second language at the start of school? Who should be evaluated with respect to whom? In my opinion, we need multiple reference points for bilinguals, and I believe Iglesias's project is developing them.

Question 3: Is Infant Bilingualism Desirable?

What is the best way to become bilingual? Is infant bilingualism superior to sequential bilingualism? Is bilingualism a desirable goal for all children?

The Spanish-speaking community in this country, by and large, does not appear to favor the idea of infant bilinguals. In all of our studies, if we were not specifically selecting for certain language backgrounds, fewer than 15 percent of our subjects had learned their two languages at the same time from birth, even among children born in this country where presumably both alternatives may be available. Most families speak Spanish to infants in the home (even when they use English with other family members) and let the community teach English later. Is there a logic to this?

In a study of older children (Oller and Eilers, in press, with Multilingual Matters), we found that children who had only Spanish in the home as infants and until age five had stronger Spanish skills at age ten, even without Spanish instruction in school, than children who had been introduced to English before age two. In fact, the group of early bilingual learners had very weak Spanish skills by age ten unless they had significant instruction in Spanish in school. This suggests that the practice of speaking only Spanish in the home may be justified as a strategy for ensuring bilingualism later in life, especially given that there are so few venues in the United States for Spanish instruction for children, even in Miami. Note that in that same study, the English skills of the two groups at age ten were equal.

Ironically, bilingual development suffers the effects of two completely contradictory myths. One myth holds that learning two languages is too hard—that children will learn better and faster if they concentrate on only one language, usually the mainstream language. (In the United States, that's English Only.) The other myth holds that children learn languages so easily and naturally that nothing special needs to be done to foster the growth of two languages. When parents believe this way, they may fail to provide the proper bilingual learning circumstances and then be surprised or disappointed when children are not fully bilingual. The first myth is especially prevalent in cases of handicap. It certainly makes some common sense, but there are not, to our knowledge, any data to support it.

The study of toddler word learning described above, although it is too small to answer the question statistically, may point the way toward a guideline. All the families recruited for our longitudinal study of bilingual infants had planned to expose their children equally to Spanish and English from birth, and the circumstances of their households seemed adequate to support their intention. In fact, almost no one did that, most favoring one language or the other in their households. Nine of the twenty-four families experienced shifts in the balance between the languages spoken in the house (occasioned by a change of jobs, for example, or by changes in the relatives living in the house) and we carefully charted those shifts.

Tracking both environment and vocabulary growth over time, we found an identifiable and proportional effect of amount of exposure in a language on the children's learning in that language. The number of hours per week spent in interaction with speakers of a given language was directly reflected in the balance of words learned in each language (Pearson et al. 1997). It was not a perfect correlation, because there are affective factors

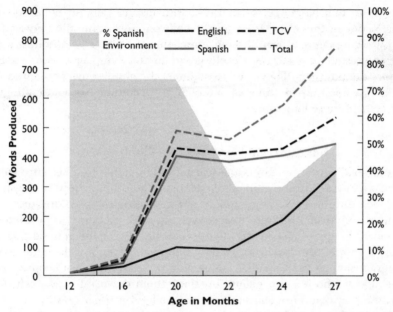

Figure 15.6. "Child 9" Language Development in English, Spanish, and Both Languages Together Over Time
SOURCE: Pearson and Fernández 1994, p. 632)

involved in the use of the languages, and it took more exposure in Spanish than in English to get an equivalent percentage of vocabulary. When changes took place, we observed about a two-month lag before we saw the effect. That may in part be an effect of how frequently we were making our observations, but Figure 15.6 (Pearson and Fernández, 1994, p.632) shows how dramatic the effect could be.

One can see from this chart that a dramatic drop in percent of Spanish input between twenty and twenty-two months resulted in a halt to the child's vocabulary growth in Spanish in that reporting period. The associated rise in English input did not seem to have an effect during that reporting period but was seen in the following period, when the child began to add English words. This child's graph shows the most dramatic and most visible changes (of the nine children in our sample with changes in their input), but all children's graphs showed a clear response to those changes.

At every level of exposure to the languages, the children learned in both languages, but 20 percent of the child's time (about seventeen hours per week) was rarely enough for it not to be a struggle. Those children were never as comfortable in that language, and it was difficult to collect our full sample in that language. By contrast, with just 30 percent of the child's time in one or the other language, the children were generally comfortable in both languages. It would seem, then, that if parents or administrators are interested in fostering development in two languages, they cannot ignore the numbers. They need to engineer the child's environment so she or he spends enough time in interaction, preferably with monolingual speakers of those languages.

Was Any Child Unable to Learn Two Languages?

In our small study, no. Everyone learned bilingually—to a certain extent. Even a Down syndrome child and a deaf child in other groups of the study were learning in both languages, at age-appropriate levels for Down syndrome and deaf children, respectively. Would everyone who tried to become bilingual succeed? We do not have figures for the general population of people who "tried to become bilingual." Even a well-documented program such as the Canadian immersion program does not keep records of children who left the system, breaking them down into those who left because they could not learn and those who left for other reasons.

Even with our self-selected sample of highly motivated families, there were a number of special cases where the child may not end up bilingual despite being "successfully" bilingual as an infant. One child developed at age three a progressive hearing loss that was not diagnosed until she was almost five. She was delayed in English at that point, and her parents were working hard to enrich her English environment at the expense of Spanish. We also had one child whose number of words in both languages combined was below the criteria for suspected language delay: fewer than fifty words at age 2 (Rescorla 1989). As it happened, this child had a language-delayed older brother who had given up trying to learn Spanish when he went to school and needed to expend so much effort learning to read. There is a good chance that our subject will also be a language-impaired child and will leave his Spanish behind. Just as the brother's difficulties did not disappear when he dropped Spanish (because the Spanish did not cause the impairment) it is unlikely that our subject's difficulties will disappear either. A third child (Figure 15.6) was a star lexically in both languages, but his father felt excluded from the child's Spanish activities and at 24 months rearranged the linguistic organization of the child's life to include little Spanish.

In a variety of circumstances, then, bilingual learning can lose out. A controlled study of the success rates of bilingual efforts, though, is not likely, because random assignment to groups for life is not an ethical option open to scholars.

The natural experiment, though, is ongoing, and Latino infants are major participants. Large political and social forces will determine how language groups coexist and prosper. And the fate of the languages will be like a barometer of those relations. Language scholars have a role to play in this scenario. On a linguistic level, they work to understand the phenomenon of bilingualism for itself and for what it tells us about language development in general. They also have a social responsibility to investigate the accuracy of received opinions and prejudices and to provide tools for educators and language pathologists who work with bilinguals.

It is an unspeakable crime against humanity willfully to deprive a child of the natural environment for learning a first language. Fortunately, it is also very difficult to do so, and we have only rarely witnessed a case like that of Genie, a feral child in 1970s Los Angeles (Curtiss 1977; Rymer 1993). It is nowhere near so heinous to deprive a child of the opportunity to develop a second or third language. Still, it makes no sense not to provide the little extra that it takes to foster in children development of the second language when it is within our power, especially when that language can carry such a large portion of our cultural heritage and can give them so much pleasure.

NOTE

This research was supported in part by grants 5 RO1 DC00484, NIH/NIDCD, and 1 RO1 HD30762/01 NNIE-SBIR to D. K. Oller and R. E. Eilers.

REFERENCES

Curtiss, S. 1977. *Genie: A psycholinguistic study of a modern-day "wild child"* New York: Academic Press.

De Boysson-Bardies, B., and Vihman, M. 1991. Adaptation to language: Evidence from babbling and first words in four languages. *Language* 67, 297–319.

Fenson, L., Dale, P. S., Reznick, J. S., Thal, D., Bates, E., Hartung, J. P., Pethick, S., and Reilly, J. S. 1991. *Technical manual for the MacArthur Communicative Development Inventories.* San Diego, CA: San Diego State University.

Hakuta, K. 1986. *Mirror of language: The debate on bilingualism.* New York: Basic Books.

Iglesias, A., Pena, E., Gutierrez-Clellen, V. F., Bedore, L., and Goldstein, B. 1999. *Development of a language test for bilingual Spanish-English-speaking children.* Symposium presented at the Annual Meeting of the American Speech, Language, and Hearing, and Association, San Francisco.

Jackson-Maldonado, D., and Bates, E. 1988. *Inventario del desarrollo de las habilidades communicativas* [Communicative Development Skills Inventory]. San Diego: University of California, Center for Research in Language.

Locke, J. 1983. *Phonological Acquisition and Change.* New York: Academic Press.

Navarro, A. M. 1998. *Phonetic effects of the ambient language in early speech: Comparisons of monolingual- and bilingual-learning children.* Ph.D. diss., University of Miami, Interdepartmental.

Navarro, A. M., Pearson, B. Z., Cobo-Lewis, A. B., and Oller, D. K. 1995. *Assessment of phonological development in bilingual children at age 36 months: Comparison to monolinguals in each language.* Paper presented at the annual meeting of the American Speech, Language, and Hearing Association, Orlando, FL.

Navarro, A. M., Pearson, B. Z., Cobo-Lewis, A. B., and Oller, D. K. 1998. Identifying the language spoken by 26-month-old monolingual- and bilingual-learning babies in a no-context situation. In *Proceedings of the 22nd Annual Boston University Conference on Language Development*, Vol. 2, A. Greenhill, M. Hughes, H. Littlefield, and H. Walsh, eds. Somerville, MA: Cascadilla Press, pp. 557–568.

Navarro, A. M., Pearson, B. Z., Oller, D. K., and Cobo-Lewis, A. B. 1998. Where's the drift in "babbling drift?" Or, identifying the language spoken by 26-month-olds in a no-context situation. Poster presented at the American Association for Applied Linguistics Annual Meeting, Seattle, WA.

Oller, D. K., and Eilers, in press (with Multilingual Matters). *Language and literacy development in bilingual children.* Poster Symposium presented at the Society for Research in Child Development, Biennial Meeting, Washington, DC.

Oller, D. K., Eilers, R. E., Urbano, R., and Cobo-Lewis, A. B. 1997. Development of precursors to speech in infants exposed to two languages. *Journal of Child Language* 24:407–425.

Pearson, B. Z. 1998. Assessing lexical development in bilingual babies and toddlers. *International Journal of Bilingualism* 2:347–372 (special issue on bilingual acquisition, ed. A. DeHouwer).

Pearson, B. Z., and Fernández, S. 1994. Patterns of interaction in the lexical growth in two languages of bilingual infants and toddlers. *Language Learning* 44: 617–653.

Pearson, B. Z., Fernández, S., Lewedag, V., and Oller, D. K. 1997. Input factors affecting lexical learning by bilingual infants (ages 10 to 30 months). *Applied Psycholinguistics* 18:41–58.

Pearson, B. Z., Fernández, S., and Oller, D. K. 1993; 1995. Lexical development in simultaneous bilingual infants: Comparison to monolinguals. *Language Learning* 43:93–120. Reprinted in *Lexical issues in second language learning*, ed. B. Harley. Toronto, Canada: OISE, pp. 31–57.

Pearson, B. Z., Umbel, V. M., Andrews de Flores, P., and Cobo-Lewis, A. B. 1999. Measuring cross-language vocabulary in childhood bilinguals at different stages of development. Poster presented to the 1999 Texas Research Symposium on Language Diversity, Austin, TX.

Rescorla, L. 1989. The Language Development Survey: A screening tool for delayed language in toddlers. *Journal of Speech and Hearing Disorders*, 54:587–599.

Rymer, R. 1993. *Genie: An abused child's flight from silence.* New York: HarperCollins.

Wetherby, A. and Goldstein, H. 1999. *The First Words Project: How early can we identify children with communication disorders?* Symposium presented at the Annual Meeting of the American Speech, Language, and Hearing Association, San Francisco, http://firstwords.fsu.edu

Chapter 16

Latin@ Languages and Identities

Ana Celia Zentella

In the autumns of 1999 and 2000, when the New York Yankees won what my baseball-addicted husband refers to as the "World Serious," Puerto Ricans on the island and throughout the United States celebrated the feats of native sons Bernie Williams and Jorge Posada, while Panamanians cheered for Mariano Rivera and Cubans boasted about el Duque. Similarly, Latin@s everywhere rooted for their compatriots on other teams, often crossing leagues to do so. And when Sammy Sosa fought his home-run battles with Mark McGuire, they crossed national boundaries in their proud support of Sosa, a Dominican. Latin@s also cross national boundaries to unite with U.S. society as a whole in their love of baseball and other national pastimes and, principally, in their support of democratic institutions. Shifting among several identities—for example, one linked to a specific nation in Latin America, another linked to a pan-Latin@ formation in the United States, another linked to the ideals of the United States, and still others identified with local cities, neighborhoods, *bloques* (blocks), and individual gender, racial, and class classifications—is commonplace for U.S. Latin@s. This in spite of the fact that critics denounce hybrid identities as evidence of cognitive confusion, as watered-down versions of one culture or another, and even as unpatriotic abandonment of a core culture (Hirsch 1988).

Language, the medium through which all culture is learned and transmitted, is a powerful lens through which we can detect the ways in which Latin@s use different voices to speak as members of different groups at different times, and even at the same time. The varieties of Spanish spoken by national-origin groups serve as nationalist flags that symbolize each group's unique identity as Puerto Rican, Mexican, Dominican, Cuban, and so on. Regional borders surface in remarks such as "She speaks Puerto Rican" and

"I speak Dominican," as though separate languages existed. Those borders recede when the Spanish language is embraced as a common denominator, to such an extent that *Spanish speakers* or *hispano hablantes* may be less problematic as a generic group label than *Latin@* or *Hispanic*.[1] In the United States, Latin@ bilinguals often blur the boundaries between Spanish and English to facilitate the adoption of new words and ways of speaking that reflect new ethnic and racial identities. To help us understand how linguistic codes help construct identities, including how and where the boundaries between linguistic codes are drawn, I have advocated an anthropolitical linguistics (Zentella 1995; 1997). Anthropolitical linguistics assumes that the ways in which Latin@s in the United States speak English and Spanish cannot be divorced from socioeconomic and political realities. Of particular importance is the dominant language ideology that equates working-class Spanish-speaking Latin@s with poverty and academic failure and defines their Spanish-English bilingual children as linguistically deficient and cognitively confused. Urciuoli's insightful study of New York Puerto Ricans documents how Spanish and any traces of Spanish in a speaker's English "assigns working class speakers to a race/class location in which people are assumed to be ignorant, disordered, and all the other stereotypes associated with the working class, thus robbing them of symbolic capital" (Urciuoli 1996). The resulting conflict is a classic example of what Puerto Ricans would describe as *palo si voga, palo si no voga* ("damned if you do, damned if you don't").[2] Whether you speak Spanish or abandon it for a Latin@ variety of English, you cannot escape being identified as disordered and ignorant, in need of control. Is there no way out? How do immigrant parents and their children in *barrios* across the nation respond to linguistic ideologies of purity that translate into social discrimination? In search of acceptance as "real Americans," many strive to acquire a variety of English that does not identify them as Latin@ and to leave Spanish behind. But others are throwing off straitjacket notions about "good English," ideal bilinguals, and inviolable language boundaries and cultural identities. They are telling us about being Latin@ *in* Latin@.

What Latin@s are saying, and how they are using their languages and dialects in a Latin@ way to say it, is a joint product of (1) linguistic behaviors and attitudes that are brought from the homeland and transformed in the new land and (2) others that are created in the United States. As Celia Falicov (this volume) points out, adaptation to the trauma of migration involves the creation of cultural spaces and "pockets of remembrance" that facilitate continuity *and* change. Latin@ languages reflect and transmit this new "dual vision." The variety of Spanish that is shared with compatriots eases the struggle of adaptation, while a growing familiarity with diverse types of Spanish and English smoothes their integration into larger communities. But adaptation and integration, so essential to any group's well-being, are severely impeded by a Hispanophobia in the dominant society that undermines the cultural and linguistic capital of Latin@s via a process of *chiquita*-fication, or diminishment and dismissal of their verbal repertoire. (Zentella 1995; 1997). In studies of Latin@s throughout the United States, two aspects of *chiquita*-fication are a common motif: the dissing of dialects and Spanglish bashing.[3]

THE *CHIQUITA*-FICATION OF VARIETIES OF U.S. SPANISH

"Dissing" the Dialects

The myth that "the only real Spanish is spoken in Spain" is widely propagated, even by language teachers and others who would never dare claim that "the only real English is spoken in England." Such a myth ignores the extent of dialectal diversity that exists in Spain and dismisses and disrespects about 90 percent of the world's Spanish speakers, some 400 million people throughout Latin America, as though their dialects were not rule-governed and subject to standardization by the Royal Spanish Academy. The United States is the fourth largest Spanish-speaking country in the world, and it too has a local chapter of the Royal Academy. Mexican and Caribbean Spanish varieties predominate; 66 percent of U.S. Latin@s are of Mexican origin, and another 18 percent are from Puerto Rico, Cuba, and the Dominican Republic. The principal contrasts between Mexican and Caribbean Spanish correspond to those between the *tierras altas* ("highlands") and the *tierras bajas* ("lowlands") of Latin America. The lowlands or coastal areas include the Caribbean, the Atlantic and Pacific coasts of Mexico, Central America's Pacific coast, Venezuela, and the Pacific coast of South America from Colombia to northern Chile. The highlands are the remaining, interior regions. A renowned Chilean linguist, Angel Rosenblat, distinguished these dialect areas, somewhat comically, on the basis of diet:

> Yo las distingo, de manera caricaturesca, por el régimen alimenticio: las tierras altas se comen las vocales, las tierras bajas se comen las consonantes. (Rosenblat 1970, p. 39)
>
> (I distinguish them, in a caricature-like manner, by their diet: the highlands eat [drop] their vowels, the lowlands eat their consonants.)

Specifically, in the Caribbean and throughout the lowlands, especially in informal speech, /s/ may be aspirated when it is in syllable-final position, as in (1a) following, where aspiration is indicated by /h/, or it may be deleted, as in (1b). Deletion is highest in the Dominican Republic, where it is favored in formal and informal speech by all social groups (Terrell 1982). These pronunciations contrast with the retention of /s/ at the end of syllables in the interior of Mexico, Central America, and South America (see 1c, below).

Pues, es un placer estar con ustedes.
(Well, it's a pleasure to be here with you [plural].)

(1a) /pueh eh un plaser ehtar con uhtedeh/
(1b) /pue e un plaser etar con utede/

Caribbean Spanish has been labeled "radical" and is stigmatized because of its final-segment deletion, unlike the "conservative" dialects of Bogotá, Mexico City, Lima and other highland centers (Guitart 1982). But Puerto Ricans, Dominicans, and Cubans retain unstressed vowels that highlanders contract. It is easy to identify *DF-eños* (people from the Distrito Federal— that is, Mexico City) because they produce mere traces of most vowels, symbolized by the apostrophes in (1c):

(1c) /p' 'sun pl'ser 'star con 'sted's/

Another irony is that although the aspiration or deletion of final /s/ is discredited, the aspiration of /s/ at the beginning of a syllable or between vowels (initial /s/), which occurs in the central highlands of Colombia, is ignored. Even highly educated *cachacos* (Colombians from the central highlands) say /nohotros/ instead of /nosotros/ for *nosotros* ("we") and aspirate the first /s-/ in words with more than one, for example, *asesino* /ahesino/ ("assassin") (Lipski 1994). Indeed, "...central Colombia is unique in the Spanish-speaking world in reducing /s/ more frequently in syllable-initial than in syllable-final position" (Lipski 1994, p. 209). Nor is Colombia free of final /s/ aspiration or deletion, both of which are common in the *costeño* ("coastal") Spanish spoken in Cartagena and Barranquilla on the Caribbean coast and along the Pacific coast. Yet Colombians in New York City, most of whom are not from the coast, think very highly of Colombian Spanish and very little of Caribbean Spanish, as we demonstrate below.

The tyranny of syllable-final /s/ exemplifies the semiotic processes of iconicity, recursiveness, and erasure that Irvine and Gal have identified as fundamental in the shaping of language ideologies. Unearthing those processes reveals "the ideas with which participants and observers frame their understanding of linguistic varieties and the differences among them, and map those understandings onto people, events and activities that are significant to them" (Irvine and Gal 1999, p. 35). Linguistic differences as simple as the presence or absence of an /s/ at the end of a syllable can become identified with superiority or inferiority, and those judgments are extended to related features and speakers in a recursive fashion. The icon of "good/pure/real Spanish" is sustained by praising speakers of dialects that retain syllable-final /s/ and criticizing those who do not. Other differences that challenge the validity of the icon, even one as closely related as the aspiration or deletion of syllable-initial /s/, are erased, and features and speakers aligned with the dominant icon are foregrounded and ascribed positive attributes, in contrast with their deviant "opposites." The origins of this particular icon can be traced to the history of the arrival of Spanish in the Americas.

The phonology of Caribbean Spanish and that of other coastal areas are direct descendants of the pronunciations brought to Caribbean ports by Spanish sailors and colonizers from the ports of southern Spain and the Canary Islands in the late fifteenth to nineteenth centuries. It still sounds similar to what is spoken in Andalucía and Las Canarias today. The regions of Mexico and Central and South America that built their principal centers of power upon the cities of the Indians they conquered were most influenced by Indian languages and by the northern Spanish dialects of administrators, dialects that retained syllable-final /s/ (Canfield 1981). Add to this picture several centuries of an intense African slave presence in the coastal/lowland areas, and the roots of the iconicity of a devalued Caribbean Spanish and a prestigious highland Spanish become evident. Today, racial and class profiles continue to play a significant role in the recursiveness of positive or negative linguistic and cultural identities and in the erasure of features that do not fit the stereotypes. For example, the Spanish of light-skinned Cubans who are financially well off does not suffer the same sweeping condemnation as that of darker, working-class Puerto Ricans or Dominicans, despite their linguistic similarities (Zentella 1990a). Social factors often determine linguistic judgments in highly selective and prejudicial ways.[4]

The levels of linguistic security or insecurity that speakers of Spanish experience as a result of popular stereotypes about the dialects of their homeland can have important repercussions for their sense of self-worth and group pride. Accordingly, speakers of stigmatized dialects may try to adopt a more prestigious variety, or shift to English altogether, unless other, more powerful mitigating factors are at work. Dominican linguistic insecurity is a case in point. More than three-fourths (80 percent) of a diverse group of Dominicans in New York City ($n = 50$), when asked—by a compatriot—whether Dominican Spanish should be taught in United States schools, disagreed. Most agreed with the majority of the Cubans ($n = 36$) and Puerto Ricans ($n = 82$), who thought that it would be best to teach a more general Spanish than that of their group (Zentella 1990a). But the primary reason more than one-third of the Dominicans gave was that Dominican Spanish is *incorrecto* ("incorrect") or *malo* ("bad"). In stark contrast, the majority (64 percent) of the Colombians ($n = 51$) thought that Colombian Spanish should be taught in United States schools, principally because, in their view, it is correct Spanish. Only 2 percent offered a negative opinion of their dialect as a reason for not teaching it in the schools (Zentella 1999).

Dominicans and Colombians also displayed the highest levels of linguistic insecurity and security, respectively, when they were asked whether they would consider it a compliment if they were told they spoke Spanish like one of their group. Only 3 percent of the Colombians said they would not consider it a compliment, but 15 percent of the Dominicans said they would be offended. These data suggest that Dominicans are likely to adopt a conservative dialect or drop Spanish altogether to avoid being identified as Dominican. However, all of the Dominican consultants spoke like Dominicans throughout their hour-long interviews, and 94 percent said that they wanted their children to learn English and Spanish.

Sociolinguists often find that the overt expression of negative attitudes toward a stigmatized dialect conflicts with covert attitudes that favor its perpetuation (Labov 1972; Eckert 1989; Macaulay 1997). Toribio (2000) suggests that Dominicans, who are predominantly mulattoes, may hold on to Spanish more than other groups because Spanish serves to identify them as non-Haitian in the Dominican Republic and as non–African American in the United States. In my experience, in New York and other northeastern cities, Dominican Spanish also serves to unite Dominicans and to distinguish them from other dark and poor Caribbean Spanish speakers and from English-speaking Puerto Ricans.[5] Exceptions are not hard to find. There are young Dominicans who choose a "cool" black identity and speak only AAVE (African American vernacular English); one Dominican teenager told her Dominican boyfriend that she was glad he did not speak Spanish because "I can't stand hicks." In the end, speakers shape ideologies brought from the homeland in ways that help them make sense of situations and groups they encounter in specific United States locales. All the changes wrought in different areas and eras, and by different generations, genders, classes, or races, have yet to be analyzed for any one group of Latin@s. The partial portraits that we do have indicate that some members of the second generation learn to communicate in ways that resist the "*chiquita*-fication" of their language skills.

New York Puerto Ricans from El Bloque

Being raised in *el bloque* ("the block"), a working-class Puerto Rican community in *El Barrio*/East Harlem, is a bilingual and multidialectal experience (Zentella 1997). Between 1979 and 1989, the children of *el bloque* acquired several dialects of English and Spanish, principally the New York Puerto Rican English of the second generation (which is not limited to Puerto Ricans but is, rather, the way of speaking of most second-generation working-class Latin@s in the northeast), and the AAVE of their black friends. Some learned standard New York English as foster children in mid-dle-class homes in Long Island, and a few learned working-class Italian American English from the descendants of *El Barrio*'s heyday as an Italian stronghold. In Spanish, *el bloque's* children interacted primarily with work-ing-class speakers of popular Puerto Rican Spanish, although several resi-dents with high school diplomas from the island also spoke standard Puerto Rican Spanish. In addition, some *bodegueros dominicanos* ("Domini-can grocery store owners") spoke popular Dominican Spanish, and for a while in the early 1980s, unexpected arrivals from Mariel added their *cubanismos* ("Cuban expressions") to the bilingual and multidialectal mix. Since the late 1980s, Mexicans from Puebla have been moving into *El Barrio,* and they have been converting many *cuchifrito* (traditional Puerto Rican food) stands into *taquerías* ("taco stands").[6] Mexican–Puerto Rican mixes in foods, families, and languages are under way, such as those that took place on a small scale when my Puerto Rican mother and Mexican father met and married in Harlem in the late 1920s, and those that have been occurring more recently, on a larger scale, among Mexicans and Puerto Ricans in Chicago.

Children in neighborhoods like *el bloque* learn to negotiate the linguistic diversity that surrounds them in keeping with the central cultural norm of *respeto* ("respect"), which requires that the young defer to their elders and accommodate the linguistic abilities of their addressees wherever possible. Those who are in regular contact with monolingual Spanish and English speakers learn to switch rapidly from one to the other. For example, a bilin-gual eight-year-old told her English-dominant friend that a younger boy had borrowed her bicycle without permission. Then she complained to the boy's mother in Spanish, challenged the child's countercharge in English, and finished off her protest—directed at the child and his mother—in Spanish. This ability to alternate among several linguistic codes in rapid succession for different people is extended to in-group talk with the same person, a fellow bilingual, and switching becomes their badge of member-ship in a bilingual community. Bilinguals may switch languages for com-plete sentences or for parts of a sentence, often performing what Le Page and Tabouret-Keller (1985) refer to as "acts of identity." Mixing several varieties of Spanish and English is a graphic way of showing that they have a foot in more than one world, and they are most at ease when they can incorporate all of them. A criticism like "Blanca be actin' big an' bad" in the midst of a Spanish and English conversation clearly calls upon the speakers' knowledge of African American models of tough or cool behav-ior, as well as on the grammatical meaning of habitual *be.* Similarly, the insertion of *Bendito* (literally "blessed") conveys a traditional Puerto Rican lament, and *Qué vaina* (akin to "What a drag") and *Andale* (akin to "OK") touch base with Dominicans and Mexicans, respectively. Given the richness of the identifications that can be incorporated, it is no wonder that some

Latin@s are following the lead of creative writers by embracing both the practice of "Spanglish"—and the term itself—with pride.

SPANGLISH BASHING

Ironically, while educators look for ways to incorporate multiculturalism in the classroom, the linguistic dexterity that children from communities such as *el bloque* bring to school, which reflects a lived multiculturalism, is misunderstood and maligned by teachers who usually have a more limited verbal repertoire than their students. Second-generation Latin@s are accused of not knowing Spanish *or* English and of corrupting both. Code switchers are characterized as lazy, sloppy, and cognitively confused (see Acosta-Belén 1975; Walsh 1991), and debates about semilingualism and alingualism are revived (see Skutnabb-Kangas 1984). Pejorative references to "Spanglish" (or to "Tex-Mex" in the Southwest) conjure up images of a linguistic mish-mash, a deficient code spoken by deficient speakers and responsible for their academic failure. At the root of the problem is a view of languages merely as separate sets of rules, not as flexible symbolic systems of communication that are enmeshed with the speakers' identities and the communicative context.

This narrow view of "bilingualism as code" instead of "bilingualism as practice," to use Urciuoli's (1985) terms, is complemented by an idealized view of bilinguals that harks back to Weinreich's outdated opinion that: "the ideal bilingual switches from one language to the other according to appropriate changes in the speech situation but not in an unchanged speech situation and certainly not within a single sentence" (Weinreich 1968, p. 73). But is the ideal bilingual really no more than a traffic cop who polices languages, keeping them in separate lanes? Is she or he just two monolinguals joined at the neck and sharing one tongue? In reality, there are multiple ways of "doing being bilingual" (Auer 1984, p. 7). In New York City's Puerto Rican community, and throughout the United States wherever there is intense and prolonged contact among distinct networks and generations of Latin@s, it is precisely the ability to use English and Spanish in the same sentence and situation that identifies the most effective bilinguals (Gumperz and Hernández-Chávez 1975; Poplack 1980; Otheguy, García, and Fernández 1989; Valdés 1976, 1981; Zentella 1983). In these communities, the rhythm and rules of "doing being bilingual" require skills reminiscent of those of an expert *salsa* dancer or basketball player. If they are acquired in infancy, as part of Bilingual First Language Acquisition (see De Houwer 1995), then by the elementary school years new partners share a wealth of moves and can follow each other without missing a linguistic beat or dropping the conversational ball.

Concerned about the damage being done to Latin@s by negative evaluations of their ways of speaking, sociolinguists have spent decades trying to allay the fears of parents, teachers, pediatricians, and speech therapists. We have identified complex linguistic constraints and syntactic hierarchies that Latin@ code switchers of all backgrounds acquire and honor and have documented how Spanglish speakers ably juggle two grammars without harming either one. (Poplack and Sankoff 1988; Lipski 1978, 1985; Zentella 1983). Indeed, we have shown that rule-governed code switching can serve as a diagnostic of normal language development. (For example, the only child of *el bloque* who did not comply with the linguistic constraints that the code switchers acquired was also the only one evaluated as language-disabled by school psychologists). But our efforts to combat unjust evaluations of bilinguals based on monolingual norms, by emphasizing "the careful code switcher in control of ti . rules," may have inadvertently reinforced the notion of fixed boundaries between separate languages. If so, then we have done a disservice to the creativity of Spanglish speakers who incorporate English words into Spanish, transform Spanish words along English models, and take every advantage of the double entendres that are bilingualism's forte (Zentella, in press).

It is, after all, in the borrowings and criss-crossings of forms and meanings that the hybrid identity of Latin@s is most manifest. The new creations that Latin@s have added to Spanish usually reflect cultural items that are unknown or different in Latin America. Technology produces many *anglicismos* ("anglicisms"), such as *la compyuta/computadora* ("the computer"), *bipéame* ("beep me"), and *tu emilio* ("your e-mail"), which flourish despite prescriptivist pronouncements of standard Spanish versions that are largely unknown in the United States or Latin America. Other borrowings reflect the daily lives of most workers: *el bos/la bosa* ("the boss," male/female), *fultaim/partaim/overtaim* ("full-time/part-time/overtime"), *el cheque* ("the paycheck," "the restaurant bill"), *los biles* ("the bills"), and *trobol* ("trouble"). Most linguistic loans are shared across the country—for example, *chiriona* ("cheater") is heard on the playgrounds of Los Angeles and New York City, but some take different shapes or genders in the Spanish of different groups—for example *la troca* ("the truck") of the *mexicanos* in the Southwest is *el tro* for the Caribbeans in the Northeast. Monolinguals may know Spanish words for the borrowed items, but their children may think that the anglicism *is* the original Spanish word (Acosta-Belén 1975). On the other hand, misguided purists who go overboard try to avoid or expunge words that have been part of Spanish for centuries—such as *estufa* ("stove")—just because it sounds like English! Most immigrants, however, begin to pick up the new vocabulary within days of their arrival, just as they would learn the regionalisms in any Spanish-speaking country, and by the time they visit home, they find it a strain to talk without them. Their Spanish-ized English loans are part of the reason why new identity labels are created for and by them. Such terms as *los chicanos, nuyoricans/neorriqueños, Dominican Yorks, Yunis* (from Ecuador, perhaps based on "United") capture the linguistic and cultural transformations that immigrants experience. In some cases, these labels are viewed as epithets and/or as divisive, but in others, young Latin@s are engaging in a process of semantic inversion that turns demeaning definitions into empowering and unifying identifiers. Creative writers are in the vanguard of the explicit defense of this process; see especially Algarín and Piñero (1975) and Anzaldúa (1987).

Just as Latin@ Spanish is influenced by English, Latin@ English has a uniquely Spanish flavor, aided and abetted by the similarities between many words with Latin roots in Spanish and English. False cognates, such as "library" and *librería* ("bookstore"), "application" and *aplicación* ("application, as of veneer or varnish"), and "embarrass" and *embarazar* ("to impregnate"), encourage calquing, the transfer of additional or new meanings and/or functions that a Spanish monolingual would find hard to grasp (Otheguy 1993). Word-for-word translations are easier to spot, such as when a Spanish-dominant Latin@ "makes (*hace*) a question" or "wins (*gana*) X dollars per hour." As Gina Valdés's poem "English con Salsa" makes clear, immigrants are leaving their imprint on English, transforming ESL (English as a second language) classes into "English surely Latinized" (Valdés 1994, p. 3). Even Latina@s who are English monolinguals may "get down from (*bajar*) the car" or "throw a fart" (*tirar un pe'o*), oblivious to the traces of Spanish in English. Of course, Latin@ English and Spanish and Spanglish can be mined purposefully for great comic effect. Only bilinguals can follow and truly appreciate the overlapping, upside-down twists and turns that produce *cuellando* ("necking") and *Entre entre y tome una silla* ("Come in and sit down," but literally "Between between and drink a chair") and enable them to recognize Placid Sunday (*Plácido Domingo*) and July Churches (*Julio Iglesias*).

An additional inspiration stems from the influence of AAVE lexicon; New York's Latin@s can *frontear* ("front," or act like something they are not), *tripear* ("trip," or act crazy), and *gufear* ("goof," or fool around), when they are not *chiliando* ("chilling," or taking it easy). Close "inner sphere relations" (Urciuoli 1996) with African Americans may be leaving their mark on the Spanish grammar of New York's Latin@s. Under the influence of AAVE's "preterite had" (Rickford and Théberge 1996), which produces sentences such as "I had went" in place of "I went," members of *el bloque* translated sentences that require the pluperfect into the preterite, for example, "She had seen him" became "Ella lo vió" (She saw him) (Zentella 1997).

The extent to which English has affected Spanish grammar, beyond the lexicon, is much debated. Some linguists insist that there is "no case for convergence" (Pousada and Poplack 1982), and others point out that some of the changes attributed to English are occurring in Spanish-speaking countries where there is little English influence (Silva-Corvalán 1989). The debated features in the Spanish of English-dominant Latin@s include the use of *estar* where *ser* is customary, as in *Está morena* ("She is olive-skinned," not a temporary state) (Silva-Corvalán 1986), progressive Spanish forms that translate English gerunds, as in *Tomando leche es saludable* ("Drinking milk is healthful" (Lantolf 1983), a decrease in certain subjunctives (Ocampo 1990), blurring the distinction between the preterite and the imperfect (Silva-Corvalán 1994; Zentella 1997), and the inclusion of optional and/or redundant prepositions (Lipski 1988), as in *Ella estuvo en el tercer grado cuando ella vivió acá* ("She was in the third grade when she lived here"). More subtle changes occur when grammatical distinctions or usages are lost in ways that emulate English patterns, although what remains is not incorrect Spanish. Examples include a decline in postverbal subjects (Silva-Corvalán 1994), as in *Los americanos dicen* instead of *Dicen los americanos* ("The Americans say"), and the elimination of the progressive meaning of the Spanish present tense, so that "*¿Qué hacen ellos?*" means only "What do they do (for a living)?" not "What are they doing (at this moment)?" (Klein 1980).

Whatever their source, and whatever their impact on Spanish grammar, these features undeniably contribute to the unique flavor of Spanish in the United States. Some may take hold and others may succumb to the standardization pressures imposed by Spanish teachers or educated immigrants. Among the second and third generations, however, Spanish is disappearing altogether because parents are raising their children in English, actively or passively. Moreover, the Spanish of children who are in the process of acquiring the language is often ridiculed because of their English borrowings and because their grammar is underdeveloped. The seven-year-old New Jersey Mexican who told me, "*Cuando yo era (tenía) seis yo todavía fue a Mexico*" ("When I was [*ser* instead of *tener*] six, I still went [third person singular] to Mexico") and the teenagers from *el bloque* whose conversations were limited to one-third of the tenses of Spanish, need time and support to develop their second language. But the net effect of dialect dissing, Spanglish bashing, the Hispanophobia that insists that only English be used in the schools and workplaces, and the "Mock Spanish" spoken by Anglos that makes fun of Spanish speakers ("no problemo") (Hill 1995), is the promotion of language shift. Latin@s who end up convinced that their Spanish is bad or *mata'o* ("killed"), and that "real Americans" are English monolinguals, rush to adopt English and eventually do kill off their Spanish. To make matters worse, the repercussions for the successful development of their English can be severe (Cummins 1981).

As a result, despite the continued influx of monolingual immigrants, Hispanics are undergoing language loss similar to, and even exceeding, that of other groups in U.S. history (Veltman 2000). Nationwide, more than 60 percent of the Latin@ population spoke English well or very well in 1990, and 22 percent of them were monolingual in English. Immigrants shift to English as their customary language within 15 years of arrival, but among the U.S.-born, who constitute the majority (64 percent), language loss is advanced. *El bloque* is a case in point. In 1979, 69 percent of the children were bilingual, but by 1993 that figure had declined to 29 percent; the remainder were either English-dominant or monolingual in English (Zentella 2000). Contrary to the inflammatory charges made by proponents of "English-only" laws, who claim that Latin@s do not know English and do not want to learn it, the English language is in no danger of being supplanted by Spanish or any other language. Instead, Spanish is being lost.

Does the loss of Spanish mean the loss of Latin@ identity? Not necessarily, because Latin@ identities are being created in and communicated via several dialects of English that reflect specific national origins; Chicano English is the best documented (Penfield and Ornstein Galicia 1985). But if one can be Latin@ in English only, then being Latin@ in the United States cannot be the same as being Mexican, Dominican, Puerto Rican, Cuban, and so on in the homeland. Yet the majority of United States Latin@s identify primarily with their ancestral land (de la Garza et al. 1992). Not surprisingly, *latinoamericanos* challenge the membership claims of those who cannot participate in the culture with its Spanish-speaking members. For them, being Mexican, Puerto Rican, Dominican, Cuban, and so on requires being it *in Spanish*—in one of the dialects spoken in that country. Instead, U.S. Latin@s of all generations are redefining their native cultures, without a language requirement. In interviews with 1,018 Latin@s in New York City (a convenience sample), 84 percent of the U.S. born ($n = 510$) and 67 percent of those born in Latin America ($n = 508$), agreed that someone could be a Puerto Rican/Dominican/etc. "without knowing Spanish."[7] For the majority of those interviewed, Spanish was not an indispensable part of their culture. They based their identity on family origins ("If your parents/grandparents are from there"), socialization ("Because that's how they were raised"), and/or personal feelings ("Because that's what I am, what I feel like"). Their criteria allow English monolinguals to be incorporated into the cultural group, as an extension of *la familia*. When they move out of their *barrios* and/or are confronted by their Latin American "compatriots," they may make distinctions between themselves and the "real" Puerto Ricans / Dominicans / Mexicans, etc. (Zentella 1990b). In effect, some feel they are neither real Americans nor real members of their ancestral culture. But others are finding the "way out" that I referred to at the beginning of this chapter, by embracing "being both/and" (Estéves 1984).

THE LANGUAGE AND IDENTITY PART OF THE LATIN@ AGENDA
FOR THE TWENTY-FIRST CENTURY

Latin@s experience distinct and changing realities and are subject to con-flicting ideologies that determine the nature and extent of their cultural and linguistic diversity. Research to date has shed enough light on the mul-tiple identities that can exist even within one family or a network of friends to prove the limitations of applying such blanket terms as the *Hispanic community*, the *Latino community*, or *Spanish-speakers* as though a monolithic group existed. Much more remains to be done. The lifespan of the hybrid identities that Latin@ youths acquire as members of overlapping commu-nities is unknown. Are they merely temporary linguistic and cultural "cross-ings" that die out when family and work obligations take center stage, as Rampton (1995) found in his study of British youth, or do they last long enough to transform the adult generations? Also, what is the role of global-ism? Does it foster or require transnational identities that will think globally but act locally—an international version of "being both/and"? And will globalism break down or strengthen the stranglehold of prescriptive lan-guage standards? The effects of media and technology on these issues are especially interesting but have been little studied.[8]

Theoretically challenging linguistic analyses, including assessment of the validity of constructs that insist on the impermeability of grammars despite the demonstrable syncretism of cultures and the abundant evi-dence of mixed languages (Thomason 1995), require a larger cadre of trained bilingual and bidialectal linguists than is currently available. Con-sequently, a key part of our agenda must address the training of Latin@ scholars, many more of whom might be attracted if our research commit-ted itself to making a real difference in Latin@ communities. In this regard, the work on language, identity, and education is crucial. Despite an emphasis on "rule-governed" bilinguals that may have misfired, I am proud to have taken part in attempts to help parents and educators appreciate the bilingual skills of code switchers and build upon these skills in their efforts to expand students' verbal repertoires. In the current climate, it is neces-sary to become more politically involved, on behalf of children like those in the exemplary bilingual school in Tucson who required counseling after Arizona passed, in November 2000, an English-only bill that will eliminate their successful program (González 2000). The legal attack on bilingual education was spearheaded by Ronald Unz, a multimillionaire member of the advisory board of the Center for Equal Opportunity, which is dedicated to eliminating all affirmative action programs. By playing on anti-Hispanic sentiment, Unz and his supporters first succeeded in California in 1998: Proposition 227 mandated English-only instruction. Arizona was targeted in 2000, and New York and Massachusetts were targeted for 2001 and 2002, respectively. The debate has become particularly virulent in the national media, and Latin@ scholars need to respond from the perspective of their various disciplines, as well as to organize within their academic circles and communities. It will take a concerted national effort to challenge the inevitability of language shift and to change the "nationalist language ideology" that surfaces in daily newspapers and in radio and TV commentaries.[9] This distorted ideology keeps the nation from addressing the fact that more than half of all U.S. teachers teach students whose proficiency in English is limited, and most of whom are Latin@s, but only 20 percent of all teachers have the necessary training in language-teaching methods (Riley 2000). Studies that place individuals in the day-to-day networks and experiences that shape their languages are essential to our arguments, but we must address the political and social conditions that determine linguistic and cultural capital as well. The stakes are very high. The educational future of Latin@ children and the economic viability of Latin@ communities are at risk, but these are not the only beneficiaries. The nation's linguistic and cultural frontiers must be opened for the good of all residents.

NOTES

1. *Latino* suggests that Portuguese-speaking Brazilians should be included, and *Hispanic* is rejected by many outside of New Mexico because it suggests an exclusive link with Spain (Hispania). *Spanish speakers* or *hispano hablantes* is not a perfect solution either, because it excludes the monolingual, English-speaking members of the second and third generations.

2. Literally, "You're beaten [with a stick] if you row and you're beaten if you don't row."

3. "Dissing" is the African American term for dismissive and/or disrespectful behavior. For recent overviews of Central American, Cuban, Mexican, and Puerto Rican experiences with language in the United States, consult the chapters by Lipski; Otheguy, García and Roca; Valdés; and Zentella in McKay and Wong 2000.

4. A similar contradiction divides upper-class British and New England English from working-class New York English. The former dialects enjoy high status despite their deletion of /r/ after vowels, as when *lord* and *Harvard* sound like *laud* and "Ha-vad," but working-class New York City English enjoys low status, in part because it deletes the same r, as in "New Yawk."

5. When one U.S.-born Dominican preteen was asked why he identified himself as Puerto Rican, he gave two reasons: (1) he did not like merengue and (2) he did not speak Spanish.

6. Linguistic misunderstandings occur when Puerto Ricans, who do not know the origin of the majority of the Mexicans, comment, when they see businesses labeled *Puebla*, that the word should end in an *o*.

7. The interviews were conducted by Hunter College undergraduates between 1996 and 1998, and the data were tabulated with the help of Andres Olvet.

8. In Chicago, Mexican American teens are ferreting out identities on the Internet. For example, *chale* signals a Mexico City working-class background, the "cholo types" from California "talk real ghetto," and *vos* is used by both Chileans

and Argentineans but the "Chilenos are really nice" whereas the Argentineans "are like . . . conceited. . . . They think they're too . . . good for you" (Cohen 2000).

9. In one Iowa daily, 46 percent of the language-related letters published in 1997–1998 reflected intolerance of linguistic diversity: "Go, English-speaking people! If people come from a different country over to ours they should speak English" (Haslett 2000).

REFERENCES

Acosta-Belén, E. 1975. Spanglish: A case of languages in contact. In *New Directions in second-language learning, teaching and bilingual education,* ed. M. Burt and H. Dulay. Washington, DC: TESOL, 151–158.

Algarín, M., and M. Piñero, eds. 1975. *Nuyorican poetry.* New York: William Morrow.

Anzaldúa, G. C. 1987. *Borderlands/La Frontera: The new mestiza.* San Francisco: Spinsters/Aunt Lute.

Auer, P. 1984. *Bilingual conversation.* Amsterdam: John Benjamins.

Canfield, L. 1981. *Spanish pronunciation in the Americas.* Chicago: University of Chicago Press.

Cohen, J. 2000. Global links from the postindustrial heartland: Mexican American high school girls, literacy, and the Internet. Paper presented at the annual meeting of the American Anthropological Association (AAA), San Francisco, November 17.

Cummins, J. 1981. The role of primary language development in promoting educational success for language minority students. In *Schooling and language minority students: A theoretical framework.* Los Angeles: California State University, Evaluation, Dissemination and Assessment Center, California State Department of Education, Office of Bilingual, Bicultural Education, pp. 3–50.

De Houwer, A. 1995. Bilingual language acquisition. In *Handbook on child language,* ed. P. Fletcher and B. MacWhinney. Cambridge, MA: Basil Blackwell.

De la Garza, R., A. Falcón, C. García, and J. García. 1992. *Latino national political survey: Summary of findings.* New York: Institute for Puerto Rican Policy.

Eckert, P. 1989. Jocks and burnouts: Social categories and identities in high school. New York: Teachers College Press.

Estéves, S. M. 1984. *Tropical rain: A bilingual downpour.* New York: African Caribbean Poetry Theater.

González, N. 2000. Telling tales out of school: Language ideologies in a dual language immersion program. Paper presented at the annual meeting of the AAA, San Francisco, November 18.

Guitart, J. 1982. Conservative versus radical dialects in Spanish: Implications for language instruction. In *Bilingual education for Hispanic students in the United States,* ed. J. Fishman and G. Keller. New York: Teachers College, Columbia University, pp. 167–190.

Gumperz, J. J. and Hernández-Chávez, E. 1975. Cognitive aspects of bilingual communication. In *El lenguaje de los Chicanos,* ed. E. Hernández-Chávez, A. Cohen, and A. Beltramo. Arlington, VA: Center for Applied Linguistics, pp. 154–163.

Haslett, K. 2000. Language ideologies of a Midwestern town: Shaping the learning experience of Latino/a students. Paper presented at the annual meeting of the AAA, San Francisco, November 15.

Hill, Jane, 1995. Language, race, and white public space. *American Anthropologist:* 680-689.

Hirsch, E. D. 1988. *Cultural literacy: What every American needs to know.* New York: Vintage Books.

Irvine, J., and S. Gal. 1999. Language ideology and linguistic differentiation. In *Regimes of language,* ed. P. Kroskrity. Santa Fe, NM: School of American Research, p. 35.

Klein, F. 1980. A quantitative study of syntactic and pragmatic indications of change in the Spanish of bilinguals in the United States. In *Locating language in time and space,* ed. W. Labov. New York: Academic Press.

Labov, W. 1972. *Sociolinguistic patterns.* Philadelphia: University of Pennsylvania Press.

Lantolf, J. 1983. Toward a comparative dialectology of U.S. Spanish. In *Spanish in the U.S. setting: Beyond the Southwest,* ed. Lucía Elías-Olivares. Rosslyn, VA: National Clearinghouse for Bilingual Education.

Le Page, R. B. and Tabouret-Keller, A. 1985. *Acts of identity: Creole-based approaches to language and ethnicity.* Cambridge: Cambridge University Press.

Lipski, J. M. 1978. Code switching and bilingual competence. In *Aspects of bilingualism,* ed. M. Paradis. Columbia, SC: Hornbeam Press, pp. 250–264.

———. 1985. *Linguistic aspects of Spanish-English language switching.* Tempe: Arizona State University, Center for Latin American Studies.

———. 1988. Creoloid phenomena in the Spanish of transitional bilinguals. Paper presented at *El español en los Estados Unidos IX,* Florida International University, Miami.

———. 1994. *Latin American Spanish.* London/New York: Longmans.

———. 2000. The linguistic situation of Central Americans. In *New immigrants in the United States: Background for second language educators,* ed. Mckay and Wong. Cambridge: Cambridge University Press, pp.189–215.

Macaulay, R. 1997. Standards and variation in urban speech; Examples from Lowland Scots. Amsterdam/Philadelphia: John Benjamins.

McKay, S., and S. Wong, eds. 2000. *New immigrants in the United States: Background for second language educators.* Cambridge: Cambridge University Press.

Ocampo, F. 1990. El subjuntivo en tres generaciones de hablantes bilingües. In *Spanish in the United States: Sociolinguistic issues,* ed. J. Bergen. Washington, DC: Georgetown University Press, pp. 39–48.

Otheguy, R. 1993. A reconsideration of the notion of loan translation in the analysis of U.S. Spanish. In *Spanish in the United States: Linguistic contact and diversity,* ed. A. Roca and J. Lipski. Berlin: Mouton de Gruyter.

Otheguy, R., García, O., and Fernández, M. 1989. Transferring, switching and modeling in West New York Spanish: An intergenerational study. *International Journal of the Sociology of Language* 79:41–92.

Otheguy, R., García, O., and Roca, A. 2000. Speaking in Cuban: The language of Cuban Americans. In *Bilingual education for Hispanic students in the United States,* ed. McKay and Wong. New York: Teachers College, Columbia University, pp. 165–188.

Penfield, J., and J. Ornstein-Galicia. 1985. *Chicano English: An ethnic contact dialect.* Amsterdam/Philadelphia: John Benjamins.

Poplack, S. 1980. Sometimes I'll start a sentence in Spanish y termino en español: Toward a typology of code-switching. *Linguistics* 18:581–616.

Poplack, S., and Sankoff, D. 1988. Code-switching. In *Sociolinguistics: An international handbook of language and society,* ed. U. Ammon, N. Dittmar, and K. J. Mattheier. Berlin: Mouton de Gruyter.

Pousada, A., and Poplack, S. 1982. No case for convergence: The Puerto Rican Spanish verb system in a language contact situation. In *Bilingual education for Hispanic students in the United States,* ed. J. Fishman and G. Keller. New York: Teachers College, Columbia University, pp. 207–240.

Rampton, B. 1995. *Crossing: Language and ethnicity among adolescents.* New York: Longmans.

Rickford, J., and C. Théberge. 1996. Preterit *had* in the narratives of African American adolescents. *American Speech* 71:

Riley, R. 2000. Riley endorses two-way bilingual education. *http:washingtonpost.com /wp-dyn/articles/A17242-2000Mar15.html.*

Rosenblat, A. 1970. La diversidad lingüística americana. In *El español de América,* R. del Rosario, ed. Sharon, CT: Troutman Press, pp. 132–140.

Silva-Corvalán, C. 1986. Bilingualism and language change: The extension of *estar* in Los Angeles Spanish. *Language* 62:587–608.

———. 1989: Past and present perspectives on language change in U.S Spanish. In *U.S. Spanish: The language of Latinos* (Special issue). *International Journal of the Sociology of Language,* ed. I. Wherritt and O. García. 79:53–66.

———. 1994. *Language contact and change: Spanish in Los Angeles.* New York: Oxford University Press.

Skutnabb-Kangas, T. 1984. *Bilingualism or not: The education of minorities.* Clevedon, England: Multilingual Matters.

Terrell, T. 1982. Relexificación en el español dominicano: Implicaciones para la educación. In *El español del Caribe: Ponencias del VI simposio de dialectología,* ed. Orlando Alba. Santiago, Dominican Republic: Universidad Católica Madre y Maestra.

Thomason, S. 1995. Language mixture: Ordinary processes, extraordinary results. In *Spanish in four continents,* ed. Silva-Corvalán, C. Washington, DC: Georgetown University Press.

Toribio, A. J. 2000. Language variation and the linguistic enactment of identity among Dominicans. *Linguistics* 38(6):1133–1159.

Urciuoli, B. 1985. Bilingualism as code and bilingualism as practice. *Anthropological Linguistics* Winter: 363–386.

———. 1996. *Exposing prejudice: Puerto Rican experiences of language, race, and class.* Boulder, CO: Westview.

Valdés, G. 1994. *Cool salsa: Bilingual poems on growing up Latino in the United States.* New York: Fawcett Juniper.

Valdés, G. 1976. Social interaction and code switching patterns: A case study of Spanish-English alternation. In *Bilingualism in the bicentennial and beyond,* ed. G. Keller, R. Teschner, and S. Viera. Jamaica, NY: Bilingual Press.

————. 1981. Code switching as a deliberate verbal strategy: A microanalysis of direct and indirect requests among Chicano bilingual speakers. In *Latino language and communicative behavior*, ed. R. P. Durán. Norwood, NJ: Ablex Press, pp. 95–108.

————. 2000. Bilingualism and language use among Mexican Americans. In *New immigrants in the United States: Background for second language educators*, ed. Mckay and Wong. Cambridge: Cambridge University Press, pp. 99–136.

Veltman, C. 2000. The American linguistic mosaic: Understanding language shift in the United States. In *New immigrants in the United States: Background for second language educators*, ed. McKay and Wong. Cambridge: Cambridge University Press, 58–94.

Walsh, C. E. 1991: *Pedagogy and the struggle for voice: Issues of language, power, and schooling for Puerto Ricans*. New York: Bergin & Garvey.

Weinrich, U. 1968. *Languages in Contact*. The Hague: Mouton. First edition published 1953.

Zentella, A. C. 1983. *"Tá bien, you could answer me en cualquier idioma"*: Puerto Rican code switching in bilingual classrooms. In *Latino language and communicative behavior*, ed. Richard Durán. Norwood, NJ: Ablex Press.

————. 1990a. Lexical leveling in four New York City Spanish dialects: Linguistic and social factors, *Hispania*, 73,(4):1094–1105.

————. 1990b. Returned migration, language, and identity: Puerto Rican bilinguals in dos worlds/two mundos. In *Spanish in the U.S.A.: New quandaries and prospects*, ed. Florian Coulmas. *International Journal of the Sociology of Language*, No. 10.

————. 1995. The '*chiquita*-fication' of U.S. Latinos and their languages, or Why we need an anthro-political linguistics. *SALSA III: The Proceedings of the Symposium about Language and Society at Austin*. Austin, TX: Department of Linguistics, pp. 1–18.

————. 1997. *Growing up bilingual: Puerto Rican children in New York*, Malden, MA: Blackwell.

————. 1999. Who speaks the best Spanish? Linguistic (in)security of Latin@s in New York City. Paper presented at the School of American Research, Santa Fe, April 21.

————. 2000. Puerto Ricans in the U.S.: Confronting the linguistic repercussions of colonialism. In *New immigrants in the United States: Background for second language educators*, ed. McKay and Wong. Cambridge: Cambridge University Press, pp. 137–164.

————. In press. "José, can you see? Latin@ responses to racist discourse." In *Bilingual blues*, ed. D. Sommer. Palgrave/St. Martin's Press. *Journal of the Center for Latin American Studies*, Harvard University.

Chapter 17

Learning English in California
Guideposts for the Nation

Patricia Gándara

Political events in California often have repercussions for the rest of the nation. Recently, California has been the site of intense legal battles over the education of its English learners, and events in the state have already affected a number of other states with large populations of English learners. This chapter offers a history of the politics and policies that have governed the education of English learners in the state over the last several decades. It reviews the effects of the most recent legal skirmish over limited-English-proficient students and predicts short- and longer-term outcomes that may result both for California and for the nation. Finally, the chapter looks to the future of education for English learners and suggests critical areas of research that may aid in constructing more enlightened educational policies for these students.

A BRIEF HISTORY OF BILINGUAL EDUCATION POLICY IN CALIFORNIA

California, through its initiative process, has been at the forefront of several national political movements in the last few decades. The passage of Proposition 13[1] in 1978 launched the famous tax revolt that swept the country during the early 1980s. Proposition 209,[2] passed by California voters in 1996, began a national backlash against affirmative action that continues unabated today. Most recently, Proposition 227, the antibilingual initiative that was passed in 1998, has set the stage for a showdown on bilingual education in a number of other states, including Colorado, Arizona, and possibly Massachusetts.

California has, on occasion, also been the site of progressive politics. It was one of the first states in the nation to enact a comprehensive bilingual-education bill: the Chacon-Moscone Bilingual-Bicultural Education Act of

LI → L2   LI + L2

Figure 17.1. Language Goals

1976, which gave schools detailed instructions about the type of language support that should be provided for English learners. California's legislation was stimulated by the Supreme Court case in 1974 ruling in *Lau* v. *Nichols*, which required schools to give limited-English-proficient students access to the same instruction that all other children received. The legislation recognized that limited-English-proficient students do "not have the English language skills necessary to benefit from instruction only in English at a level substantially equivalent to pupils whose primary language is English." Thus, "The Legislature ... declare[d] that the primary goal of all programs under this article [was], as effectively and efficiently as possible, to develop in each child fluency in English" (California Education Code, 1976, Section 52161). The preferred means for doing so was through early use of the primary language, with a planned transition into English-only instruction. Although the act did not specify when this transition should occur, the expectation came to be that students would be mainstreamed into an English-only classroom by the fourth grade.

Although this 1976 legislation was clearly progressive in its time, it also framed the challenge facing English learners as primarily a *language problem*, and it framed the solution to this problem as transitional bilingual education (TBE). From a theoretical perspective, there are at least three possible goals of bilingual education: (1) the teaching of language, (2) the fostering of positive intercultural relations, and (3) the enhancing of academic or cognitive development. Each of these goals can also be represented on a continuum. For example, the teaching of language can be conceptualized as simply transitioning an individual from her or his native language into a second language as efficiently as possible. This represents the far-left end of a continuum. At the other end of the continuum is the possibility of the individual's becoming fully bilingual and biliterate and therefore having the ability to communicate in two languages. See Figure 17.1.

In terms of intercultural relations, the far-left end of the continuum represents simply knowledge of one's own culture in the context of the mainstream culture; this is thought to support higher self-esteem (Spencer and Markstrom-Adams 1990). At the other end of the continuum is a fully bicultural or multicultural orientation, in which both members of the mainstream culture and members of the minority culture are taught to value and appreciate each other's culture and language and are encouraged to incorporate features of both into multicultural social identities (Rotherham-Borus 1994; Cazabon, Lambert, and Hall 1993). It has been argued that this orientation can reduce prejudice and ethnic stereotyping

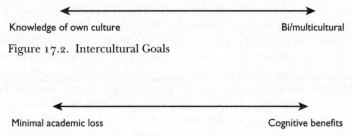

Knowledge of own culture   Bi/multicultural

Figure 17.2. Intercultural Goals

Minimal academic loss   Cognitive benefits

Figure 17.3. Cognitive and Academic Goals

and enhance intergroup relations (Lindholm 1994; Freeman 1998; Genesee and Gándara 1999). See Figure 17.2.

Finally, with respect to academic or cognitive competence, bilingual education can, at the far-left end of the continuum, simply help to prevent learning losses by providing instruction in the primary language in some or all subjects while the individual is transitioning into the second language. At the other end of a continuum, bilingual education can offer true cognitive advantages to students who are fully bilingual and biliterate, resulting in certain types of academic superiority over monolinguals (August and Hakuta 1997; Reynolds, 1991). See Figure 17.3.

The California legislation, much like legislation in other states, provided for a program that could generally be located at the left end of the continuum in all three goal areas. All transitional bilingual-education programs, no matter how effective they are in helping students to join the academic mainstream, implicitly foster prejudice against non-English languages because transitional programs are based on the "language as problem" model (Ruiz 1984). The children's non-English language is something to be dispensed with, and transitioned out of, as quickly as possible. Alternative conceptualizations of language difference include "language as a resource" (Ruiz 1984) models that build on students' native languages as an avenue to enhanced academic competencies. Dual-language programs, for example, adopt the position that non-English languages are a resource for English learners and an enrichment for English speakers. By valuing the non-English language in the curriculum, such programs give that language—and its speakers—greater prestige, thus simultaneously addressing issues of intergroup relations.

California's legislation, like most legislation nationwide, was largely silent on issues of intercultural relations and academic development. Included were specific provisions for instruction in the "development of an understanding of the history and culture of California and the United States, as well as an understanding of customs and values of the cultures associated with the languages being taught" (California Education Code, 1976, Section 52163). However, nowhere in the legislation were there specific provisions for the cultural components of instruction, nor did the act provide any objectives for such cross-cultural instruction. Certainly there was no mention of a goal of reducing intercultural conflict through these programs, although it might be inferred from the program's inclusion of instruction in both the U.S. culture and the culture of the students. Nonetheless, because the program targeted the instruction of English learners, it appears that cross-cultural understanding was meant to apply, for the most part, to English learners, not to English speakers.

The act also specified that, to the greatest extent possible, no less than one-third of the students in a bilingual-education classroom should be fluent English-speaking students (California Education Code 1976, Section 52167). (The law did *not* specify that these children should be of the dominant cultural group, although this was clearly inferred by many school personnel.) It was thought that the presence of such students would provide important English models for the English learners. Unlike the Canadian experiments with immersion education, to which U.S. bilingual education is often compared, California's program did not have a goal of furthering more positive attitudes toward minority-language speakers (Genesee and Gándara 1999). In fact, the law did not specify any benefits that should accrue to the English speakers in these classrooms, and in the absence of any intent to provide for the *development* of the primary language (in this case nearly always Spanish), there was little reason for the parents of English speakers to want their children to be in such a classroom. In most cases, English speakers would not be exposed to sufficient Spanish to develop any true facility in the language, and Spanish speakers were encouraged to transition to English as quickly as possible. In this context, many parents of English speakers complained that learning was slowed down to accommodate the children who did not speak English and that their children derived no benefit from being in these classes. It became difficult to find sufficient numbers of English-speaking students to fulfill the one-third rule. For this reason, and, because resources were usually inadequate to meet even the needs of the English-learner population, most programs simply did not adhere to that rule. Thus, not only did these programs, as they were conceived, offer no clear means of enhancing intercultural communication, but in some cases they actually contributed to intercultural strife, pitting the needs of English speakers against those of English learners. Moreover, they sometimes increased tensions between African Americans and Latinos because of the perception that bilingual education, by clustering English learners into separate programs, undermined desegregation efforts (Donato 1997).

The focus on language as *the* problem that needed to be remediated, with the goal of transitioning students to English "as efficiently as possible," also meant that academic achievement was not articulated as an important goal

for these programs. Therefore, a minimum threshold of academic competence was established for students to exit from the programs. This was often
far below the median academic performance of all students in the district or
state.[3] Although the arguments for incorporating the primary language into
students' instruction were predicated on a belief that doing so made access
to the standard curriculum possible during the time students were learning
English, bilingual education, as conceived of in California law and regulations, was not designed to focus on academic achievement. Its main purpose
was always simply to transition students into English.

Not surprisingly, this instructional policy was never without controversy.
Bilingual advocates believed the program did too little to promote either
academic competence or dual language facility, and English-only proponents decried any use of the primary language, believing that it delayed
students' entry into the mainstream of schooling. By 1986 the existing California bilingual-education legislation had "sunsetted" (was not reauthor-
ized), so these programs continued under the authority of Department of
Education regulations, which were shaped largely by federal requirements.
Over the years there were numerous attempts to modify the law and to
abandon the practice of primary-language instruction, but none of these
attempts was ultimately successful.

In part because of the controversy generated by bilingual education,
no policy was ever adopted to provide certified bilingual teachers for all
English learners. Moreover, although a few school districts provided small
financial bonuses for teachers with bilingual credentials, no statewide incentive policy was ever adopted to recruit sufficient numbers of bilingual
teachers. Thus, by the time the Chacon-Moscone Act sunsetted, only about
one-third of the students who were eligible for a bilingual program were
able to be placed with a bilingual teacher.

CALIFORNIA'S PROPOSITION 227

It was in this context that Proposition 227 came onto the California political
scene. Proponents of Proposition 227 contended that bilingual education
had failed and therefore should be abandoned as a pedagogical strategy. As
evidence for its failure, they cited the continuing underachievement of English learners and the failure of programs to reclassify more than 5 percent of
limited-English-proficient students to fluent-English-proficient status annually. Bilingual-education advocates countered that, in addition to being
inaccurate, the 5 percent figure was calculated from an ever-growing base
of students, because the population of English learners in California had
been mushrooming for two decades. More important, however, they noted
that because of the lack of sufficient numbers of qualified teachers, most
English learners were not enrolled in bilingual programs so their academic

underachievement could not be attributed to any failure of these programs. Nonetheless, Proposition 227 was passed by the voters of California in June 1998. It became law immediately, requiring that schools implement its provisions in the 1998–1999 school year.

Proposition 227 required that "all children in California public schools shall be taught English by being taught in English." The mandated pedagogical strategy was to place English learners for a period not normally to exceed one year in "sheltered English immersion" classes. These are defined in the law as multiage classrooms with students at the same level of English proficiency in which the focus of instruction is the development of English-language skills. The only exception to the English-only mandate was to be in cases in which parents sought a specific waiver of the English-only program for their children. According to Proposition 227, waivers could be allowed on the basis of one of three conditions: (1) the child already knew English; (2) the child was over ten years of age, and school staff believed that another approach might be better suited to the student; or (3) school staff determined that the child had special needs that could be better met in an alternative program.

Proposition 227 took a unique approach to ensuring implementation, an approach that had serious implications for schools and teachers. It provided that any educator who willfully and repeatedly refused to implement the law could be personally sued in court. Thus, in order to avoid legal liability, it was critical that teachers and administrators understand completely the provisions and restrictions of the law. However, the language of Proposition 227 left much to interpretation. For example, it was not clear what the course of action should be if students needed more than one year of specialized instruction (which virtually all of the research on language acquisition contends would be the case[4]); how much primary language might be acceptable under the law in the "sheltered English immersion" classroom; or how much discretion schools or districts had in granting or denying parental exception waivers. The State Board of Education issued regulations clarifying some of these matters in October 1998. However, because schools had to implement the law in September, when most began the new school year, these clarifications came too late to provide guidance in the early stages of implementation.

The Context of Proposition 227: Reform Run Amok

A major theme in the implementation of Proposition 227 is the extent to which it has been affected by other school reform efforts. Proposition 227 was enacted in what has been the most active period of education reform in California in recent times. During the same period, class size reduction, which began in 1996 with two grades, was expanded to include all of the primary grades (thus creating an enormous demand for new teachers);

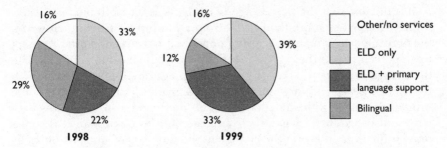

Figure 17.4. Instructional Services for English-language learners before and after Proposition 227
SOURCE: Rumberger and Gándara 2000

new curricular standards were introduced into the schools; a high-stakes testing program was implemented; and new restrictions against social promotion were enacted that could result in the retention of large numbers of students who do not meet grade-level standards. Teachers have had to respond to all of these mandates, often without having had adequate training themselves to address the needs of English learners.

The plethora of reforms have the potential to work at cross-purposes, for children in general, but especially for English learners. For example, imposing strict new curricular standards at the same time that statewide testing is implemented, without devoting any attention to the curriculum provided for English learners, has left many teachers wondering how best to prepare these students to meet the challenges that the testing imposes. Expanding class size reduction to more grades increased the demand for teachers and required school districts to hire many new, untrained, and inexperienced teachers who were often assigned to classrooms serving English learners. Trying without any specific training to juggle new standards, a high-stakes test, and a roomful of students who do not speak English has proved to be a daunting—and sometimes demoralizing—task for many teachers.

How Proposition 227 Has Affected California Schools

The extent to which Proposition 227 has influenced the schooling of English learners, who constitute one-fourth of all the state's public school children, is difficult to measure precisely because school and classroom practices have been affected by so many recent mandates. Some facts, however, are indisputable. Fewer children are receiving instruction from bilingual teachers than before the enactment of Proposition 227, and fewer are assigned to classrooms in which the primary language is used for academic instruction. See Figure 17.4.

It is notable that the percentage of students assigned to bilingual class-rooms dropped by more than half—from 29 to just 12 percent. However, the percentage of students receiving only English instruction grew from 33 to 39 percent. Thus the category that expanded the most to accommodate the change in policy was that of English language development (ELD) with primary-language support.[5] In other words, many classrooms utilize some primary language with students, although the manner in which this happens and its extent vary greatly from classroom to classroom. It is sometimes difficult to interpret the change in the numbers of students officially assigned to one program or another, because those numbers may obscure more than they reveal. For example, some schools and districts complied with Proposition 227 by creating their own interpretations of phrases such as *overwhelmingly in English*. Thus they might have been provided students "in structured English immersion" classrooms with 52 percent of their instruction in English, meeting their own definition of *overwhelming*. Another strategy was to provide "preinstructional activities" and "review sessions" in the primary language, reserving the actual instructional time for English only. An administrator in one large district described the challenge of defining *overwhelmingly in English* in a way that met legal, though not necessarily instructional, objectives:

> [T]he state board of education has allowed districts in California to interpret that based on their own criteria as long as it's overwhelmingly in English. And so the district has determined that 60 percent of the time you have to teach in English, and 40 percent in Spanish or whatever it is. 60-40, 70-30, 80-20, 90-10, I've heard it all. And it all adds up to the point now that districts in California are forced to come up with a working definition based on the legal interpretations, not based on the instructional needs of the child. (Gándara et al. 2000)

A second change that we have noted is the pervasive concern about helping children to get ready for English testing no matter what type of classroom they are in. In separate studies in California schools that have been coordinated by the Linguistic Minority Research Institute,[6] we found a consistent pattern of erosion of strong literacy practices in favor of "bottom line" instruction aimed at yielding short-term gains on statewide tests in English. Often teachers commented that they did not feel good about what they were doing—leapfrogging much of the normal literacy instruction to go directly to English word recognition or phonics bereft of meaning or context. However, they worried greatly that if they spent time orienting the children to broader literacy activities, they risked jeopardizing students' English test scores. One teacher described her situation in the following words:

> I feel like the children are forced into silence. Really . . . they're really not getting the opportunity to express themselves as they normally would were they

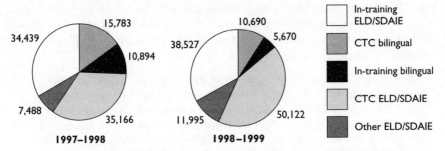

Figure 17.5. Number of Teachers Providing Instructional Services for English Learners, by Certification, before and after Proposition 227
SOURCE: Gándara et al. 2000

in a bilingual classroom. And I, I feel sorry for them . . . I really do. I think that it's very unfair. I don't think they're receiving an equal opportunity, equal education in the sense that they're really not learning to read. . . . They're learning to decode. [And] their decoding skills are coming along nicely, but the problem is that second language acquisition, it takes time. And you know the district expects us to move these children from ELD level 1 to ELD level 4 in a matter of one year, with ELD level 4 then you can begin to present instruction of all the subjects in English (Gándara et al. 2000).

The impact of Proposition 227 that will probably have the longest-term policy consequences is its effect on utilization of the teaching force. Figure 17.5 shows the numbers of teachers serving as bilingual teachers, and the numbers of those in training for bilingual positions, prior to Proposition 227 and in its aftermath.

In 1998, before the passage of Proposition 227, almost 16,000 certificated bilingual teachers were providing instruction to English learners. After the passage of Proposition 227, this number had been reduced by one-third, to 10,690. Perhaps even more important, there were 10,894 teachers in the pipeline for bilingual credentials working in California schools in 1998, whereas in 1999, after the passage of Proposition 227, that number had been reduced by half to 5,670. Some portion of those teachers may still be pursuing their bilingual credentials, but without the perception that there is a demand for their services, it is not clear what incentive they have to continue to devote the additional time and effort necessary to acquire these specialized credentials.

Both the October 1998 memorandum from the state Board of Education and a fact sheet released by the Commission on Teacher Credentialing in the same month restated the importance of maintaining bilingual teachers in classrooms serving English learners. And this same commission reported that in a survey of districts after the passage of Proposition 227, all intended to continue hiring "as many as they can find."[7] Nonetheless, this is not the message articulated in some of the districts that chose to abandon primary-language instruction. One rural administrator explained the position of his district as follows:

> One thing I didn't mention earlier, and this may apply to several different questions, I'll just tell what it is—we no longer have to worry about that B-CLAD [bilingual credential]. That, you know, writing that annual staffing plan was just, it was futile! Because there's just no way you're going to get people to get their B-CLAD and that's what the law requires, that these people, if they have any students, which, in our district, is all over the place, they gotta be working towards their B-CLAD. It's not going to happen! And so, what's nice is, we don't have to play with that anymore (Gándara et al. 2000).

We think it quite possible that administrators in school districts that were not supportive of primary-language instruction before Proposition 227, and who used passage of the initiative as a reason to dismantle their programs immediately, may respond to official surveys with what they consider to be a bureaucratically correct answer. However, what they do and what they say may differ considerably.

Proposition 227 in the Context of the California Teacher Crisis

Two major reports have recently called attention to the crisis that California faces in providing a qualified teacher for every student in the state, largely as a result of the class size reduction initiatives (Shields et al. 1999; Betts, Rueben and Danenberg 2000). Current estimates are that 10 percent of teachers in California are teaching without proper authorization—they are not credentialed to teach. However, the distribution of these teachers is far from even. In fact, schools in high-income areas are likely to have no teachers in the classroom who lack teaching credentials, whereas in schools in low-income and minority areas, as many as 25 or 30 percent of the teachers may be without credentials. Not only are these teacher uncredentialed, but most are without any experience in the classroom. The students most likely to be taught by uncredentialed teachers are English learners. Figure 17.6 shows the distribution of uncredentialed teachers in the year prior to the onset of class size reduction, and in the year after, by percentage of English learners in the school.

Before the passage of Proposition 227, major inequities were noted in different students' access to credentialed teachers in California. English learners were then, and are now, the most likely to be taught by a teacher without any credentials. The difference now, however, is that much more is being asked of teachers, including the implementation of a new law that

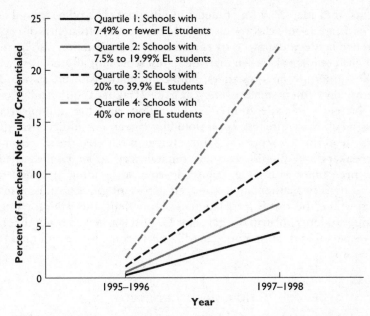

Figure 17.6. Percentage of Teachers without Credentials by Percent EL, Before and After Class Size Reduction
SOURCE: Rumberger and Gándara 2000

mandates a type of instruction about which there is considerable confusion, few related resource materials, and little help in interpretation.

Initial Academic Outcomes

More than two years after the passage of Proposition 227, the pundits and the policymakers are anxiously making pronouncements about its effects on California's English learners. Ron Unz, the author of the initiative, and his colleagues have declared it a success on the basis that the redesignation rates from limited-English-proficient (LEP) to fluent-English-proficiency (FEP) increased from 7 to 7.6 percent in the year following implementation. They have also noted that standardized test scores are up for LEP students across the state. However, this is scant evidence on which to claim success. Proposition 227 was based on its author's contention that LEP students normally should need no more than one year of English instruction in order to join the mainstream, which claim suggests that all but a few students would be redesignated to FEP status at the end of one year. An increase of less than one percentage point would appear to fall far short of this goal. Moreover, although test scores did indeed increase for LEP students, they increased for students in bilingual classrooms as well as for those in English-only classrooms, and there was no consistently discernible difference between the two (Orr et al. 2000). Moreover, they also increased for English-only speakers. An increase in test scores for all students was predictable under any circumstances; simple familiarity with the standardized test normally confers small year-to-year gains (Hakuta 1999). And given the large increases in expenditures on education, and the multiple reform efforts, a failure to raise test scores would have been very difficult to explain.

In spite of the test score gains, however, gaps between the scores of English speakers and English learners remain very large: English speakers score three times as high as English learners in reading and more than twice as high in mathematics, averaged across all grades. And, in mathematics, where the test is least language-dependent, the *gains* for English-speaking students outstrip the gains for English learners, a result that raises the prospect that the test score gap will only become wider with time (Gándara 2000).

HOW DID WE GET HERE?

It could be argued that California's present situation was highly predictable, given the decisions that it made more than two decades ago. It built a bilingual program founded on the notion that for English learners, language is *the problem*. The bilingual program, therefore, was constructed to solve that problem by transitioning these students "as efficiently as possible" into an English-only curriculum. The famed Swiss psychologist Jean Piaget, who studied the cognitive development of children, characterized American psychology as being obsessed with one question: *Can it (development) be speeded up?* He dubbed this "the American question." It is not surprising, then, that once there was consensus that language was the problem, the logical next question would be how quickly the problem could be resolved.

Every major evaluation of bilingual education has been asked to answer the same question: Which program most efficiently moves English learners into the mainstream of English instruction? Achievement has been measured only in the context of the amount of time it was presumed that children should take to complete the transition to English. Thus the most carefully conducted and comprehensive study of bilingual education was given only four years to establish whether there were achievement differences among children in different program types. Although Ramirez, Yuen, and Ramey (1991) found that the learning slope was steeper for the children in primary-language instruction, it was never possible to test the long-term effects of the instruction, in good part because the underlying assumption was that there should *be* no "long term" for bilingual instruction.

Achievement was of interest only within the framework of an "efficient" program that produced English-only speakers.

Because the commitment to instruction in two languages has been weak, and because the mark of program success has been the rapidity with which programs are able to dispense with primary-language instruction, development of a corps of teachers with strong skills in the science and methods of learning and using two languages has never been a truly serious objective in California. Bilingual teachers have been viewed as expedient—useful up to a point, but not essential. Millions of dollars have been spent on evaluating the effectiveness of *programs* rather than the effectiveness of *teaching strategies* (August and Hakuta 1997). The assumption has been that teacher competencies are not critical if we can just identify the silver-bullet program. Of course, decades of research on classroom learning have pointed to one conclusion: nothing matters more in school than the quality of the teacher (Shields et al. 1999; Haycock 1998). One wonders why it is not obvious that the same would hold true in a bilingual classroom.

The present circumstances can also be traced to the fact that most bilingual programs were not designed to focus on intercultural relations or academic achievement. California's bilingual-education law indicated that English learners were to learn something of their own culture, ostensibly to enhance their self-concept, but nothing in the law suggested that native English speakers should know anything about the English learners' culture. It is difficult to feel proud of one's cultural heritage when everyone else is ignorant of it. A primary reason for Canada's success with French-immersion programs is that they are geared toward helping the children of the dominant culture appreciate the language and culture *of the minority group* (Genesee and Gándara 1999).

It is telling as well that while the country wrung its hands over the low academic achievement of America's students, little was said about the much lower achievement of English learners. In fact, most testing programs have been reluctant even to measure it. The assumption has been that because the problem is language, once that is "fixed," the students' achievement will rise to meet that of their English-speaking peers. In fact, this does not happen. A recent study examined the influence of language background and other factors on the 1998 SAT-9 test performance of 26,126 second-, third-, and fourth-grade California students.[8] The study first examined the independent effects of language background and poverty on student achievement (see Figure 17.7, left panel).

The researchers found that poverty affects the achievement of all students, regardless of their language background, but because the majority of English learners are poor, they are at a particular disadvantage in school. The study next examined the impact of language background and ethnicity on student achievement (see Figure 17.7, right panel). Even Hispanic

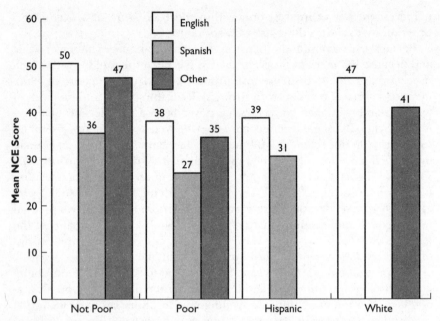

Figure 17.7. 1999 SAT-9 Reading Scores by Language Background and Poverty, Hispanics and Whites
SOURCE: Mitchell and Mitchell 1999

students from English-speaking backgrounds had significantly lower test scores than white students from English-speaking backgrounds. This suggests that because something other than English proficiency must be accounting for the differences, merely improving students' English proficiency is unlikely to raise their achievement to the levels of white, native-English speakers. Similarly, in a review of studies of high-quality programs of various types, we could identify none that showed that English learners ever achieved the same level of English-reading proficiency as their more advantaged native-English-speaking peers (Gándara 1997).

WHERE WE ARE GOING

California's social policy has been, for good or for ill, a harbinger of things to come in other states. Arizona, Colorado, and Massachusetts, in particular, are now poised to reexamine their instructional policies for English learners. California's bilingual programs have not differed greatly from the programs offered in these states, and it is probably safe to assume that similar political issues will be visited by these other states as well. It may therefore be instructive to assess the policy dimensions of recent events in California as a means of initiating a national conversation on the education of English learners.

The Extraordinary Impact of Testing on Instructional Policy

High standards can be a very good thing, and they can be used as a policy tool to level the playing field for Latino students. The more transparent the standards are, the greater the likelihood that the Latino community can exert pressure to ensure that equal educational opportunities are provided in their schools. Futhermore, tests that are tied to these standards are an important means of holding schools accountable for giving students an opportunity to meet these standards. However, when testing does not take into account the curricular needs of English learners, it can have a very negative impact on instructional practice. We have seen that the blanket policy of testing all students in English (except those who have been in U.S. schools for less than one year), and tying the test results to sanctions and rewards for schools and students, has had the effect of distorting pedagogy in the classroom. Because teachers know that students who do not perform well on the tests *in English* can suffer penalties (for example, they can be held back a grade), we have seen a dilution of good literacy instruction in favor of an exclusive focus on phonics, decoding, and English vocabulary. We have seen bilingual teachers set aside broader literacy activities—storytelling, story sequencing activities, reading for meaning, journal writing, and vocabulary development in the primary language—to focus exclusively on skills that would be tested on the standardized English test. Past research suggests that this may well produce short-term gains on test scores at the expense of deeper comprehension—a skill that will be tested in later grades, and one that is fundamental to more complex learning.

To the extent that standardized testing focuses solely on English skills, this is what teachers will endeavor to cultivate. Unfortunately, this may not be in the best interests of many English learners in the first several years of their schooling. It also sends the strongest possible message to schools that the only thing that counts is skills that are assessible in English. Deep and complex understandings of subject matter, framed in another language, are not valued. This is particularly worrisome because it may overlook some of our academically strongest students—those who come to American schools with a good academic foundation in their primary language and whose families have prepared them in important ways in the language of the home.

The Impact of Language Policy on the Preparation of Bilingual Teachers

One of the great ironies of the success of Proposition 227 is that its implementation relies to a great extent on the availability of teachers with good knowledge of the learning needs of English learners, and this generally means bilingual teachers. The meager research on "structured immersion" or "sheltered English" approaches concludes that teachers should be able to reinforce and help explain lessons and to check for understanding in the primary language, even if this is done minimally (Gersten and

Woodward 1985; Krashen 1991). Sheltered English is, in fact, a strategy recommended for use by bilingual teachers who are able to shape instruction in terms of the linguistic needs of the child (Walqui-van Lier n.d.). In the absence of a well-developed pedagogy, which structured English immersion does not have, bilingual teachers are best equipped with the training necessary to provide responsive instruction for English learners. However, the success of Proposition 227 has seriously undermined the market incentives for teachers to pursue bilingual credentials. All the evidence suggests that the most immediate impact of the initiative has been to reduce the supply of such teachers for the present and into the future. If this proves to be the case, the state will have lowered the bar on teacher standards for English learners at the same time that it is attempting to raise the bar for all other teachers. The very students who are likely to perform at the lowest levels, and who are therefore the most in need of excellent teaching, will continue to be the least likely to receive it. Thus the proposition's negative impact on the teacher corps may be its most profound and lasting legacy. Moreover, the erosion of the infrastructure of bilingual personnel—both in the classroom and in administrative positions—may make it very difficult to respond to alternative pedagogies.

A Hopeful Sign

Taking their cue from the Canadian experience, many researchers and policymakers have believed for some time that the most effective strategy for meeting the needs of English learners may well be through dual-immersion or two-way bilingual programs. These programs have the advantage that they incorporate the three core theoretical goals of bilingual instruction: academic enrichment, enhanced intercultural relations, and competence in two languages. They do this by combining English speakers and English learners in the same classroom with a curriculum that is taught in both languages but in proportions that balance issues of social power and linguistic hegemony. The goal of such programs is to produce students who are culturally and academically competent in two languages and who value cultural diversity.

When the current superintendent of public instruction in California came into office in 1994, she articulated a goal of providing the opportunity for all children to learn two languages, and polls of parent attitudes show strong support for such curricular innovation in the public schools (Huddy and Sears 1990; Krashen 1996). However, the din of political rhetoric assailing bilingual education drowned out the voices raised in defense of a more progressive education agenda that viewed language as an asset rather than a liability. In March 2000, then Secretary of Education Richard Riley went on record as supporting a major initiative to increase fourfold the number of dual-language programs nationwide over the next five years; he also pledged to provide the financial support to make this a reality. Riley was quoted as saying, "I think it is high time we begin to treat language skills as the asset they are, particularly in this global economy" (Cooper 2000). According to the Center for Applied Linguistics, California, in spite of Proposition 227, is the state with the largest number of dual-language programs, 83. However, with California set on a course to dismantle its bilingual-education infrastructure, the question at hand is whether it is already too late for this state to respond to the call for a language policy that makes educational, social, and economic sense.

TOWARD A NEW RESEARCH AGENDA

Perhaps unwittingly, or perhaps because of the narrow visions and political constraints of the times, past research has largely played into a political agenda that was never intended to treat multilingualism as a real possible outcome for English learners. Thus, studies have tried diligently to answer questions such as "Which program most efficiently moves English learners out of their primary language and into the English-only mainstream?" and "How can we attract more 'good' (no mention of linguistically or culturally competent) teachers for English learners?" However, if we are to heed the concerns of Gene García when he asserts that teachers must pay attention to both the roots and the wings of our English learners, as well those of Luis Moll and Richard Ruiz (Chapter 18) when they admonish educators to build on the cultural resources in students' communities, then we must shift the dominant research paradigm in the education of English learners. Among the questions that must be to explored are

1. In what ways does multilingualism contribute to greater academic and cultural competence in children from all backgrounds?
2. In what ways does multilingualism contribute to the social and economic benefit of the state and nation?
3. How do multilingual teachers who share knowledge of their students' cultural backgrounds and experiences differ in their instructional effectiveness from teachers who lack these attributes?
4. How can we build educational programs that enhance the possibility of true multilingualism for all students?

NOTES

1. Proposition 13 limited the property tax in California to 1 percent of assessed value for both residential and commercial properties. Proposition 13 gradually eroded the property tax base and resulted in the state's having to take over the major funding of many local public services, including education. After the passage

of Proposition 13 in California, a number of other states passed similar legislation reducing property taxes.

2. Proposition 209 was backed by the University of California regent Ward Connerly, who the year before had successfully engineered a majority vote of the University of California regents in favor of barring the use of race, ethnicity, or gender in consideration of candidates for admission to the university. Proposition 209 extended this bar to state employment and contracting, as well as enacting, the prohibition against the use of affirmative action for admission to all state-supported educational institutions.

3. Multiple criteria are used to classify students from limited-English to English-proficient status. These multiple criteria, at the discretion of local districts, commonly consist of passing an English-proficiency test, being recommended by a teacher, and scoring at or near the 36th percentile on an academic achievement test in English.

4. See, for example, K. Hakuta, *How Long Does It Take to Learn English?* (Santa Barbara: University of California Linguistic Minority Research Institute, 1999). Available on the World Wide Web at **http://www.lmrinet.ucsb.edu**

5. The designation ELD, "English language development," is used by the state Department of Education to include all programs that focus on the use of English for the purposes of instruction. It incorporates the "structured English immersion" program cited in the Proposition 227 initiative, as well as similar programs that go by other names, such as "sheltered English" and SDAIE (specially designed academic instruction in English).

6. The UC LMRI coordinated data collection and analysis of the effects of proposition 227 in sixteen school districts and twenty-two schools in California during 1998–1999. Researchers from the UC Berkeley, UCLA, and UC Davis campuses were involved in the study, which has been released as Gándara et al. (2000).

7. *Proposition 227: A Fact Sheet That Focuses on CLAD/BCLAD Teacher Preparation.* Office of Policy and Programs, California Commission on Teacher Credentialing, October 1998

8. Douglas E. Mitchell and Ross Mitchell, *The Impact of California's Class-size Reduction Initiative on Student Achievement: Detailed Findings from Eight School Districts* (Riverside: California Educational Research Cooperative, 1999). Available on the World Wide Web at **http://cerc.ucr.edu/publications**

REFERENCES

August, D., and Hakuta, K. (1997). *Improving the Schooling of Language Minority Students.* Washington, DC: National Research Council, National Academy Press.

Betts, J., Rueben, K., and Danenberg, A. (2000). *Equal Resources, Equal Outcomes? The Distribution of School Resources and Student Achievement in California.* San Francisco: The Public Policy Institute of California.

Cazabon, M., Lambert, W., and Hall, G. (1993). *Two-Way Bilingual Education: A Progress Report on the Los Amigos Program.* Santa Cruz, CA: National Center for Research on Cultural Diversity and Second Language Learning.

Cooper, K. (2000). Riley endorses two-way bilingual education. *Washington Post,* March 16, 2000, p. A2.

Donato, R. (1997). *The Other Struggle for Equality: Mexican Americans during the Civil Rights Era.* Albany: SUNY Press.

Freeman, R. (1998). *Bilingual Education and Social Change.* Clevedon, England: Multilingual Matters.

Gándara, P. (1997). *Review of the Research on the Instruction of Limited English Proficient Students.* Santa Barbara, CA: Linguistic Minority Research Institute. Available on the World Wide Web at **www.lmrinet.ucsb.edu**

Gándara, P. (2000). In the aftermath of the storm: English learners in the post-227 era. *Bilingual Research Journal,* 24:1–13.

Gándara, P., Maxwell-Jolly, J., García, E., Asato, J., Gutiérrez, K., Stritikus, T., and Curry, J. (2000). *The Effects of Proposition 227 on the Instruction of English Learners. A Policy Brief.* Santa Barbara and Davis, CA: The Linguistic Minority Research Institute, Eduation Policy Center.

Genesee, F., and Gándara, P. (1999). Bilingual education programs: A cross-national perspective. *Journal of Social Issues* 55:665–685.

Gersten, R., and Woodward, J. (1985). A case for structured immersion, *Educational Leadership* 75:24–9.

Hakuta, K. (1999). *What Legitimate Inferences Can Be Made from the 1999 Release of SAT-9 Scores with Respect to the Impact of Proposition 227 on the Performance of LEP Students?* Available on the World Wide Web at **http://www.stanford.edu/~hakuta /SAT9/index.htm**

Haycock, K. (1998). *Good Teachers Matter . . . A Lot.* Santa Cruz, CA: Center for the Future of Teaching and Learning.

Huddy, L., and Sears, D. (1990). Qualified public support for bilingual education: Some policy implications. *Annals of the American Academy of Political and Social Science* 508:119–134.

Krashen, S. (1991). Bilingual education: A focus on current research. *Occasional Papers in Bilingual Education* 3 (Spring).

Krashen, S. (1996) Surveys of opinions on bilingual education: Some current issues. *Bilingual Research Journal* 20:411–431.

Lindholm, K. (1994). Promoting positive cross cultural attitudes and perceived competence in culturally and linguistically diverse classrooms. In *Cultural Diversity in Schools,* ed. R. DeVillar, C. Faltis, and J. Cummins. Albany: SUNY Press.

Mitchell, D., and Mitchell R. (1999). *The Impact of California's Class-size Reduction Initiative on Student Achievement: Detailed Findings from Eight School Districts.* Riverside: California Educational Research Center, University of California.

Orr, J., Butler, Y., Bousquet, M., and Hakuta, K. (2000). What Can We Learn about the Impact of Proposition 227 from SAT-9 Scores? An Analysis of Results from 2000. Available on the World Wide Web at **http://www.stanford.edu/~hakuta /SAT9/SAT9_2000**

Ramirez, J. D., Yuen, S. D., and Ramey, D. R. (1991). Longitudinal study of structured English immersion strategy, early-exit and late-exit transitional bilingual education programs for language-minority children. *Final Report to the U.S. Department of Education.* Executive Summary and Vols. I and II. San Mateo, CA: Aguirre International.

Reynolds, A. (1991). *Bilingualism, Multiculturalism, and Second Language Learning.* Hillsdale, NJ: Erlbaum.

Rotherham-Borus, M. (1994). Bicultural reference group orientations and adjustment. In *Ethnic Identity,* ed. M. Bernal and G. Knight. Albany: SUNY Press.

Ruiz, R. (1984). Orientations in language planning. *Journal of the National Association of Bilingual Education* 2:15–34.

Rumberger, R., and Gándara, P. (2000). The schooling of English learners. In *Crucial Issues in California Education 2000: Are the Reform Pieces Fitting Together?* ed. G. Hayward and E. Burr. Berkeley and Palo Alto, CA: Policy Analysis for California Education (PACE).

Shields, P., Esch, C., Humphrey, D., Young, V., Gaston, M., and Hunt, H. (1999). *The Status of the Teaching Profession: Research Findings and Policy Recommendations.* Santa Cruz, CA: The Center for the Future of Teaching and Learning.

Spencer, M., and Markstrom-Adams, C. (1990). Identity processes among racial and ethnic minority children in America. *Child Development* 61:290–310.

Walqui-van Lier, A. (n.d.) *Doing Sheltered English Right.* Palo Alto, CA: Stanford University.

Commentary

Maria S. Carlo and Catherine E. Snow

The three chapters on which it is our privilege to comment define the key research questions at the center of an agenda for Latino research quite differently. Barbara Zurer Pearson's paper focuses on the conditions under which young Latino children can become bilingual and on what language skills in Spanish and English they actually achieve under varying circumstances. Her paper makes it clear that widely held beliefs that bilingual children are deficient in their language knowledge are an artifact of monolingual bias in measurement instruments. At the same time, she points out that children growing up bilingual do not magically learn twice as much as children growing up monolingual—one needs to take both their languages into account to get a good picture of their language proficiency. Ana Celia Zentella's paper explores the intricate bidirectional relationships between language use and personal/cultural identities. She poses questions about the degree to which the recent history of Latinos in the United States, with its features of hybrid identity and characteristic communitywide language-use patterns, will persist in characterizing future generations. She also questions traditional linguistic definitions of language as incapable of explaining the hybrid language varieties that bilingual communities create, noting as well that linguists from outside these communities will be unable to provide descriptively adequate characterizations of their language use. Patricia Gándara tells the depressing story of bilingual-education policy in California, offering this story as a warning to other states with large numbers of Spanish speakers. She formulates a series of questions emphasizing the benefits of bilingualism and criticizes most research evaluating bilingual education for focusing only on short-term accomplishments in English.

These three thought-provoking contributions interject the crucial dimension of language into the larger conversation represented in this volume about the Latino experience. The linguistic dimension is too often neglected in discussions of cultural contact, migration, assimilation, and even academic achievement.

Although the three research agendas proposed in these chapters are of great interest and value, each is (of course) also a product of the disciplinary tradition within which it has been carried out and of the resulting focus on a particular approach to analyzing language. Following any of the three agendas proposed in these chapters would enhance our knowledge, but connecting the disciplinary perspectives behind these three agendas would enrich all of them. We would argue that a Latino-focused agenda for language research in the twenty-first century calls for programs of research that allow interdisciplinary collaborations and that bring together everything we know about a bilingual's knowledge, the linguistic environment he or she functions in, and the ideological contexts that affect both individuals and language environments. Within the disciplinary tradition of psycholinguistics, Pearson's focus on an analysis of language capacities enables her to measure varying degrees of skill but makes it hard to attend adequately to the larger political and social context in which the children are learning. Within the tradition of sociolinguistics and linguistic anthropology, Zentella is able to highlight the creative and adaptive dimensions of language use, but the group focus of sociolinguistic analysis comes at the expense of attending to differences in skill level among the speakers being studied. Gándara's policy-based analysis defines the challenge of providing an adequate education for Latino children as one of a particular program design and access to bilingual teachers without being able to incorporate data about determinants of high quality and effectiveness within and across program types.

Pearson's analysis of bilingual development would be much enhanced by the careful description of the language context provided by Zentella's sociolinguistic methods, and of the language policies identified by Gándara that have had an impact on these children's parents' skills in Spanish and English as well as on the use of Spanish and English in their immediate environment. Zentella's anthropolitical descriptions of language use would be enriched if actual language proficiency measures were available on her informants. For example, although her description of code switching as an identity move is convincing for many cases, one wonders what other purposes code switching might be called upon to serve, such as conveying one's message more precisely by using a lexical item from the other language. Gándara's analysis of instructional programs would benefit from recognition that (1) a child's proficiency in the home language and the school language interacts with the specifics of the instruction offered to determine outcomes, and (2) the instruction offered responds to the issues of context and of identity that Zentella notes. Having a bilingual teacher—

clearly an advantage for the Spanish-speaking child—does not however, preclude exposure to the damaging ideologies about language "quality" that Zentella identifies, because these ideologies permeate the Spanish-speaking as well as the English-speaking world. Furthermore, teacher knowledge about children's learning, about literacy, and about instructional options influences child outcomes as powerfully as does sharing a home language.

All three of these papers start from the assumption, which we share, that children who know Spanish well should have an advantage in U.S. schools—if only the schools could build on their knowledge effectively. Helping schools help Spanish-speaking children learn English and acquire literacy in both Spanish and English requires (1) understanding the circumstances under which robust knowledge of Spanish develops in Latinos growing up in the United States, and (2) having a well-articulated theory of how skills derived from Spanish knowledge might support the acquisition of English language and literacy. These three papers all help us understand the many influences that need to be taken into account in exploring these issues. Pearson points out that acquiring high levels of Spanish skill requires an environment that is structured to provide rich experiences with Spanish; such knowledge does not come automatically just from having a Spanish-speaking parent or teacher or from living in a Latino neighborhood. Zentella highlights the beliefs and attitudes of the larger society that can undermine high proficiency in Spanish, and Gándara points out the policy shifts that have disrupted both Spanish learning and optimal cross-language transfer for children in California. Ideally, bilingual teachers can capitalize on their own knowledge of Spanish and on their bilingual experiences to promote cross-language transfer in their students. Unfortunately, the research base available to guide teachers in making decisions about when to introduce English, when to introduce what sorts of literacy experiences in English, and how to teach explicitly for transfer is inadequate. We would add these topics to the Latino research agenda for the twenty-first century.

Chapter 18

The Schooling of Latino Children

Luis C. Moll and Richard Ruiz

In perhaps no other domain of society is the growth of the Latino population in the United States more marked than in education. Latino students, along with African Americans, now constitute the majority in the principal urban school districts, and their growing presence is also becoming noticeable in rural schools (Young 1999). The purpose of this chapter is to summarize some major issues related to the schooling of Latino students in the United States, a challenging task given the variability of this population, its wide geographic dispersal, and the complexity of the topic.[1] We start by providing an overview of the sociohistorical context of the education of Latino students, for it reveals issues of coercion and control that are still very much a part of the contemporary scene. This education must also be understood in relation to the social class characteristics of the population, because it is this factor, more than any other, that determines the nature of their schooling.

In order to illustrate briefly the most pressing educational issues, we will develop a "case example" of one school district, the Los Angeles Unified School District (LAUSD), the second largest in the country. We claim that the issues revealed through this example arise in other regions of the country as well, although with much diversity in how they are manifested and addressed. We then propose the concept of "educational sovereignty" as a means of challenging the legacy of control and imposition that characterizes the education of Latino students in this country.[2] Educational sovereignty means that communities create their own infrastructures for development, including mechanisms for the education of their children that capitalize on rather than devalue their cultural resources. It will be their prerogative to invite others, including those in the academic community, to participate in such a creation. These forms of education must address

Latino self-interest or self-determination, while limiting the influence of the anglocentric whims of the majority that historically have shaped their schooling. We conclude this chapter by presenting some themes that may help shape any future educational-research agenda for Latino students.

SOCIOHISTORICAL CONTEXT

Latinos have a varied history in the United States, and that variation has been used to explain their schooling achievement. Relatively recent immigrant groups from Central and South America and the Caribbean exhibit some of the characteristics posited by Ogbu and his colleagues (Gibson and Ogbu 1991) for immigrant groups historically: a sense of appreciation for their host country, a need to acculturate to a new set of norms and values, and allegiance to a political system that may require great adjustments on their part. Such groups may be expected to acquiesce to the expectation that they "become Americans" as quickly as possible, with the school as primary agent of the transformation. Although school achievement levels for these groups have in general been low, studies suggest variations depending on such factors as age on arrival, previous schooling experiences, the existence of social support networks within the receiving community, effort expended on studies, and social class (see, for example, Rumbaut 1999).

Other immigrant Latinos have higher achievement levels, both in school and in social mobility. This is especially true for Cubans, whose arrival in large numbers in this country (principally south Florida) coincided with the Cuban Revolution of the late 1950s. Although there was little in the way of a support infrastructure for them in place, their relatively high economic standing and (therefore) extensive schooling experience helped them create networks of support for themselves.[3] Moreover, and perhaps most important, their strong anticommunist sentiments fitted well with the emerging U.S. ideological phobias of that era. The U.S. interest in demonstrating the superiority of democratic capitalism over the socialist system compelled the government to promote and sustain (through the infusion of billions of dollars) social supports, including school programs, that would ensure the new arrivals' success. It is not accidental that the first— and in some ways still the best—bilingual programs for Spanish speakers in public schools were developed in Dade County with the full blessing of the government and with support from local, state, and national agencies and foundations.

The situation is very different for two other major Latino groups, who have a much longer history in this country and by and large do not consider themselves "immigrants." Puerto Rico became a possession of the United States at the turn of the twentieth century (1898). The major migration to the mainland, primarily to New York City, commenced in the

1950s and extended, with considerable fluctuations, through the 1960s and beyond; thus Puerto Ricans became the dominant Latino population of the northeastern coast of the United States (Carrasquillo and Sánchez-Korrol 1996; Rodríguez 1995). The status of Puerto Ricans as citizens has been tenuous from the beginning and remains contentious today, given the continuing U.S. colonial domination and ongoing discussions of statehood or independence for the island. In general, Puerto Ricans in the United States have had low school achievement and socioeconomic mobility (Nieto 1999).

Similarly, Mexican Americans (or Chicanos) also exhibit low achievement and mobility (García 1995). Their history in North America predates that of any other Latino group, a fact that is not lost on many within the community (Gutierrez 1995). Upon the signing of the Treaty of Guadalupe-Hidalgo in 1848, Mexicans became Mexican Americans with the stroke of a pen. The treaty gave this country nearly half of Mexico's territory, what are now the states (or parts thereof) of Texas, New Mexico, Arizona, Colorado, Utah, Nevada, and California. As Anglo Americans occupied the new territories, motivated by the mining for gold in California and the rapid spread of railroad lines and commerce, the ideology of white supremacy followed, under the philosophical guise of "manifest destiny," providing justification for the displacement not only of lands and property but also of language and culture (Vélez-Ibáñez 1997).

The schools played an important role in facilitating the Anglo American dominance of new territories, in both the occupation of the Southwest and the colonization of Puerto Rico (for the latter, see Cabán 1999). In the Southwest, the schools used two primary methods of social control, both intended to preserve the status quo by denying the Mexican population the knowledge necessary to protect its political and economic rights and to advance economically in society (see Spring 1997, pp. 82–89). One method was exclusion from schooling, which entailed not enforcing the compulsory school laws. The second method (more relevant for our present purposes) was to control the content and purpose of schooling. Public officials wanted Mexican children in schools but segregated so that they could be controlled and indoctrinated—so that they could be "Americanized," learn English, and rid themselves of their native language and customs, which the officials deemed detrimental to assimilation and to the maintenance of a unified nation. This strategy springs from the same ideology used to justify the separate schooling of Indian and African American children. And it is the same strategy pursued today in California and other states through initiatives designed to eliminate bilingual education, to impose a highly controlled English monolingual education, and to make it illegal to use languages other than English in school.

This dual strategy of exclusion and condemnation, divesting Latino students of their primary resources—their language and culture—is what Valenzuela (1999) has called "subtractive schooling." This form of schooling has become a major feature of the education of poor and working-class Latino students all over the country. It results in disdain for what one knows and what one is, influences children's attitudes toward knowledge, and undermines their personal competence. That is, subtractive schooling creates a social distance between the students and the world of school knowledge. It creates the impression that someone else possesses great knowledge and expertise, whereas, in contrast, one is unskilled and incompetent—that one's language and knowledge are inadequate because they are not privileged (formalized and accorded special status) by the school. This mind-set (the superiority of the other and the inferiority of one's own) is accepted as "natural," as just the way things are. It is considered "common sense," and it easily becomes self-imposed (cf. Banks 1994).

Consequently, some students even appropriate the ideology that learning English at all costs is the way to guarantee success in life. The result is the great illusion of American education: that to learn English (and have academic success), it is necessary to shed Spanish and the intimate social relations created through that language. The logical extension of this ideology is the overwhelming obsession, as manifested in the schools and in the current laws in various states, with teaching the children English "as quickly as possible," *to the detriment of critical subject matter learning.* As a consequence, we are left with the impression that these children are either unable or unwilling to learn English, although all recent studies suggest otherwise (López 1999; Rumbaut 1999).

Our claim, then, is that the control and coercion exemplified by subtractive forms of schooling are a major feature of the schooling of Latino students, especially given their working-class status. Further, the pervasiveness of this form of schooling is reinforced by both current educational policies and language ideologies about English and Spanish. We now turn to an example from LAUSD to illustrate these issues in a contemporary urban context (cf. Walsh 1998).

LOS ANGELES: A PROTOTYPE OF ISSUES

The Los Angeles metropolitan area has undergone major demographic shifts during the last two decades, most prominently the increase of the Latino population, both immigrant and U.S.-born, and of other immigrant populations. Rumbaut (1998) has estimated that 62 percent of the population of Los Angeles County, or approximately 6 million people, are of "immigrant stock," most of them Latinos. A current estimate is that the

Latino population of the city and county of Los Angeles ranges from 40 to 45 percent of the total population. In the county this percentage represents a total of about 4,240,000 people, the majority population of Los Angeles, and about 40 percent of them are of school age (from birth to ages seventeen); moreover, about 63 percent of young children (from birth to age five) in the county are Latinos (Children Now 1999).

The great majority of this population, be they recent immigrants or of second-generation or other vintage, is working-class or poor (Ong and Blumenberg 1996). In fact, Ortíz (1996) has suggested that because of broader social and economic factors, the Mexican-origin population of Los Angeles, which is approximately 80 percent of the overall Latino population, may be mired in a "permanent" low working-class status (cf. Myers 1998). This low socioeconomic standing has major implications for the schooling of children, an issue to which we shall return.

The Latino student population of the Los Angeles Unified School District (LAUSD), according to state data (1998–1999), numbers approximately half a million students (480,655), or 69 percent of the total student population; the Anglo student population is 10.5 percent (73,321).[4] Therefore, this school district is approximately 90 percent "minority," if such a term is still applicable. Furthermore, 74 percent of students in the district are eligible for free or reduced-cost lunch services, an index of poverty. In addition, of the total number of students in the district (695,885), approximately half (45.9 percent) are designated as limited-English-proficient (LEP), about 300,000 of these students being Spanish speakers. Nearly all of these LEP students (95 percent) are in the free or reduced-cost lunch program; hence they are among the poorest students in the district.

The teaching corps, however, remains largely white (49.4 percent), with 23.6 percent Latino and 14.7 percent African American members. Statewide, we should point out, the discrepancies are larger: the Latino student population is at 41 percent (37.8 percent are white), whereas 76.2 percent of teachers are white and only 12.1 percent are Latinos. Thus Latinos constitute the majority of students at LAUSD and statewide, and they are largely working-class and poor, but the teaching corps is primarily white and middle-class—and English monolingual as well.[5]

The academic performance of the Latino students is generally low. The dropout rate (grades 9–12) for Latinos, and for African Americans, exceeds 20 percent, a figure that also reflects the national trend. In addition, the national percentile rank of test scores for all Latino students (collectively) is considerably below the national average, even when the LEP scores are excluded. These high dropout rates and low achievement rates are a consistent finding in all school districts nationally that have comparable socioeconomic profiles. However, within LAUSD, even taking this profile into account, about 41 percent of the Latino students (46 percent for all students in the district; 30 percent countywide) who graduate are eligible for entrance into the University of California or California State University system. This percentage is clearly a positive development, although the white graduates' percentage of eligibility is much higher at 57 percent, a significant difference.

In addition to these general characteristics of the district, there are other interrelated issues that help capture the Gestalt of the educational situation of Latino students in this district and, by implication, elsewhere in the country as well.[6] We will mention only two of them for illustration purposes. The most recent is the passage (on June 2, 1998) of Proposition 227 banning bilingual education (see Chapter 17 in this volume). This proposition is part of an insidious pattern of oppressive actions aimed at Latinos—maneuvers that have successfully circumvented legislative channels where Latinos may hold some leverage, especially in California (Santoro 1999). The extent to which this proposition represents a quasicolonial imposition on the Latino population of Los Angeles is made clear by the following figures: 68 percent of Latinos in Los Angeles favor bilingual education; this figure increases to 88 percent when respondents are limited to those parents with children in the classrooms of the city (Crawford 1999). Consider the coercive ideological context that such a law perpetuates, establishing Spanish as a pariah language in the schools, privileging English exclusively, and demonstrating clearly how only the interests that an elite Anglo monolingual community deems worthwhile can be represented in the schools.

A second issue is the prominence of reductionist pedagogies as illustrated by the phonics reading mandates. These mandates require, under penalty of law, employing English-language phonic drills as the *only* way to teach beginning reading, usually as part of a highly rigid and prescriptive packaged curriculum imposed on teachers and students (for a critique, see Smith 1999). The intent is to reduce or eliminate teacher autonomy by dictating what and how they teach. This includes reducing any flexibility teachers might otherwise have to develop meaning-based literacy innovations to help the students. This reading agenda, which excludes all but certain forms of positivist research from funding and marginalizes all those who do not toe the ideological line of a particular model of reductionist reading research (Allington and Haley 1999; Taylor 1998), also removes the possibility of biliteracy approaches that have great promise for bilingual children.

The key point is that these are not just isolated issues that coincide. It is vital to recognize the organized political forces that guide these activities as part of a broader ideological coalition and an urgent agenda to control schools. Our claim is that this situation, whatever varied form it takes, represents several steps backward for Latino students in the United States—a population that is overwhelmingly working-class and poor, is growing demographically, and is daily suffering the consequences of increasing numbers and its low position in the social order.

EDUCATIONAL SOVEREIGNTY

In what follows we present two promising responses to the encapsulation of schooling by dominant policies, practices, and ideologies. We use the term *educational sovereignty* to capture the need to challenge the arbitrary authority of the white power structure to determine the essence of education for Latino students. In particular, we emphasize the type of agency that considers the schooling of Latino children within a larger education ecology and that respects and responds to the values of education possessed by Latino families (see Goldenberg and Gallimore 1995; Ruiz 1997). This larger ecology includes not only the schools but also the social relationships and cultural resources found in local households and other community settings.

The emphasis is on challenging the ideological and structural constraints that are so dominant in the schooling of Latino children through a strategic and vigorous agency that builds on the culturally grounded resources of children, families, and communities.

Mediating Institutional Arrangements.   One line of study is the reorganization of the schooling experience itself to mediate ingrained structural constraints. An important example is provided by the work of Mehan and colleagues (Mehan et al. 1996) on a teacher-initiated innovation, a three-year "untracking" program known as AVID (Advancement via Individual Determination). This work featured two key elements. One was the placement of students within a regular academic track, requiring that they take courses that lead to college admission. A second element was providing the "social scaffolds" necessary to ensure that the students would succeed within these courses (cf. Lee and Smith 1999). In particular, this social support included rigorous, weekly academic tutoring, with explicit instruction on note taking, test taking, and study strategies. It also included teacher advocacy on the students' behalf, the creation of social networks that facilitated acquiring the knowledge and wherewithal necessary to deal with the school culture, and acquaintance of the students with the procedural knowledge they needed to deal with college applications and admission.

Another central factor in the success of the Latino (and African American) low-income students was the development of an "academic identity." This identity featured the formation of academically oriented associations among students, while dealing with potentially incompatible social identities and relationships. Just as important, both students and teachers developed a "critical consciousness" about race, class, and school politics and about resistance to the innovation as manifested either in or out of school (see Hubbard and Mehan, in press). In all, of the sample ($n = 248$) studied by Mehan and his colleagues in San Diego, 88 percent graduated to a college education (48 percent in four-year colleges, 40 percent in two-year colleges), with the highest proportion of college attendance among the students from low-income and working-class families.

Other examples of school-based changes to provide additive forms of schooling for Latino students include "maintenance" bilingual education and dual-language programs (Brisk 1998), the school reorganization research of Goldenberg and Sullivan (1994), and the dual-language school in Tucson documented by Smith (2000).

Activating Cultural Resources. There are forms of schooling that deliberately attempt to build upon the resources of the students and their communities in doing academic work. One example is our collaborative research on "funds of knowledge," those bodies of knowledge developed socially and historically by households. This work, which was conducted mostly in working-class, Latino neighborhoods and schools in Tucson, Arizona, has been particularly successful in helping teachers approach, understand, and define their school's community in terms of these funds of knowledge (Moll and González 1997; Mercado and Moll 1997). The teachers in these studies visit their students' households to learn from the families; they are convinced that it is of great value to understand the ways in which people generate knowledge as they engage life. This work by implication debunks the preconception that working-class Latino households lack worthwhile knowledge and experiences, replacing it with the assumption that the knowledge and experiences of the children and their families can be identified, documented, and accessed for teaching. This view of households as possessing valuable resources for learning changes radically how the students are perceived, talked about, and taught.

Other work features schools with curricula that critically engage community needs and realities (Rivera and Pedraza 2000; Ramos-Zayas 1998), and the creation of alliances between teachers and families in support of schooling (Delgado-Gaitán 1990; Rodríguez-Brown and Mulhern 1993; Paratore, Melzi, and Krol-Sinclair 1999). Still other innovations feature community-based alliances among social and educational institutions to create nonschool settings for the learning and development of children and adults. Outstanding efforts include those of Vásquez (1994) and Gutiérrez, Baquedano-López, and Alvarez (in press). There are also community-based settings specially created for the personal and intellectual development of women. These include work reported by Andrade, González, Le Denmat, and Moll (2000), Benmayor, Torruellas, and Juarbe (1997), and Rivera (in press).

ANTICIPATING RESEARCH THEMES

In this final section we project three themes that might help shape a future educational agenda for Latino students. These themes emphasize the need to create strategic alliances in enhancing the educational landscape of these students, especially in the changing demographic context of the United States, and the need to stimulate new theoretical thinking about educational issues.

Interethnic Coalitions.   The character and dimension of the schooling of Latinos should be analyzed not independently, as is usually the case, but rather in relation to the situation of African American children, for they share similar political environments and colonial forms of education. Clearly, the degree of similarity may vary considerably with the urban area, the political and economic history and arrangements, and the specific social issues that arise (Rodríguez 1999). Just as clearly, however, education is an issue that lends itself to intergroup analysis and action, because schools remain crucial institutions for both Latino and African American communities.

Transnational Dynamics.   This issue reflects one of the most important developments in Latino communities across the country. It refers to the proliferation of social networks that facilitate more or less continuous links between the society of origin and the society where the immigrants have settled. Although they are not a new phenomenon, these transnational communities may have a new character given the large number of people involved and, especially, the new modes of communication (Portes 1999).

The social, economic, or political activities that these international social networks facilitate may have implications for the formation of identities and for education. One such effect may be the creation of a strong "linguistic marketplace" where language proficiency is seen as real capital in the global economy, thus establishing the desirability of bilingualism and biliteracy for all populations, but especially for Latinos (Fradd 1999; Skutnabb-Kangas 1999). In a sense, these transnational activities extend the borders of the countries in question, and in this context, Latinos in the United States are hardly a minority. Instead, they are part of a much larger and international community.

Linguistic Human Rights.   The last few years of the twentieth century saw a virtual explosion in scholarly interest in the issue of how to extend rights to language-minority communities, especially those in large, multinational states (Kontra et al. 1999). Although this interest emerged most dramatically out of concern for saving the world's dying indigenous languages (Krauss 1992), it has been broadened to portray the language rights of immigrant and other minority communities as essential civil rights, regardless of the status of the languages (Hernández-Chávez 1995). This will surely be a matter of great concern with respect to Latinos in the United States as the Spanish-speaking population grows to be the largest minority group in the country.

CONCLUSION

The discussion of the schooling of Latino students that is presented in this chapter is designed to provide an overview of the sociohistorical context of this schooling, and a summary of the most important contemporary issues that help perpetuate disabling pedagogical conditions. In response, we proposed the concept of educational sovereignty as the mediating agency needed to challenge such conditions. This educational sovereignty must (1) attend to the larger historical structures and ideologies of schooling, with the goal of making educational constraints, especially those related to social class, visible and unstable, (2) teaching and learning as part of a broader education ecology, (3) and tap into existing social and cultural resources in schools, households, and communities in promoting change.

We are well aware of the difficulty of the task for those who want to change the fortunes of schooling for Latino children. Concerted efforts, combined with the disposition to challenge the constraining ideologies and practices that characterize the educational status quo for Latino children, are the minimal requirements to produce such change.

NOTES

1. For present purposes, we limit our comments to K–12 schooling in public schools (see Chapa, this volume, for issues that arise in higher education).

2. Our use of the term *educational sovereignty* was inspired by the work of colleagues doing research in and with indigenous communities (such as Warner 1999; see also Henze and Davis 1999; Lomawaima 2000).

3. There has been considerable variation, especially in terms of social class, in the different waves of Cuban immigration (Pedraza 1996); we are referring here to the dominant, first wave of wealthy and highly educated refugees.

4. Unless otherwise indicated, all LAUSD figures are from the California State Department of Education Web site. See **goldmine.cade.gov and ed-data.k12.ca.us /dev/District.asp**

5. The middle-class status of the teachers is an estimate based on their reported salaries and levels of education. LAUSD teachers must be college graduates, and they earn between $32,569 (entry level) and $61,169. Source: **certificated.lausd .k12.ca.us/cert/info/ Teaching_in_L.A/ teaching_in_l.a..html**

6. There are several important issues that we do not discuss for lack of space, such as differential school financial resources by social class, school segregation, tracking, disproportionate special-education referrals, bias in high-stakes testing, violence, and harassment by immigration officials. All of these issues form part of the daily reality of the schooling of Latino children.

REFERENCES

Allington, R., and Haley, W. J. (1999). The politics of literacy teaching. *Educational Researcher* 28(8):4–12.

Andrade, R., González Le Denmat, H., and Moll, L. C. (2000). El grupo de Las Señoras: Creating consciousness through literature. In *Challenging a single standard*, ed. M. Gallego and S. Hollingsworth. New York: Teachers College Press, pp. 271–284.

Banks, J. (1994). *Multiethnic education.* Boston: Allyn & Bacon.

Benmayor, R., Torruellas, R. M., and Juarbe, A. L. (1997). Claiming cultural citizenship in East Harlem. In *Latino cultural citizenship*, ed. W. Flores and R. Benmayor. Boston: Beacon, pp. 152–209.

Brisk, M. E. (1998). *Bilingual education.* Mahwah, NJ: Erlbaum.

Cabán, L. (1999). *Constructing a colonized people.* Boulder, CO: Westview.

Carrasquillo, H., and Sánchez-Korrol, V. (1996). Migration, community, and culture. In *Origins and destinies*, ed. S. Pedraza and R. G. Rumbaut. Belmont, CA: Wadsworth, pp. 98–109.

Children Now (1999). *California county data book.* Los Angeles, CA: Children Now.

Crawford, J. (1999). *Bilingual education*, 4th ed. Los Angeles: Bilingual Educational Services.

Delgado-Gaitán, C. (1990). *Literacy for empowerment.* New York: Falmer.

Fradd, S. (ed.). (1999). *Creating Florida's multilingual global workforce.* Gainesville, FL: Institute for the Advanced Study of Communication Processes.

García, E. (1995). Educating Mexican American students. In *Handbook of research on multicultural education*, ed. J. Banks and C. McGee Banks. New York: Macmillan, pp. 372–387.

Gibson, E., and Ogbu, J. (eds.). (1991). *Minority status and schooling.* New York: Garland.

Goldenberg, C. (1996). Latin American Immigration and U.S. schools. *Social Policy Report: Society for Research in Child Development* 10(1):1–30.

Goldenberg, C., and Gallimore, R. (1995). Immigrant Latino parents' values and beliefs about their children's education. In *Advances in motivation and achievement*, ed. P. R. Pintrich and M. Maehr. Greenwich, CT: JAI Press, pp. 183–228.

Goldenberg, C., and Sullivan, J. (1994). *Making change happen in a language-minority school* (EPR #13). Washington, DC: Center for Applied Linguistics.

Gutiérrez, R. (1995). Historical and social science research on Mexican Amercians. In *Handbook of research on multicultural education*, ed. J. Banks and C. McGee Banks. New York: Macmillan, pp. 203–222.

Gutiérrez, K. D., Baquedano-López, P., and Alvarez, H. H. (In press). A cultural-historical approach to collaboration. *Theory into Practice.*

Henze, R., & Davis, K. (eds.). (1999). Authenticity and identity: Lessons from indigenous language education (Theme issue). *Anthropology and Education Quarterly* 30(1)3–21:

Hernández-Chávez, E. (1995). Language policy in the United States. In *Linguistic human rights*, ed. T. Skutnabb-Kangas and R. Phillipson. Berlin: Mouton de Gruyter, pp. 141–158.

Hubbard, L., and Mehan, H. (In press). Race and reform. *Journal of Negro Education.*

Kontra, M., Phillipson, R. Skutnabb-Kangas, T., and Varady, I. (eds.) (1999). *Language: A right and a resource*. Budapest: Central European University Press.

Krauss, M. (1992). The world's languages in crisis. *Language* 68:4–10.

Lee, V., and Smith, J. (1999). Social support and achievement for young adolescents in Chicago. *American Educational Research Journal* 36(4):907–945.

Lomawaima, K. T. (2000). Tribal sovereigns: Reframing research in American Indian communities. *Harvard Educational Review* 27(1):1–21.

López, D. (1999). Social and linguistics aspects of assimilation today. In *The handbook of international migration*, ed. C. Hirschman, P. Kasinitz, and J. DeWind. New York: Russell Sage Foundation, pp. 212–222.

Mehan, H., Villanueva, I., Hubbard, L., and Lintz, A. (1996). *Constructing school success*. Cambridge: Cambridge University Press.

Mercado, C., and Moll, L. C. (1997). The study of funds of knowledge. *Centro* 9(9):26–42.

Moll, L. C., and González, N. (1997). Teachers as social scientists. In *Race, ethnicity and multiculturalism*, ed. P. M. Hall. New York: Garland, pp. 89–114.

Myers, D. (1998). Dimensions of economic adaptation by Mexican-origin men. In *Crossings*, ed. M. Suárez-Orozco. Cambridge, MA: Harvard University Press, pp. 157–200.

Nieto, S. (ed.). (1999). *Puerto Rican students in U.S. schools*. Mahwah, NJ: Erlbaum.

Ong, P., and Blumenberg, E. (1996). Income and racial inequality in Los Angeles. In *The city: Los Angeles and urban theory at the end of the twentieth century*, ed. A. Scott and E. Soja. Berkeley: University of California Press, pp. 311–35.

Ortíz, V. (1996). The Mexican-origin population: Permanent working class or emerging middle class? In *Ethnic Los Angeles*, ed. R. Waldinger and M. Bozorgmehr. New York: Russell Sage Foundation, pp. 247–278.

Paratore, J., Melzi, G., and Krol-Sinclair, B. (1999). *What should we expect of family literacy? Experiences of Latino children whose parents participate in an intergenerational project*. Chicago, IL: International Reading Association and National Reading Conference.

Pedraza, S. (1996). Cuba's refugees: Manifold migrations. In *Origins and destinies*, ed. S. Pedraza and R. G. Rumbaut. Belmont, CA: Wadsworth, pp. 263–279.

Portes, A. (1999). Immigration theory for a new century. In *The handbook of international migration*, ed. C. Hirschman, P. Kasinitz, and J. DeWind. New York: Russell Sage Foundation, pp. 21–32.

Ramos-Zayas, A. Y. (1998). Nationalist ideologies, neighborhood-based activism, and educational spaces in Puerto Rican Chicago. *Harvard Educational Review* 68(2):164–192.

Rivera, K. (In press). From developing one's voice to making oneself heard. In *Socio-political perspectives on language policy and language planning*, ed. T. Huebner, K. Davis, and J. LoBianco. Amsterdam/Philadelphia: Benjamins.

Rivera, M., and Pedraza, P. (2000). The spirit of a Latino/a quest: Transforming education for community self-determination and social change. In *Puerto Rican students in U.S. schools*, ed. S. Nieto. Mahwah, NJ: Erlbaum, pp.223–243.

Rodríguez, C. (1995). Puerto Ricans in historical and social science research. In *Handbook of research on multicultural education*, ed. J. Banks and C. McGee Banks. New York: Macmillan, pp. 223–244.

Rodríguez, N. (1999). U.S. immigration and changing relations between African Americans and Latinos. In *The handbook of international migration*, ed. C. Hirschman, P. Kasinitz, and J. DeWind. New York: Russell Sage Foundation, pp. 423–432.

Rodríguez-Brown, F., and Mulhern, M. (1993). Fostering critical literacy through family literacy. *Bilingual Research Journal* 17(3):1–16.

Ruiz, R. (1997). The empowerment of language minority students. In *Latinos and education*, ed. A. Darder, R. Torres, & H. Gutiérrez. New York: Routledge, pp. 319–328.

Rumbaut, R. (1998). *Transformations.* Paper presented at the Annual Meeting of the Eastern Sociological Society, Philadelphia, March 21.

Rumbaut, R. (1999). Assimilation and its discontents. In *The handbook of international migration*, ed. C. Hirschman, P. Kasinitz, and J. DeWind. New York: Russell Sage Foundation, pp. 172–195.

Santoro, W. (1999). Conventional politics takes center stage: The Latino struggle against English-only laws. *Social Forces* 77(3):887–909.

Skutnabb-Kangas, T. (1999). Linguistic diversity, human rights and the "free"market. In *Language: A right and a resource*, ed. M. Kontra et al. Budapest: Central European University Press, pp. 187–222.

Smith, F. (1999). Why systematic phonics and phonemic awareness instruction constitute an educational hazard. *Language Arts* 77(2):150–155.

Smith, P. (2000). *Community as resource for minority language learning.* Ph.D. diss., University of Arizona.

Spring, J. (1997). *Deculturalization and the struggle for equality.* 2d ed. New York: McGraw-Hill.

Taylor, D. (1998). *Beginning to read and the spin doctors of science.* Urbana, IL: National Council of Teachers of English.

Valenzuela, A. (1999). *Subtractive schooling.* Albany, New York: State University of New York Press.

Vásquez, O. (1994). The magic of La Clase Mágica. *Australian Journal of Language and Literacy,* 17(2):120–128.

Vélez-Ibáñez, C. (1997). *Border visions.* Tucson: University of Arizona Press.

Walsh, C. (1998). "Staging encounters": The educational decline of U.S. Puerto Ricans in [Post]-colonial perspective. *Harvard Educational Review,* 68(2):218–243.

Warner, S. L. N. (1999). Kuleana: The right, responsibility, and authority of indigenous peoples to speak and make decisions for themselves in language and cultural revitalization. *Anthropology and Education Quarterly* 30(1):68–93.

Young, B. (1999). *Characteristics of the 100 Largest Public Elementary and Secondary School Districts in the United States: 1997–98,* NCES 1999-318. Washington, DC: U.S. Department of Education, National Center for Education Statistics.

Chapter 19

Affirmative Action, X Percent Plans, and Latino Access to Higher Education in the Twenty-first Century

Jorge Chapa

Affirmative action in higher education is under attack across the nation. It has been stopped by litigation, popular referenda and executive decisions in Texas, California, Washington, and Florida, and it is under similar attack in many other states. The intensity of these attacks threatens to undermine the educational, economic, and political gains Latinos have made very recently. The rapid growth of the Latino population and its much more modest growth in institutional influence have probably both served to motivate this attack. In Texas, affirmative action was dismantled by the decision of the Fifth Circuit Court of Appeals in the Hopwood case (to learn more about Hopwood see Chapa and Lazaro 1998). In California, affirmative action in higher education admissions was ended by Proposition 209.

More than half of the nation's Latinos live in Texas and California, and without effective interventions, Latino participation in selective institutions of higher education will decrease. Even with access to affirmative action programs before they were halted in these two states, Latinos were severely underrepresented in the selective institutions of higher education that have highly competitive admissions. Without affirmative action, Latino chances for participation in higher education now appear to be severely limited. This limitation on Latino participation in higher education comes at a time when Latino undergraduate enrollments in higher education are expected to increase from 11 percent of the total in 2000 to 15 percent in 2015 (Carnevale 2000, pp. 59–72). However, preliminary indications that the top 10 percent plan in Texas has had a positive impact on Latino participation at the state's most selective public institutions of higher education may provide a reason for at least a little optimism.

The goal of this chapter is to examine the prospects for increasing Latino representation in higher education in a post-affirmative-action context. We will first define our terms and the present evidence that affirmative action programs for Latinos can be solidly justified. George Curry says that the U.S. Civil Rights Commission has defined affirmative action as "any measure, beyond simple termination of a discriminatory practice, *which permits the consideration of race, national origin, sex, or disability,* along with other criteria, and which is adopted to provide opportunities to a class of qualified individuals who have either historically or actually been denied those opportunities, and to prevent the recurrence of discrimination in the future" (Curry 1996, p. xiv, emphasis added).

This definition is particularly helpful in discussing student affirmative action programs because there are many different types of such programs with a vast range in scale and scope. (Employment-focused affirmative action programs are much more narrowly constrained by law and regulation.)

Affirmative action rests on the principle that merely prohibiting discrimination is not enough to bring about increased economic and educational opportunities for the victims of past and continuing unequal treatment. Moreover, because these programs were intended to help overcome past discrimination on the basis of race and national origin, they were also intended to consider race and national origin explicitly in bestowing their benefits. It is exactly this inherent feature of affirmative action that has generated controversy and has been the most vulnerable to successful legal and political attacks.

WHY LATINO HIGHER-EDUCATION AFFIRMATIVE ACTION PROGRAMS ARE JUSTIFIED

One compelling justification for affirmative action is that so many Latinos have been relegated to separate, unequal, and inferior public educational facilities. Latinos are becoming a major population group in several states and many cities. Their youthful age distribution will result in an even higher proportion of Latinos among the school-age population and the preschool population. School segregation has been, and continues to be, a major obstacle to the attainment of equal educational opportunity for a substantial proportion of Latino students. Several authors have traced the roots and contemporary conditions of segregation faced by Latino students and have underscored the undeniable link between ethnic isolation and limited educational opportunities. Given the recent increases in immigration, the high birthrate of Latinos, and the general lack of support for desegregation efforts, school segregation of Latinos is on the rise. In fact, segregation of Hispanics has been so dramatic that these students now have the unfortunate distinction of being the most segregated ethnic/racial group in our nation's schools (Orfield and Yun 1999).

The link between school segregation and adverse learning and achievement outcomes are easy to find. Observed correlations between segregation and educational outcomes are negative and robust. As the Latino student body increases in size and concentration, several schooling problems likewise increase. Achievement scores on standardized tests at all grade levels decline. At the secondary level, when segregation increases, the dropout rate rises, the number of college preparatory courses offered decreases, the percentage of students taking college entrance examinations decreases, and the average college admissions test scores decline. Suffice it to say that there is a clear and direct implication here for postsecondary schooling. The segregation of school-age Latinos is highly related to their very low participation in higher education (Orfield and Yun 1999; Orfield et al. 1997).

In the mid-1990s, after decades of litigation and legislation, Texas minimized the extreme and gross inequities in per capita funding in K-12 public schools in the mid-1990s. (Chapa et al. forthcoming). Before then, per capita education expenditures were largely determined by property values in each school district. Latino and African American students were overwhelmingly concentrated in poor districts and in schools with low per capita expenditures. These efforts were the consequence of the 1989 Texas Supreme Court decision in *Edgewood Independent School District* v. *Kirby*. The justices mention that even though poor districts had higher property tax rates than wealthy districts, schools in the poorest district had only $2,112 per student, compared to $19,333 in the wealthiest district. As was pointed out when that case was heard, disparities of this magnitude do indeed matter.

> The amount of money spent on a student's education has a real and meaningful impact on the educational opportunity offered that student. High wealth districts are able to provide...more extensive curricula, more up-to-date technological equipment, better libraries and library personnel, teacher aides, counseling services, lower student–teacher ratios, better facilities, parental involvement programs, and drop-out prevention programs. They are also better able to attract and retain experienced teachers and administrators.
>
> The differences in the quality of education programs offered are dramatic. For example, San Elizario ISD offers no foreign language, no prekindergarten program, no chemistry, no physics, no calculus and no college preparatory or honors program. It also offers virtually no extra-curricular activities such as band, debate or football.... In many instances, wealthy and poor districts are found contiguous to one another within the same county. (*Edgewood* v. *Kirby* 1989, p. 393)

Students who are now in high school attended elementary schools characterized by disparities of this magnitude. Moreover, significant inequalities are still to be found in Texas public education. The Southern Regional

TABLE 19.1. Average Percentage of Texas High School Students
Taking Advanced Placement Courses in 1997, by Type of Campus

Category	All Schools in Data Set— Average for Texas	Top-50 UT Austin Feeder Schools	50 High Schools with Highest Dropout Rate	Schools with at Least 50 Percent Black/ Hispanic Enrollment	Schools with at Least 50 Percent Economically Disadvantaged Enrollment
All students	17.51	22.93	13.12	14.75	14.48
White	21.60	25.14	18.13	21.71	21.02
Hispanic	12.35	14.06	10.72	11.76	12.68
African American	11.37	12.73	9.79	10.80	10.68
Asian American	31.79	35.92	24.79	28.98	27.59
Economically disadvantaged	10.28	10.79	10.17	10.59	12.38

SOURCE: Analysis of Texas Education Agency from Chapa et al. (forthcoming)

Education Board reported in 1994 that only 37 percent of public high schools in Texas offered advanced placement (AP) courses (Southern Regional Education Board 1994). Although there has been a rapid increase in the number of students taking AP courses, Table 19.1 shows that there are still large differences in the proportions of high school students from different racial groups who took advanced placement courses in 1997. These differences are due in part to the lesser availability of advanced placement courses in schools with concentrations of poor and minority students and in part to the fact that fewer minorities take advantage of AP courses even when they are available. However, the students on whom Table 19.1 is based started high school before funding was equalized.

Table 19.1 also identifies a category referred to as the "top-50 UT Austin feeder schools." These schools were identified from College Board data. Our analysis showed that a disproportionately large proportion of the applicants who sent SAT scores to the University of Texas at Austin graduated from 50 of the state's 1,150 high schools. Graduates from a handful of high schools in wealthy areas dominated the UT applicant pool. At one extreme, half of the seniors in Plano High School, which serves the richest school district in the state, sent SAT scores to UT Austin. At the other extreme, hundreds of Texas high schools did not send any students to UT Austin. It should be no surprise, then, that the top-50 UT Austin feeder schools had the highest proportion of students taking AP courses.

Further confirmation that public higher education in Texas is becoming gentrified can be seen in the fact that according to the UT Office of Admissions Research Web site, the median family income of the fall 1997 entering freshmen was $61,000. Undergraduates from low-income homes have a very low retention rate at UT. Therefore, the median family income of students who complete a BA is likely to be even higher than $61,000. This is about twice the median family income in Texas. At the other extreme of the opportunity structure, hundreds of high schools send one or two students to UT, and hundreds more send none. Even with school expenditures more or less equalized across schools in poor and wealthy areas, the children of wealthy parents are still going to have tremendous educational advantages both in terms of access to public resources and in terms of the benefits that their parents' wealth can buy. SAT prep courses offer one example. In the 1999–2000 academic year, one school district in Bexar County offered SAT prep courses only at the high school campus in the wealthiest area, because that was the only campus where the parents demanded such a program. These parents would also be the ones best able to afford private SAT preparation classes (Cardenas, 2000).

It was also in the mid-1990s that the state of Texas began to reduce similarly gross disparities in Latino access to public higher education programs. Like the elementary and secondary school finance system, the system for funding higher education in Texas had a negative impact on poor minorities. The counties on the Texas-Mexico border have a majority Latino population and are also among the poorest counties in the United States. Texas spent $46 per capita on higher education in this region while the rest of the state received an average of $96 per capita. This region stretches almost 800 miles from El Paso to Corpus Christi and includes San Antonio. In this vast area, the state had provided no graduate or professional education programs (Jones and Kauffman 1994).

Despite its history of providing second-class educational opportunities for Latinos, it does seem that Texas may finally be on the road toward providing an adequate public K–12 education to all its residents. However, a legacy of more than a century of discrimination cannot be erased overnight, and not all of the reforms will necessarily be either beneficial for Latinos or implemented in a reasonable manner. For example, it is possible to support accountability in public education and still be skeptical about a policy requiring that students be required to pass a test in order to graduate from high school, Linda McNeil and Angela Valenzuela have amply demonstrated the severe disparate impact of this practice on blacks and Latinos (McNeil and Valenzuela 2000). Furthermore, although there have been improvements in the geographic distribution of higher education facilities and a significant expansion of the higher education facilities in the border counties, large discrepancies remain.

The disparities between Anglo and Latino educational opportunities may have been the largest in Texas, but Latinos in California and other states have also had unequal access to public education resources. These disparities are documented in Gonzalez 1996 and Camarillo 1999. For Latinos, the educational playing field was sufficiently uneven to have limited the opportunities for many Latinos still in the higher education pipeline today. Note that the American Civil Liberties Union has filed a lawsuit seeking to bar the consideration of AP courses in admissions decisions on the grounds that the availability of such courses in California is as skewed as it is in Texas (Berthelsen 1999). For those who are willing to see it, there is plenty of evidence to support a claim for preferential treatment for Latinos in California, Texas, and many other states on the basis of opportunities denied both currently and historically. Yet despite the need and justification for affirmative action in Texas and California, it has been stopped in both states. Because affirmative action cannot presently be used to increase the participation of Latinos, we now examine some recently proposed alternatives.

PROMOTING DIVERSITY IN HIGHER EDUCATION WITHOUT AFFIRMATIVE ACTION

There are many aspects of access to higher education that have a negative impact on minorities. The first and foremost culprits are standardized tests. Because the distribution of minority scores is substantially lower than that of majority scores, any admissions or financial aid decision that is largely based on these scores will reduce minority access and participation. I am among the many who believe that these test scores are very often used inappropriately and perniciously; that is, they are assumed to have reliability, validity, and significance beyond their technical capacity. I also believe that such use wrongly discriminates against minorities. However, for any individual applicant, test scores provide a race-blind basis for selection. Any applicant who applies for a scholarship awarded on the basis of test scores and who has a high enough score, will get that scholarship regardless of his or her ethnicity. Even so, test scores are not race-neutral because disproportionately fewer minorities, including Latinos, have qualifying scores. A race-blind diversity measure would be one based on a characteristic or a set of characteristics that did not consider race or minority status but were genuinely race-neutral; in other words, they did not wrongly or unfairly exclude minorities. *A race-neutral measure would leave the same proportion of minorities in the pool after it was applied as existed in the pool before.* A merely race-blind measure, such as test scores, *can* change the racial composition of the pool after it is applied. In post-affirmative-action states such as California and Texas, a measure that had a smaller negative impact on minority participation than the current overreliance on test scores would be a welcome improvement. This is the context in which Texas's top 10 percent plan and other possible alternatives should be considered.

Texas's Top 10 Percent Plan

Texas top 10 percent plan was a consequence of the passage of House Bill (HB) 588 in 1997. This law requires all Texas public universities automatically to admit students who graduate in the top 10 percent of their class. The intended effect of the automatic admissions policy is to eliminate the use of standardized test scores as a barrier to admissions. It is still required that applicants take the Scholastic Aptitude Tests and have their SAT scores reported. However, any top 10 percent student will be admitted with any test score. Although some aspects of the top 10 percent plan pertain to all public colleges and universities in Texas, it substantially changed the admissions procedures only at the state's two most competitive undergraduate programs, the University of Texas at Austin and Texas A&M. Even at UT, it was not a major departure from recent practice. Until 1993, the automatic admission of any applicant in the top 10 percent of his or her high school class was standard practice. Beginning in 1994, a more restrictive combination of high school class rank and SAT scores was required for automatic admission. The top 10 percent plan apparently has the potential to revolutionize access to higher education in Texas and wherever else such an approach is adopted. Before the top 10 percent plan, graduates from a handful of high schools from wealthy areas (the top 50-UT Austin feeder schools discussed in connection with Table 19.1) dominated the UT applicant pool.

The top 10 percent plan has the potential to democratize access to Texas's selective public institutions and to spread the geographic origins of the UT's entering class across the state. The admissions system in place at UT before the top 10 percent plan preferentially conferred the opportunity for public higher education on those who already had all the advantages. Besides having well-educated parents with high incomes, students from the top feeder schools have the best teachers in the best facilities with the best programs, from preschool through high school. Access to advanced placement courses enable these students to earn grade-point averages (GPAs) above 4.0. (This is not possible in high schools that do not offer such courses.) They can take SAT prep courses at their public schools. And if they chose to enroll at UT, they formerly could take many of the places in the entering freshmen class. Now, however, students from every high school have a shot at a publicly supported higher education. Of course, the 10 percent plan cannot level the playing field and eliminate the disparity in resources between schools, but it makes the competition for admission more fair by placing great weight on how well a student can do *with the resources and opportunities available* to him or her.

In a state and country where minorities are typically concentrated in highly segregated schools, the top 10 percent plan also has implications for diversity. If a school is 95 percent or more Latino, as some Texas schools are, then we could expect that Latinos would be well represented in the top 10 percent. Even if Latinos are not 95 percent of the top 10 percent, the policy has apparently worked to increase the proportion of minority students at UT so that they are as well represented in the entering class as they were before the Hopwood decision ended race-conscious affirmative action in admissions and financial aid. The fall 1999 freshman class at the University of Texas had many more top 10 percent minority students and was as diverse as the class that was admitted using race-conscious affirmative action (Walker 2000). Note that the increase in minority students is not an automatic consequence of the enactment of HB 588. Texas A&M's freshman class in the fall of 1999 had far fewer minorities than was the case before Hopwood (Bahadur 2000). UT's success in recruiting more minorities under HB 588 can be attributed to vigorous recruitment efforts as well as restructured financial aid programs (Walker 2000).

The top 10 percent students entering UT in fall 1999 had lower SAT scores than the top 10 percent admitted before Hopwood. Nonetheless, the top 10 percent turned in a good academic performance, as the following excerpt from a UT Admissions Office report shows.

> HB 588 did bring a larger number of top 10% students to the university from the lowest score ranges in 1998 and 1999 when compared to 1997. This resulted in a lower mean SAT. (1997 =1246; 1998 = 1237; 1999 = 1220). However, even the lowest scoring top 10% students (<900) obtained a respectable GPA of 2.45 in 1998 and 2.57 in fall, 1999.
>
> Top 10% students outperformed their lower ranking peers in terms of freshman GPA during the 1998–99 school year (top 10% GPA = 3.23; others = 2.73). The retention rate from fall to fall semester was also higher among the top 10% than among other students (top 10% retention = 94%; others = 88%). This strong performance of top 10% students was evident across all Colleges within the University... even among the most competitive such as Business and Engineering. (Walker 2000)

As positive as this report is, there is much more we would like to know. How well are the minority top 10 percent students doing and how well are students from the underperforming schools doing? The top 10 percent plan does make it possible for poorly prepared students to be admitted to the most competitive public university in Texas. The finding that even students with SAT scores under 900 are, on the average, earning a GPA that keeps them in good standing, and that they have high retention rates, suggests that this is less of a problem now than it was under affirmative action.

However, this good news only partially addresses the efficacy of the top 10 percent plan. Indirectly, given that even top 10 percent students with low SAT scores have slightly better grades and retention rates than other students with similar scores, it does seem that the top 10 percent students who might not otherwise have been admitted are doing well. However, because HB 588 grants admission to graduates from all high schools, the key research question concerns the success rate of students from low-performing high schools—high schools that have rarely if ever successfully sent a student to—and through—UT. A closely related question is whether class rank predicts college success better than SAT scores do. To whatever degree standardized test scores measure academic aptitude, they do not measure motivation. Arguably, class rank at least reflects it.

Eligibility in a Local Context: California's Top 4 Percent Plan

Three California electoral initiatives characterize the virulently anti-Latino politics of Governor Pete Wilson's second term from 1994 to 1998: Propositions 187, 209, and 227. Proposition 187 bars undocumented immigrants from using all state services except emergency health care. It also empowers public employees to police the use of these services and turn in suspected undocumented immigrants. In 1996, Proposition 209 ended all race-conscious affirmative action programs in California state institutions, particularly higher education. Latinos had been severely underrepresented at all levels of California higher education; Prop. 209 removed any hope of improvement. Finally, in 1998, Proposition 227 ended bilingual-education programs in California, the state with the greatest number and percent of children with limited English proficiency or with non-English-language backgrounds. (See Chapters 17 and 18 in this volume for more on California's educational problems.)

In California, affirmative action programs that were intended to improve successful access to K–12 and higher education were stopped by a plebiscite rather than a court order, but the result was the same as in Texas: a sharp decrease in the number of minority students admitted to the competitive and selective public higher education programs. For example, at UC Berkeley, the number of African Americans in the fall entering class declined from 252 in 1997 to 122 in the fall of 1999. For Chicanos, the most underrepresented Latinos, fall enrollments fell from 385 in 1997 to 219 in 1999 (Center for Latino Policy Research 2000).

California's master plan for higher education dictates that the University of California (UC) system shall educate the top 12.5 percent of the *state's* high school graduates. However, this is very different from Texas's top 10 percent plan, which applies to the graduating class of *each* high school. In California, the top 12.5 percent are drawn from all statewide high school graduates pooled together. The California procedure markedly favors the students at high schools with the most resources and the most rigorous academic programs. Not surprisingly, this procedure also has a negative impact on minority students. Only 3.3 percent of blacks and 3.8 percent of Latinos are eligible by virtue of being in the top 12.5 percent statewide pool. But 6.6 percent of blacks and 7.2 percent of Latinos would become eligible if the top 12.5 percent of each high school were eligible (Geiser 1998). When California State Senator Teresa Hughes proposed a state constitutional amendment that would admit the top 12.5 percent of each high school to UC, it failed to be enacted.

UC *did* adopt a top 4 percent plan, but this was not really a plan to increase diversity. It was primarily a way to increase the size of the pool to the mandated 12.5 percent level without "lowering standards." The statewide pool is determined on the basis of standardized test scores, grade-point average, and curriculum. Because of declining test scores, by 1998 the standards that had previously been met by the top 12.5 percent of all California high school graduates were now met by only 11.1 percent. In order to fulfill its mandate, UC had to increase the size of the pool. The obvious way to do this would have been lower grade and/or test score requirements to whatever level was necessary to identify 12.5 percent of the statewide pool. Certainly, this would be an unpalatable undertaking. Including the top 4 percent of the graduates of each high school made it possible to avoid this, threw a sop to the supporters of the Hughes Amendment, and brought the size of the pool back up to 12.5 percent. (The reason why 11.1 percent plus 4 percent equals 12.5 percent is that many of the top 4 percent of each high school are already part of the statewide eligibility pool defined in terms of test scores and grades.) In terms of diversity, African Americans would constitute only 2 percent of the UC-eligible pool whether it were identified via the top 4 percent plan or the 12.5 percent statewide pool. In simulations, Latino eligibility increases by one percentage point to comprise 10 percent of all eligible students under the top 4 percent compared to the statewide pool. (This paragraph is the author's analysis of data presented in Geiser 1998.)

Given the imprecise nature of simulations, California's top 4 percent plan may or may not result in any increase in UC's Latino enrollments. However, it does create a very important opportunity for students who do not attend top high schools—and it will yield information of great interest to researchers. It makes the competition for eligibility more fair, because all students are compared to other students in the same high school with the same access to funding and resources. Students from high schools that rarely if ever send students to UC now have an opportunity to be admitted. The research question is simply whether they can do the work required to stay in college and graduate. If the students from low-performing high

TABLE 19.2. Conceptual Schema Identifying
Errors Possible in Admissions Decisions

	Applicant Qualifications	
Admissions Decision	Qualified	Unqualified
Reject Applicant	Type A Error	Correct Decision
Accept Applicant	Correct Decision	Type B Error
	Test score bias results in qualified minority applicants being wrongly rejected.	Top X percent plans wrongly admit unqualified students from low-performing schools.

schools succeed, their achievement will provide an effective argument for increasing the percentage of students admitted on the basis of their class rank rather than their test scores.

RESEARCH PARADIGM FOR X PERCENT PLANS

Admissions programs like the top 10 percent plan have been adopted in a number of states. It will be crucially important to assess the positive and negative consequences of these plans and compare them to the admissions systems they replace. The foregoing sections of this chapter have posed specific research questions about the Texas and California plans. Here I would like to propose one aspect of a research paradigm for investigating the "errors" made by using X percent plans versus traditional admissions procedures that put undue weight on standardized test scores and give unfair advantage to students who attend high schools that offer exceptional resources and learning opportunities. There are two types of errors that any fair and rational admissions system would seek to avoid. In direct analogy to the Type I error / Type II error framework used in the formal statistical analysis of hypothesis testing, Table 19.2 identifies Type A and Type B errors. Type A errors occur when qualified applicants are wrongly denied admission. I believe that such errors are common when standardized test scores are used inappropriately and are accorded too much weight in the decision. Furthermore, given that racial and ethnic bias affects test scores, errors of this type have a greater negative impact on minority applicants. Type B errors occur when unqualified applicants are admitted, which may be more likely to occur with X percent plans. Table 19.2 presents a preliminary and simplistic conceptual schema for these two types of errors. Refining these concepts and measuring their magnitude is a high-priority research issue.

Until we are able to do this research, I am willing to speculate that the frequency of Type B errors will be less of a problem than commonly imagined. Many have claimed that X percent plans increase the possibility of Type B errors, but note that this has not been the case with Texas's top 10 percent plan. Minorities and low-income students encounter many obstacles and barriers that keep them from matriculating in competitive higher education programs. Typically, the home, neighborhood, and school environments of these students are devoid of accurate or encouraging information about higher education. In fact, the opposite is very often true. I hypothesize that it will be the exceptional top 10 percent students from low-performing schools who take advantage of these opportunities. The top 10 percent plan offers a way to identify students with drive and determination, and it permits them to go to a competitive college if they also surmount all the other barriers they still must face and overcome.

If the student is not really able to do college-level work, there will be many opportunities over a long period for the student to hear this message from teachers, counselors, and so on. Plans such as the top 10 percent in Texas offer an opportunity for low-performing schools and their students to get some very useful feedback. If the best students from such a high school all flunk out during their first semester at the university, changes need to be made at the high school. This information can be used by the students and the school to overcome the deficiencies in the curriculum. Moreover, this plan reinforces the importance of the material taught in school every day, rather than overemphasizing the one shot the student gets at taking a standardized test that is unfamiliar in format and content.

My enthusiasm for the top 10 percent plan has to be put in context. Race-conscious affirmative action in Texas ended abruptly and completely. The specifics of the Fifth Circuit Court's Hopwood decision and of Texas Attorney General Dan Morales's interpretation of this decision made it quite possible for any university administrator who *did* act affirmatively and made race-conscious admissions or financial aid decisions to be personally liable for actual and punitive damages, and for legal expenses, should these decisions be challenged in a lawsuit (see Chapa and Lazaro 1998). Affirmative action was dead, and any race-conscious alternative would have been stillborn. Compared to a total absence of diversity programs in higher education, the top 10 percent plan looks very good indeed.

In California, affirmative action ended as a result of the passage of a ballot initiative, Prop. 209. The top 4 percent plan will not have much of an impact on the diversity of the student body entering UC, but the plan does create a framework for comparing students within the context of the educational opportunities available to them. California's top 4 percent plan may help students from high schools without AP courses, and in this way it somewhat democratizes access to competitive institutions of higher education in California.

Top X percent plans may also decrease minority enrollment, depending on the magnitude of X and on the demographics of the high schools. Perhaps all of these plans should be seen as steps toward the development of race-blind and race-neutral admissions and financial aid systems that minimized both Type A and Type B errors. These plans also offer the opportunity to coordinate high school curricula with college requirements and possibly to improve the quality of college prep curricula at low-performing schools. Ultimately, the ideal system would correctly identify all eligible students and give them equal access and an equal chance to succeed.

REFERENCES

Bahadur, Gajutra. 2000. "Top 10% Admissions Rule Praised." *Austin American Statesman*. May 24, pp. B1, B5.

Berthelsen, Christian. 1999. "Suit Says Advanced-Placement Classes Show Bias." *Chronicle of Higher Education*. July 28. (**www.chronicle.com**).

California Secretary of State's Office. 1996. "Analysis of Proposition 209." *California Legislative Analyst*.

Camarillo, Albert. 1999. "Expert Report of Albert M. Camarillo." *Exhibit in Gratz et al. v. Bollinger et al.*, No. 97-75321 (E.D. Mich.). **http://www.umich.edu/~urel/admissions/legal/expert/camarill.html**

Cardenas, Blandina. 2000. "Presentation to the Meeting of ENLACE Planning Grantees." San Antonio, TX. February.

Carnevale, Anthony P. 2000. *Education = Success: Empowering Hispanic Youth and Adults*. Princeton, NJ: Educational Testing Sevice.

Center for Latino Policy Research. 2000. "Statistics on the Status of Latinos and Higher Education in California and Texas." Spring 2000 Berkeley Research Symposium. University of California, Berkeley.

Chapa, Jorge, et al. (forthcoming). "Diversity in Texas Higher Education after Hopwood—Problems and Prospects." Michigan State University.

Chapa, Jorge, and Vincent Lazaro. 1998. "Hopwood in Texas: The Untimely End of Affirmative Action." In *Chilling Admissions*, ed. Gary Orfield and Edward Miller. Cambridge, MA: Harvard Civil Rights Project.

Curry, George (ed.). 1996. *The Affirmative Action Debate*. Reading, MA: Addison-Wesley.

Edgewood v. Kirby, Texas Supreme Court. 777 SW 2d 391 (Texas 1989), p. 393.

Geiser, Saul. 1998. "Redefining UC's Eligibility Pool to Include a Percentage of Students from Each High School: Summary of Simulation Results." (mimeo). University of California Office of the President: Student Academic Services.

Gonzalez, Gilbert G. 1996. "A Brief Review of Chicano Educational History in California: A Legacy of Inequality." In *Strategic Interventions in Education: Expanding the Latino/Latina Pipeline*, ed. Aida Hurtado, Richard Figueroa and Eugene E. Garcia. University of California Latino Eligibility Study, University of California, Santa Cruz.

Grutter et al. v. *Bollinger et al.*, No. 97-75928 (E.D. Mich.), available through (**www .umich.edu/~urel/admissions/legal/**).

Hopwood v. *State of Texas*. U.S. Court of Appeals, Fifth Circuit. 78 F.3d 932 (1996).

Jones, Richard C., and Albert Kauffman, 1994. "Accessibility to Comprehensive Higher Education in Texas." *Social Science Journal.* 31(3):263–283.

Murdoch, S., B. Pecotte, M. McGehee, P. Pope, and R. Bailey. 1998. "An Assessment of Potential Needs Unmet and Opportunities Lost as a Result of *Hopwood.*" Paper presented at the second annual Texas A&M Hopwood Conference, February 12, College Station, Texas.

McNeil, Linda and Angela Valenzuela. 2000. "The Harmful Impact of the TAAS System of Testing in Texas: Beneath the Accountability Rhetoric." Center for Education, Rice University, Houston, Texas, Occasional Papers Series, Volume 1, Issue 1, April 2000 **http://www.ruf.rice.edu/~ctreduc/TAASArticle.pdf**

Orfield, Gary, et al. 1997. "City-Suburban Desegregation: Parent and Student Perspectives in Metropolitan Boston." The Civil Rights Project, Harvard University. **http://www.law.harvard.edu/groups/civilrights/publications/metbody.html**

Orfield, Gary, and John T. Yun. 1999. "Resegregation in American Schools" The Civil Rights Project, Harvard University. **http://www.law.harvard.edu/groups /civilrights/publications/resegregation99.html**

Robison, Clay. 1997. "Texas 2-Step: Preferences, No—Affirmative Action, Yes." *Houston Chronicle*, November 16, final edition.

Southern Education Foundation. 1995. *Redeeming the American Promise: Report of the Panel on Educational Opportunity and Postsecondary Desegregation.* Atlanta, GA: Southern Education Foundation.

Southern Regional Educational Board, Educational Benchmarks 1994. n.d., p. 19. Atlanta, GA.

The Texas Higher Education Coordinating Board. 1998. "The Texas Plan for Equal Education Opportunity: A Brief History." **http://www.thecb.state.tx.us /divisions/ane/PlanHistory.htm**

Walker, Bruce. 2000. "The Implementation and Results of HB 588 at the University of Texas at Austin." Report 2 (updated January 17, 2000). **http://www.utexas .edu/student/research/reports/admissions/HB58820000126.html**

Commentary

Gary Orfield

There is very little national attention being devoted to what may be the most decisive set of social choices now being made in the United States. The United States is in the midst of a demographic revolution, which our Census Bureau believes will lead to a Latino population of 100 million people by midcentury. This population, which will be far larger than that of any European country and several times the population of Canada, is growing prodigiously. It is also heavily concentrated in the large metropolitan areas of a huge "postindustrial" society increasingly dominated by "knowledge-based" employment, but it is not connecting effectively with the educational system. Nine-tenths of Latinos lived in metropolitan areas in 2000. Unless this connection is made, the Latino community, which by midcentury will be some three times as large as the present black community, will be severely excluded. In fact, a number of current trends and policy decisions threaten to make a bad situation worse.

In spite of this demographic outlook, there are no plans, no set of policies, and no serious proposals on the table in Washington or in state capitals that most experts believe would have any chance of bringing Latinos into the educational mainstream. It is policy by nonpolicy. None of the goals set for equalizing educational success for minority students by 2000 in the "Goals 2000" legislation, and in the agreement between the president and the governors in 1989, have been realized. In fact, some of the most important gaps between Latinos and non-Hispanic whites and Asians have actually widened during this period. To add insult to injury, state and federal officials have adopted a number of policies very likely to make things even worse (see Chapters 17 and 19 in this volume). Some states have adopted racially polarized referenda, spurred by white fears of the demographic revolution and by political leaders scapegoating the growth

TABLE 1. Public School Enrollment Changes, 1968–1998 (in millions)

	1968	1980	1994	1996	1998	Change from 1968 to 1998
Hispanics	2.00	3.18	5.57	6.38	6.90	+4.38 (219%)
Anglos	34.70	29.16	28.46	29.11	28.93	−5.59 (−16%)
Blacks	6.28	6.42	7.13	7.69	7.91	+1.41 (22 %)

SOURCES: DBS Corp., 1982, 1987; Gary Orfield, Rosemary George, and Amy Orfield, "Racial Change in U.S. School Enrollments, 1968–84," paper presented at the National Conference on School Desegregation, University of Chicago, 1986. National Center for Education Statistics, U.S. Department of Education, Common Core of Data.

of the Latino population as the cause for economic and other problems-desperately seeking "wedge issues" to hold on to white votes (see Chapter 8 in this volume). It is a strategy much like the race-baiting techniques used for decades in the American South to convince poor whites to vote against their economic interests in order to defend their racial prerogatives.[1] This political crisis reached a high point of polarization in California in the 1990s, but it is also intimately related to national struggles that began in the 1960s over the role of the courts, civil rights laws, and race-conscious policies in addressing minority inequality and exclusion.[2]

Latino students, whose numbers have exploded since national data were first collected in the late 1960s, are by far the least successful group of students in finishing high school, and their access to college is declining. The number of Latino students in the country grew an incredible 219 percent in just two decades. The Latino enrollment grew 4.4 million while the Anglo enrollment fell 5.6 million (see Table 1). This in a country where workers without postsecondary education have much lower real incomes than similar workers had a quarter-century ago. In the new knowledge-intensive economy, all the gains of prosperity have gone to people with advanced education. As Suárez-Orozco and Páez outline in their introduction to this volume, Latinos have migrated in great numbers, mostly to escape poverty and to gain opportunity, but huge numbers are working full-time but still living in poverty and finding themselves unable to launch their children into the American middle class. Families and communities that do not obtain educational credentials in this situation are very likely to face extremely severe economic and social problems. During the twenty-four years from 1973 to 1997, young families headed by high school dropouts experienced a 33.6 percent decline in real income as the relationship between education and income became much more dramatic in American society. Half of those young families were living under the poverty line, compared to 24 percent of those headed by a high school graduate and 2.5 percent of those headed by a college graduate.[3] Among the nation's young adults in the fall of 1999, only 54.9 percent of Latinos had high school diplomas.[4] In the parts of the country that are becoming predominantly Latino, the entire future of the area may be at stake.

With the exception of the Puerto Ricans, who unfortunately came to New York after that city had become an early leader in the turn toward a postindustrial economy, the Latino immigration was largely into areas that had a very healthy market for low-skilled labor for a long time. In Chicago, the great midwestern center of migration, there were jobs in the steel mills, the railroads, the stockyards, and the industrial plants of what was the world's largest industrial center after World War II. In the sunbelt, from Florida to Texas to the Southwest and California, Latinos were migrating into booms that lasted for decades. There was a vast demand for workers who were ready to work hard in dirty jobs, and no one asked much about their schooling. Then things changed. In the 1970s, Chicago was devastated by industrial shutdowns, the oil crisis hit Texas in the 1980s, and California finally faced its first severe economic downturn in sixty years in the early 1990s. The 1994 ratification of the North American Free Trade Agreement put low-wage industrial workers in the Southwest in direct competition with much lower-wage workers across the border in Mexico. Both California and Texas experienced significant net job loss and downward pressure on wages in such jobs.[5]

The vulnerability of communities that worked hard but were uneducated became very painfully evident when these changes came. Too often the only choices were working and still being poor in dead-end or off-the-books jobs, living on welfare, or entering the underground or criminal economy. Suddenly, populations famous for strong families and self-reliance experienced terrible social tensions and had to ask for help. Clear symptoms of social pathology and isolation from the mainstream intensified. Crime became more serious. This accounts for some of the frightening findings of decline between the first and subsequent generations for some immigrants, where the parents had taken the dramatic and very difficult step of leaving their homeland for what they saw as a better life for the family. But the children saw only the barrio, dysfunctional schools, and burgeoning gangs, and with little hope, they often fell into destructive patterns. The U.S. Justice Department now projects that one-sixth of young Latino men will spend time in prison.[6] Obviously, this is a community in crisis in which the attainment of reasonable levels of education is an absolute necessity.

The vast immigration of poor people with very low educational levels from Mexico and Central America was, of course, one of the great challenges the schools faced. School-age children of immigrants in the United

States soared from 3.5 to 8.6 million between 1970 and 1995, surpassing the nation's black enrollment. By 1997 they accounted for 19 percent of the nation's students. More than an eighth (13.3 percent) of students came from a home where a foreign language was spoken, almost three-fourths of them from Spanish-speaking homes. In California, 27 percent of all students were from Spanish-speaking homes.[7] It is not surprising that these huge numbers drew a great deal of attention in Latino education to issues of immigration and language, even though most immigrant children—and the great majority of children of immigrants born in the United States—are not classified as limited English proficient (LEP) and do not receive bilingual or other special language instruction.[8] Chapters 17 and 18 in this volume focus primarily on this problem, as has the national debate over instruction of Latinos.

Latinos have been beneficiaries of programs from the civil rights era, but those programs began to shut down just as there was an exponential increase in the numbers of Latino students who needed them (see Chapter 19 in this volume). The 1960s and early 1970s brought large programs for preschool and early elementary education (Title I), bilingual education and the court decisions, regulations, and state laws supporting it, the first major financial aid for college for low-income students, the TRIO college outreach programs, desegregation, affirmative action admissions, minority scholarships, affirmative recruitment of minority teachers and professors, the creation of Latino research centers, and many other efforts. There was a huge expansion of the supply of spaces in open-access public colleges and universities charging low tuitions. Outside of education there were major efforts to expand voting rights, outlaw discrimination in housing, and provide health care for the poor. This period brought early recognition of the educational crisis facing Latinos; created a core of law, policy, and theory that has set much of the agenda since; and brought substantial increases in participation, achievement, and graduation for Latino students. The period also brought a tidal wave of new Latino immigration into the United States, a tide that seems likely to continue to roll for many years.

Tragically for Latino families, their great growth in numbers has come during a period of cutbacks in government services and investment in the young and of dramatic reversals in policies on civil rights. The Latino community has the largest and youngest families, so its future is peculiarly influenced by these decisions. During the time of dramatic growth of the Latino population, social policy debates have increasingly narrowed into arguments about Social Security and Medicare, both programs for the elderly. The huge investments in expansion of low-cost colleges from the 1950s to the 1970s has given way to a major shift of costs to students, with soaring tuition, increasing competition for spaces, and test-driven selectivity. The dream of providing low-income minority students with access to middle-class, white schools has given way to resegregation. For almost two decades now, the basic policy model has assumed that administering highly demanding tests that many students in inferior schools flunk will somehow lead those schools to perform better. During this same time, strong outreach for Latino teachers has been replaced, in many states, by teacher exams that sharply reduce Latino certification.

As Gándara (Chapter 17) notes, the political reaction against equity in education has been most intense in California, a state that enrolls almost a third of all Latino students in the country. It is a state well along the path to becoming majority-Latino, but it still has a small minority of Latino voters (see Chapter 20 in this volume). California produced Richard Nixon and Ronald Reagan, the two presidents who played the leading role in ending the civil rights era and setting the nation on a far more conservative course in terms of the equal opportunity agenda of the federal government. It also produced the governor, Pete Wilson, who led the most explicitly anti-immigrant movement of the late twentieth century. California voters adopted a series of propositions against fair housing, school desegregation, the rights of immigrants, affirmative action, and bilingual education.[9]

The prohibition of any kind of meaningful bilingual education and the bitter attack on efforts to retain Spanish in school instruction were body blows to the only major policy response to Latino educational problems. They were an assault on the efforts of a great many Latino professionals who worked in bilingual classrooms and schools. They were also a direct cultural insult to many Latino parents and professionals who valued Spanish and saw it as a key link to their history and culture. In that light, Chapters 17 and 18 of this volume clearly reflect the profound disillusionment felt by many Latino intellectuals concerning this period of dramatic reversals. These scholars see the reversals that have occurred in the state. They particularly focus attention on the enactment of the antibilingual Proposition 227 in 1998 as a serious attack on Latino education and the Latino community. The enactment of a similar proposition in Arizona in 2000 and efforts to limit the period of language instruction in other states and in federal law illustrate the pernicious spread of that movement.

The authors of these chapters see bilingual education as central to preserving the prospects of Hispanic students. Together with other major researchers in the field, they believe that a successful transition to a second language cannot be accomplished in a short period of time. They defend the vision of a society in which the Spanish language is seen as an asset—something to be nurtured together with English—not as a liability to be shed as rapidly as possible.

Moll and Ruiz writing in this section of the book, advocate two-way bilingual or dual-immersion programs in which both English-speaking and Spanish-speaking children learn from each other in settings where both languages and cultures are respected. It is a new vision of the kind of just society sought by the civil rights movement. It incorporates diverse languages and nationalities into what was originally a black-and-white picture. I believe that two-way bilingual or dual-immersion schools offer important possibilities. The endorsement by Clinton administration Education Secretary Richard Riley was a positive sign, as is the fact that these schools were exempted from the bilingual limits of the California proposition.

The underlying reality is that fluency in two languages—especially English and Spanish—is already an important economic asset for employment in some parts of the country, and it will surely be an asset in many more regions as the demographic revolution proceeds. We should be creating schools that will help prepare students for the bilingual society that is rapidly developing. With the rise of Latino numbers and political power, bilingualism may soon be defined as an asset for college admissions and (eventually perhaps) as a prerequisite for government employment in state and local government. At present, however, the approach remains very limited. It also faces the practical limitations of implemention in large, segregated, low-income areas where it is very unlikely that fluent English speakers will be tempted to enroll in low-achieving barrio schools.

Instead of witnessing an active pursuit of a positive vision, however, the situation in Latino education at the beginning of the twenty-first century was grim. Policy was moving in a negative direction on all dimensions, and Latino students were becoming increasingly isolated in highly inferior schools while educational requirements for either jobs or higher education were escalating. Furthermore, positive efforts to aid minority students were being dismantled and replaced by increasing reliance on assessment systems that strongly reflect students' family background and tend to perpetuate inequalities (see Chapa's remarks in this section).

It is not surprising that Latino intellectuals at the beginning of the twenty-first century find it deeply frustrating that their community faces reactionary policies and prejudice just when it most needs welcome and support for its youth. Patricia Gándara, one of California's most skillful education policy analysts and researchers, explores in great detail how an array of political decisions has constrained the efforts of teachers and schools to address the very severe problems of Latino children. The implementation of Proposition 227 sharply reduced bilingual instruction, but it also very rapidly reduced the number of teachers training in the field. The supply of teachers for Latino students was further limited by the implementation of teacher tests that tended to screen out Latinos disproportionately. As Moll and Ruiz convincingly argue, whatever approach is taken in the future to teach non-English-speaking students, it will obviously be important to have teachers who can understand English-language development for LEP students and who can communicate effectively with those students and their parents.

These scholars also note that the impact of other reform initiatives may be even more devastating to Latino students. After California's Latino voters turned out to help oust a hostile Republican governor, Pete Wilson, the new Democratic governor, Gray Davis, whose election was strongly aided by Latino voters, pushed through the legislature a policy of high-stakes testing in English. Under this testing policy, skills in English-language tests become the only real measure of school success and accountability, and massive numbers of Latino students are threatened with failure and denial of diplomas raising the state high dropout rate. This is driving teachers and principals to radically devalue and limit any instruction in a student's native language and to prevent bilingual teachers from using the full range of their teaching skills. This is an illustration of the way in which seemingly attractive policies, implemented without consideration of the real situation of Latino youth, can end up making things worse.

Another striking example occurred when the state suddenly decided to reduce class size (an excellent idea) without coming to terms with the fact that many Latino schools were already wanting in qualified teachers and did not have enough rooms even for their larger classes. When underqualified teachers must be hired and put in spaces that lack classroom necessities, the value of an expensive reform is radically reduced. Policies need to be based on an informed understanding of Latino realities.

These chapters are excellent contributions, but, of course, they deal with only some aspects of a vast topic. As the research and policy debates continue to develop in this field, I believe that we will see intense interest in a number of additional topics and that there will be an effort to connect the Latino educational crisis more directly with a broader crisis in education for poor and minority children across the United States. The United States is in reality a metropolitan society (eighty percent of our people were in metropolitan areas by 2000) that exhibits highly segregated residential and educational patterns for Latino and black youth. These patterns lock those students—and almost no white students—into highly impoverished schools that are often overwhelmed by failure and demoralization, leading teachers and administrators to abandon them as rapidly as possible. These are often schools where the families move frequently and there is little stability in student enrollment. The truth is that in spite of a few remarkable successes achieved by powerful principals and committed faculties, these schools tend to be inferior in almost every way. Existing interventions are too weak to make much difference in most cases. In fact, the huge federal Title I program has shown little evidence of success in changing outcomes. Although there are programs and policies that do make a difference, the schools still tend to be seriously substandard even after a full intervention.

One of the things that became clear in a recent roundtable on bilingual education at the Harvard Civil Rights Project was that successfully implementing bilingual education or any complex school improvement strategy requires having a school that is functioning at least reasonably well. Many schools that serve Latino and other isolated minority children are not minimally adequate. Many issues cry out for serious examination: Why are English-speaking Latino students doing so badly in schools, even in the second and third generations? Their problems are not modern language. What forms of desegregation and magnets work for Latino students of various backgrounds? Under what policies and conditions do they work best? What is—and what should be—the contribution of parochial and charter schools? What can be done about tracking, poor course selection, and negative peer group influences? What kinds of counseling and precollegiate interventions work best? To what degree are very high dropout rates related to inappropriate test requirements? How should we measure English-language development within bilingual programs, and how should we assess content? What kinds of secondary reforms increase retention and graduation from high school? What are the central barriers to higher education, and what do we know about the success of interventions ranging from targeted financial aid to ending admissions tests? What kinds of teacher training are most helpful in preparing teachers to teach Latino children successfully and relate effectively to their parents and communities? We are facing a transformation in American society, and we need a very ambitious program of research and experimentation to help if we are to find a responsible educational path. The contributions in this volume are an important step in that direction.

Finally, it is important to consider the Latino experience in a still broader context. The tendency today is for each group to look inward at its own problems rather than to look across the society and see commonalities, even though that may be essential to building coalitions for change. Many of the problems that face Latino students also face African Americans, American Indians, Asian refugee communities, and communities of poor whites, usually found in rural America. For example, all of these groups also face serious problems in acquiring the "standard" or academic English needed for higher education, and policies on English-language development could well help them if broadly conceived. If we are to prevent these demands for change from being dismissed by those who simply blame the particular minority community for its failure to value education or its bad behavior, it is important to show that the problems are broader and systemic and that they merit serious consideration. If fragmentation between black and Latino communities, now vying for leadership positions in many urban school districts, is to be limited or reversed, both groups will have to come to understand the needs they share, as well as the special circumstances and problems and assets of each group. Very little work of this sort is now being done. But as it evolves, it will be an important contribution to the creation of clearer goals and to the marshaling of stronger support for policies that will benefit all.

NOTES

1. V. O. Key, Jr., *Southern Politics in State and Nation* (New York: Knopf, 1949); Dan T. Carter, *The Politics of Rage: George Wallace, the Origins of the New Conservatism, and the Transformation of American Politics* (New York: Simon and Schuster, 1995); Robert Huckfeldt and Carol Weitzel Kohfeld, *Race and the Decline of Class in American Politics* (Urbana: University of Illinois Press, 1989).

2. Gary Orfield, "Politics Matters: Educational Policy and Latino Students," in Jose E. Moreno, ed., *The Elusive Quest for Equality: 150 Years of Chicano/Chicana Education* (Cambridge, MA: Harvard Education Review, 1999), pp. 111–21; Lydia Chavez, *The Color Bind: California's Battle to End Affirmative Action* (Berkeley: University of California Press, 1998).

3. Samuel Halperin, ed., *The Forgotten Half Revisited* (Washington, DC: American Youth Policy Forum, 1998), pp. 13–15.

4. Another 8.5 percent reported a high school equivalency diploma such as a GED. These examinations have not been shown to produce the same results in the job market. See Phillip Kaufman et al. *Dropout Rates in the United States* (Washington, DC: National Center for Education Statistics, 2001), p. 19.

5. Robert E. Scott, "NAFTA's Pain Deepens: Job Destruction Accelerates with Losses in Every State," Economic Policy Institute Issue Brief, November 1999, p 4.

6. Thomas P. Bonczar and Allen J. Beck, *Lifetime Likelihood of Going to State or Federal Prison* NCJ-160092. Washington, DC: Office of Justice Programs, March 1997, p. 2.

7. Jorge Ruiz-de-Velasco and Michael Fix, *Overlooked and Underserved: Immigrant Students in U.S. Secondary Schools* Washington, DC: Urban Institute, 2000.

8. Ibid., pp. 12–14.

9. Orfield. 1999.

Chapter 20

Forever Seen as New

Latino Participation in American Elections

Louis DeSipio and Rodolfo O. de la Garza

With each presidential election, the media and the punditocracy discover Latinos anew.[1] Rapid growth in their numbers presage rapid growth in votes and influence. High levels of immigration and previous quiescence among the U.S.-born suggest something new, mysterious—and for some—dangerous. Concentration in electoral-college-rich states such as California, New York, Texas, Florida, and Illinois allow scenarios to emerge wherein presidential candidates must cater to Latino voters to win. Despite these recurring predictions, each election is followed by a somewhat disappointing review in which the Latino promise is not met and in which ongoing problems (most notably low turnout) are advanced as easy explanations.

In this chapter, we explore this notion of "newness" in the Latino electorate with an eye to the future Latino vote. We examine themes wherein outside observers or scholars anticipate change in Latino voting or influence, and we assess whether the phenomenon in question is truly new. Our analysis is informed by three studies of Latinos and national election cycles (de la Garza and DeSipio 1992; de la Garza and DeSipio 1996; de la Garza and DeSipio 1999), one of Latinos and local elections (de la Garza, Menchaca, and DeSipio 1994) and some initial observations about the 2000 elections. We assess the "newness" of Latino demography, naturalization, non-naturalized immigrants, partisanship, geographic concentration, elite resources and institutions, issues, and dual nationality. What will emerge is a picture of a national electorate that is experiencing incremental growth, but no dramatic changes, at the beginning of the twenty-first century.

We study elections for a specific reason. Elections in democratic systems offer politically marginalized populations the opportunity to exert some influence on the selection of leaders and the direction of public policy.

Clearly, voting is just one way of exerting influence, but unlike many others—such as making campaign contributions, lobbying, taking part in personal networks, and running for office—it offers the poor, less well educated, and less politically sophisticated an opportunity to participate at high levels. Historically, the vote was used by immigrants and their U.S.-born children and grandchildren to assert their status in American society. With the decline in electoral participation among all segments of the population in the late twentieth century, elections provide a less important resource for immigrant and ethnic populations than in the past. Despite this decline, and the concomitant decline in popular attention to elections, they provide the single greatest opportunity for a population such as Latinos to influence the nation's politics.

We should also note what we are *not* doing in this chapter. Our focus is national elections and the national Latino electorate. Certainly, much is also happening at the local level, and we do not seek to minimize the value of studying these important local processes, but we cannot explore local experiences here. National Latino politics of the future will certainly reflect blending of local political environments with the patterns that we identify here, but they will have to be the subject of future studies.

DEMOGRAPHY

The rapid growth of the Latino population in the past thirty years has raised popular expectations for its political impact. Now numbering more than 35 million and soon to overtake African Americans as the nation's largest minority, Latinos are often the subject of naive predictions for their imminent domination of politics and society (de la Garza 1996a). The electorate, of course, is much smaller than the total population: just one in six Latinos votes.

Much of the gap between rates of electoral participation for Latino and Anglo citizens can be explained by simple demographics. Among all populations, the young, the less well educated, and the low-income are less likely to vote. All of these groups are disproportionately represented among Latinos. Remedies for the impact on turnout of youth, limited education, and low-income are less clear. Community-wide mobilization, such as that which the African American community experienced as a result of the civil rights movement, can overcome these impediments to participation. Without such mobilization, however, Latinos are likely to continue to experience lower-than-average rates of participation, despite the steady growth in the number of Latino voters from election to election.

One of these traits—youth—has a natural remedy, aging. At present, Latinos are approximately nine years younger than the average non-Hispanic white. Immigration and high birth rates will keep Latino voting rates low, but increasing numbers of Latinos will enter their forties and fifties, the ages that see peak voting in all populations. Today, approximately 6.3 million Latinos are forty-five or older. This number will increase to 11.0 million by 2010 and to 20.7 million by 2030 (U.S. Bureau of the Census 1996). Income and education levels are also rising, particularly among the U.S.-born (de la Garza 1996b). However, these slow gains could disappear if the U.S. economy were to deteriorate. For the time being, the steady aging of the Latino population and the growth of an educated middle class spur an increase of 10 to 15 percent every four years in the number of Latinos who turn out to vote.

Electoral growth, however, does not guarantee increased Latino influence. In 1996, for example, the Latino electorate had grown by 16 percent over 1992, and the impact of this growth in the Latino share of the electorate was magnified by a decline in the Anglo electorate. Yet Latino voters were influential in more states in 1992 when the election was closer and more states where many Latinos lived were crucial to the outcome. Thus, increasing the size of the electorate is an important goal, but it is not directly related to influence.

Over time, an increase in the size of the Latino electorate could bring people with different positions or interests into the electorate. This happened, for instance, as Cuban Americans began to vote, reducing the Democratic share of the Latino electorate. Looking to the future, electoral growth spurred by increasing incomes among Latinos would probably increase the Republican share of the electorate. On the other hand, as Latinos age, health care and Social Security could assume a central position in the issue agenda of Latino voters in a way that they do not today. These have long been Democratic issues, and their increased salience could strengthen Latino Democratic ties.

The ongoing slow growth in the number of Latinos who vote could, of course, speed up if an issue or a leader were to mobilize current nonparticipants. This appears to have occurred in California over the last six years in response to increases in nativist and anti-Latino rhetoric on the part of state Republican leaders (Pachon, with Sánchez and Falcon 1999). Two components of the Latino nonvoting population that would be promising targets for such mobilization are registered voters who do not vote (they numbered approximately 1.6 million in 1996) and the newly naturalized.

NATURALIZED CITIZENS

Whereas demographic limits on electoral participation affect all groups, a second characteristic disproportionately affects Latinos. Noncitizens total

39 percent of Latino adults and are the largest potential new electorate among Latinos (DeSipio 1996a). Any effort to mobilize them, however, must begin by encouraging naturalization, because noncitizens are barred from voting in virtually all elections.

In the mid-1990s, naturalization began to surge. The reasons for this growth have been analyzed elsewhere (DeSipio 1996b). What is important for our purposes, is the result: approximately 2.4 million Latinos became naturalized citizens between 1995 and 2001 (they were joined by approximately 2.6 million non-Latino new citizens). These 2.4 million new Latino citizens are potentially influential for several reasons. First, if they were all to join the electorate (an unlikely scenario), they would add almost 50 percent to the existing Latino vote overnight. Second, the newly naturalized are concentrated in a few states, so their impact would be magnified. Finally, many became naturalized at least in part in response to government efforts to limit the rights of immigrants, so there was a political dimension to the decisions made by many such citizens.

The reality, however, is that these naturalized citizens face the same barriers that U.S.-born Latinos do. Demographics limit the numbers who vote. They also face an additional barrier unique to their immigrant origins: they are less familiar with American politics and need more assistance in engaging in the electoral process. Surveys that compare naturalized Latino citizens to the U.S.-born and that control for sociodemographic characteristics show that immigrants are *less* likely than the U.S.-born to register or vote (DeSipio 1997; DeSipio and Jerit 1991, Minnite, Holdaway, and Hayduk 1999). In all likelihood, no more than 40 percent of these newly naturalized citizens will become regular voters. Even so, however, naturalized Latinos can still make up a "new" electorate—or at least a new source of growth in Latino turnout.

The voice of the naturalized Latinos who do vote will probably not differ considerably from that of the U.S.-born, so their newness will be limited to new numbers and will not include new policy or partisan positions. Survey evidence suggests that the views of naturalized Latinos are broadly united with those of the current Latino electorate. Like the U.S.-born, they are strong partisans. Among Mexican Americans, the naturalized are even more likely to be Democrats than the strongly Democratic U.S.-born Mexican American population. Their numbers also make the naturalized likely to be "junior partners" with the U.S.-born. In no state do the naturalized make up a majority. Florida comes the closest; there, the naturalized account for approximately 46 percent of Latino adults. At the other extreme, less than 20 percent of the adult Latino citizens in Arizona and Texas are naturalized.

NON-NATURALIZED IMMIGRANTS

What of the remaining (non-naturalized) Latino immigrants? Do they offer the foundation for an expanding new electorate? The answer is yes, but their impact will be felt slowly. Approximately 1.1 million Latinos (including 7.7 million adults) were not U.S. citizens in 1999. Of these, more than 4 million were undocumented, so there were approximately four million permanent residents. Of these 1.6 million immigrated in the past five years and thus are presently ineligible for naturalization. The remaining 2.4 million naturalization-eligible Latino immigrants are a pool for further growth in the Latino electorate.

In all likelihood, however, this remaining pool of Latino immigrants will be slow to become naturalized. A unique set of pressures and incentives encouraged most of the eligible who were immigrants interested in citizenship to seek naturalization in the late 1990s. Those who did not do so will require added encouragement to pursue citizenship now.

In sum, naturalized citizens and future naturalizees do have some "new" elements, but without renewed and pervasive mobilization, their contribution will be to add to the ongoing gradual increase in the Latino electorate. Because their policy and partisan preferences are broadly congruent with those of existing Latino electorates, they will serve as a pool for an incremental growth that maintains existing cohesiveness.

PARTISANSHIP

As they campaigned in 2000, both George Bush and John McCain could make a claim that no Republican seeking the presidency had ever been able to make before. In their most recent campaign, they could boast, they did well among Latinos. Bush could show one exit poll in his 1991 gubernatorial race that had him winning 41 percent of Latino votes. McCain did even better, having been elected to the Senate with 52 percent of the Latino vote. For many observers, this phenomenon indicated a movement of Latinos into the Republican camp—or at least a new willingness among Latinos to "swing" to the Republicans under the right circumstances.

Despite these exceptions, Latinos continue to exhibit a long-standing pattern of strong, primarily Democratic partisanship. One of Latinos' strengths in negotiating their place in electoral politics is that they do not swing and, instead, make up a core Democratic electorate in the states where they are concentrated. The exception to this rule, of course, is Florida, but there Latinos are equally loyal Republicans.

Although this assertion of strong Latino partisanship may seem to fly in the face of the current conventional wisdom, we would offer as evidence two important considerations. First, opinion polls of Latinos show little movement among Democratic Latinos to the Republican party. Recent polls show Latino Republican partisanship at roughly the rates seen through the 1980s and 1990s. Second, exit polls in Latino communities, which are used as the foundation for arguments that Latinos are shifting their partisan allegiances, are frequently flawed (Shaw, de la Garza, and Lee 2000). Their samples are small and they oversample middle-class and suburbanized Latinos.

For most of the contemporary era, non-Cuban Latinos have been solid Democrats, and recent polling indicates that this pattern continues to hold (*San Jose Mercury News* 2000). Since the 1970s, Cubans have been solid Republicans. In both cases, their rates of partisanship exceed 60 percent. Few Democrats report that they used to be Republicans, whereas approximately one-third of Republicans report being former Democrats (de la Garza et al. 1992, Table 1.25). There are several causes of these Democratic-to-Republican partisan shifts, but only one is operating at this writing. Some Cuban Americans originally joined the Democratic party but became Republicans as the Democrats came to be perceived as softer on Fidel Castro and Cuba (and as the state and local Republican parties in Florida offered greater opportunities for influence and elective office). A second group of Republican converts includes southwestern—particularly Texan—Latinos who were wooed to the Republican party by the Reagan candidacies. The final source of partisan shift is class-based and, unlike the others, continues. Upper-income Mexican Americans and Puerto Ricans are somewhat more likely to be Republicans than are lower-income Mexican Americans and Puerto Ricans. That said, they are much more likely to be Democrats than are Anglos at comparable income levels. As Latino incomes rise, there will be more of these "new" Latino Republicans.

In sum, we see little evidence of a partisan shift to build a new Latino electorate in the short term. Issues and mobilization exogenous to the Latino community may arise and drive Latinos to or away from one of the parties (Proposition 117 and the Contract with America, for example, drove Latinos away from the Republicans), but their steady state is solid support for the Democrats.

CONCENTRATION

Latinos are more geographically concentrated than Anglos and are becoming even more concentrated. Some argue that this concentration boosts Latino empowerment. We find that its minuses may well outweigh its plusses. Let's consider both.

Instead of having a national election for the presidency, the electoral college reflects fifty state elections, in which most states award all of their delegates to the candidate who receives the most votes. Any concentrated electorate that can secure a state for a candidate exerts a form of influence that would be lost if each vote were tallied nationally. Latinos benefit from concentrating most of their numbers in just nine states and from having cohesive voting patterns in each. Latino advocates are quick to observe that Latinos are concentrated in states that elect three-quarters of the electors needed to win the presidency.

Concentration also entails a cost in national elections. No campaign runs equal efforts in all fifty states. Rather, campaigns calculate how they can best spend their money. Little is spent in states that are probable losses *or* in states where victory is very likely. Money and time are focused on the competitive states so that a winning margin of 270 electoral votes can be earned. In 1996, for example, Bob Dole recognized that he would almost certainly be defeated in California, New York, and Illinois, and consequently he spent little money there. President Clinton realized that he could win nationally without Texas and therefore neglected it. Thus, despite Latinos' concentration in states rich in delegates to the electoral college, neither party invested much in mobilizing them. This pattern is repeated in local elections, many of which are noncompetitive as a result of incumbency or partisan advantages.

In the short run, then, concentration is an advantage only in states or other electoral districts that are competitive. In the longer run, areas of concentration can become the sites of sustained multiyear mobilization efforts targeted not just at a specific campaign or election cycle. Efforts such as these, which make concentration an advantage, require leadership and resources that have been absent from most Latino outreach in recent years.

ELITE RESOURCES AND INSTITUTIONS

Although it has been little studied, one genuinely new phenomenon in Latino electoral participation is the rise of a new cadre of Latino elites and new institutions to shape candidate outreach to Latinos. The new elites are made up primarily of young, highly educated Latinos who have begun to populate campaigns. In the process, they have drawn attention to Latino issues and have educated non-Latino candidates about Latino communities. Institutional development has been slower but will probably expand in the next decade. These institutions include Latino political action committees (PACs) and Latino organizations within the national and state political parties.

Latinos have long been involved in electoral campaign management—at the state level since the 1930s (Pycior 1997) and at the national level since 1960 (García 2000). In this earlier era, however, the Latinos who were involved were isolated and relegated to narrow roles mobilizing Latinos.

In the 1990s, the story has changed dramatically. Latino campaign operatives have increased in numbers. More important, some campaigns have tapped Latinos for jobs dealing with all aspects of elections. Most notable among these were the 1992 and 1996 Clinton campaigns, in which Latinos made up as much as 20 percent of the campaign staff and played diverse roles. Many of these staffers went on to prominent positions within the administration, including Deputy Chief of Staff Maria Echaveste.

Institutions have been slower to develop. Several Latino PACs have been established to much fanfare with the goal of promoting Latino candidates and issues. There is no evidence, however, that they raised much money or had much influence. Undoubtedly, as Latinos gain wealth and status, such efforts will expand.

Each of the parties has also created a network of Latino influentials. This form of institutional elite organization is much better entrenched in the Republican party, where it has existed since the 1910s. It includes leadership training for local Latino Republican leaders, frequent fax updates on policy issues in Washington, and a ready network for state and national Republican candidates to tap when they realize that they need Latino votes. The Democrats, perhaps not so well financed, have made less of an investment in this area.

In addition to the formal networks of Latino elites, in some states informal structures have also emerged that make demands for increased Latino electoral representation. Democratic Latinos in California are perhaps the best example of this phenomenon. Beginning in the mid-1990s, senior Latino Democrats, with the tacit support of non-Latino Democrats, began to assert that certain state legislative seats were "Latino." These Latino-designated seats were off limits to non-Latinos, or at least to non-Latinos who expected support from the state party. A system such as this works only if the Latinos who win in the primaries are able to win the seat in the general election. In California they have done so, and this informal network has, in a very fundamental sense, reasserted Democratic dominance in the legislature and built a foundation for Latinos to move into the legislative leadership and the lieutenant governorship.

The increase in the number of Latino votes and the opportunities for these votes to prove influential in electoral outcomes paves the way for expansion in the role of elite resources and institutions. This growth will be spurred by the talent pool of skilled Latino politicos who seek both influence in campaigns and a voice on Latino issues. Thus, although the phenomenon of elite institutions and resources is not new, its potential for influence is, and it merits continuing scholarly appraisal.

ISSUES

In our studies of Latinos and national elections, we make a dedicated effort to identify issues that are important to Latino communities or that are used as a means to connect national candidates to Latinos. After each election, we observe that the issue agenda of Latinos is similar to that of the population as a whole. There are certainly exceptions on the national level (for example, some Latinos took umbrage at George Bush's reference to his Mexican American grandchildren as "the little brown ones") and state-specific exceptions, but for the most part Latinos are concerned with the same issues as Anglos.

Perhaps this finding should not surprise us. The issue agenda of the Latino community has been consistent ever since reliable surveys of its opinions have been taken; the issues of concern to Latinos are primarily U.S. domestic policies. When asked about the *most* important issue the nation or their city faces, Latinos consistently identify social issues. Primary among these social issues are those related to education. Next most important are economic issues and public-safety issues. It is also instructive to observe what does *not* top the issue agenda of Latinos. Latino-specific issues (such as the need for Latino unity and issues related to community leadership) are seldom the *most* important issues. Issues related to countries of origin or ancestry are unimportant, as is immigration policy.

Obviously, people are concerned about a number of issues, not just about a "most important issue." Here, perhaps, changes have occurred over the past twelve years, and we would expect this pattern to continue. Issues related to immigrant settlement, to the provision of state resources for the incorporation of new members, and to economic adjustment have increased in importance. This new pattern appeared most dramatically in the 1996 election (after Proposition 117, the welfare reform bill, and the immigration reform bill).

DUAL NATIONALITY

A final factor that may create a "new" Latino vote is the efforts by several Latin American nations to establish dual nationality for their émigrés and, in some cases, for the U.S.-born children of their émigrés (Jones-Correa 2000). The exact forms of dual nationality vary, and some countries even offer the opportunity to vote in the country of origin/ancestry. To the extent that Latinos take advantage of these opportunities and to the extent that these opportunities stimulate voting in the home countries, they will create a new Latino electorate, though one that is focused elsewhere. There is little hard evidence on this question, but we expect that a relatively few Latinos will take advantage of opportunities for dual nationality. The one piece of available evidence confirms this hypothesis. To date, the number of Mexicans who have applied for dual nationality number just 25,000 out of an eligible pool estimated by Mexico to exceed 7,000,000.

Perhaps the more interesting question is what would happen if more were to take advantage of these opportunities. Would such a pool of active, voluntary dual nationals change the composition or size of the Latino vote? Again, we must speculate. Several studies of the political attitudes of U.S. Latino communities indicate that in areas where there is conflict between U.S. interests and the interests of their countries of origin or ancestry, Latinos support the U.S. position (de la Garza and DeSipio 1991; de la Garza et al. 1991). The evidence is most developed in terms of Mexican immigrants and Mexican Americans. On issues where the two nations have different views, Mexican Americans take positions much closer to those of the United States. Although the evidence is somewhat less developed for other Latin American countries, the survey data that do exist indicate that U.S. Latinos understand binational relations through a lens shaped by U.S. policy makers (de la Garza et al. 1991).

Will dual nationality change this equation? Possibly, especially if it is accompanied by an active campaign to incorporate U.S. nationals. But what would seem more likely is that dual nationals will try to influence their countries of ancestry/origin by espousing policy views shaped by U.S. public opinion. It is unlikely that this new political voice will be well received by these countries.

CONCLUSIONS

In the continual search for what is new in the Latino electorate, there is a tendency to neglect the incremental but steady changes that shape Latino politics. Latino votes have become increasingly sought by candidates and parties. These votes do occasionally determine outcomes, although when they do, they are usually determined by factors exogenous to the Latino community. Both parties have designed Latino-specific outreach strategies and dedicated resources to winning Latino votes, and Latinos have become more centrally positioned in campaigns and elite networks. As a result, candidates are somewhat less likely to speak from ignorance when they address Latino issues. Although we have not discussed it here, the number of Latino elected and appointed officials has grown. When the Voting Rights Act was extended to Latinos in 1975, they were not a nationally influential electorate; today they are. What we find, however, is not a single, dramatic change but incremental change and growth in the electorate. We expect this pattern to continue, but we do not anticipate a sudden burst of new Latino electoral empowerment.

This increase in the importance of the Latino electorate is not the result of mobilization among all Latinos or all Latino citizens. Instead, Latinos have followed the pattern of Anglos: voting is more common among the educationally and economically advantaged. For a truly new Latino electorate to emerge, this pattern would have to change, and mobilization would have to extend to all segments of the Latino electorate. Survey data indicate that even if this were to occur, such a broad-based mobilization would not appreciably change the issue focus of Latino electorates, just likelihood of their influencing electoral outcomes.

Will Latinos play a central role in the outcomes of upcoming national elections? The answer to this question is found primarily outside of the Latino community. The incremental growth in Latino electorates makes it, all other factors remaining constant, slightly more likely each presidential election cycle. But the final answer will be determined each election year. Latinos will be important if the race comes down to the states where their numbers are concentrated, if one or both of the candidates see Latino votes as central to their ability to win those states, and if one or both of the candidates dedicate resources to winning Latinos' votes (or to preventing the other candidate from winning their votes). In this scenario, their votes could make the difference. The candidates and parties now possess the expertise to structure a campaign to win their votes. In this scenario, their strong partisanship and state-level cohesion make them an inviting target relative to other electorates.

NOTE

1. We use the terms *Latino* and *Hispanic* interchangeably to identify individuals who trace their origin or ancestry to the Spanish-speaking countries of Latin America or the Caribbean. We would like to thank Chuck Haynes and the Public Policy Clinics of the University of Texas Department of Government for research assistance with this chapter.

REFERENCES

de la Garza, Rodolfo O. 1996a. "El Cuento de los Números and Other Latino Political Myths." In *Su Voto es Su Voz: Latino Politics in California*, ed. Aníbal Yáñez-Chávez. San Diego: Center or U.S. Mexican Studies, University of California, San Diego, pp. 11–32.

———. 1996b. "The Effects of Primordial Claims, Immigration, and the Voting Rights Act on Mexican American Sociopolitical Incorporation." In *The Politics of Minority Coalitions: Race, Ethnicity, and Shared Uncertainties*, ed. Wilbur C. Rich. Westport, CT: Praeger Publishers, pp. 163–176.

de la Garza, Rodolfo O., and Louis DeSipio. 1992. *From Rhetoric to Reality: Latino Politics in the 1911 Elections*. Boulder, CO: Westview.

———, eds. 1996. *Ethnic Ironies: Latino Politics in the 1992 Elections*. Boulder, CO: Westview.

———. 1991. "Interests Not Passions: Mexican American Attitudes toward Mexico, Immigration from Mexico, and Issues Shaping U.S.–Mexico Relations." *International Migration Review* 32(2) (Summer): 401–422.

———, eds. 1999. *Awash in the Mainstream: Latino Politics in the 1996 Elections*. Boulder, CO: Westview.

de la Garza, Rodolfo O., Louis DeSipio, F. Chris García, John A. García, and Angelo Falcón. 1992. *Latino Voices: Mexican, Puerto Rican, and Cuban Perspectives on American Politics.* Boulder, CO: Westview.

de la Garza, Rodolfo O., Martha Menchaca, and Louis DeSipio, eds. 1994. *Barrio Ballots: Latino Politics in the 1990 Election.* Boulder, CO: Westview.

de la Garza, Rodolfo O., Manuel Orozco, Harry Pachon, and Adrian Pantoja. 1991. *Family Ties and Ethnic Lobbies: Latino Relations with Latin America.* Claremont, CA: Tomás Rivera Policy Institute.

DeSipio, Louis. 1996a. *Counting on the Latino Vote: Latinos as a New Electorate.* Charlottesville, VA: University Press of Virginia.

———. 1996b. "After Proposition 117, the Deluge: Reforming Naturalization Administration While Making Good Citizens." *Harvard Journal of Hispanic Policy* 9:7–24.

———. 1997. "Making Citizens or Good Citizens? Naturalization as a Predictor of Organizational and Electoral Behavior among Latino Immigrants." *Hispanic Journal of Behavioral Sciences* 11(2) (May): 194–213.

DeSipio, Louis, and Jennifer Jerit. 1991. "Voluntary Citizens and Democratic Participation: Political Behaviors among Naturalized U.S. Citizens." Paper prepared for presentation at the Midwest Political Science Association meetings. April. Chicago.

García, Ignacio. 2000. *Viva Kennedy: Mexican Americans in Search of Camelot.* College Station: Texas A&M University Press.

Jones-Correa, Michael. 2000. *Under Two Flags: Dual Nationality in Latin America and Its Consequences for the United States.* Cambridge, MA: David Rockefeller Center for Latin American Studies.

Minnite, Lorraine C., Jennifer Holdaway, and Ronald Hayduk. 1999. "Political Incorporation of Immigrants in New York." Paper prepared for presentation at the annual meetings of the American Political Science Association. September. Atlanta.

Pachon, Harry, with Lupe Sánchez and Dennis Falcon. 1999. "California Latino Politics and the 1996 Elections: From Potential to Reality." In *Awash in the Mainstream: Latino Politics in the 1996 Elections,* ed. Rodolfo O. de la Garza and Louis DeSipio. Boulder, CO: Westview, pp. 167–190.

Pycior, Julie Leininger. 1997. *LBJ and Mexican Americans: The Paradox of Power.* Austin: University of Texas Press.

San Jose Mercury News. 2000. "Special Report: A Mercury News Poll of Latinos." **http://www.mercurycenter.com/local/center/polldata.htm**.

Shaw, Daron, Rodolfo O. de la Garza, and Jongho Lee. 2000. "Examining Latino Turnout in 1996: A Three States, Validated Survey Approach." *American Journal of Political Science* 44(2) (April): 339–346.

U.S. Bureau of the Census. 1996. *Population Projections of the United States by Age, Sex, Race, and Hispanic Origin: 1995 to 2050.* Current Population Reports, Series P-25, No. 1130.

Chapter 21

Gender and Citizenship in Latino Political Participation

Lisa J. Montoya

Latinos are as likely to participate in nonelectoral activities as Anglos after controlling for socioeconomic status (Wolfinger and Rosenstone 1980; Uhlaner, Cain, and Kiewiet 1989; DeSipio 1996).[1] However, the raw numbers paint quite a different picture. Without controlling for sociodemographics, Latinos participate much less in most nonelectoral activities. The participation gap begs the question of how Latinos might be influenced so as to participate more in politics. This paper examines the most important influences on political participation and their varying influences on Latino subpopulations. Given that the social and political contexts of men and women and of citizens and noncitizens can be dramatically different, a focus on these cleavages should help us understand what strategies and institutions are most effective for mobilizing the Latino polity. I find that the influences on participation differ between Latino men and women but are similar between citizens and noncitizens. I argue that organizations play a critical role in mobilizing Latinos and urge more data gathering and research on the roles of elites, schools, and voluntary associations in mobilization.

The measure of political participation analyzed here is a set of actions in which most citizens and denizens have some opportunity to participate. These actions include signing a petition, writing a letter to a public official, attending a public meeting, wearing a campaign button, attending political meetings, working for a party or a candidate, and contributing money to an individual candidate or a political party. Using OLS regression, I estimated models for Mexican, Puerto Rican, and Cuban men and women, assessing differences within and across national-origin groups. For citizens and noncitizens, I estimated a similar model on Mexicans and Cubans only.

A focus on different subpopulations acknowledges explicitly that political participation occurs in a social and political context. Those who have resources participate more, whereas those who have fewer resources participate less or not at all. More than that, political opportunity arises out of many situations, including work, voluntary organizations, churches, and schools; those with a broader social network will undoubtedly have more opportunities for political participation. Studying participation among Latinos helps us understand the mechanisms or paths through which Latinos are motivated to participate in politics. If the paths are the same, then we would expect that, all other things being equal, mobilization strategies would be equally effective for men and women and for citizens and noncitizens. If the paths are not the same, then multiple strategies might be developed to mobilize various Latino subpopulations.

Studying differences in participation also provides a snapshot of the process of civic incorporation. If, for example, even after controlling for resources, mobilization, and socioeconomic status, we find that women are less likely to participate in politics, then we can infer that the transmission of civic values is being disrupted in some way, perhaps through a slower process of ethnic acculturation. A more likely scenario is that Latinas participate at about the same rate as men and that women who have the most exposure to higher education and to the work environment demonstrate higher levels of participation, after controlling for other relevant variables. This result would lead us to conclude that civic incorporation is proceeding at equal rates for men and women. It would not necessarily tell us, however, whether civic incorporation happens in the same way for Latino men and women.

I compare citizens and noncitizens because noncitizens exhibit substantially lower levels of participation. Thus a comparison of citizens and noncitizens highlights the differences between very different segments of the population. Further, many Latino immigrants do not pursue naturalization when they become eligible. They live in the United States, buy homes, establish businesses, and raise children without the benefit of citizenship. Still, at least some are politically active. What can be done to mobilize more of these denizens?[2]

This paper is organized as follows. First, I present the literature on political participation focusing on Latinos, gender and citizenship. Second, I discuss the data—the Latino National Political Survey (LNPS)—and methodology. Next I briefly compare Latino and Anglo participation to place Latinos in context and then present the analyses for both gender and citizenship. Finally, the conclusion discusses the policy implications of the results and offers suggestions for future research.

LITERATURE ON POLITICAL PARTICIPATION

Early studies on participation emphasized the role of socioeconomic indicators in predicting political activity (Verba and Nie 1972): education and, to a lesser extent, income were the most common measures. Subsequent work on Latinos reifies the role of socioeconomic status (SES) in predicting participation (Hero and Campbell 1996; Lien 1994; Uhlaner, Cain, and Kiewiet 1989; Calvo and Rosenstone 1989; Garcia and Arce 1988; Welch, Comer, and Steinman 1975). During the same period, scholars studying Latinos were also considering the role of ethnic political consciousness as a predictor of participation (Dale 1979; Antunes and Gaitz 1975). Our understanding of participation has grown substantially since Verba and Nie's early work, and a number of other important determinants have been found, including life-cycle and situational variables, political engagement, and mobilization. Life-cycle and situational variables include age, gender, marital status, ethnicity, and citizenship (Milbrath and Goel 1977). Political engagement reflects the psychological predisposition to participation and is assessed in terms of measures of interest in politics and following politics (Verba, Schlozman, and Brady 1995). Mobilization— via the social networks that yield invitations for continued or new participation—can be the result of personal interactions or organizational membership and activity. More significantly, an understanding of how elites mobilize people on specific issues and campaigns explains the ebb and flow of political activity (Rosenstone and Hansen 1993). For Latinos, organizational memberships increase participation, and even passive membership has a positive effect (Diaz 1996; Wrinkle et al. 1996).

A more developed understanding of the determinants of participation is embodied in the civic voluntarism model, which uses resources, political engagement, and networks (or mobilization) to explain participation in politics (Verba, Schlozman, and Brady 1995). This model expands the list of resources that are important to politics to include skills attained through work, voluntary associations, and churches and free time. It also recasts the role of organizations by arguing that membership alone does not increase participation. Rather, it is the skill one attains in a voluntary association or the opportunity one receives in the social context of an organization that influences participation.[3] Using this model, Schlozman, Burns, and Verba ask whether the constellation of influences on political participation is the same for men and women. They find the influences to be similar except that membership in voluntary, nonpolitical associations has an effect on women but not on men (1994, pp. 978–79).

Although the extant research on Latinos is not extensive, it demonstrates that Latinos are subject to the same influences on political participation as the rest of the U.S. population, with only a few anticipated additions. Because many Latinos are immigrants, situational variables (including naturalization and ability to speak English) are also important predictors.

DATA AND METHODOLOGY

Data for this study are taken from the Latino National Political Survey (LNPS), a national sample of Mexicans, Puerto Ricans, Cubans, and other Latinos conducted in 1989 and 1990 (see de la Garza et al. 1992 for a complete description of survey methodology). Its sample is drawn from forty "Standard Metropolitan Statistical Areas" and from communities across the socioeconomic spectrum. The survey defined a respondent as Latino if "he or she, one parent, or two grandparents were solely of Mexican, Puerto Rican, or Cuban ancestry" (de la Garza et al. 1992). The data are representative of 91 percent of Mexicans, Puerto Ricans, and Cubans in the United States. The data are not representative of those Latinos who reside in states where less than 5 percent of the population is Latino. The data also include an Anglo comparison group. This Anglo subsample is representative of those Anglos who live in neighborhoods where Latinos live, not of all Anglos in the United States. For the purposes of this chapter, determination of ethnicity is based on the national-origin identity of respondents. The sample in this study is composed of 2,676 Latino citizen and noncitizen respondents, including 1,546 Mexicans, 589 Puerto Ricans, and 682 Cubans. All other Latinos (from Central or South America) in the sample are excluded.

Ordinary least-squares regression is used to estimate the participation model. For the gender analysis, each model is estimated separately for Mexicans, Puerto Ricans, and Cubans. The citizenship model is estimated only for Cubans and Mexicans because Puerto Ricans are citizens.

The independent variable is a scale of nonelectoral activities that probe the ways in which people make their views known. The question is as follows.

We would like to find out about some of the things people in the U.S. do to make their views known. Which of the activities listed on this card, if any, have you done in the past twelve months?

a) signed a petition regarding an issue or problem that concerns you?

b) written a letter, telephoned or sent a telegram to an editor or public official regarding issues that concern you?

c) attended a public meeting?

d) worn a campaign button, put a campaign sticker on your car, or placed a sign in your window or in front of your house?

e) gone to any political meetings, rallies, speeches, or dinners in support of a particular candidate?

f) worked either for pay or on a volunteer basis for a party or a candidate running for office?

g) contributed money to *an individual candidate*, a political party, or some other political organization supporting a candidate or an issue in an election?

This paper uses predictors based on socioeconomic status, resources, mobilization, political engagement, and life-cycle and situational measures to examine fully the effect of gender and citizenship on participation (see the Appendix to this chapter for a complete description of these variables). Socioeconomic status is operationalized by education and income. Resources are operationalized by workplace skills acquired that facilitate political activity. Further, skills developed in any organizational or work setting were transferable to politics. Mobilization is operationalized by respondent membership in voluntary organizations, by parental school involvement, and by frequency of church attendance. Although it may seem tautological to measure some forms of participation with others, the independent variables used here are theoretically and practically distinct from those included in the dependent variable. Political engagement is operationalized by asking how often respondents follow politics and whether they are likely to help solve a problem in their neighborhood or city. Life-cycle and situational measures are age, facility with English, and citizenship status.[4]

COMPARISON OF LATINO AND ANGLO PARTICIPATION

To place Latino participation levels in context, I begin my analysis by comparing Latinos and Anglos from the LNPS with a national sample from the civic voluntarism study (conducted by Verba, Schlozman, and Brady (1995).[5] Participation rates among Latinos are far below the rates for Anglos. This is due in part to citizenship. Of the 17.4 million Latinos in the nine states most heavily populated with Latinos, 44 percent (7.6 million) are noncitizens (Tomás Rivera Center 1996, pp. 2–3). Noncitizens may not vote and are unlikely to participate in other electoral activities.[6] They are also unlikely to engage in activities that might expose their illegal status to immigration authorities, and this reluctance limits their participation in nonelectoral activities as well. Among Latino citizens, participation rates are also low compared with Anglos. To illustrate these differences, Table 21.1 presents the mean political acts by income for four populations and two data sets. From the LNPS, the table provides data for all Latinos, Latino citizens, and Anglos. From the civic voluntarism study, the table provides data for U.S. citizens. The summary measure consists of eight political acts: voting, volunteering for a campaign, making a campaign contribution, contacting a public official, attending a rally or protest, attending a school

TABLE 21.1. Mean Political Acts (Number of Acts
Out of a Possible Eight) by Income and Ethnicity

	Latino National Political Study			
	Latinos		Anglos in	U.S. Population[2] (civic voluntarism study data)
Income	All Latinos	Citizens Only	Subsample[1]	
All income (total population)	0.9	1.2	1.5	2.1
Under $15,000	0.8	1.0	1.3	1.3
$15–34,999	0.8	1.1	1.5	1.9
$35–49,999	1.4	1.7	1.7	2.4
$50–74,999	1.2	1.4	2.0	2.9
$75,000 and above[3]	1.9	2.1	1.9	3.0
($125,000 and above)	Not available	Not available	Not available	3.4

[1]The Anglo subsample is representative of Anglos who live in close proximity to Latinos.
[2]Data from Verba, Schlozman, and Brady (1995, p. 188) are weighted and include Latinos and African Americans.
[3]This category is $75,000 to $124,999 for the Verba et al. study.
SOURCE: Latino National Political Study (LNPS)

board meeting, working to solve a problem in one's neighborhood or community, and being a member of a social organization that takes positions on political and social issues.

Among all Latinos, the mean number of acts is 0.9, less than one act, on average, out of eight possible acts. When Latino citizens alone are examined, the average number of acts increases to 1.2. The Anglos in the LNPS are somewhat more active, with an average of 1.5 acts, and the U.S. sample shows that the average number of political acts for the population overall is 2.1.

Table 21.1 shows the influence of resources on participation and illustrates the limits of relying solely on resources as an explanation. The table confirms that as income increases, so does participation. Beginning with respondents whose income is under $15,000 annually, there is little difference between Latino citizens and Anglos in the LNPS and between Latino citizens and the overall population in the civic voluntarism study. With so few resources to expend on politics, ethnicity has little impact. But once people have some free time and discretionary income—that is, once they have some resources—political socialization, context, and opportunity all become more important predictors of participation. Between $15,000 and $34,999 in annual income, Anglos in the LNPS lag behind the civic voluntarism study by only half as much as Latino citizens. Perhaps the

Anglos are asked more often to attend a rally or join an organization, and because they have the free time or are able to pay the organization dues, they become more active than their Latino neighbors. At the next income level, $35,000 to $49,999, the additional income equalizes participation between Latino citizens and Anglos in the LNPS, but both lag behind the civic voluntarism study by .7 act. The Latinos and Anglos in the LNPS live in neighborhoods where the context is less supportive of political participation than in other neighborhoods with similar resources. Above $50,000, the additional availability of resources increases the participation of both Latino citizens and Anglos; however, the gap between these groups and the civil voluntarism study are greater than ever. Despite similar income, the neighborhood and work contexts of Latinos are not as likely to foster political opportunity or activity.

This comparison between the LNPS data and the civic voluntarism data suggests that, despite similar economic resources, the neighborhood and work contexts of Latinos are less likely to produce political opportunity or activity. Now we consider whether the Latino context differs between men and women and between citizens and noncitizens.

BIVARIATE AND MULTIVARIATE ANALYSIS

Gender

We begin with a brief summary of the frequency with which Latino and Anglo men and women engage in seven political activities, the activities that constitute our measure of political participation.

The most striking feature of Table 21.2 is unrelated to gender or citizenship; it is the difference between the levels of Anglo and Latino participation. First, Anglos participate substantially more than Latinos in all but one category (volunteer for a political candidate). Second, even for the least costly political acts—signing a petition, for example—the highest level reported in the table is 50 percent. This act, in particular, is a good indicator of political opportunity. Usually, one signs a petition only when one is asked to do so. For activities requiring more substantial investments of time, the highest rate reported is 25 percent.

With few exceptions, there are only small differences in participation by gender, although men still participate more overall. By national origin, however, different patterns emerge when we examine gender. Mexican women are more likely than men to participate, but for Puerto Ricans, men participate more. Cubans participate at roughly equal rates, and Anglo men participate more than Anglo women. Overall, men are more likely to make campaign contributions, and women do not lead in any category of participation. Among Latinas, Mexican women are slightly more participatory

TABLE 21.2. Making Views Known, Latinos and Anglos, 1989

Political Act	Mexicans		Puerto Ricans		Cubans		Anglos	
	W	M	W	M	W	M	W	M
Sign a petition (%)	21	19	16	21	11	11	42	50+
Write a letter, call an official (%)	10	8	9	7	7	9	21	25
Attend public meeting (%)	14	11*	12	18*	5	7	23	25
Wear campaign button, attach bumper sticker, erect house sign	13	12	13	16	10	10	19	18
Attend political rallies/speeches	6	7	7	7	4	5	10	8
Volunteer for a political candidate	5	5	5	3	3	3	4	5
Make a campaign contribution	4	7	4	6	4	4	9	17*

KEY: * significant at .05 level
       W = women, M = men
SOURCE: Latino National Political Survey

overall. In sum, Latino participation is low overall and does not differ significantly by gender.

Now we examine the multivariate results to see whether the influences on Latina participation are different from the influences on Latino participation. Table 21.2 provides the OLS results for each of the national-origin groups. Note that each model explains a moderate amount of variance and that the constants are negative for both Mexicans and Puerto Ricans. In this instance, a negative constant means there is a bias against participation. In other words, there would have to be considerable levels of activity or of attributes positively associated with the participation measures before a prediction of participation could be made. The bias against participation is most pronounced among Puerto Ricans.

Table 21.3 presents the multivariate results for Latino political participation by gender and national origin. A summary view shows that Mexican men and women are more similar than either Puerto Rican or Cuban men and women. Education, work skills, organizational and school participation, and solving neighborhood problems predict participation for Mexican men and women alike. The four predictors that distinguish Mexican women from Mexican men indicate that women face additional barriers to political participation. Given that politics remains largely the province of men, Mexican women participate only when they have additional monetary resources to do so. Women also remain less interested in politics than are men on average (Bennett and Bennett 1989), so it is the more informed Mexican women who are politically active. Mexican women become more active as they age, and Mexican women are more likely to participate if they are proficient in English. None of these factors appears

TABLE 21.3. Latino Political Participation
by National Origin and Gender, OLS Regression

Variable	Mexicans Women	Men	Puerto Ricans Women	Men	Cubans Women	Men
Education	.04**	.04**	.05*	.06*	.01	−.03
	(.01)	(.01)	(.02)	(.03)	(.01)	(.02)
Income	.02*	−.01	−.02	.05+	.03+	.003
	(.01)	(.01)	(.02)	(.03)	(.02)	(.022)
Age	.006*	.004	.005	.019**	−.002	.001
	(.003)	(.004)	(.005)	(.006)	(.003)	(.004)
Language						
Bilingual	−.18+	.05	.38+	−.09	−.25	−.33
	(.10)	(.13)	(.22)	(.23)	(.25)	(.27)
Spanish-speaking	−.36**	−.15	.39+	−.31)	−.30	−.46+
	(.12)	(.14)	(.24)	(.29	(.25)	(.26)
Work skills	.06+	.19***	.19***	.09	.16***	.05
	(.03)	(.04)	(.05)	(.06)	(.04)	(.06)
Following politics	.07+	.03	.06	.03	.06	.12*
	(.04)	(.05)	(.06)	(.07)	(.04)	(.06)
Church attendance	−.07	−.08	.18	.49*	−.01	−24.
	(.10)	(.11)	(.17)	(.21)	(.12)	(.16)
Organizational	.13**	.29***	.18+	.01	.16**	.31***
participation	(.05)	(.06)	(.10)	(.11)	(.05)	(.09)
School participation	.20***	.19***	.17***	.07	.10*	.02
	(.03)	(.04)	(.04)	(.06)	(.04)	(.07)
Solving neighborhood	1.22***	1.42***	1.52***	1.14***	1.23***	1.09***
problems	(.12)	(.15)	(.20)	(.22)	(.20)	(.27)
Constant	−.51*	−.36	−1.03*	−1.30*	.30	.40
	(.24)	(.32)	(.43)	(.58)	(.36)	(.45)
Adj R^2 =	.38	.46	.36	.35	.39	.20
N =	877	669	374	215	387	294
F =	39.25**	44.27***	15.58***	9.21***	19.54***	6.58***

Unstandardized regression coefficient (standard error).
KEY: $+ p < .10$; $* p < .05$; $** p < .01$; $*** p < .001$. See Appendix for explanation of variables.
SOURCE: Latino National Political Survey (de la Garza et al. 1992)

to matter for Mexican men. Puerto Rican women are mobilized by a wider array of organizational factors than their male counterparts. Among Cubans, women who have higher incomes, who have work skills, and who participate in schools and associations are more likely to be politically engaged. In contrast, men are influenced only by their interest in politics, their organizational associations, and their political efficacy.

What emerges is that the predictors for women's participation are more consistent than for men's across national origin. The effects of work skills and organizations show the influences on working women and women who stay at home. Many Latinas work in pink-collar or clerical positions and thus are more likely than their male counterparts to develop skills that are transferable to politics. For Latinas who stay at home, their participation in schools, charities, and social organizations is a source of political information and mobilization—opportunities that men often have through work situations.

The role of the Spanish language in political culture reveals itself here. Spanish-speaking and bilingual Mexican women are less likely to participate than English-dominant Mexican women. In contrast, bilingual and Spanish-speaking Puerto Rican women are more likely to participate than their English-speaking sisters. English makes Mexican women insiders and Puerto Rican women outsiders.

Overall, the organizational variables and workplace skills are the most consistent predictors across gender and national origin. Participation in unions, work or social groups, charities, and ethnic associations promote other forms of participation because they are settings for information sharing and mobilization. Those who have had experience writing letters and contacting officials on behalf of a group will do so independently when a political issue is important to them. Solving neighborhood problems is also a consistent measure across all groups.

Each model explains a moderate amount of variance. Note that the constants are negative for both Mexicans and Puerto Ricans. In this instance, a negative constant means there is a bias against participation. In other words, there would have to be considerable levels of activity or of attributes positively associated with the participation measures before a prediction of participation could be made.

Are there different paths to participation among Latino men and women? Yes. The distinctions are most clear among Cuban men and women. Cuban women who have some financial autonomy, work skills, and the time to become involved in associations (especially schools) are more likely to participate. We could interpret this set of characteristics as affluence, but it is a gendered affluence because the same qualities do not also predict male participation. In addition, the skills acquired in the workplace help Latinas to participate but do not consistently help Latinos.

Two conclusions can be drawn from the inconsistency of predictors across the Latino male populations. (1) Politics is structured differently in Mexican, Puerto Rican, and Cuban communities. Puerto Rican and Cuban politics thrives more in ethnic enclaves than Mexican politics does. (2) The social context of Latinos may be broader and more diverse than the social context of Latinas, and the factors affecting Latino political participation may consequently be equally diverse.

What approaches do these results suggest for mobilizing Latinos? Reaching out to Latino men and women through existing organizations is a sure-fire approach to mobilization. In particular, women can be mobilized more effectively through schools. More must be done by using existing voluntary associations. For Mexican women, promoting English will also help to increase participation. However, for Puerto Rican women, Spanish fluency remains an advantage. As the U.S.-born generation of Puerto Ricans ages, however, Spanish fluency may become less important.

Citizens and Noncitizens

We now turn to citizens and noncitizens who report engaging in at least one political act. Approximately 50 percent of U.S.-born Mexicans and Cubans reported at least one form of participation, compared with 62 percent of their Anglo neighbors. We would expect noncitizen participation rates to be lower, but over 75 percent of the noncitizen respondents reported having lived in the United States six years or more—enough time to be eligible for citizenship and voting. Despite many years of exposure to the U.S. civic culture, noncitizen Mexican and Cuban participation rates are 13 and 14 percent, respectively. Even when noncitizens had resided in the United States for ten years or more, no more than 15 to 22 percent of them reported engaging in political activity.

In Table 21.4, we examine the predictors of participation for citizens and noncitizens. Bear in mind that the noncitizens for whom data are reported in Table 21.4 are distinct populations. The Mexican noncitizens are legal residents or undocumented immigrants who have come to the United States to join or raise a family and to work, mainly in unskilled or semiskilled industries. Many intend to stay in the United States although they return to Mexico when possible. The Cuban noncitizens came to the United States as political refugees. They received government assistance with resettlement, and few return to Cuba even to visit (see Chapter 3 in, this volume). The vast majority of these Cuban noncitizens have been in the United States for at least fifteen years, and many have settled in Miami's Cuban enclave where they could benefit from a cohesive network of social and economic ties.

The results shown in Table 21.4 suggest that the predictors of participation for Mexican citizens and noncitizens are strikingly similar. Higher educational attainment, work skills, organizational and school participation, and the ability to solve neighborhood problems all determine whether

TABLE 21.4. Latino Participation by National
Origin and Citizenship Status, OLS Regression

Variable	Mexicans		Cubans	
	Citizens	Noncitizens	Citizens	Noncitizens
Education	.06**	.024**	−.009	−.03*
	(.02)	(.009)	(.02)	(.01)
Income	.02+	−.02*	.008	.01
	(.01)	(.01)	(.02)	(.01)
Age	.005	.002	.001	−.005+
	(.004)	(.003)	(.005)	(.02)
Language				
Bilingual	−.03	.59*	−.28	.20
	(.11)	(.25)	(.25)	(.4)
Spanish-speaking	−.15	.32	−.40	.27
	(.19)	(.24)	(.24)	(.33)
Work skills	.10**	.10***	.10*	.07
	(.03)	(.03)	(.05)	(.04)
Following politics	.10*	.003	.10	.08*
	(.05)	(.028)	(.07)	(.03)
Church attendance	−.08	−.05	−.26	.04
	(.12)	(.07)	(.19)	(.10)
Organizational participation	.16***	.17***	.17**	.22*
	(.05)	(.05)	(.06)	(.10)
School participation	.24***	.13***	.10+	.01
	(.04)	(.03)	(.05)	(.05)
Solving neighborhood problems	1.37***	.99***	1.67***	.52**
	(.12)	(.13)	(.24)	(.20)
Constant	−.99***	−.43	.23	.05
	(.31)	(.29)	(.48)	(.39)
Adj R^2 =	.39	.29	.35	.08
N =	885	661	306	375
F =	42.70***	20.65***	14.19***	3.38***

Unstandardized regression coefficient (standard error).
KEY: + p < .10; * p < .05; ** p < .01; *** p < .001. See Appendix for explanation of variables.
SOURCE: Latino National Political Survey

Mexican citizens and noncitizens will participate. Only two variables distinguish Mexican citizens from noncitizens. Mexican citizens are influenced by their interest in politics, whereas noncitizens participate more if they are bilingual. From this vantage point, Spanish-dominant speakers are at a disadvantage.

Fewer of the predictors are significant in the Cuban case, and only two—organizational participation and solving neighborhood problems—are significant for citizens and noncitizens. But these two predictors are also some of the strongest predictors for Mexicans. For Cuban citizens, the constellation of significant predictors highlights the role of the enclave in Cuban participation. Associational ties and skills promote participation. Those with few group connections or without such abilities are less likely to be active. Political participants are bilingual or English-dominant; there is a statistically significant negative effect for Spanish speakers. The ethnic enclave model is less convincing for noncitizen Cubans. Instead, resources available, life-cycle variables, and associational variables explain participation.

The model predicts a modest amount of variance. The constants in both the Mexican models are negative, indicating a strong bias against participation. Overall, voluntary organizations, school activities, the ability to help solve neighborhood problems, and work skills are the strongest and most consistent predictors of participation across these populations. For Mexicans, the only important differences among citizens and noncitizens are facility with English and political interest, both of which are more likely (though not guaranteed) to increase as immigrants become more established and through marriage, children, and home ownership. For Cubans, age has a negative effect and schools have no effect on participation. This suggests that noncitizens are either much younger or much older than citizen Cubans. Their lower level of participation shows that they have fewer established connections to the U.S. polity.

The results shown in Table 21.4 demonstrate that mobilization strategies focusing on organizations and schools would be influential, but they offer no insight into how mobilization strategies could be customized to reach out to noncitizens. In Table 21.5, I propose a final model, looking only at noncitizens by income level. When income is controlled for, other differences among noncitizens might emerge that suggest distinctive mobilization strategies. Noncitizens are categorized as low-, medium-, or high-income.[7]

The results show that the only predictors of participation among low-income noncitizens are political efficacy and organizational participation. As income rises, other life-cycle, situational and resource variables become important.

Are the paths to participation different between Latino citizens and noncitizens? No. In the aggregate, the paths are similar. However, for lower-income noncitizens, given that they have few resources or skills, the role of organizations is central. As income rises among noncitizens, facility with English and level of education become significant. For high-income noncitizens, bilingualism and Spanish dominance are both predictors of political

TABLE 21.5. Latino Participation by Income,
Noncitizens Only, OLS Regression

| Variable | Noncitizen Latinos | | | |
	All	Low-Income	Medium-Income	High-Income
Education	.01+	−.004	.04**	−.002**
	(.007)	(.008)	(.01)	(.02)
Income	−.006	NA	NA	NA
	(.007)			
Age	−.003	−.005	−.01**	−.01+
	(.002)	(.002)	(.003)	(.007)
Language				
Bilingual	.49**	.09	.50+	1.8***
	(.18)	(.32)	(.27)	(.43)
Spanish-speaking	.43*	.17	.37	1.62***
	(.18)	(.31)	(.26)	(.43)
Work skills	.08***	.05	.007	−.09
	(.02)	(.04)	(.04)	(.06)
Following politics	.05+	.04	.04	.10
	(.02)	(.03)	(.04)	(.08)
Church attendance	−.13*	−.06	−.06	−.21
	(.06)	(.07)	(.11)	(.17)
Organizational participation	.19***	.22**	−.07	.28***
	(.04)	(.06)	(.08)	(.08)
School participation	.07**	.03	.06	.15+
	(.02)	(.03)	(.04)	(.08)
Solving neighborhood problems	.65***	.24+	.50*	2.20***
	(.11)	(.14)	(.22)	(.32)
Constant	−.43*	−.07	.27	−1.42**
	(.21)	(.33)	(.34)	(.50)
Adj R^2 =	.18	.05	.12	.61
N =	1076	521	317	125
F =	17.04***	3.22***	4.72***	17.00***

Unstandardized regression coefficient (standard error)
KEY: + p < .10; * p < .05; ** p < .01; *** p < .001. See Appendix for explanation of variables.
NA = Not applicable
SOURCE: Latino National Political Survey

activity. These somewhat contradictory results confirm that noncitizen Latinos live with other immigrants in a Spanish-dominant environment. Those with the time, resources, interest, and leadership skills may not need to speak English to be active in politics. Bilingualism enhances one's ability to be a leader, however, because it enables one to be a spokesperson.

What approaches do these results suggest for mobilizing Latino noncitizens? For noncitizens with the fewest resources, reaching out through organizations they trust is a first step. Afterward, providing information and political opportunity and helping to build skills that can be transferred to politics will also promote political activity.

CONCLUSION

For Latino women and men, the paths to political participation are different; for citizens and noncitizens, the paths are increasingly similar as noncitizens attain greater resources. The most consistent predictor of Latino participation has been the mobilization role of membership in organizations. Even though we do not know just how organizational memberships contribute to political participation, the evidence presented here suggests that for lower-income noncitizens, with few resources or skills, the role of organizations is central. As income rises among noncitizens, English ability and educational attainment become important predictors. The evidence further suggests that the schools are fertile ground for encouraging Latino, and particularly Latina, participation. More generally, women's participation was influenced by financial means, work skills, and the time to become involved in associations—gendered measures of affluence. In addition, Mexican women will benefit from learning English.

In sum, a long-term approach to encouraging more general participation would be (1) to encourage activities in schools and other fundamental institutions as a training ground for continued and increased civic participation and (2) to promote learning English.

This research maps the macro effects of the predictors of participation. It does not reveal details about the micro processes that are the most successful promoters of participation. In order to do this, research should focus more on the roles of organizations, elites, and the media in mobilizing Latinos. With richer information about organizational participation, scholars can determine to what extent organizations build skills, provide opportunity, or promote information and discussion. Data sources should ask in a systematic way whether and with whom people discuss politics, whether individuals are asked to participate, and by whom.[8]

Another avenue of research is to understand better the relationship between skills acquisition at work and in organizations.[9] Are skilled people joining organizations? Or are organization members learning new skills and using them in their volunteer associations? The answer is probably both, but among stay-at-home women and noncitizens who have fewer opportunities for political mobilization, I suspect that membership comes before skills acquisition. This means that greater involvement within organizations can help promote participation in the long run.

A third research area would be to pursue strong models and strategies for using schools as organizing institutions for participation. There are advantages and disadvantages to focusing on schools. One advantage is that schools are a focal point of family life and that parents are becoming increasingly involved in schools. A disadvantage is that parents leave schools as their children age. In this respect, schools are not as stable in their membership as churches. Schools also provide limited occasions when parents gather together for discussion or information exchange. The most frequent such events are school board meetings and parent association meetings, which tend to have their own political agendas. Smaller or more informal groups of parents might be a better focus of future research.

These richly contextual data are rare in political science, as Jan Leighley (1995) has noted. But if we are to advance the study of Latino politics and political participation in general, research should extend beyond the study of the vote. To be sure, there is logic to the focus on voting; a responsible citizen in the eyes of the civic culture is at the very least a voter. Still, the range and impact of other forms of political participation and their predictors are so great that they require further study.

APPENDIX

Resources

Education: measured in number of years of education, range 1–17.
Income: measured as a categorical variable in increments of $5,000.
Work skills: Scale of responses to skills completed on the job. A positive
response was recorded as a 1. Over the past month, have you had
to do any of the following as part of your job: write a letter, make
a telephone call to someone you do not know personally, take part
in a meeting where decisions are made, give a presentation or talk,
get in touch with a government official?

Situational/Life-Cycle Variables

Age: age at time of interview
Gender: 0 = male, 1 = female
Citizen: 0 = not a citizen, 1 = citizen
Bilingual: Combination of questions assessing language ability. 1 = both
languages equally, 0 = all else.
Spanish: Combination of questions assessing language ability. 1 = only
Spanish, more Spanish than English, 0 = all else.

Political Engagement

Solving neighborhood problems: 1 = yes to the question "During the last twelve months, have you worked or cooperated with others to try to solve a problem affecting your city or neighborhood?" 0 = no.

Following politics: Would you say that you follow what's going on in politics and public affairs: never (1), hardly at all (2), only now and then (3), some of the time (4), most of the time (5)?

Mobilization

Church attendance: How often do you attend religious services? 1 = almost every week or more, 0 = never, almost never, a few times a year, or once or twice a month.

Organizational participation: Scale of membership in voluntary organizations. Respondents could name up to four organizations in each category. A membership is recorded as 1. No membership is recorded as 0. Please tell me the names of any organizations you have belonged to in the past twelve months that are: (1) unions, associations, or groups associated with work, business, or professions; (2) charities, religious organizations, or other organizations that look after people such as the elderly, handicapped children, or similar groups; (3) concerned with social issues, such as reducing taxes, protecting the environment, promoting prayer in schools, or any other cause; (4) sports, recreation, community, neighborhood, school, cultural, or youth organizations, (5) Hispanic organizations. Range 0–20.

School participation: Scale of involvement in school activities. A positive response to each activity was recorded as 1. A negative response was recorded as 0. Here are some ways that people get involved in the schools. Other than when you were a student, have you: met with a teacher or teachers, attended a PTA meeting, met with the school principal, attended a meeting of the school board, voted in a school board election? Range 0–5.

NOTES

The author gratefully acknowledges the assistance of Marcelo Suárez-Orozco, Michael Jones-Correa, Jorge Dominguez, Rodolfo de la Garza, Gary Freeman, Louis DeSipio, and Yvonne Montoya. This research is supported by a grant from the Social Science Research Council and the InterUniversity Program for Latino Research and by the Texas Public Policy Clinic. The data used in this paper are available from the ICPSR. Analysis was conducted using SPSS. Documentation for replication can be obtained from the author. Comments may be directed to the author at the Department of Government, University of Texas at Austin, Austin, TX 78712 or at **lmontoya@mail.la.utexas.edu** .

1. The term Latino refers to those who have immigrated from, or trace their ancestry to, Spanish-speaking countries of Latin America and the Caribbean. The terms *Anglo* and *White* will be used interchangeably to refer to non-Hispanic whites.

2. The National Association of Latino Elected and Appointed Officials and other groups have mobilized to encourage eligible Latinos to naturalize, but the number who have not become naturalized remains high. For a thorough discussion of the literature, see Michael Jones-Correa (1998) and Louis DeSipio (1996).

3. The LNPS did not ask about skills developed in organizations, so it is not possible to assess the impact of organizational memberships versus skills developed in organizations.

4. Three variables that could disproportionately affect women are indicators of free time, the presence of children, and attitudes on women's autonomy. Preschool children, in particular, have an effect on the time a parent devotes to other activities (Verba, Schlozman, and Brady 1995, pp. 293-94). Finally, attitudes on women's autonomy might also help to predict which women are most likely to engage in political activity (Carroll 1988). A measure of political opportunity would have been helpful for both noncitizens and women. People may not participate simply because they are not asked (Leighley 1995, p. 191). It might have been profitable to include these variables in place of or in addition to those noted above, but they were unavailable in the LNPS.

5. Both studies used nearly identical wording in these questions, but there were two differences. First, the Verba instrument asked about membership or meeting attendance on any board, whereas the LNPS asked about meeting attendance only at school boards. Thus LNPS is likely to overstate Latino board participation, compared with the measure in the Verba instrument. Second, the Verba study asks about membership in political organizations, whereas the LNPS asks about organizations concerned with social issues such as reducing taxes, protecting the environment, promoting prayer in schools, or any other cause. Thus the LNPS probably overstates Latino participation, compared with the Verba instrument, because Latinos are more active in voluntary and community organizations than in any other form of civic activism.

6. See Chapter 20 in this volume for a discussion of Latinos in electoral politics.

7. Low-income = less than $20,000 per household per year. Medium-income = $20,000-40,000 per household per year. High-income = above $40,000 per household per year.

8. The LNPS asked many of these questions.

9. I am indebted to Marcelo Suárez-Orozco for this suggestion.

REFERENCES

Andersen, Kristi. 1975. "Working Women and Political Participation, 1952–1972." *American Journal of Political Science* 19:439–453.

Antunes, George, and Charles Gaitz. 1975. "Ethnicity and Participation: A Study of Mexican-Americans, Blacks, and Whites." *American Journal of Sociology* 80: 1192–1211.

Bennett, Stephen Earl, and Linda L. M. Bennett. 1989. "Enduring Gender Differences in Political Interest." *American Politics Quarterly* 17(1):105–122.

Calvo and Rosenstone. 1989. *Hispanic Political Participation.* San Antonio, TX: Southwest Voter Research Institute.

Carroll, Susan J. 1988. "Women's Autonomy and the Gender Gap: 1980 and 1982." In *The Politics of the Gender Gap: The Social Construction of Political Influence,* ed. C. M. Mueller. Newbury Park, CA: Sage.

Clark, Cal, and Janet Clark. 1986. "Models of Gender and Political Participation in the United States." *Women and Politics* 6:5–25.

Conway, Margaret M. 1985. *Political Participation in the United States.* Washington, DC: Congressional Quarterly Press.

Diaz, William. 1996. "Latino Participation in America: Associational and Political Roles." *Hispanic Journal of Behavioral Sciences* 18(2):154–174.

de la Garza, Rodolfo, Louis DeSipio, F. Chris Garcia, John Garcia, and Angelo Falcon. 1992. *Latino Voices.* Boulder, CO: Westview.

DeSipio, Louis. 1996. *Counting on the Latino Vote.* Charlottesville: University of Virginia Press.

Garcia, John A, and Carlos H. Arce. 1988. "Political Orientations and Behaviors of Chicanos: Trying to Make Sense Out of Attitudes and Participation." In *Latinos and the Political System,* ed. F. Chris Garcia. Notre Dame, IN: University of Notre Dame Press.

Hayes, Bernadette, and Clive Bean. 1993. "Gender and Local Political Interest: Some International Comparisons." *Political Studies* 41: 672–682.

Hero, Rodney, and Anne Campbell. 1996. "Understanding Latino Political Participation: Exploring the Evidence from the Latino National Political Survey." *Hispanic Journal of Behavioral Sciences* 18(2):129–141.

Jennings, M. Kent. 1983. "Gender Roles and Inequalities in Political Participation: Results from an Eight Nation Study." *Western Political Quarterly* 36:364–385.

Jones-Correa, Michael. 1998. *Between Two Nations: The Political Predicament of Latinos in New York City.* New York: Cornell University Press.

Leighley, Jan. 1995. "Attitudes, Opportunities, and Incentives: A field essay on political participation." *Political Research Quarterly* 48: 181–209.

Lien, Pei-te. 1994. "Ethnicity and Political Participation: A Comparison between Asian and Mexican Americans." *Political Behavior* 16(2):237–264.

Milbrath L. W., and Goel, M. L. 1977. *Political Participation* 2nd ed. Chicago: Rand McNally.

Nelson, Dale. 1979. "Ethnicity and Socioeconomic Status as Sources of Participation: The Case for Ethnic Political Culture." *American Political Science Review* 73(4):1024–1038.

Rosenstone, Steven, and John Mark Hansen. 1993. *Mobilization, Participation, and Democracy in America.* New York: Macmillan.

Schlozman, Kay Lehman, Nancy Burns, and Sid Verba. 1994. "Gender and the Pathways to Participation: The Role of Resources." *Journal of Politics* 56: 963–990.

Stanley, Harold W. and Richard Niemi. 1992. *Vital Statistics on American Politics.* Washington, DC: CQ Press.

Tomás Rivera Center. 1996. *The Latino Vote at Mid-Decade.* Claremont, CA: Tomás Rivera Center.

Uhlaner, Carole, Bruce Cain, and Roderick Kiewiet. 1989. "Political Participation of Ethnic Minorities in the 1980s." *Political Behavior* 11(3):195–232.

Verba, Sid, and Norman Nie. 1972. *Participation in America: Political Democracy and Social Equality.* New York: Harper & Row.

Verba, Sid, Kay Lehman Schlozman, and Henry Brady. 1995. *Voice and Equality: Civic Voluntarism in American Politics.* Cambridge, MA: Harvard University Press.

Welch, Susan, and Lee Sigelman. 1989. "A Black Gender Gap?" *Social Science Quarterly.* 70(1):120–133.

Welch, Susan, John Comer, and Michael Steinman. 1975. "Ethnic Differences in Political and Social Participation: A Comparison of Some Anglo and Mexican Americans." *Pacific Sociological Review.* 18:361–382.

———. 1992. "A Gender Gap among Hispanics? A Comparison with Blacks and Anglos." *Western Political Quarterly* 45(1):181–199.

Wolfinger, Raymond, and Steven Rosenstone. 1980. *Who Votes?* New Haven, CT: Yale University Press.

Wrinkle, Robert D., Joseph Stewart, Jr., J. L. Polinard, Kenneth J. Meier, and John R. Arvizu. 1996. "Ethnicity and Nonelectoral Political Participation." *Hispanic Journal of Behavioral Sciences.* 18(2):142–153.

Commentary

Jorge I. Domínguez

Latinos are not from the other side of the Moon. In important respects they resemble other Americans in their political preferences and behavior. The interesting and thoughtful chapters by Louis DeSipio and Rodolfo de la Garza and by Lisa Montoya call attention to various fundamental similarities. Three of these should be highlighted.

First, the issue preferences of many Latinos are very much like those of other U.S. citizens. The social and economic issues that are important to the electorate as a whole are the same issues that matter to Latinos. Second, Latinos for the most part do not care about the governments of the countries from which they came; in fact, some Latinos profess intense dislike of and opposition to the governments of the lands of their birth. Latinos are much more concerned about issues within the United States than they are about issues in their ancestral homelands. Latinos are not agents of foreign powers, nor are they likely to become so. Third, the factors that explain the political attitudes and behavior of Latinos, as Montoya in particular makes clear, are the same as those that explain the political attitudes and behavior of other U.S. citizens. These include the impact of socioeconomic status, the quality and diffusion of work skills, the extent and intensity of organizational membership, and so forth.

Even so, Latinos are distinctive along several important dimensions. First and most obviously, Latinos tend to be poorer and less well educated than other U.S. citizens. Most Latinos in the mainland United States (other than Cuban Americans) show lower levels of political participation than is typical in the United States. Second, Latinos are highly partisan and show remarkable stability in their patterns of partisanship. In this respect, they also differ from the median non-Latino U.S. citizen. Most Latinos are strong and consistent Democrats. Even upper-income and highly educated

Latinos are more likely to be Democrats than are non-Latino U.S. citizens with comparable levels of income and education. Cuban Americans are the only Latinos who are much more likely to be Republicans, and they too are strong and consistent partisans.

Latinos' issue preferences cluster in distinct ways as well, although this evidence comes mainly from public-opinion polling in the state of California. By very lopsided margins, as DeSipio and de la Garza note, California Latinos support universal health care, gun control, and school vouchers and oppose legal abortion. This clustering is unusual in the politics of the United States at large, where those who favor universal health care and gun control by such overwhelming margins are often political liberals who are more likely to oppose school vouchers and to favor legal abortion. This Latino attitudinal cluster and the Latino patterns of high and stable partisanship have a much stronger echo in Europe than in the United States. In some ways, U.S. Latinos resemble European Christian Democrats.

Like European Christian Democrats, U.S. Latinos believe that the power of the national state can be harnessed to accomplish laudable and useful goals. Cuban Americans, share this preference for a strong and activist state. Most Cuban Americans are virulently anticommunist, which associates them politically with the antistatist Republican right. Yet the key point is that Cuban Americans support a muscular state to defeat Fidel Castro, open the United States to more Cuban migrants pending that outcome, and fund generous Social Security benefits for a rapidly aging community.

Much is known about the attitudes and behavior of U.S. Latinos, and much remains to be learned. For example, DeSipio and de la Garza argue that election campaigns matter. They explain whether Latinos do or do not support certain candidates at various times as a function of effective or ineffective campaign practices from some candidates. Yet there is a body of literature on elections in the United States and Western Europe that argues that campaigns matter little. According to this view, campaigns are poor vehicles for getting voters to change their minds. Instead, campaigns serve principally to reinforce views—to remind Cuban Americans, for example, that they should love George W. Bush. Thus an alternative explanation for the lack of Latino support for the Bob Dole presidential election bid in 1996 is that it had rather little to do with Dole or Clinton campaign tactics. Instead, Latinos might have flocked to Democratic party candidates in 1996 in response to the "issue earthquake" triggered by California Republican Governor Pete Wilson's anti-immigrant campaign, which was emulated at the national level by the Republican majorities in Congress after the large Republican victory in the 1994 congressional elections. That is, the Republican governor of the state that hosts the largest number of U.S. Latinos and the Republican Congress manufactured the political salience of a relatively dormant issue; in response to this new salience, Latinos (other than Cuban Americans) stampeded to become naturalized U.S. citizens and to vote Democratic.

How homogeneous is the U.S. population of Latin American origin? Montoya persuasively emphasizes differences in political behavior between Latinos and Latinas, but her data suggest that even Latinas differ greatly among themselves. In particular, Mexican American women are unlike other Latinas in important respects. Income and reliance on the use of the Spanish language shape the political participation of Mexican American women; these factors are much less significant for Puerto Rican and Cuban American women. The extent and quality of work skills provide one of the more powerful explanations for the behavior of Puerto Rican and Cuban American women, but they explain little about the behavior of Mexican American women. School participation is the only statistically significant explanatory variable that affects the political behavior of all Latina subgroups and that also distinguishes Latinas from most Latinos (though not from Mexican American males).

Consequently, one fruitful avenue for further research on the political behavior of Latinos would be to understand the differences among them. Scholars should seek to explain a puzzle about Puerto Rican political participation: Puerto Ricans display a very low level of political participation in the mainland United States, yet on the island of Puerto Rico they demonstrate the highest level of political participation under the U.S. flag. Puerto Rican rates of electoral turnout resemble those of high-voting Europeans, not those of U.S. citizens. One possible explanation for this discrepancy is that political parties in Puerto Rico are well organized to get out the vote in every nook and cranny of the island, whereas neither major political party in the United States mobilizes Puerto Ricans to the same extent.

Another interesting avenue of research might be to examine the dense organizational network of immigrants from the Dominican Republic. In Washington Heights, New York, and in Jamaica Plain, Boston (among other sites), Dominicans exhibit a disciplined partisanship linked to the political parties of their homeland but also, increasingly, to the U.S. Democratic party. Dominicans have also nurtured small businesses that cater to their community in language, intonation, and buying habits. A less salutary aspect of this flowering of organization is the rapid development of criminal gangs within Dominican communities. All of these—individuals, families, community groups, political parties, small businesses, and gangs—engage in complex transnational relations, sending remittances home and helping to shape and reshape behavior in the Dominican Republic and the United States.

The U.S. Latino population is changing in many important ways. It is growing very rapidly, as various chapters in this book attest. But it is also deeply differentiated. Rapid naturalization rates marked the Mexican

American community in the 1990s, but naturalization is not an issue for Puerto Ricans, all of whom are U.S. citizens. Many Latinos are transforming the demographic composition of public schools in the United States, but for Cuban-Americans, the aging of their community is a comparably central concern. The impact of Latinos on the politics of California differs greatly from their impact on the politics of Texas. In Texas, the ratio of Latino citizens to Latino noncitizens is 3:1; in California, it is only 1:1.

Latinos illustrate the importance of considering the nature of Americanness. Social scientists and ordinary citizens must think more about how this rapidly growing subgroup of the population of the United States engages with the rest of the nation. What Latinos care about, think, and feel is too important to leave for the consideration of Latinos alone.

NOTE

I am grateful to Magda Hinojosa for her excellent note-taking of my oral remarks at the conference where these notions were first presented.

Epilogue

Problematic Paradigms

Racial Diversity and Corporate
Identity in the Latino Community

Silvio Torres-Saillant

BORDERS THAT EXIST

The presumption of a seamless, unproblematic Latino identity militates against the unity that U.S. Hispanic communities could and should forge in order to increase their levels of empowerment in American society. The potential for building coalitions, fashioning collaborative agendas, and joining forces in causes of common interest can become a reality only through serious reflection, inclusive dialogue, and tactful planning. Simply to assume Latino unity is to forgo the hard work, long time, and deep thought that bringing it about will take. A good number of scholars and intellectuals have already warned against the danger of uncritically embracing homogenizing discourses in defining the Hispanic subsection of the American population (Klor de Alva, West, and Shorris 1988; Oboler 1995; Flores and Yudice 1993; Davis 2000). Juan Flores and George Yudice have described Hispanics in the United States as a "very heterogeneous medley of races and nationalities," composing not "even a relatively homogeneous 'ethnicity'" (p. 199). These authors and many others have abundantly shown that promoting totalizing representations of the Latino community overlooks the differentiated cultural contributions and the particular social legacy that each individual subgroup has brought to the large canvas of American society. The disadvantages have thus far been articulated in terms of the levels of material or symbolic power that a homogenizing representation can cause Hispanics to lose or fail to acquire vis-à-vis American society's non-Latino political and economic mainstream. But no one, to my knowledge, has alerted us to what is perhaps an even graver danger: the debilitating impact that such representations can have on the ability of individual subgroups to fend off intra-Latino injustices.

Given the varied circumstances under which the various subgroups entered the United States, as well as the differing "ages" of their relationships with this country, at least these subgroups' economic and political leaderships differ in visibility, access to resources, and levels of empowerment. Differing levels of empowerment imply, of course, unequal degrees of vulnerability. Divides may exist even within Latinos of the same national origin if obstacles such as race and class intervene. Narrating his experiences in Tampa, Florida, in the 1930s, the U.S.-born black Cuban Evelio Grillo recalls that "black Cubans and white Cubans lived apart from one another in Ybor City" (Grillo 2000, p. 9). Not only does Grillo not remember ever "playing with a single white Cuban child" when he was a kid, but he, unlike his white Cuban compatriots, also had doors of opportunity slammed on him by Jim Crow America because of his color. "I don't know of any black Cuban college graduate of my generation, and of all the generations preceding desegregation, who is not a graduate of a historically black college," says Grillo, who recalls that even in matters of carnal love, the racial difference between black Cubans and white Cubans outweighed their shared national origin. Thus for black Cubans, dating almost exclusively involved "eligible black American counterparts" (pp. 9–12). A Cuban American scholar who has studied this period notes the irony inherent in the fact that Círculo Cubano and Unión Martí-Maceo, the mutual aid societies that serve Tampa's white and black Cubans, respectively, both engaged in centennial celebrations in 1999–2000 as both approached the hundredth anniversaries of the "respective clubs (and their memberships' [racial] separation) in significantly different ways" (Dworkin y Mendez 2000, p. xii). That is, they reflect even today their unequal condition, an enduring legacy of the fact that one group had to bear the brunt of Jim Crow policies while the other did not. Clearly, these examples of inter- and intra-group divisions among the multiple segments that make up the Latino community argue that we should apply a measure of caution when formulating claims about panethnic Latino identity.

With this background in mind, I would like to suggest that current assertions of a harmonious panethnic Latino identity have the potential to perpetuate intra-Latino exclusions and injustices, thus preventing the emergence of a genuine sense of community among the various Hispanic groups that form part of the U.S. population. A corollary to this critique will be an argument against locating Latino identity in the obtuse vastness of panhemispheric or intercontinental cultural spheres. I argue that borders exist, the global economy notwithstanding and despite the transnational dynamics that self-proclaimed postmoderns point to as indicative of the demise of the nation-state. I insist on the need to separate Latin American from Latino identity, especially given the legacy of racial inequality in countries south of the Rio Grande. In so doing, I reject the seductive

fusion of the Latin South and the Latino North encouraged by the Hispanic subsection of corporate America.

IMPERIAL CONTIGUITY AND LATINO UNITY

Like any other minority, Latinos lack the freedom to choose the way the
larger society configures their ethnic affiliation. Richard Delgado is not far
off the mark when he says that "membership in a racial minority can be
considered neither self-induced, like alcoholism or prostitution, nor alter-
able" (1995, p. 159). We do not need to repeat the work of documenting
the process whereby people with disparate Latin American origins gradually
fell under the single homogenizing label of Hispanic or Latino, which
Suzanne Oboler has done remarkably well in her *Ethnic Labels, Latino Lives*
(1995). But preceding the history of the nomenclature that Oboler maps
in her study, there is an earlier imperial history that describes the expansionist imperative of the United States. The logic of self-defense sounded
by President James Monroe in his 1823 speech evolved in time into a
self-assured affirmation of America's right to expand by virtue of what eventually became known as manifest destiny. With the 1846 U.S. invasion of
Mexico under President James Polk, an action that would lead to the acquisition of Arizona, California, Colorado, New Mexico, and Utah two years
later, American might proved its dexterity at gliding over coterminous
nation-states. But the U.S. defeat in 1898 of the older Spanish empire,
which entailed the domination of several overseas territories, showed that
irresistible power could make up for the inconvenience of great distances.
In this sense, in a speech delivered on September 16, 1898, Indiana Senator Albert J. Beveridge resignified the idea of contiguity. He said, "The
ocean does not separate us from lands of our duty and desire—the oceans
join us, a river never to be dredged, a canal never to be repaired. Steam
joins us; electricity joins us—the very elements are in league with our destiny. Cuba not contiguous! Puerto Rico not contiguous! Hawaii and the
Philippines not contiguous! Our navy will make them contiguous. . . .
American speed, American guns, American heart and brain and nerve will
keep them contiguous forever" (Beveridge 1971, p. 333).

The contiguity created by American imperial expansion, whether over
coterminous territories or across transoceanic land masses, created the
historical grounds for the presence of Hispanic communities in the United
States. The awareness that one is in the United States today as a result of
the defeat suffered by one's forebears, or the understanding that one's
original homeland has existed for over a century in a position of sub-
servience vis-à-vis American power in the hemisphere, does seem to create
a sense of commonality. Latinos in the United States are a composite of
diverse historical realities, national experiences, and collective existential

traumas.[1] Before entering American society from the native land, which for each distinct group corresponded to different sociohistorical and geopolitical events, one did not see oneself as Latino or Hispanic but as Puerto Rican, Cuban, Colombian, or Dominican, to name only a few of the Latino groups that are most visible in my current base of operation, New York. As members of a diaspora, however, we have become unified in significant ways. We share the experience of having been uprooted by large socioeconomic forces from our original homelands. We come from societies with a history of unequal association with the United States, a country that has influenced and sometimes even dictated political behavior in Latin America. The image of "backyard," often invoked by U.S. policy makers to identify Latin America's geographic proximity to the United States, entails a qualitative view that construes the region not as partner but as subordinate.

By the third decade of the twentieth century, a good many Latin American nations already had experienced, through the incursion of U.S. armed forces into their territory, the concrete inequality of their relationship with their North American neighbor. They had also become acquainted with the views that often informed these military invasions. For instance, Senator Beveridge, speaking before the U.S. Senate in 1901, had declared, "God has made us the master organizers of the world to establish systems where chaos reigns.... He has made us adept in government that we may administer government among savages and senile people" (Welles 1966, p. 916). Similarly, President Theodore Roosevelt is known to have publicly decried the Cubans', Dominicans', Haitians', and Nicaraguans' conduct of their political lives. The famous "corollary to the Monroe Doctrine" in Roosevelt's annual message to Congress in 1904 hints at the U.S. sense of moral and political superiority to the peoples of Latin America: "Chronic wrongdoing or an impotence which results in a general loosening of the ties of civilized society, may in America, as elsewhere, ultimately require intervention by some civilized nation, and in the Western Hemisphere the adherence of the United States to the Monroe Doctrine may force the United States, however reluctantly, in flagrant cases of such wrongdoing or impotence, to the exercise of an international police power" (cited in Black 1988, p. 23).

The preceding background largely explains the political, economic, and cultural "otherness" to which U.S. Hispanics typically find themselves relegated with respect to the dominant social structure. The awareness of this otherness leads us to assert our commonality with those who share our history of defeat, particularly when we can claim linguistic, religious, and regional links among our various national groups. The experience of diasporic uprooting and the sense of living outside the dominant realm of the receiving society permeate our Latino identity. For even though Mexicans, Puerto Ricans, and Dominicans became ethnic communities in the United

States through profoundly different processes, we are bound by political imperatives to see ourselves as one. Ironically, Simón Bolívar's desideratum of a unified Latin American nation and the ideal upheld by Eugenio María de Hostos of an Antillean federation find in us a strange kind of fulfillment. We have come to articulate a collective identity not in our native homelands, as Bolívar and Hostos had dreamed, but within the insecure space of the diaspora. The feeling that ours is a contested terrain—that we do not inherit our social space but must carve it out for ourselves in the face of adversity—leads us to lift the banner of our oneness despite differences in the circumstances under which each of our distinct groups became part of the United States. The language of unity in this case functions as an instrument of survival.

LEVELS OF LATINO MARGINALITY

The foregoing emphasis on the historical, contingent nature of the presumed Latino unity seeks to suggest that the need for unitary political practices does not translate automatically or unproblematically into ontological sameness. The distinct subgroups that make up the U.S. population that is labeled Hispanic are neither identical nor equal. Let us, for argument's sake, concentrate on the dynamic of epistemological inequality among the various subgroups. Dominicans provide an illustrative case. A disdain for Dominican knowledge is evident in several of the overviews, surveys, and compilations that purport to cover holistically the history, culture, and contributions of Latinos in American society. Because such panoramic vistas are normally penned or coordinated by authors who belong to the Latino subgroups that enjoy greater socioeconomic and political empowerment, it makes sense that they should either omit any mention of the Dominican portion of the Latino experience or dispatch it briefly and superficially. The same logic applies here as with the rapport between dominant and dependent nation-states. Studying the experiences of the larger and better-positioned portions of the Latino population—the "meaningful" parts that can stand for the whole—seems to lessen the need for complex and in-depth coverage of the smaller and weaker portions.

Witness the coverage that Antonia Darder and Rodolfo D. Torres pursue in their collection *The Latino Reader: Culture, Economy, and Society* (1998). The book includes no chapter on, and no extended consideration of, the Dominican experience. The editors proceed as though they deemed knowledge about the life of that subgroup irrelevant to understanding the Latino community. The exclusion of Dominicans, as authors and as subject matter, from the 94-chapter anthology *The Latino/a Condition: A Critical Reader* (1998) edited by the scholars Richard Delgado and Jean Stefancic seems to say no less. From the perspective of the major Latino subgroups, then, the experience of the lesser groups does not promise to yield knowledge capable of transcending the limits of such a community. We see here a case of what could be called intracolonial epistemological inequality that leaves Dominicans out of the master narrative of the Latino experience. In addition to omitting Dominicans, the dynamic also manifests itself as a casual treatment of the lesser group. When *Washington Post* journalist Roberto Suro writes a book on Latinos his Dominican chapter is devoted to rebuking the community's leaders for not attacking with sufficient energy the drug problem in their midst and for not being proactive in circumventing the limits of the enclave economy (Suro 1998, pp. 197, 202–203). Exhibiting a similar sense of superiority, Univision anchorman Jorge Ramos assigns himself the poetic license to coin his own genteelisms to name Dominicans: "Portodominicans" (portodominicanos) for those living in Puerto Rico and "Neodominicans" (neodominicanos) for those living in New York (Ramos 2000, pp. 179–185). I cannot help but conjecture that if this Mexican brother had been writing about a group with a greater degree of power vis-à-vis the other Latino subgroups, he would have consulted appropriate sources to find out what the members of the community actually call themselves, instead of inflicting on them his own flair for neologistic acrobatics.

By the same token, *New York Daily News* journalist Juan González, the author of the book *Harvest of Empire: A History of Latinos in the United States* (2000), does not invest in Dominicans anywhere near the intellectual labor apparent in his coverage of Chicanos and Puerto Ricans. For Chicanos and Puerto Ricans, González draws amply from the existing scholarship on the lives of those communities in the United States. As a result, he writes competently on them. But in the case of Dominicans, he seems to have felt no compulsion to consult the bibliography that U.S. Dominicans have generated, most of which has been annotated by Sarah Aponte (1999). Apparently confident that he could discern the intricacies of the Dominican experience without the aid of the work done by Dominican American scholars, and disdaining the archival resources of the City University of New York's Dominican Studies Institute, González proceeds to explain the community *ex-nihilo,* basing his account largely on scanty reading and several interviews with Dominican New Yorkers. Not surprisingly, his Dominican chapter is fraught with intellectual poverty. A Dominican reader would indeed find it very hard to concur with Juan Flores's assessment of *Harvest of Empire* as "no doubt the most wide-ranging, engaging, and critically reflective book about Latinos to date" (Flores 2000, p. 43). A piece of irony here: *Magic Urbanism* (2000), an overview of Latinos written by the distinguished Anglo author Mike Davis, stands out as the only one among such efforts that shows an interest in accessing the knowledge produced by Dominican scholars and integrating it into the larger panethnic conversation. Perhaps Anglo colleagues, unencumbered by membership in any of the individual subgroups, have at present a better chance than Hispanics to look panoptically at Latinos, ensuring that no subgroup is left out of the picture.

WHITE-SUPREMACIST HYBRIDITY

The reiterative musings about borderlessness, hybridity, and transnational dynamics that pervade recent scholarly production on the Latino experience have only ostensibly celebrated diversity. The exclusionary ideological structures that lie at the core of corporate identity formulations in the community remain virtually unchallenged. The academia, the media, and the consumer market for the most part have rallied around the consensus that promotes the notion that U.S. Hispanics constitute a seamless unit. Few have stopped to consider the resonance of that view with the elitist, Eurocentric, and white-supremacist ideas on *hispanidad* that cohered in the minds of the Latin American intelligentsia of the generation that witnessed and mourned the change of imperial guard that took place in 1898 in the Western Hemisphere. Although they paid lip service to the virtues of *mestizaje*, the celebrants of *hispanidad* (or *latinidad*) in practice supported negrophobic and anti-Indian regimes. José Martí may have denied the existence of "races" in an often-cited 1894 essay, arguing for the essential, unquestionable humanity of all peoples, but to think of his view as common to many Latin American intellectuals at the time would be erroneous.

This warning matters especially, given the present context in which, spurred by the recognition of a certain geopolitical and economic interdependence between the United States and Latin America, many Latino scholars find it natural to proclaim their intellectual kinship to a history of ideas rooted in the Iberian side of the hemisphere. The distinguished scholar Frank Bonilla, who has himself invested enormous energy in creating bridges of intellectual communication between Latin Americans in the South and Latinos in the North, has borne witness to serious obstacles that have emerged at given moments, sometimes even connected to our varying ways of understanding key concepts such as ethnicity, culture, and racism (Bonilla 1998, p. 224). Many colleagues accept too quickly the view that the Spanish-speaking world has a less racialized and more humane understanding of difference among human beings. A 1996 conversation on the topic of race relations between Latino scholar Jorge Klor de Alva and African American essayist Cornel West, moderated by Earl Shorris, left little doubt that Klor de Alva felt that his privileging linguistic background and culture to define U.S. Hispanics constituted a more accurate rendition of social identity than his African American colleague's focus on blackness to speak of his community (*Harper's* 1996, p. 55). Latino colleagues at times can hardly conceal their pride at the thought that their culture is less racist than that of the Anglos. As Nicolás Kanellos would put it, "[Although] 'race' distinctions and prejudice exist in Spanish America, they do not take, nor ever have they taken, the form of institutionalized discrimination as in the United States; they are more subtly expressed (some glaring exceptions are to be found in the history of Cuba and Puerto Rico under U.S. domination)" (Kanellos 1998, p. 178).

I would be less sanguine about exonerating Latin America of official, institutionalized racial misconduct, especially in light of the many countries in the region that at various points in history specified a preference for whites in their immigration legislation. Jorge Cañízares Esguerra has even advanced the idea that modern racism originated in Latin America. He contends "that the science of race, with its emphasis on behavioral-cultural variations, and its obsession with creating homogenizing and essentializing categories, was first articulated in colonial Spanish America in the seventeenth century, not in nineteenth-century Europe" (Cañízares Esguerra 1999, p. 35). At any rate, without clear, tangible institutional barriers exacerbating the subjugation of particular racial communities, one would be hard put to explain most of the violent racial clashes that Latin America has witnessed (the 1912 uprising of blacks and their subsequent mass killing in Cuba stand out as a particularly glaring example).

The following incident comes to mind. In the evening of Thursday, February 25, 2000, a Haitian-descended Dominican woman named Sonia Pierre suffered abuse upon entering the United States through JFK Airport in New York City. She had traveled to the North in her capacity as head of the Santo Domingo–based Dominican-Haitian Women's Movement (MUDHA). A guest at a national conference organized by the group Dominicans 2000 at City College, which featured First Lady Hilary Rodham Clinton among the keynote speakers, Pierre had come prepared to enlighten the audience regarding the plight of Dominican-born children of Haitian parents whom Dominican government authorities have thus far denied the right of citizenship on the basis of their ethnicity. She came loaded with data to show the extent to which the intellectual heirs of the Trujillo dictatorship would go in publicly declaring Haitian ancestry to be antithetical to and incompatible with the very concept of Dominicanness. She could not possibly have imagined that the affronts she suffered daily as a member of a despised community in the Dominican Republic would follow her all the way to JFK. After all, what do "Americans" know about ethnic tensions in the Caribbean island of Hispaniola? However, Pierre had the misfortune to be received at the immigration checkpoint not by an Anglo but by a Latina INS agent, a Dominican-descended U.S. citizen with the name Goico on her tag. When Pierre presented her passport and other qualifying papers, Ms. Goico challenged their authenticity and accused her of forgery. She felt confident that from a look at Sonia's "Haitian appearance" (that is, her coarse hair untamed by relaxers and her negroid facial features), she could tell that the passenger was a Haitian trying to pass for Dominican. The last name Pierre did not help, of course. The letter of invitation from the conference organizers did not suffice. An overwhelming amount of documentation, a close examination of the papers suspected to have been forged, and lengthy interviews with several INS officers ensued before Pierre, after nearly two hours of excruciating detention, was allowed to proceed without receiving an apology from Ms. Goico.

Ms. Goico's anti-Haitian antipathy corresponds to a prediasporic experience in Dominican society, dating back to an earlier milieu that encouraged hatred for the neighbors on the other side of the island of Hispaniola. Dominican anti-Haitianism gradually fades in the diaspora, especially among people with some community involvement. Community activism brings Haitians and Dominicans together as they, free from the supervision of the State that fueled their ethnic antipathy, learn to recognize each other as allies in a common struggle for survival as minorities of color. The affirmation of her difference as a person of color who recognized herself as an "other" with respect to the Anglo norm would have fostered in Ms. Goico a sense of kinship with other Caribbean people, Haitians included, as well as with African Americans and other nonwhite ethnic groups. Apparently having been deprived of such an enlightened background, Ms. Goico clung to the negrophobia and the anti-Haitian sentiments that formed part of her "education" on matters related to nation, cultural identity, and Dominicanness in the home country during the Trujillo and Balaguer regimes. Importing her original homeland's racial hang-ups, she forgot herself. Entrusted, as an INS officer, with the task of guarding the U.S. statutory border against illegal entrants, she instead spent nearly two hours trying to bar a Haitian ethnic from entering the space of Dominicanness. She thus trampled the civil rights of a human being and momentarily deprived her victim of the protection that U.S. law guarantees.

I believe this incident illustrates the extent to which blurring the boundaries between the Latin American South and the Latino North can complicate the process of cultural and political self-definition of U.S. Hispanics. Should that blurring take place, the Latino community would abdicate its position as a vanguard committed to the further democratization of the United States. For we can play that role creditably only when we free ourselves from the influence of those aspects of our Latin American background that militate against equality and justice.

I do not see Ms. Goico as a unique or isolated case. Her ethnic antipathy matches that of a good many individuals in the Latin American population. Nor is she alone in importing to the Latino North a hatred that belongs in a specific part of the Latin American South. I see a parallel in the racial misconduct of the business executives who control the TV programs that Spanish-speaking Hispanics watch. Just as Ms. Goico has not rid herself of a deleterious racial ideology she inherited from her home country, so do the corporate leaders behind Univisión and Telemundo resist allowing black and Indian faces to appear before the cameras even in these postdesegregation United States. One could surmise that in an applicant's effort to land a job as a newscaster on a Spanish-speaking TV station or network, Scandinavian ancestry would be very helpful. Conversely, displaying the Indian features of nineteenth-century Mexican president Benito Juárez or the black features of Cuban independence leader Antonio Maceo would seriously reduce the applicant's chances. Anyone who watches Hispanic TV in the United States will easily recognize the white-supremacist value system that governs the way mass-media corporations promote the collective visage of the Latino community. It is through the white faces of our anchorpersons that Hispanic TV networks have chosen visually to represent the homogeneity that our corporate identity is supposed to embody.

I argue against embracing uncritically the notion that U.S. Hispanics are unified by the all-powerful bond of a shared linguistic heritage and a common culture, precisely because such a view impairs our ability to combat the anti-Indian and negrophobic traditions we inherit from Latin America. The claim that Latinos constitute one big happy family conceals the tensions, inequities, and injustices in our midst, contributing to a conceptual ambience that legitimizes the absence of black and Indian faces and voices from Latino fora. The operating logic seems to be that, because everyone in our polychromatic community is really the same, everyone is inherently represented even when only one color continues to peer out at us from the tube. Public visibility translates into intellectual representation. In a related observation, individuals with pronounced indigenous features seldom appear in Latino academic forums, speaking as producers of knowledge and as the intellectual equals of their colleagues. To enjoy such a privilege, an Indian would normally have to achieve a distinction comparable to that of Nobel Prize winner Rigoberta Menchú. Characteristically, the Mexican American essayist Richard Rodriguez, the one Latino thinker with perceptible Indian features who enjoys intellectual prominence, has attained his celebrity through Anglophone mainstream media venues such as PBS, not through the Hispanic venues of Univisión or Telemundo. He begins one of his essays by evoking a time when he "used to stare at the Indian in the mirror. The wide nostrils. The thick lips. . . . Such a long face—such a long nose—sculpted by indifferent, blunt thumbs, and of such common clay. No one in my family had a face as dark or as Indian as mine" (Rodriguez 1991, p. 535).

The Univisión TV station Channel 41, which serves New York, New Jersey, and Connecticut, has lately been airing a well-orchestrated publicity campaign that sings the praises of our common *hispanidad*. The campaign features many popular entertainers from the music industry. Their song insistently dwells on the language, the culture, and the traditions that make us *una sola familia*. Although I am intellectually skeptical about the views propounded by the whole campaign, I have reacted most viscerally to the one spot that in my view most abusively mocks historical truth, scoffing at the suffering of the conquered. The spot I have in mind features an Andean band made up of *indios* who enthusiastically sing the praises of *hispanidad* and our shared Spanish heritage. The spot displays utter disregard for the grief of the indigenous populations of South America and the rest of the hemisphere who fell under the genocidal hand of the old Spanish empire that invaded their land. Such historical amnesia also has the effect of completely exculpating the Latin American ruling elites responsible for perpetrating great evils against Indians since independence from Spain. At least from the time of Argentinean statesman Domingo Sarmiento onward, anti-Indian scorn has too often entered the official discourse of Latin American nations and influenced public policy, with dire consequences for the indigenous populations. The moving story told by the film *El Norte*, which dramatizes the plight of aboriginal peasants who have to flee their native Guatemalan home in order to save themselves, testifies to the resilience of anti-Indian violence in contemporary Latin America.

For Univisión to have Indians appear on TV praising the glory of our presumably common Spanish heritage is to mock the victims of a continuous five-century genocide in Latin America. By the same token, when the aforementioned publicity campaign has Afro-Cuban star Celia Cruz adding her voice to the praise of the common culture, traditions, and Spanish language that make all Hispanics *una sola familia*, one wonders whether she is aware of the negrophobic and anti-Indian project she is legitimizing. As *Washington Post* journalist Michael A. Fletcher has recently noted, Afro Latinos or indigenous people are rarely cast in Spanish-language television shows in the United States, and the few that are "most often play demeaning roles." In the widely popular "telenovelas," the soap operas, "darker skinned people most often play maids, gardeners, chauffeurs or dabblers in witchcraft" (Fletcher 2000). Because of her blackness, the popular New York–based radio personality Malín Falú, producer of a long-running talk show on WADO, has confronted insurmountable barriers in her attempts to land jobs in Spanish-language television in the United States. The Tomás Rivera Policy Institute surveyed 4,000 Latino members of the Screen Actors Guild to learn that the majority of the respondents thought dark skin was a liability for any Latino actor who hoped to get opportunities in Spanish-language television productions (Fletcher 2000).

I had occasion to raise the issue of race with the former president and CEO of Univisión, Henry G. Cisneros, when he, in the role of keynote speaker, addressed the participants in a major Latino studies conference held at Harvard University in April 2000. At the end of his speech, I courteously asked him whether, from his influential position in the network, he "envisioned a time in the near future when one would not have to be *güero* to serve as an anchorperson in Univisión." After much circumlocution, Cisneros did not really commit himself to an answer, but he did reassure his audience that network managers had been looking seriously into the issue of representation. He urged us to look for evidence of their concern in the composition of the live audience that appears in the very successful *Show de Cristina*, which is hosted by the Cuban Cristina Saralegui, the author of a memoir significantly entitled *Cristina! Confidencias de una rubia* (1998) [*Confessions of a Blond*]. Cisneros also said that the cast in the early-morning variety show "Despierta América" reflects a concern with representing diversity, a clear allusion to Rafael José, a Puerto Rican mulatto featured among the hosts at the time. Clearly I had posed a difficult question, and the answer Cisneros gave was no more satifsfactory than that of Telemundo spokesperson Ted Guefen, who, fumbling for evidence to show his network's concern for racial inclusiveness, cited the case of the successful show "Xica," a soap opera based on the life of a nineteenth-century Afro-Brazilian slave who used her sexual prowess to earn her freedom and climb socially. The Brazilian-made program, noted for risqué love scenes, features the hypersexualized young actress Tais Araujo, reportedly the first black actress ever to land a leading role in a Latin American soap opera.

Cisneros trod on firmer rhetorical ground in answering the second part of my question, wherein I inquired whether Univisión was planning to change the objectionable scenario depicted by the telenovelas, which invariably present blacks and Indians as housemaids or servants. He immediately absolved his network of any responsibility for those portrayals by quickly responding, "We have no control over what goes into the telenovelas because they are made in Mexico." A natural follow-up question would have demanded further satisfaction; as the telenovela producers' client, the network ought to have the power to influence the merchandise it purchases. But the follow-up became unnecessary as Cisneros proceeded to expound on the importance of the telenovelas as the network's number-one revenue-producing venture. Thanks to the telenovelas, Univisión has often gotten a greater share of the national market than the major English-language television networks. "Without them," the former HUD Secretary said, "we would be out of business," emphasizing that Univisión has to see itself first and foremost as a profit-making enterprise. Cisneros unambiguously pointed out that because the telenovelas bring in such great profits the way they are currently made, the network could not take any chances by altering the nature or the texture of the shows. His answer also reflected the conviction that Mexican society is less preoccupied with racial sensitivity than the United States.

LATINO CORPORATE IDENTITY AND THE CORPORATIONS

Whether Latino scholars and artists know it or not, their remaining loyal to a holistic view of Latino identity perfectly serves the economic interests of the Latino portion of corporate America. When over 30 million people can see themselves as a unit, sharing values, language, culture, and aspirations, capital can accumulate more rapidly. Businesses can target their publicity campaigns and marketing strategies with greater precision. The 17.3 million Spanish-speaking Hispanics willing and able to watch television, listen to the radio, and read newspapers, are a gold mine that business is eager to tap into. Spanish speakers in the U.S. population outnumber speakers of the most numerous among the other "foreign" language speakers ten times over. Hispanic buying power by 1999 had reached $348 billion a year, up 65 percent since 1990, according to the Selig Center for Economic Growth of the University of Georgia (Sleeper 1999, p. 10). One can therefore understand the insistence with which Univisión and Telemundo promote the idea of U.S. Hispanics as an ethnically and culturally homogeneous people. The premise clearly informs Univisión's extremely successful variety program *Sábado Gigante*, hosted by the Chilean TV announcer Mario Kreuzberger, who is popularly known as Don Francisco. The same applies to the talk show *Cristina*, hosted by Saralegui. Vigorously embracing the view that U.S. Hispanics have a common heritage that makes them one people, these shows also exhibit the all-encompassing hemispheric notion that Hispanics North and South share one worldview. The most successful of the shows air in almost every city of Latin America as well as in the United States, and some, such as *Sábado Gigante*, are produced alternately in Latin America and the United States (Fox 1997, pp. 47–49).

Media executives have a huge stake in ensuring that U.S. Hispanics see themselves as one, for these executives can use their power over the community's perceptions and opinions as a bargaining tool in their competition with their corporate counterparts. Raul Alarcón, president of the Spanish Broadcasting System, and Jesus Chavarria, publisher of *Hispanic Business*, have complained about major advertisers who in their view distribute advertising dollars unfairly to the advantage of Anglo companies. They cite such examples as the "Miami Univisión TV station Channel 23, which is ranked number one in terms of ratings but receives considerably less advertising revenue than other TV stations in its market" (Dougherty 1999, p. 26). In response to that perceived unfairness, Hispanic media executives have joined their African American counterparts, with the support of political leaders and legislators, in creating the Madison Avenue Initiative to advance the interests of minority-owned media companies. They can wield no greater weapon, however, than the assurance that they have a unified Hispanic community backing them. The corporate leadership gains a competitive edge when Latinos subscribe to a corporate identity. Counting on a homogeneous community supportive of their business interests, the Hispanic media executives can then exert greater pressure as they step up their demand for a larger piece of the economic pie. They can invoke "the community" to advance their ends. They have even gone as far as threatening to "engage in boycotts," as was made clear by a New York Latino legislator who, siding with the Hispanic media executives, asserted that advertisers that "continue to ignore" our community "can suffer economic casualties" (Dougherty 1999, p. 28). Nor do these Hispanic media executives have any doubt about their own ability to forge a sense of pan-Latino identity, because, in the words of the publisher of *The Miami Herald* and *El Nuevo Herald,* Alberto Ibarguen, "technology and economic forces" have the power to define "community identity" (Sleeper 1999, p. 3). Also, in as much as, for them, North and South have fused into one market, it is in their best interest to promote panhemispheric visions of Latino identity. As Ibarguen has said, "Miami is the central communication point for all of the Caribbean and much of South America. . . . Television, ad agencies, banks, music recording companies all have their Latin American headquarters here" (Sleeper 1999, p. 3).

RESTORING BORDERS TEMPORARILY

I hope the foregoing makes clear that both the homogenizing views of Latino identity and the panhemispheric compulsion to erase the dividing line between the Latin South American and the Latino North coincide with the figurations promoted by powerful economic interests in the mass media and other market forces, as well as with political structures. Latin American governments and corporate leaders have become cognizant of the growing economic value of keeping their diasporas loyal to their lands of origin in order to preserve the constant flow of remittances. They may also hope to prevail on diasporic communities to advocate in favor of the interests of the ancestral country in the context of U.S. foreign policy. Those governments and corporate sectors will certainly encourage consolidation of panhemispheric Latino/Hispanic identity. These governments, along with corporations on both sides of the Rio Grande, are likely to relish an idea of Hispanic/Latino identity akin to that recently proposed by Cuban-born philosophy scholar Jorge J. E. Gracia, which is not only panhemispheric, spanning both North and South, but also transatlantic, covering practically the entire globe. Gracia describes Hispanics as "the people of Iberia, Latin America, and some segments of the population in the United States, after 1492, and the descendants of these peoples anywhere in the world as long as they preserve close ties to them" (Gracia 2000, p. 52). I believe that this formulation confounds rather than clarifies the issues involved in the debate on Latino identity. Gracia concerns himself with what he calls "the total Hispanic/Latino population in the world," which is connected by the unifying thread of Spanish as its "lingua franca" as well as by shared "origin, culture, and values" in the context of a long history of *mestizaje* (Gracia 2000, pp. ix, 128–129). Yet the debate in the U.S. academy has been predicated on an understanding of Latinos as a U.S. ethnic minority, the only conceptual location where it could possibly make sense. It is only in the United States that Dominicans and Guatemalans can come to see themselves as Hispanics or Latinos. In that respect, we can say, with Harvard political scientist Jorge Dominguez, that "Latinos are a problematique of Americanness."[2]

However, despite his unfortunate thesis, Gracia insightfully construes the notion of Hispanic as one that refers to "a group of people who have no common elements considered as a whole" and justifies their "unity" as "not a unity of commonality" but "a historical unity founded on relations" (p. 50). Similarly, although he describes Hispanic unity as resembling that of a family, a figure that he draws from Wittgenstein, he cautiously explains that "the metaphor of the family must be taken broadly to avoid any understanding of it as requiring genetic ties. . . . Indeed, the very foundation of a family, marriage, takes place between people who are added to a family through contract, not genesis" (p. 50). Here Gracia allies himself conceptually with what is arguably the most sober approach to defining the nature of ethnic identification. Many scholars today would agree that "it is primarily the political community, no matter how artificial, that inspires the belief in common ethnicity," as established early in the twentieth century by Max Weber, who contended further that "palpable differences do not exclude sentiments of common ethnicity" (Weber 1965, pp. 306–307). This understanding of ethnic identification corresponds almost entirely with the idea of a minority group, which, one might recall, does not necessarily depend on numbers. As Louis Wirth argued decades ago, a group may outnumber another and yet remain a minority by virtue of its social, political, and economic subordination (Wirth 1965, p. 310). A minority defines itself by its unequal status vis-à-vis "a corresponding dominant group enjoying higher social status and greater privilege" as well as by its "exclusion from full participation in the life of society" (Wirth, p. 309).

In keeping with Gracia's useful caveat, then, and focusing strictly on the historical relations—that is, the material conditions, the social forces, and the political dynamics that frame the experience of Latinos—one might perhaps explore ways of speaking about U.S. Hispanics holistically without

450 SILVIO TORRES-SAILLANT

imposing a priori notions of homogenity. As in the case of Dominicans discussed earlier, essentialistic claims will not take us very far in this conversation. Definers of the essential features "shared by most Hispanics independent of their national background, birthplace, dominant language, or
any other sociodemographic characteristic" have placed too great a demand
on our imagination (Marin and Marin 1991, p. 2). To claim, for instance,
that Rosa, a descendant of Spanish settlers in New Mexico who no longer
speaks Spanish, is ontologically indistinguishable from José, an undocumented Nicaraguan who has just arrived in the United States, is to rely
unduly on the power of so-called cultural values (p. 2). Scholars Gerardo
Marin and Barbara VanOss Marin speak unambiguously of "the common
cultural values that remain strong and personally significant across generations and that may lead both Rosa and José to think of themselves as sharing 'something' that they do not share with non-Hispanic residents of the
United States" (p. 2).

Marin and Marin attribute to Latinos the quality of "familism"—a
"strong identification with and attachment to their nuclear and extended
family" which these theorists regard as one of the most important culture-
specific values of Hispanics (p. 13). Such arguments would be stronger if
these authors were to supplement their findings with comparative data that
would show whether Latinos in fact cherish their relatives appreciably
more than other groups, such as Irish Americans, Italian Americans,
African Americans, and Jews. Indeed, a number of scholars have argued
that immigration and displacement are highly stressful to Latino families—
a point well made in Chapters 13 and 14 in this volume and by other
authors. David Abalos, for example, has argued that the disquieting levels
of disruption affecting the Latino family are a consequence of migration,
displacement, and the trauma that ensues (1993, p. 54). Most disconcert-
ing among the sources of stress affecting the family unit is a variable that
one could describe as "cultural" because it is grounded in the place of male
authority in the traditional Spanish family (see Chapter 13 in this volume).
Abalos highlights the place of male privilege and the patriarchal system
that informs the politics of sexism in the Latino family with dehumanizing
consequences for both men and women (p. 53). Given this scenario, rather
than highlighting "familism" as a special quality of the community, we
might more convincingly assert that the institution of the family may be in
no better shape among Latinos than among any other subsection of the
country's population.

THE TENUOUS TIES THAT BIND

We can rest assured that, whatever its problems, the idea of a pan-Latino
community with a claim to some kind of wholeness is here to stay (Torres

2000; Oboler 2000). We therefore face the challenge of articulating an all-encompassing narrative that might historicize the U.S. Hispanic experience, all national groups and ethnic constituencies included. But we must remain acutely aware of the problematic paradigms that inform our effort. Perhaps we ought to start by avoiding any query that might point to the interstices of the Latino soul. Essentialistic claims will take us nowhere, as Klor de Alva warned over a decade ago, urging us to reflect on the importance of class differences within the Latino community. Equating "class" with "culture," he questioned the very existence of "such thing as *the* Hispanic family" because in his view family, kinship, and gender roles all vary along socioeconomic and generational lines (Klor de Alva 1988, pp. 116, 122). It follows, that "the poor inhabit a different cultural and socioeconomic world" from other strata of society among Latinos as among any other portion of the U.S. population (p. 116). Along with many other colleagues from colleges and universities throughout the United States, I have joined the Recovering the U.S. Hispanic Literary Heritage Project, an effort spearheaded by Nicolás Kanellos at the University of Houston that seeks to map the literary and intellectual presence of Hispanics in this country from the beginning of the conquest in the early 1500s to 1960. But I would caution against letting white-supremacist instincts shape the contours of the totalizing narrative we construct.

No doubt we could benefit from devising a historiographic model that enables us to claim a North American heritage that goes back to the colonial period, spanning the exploits of explorers such as Juan Ponce de León and Hernando de Soto, along with literary and historical texts produced by the likes of Alvar Núñez Cabeza de Vaca and Gaspar Pérez de Villagrá. But we might wish to think twice before concurring with Carlos G. Vélez-Ibáñez in accepting Cabeza de Vaca as "the first Chicano" writer (1996, p. 213). The basis for this rather rapid affirmation is the author's understanding of the sociocultural sameness of the conqueror and the conquered. He asserts, for instance, that the majority of the "Hispanos/Mexicans who migrated north from New Spain after the post-Pueblo Revolt of 1680 were primarily crafts people and agropastoralists who had more in common with the Pueblo peoples than they did with the upper reaches of the peninsular caste/class sector" (p. 266). One wonders whether such a view of the fundamental similarity between the native peoples and the invaders during the colonial transaction in what is now the Southwest of the United States might not lie at the core of the practice of erasing difference when imagining Latino history. One thinks of examples such as a 1972 overview that closed with sixty biographical sketches of Hispanic individuals from Juan de Oñate to Herman Badillo and mentioned not one Indian or black, not even Estevan, the black Moor who came in the expedition that brought the author of *Naufragios* to the North (Alford 1972).

Clearly, we must come to terms with our traumatic past. We must also acknowledge as cultural progenitors the indigenous population who suffered the consequences of that early Hispanic presence in what is now the United States. We inherit a racist imaginary from both Latin and Anglo America, and we must try to keep it from dictating the logic of our remembering as we construct a Latino history. Given the pervasiveness of that pernicious imaginary, I propose that we protect ourselves by instituting analytic safeguards in our models. Specifically, I recommend that we once and for all admit the utility of borders—those confines that initially at least, enable people to recognize one another in their difference. I would urge us temporarily to erect intra-Latino borders so that the differentiated experiences of specific national groups can come to light. I believe it is as wrong to demonize borders as it is to pastoralize the common linguistic heritage that by some unexplained mutation turns all our disparate national and ethnic groups into one big happy family. We need to pause for a moment and begin to train our eyes on unearthing the distinct histories of all the Latino subgroups that make up the U.S. Hispanic population, going beyond the exclusive focus on Chicanos, Puerto Ricans, and Cubans. A serious effort also needs to be made to determine the exact location of Brazilians within the larger spectrum of U.S. communities sharing a Latin American heritage. Even if the term *Hispanic* would tend to leave Brazilians out, the term *Latino* would seem to allow for their inclusion (Margolis 1998, pp. 103–104).

Similarly, I can see great utility in isolating those ethnic identity zones that trespass the boundaries of what David A. Hollinger calls "the ethnoracial pentagon," the five communities of descent into which the U.S. population is divided for census purposes (Hollinger 1995, p. 8). I think we can learn a great deal by looking closely at the differentiated experiences of white Latinos, Indian Latinos, Asian Latinos, and Afro-Latinos. I find no mere coincidence in the fact that the blacker components of the U.S. Hispanic population have recently become more visible in Latino forums just as initiatives have emerged for highlighting the Afro-Latino experience. In mid-September 1999, the White House hosted a program aimed at addressing the concerns of the African-descended portion of the Latino community. Concurrently with the White House activities, and extending through October 12, the Smithsonian Institution's National Portrait Gallery also devoted its Latino Festival Program to the differentiated experience of Afro-Latinos. As a result, Dominicans, who seldom get invited to national conversations about the Latino agenda, enjoyed inclusion in panels and had a chance to participate. This example suggests to me that by creating structures designed to examine intra-Latino difference, we can achieve greater inclusiveness than we have at present. Such structures can help us counteract the omnipresence of our white-supremacist education. I believe that temporarily erecting intra-Latino borders can lead to our self-recognition in our complex diversity. These borders can help us discern our own internal oppressions, making us accountable for the same principles of equality and justice by which we purport to judge the behavior of Anglo society. Recognizing our differences and understanding the tensions that often mark our rapport, we might develop the skill to see one another clearly, protect ourselves from too facile an identification with one another, rectify our tendency to stand in the way of one another's progress, and come to respect one another. With that goal securely achieved, it will then be realistic for us to aspire to federate our distinct constituencies and communities with the purpose of actually becoming, eventually, that one big family striving together in pursuit of common happiness.

NOTES

1. The remainder of this paragraph and the four that follow reproduce almost verbatim the second section of my essay "Visions of Dominicanness in the United States" (Torres-Saillant 1998, pp. 139–152).

2. Comment made as part of his remarks when he served as discussant to a panel in the April 2000 Latino studies conference at Harvard.

REFERENCES

Abalos, David T. *The Latino Family and the Politics of Transformation*. Westport and London: Greenwood Press, 1993.

Alford, Harold J. *The Proud Peoples: The Heritage and Culture of Spanish-Speaking People in the United States*. New York: McKay, 1972.

Aponte, Sarah. *Dominican Migration to the United States, 1971–1997: An Annotated Bibliography*. Dominican Research Monographs. New York: CUNY Dominican Studies Institute, 1999.

Beveridge, Albert J. "Beveridge Trumpets Imperialism." In *To Serve the Devil*, vol. 2, edited by Paul Jacobs and Saul Landau with Eve Pell. New York: Vintage Books, 1971.

Black, George. *The Good Neighbor: How the United States Wrote the History of Central America and the Caribbean*. New York: Pantheon, 1988.

Bonilla, Frank. "Rethinking Latino/Latin American Interdependence: New Knowing, New Practice." In *Borderless Borders: U.S. Latinos, Latino Americans, and the Paradox of Interdependence*, edited by Frank Bonilla et al. Philadelphia: Temple University Press, 1998, pp. 217–230.

Cañízares Esguerra, Jorge. "New World, New Stars: Patriotic Astrology and the Invention of Indian and Creole Bodies in Colonial Spanish America, 1600–1650." *American Historical Review* 104.1 (February 1999): 33–68.

Darder, Antonia, and Rodolfo D. Torres, eds. *The Latino Studies Reader: Culture, Economy, and Society*. Malden & Oxford: Blackwell Publishers, 1998.

Davis, Mike. *Magical Urbanism: Latinos Reinvent the U.S. City.* London and New York: Verso, 2000.

Delgado, Richard. "Words That Wound: A Tort Action for Racial Insults, Epithets, and Name-Calling." *Critical Race Theory: The Cutting Edge,* edited by Richard Delgado. Philadelphia: Temple University Press, 1995, pp. 159–168.

Delgado, Richard, and Jean Stefancic. *The Latino/a Condition: A Critical Reader.* New York: New York University Press, 1998.

Dougherty, Tim. "Media versus Minorities." *Hispanic Business* October 1999, pp. 26–28.

Dworkin y Mendez, Kenya. "Introduction." In Evelio Grillo, *Black Cuban, Black American: A Memoir.* Houston: Arte Público Press, 2000, pp. vii–xiv.

Flores, Juan, and George Yudice. *Divided Borders: Essays in Puerto Rican Identity.* Houston: Arte Público Press, 1993.

Flores, Juan. "Review of *Harvest of Empire: A History of Latinos in America* by Juan González." *Color Lines: Race Culture Action* 3.3 (Fall 2000): 43.

Fletcher, Michael A. "Latino Actors Cite Color Barrier in U.S." *Boston Sunday Globe,* August 2000.

Fox, Geoffrey. *The Hispanic Nation: Culture, Politics, and the Construction of Identity.* Tucson: University of Arizona Press, 1997.

Gonzalez, Juan. *Harvest of Empire: A History of Latinos in America.* New York: Viking, 2000.

Gracia, Jorge J. E. *Hispanic/Latino Identity: A Philosophical Perspective.* Malden and Oxford: Blackwell, 2000.

Grillo, Evelio. *Black Cuban, Black American: A Memoir.* Introduction by Kenya Dworkin y Mendez. Houston: Arte Público Press, 2000.

Hollinger, David A. *Postethnic America: Beyond Multiculturalism.* New York: Basic Books, 1995.

Kanellos, Nicolás. "Hispanics and Race." In *Reference Library of Hispanic America,* vol. 1, edited by Nicolás Kanellos. Detroit: Gale Research, 1998, pp. 176–184.

Klor de Alva, J. Jorge. "Telling Hispanics Apart: Latino Sociocultural Diversity." In *The Hispanic Experience in the United States: Contemporary Issues and Perspectives,* edited by Edna Costa Belen and Barbara R. Sjostrom. New York: Praeger, 1988, pp. 107–136.

Klor de Alva, J. Jorge, Cornel West, and Earl Shorris. "Our Next Race Question: The Uneasiness Between Blacks and Latinos." In *The Latino Studies Reader: Culture, Economy and Society,* edited by Antonia Darder and Rodolfo D. Torres. Malden and Oxford: Blackwell, 1998, pp. 180–189.

Margolis, Maxine L. *An Invisible Minority: Brazilians in New York City.* New Immigrants Series. Boston: Allyn & Bacon, 1998.

Marin, Gerardo, and Barbara VanOss Marin. *Research with Hispanic Populations.* Vol. 23. Applied Research Methods Series. Newbury Park: Sage Publications, 1991.

Oboler, Suzanne. *Ethnic Labels, Latino Lives: Identity and the Politics of (Re)Presentation in the United States.* Minneapolis and London: University of Minnesota Press, 1995.

Oboler, Suzanne. "Contemporary Constructions of Latino Identity: Rethinking the Discourse in Race Relations in the United States." Paper presented at the conference on Emerging Trends and Interdisciplinary Discourses in Latino Studies. Latino Studies Program, Cornell University, April 14–15, 2000.

Ramos, Jorge. *La otra cara de América: Historias de los inmigrantes latinoamericanos que están cambiando a Estados Unidos.* Mexico, DF: Editorial Grijalbo, 2000.

Rodriguez, Richard. "Mixed Blood: Columbus's Legacy: A World Made Mestizo." Originally in *Harper's* 1991. Reprinted in *Progressions: Readings for Writers*, edited by Betsy S. Wilbert. New York and London: Norton, 1998, pp. 535–549.

Saralegui, Cristina. *Cristina! Confidencias de una rubia.* New York. Warner Books, 1998.

Sleeper, Jim. *Should American Journalism Make Us American?* Cambridge, MA: Joan Shorenstein Center on the Press, Politics and Public Policy and the John F. Kennedy School of Government, Harvard University, 1999. (15 pp. pamphlet)

Suro, Roberto. *Strangers among US: Latino Lives in a Changing America.* New York: Knopf, 1998.

Torres, Andrés. "Latino Cultural Identity and Political Participation: Scanning the Recent Literature." Paper presented at the conference on Emerging Trends and Interdisciplinary Discourses in Latino Studies. Latino Studies Program, Cornell University. April 14–15, 2000.

Torres-Saillant, Silvio. "Visions of Dominicanness in the United States." In *Borderless Borders: U.S. Latinos, Latin Americans, and the Paradox of Interdependence*, edited by Frank Bonilla et al. Philadelphia: Temple University Press, 1998, pp. 139–152.

Vélez-Ibáñez, Carlos G. *Border Visions: Mexican Cultures of the Southwestern United States.* Tucson: University of Arizona Press, 1996.

Weber, Max. "Ethnic Groups." *In Theories of Society: Foundations of Modern Sociological Theory*, edited by Talcott Parsons et al. One-volume edition. New York: The Free Press, 1965, pp. 305–309.

Welles, Sumner. *Naboth's Vineyard: The Dominican Republic, 1844–1924.* Mamaroneck, NY: Paul P. Appel, 1966, p. 916.

Wirth Louis. "The Problem of Minority Groups." In *Theories of Society: Foundations of Modern Sociological Theory*, edited by Talcott Parsons et al. One-volume edition. New York: The Free Press, 1965, pp. 309–315.

Afterword

American Projections

Doris Sommer

Percentages, concentrations, rates of intermarriage, language loss, economic bracket—these are the terms for projections about Latin@s in the twenty-first century. We see them as pie graphs and as bar graphs, as causes for hope, concern, and relief, and as motives for denial for those who would rather not see the sea change. I cannot add to the able contributions by demographers and by social scientists in general. Instead, the opportunity to reflect on the chapters in this volume enables me to consider another kind of *projection*—not the statistical extrapolation but the collective fantasy that shores up a denial of statistical effects, the fantasy of monological and monocultural nationhood in this country of diverse and continuing immigration. It projects the real America onto a space elsewhere or into a future time beyond cultural and racial differences.

"What's the best thing about New York?" a popular riddle asks.

"The best thing about the City is that it's so close to the United States!"

The funny thing about this joke is the ease with which it travels and substitutes one city for another. The joke about America being elsewhere brings a laugh in and about Miami, Los Angeles, San Francisco, and even Chicago, far from the coastlines where moorings can float and communities stay awash in foreign cultures. Where is the real "America" except in diminishing pockets and in deluded projections? I confess a preference for the New York version of the riddle, given the island's geographic independence, something like Great Britain's ironic distance from the rest of Europe. But there may be richer pockets of "un-American" cultural activity close to America's heartland, simply because the monological imaginary will find real obstacles where it least suspected them. In Dodge City, Kansas, for example, half of the schoolchildren come from non-English-speaking homes; and the underpopulated, 96 percent white state of Iowa, for another example, has recently legislated incentives for immigrants in the hope of becoming the "Ellis Island of the Midwest" (Pam Belluk, *New York Times*, August 28, 2000, p. 1).

Throughout the United States, monologism is losing its descriptive power. It is a country that now claims to speak one language (after a long history of multilingualism that apparently ended during the paranoia of World War I), although visitors will hear several languages in any of the cities mentioned above and in many others, including the Boston that François Grosjean described almost 20 years ago in *Life with Two Languages* (Boston: Harvard, University Press, 1982). Maybe the denial of diversity is predictable, to follow the tone of his book. Its preface to the international review of the discords between language use and official language policy concludes that "there is probably a larger proportion of bilinguals in monolingual nations than in bilingual and multilingual countries." Grosjean was writing from and about the United States, among other ideally, but impossibly, coherent countries.

Some dangerous idealists don't stop projecting. "After leading the revolt against bilingual education in California, Ron Unz would like to see one in New York City" (John Tierney, *New York Times*, August 16, 1999). A year later, the *Times* allays the fears of critics who apparently worried that Hispanic children couldn't learn in English-only schools: "Two years after Californians voted to end bilingual education and force a million Spanish-speaking students to immerse themselves in English as if it were a cold bath, those students are improving in reading and other subjects at often striking rates" (Jacques Steinberg, *New York Times*, August 20, 2000). This glibness about cold-bath cures, as though Spanish were dirt or a disease, ignores several losses and the dangers that follow from loss. One loss is to the children and their families, because Spanish is not only a vehicle for learning lessons in school (a context in which it is perhaps replaceable by English) but also an international code that could foster communication, commerce, and create interaction with fellow Spanish speakers in almost two dozen countries. Another loss is that of something beyond, or alongside, the rational functions and advantages of a second language. It is the children's loss of the range of affective, respectful, intimate, and generally performative registers of a second home, or subaltern language. "Indeed the conflict has been not just between two languages, but between two quite different conceptions of language," Terry Eagleton says about a different example of doubling, "since the English empiricist conception of language as representational has never had much appeal to the more linguistically performative Irish. The Irish have on the whole, in the manner of subaltern peoples, tended to see language as strategic, conative, rhetorical rather than cognitive, and there is a theological dimension to this suspicion of representationalism."[1] And a third loss has the broadest consequences for all of us; it is the loss of difference itself—one kind of difference that democracy depends on.

To say that difference is good for democracy is a bold way of putting the healthful side effects of home-grown diversity and of immigration. Immigration, regional ethnic, and gender rights upset the stubborn compact between (ethnic) nation and the constitutional state, and they stretch liberal practices toward a greater realization of liberalism's own promises. Universalism itself depends on difference, to follow Ernesto Laclau's provocative formulation, which some critical legal scholars share.[2] The universal has survived classical philosophy's dismissal of particularity as deviation, and it has outlived a European Enlightenment that conflated universal (subject, class, culture) with particular (French) incarnations. Today's universalism is a paradox for the past, because it is grounded in particularist demands. They unmoor universalism from any fixed cultural content and keep it open to an "always receding horizon."[3] The corollary paradox of democracy, Laclau admits without embarrassment, is that it requires unity but depends on diversity. Tension and ambiguity are structural to democracy, which neither Habermas's ideal of communication nor Lyotard's lament over an impasse can acknowledge. The point of politics is to win ground and rights from centers of power, not to dispense with the power that invites struggle.[4] This is perhaps the closest that political philosophy comes to appreciating antagonism as democracy's normal condition.

There is no doubt that student advances in English should be celebrated, but the unfounded assumption that these advances are possible only with the loss of Spanish begs comparative questions: Is bilingualism a liability if the other language is French or German? Are bilingual children at risk of learning in neither language if they come from the middle class? Has Spanish been racialized and stigmatized to the point where white speakers are told that "they don't look Spanish"? Training America's ears to hear the same kinds of advantages of one language in the sounds of another will be an almost technical challenge that will bring broad, conceptual rewards.

In Spanish, the concept of America has always been polyglot, complex, baroque, excessive, overloaded. The very fact of the conquest brought cultures into crises of self-definition and produced the supplements that show how unstable or insufficient the "original" culture had been. European baroque art and thought were anxious responses to the shock of discovering America, a vast and variously sophisticated world that took no notice and had no need of Europe. Half a millennium later, after various migratory movements and shifting borders (when the United States grew by shrinking Mexico and then overtaking Puerto Rico) have continued to refresh the baroque patterns of America, and its culture and politics have become ever more complicated. To recognize them as beautiful, we will need some training beyond a classical taste for unity. The chapters in this book offer important lessons.

Silvio Torres-Saillant calls threads of these baroque patterns "problematic paradigms." He appreciates the ways in which Hispanics in the United States "have advanced the cause of human justice" by stretching the working definitions of citizenship, as they mark their difference from the dominant society and also mark their legitimate place inside the country. On the other, paradoxical, side of ethnic markings, Torres-Saillant complains, Hispanics tend to override (not to say whitewash) the differences in origin, race, and class among constitutive groups and to cultivate the same kind of colorblindness that makes Anglo conservatives indifferent to racial discrimination. The projections of *one-derland,* in other words, are also dangerous fantasies for Latinos. This should not surprise us, because their Latin American countries of origin practiced similar simplifications: José Martí, among other nation builders, wished away internal differences as obstacles to national consolidation.

How does one imagine a future without the help of narratives? And how does one imagine possibilities without the risks of juxtapositions and relationships that characterize language arts? Along with the other scholars in this book, and in the same spirit that stimulates Nestor García Canclini's *Imagined Globalization* (Buenos Aires, Paidós, 2000), I recommend that we grasp all opportunities to tell productive, democratic, creative stories about the future—to fulfill the promise of a flexible and capacious America.

NOTES

1. Terry Eagleton, "Postcolonialism: The Case of Ireland," in David Bennett, *Multicultural States: Rethinking Difference and Identity,* (London: Routledge, 1999), p. 128.

2. See Neil Gotanda, "A Critique of 'Our Constitution Is Color-Blind,'" *Stanford Law Review* 44 (1) (November 1991) 1–68. Citing Robert Paul Wolff, in *Beyond Tolerance in A Critique of Pure Tolerance* 4, 17 (ed. Robert Paul Wolff, Barrington Moore, Jr. and Herbert Marcuse, 1965), Gotanda defends racial-cultural diversity as a positive good in the polity, rather than something merely to be tolerated and benignly overlooked (p. 53). Gotanda also quotes Justice Brennan, whose decision in *Metro Broadcasting* v. *FCC* draws from *Regents of University of California* v. *Bakke.* "Just as a 'diverse student body' contributing to a 'robust exchange of ideas' is a 'constitutionally permissible goal' on which a race-conscious university admissions program may be predicated, the diversity of views and information on the airwaves serves important First Amendment values. The benefits of such diversity are not limited to the members of minority groups . . . ; rather, the benefits redound to all members of the viewing and listening audience" (p.57). Thanks to Susan Keller for directing me to this article.

3. Ernesto Laclau, "Universalism, Particularism and the Question of Identity," in *The Identity In Question*, ed. John Rajchman (New York: Routledge, 1995), pp. 93–108. Judith Butler cautiously agrees that universality can be a site of translation. See Seyla Benhabib, Judith Butler, Drucilla Cornell, and Nancy Fraser, introduction by Linda Nicholson, *Feminist Contentions: A Philosophical Exchange* (New York: Routledge, 1995) p. 130: "[T]he universal is always culturally articulated, and the complex process of learning how to read . . . is not something any of us can do outside of the difficult process of cultural translation [but definition is in the process of defining, *el camino se hace al caminar*] . . . the terms made to stand for one another are transformed in the process, and where the movement of that unanticipated transformation establishes the universal as that which is yet to be achieved and which, in order to resist domestication, may never be fully or finally achievable."

See also Butler's "Sovereign Performatives in the Contemporary Scene of Utterance" forthcoming in *Critical Inquiry*, where she argues for the efficacy of "performative contradictions" in the contestatory translations of "universal." *Performative contradiction* is a term Habermas had used to discredit Foucault's critique of reason via reason. See Jürgen Habermas, *The Philosophical Discourse of Modernity*, ed. Frederick Lawrence (Cambridge, MA: M.I.T. Press, 1987), Introduction by Thomas McCarthy, p. xv. I'm not sure, however, how different in practice is Butler's project of open-ended translation from Habermas's pursuit of the universal as an ideal. *Philosophical Discourses*, p. 198. Who could ever reach an ideal? And yet, in the heuristic spirit of Seyla Benhabib's work, how can one have a political engagement without imagining ideals?

Homi K. Bhabha also makes translation the site of the movable nature of modernity in general. See *The Location of Culture* (New York: Routledge, 1994). See especially pp. 32 and 242. Translation is the favored strategy for keeping the promise of modernity usably alive.

4. Judith Butler, Ernesto Laclau, and Slavoj Žižek, *Hegemony, Universality, Contingency* (London, Verso, 2000).

NOTES ON CONTRIBUTORS

Ricardo C. Ainslie is professor in the Counseling Psychology Doctoral Training Program at the University of Texas at Austin.

Elaine Bernard is executive director of the Trade Union Program at Harvard University.

E. Richard Brown is professor of public health in the School of Public Health and director of the Center for Health Policy Research at the University of California, Los Angeles.

María S. Carlo is assistant professor of education at Harvard University.

Jorge Chapa is professor and founding director of Latino Studies at Indiana University, Bloomington.

John H. Coatsworth is professor of history, Monroe Gutman Professor of Latin American Affairs, and director of the David Rockefeller Center for Latin American Studies at Harvard University.

Wayne A. Cornelius is professor of political science, adjunct professor of International Relations and Pacific Studies, and Theodore E. Gildred Chair in U.S.-Mexican Relations at the University of California at San Diego.

Rodolfo O. de la Garza is professor of political science at Columbia University.

Louis DeSipio is associate professor of political science and interim director of the Latina/Latino Studies Program at the University of Illinois at Urbana-Champaign.

Jorge I. Domínguez is Harvard College professor, Clarence Dillon Professor of International Affairs, and director of the Weatherhead Center for International Affairs at Harvard University.

Celia Jaes Falicov is associate clinical professor in the Department of Psychiatry at the Univeristy of California, San Diego.

Paul Farmer is professor of medical anthropology in the Department of Social Medicine and co-director of the Program in Infectious Disease and Social Change at Harvard Medical School.

Juan Flores is professor of Latin American and Hispanic Caribbean Studies at City University of New York.

Patricia Gándara is associate professor of education at the University of California, Davis.

Merilee S. Grindle is Edward S. Mason Professor of Development at the Kennedy School of Government at Harvard University.

Jacqueline Hagan is associate professor of sociology and co-director of the Center for Immigration Research at the University of Houston.

David E. Hayes-Bautista is professor of Medicine and director of the Center for the Study of Latino Health at the School of Medicine, University of California, Los Angeles.

Pierette Hondagneu-Sotelo is associate professor of sociology and the Program in American Studies and Ethnicity at the University of Southern California.

Peggy Levitt is associate professor of sociology at Wellesley College.

Luis C. Moll is professor of language, reading, and culture at the University of Arizona.

Lisa J. Montoya is lecturer at the Center for Mexican-American Studies at the University of Texas at Austin.

Gary Orfield is professor of education and social policy at Harvard University.

Mariela Páez received her doctorate in 2001 from the Harvard Graduate School of Education and is currently working as a researcher at Harvard University.

Nestor Rodríguez is associate professor of sociology and co-director of the Center for Immigration Research at the University of Houston.

Richard Ruiz is professor of language, reading, and culture at the University of Arizona.

George J. Sanchez is associate professor of history and the Program in American Studies and Ethnicity at the University of Southern California.

Robert C. Smith is assistant professor of sociology at Barnard College.

Catherine E. Snow is Henry Lee Shattuck Professor of Education at the Harvard Graduate School of Education.

Doris Sommer is professor of Latin American literature at Harvard University.

Alex Stepick is professor of sociology and anthropology and director of the Immigration and Ethnicity Institute at Florida International University.

Carol Dutton Stepick is field research director at the Immigration and Ethnicity Institute at Florida International University.

Carola Suárez-Orozco is co-director of the Harvard Immigration Project and senior research associate and lecturer in human development and psychology at the Harvard Graduate School of Education.

Marcelo M. Suárez-Orozco is Victor S. Thomas Professor of Education at Harvard. He is also co-director of the Harvard Immigration Projects, chair of the Interfaculty Committee on Latino Studies, and a member of the Executive Committee of the David Rockefeller Center for Latin American Studies.

Silvio Torres-Saillant is associate professor of English at Syracuse University and director of the CUNY Dominican Studies Institute at City College of New York.

John Trumpbour is research director of the Trade Union Program at Harvard University.

Diego Vigil is professor of criminology, law, and society at the University of California, Irvine.

Mary C. Waters is Harvard College Professor and professor of sociology at Harvard University.

Hongjian Yu is associate director of the Center for Health Policy Research at the University of California, Los Angeles.

Ana Celia Zentella is professor of ethnic studies at the University of California, San Diego.

Barbara Zurer Pearson is research project manager in the Department of Communication Disorders at the University of Massachusetts, Amherst.

INDEX

Compositor: Michael Bass & Associates
Text: 10/12 ITC New Baskerville
Display: ITC New Baskerville
Printer and binder: Maple-Vail Manufacturing Group